NONVERBAL COMMUNICATION
THE UNSPOKEN DIALOGUE

NONVERBAL COMMUNICATION

THE UNSPOKEN DIALOGUE

SECOND EDITION

Judee K. Burgoon
University of Arizona

David B. Buller
University of Arizona

W. Gill Woodall
University of New Mexico

THE McGRAW-HILL COMPANIES, INC.

New York St. Louis San Francisco Auckland Bogotá Caracas Lisbon
London Madrid Mexico City Milan Montreal New Delhi
San Juan Singapore Sydney Tokyo Toronto

McGraw-Hill

A Division of The **McGraw·Hill** Companies

NONVERBAL COMMUNICATION
The Unspoken Dialogue

Acknowledgments appear on pages 510–511, and on this page by reference.

 This book is printed on recycled, acid-free paper containing 10% postconsumer waste.

1 2 3 4 5 6 7 8 9 0 FGR FGR 9 0 9 8 7 6 5

ISBN 0-07-008995-7

This book was set in Times Roman by ComCom, Inc.
The editors were Marjorie Byers and John F. Morriss;
the production supervisor was Paula Keller.
The cover was designed by Joan Greenfield.
The photo editor was Kathy Bendo;
the photo researcher was Elyse Rieder.
Project supervision was done by The Total Book.
Quebecor Printing/Fairfield was printer and binder.

Library of Congress Cataloging-in-Publication Data

Burgoon, Judee K.
    Nonverbal communication: the unspoken dialogue / Judee Burgoon,
David Buller, W. Gill Woodall. — 2 ed.
      p.   cm.
    Includes bibliographical references and index.
    ISBN 0-07-008995-7
    1. Nonverbal communication (Psychology)   I. Buller, David B.
II. Woodall, William Gill (date)   III. Title.
BF637.N66B87 1996
153.6'9—dc20
                                 95-39796

ABOUT THE AUTHORS

JUDEE K. BURGOON is Professor and Director of Graduate Studies in communication at the University of Arizona, where she specializes in nonverbal communication, interpersonal relationship management, and research methods. She has held appointments in communication previously at Michigan State University, the University of Florida, and Hunter College and as a visiting scholar in psychology at Harvard University. Dr. Burgoon's research and writing credits include seven books and monographs (*Small Group Communication: A Functional Approach,* with J. McCroskey & M. Burgoon; *The Unspoken Dialogue,* with T. Saine; *The World of the Working Journalist,* with M. Burgoon and others; *Mexican Americans and the Mass Media,* with B. Greenberg, M. Burgoon, & F. Korzenny; *Nonverbal Communication: The Unspoken Dialogue,* with D. Buller & G. Woodall, and *Interpersonal Adaptation: Dyadic Interaction Patterns,* with L. Stern and L. Dillman), 22 research grants, and over 140 articles, chapters, and reviews on such subjects as nonverbal and relational communication, small group communication, deception, interpersonal interaction patterns, and research methods. The recipient of numerous teaching and research awards, Dr. Burgoon is a frequent guest lecturer and consultant to industry.

DAVID B. BULLER is Associate Professor of communication at the University of Arizona. He is also the Director of the Behavioral Sciences Section at the Arizona Cancer Center. Professor Buller received his Ph.D. in communication at Michigan State University and was previously a member of the speech communication faculty at Texas Tech University. Professor Buller is the author of many publications in journals and has edited volumes on nonverbal communication and social influence, deception in interpersonal exchanges, and health behavior change. His research is supported by grants from the U.S. Army Research Institute and Office, the National Cancer Institute, and the U.S. Centers for Disease Control and Prevention.

W. GILL WOODALL is Associate Professor of communication and journalism at The University of New Mexico, and also the Director of the Prevention Division of the Center on Alcoholism, Substance Abuse and Addictions *(CASAA)* at UNM. Professor Woodall received his Ph. D. in Speech Communication from the University of Florida in 1978, and was an Assistant Professor at Cleveland State University before accepting a faculty appointment at the University of New Mexico in Albuquerque. He has authored and co-authored a variety of journal articles, book chapters, and texts in the areas of nonverbal communication, communication and social cognition, comprehension of television news, and more recently, in health communication and substance abuse prevention. Dr. Woodall's research in substance abuse prevention has been funded by grants from the U.S. Dept. Of Education, and from the National Institute on Alcohol Abuse and Alcoholism of the National Institutes of Health.

To Erin, Ian, Katie, Caitlin, and Eli
who daily teach us lessons
about the unspoken dialogue
not found in books

and

To Michael, Mary, and Patricia
who have remained our partners
in the unspoken dialogue
and who continue to share its full measure
of pleasures, tribulations, and surprises

CONTENTS

PREFACE

Humans are social creatures. We spend most of our waking hours in contact with other people—learning, working, playing, courting, parenting, negotiating, buying and selling, and just plain talking. We not only communicate with people face-to-face, we watch them on television and videos, listen to them on talk radio, and interact with them via telephones, faxes, and computers. With so much of our day-to-day existence consumed by communication, it should be obvious that our ability to navigate the vicissitudes of daily living—indeed, our prospects for sustaining happy, healthy lives—depends on how well we communicate. This isn't just our opinion. A local conciliation court recently reported that for the fourteenth year in a row, the number one reported problem among troubled marriages is the lack of good communication. Successful relationships are built upon a solid foundation of communication skills.

It should be just as obvious that communication's profound impact isn't limited to off-work hours. It is also instrumental to our success or failure in the workplace. Surveys among business leaders, major employers, and employment counselors emphasize the importance of communication skills in acquiring jobs and performing effectively on the job. A study by the Administrative Management Society, for example, found that 80 percent of the managers rated communication skills as among the most important qualifications of prospective employees; 65 percent also cited interpersonal and leadership skills. A survey among women managers on strategies or techniques they credited with helping them reach their current positions further endorsed the importance of communication abilities. Rated as very or extremely important were communication skills (89 percent), personal power (78 percent), and charisma, charm, and social skills (53 percent). In another study by a college placement service, several hundred alumni reported that communication abilities were more important to their job success than the major subject they studied.

These testimonials probably pale in comparison to the vividness of your own first-hand experiences. What could be more persuasive evidence of the importance of communication than the recollection of butterflies in your stomach when you fretted about what to say on your first date, the flush of pleasure after making a well-received presentation in class, the exhilaration of receiving a job offer after a grueling interview, the satisfaction of winning an argument with your parents, or the sadness of losing a friendship over a silly disagreement? Clearly, communication plays a pivotal role in the significant—as well as insignificant—moments in your life, and a major contributor to the success or failure of communication is its nonverbal dimension.

Unfortunately, until recently, the study of nonverbal communication was dismissed as trivial or suspect, a view fueled by charlatans claiming that your every movement talks and promising to teach you how to read others like a book. Characteristic of the cynicism promoted by this popularized version of "body language" was this sardonic observation by Aldous Huxley (1954):

When it comes to any form of non-verbal education more fundamental (and more likely of some practical use) than Swedish drill, no really respectable person in any really respectable university or church will do anything about it. . . . Besides, this matter of education in the nonverbal humanities will not fit into any of the established pigeon-holes. It is not religion, not neurology, not gymnastics, not morality or civics, not even experimental psychology. This being so, the subject is for academic and ecclesiastical purposes, non-existent and may be safely ignored altogether or left, with a patronizing smile, to those whom the Pharisees of verbal orthodoxy call cranks, quacks, charlatans and unqualified amateurs. (pp. 76–77)

Much to our relief, such cynicism has abated. In fact, the respectability of studying nonverbal behavior and communication is evident in the flood of writing on the subject. What was once the "foundling child of the social sciences—disdained, neglected, even nameless" (Burgoon, 1980, p. 179) has become a legitimate area of scholarship, as documented by the publication of literally thousands of articles and books on the subject. In fact, the unceasing interest in nonverbal communication has created a state of information overload. In contrast to Huxley's gloomy assessment, knowledge about nonverbal communication now springs from such fountainheads as psychology, psychiatry, sociology, anthropology, linguistics, semiotics, and biology, in addition to the field of communication itself. Trying to make sense of this diverse body of information is no small task, especially given that scholars from different fields approach nonverbal behavior with differing perspectives, assumptions, and methodologies.

Our mission in writing this textbook has been to sift through the mounds of literature on the subject and, while attempting to be comprehensive and current, to distill the most valid and valuable information into understandable and usable principles. Because we believe that different disciplines offer unique perspectives and insights, our "take" on nonverbal communication is integrative and eclectic. It is our hope that in the process, we have escaped the plight of the three blind men trying to describe an elephant, each with only a limited experience of one part of the elephant's anatomy.

This does not mean, however, that there is no underlying perspective that unifies our orientation to nonverbal behavior. We believe that nonverbal *communication* can best be understood according to the functions—the goals and purposes—it serves. This approach, which other scholars have increasingly embraced, guided the first version of this text, *The Unspoken Dialogue* (Burgoon & Saine, 1978). We discuss the primary features of this approach in Chapters 1 and 5. Its main significance is that it combines various elements of nonverbal communication in a way people intuitively understand. It makes it easier to answer the question, "What can nonverbal communication do for me or to me?" We suspect you are far more interested in knowing how to use nonverbal communication to make a good impression on an employer, influence a group, keep a conversation going, interpret a friend's emotional expressions, or woo a mate than to know how many different ways people use eye contact or how frequently they touch. Consequently, most of this textbook is organized around the communication functions in which nonverbal behavior plays a central role. The first five chapters supply some necessary background about nonverbal codes and their relationship to verbal communication before the functions themselves can be explored fully. The remaining ten chapters are all devoted to the various purposes of nonverbal communication that loom largest in people's communication lives.

A second feature unifying our perspective on nonverbal communication is our emphasis on scientific knowledge rather than anecdotal experience. This book is dedicated to giving you the most current and comprehensive coverage of theories and research findings related to nonverbal communication and behavior. Many popular books and self-proclaimed experts promise to divulge how you can "win friends and influence people." One "authority" making the talk show circuit at the time of this printing is promoting a book entitled *Let Me See Your Body Talk,* which purports to reveal all the secrets to successful courtship. We wish the state of our knowledge were that certain. But the truth is, human behavior cannot be "read" like a book, and there are as many questions about nonverbal communication as there are answers. The cookbook approach to communication may make its promoters a bundle of money, but it is unlikely to give you a sound basis for guiding your own nonverbal messages or responding to the nonverbal behavior of others. Much of what we know about nonverbal communication is tentative because new research is daily challenging or disconfirming old beliefs while creating new ones. The best we can offer you, then, is the best of the current state of thinking and scientific evidence that is supplemented rather than replaced by anecdote and personal experience. Though the absence of abundant clear-cut prescriptions about how to behave nonverbally may be unsatisfying to some readers, we are comforted by Voltaire's statement that "doubt is a not very agreeable status but certainty is a ridiculous one."

The Plan of the Book

Although this book is intended to be reasonably comprehensive, we have organized it in a way that should permit instructors the option of using all or only part of it and to order the chapters in a sequence best suited to their sense of the unfolding story of nonverbal communication. The current organization, which is modified from the previous one, reflects our assumption that it is best to first introduce basic principles and individual codes before considering how they work together to accomplish various communication functions. Accordingly, Chapter 1 addresses definitional issue and key principles, Chapters 2 through 4 cover the structural and normative nature of the seven primary nonverbal codes, and Chapter 5 introduces the systemic relationships between nonverbal and verbal codes.

This foundational material paves the way for considering ten communication functions that nonverbal behavior serves. Chapter 6 considers the role of nonverbal communication in the production and processing of messages, which is essential to people understanding one another. Chapter 7 covers the role of nonverbal cues in defining communication situations even before people interact and how it encourages or inhibits interaction. Chapters 8 and 9 focus on how nonverbal cues reveal something about actors— how senders use them to create and signify personal identities and how receivers use them to form impressions. Chapters 10 and 11 consider the "content" of nonverbal messages—how they function to express emotions and how they define interpersonal relationships. Chapter 12 considers the interaction process itself and how nonverbal cues play a key role in regulating and organizing conversations. Finally, Chapters 13, 14, and 15 address the role of nonverbal cues in managing desired impressions, in influencing others, and in deceiving others. Naturally, we believe all of this information is important and provides the most complete picture of what nonverbal communication is and does. But it is possible to cover a subset of these topics and still obtain a good introduction to nonverbal communication.

Acknowledgments

The process of producing this book has involved the labors and contributions of many people whom we wish to acknowledge. We are grateful to Tanya Boone, Heidi Carr, Dan Freeman, Joe Grandpre, Michelle Johnson, and Christie van Riet, who assisted us with everything from library research to editing to candid appraisals of our revisions. We are also indebted to our other graduate and undergraduate students who through their curiosity and classroom discussions helped us sharpen our own thinking and organization.

We also wish to thank the following individuals for their thoughtful and helpful reviews of the book: Joseph N. Cappella, University of Pennsylvania; Howard Friedman, University of California, Riverside; Randy Koper, University of the Pacific; Beth LePoirè, California University, Santa Barbara; George Ray, Cleveland State University; Martin Remland, Westchester University; Susan Stearns, Eastern Washington University; and John Wiemann, University of California, Santa Barbara.

Finally, two people at McGraw-Hill were especially instrumental in bringing this revision to fruition. To Elyse Rieder, who offered us a cornucopia of wonderful photos from which to choose, our sincere thanks. And to Annette Bodzin, whose "take no prisoners" style overcame many obstacles to move this revision from process to product, we are most indebted.

Judee K. Burgoon
David B. Buller
W. Gill Woodall

ONE

NONVERBAL CODES: STRUCTURES, USAGE, AND INTER-RELATIONSHIPS

1

NONVERBAL COMMUNICATION

The word not spoken
goes not quite unheard.
It lingers in the eye,
in the semi-arch of brow.
A gesture of the hand
speaks pages more than words,
The echo rests in the heart
as driftwood does in sand,
To be rubbed by time
until it rots or shines.
The word not spoken
touches us as music
does the mind.

William S. Cohen (R., Maine)

This text is about "unspoken dialogue," all those messages that people exchange beyond the words themselves. Nonverbal communication pervades every human transaction, from mundane requests at the grocery store to workplace discussions of job performance to delicate international negotiations. As the poem by Senator Cohen attests, the nonverbal side of communication is crucial and often overshadows the verbal communication that is going on. Successful human relations hinge on the ability to express oneself nonverbally and to understand the nonverbal communication of others.

In this text we will explore various facets of nonverbal communication—the "codes" of which it is composed, the many kinds of messages that it can send, the purposes or functions that it can serve, and the processes whereby people generate, exchange, and interpret such messages.

THE IMPORTANCE OF NONVERBAL COMMUNICATION

Intuition tells us, and research confirms, that nonverbal communication is a major force in our lives. In fact, it has been estimated that nearly two-thirds of the meaning in any social situation is derived from nonverbal cues (Birdwhistell, 1955). A more extreme estimate touted in the popular literature is that 93 percent of all meaning is nonverbal

3

(Mehrabian & Ferris, 1967). This estimate is an overestimate, however (as discussed in Chapter 5). Regardless of the actual percentage of meaning that can be attributed to nonverbal cues, there is abundant evidence that people rely heavily on nonverbal cues to express themselves and to interpret the communicative activity of others. A convincing illustration of this appears in Box 1-1, where nonverbal cues signaled an ominous chill in diplomatic relations between the United States and Russia.

Although the significant role of nonverbal communication in daily transactions is indisputable, just why it has such influence is less understood. There appear to be several reasons for its importance.

Nonverbal communication is omnipresent. Every communicative act carries with it nonverbal components. In face-to-face conversations, in public addresses, and in televised or videotaped presentations, all the nonverbal channels come into play. Bodily actions such as gestures, facial expressions, posture, and eye contact; vocal behaviors such as pitch, loudness, and tempo; proximity and potential for touch; physical appearance cues such as attractiveness, dress, and grooming; time messages such as pacing and giving undivided attention; and surrounding furnishings and objects that may add to one's identity all play a part in creating the total communication. In telephone conversations or audiotaped presentations, fewer nonverbal channels are available, but vocal, proxemic, and temporal messages are still present. For example, the decision to talk to someone on the telephone rather than in person expresses a desire for a less involving conversation. The decision to write a nasty letter rather than confronting someone personally can be a delaying tactic that is its own message. Even when people are not talking to each other, it is possible to read nonverbal meaning in their actions. This makes every encounter between two or more people a potential nonverbal exchange, regardless of whether any verbal exchange takes place.

Nonverbal behaviors are omnipresent in another way: they are multifunctional. That is, they are part of almost every communication purpose one can imagine. For example, they may be used to create a favorable first impression, to persuade someone, to control whose turn it is to talk in a conversation, to express one's current emotional

---

BOX 1-1

A TOUCH OF FROST AFTER COLD WAR THAW

Clinton, Yeltsin exchange only silent treatment

BUDAPEST, Hungary—President Clinton and Russian President Boris Yeltsin stood apart on the same stage Monday, a day that should have brought smiles as they formalized a nuclear treaty that took nine years to negotiate and three more to nail down.

Neither ventured a word during the treaty-signing ceremony. But their body language spoke volumes—capping a month of public disputes and souring relations.

While Clinton had hearty handshakes and words of thanks for [others], he averted even eye contact with a frowning Yeltsin, who was sitting right next to him.

. . . .

The silent treatment between Clinton and Yeltsin was only the latest evidence of a recent chill in relations. . . .

Source: Katz, 1994, p. 10A.

state, to signal attraction toward someone, or to clarify the meaning of the verbal message. In fact, they may do several of these things at once. Because many different nonverbal channels can be used to send simultaneous messages, they are often pressed into service to do just that—handle multiple responsibilities in conjunction with, or as a replacement for, verbal communication.

Nonverbal behaviors may form a universal language system. Many scholars believe that nonverbal signals are part of a universally recognized and understood code. This view is evident in this statement by Edward Sapir (1928):

> We respond to gestures with an extreme alertness and, one might almost say, in accordance with an elaborate and secret code that is written nowhere, known to none and understood by all. (p. 556)

Behaviors such as smiling, crying, pointing, caressing, and staring are examples of nonverbal signals that appear to be used and understood the world over. They allow people to communicate with one another at the most basic level regardless of their familiarity with the prevailing verbal language system. Such nonverbal actions thus transcend cultural differences, forming a kind of universal language.

This capacity of nonverbal communication to cross geographic boundaries was brought home when a former student sent a postcard describing her visit to relatives in Italy. She wrote:

> As a non-Italian traveler, it is amazing how much understanding can be grasped by carefully listening to other cues one hears and sees. When sitting at the dinner table with 25 relatives, it struck me how much I relied on the nonverbals.

Clearly, not all meaning can be gleaned from nonverbal cues alone, and there are differences between and within cultures. But the fact that exclusive reliance on nonverbal cues can produce a sense of commonality and understanding in a foreign situation is testimony to their universal character. When words fail us, we can always fall back on our nonverbal communication system to achieve some minimal level of mutual exchange.

Nonverbal communication can lead to misunderstanding as well as understanding. Although nonverbal signals can help us make sense of the world, they can also cause misunderstanding. This can be tragic, as the following anecdote illustrates.

A young photographer, accustomed to working alone, was flown into a remote part of Alaska for the summer. He so prized his solitude that on a previous survival retreat, he had chastised his father for sending a search party after him. On this trip, he failed to make clear arrangements for being flown back out of the wilderness. When the weather began turning cool, his father reluctantly sent a plane looking for him. The pilot soon located the camp. As he neared it, the young man waved a red jacket liner, which to pilots is a signal to wave someone away. The young man then gave a thumbs-up gesture and walked casually to his campsite. The pilot concluded that everything was OK and flew away.

A diary the young man kept revealed a very different interpretation of the encounter. He was thrilled to see the plane, and to ensure being seen, he waved his jacket in the air. He gave the thumbs-up gesture as a sign of his elation and his victory over his growing fears. He then jaunted to his campsite, expecting the plane to land, and was totally disbelieving when it flew on. Weeks later, when the weather turned bitter cold and he ran out of firewood, the young photographer used his last bullet to take his own life. The diary was found with his frozen body.

Not all nonverbal misunderstandings have fatal or even serious consequences. But the potential for nonverbal cues to mislead and be misread is there, and such misreadings can often have a more profound impact than the accurately exchanged cues. This is especially true when people draw inferences from others' unintentional behavior. Many mistakenly believe that nonverbal behaviors all have obvious meanings and that everyone interprets nonverbal cues the same way. Recognition of the potential for misunderstanding is a prerequisite to successful communication.

Nonverbal communication has phylogenetic primacy. This is a fancy way of saying that in our development as a species, nonverbal communication predated language. Although there are numerous theories about whether vocalizations preceded gestural communication or vice versa, there is little doubt that nonverbal forms of expression preceded verbal ones (Dew & Jensen, 1977; McBride, 1975; McNeill, 1970). In that nonverbal communication came first to the species, it can be argued that we are inherently programmed to attend first and foremost to nonverbal signals. This primacy of nonverbal cues should cause us to give them more weight in interpreting communicative events, especially in times of stress, when we are more likely to revert to more primitive (phylogenetically older) response patterns. If we as humans rely more heavily on nonverbal than verbal messages, it may be because we are innately predisposed to do so.

Nonverbal communication has ontogenetic primacy. Just as members of the species first turned to nonverbal forms to communicate with one another, so, too, do individuals rely first on nonverbal means to interact with their caretakers and environment. Even before birth, the fetus in utero is already developing an awareness of its mother through the senses of touch and hearing. At birth, the infant's primary interactions with other humans continue to center on auditory and tactile sensation. Nursing, grasping, rocking, holding, crying, cooing, singing—all these experiences contribute to the infant's awakening recognition that humans communicate with one another. As the infant's vision improves, visual cues are added to the nonverbal mix; sequences of separation and contact likewise add to the understanding of spatial and temporal messages. Long before a child has begun to grasp the concept of verbal language, it has already acquired a rich communication system that is strictly nonverbal. The importance of nonverbal modes of expression at this critical and vulnerable stage of life may contribute to our continued dependence on them even though we acquire more sophisticated means of expression. We do not abandon the nonverbal system; rather, as we mature, we broaden our communicative repertoire to include more complex verbal and nonverbal forms.

Nonverbal communication has interaction primacy. Besides being the first form of communication in the history of the species and in the life span of the individual, nonverbal behavior has primacy in the opening minutes of interpersonal and mediated communication events. Before people even open their mouths, their nonverbal behaviors are supplying a wealth of information to onlookers. Everything from posture to gait to hairstyle to voice quality paints a picture for the observer and provides a frame of reference for interpreting what is said verbally. Especially important are the visual nonverbal cues, such as physical appearance and gestures, that are available at a distance. These begin working before a communicator is within speaking range. Environmental nonverbal cues may also set the stage. For instance, when the president holds a news conference, the American flag, the red carpet, and all the other symbols of the White House create an image of power; they evoke respect from the gathered press prior to the president's opening remarks. This ability of nonverbal cues to "get in the first word," so to speak, gives them a temporal primacy that may also cause their meanings to take precedence over verbal ones.

Nonverbal communication can express what verbal communication can't or shouldn't. There are many occasions when to verbalize our thoughts and feelings would be risky, rude, or inappropriate, so we use nonverbal channels instead. In the early, faltering stages of a romance, for instance, people are hesitant to commit themselves too quickly for fear of being rejected. Rather than say how they feel, people usually rely on nonverbal approaches to determine if the relationship is going to escalate. If a prolonged gaze or lingering touch is not reciprocated, one can retreat to a less intimate level without embarrassment. Similarly, nonverbal cues can be used to satirize, criticize, or leak information without the communicator being held accountable for his or her acts. (See Box 1-2.)

We entrust the expression of our most deep-seated emotions to nonverbal channels. Witness Steven Spielberg's powerful portrayal of the horrors of Auschwitz in his film *Schindler's List.* No verbal description can compare to the palpable terror evident in the faces, postures, and touches of the women and children seen clinging desperately to one another in the showers, waiting for the deadly gas to overtake them.

Nonverbal communication is trusted. Either because of the preceding reasons or in addition to them, nonverbal behaviors are assumed to be more truthful and therefore more trusted. The naive belief exists that nonverbal behaviors are spontaneous and

---

BOX 1-2

APPLICATIONS: THE COURTROOM AND THE MILITARY

Lawyers and soldiers have something in common: an ability to use nonverbal signals to send illicit information. Birdwhistell offers two illustrations:

> Take courtroom procedure, for example. The present system of restricting admissible evidence to exhibits and words still leaves the way open for the introduction of nonadmissible ideas and attitudes. The trial lawyer often is a master of the raised eyebrow, the disapproving headshake and the knowing nod. In many cases, these gestures, if translated into words, would be inadmissible as evidence. Yet, as presented, they have a definite effect on the judge and jury. (Birdwhistell, cited in Rosekrans, 1955, p. 56)

> The salute, a conventionalized movement of the right hand to the vicinity of the anterior portion of the cap or hat, could, without occasioning a court-martial, be performed in a manner which could satisfy, please or enrage the demanding officer. By shifts in stance, facial expression, the velocity or duration of the movement of salutation, and even in the selection of inappropriate contexts for the act, the soldier could dignify, ridicule, demean, seduce, insult, or promote the recipient of the salute. By often imperceptible variations in the performance of the act, he could comment upon the bravery or cowardice of his enemy or ally [or] signal his attitude toward army life. . . . (Birdwhistell, 1970, pp. 79–80)

uncontrolled, that they are "windows to the soul." As we will see, this is not necessarily true. Many nonverbal behaviors are intentionally manipulated, some for deceptive purposes, and people who are image-conscious work scrupulously to suppress expression of behaviors that make a bad impression. Nevertheless, there is a prevailing faith in the honesty and candor of nonverbal behaviors. Consequently, people believe them more readily than verbal behaviors. In fact, research shows that when verbal messages contradict nonverbal ones, adults usually believe the nonverbal message (e.g., Argyle, Alkema, & Gilmour, 1971; Argyle, Salter, Nicholson, Williams, & Burgess, 1970; Mehrabian & Wiener, 1967).

These eight reasons for the significant impact of nonverbal communication, though not exhaustive, highlight the need to understand how nonverbal communication works together with verbal communication and independently of it. Unfortunately, few of us receive formal training in this subject. Despite the emphasis placed on communication skills in elementary school, attention is devoted almost exclusively to reading and writing—in other words, to verbal communication. Ideally, nonverbal communication should be interwoven into all communication study from preschool onward as an integral part of the communication system. But since it is not, an introductory course in nonverbal communication becomes a necessity to remediate nonverbal illiteracy. Although this text is about nonverbal communication, because we are committed to a more integrated approach to verbal and nonverbal communication, you will find a variety of general communication principles and some specific findings about verbal communication throughout the book.

DEFINING NONVERBAL COMMUNICATION

So far, we have been referring to nonverbal communication as if there were some commonly accepted definition for it. In reality, there may be as many definitions of it as there are textbooks about it. Before we proceed any further, it is important that we come to a common understanding of the terminology being used. Although discussing definitional issues may seem as useful as debating how many angels can dance on the head of a pin, definitions can make quite a difference in how actions are interpreted. Consider the following scenario:

> *Girlfriend*: Our relationship's falling apart. You've become totally detached from me.
> *Boyfriend*: How can you say that? Give me just one example.
> *Girlfriend*: I'll give you several. You don't talk to me when we go out to eat together. You spend more time with your friends than you do with me. You don't look at me when we do talk, and you never hold my hand anymore.
> *Boyfriend*: You're just imagining things. I've had a lot on my mind between school and my job, but I haven't changed how I behave toward you.

She interprets his actions as nonverbal messages of distance and lack of affection. He claims his behaviors are unchanged or merely indicative of being preoccupied with other things; any "messages" are her imagination. If his actions are defined as nonverbal communication, even though he may be unaware of them or deny they have occurred, he might be faulted for communicating detachment. Under a different definition, however, she might be seen as reading too much into unintentional and noncommunicative activity. In this very practical way, then, definitions can make a difference. Box 1-3 provides another illustration.

Basic Concepts: Communication, Information, and Behavior

A starting point for arriving at a sound definition is the concept of communication itself. This term is a slippery one because people use it to refer to everything from communing with nature, to "dialoguing" with oneself, to linking computers, to transmitting by satellite.

We can begin by limiting the domain to *human* communication, that is, to exchanges between two or more people. This eliminates a lot, including intrapersonal communication, man-machine communication, and animal or animal-human communication. Apart from philosophical justifications for such exclusions, this restriction is pragmatic. It makes it far more likely that we will uncover general principles if the kinds of communication phenomena to be explained have something in common. It is difficult to find principles that explain bee signals and computer interfaces in the same way that we account for nonverbal exchanges between humans. Nevertheless, we can learn some things about human communication processes by studying nonhuman interactions, and your authors will draw on these observations when they serve as useful illustrations or analogues.

BOX 1-3

APPLICATIONS: DO DEFINITIONS MATTER?

For those involved in legal matters, the answer is a resounding yes. Consider the matter of James B. Daniels, an attorney before the Union County, New Jersey, Superior Court, whose nonverbal actions earned him a contempt citation. It seems that during early proceedings, he responded to a judge's repeated denial of his motions by shaking his head and smiling. The judge declared his behavior disrespectful and warned him that further displays of disapproval would land him in jail. The attorney apologized, excusing his behavior as "a very human response" and not intended as disrespect. But the next day, when he was overruled again, his reaction prompted the judge to hold him in contempt of court. The ruling was not based on anything the attorney said, but on what he did—"laughing, rolling his head, and throwing himself back in his chair"—all of which was noted in the court records. The attorney appealed the ruling, but it was upheld by the New Jersey Supreme Court. What orientation toward nonverbal behavior is reflected in these rulings?

In another case *(United States v. Arshad Pervez)*, a defendant in a criminal matter was seen on videotape nodding his head while being questioned by undercover agents. The government contended that his nods were an affirmative response that served as a confession of guilt. The defense argued that the nodding should not be construed as a yes but rather as typical of what listeners do during conversation and merely a gesture of attentiveness to what the agents were saying. The defense further claimed that the agents' own behavior, by reinforcing the suspect's listener response pattern, had entrapped him and filed a motion to preclude the agents from giving their interpretation of the nods. If the judge followed a sender orientation, what would the ruling be? How would it differ from receiver and message orientations?

These examples show that the way in which nonverbal communication is defined and the degree to which it is equated with verbal communication can have very real consequences.

Within the domain of human communication, most scholars agree that communication refers to a *dynamic and ongoing process* whereby *senders and receivers* exchange *messages.* Messages originate as sender cognitions that are *encoded* (transformed into signals) by *commonly understood codes* and *decoded* by receivers (the signals must be recognized, interpreted, and evaluated). Formal languages, American Sign Language, and Morse code all meet these requirements. Nonverbal codes, then, must include the same properties.

At this stage, it might seem that defining nonverbal communication is easy. But consider the following possibilities and determine for each whether you think it is a nonverbal message or not:

- wearing one red and one blue tennis shoe
- sneezing
- squinting in bright sunlight and having someone interpret it as a sign of disapproval
- unconsciously signaling depression through a slumped posture
- crying
- breaking out in a rash
- standing close to others because of a hearing impairment

Most or all of these may seem obvious instances of communication to you. To other people, none may qualify. Additional criteria are necessary to resolve the issue.

One way to clarify the matter is to distinguish among the concepts of information, behavior, and communication. Information can be thought of as *all stimuli in the environment that reduce uncertainty for the organism.* That is, information is anything people use to gain predictability about the environment and to guide their behavior. The position of the sun in the sky is information about the time of day, but one would normally not call it a message. After all, the sun did not establish its position for the purpose of signaling to observers what hour of the day it is on earth. It is simply there as an environmental stimulus from which observers can draw inferences and adjust their own behavior. Similarly, a botanist can examine blotches on a leaf and diagnose leaf blight.

Unfortunately, when the source of the information becomes a human, people are inclined to label the inference-making process as communication. For example, a red rash on a child becomes a "nonverbal message" to the doctor that the child has measles, even though the information being gleaned is no different than the leaf blight example. The child does not will the measles into being, nor can it choose to suppress their appearance. Similarly, a sneeze may be symptomatic of an allergy, and a close conversational distance may indicate a hearing problem. In the absence of other knowledge about the situation, these behaviors should be regarded only as information and not as communication. Put differently, the passive or involuntary display of cues that an observer might wish to interpret should be treated only as information and not specifically as communication. To be communication, the behavior must be *volitional* and *other-directed* (targeted to a receiver or receivers). This distinguishes it from what others have labeled informative, expressive, indicative, or incidental behavior (see Andersen, 1991; Bavelas, 1990; Ekman & Friesen, 1969b; Knapp, 1983b, 1984b; Motley, 1990).

This is not to say that communication is not informative, because it is. In fact, all communication is potentially information. But not all information is communication.

Communication is a subset of information rather than synonymous with it. In the same vein, many forms of behavior are informative, but only some qualify as communication. Here the confusion is even more likely, partly because of the perspective that regards any and all nonverbal activity as messages. If one subscribes to this view, there is no need for a separate concept of communication because it is totally redundant with behavior.

It seems more useful to distinguish between the broad category of behavior, which encompasses *any actions or reactions performed by an organism,* and the more specific category of communication. The difference is that behavior can take place without others witnessing it, responding to it, or understanding it. Typically, routine activities such as sleeping and eating would be classified as behavior rather than as communication unless they were done in a manner or context designed to turn them into statements. It is doubtful that a person taking a nap in the privacy of her own home intends to communicate something to an accidental observer; however, if she chooses to do it in the middle of a political science lecture, the publicness and inappropriateness of the act may suggest it is a message. The important point is that not every behavior should be regarded as communication; as with information, *communication is a subset of behavior, which is itself a subset of information.* The relationship is shown in Figure 1-1. This perspective reduces to a manageable level the number of things that qualify as nonverbal communication.

Perspectives: Source, Receiver, and Message

Another helpful distinction in defining nonverbal communication is the general orientation one holds on defining communication. This distinction revolves around issues of *intent, consciousness,* and *awareness.*

Source Orientation   Those who hold a source orientation believe that communication includes only those messages that the source intends to send. Unintended or unconscious messages don't count.

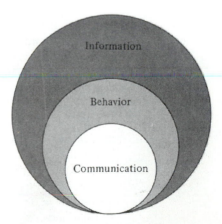

FIGURE 1-1
The relationship among information, behavior, and communication.

The issue of whether communication must be intentional or not is hotly contested (see Andersen, 1991; Kellermann, 1992; Motley, 1986, 1991; Stamp & Knapp, 1990). A major difficulty with this perspective is discerning what is or is not intentional behavior. With verbal communication, one can at least assume an intent to communicate if a person vocalizes or writes something, even if the purpose or meaning of the message itself is unclear. With nonverbal communication, determining intent is much more difficult. As Knapp, Wiemann, and Daly (1978) note:

> Some messages, for instance, are planned and sent with a high degree of conscious awareness; others seem more casually prepared; some messages are designed to look casual or unintentional; still others are more reflexive, habitual, or expressive responses; and some are "given off" rather than "given." (p. 273)

Take the case of the employer who frowns whenever an employee expresses a concern. If she denies frowning, has she communicated nonverbally? The frowning employer would probably say no; the disgruntled employee would probably say yes. And who decides whether she intended to frown or not—the source, the receiver, or some impartial observer? Taking a Freudian approach that says a person's subconscious may intentionally send messages of which the source is unaware is not very satisfying because it casts us all in the role of psychoanalyst, with no one to arbitrate between opposing opinions. As this illustrates, it is easy to disavow intent for much of what goes on nonverbally.

A related problem is that most nonverbal expressions and patterns are well-learned habits that require little forethought or conscious awareness. Just as we apply a car's brakes automatically when approaching a red light, so, too, do we perform numerous nonverbal behaviors without thinking about them. For example, we do not have to remind ourselves consciously to smile and make eye contact when greeting a friend. This low level of awareness of routine communication activity has been called *mindlessness* (Langer, 1989; see also Bavelas & Coates, 1992; Burgoon & Langer, 1995). Mindlessness does not imply that the brain is not engaged, but merely that heavy cognitive involvement is no longer required to perform these habitual communicative acts. This raises the question of whether such activity is intentional communication or not. Intent can readily be claimed when the behavior is first learned, as when a child learns not to bump into people. But whether an adult's avoidance of contact with strangers can then be regarded as a deliberate message or just an ingrained, unconscious habit is less clear. It may be that our larger goals and plans are intentional (strategic) but that the particular behaviors used to achieve them are enacted automatically (Bargh, 1989; Kellermann, 1992). For instance, we may have as a goal making someone else like us but not pay attention to the particular nonverbal behaviors we use to achieve this goal (Palmer & Simmons, 1993).

There are additional problems with trying to identify intent (Knapp et al., 1978). One is timing. During an encounter, we may not be fully aware of our actions but in retrospect may admit that we purposely committed a particular behavior, such as snubbing someone. If questioned at the time of the act, we might deny intent but at a later time concede it. This suggests that a person's own self-report of intent is of questionable value and can vary greatly, depending on when the person is asked. Another problem is that circumstances may alter whether the same behavior is seen as intentional or not. For example, you are more likely to see a "hard sell" in the glad-handing of a used car salesperson than in the same warm handshake from your friend. But if you meet the salesperson at a social event, you are less likely to attribute ulterior motives to his handshake than if you met him on the car lot. Some situations and some people cause us to be more sensitive to intent than others, and we may recognize intent when the communicator does not.

These issues demonstrate that if all behaviors for which a source disclaims responsibility or professes lack of awareness are ruled out as communication, the nonverbal domain may become overly narrow, especially considering how poorly many people monitor their own nonverbal behavior. For this reason, most nonverbal communication scholars find the source orientation unsatisfying.

Receiver Orientation   At the opposite extreme of the source orientation is the receiver orientation, which holds that anything a receiver interprets as a message is communication, regardless of source intent or awareness. This perspective originated with a highly popularized postulate of interpersonal communication that "one cannot not communicate" (Watzlawick, Beavin, & Jackson, 1967), which quickly became interpreted as "all nonverbal behavior is communicative." According to this perspective, accidental and unintended behaviors are included as long as a receiver chooses to read something into them. For example, if a hypersensitive classmate mistakes a squint for a frown and sees it as personal rejection, the receiver orientation would say communication has taken place.

The "one cannot not communicate" postulate has generated considerable debate (see Bavelas, 1990; Clevenger, 1991; Motley, 1990). Although in face-to-face contexts it may be true that our behavior signals whether or not we are willing to interact with another, many find the receiver orientation too broad. From a practical standpoint, we again face the problem of trying to derive some general principles about communication if everything from involuntary and idiosyncratic behaviors (such as allergic sneezing and frequent blinking) to physical traits over which a person has little control (such as short stature and a bowlegged gait) counts, as long as someone draws an inference from them. Imagine, too, our personal discomfort if we truly believed that all of our actions could be "read" by someone. In addition to constantly monitoring our own behaviors, we would have to be on constant alert for signs that a receiver had made something of them. Common sense tells us that not everything we do is a message.

In another respect, the receiver orientation is too narrow. Just as the sender orientation completely neglects the role of the receiver, so the receiver orientation places the decision of what constitutes communication strictly with the receiver, making the sender's role irrelevant. Given that communication entails both sender and receiver, a definition ought to take both parties into account.

Message Orientation   The third perspective is the one we advocate. Called the message orientation (Burgoon, 1980), it defines as communication only those behaviors that form a socially shared coding system. This includes behaviors that (a) are typically sent with intent, (b) are used with regularity among members of a given social community, society, or culture, (c) are typically interpreted as intentional, and (d) have consensu-ally recognized meanings. The operative terms are typically, regularity, and consensually recognized. Behaviors need not be intentional or regarded as intentional every time they are used. But they must be ones that senders routinely select when they wish to encode an intentional message and ones that receivers routinely recognize as constituents of intentionally crafted messages. They should also have a definable set of common inter-pretations associated with them (such as might be found in a dictionary) and be used frequently enough for those meanings to achieve normative status. In short, they should form the lexicon of nonverbal communication. The message orientation forms the foun-dation of the social meaning model of nonverbal behavior (see Burgoon, Buller, Hale, & deTurck, 1984; Burgoon, Coker, & Coker, 1986; Burgoon & Newton, 1991), which pro-poses that many nonverbal behaviors exert direct and powerful influence on others because of the consensual meanings they reflect.

The message orientation is similar to a position advocated by some psychologists over two decades ago. Wiener, Devoe, Rubinow, and Geller (1972) proposed that non-verbal *communication,* as distinct from nonverbal *behavior,* should entail "(a) a socially shared signal system, that is, a code, (b) an encoder who makes something public via that code, and (c) a decoder who responds systematically to that code" (p. 186). Our approach, like theirs, recognizes the need to focus on shared meanings rather than idio-syncratic behaviors. In that respect, it also overlaps with Stamp and Knapp's interac-tion perspective (1990), which holds that meanings are negotiated by both sender and receiver within the context of a particular interaction. The message orientation recog-nizes that meanings depend on both people's perspective and are constrained by con-textual features.

According to this view, an unconscious frown directed toward another could qualify as communication because people often use a frown to express displeasure and people generally interpret a frown as carrying that meaning. That same frown, however, would not qualify as communication if it occurred while a person was working alone and was merely overseen by an onlooker or could be attributed to a person's being "lost in thought." Similarly, the routine and automatic looking at another as one finishes speak-ing would qualify as communication because it is a well-understood, deliberate turn-taking signal that one wishes to relinquish the floor to another. By contrast, if a busboy at the local pizza place wears unmatched tennis shoes, such idiosyncratic behavior is unlikely to produce consistent meaning among observers. It may be informative—we may infer from it that he is a disorganized person or someone who is socially inept—but we probably will not regard this single behavior as communication. However, if it is coupled with other behaviors, such as wearing spiked blue hair and one earring, it may be taken as the busboy's attempt to make a rebellious statement. Thus, a key criterion for deciding if something is communication is whether or not a behavior or collection of behaviors generates consensual meaning.

We find the message orientation most practical for studying nonverbal communica-tion because it sidesteps the trap of trying to discern communicator intent for every action. It also avoids the problem of the relative skill, self-monitoring, and perceptive-ness of communicators in determining whether their behavior qualifies as nonverbal communication or not. The focus instead is on the message itself and what possible meanings might be entailed by a system of behaviors (although individual differences will certainly play a role in what meanings they select among possible alternatives). At a more theoretical level, this perspective also reflects your authors' belief that meanings do reside in behaviors (and texts) rather than in people. Granted, contextual information is often essential to decide which of several meanings to assign to a given behavior, and different communicators will bring different connotations and experience-shaped interpretations to a given behavior, but without some common nonverbal vocabulary and grammar, communication between people would be impossible.

This approach recognizes habitual behavior as part of communication. But it also stipulates that, to qualify as communication, a behavior must be frequently selected by communicators to convey a particular meaning and must be frequently interpreted by recipients or observers as a purposive and meaningful expression. This is what makes it part of a socially shared coding system.

Representations: Signs and Symbols

Another issue is the distinction between signs and symbols. *Signs* are anything that stand for something else and produce at least some of the responses that the referent produces (Anttila, 1972). Used in this general sense, signs include language (linguistic signs). However, for our purposes, it is more useful to limit signs to referents that are *natural and intrinsic representations* of what they signify, as in smoke being a sign of fire. Signs may *index* a relationship between meaning and form. They may be an attribute of a larger substance or process and signal its presence. For example, nonverbal emotional expressions like crying and smiling are outward manifestations of internally experienced feelings or actional tendencies (Buck, 1982). Or they may have an *iconic* relationship with the referent, in which case there is a physical resemblance between the sign and the referent. For example, a sculpture is a highly iconic sign of the person represented; a photograph is a somewhat less iconic version (because it is only two-dimensional). Another term that Cronkhite (1986) preferred to use for these kinds of completely nonarbitrary representations is *symptoms.*

By contrast, *symbols* are *arbitrarily assigned representations* that stand for something else. The word *fire* is an arbitrarily selected label or symbol for the substance of fire (unlike the iconic visual representation on campground billboards). Nonverbal symbols include such things as the hitchhiker's thumbing gesture requesting a ride, the cleric's white collar signifying a religious occupation, and the use of carpeting and wood furniture in corporate offices as a show of status.

Some people have attempted to minimize the communicative value of nonverbal behaviors by claiming that they are not symbolic. Certainly, many nonverbal behaviors are nonarbitrary and better qualify as signs than symbols. Spontaneous emotional expressions and species-wide displays such as threat stares are naturally occurring behaviors that the individual need not learn to produce or interpret. Liska (1986) called some of these behaviors *rituals*—"sign behaviors that are neither totally arbitrary nor totally symbolic" (p. 174). Such things as stylized fear expressions fall somewhere in the middle of the continuum from sign to symbol. What Knapp (1983b) referred to as expressive behaviors and Ekman and Friesen (1969b) referred to as behaviors with intrinsic meaning generally qualify as signs.

Buck (1982) made a useful distinction between our *biologically shared signal system* and our *socially shared signal system.* Biologically based displays (e.g., territorial defense, anger displays, play behavior) fall into the sign category. What sets them apart from symbolic communication is that they are involuntary, spontaneous, and indicative of emotional and motivational content. Conversely, symbolic communication (a) is voluntary and intentional, (b) has an arbitrary relationship between the reference (symbol) and the referent (the thing itself), (c) is part of a socially shared coding system, (d) has propositional content, which means that it is capable of logical analysis and can be declared true or false, and (e) is processed primarily by the left hemisphere of the brain.

While this distinction is helpful in clarifying that some nonverbal behaviors are symbolic and others are not, it does not address adequately the question of posed or controlled emotional expressions. Such expressions as feigned sadness at the death of a despised coworker are deliberate and voluntary, have socially shared meaning, and are propositional in that they can be judged true (honest) or false (deceptive), but they are not arbitrarily concocted expressions. Similarly, the smile originated as a natural expression of pleasure or affection, but the smiling face is also used symbolically to express such nonspontaneous sentiments as approval and congratulations. Moreover, one can take an essentially spontaneous expression and intentionally overintensify it (e.g., the person who gushes over a gift) or deintensify it (e.g., masking one's pleasure at besting an opponent).

Is this gesture a sign or a symbol? Is it a biological signal or a social signal? Can it be both?

Greeting rituals, at the pattern level, are symbolic but usually comprise both socially based signals (e.g., bowing) and biologically based signals (e.g., touching).

Communication Continua: A Dimensional Approach

A more useful approach to defining nonverbal communication may be to place behaviors along continua or dimensions. Nolan (1975), for example, proposed instead that verbal and nonverbal behaviors should be placed along a continuum from highly intentional, deliberate, and conscious to highly unaware and nondeliberate. Nolan referred to this as the degree of *propositionality*. The more propositional the behavior (i.e., consciously and deliberately encoded and expressing a falsifiable statement), the more communicative. Similarly, signs and symbols can be viewed as representing a continuum, a position also advanced by Cronkhite (1986). This is especially useful when we consider larger combinations of cues. While individual behaviors may have originated as natural cues, together they may be symbolic. For example, greeting rituals usually include spontaneous or posed shows of liking, semiautomatic displays of mutual gaze as a show of attentiveness, and socially prescribed forms of handshakes or hugs. The larger pattern is symbolic but comprises a combination of symbolic and nonsymbolic behaviors. Inasmuch as we typically respond to larger patterns rather than single cues, the nonarbitrary origins of individual signs may be irrelevant. What seems to be more important is that both biologically and socially based signals, whether they are signs, rituals, or symbols and have species-or culture-wide recognition, are major vehicles for communication. In fact, it is possible that the biologically based cues, because of their universal use and recognition, may be the more significant in the process of exchanging meaning between humans.

STRUCTURES AND FUNCTIONS OF NONVERBAL COMMUNICATION

The foregoing discussion should clarify somewhat that what we intend to cover as nonverbal communication includes signs and symbols that qualify as potential messages by virtue of regular and consistent use and interpretation. This becomes much more concrete if we consider the specific codes, patterns, and purposes involved.

Structures: Codes and Channels

A code is a set of signals that is usually transmitted via one particular medium or channel. Nonverbal communication codes are often defined by the human sense or senses they stimulate (e.g., the visual sense), the carrier of the signal (e.g., the human body or artifacts), or both. The various codes in combination form the structure of nonverbal communication.

Various systems have been advanced for classifying nonverbal codes and channels. One of the earliest approaches, proposed by Ruesch and Kees (1956), grouped nonverbal cues into three categories. *Sign language* included any type of gesture that replaces specific words, numbers, or punctuation marks—for example, a head tilt signaling the end of a question or holding up five fingers to say "five." *Action language* included all other body movements not used as signs. Running and eating fit this category. *Object language* incorporated the intentional or unintentional display of objects that could act as statements about their user. Everything from the personal appearance, architecture, implements, and organization of space to traces of human activity such as footprints fell under this heading. This classification system has since been discarded, in part because its categories were too gross, grouping dissimilar types of cues; in part because it omitted important facets of nonverbal communication such as vocal behavior and use of time; and in part because it cast the net too broadly in encompassing all manner of unintentional and noncommunicative behavior.

A second approach, offered by Harrison (1974), groups nonverbal communication into four categories. *Performance codes* include all nonverbal behaviors that are executed by the human body—body movement, facial expression, eye gaze, touch, and vocal activity. *Spatiotemporal codes* combine messages based on manipulation of space, distance, and time. *Artifactual codes* include any use of materials and objects to communicate. Clothing and adornment as well as architecture and arrangements of objects fit this category. A final, unique category, *mediatory codes,* is designed to account for the special effects of media when interposed between sender and receiver. For example, the camera angle used in a television commercial adds an extra nonverbal message.

A more common approach to classifying codes (e.g., Burgoon & Saine, 1978; Harper, Wiens, & Matarazzo, 1978; Knapp, 1978; Leathers, 1976; Malandro & Barker, 1983; Rosenfeld & Civikly, 1976) further differentiates them according to the transmission medium and channel used. Typically, body movement, facial activity, and gaze are combined into *kinesics,* or what is known in the popular vernacular as body language. (Some people use a separate category of *oculesics* for eye behavior.) Vocal activity forms another category known as *paralanguage* or *vocalics.* Likewise, touch is treated as a separate code called *haptics.* The use of space, called *proxemics,* and the use of time, called *chronemics,* are also usually given independent status. Finally, *physical appearance* is often separated from the use of *artifacts* (sometimes called *objectics*), and occasionally olfactory-related cues are treated as a separate category called *olfactics.*

The first seven are the ones we will study in this text. Because of their commonalities in appealing to the visual and auditory senses, kinesics, physical appearance, and vocalics will be covered in one chapter. Proxemics and haptics, which are highly interrelated in signaling approach and avoidance, will be covered in a second chapter, and chronemics and artifacts, with their strong influence on context, will be covered in a third.

Although it is necessary temporarily to decompose nonverbal communication into its component structural features, ultimately we must look at the interrelationships among codes if any understanding of nonverbal communication is to be achieved. As Cherry (1957) observed, "The human organism is one integrated whole, stimulated into responses by physical signals; it is not to be thought of as a box, carrying independent pairs of terminals labeled 'ears,' 'eyes,' 'nose,' et cetera" (pp. 127–128). Katz and Katz (1983) likewise noted that each of the nonverbal channels simultaneously sends forth a stream of information, and it is the totality of all the channels, their juxtaposition, and their degree of congruence or incongruence that produces the meaningful pattern. Like many other writers on nonverbal communication, Katz and Katz called for an integrated approach. One way to take an integrated view is to look at how the codes work together to achieve specific communication functions.

Functions: Purposes, Motives, and Goals

Functions are the purposes, motives, and goals of communication. An analysis of functions answers the question What does nonverbal communication do?

Early analyses focused on its subsidiary role to verbal communication. Ekman and Friesen (1969b) proposed five functions that became the popular view of the primary functions of nonverbal behavior. Discussed more fully in Chapter 5, where verbal and nonverbal communication are compared, they include *redundancy* (duplicating the verbal message), *substitution* (replacing the verbal message), *complementation* (amplifying or elaborating on the verbal message), *emphasis* (highlighting the verbal message), and *contradiction* (sending opposite signals of the literal meaning of the verbal message). We can update this perspective on nonverbal communication by considering its fundamental role in the encoding (production) and decoding (interpretation) of verbal messages. On the encoding side, senders rely on nonverbal cues to help them create a total message. Gestures, for example, may "prime the pump," enabling senders to find words they are searching for in memory. Conversely, creating complex verbal messages may impair nonverbal performance. On the decoding side, the use of gestures and vocal punctuation enables receivers to segment and interpret incoming messages. The presence or absence of various nonverbal channels—which occurs with computer-mediated communication, telephone conversations, and teleconferencing—can significantly affect both message production and decoding. The role of nonverbal behaviors in message production and processing is part of Chapter 5's focus on the interrelationships between verbal and nonverbal communication.

But nonverbal behaviors need not be relegated to auxiliary status. Not only do they hold equal partnership with verbal behavior in accomplishing numerous communication functions, they often operate independently in achieving key communication goals. The potential goals or functions they may fulfill are numerous (see Argyle, 1969, 1972a; Burgoon & Saine, 1978; Eisenberg & Smith, 1971; Harrison, 1974; Higginbotham & Yoder, 1982; Patterson, 1983, 1990; Scheflen, 1967; Scheflen & Scheflen, 1972; Sebeok, Hayes, & Bateson, 1964). The functions we will cover in this textbook represent a synthesis of the primary ones that have been identified and studied. Beyond their role in the *production and processing of* verbal messages (see Chapter 6), nonverbal behaviors fulfill functions related to the setting, the actors, the content, the process, and the outcomes of communication.

Before communication even begins, nonverbal cues define the setting. We refer to this as *structuring interaction,* because the nonverbal cues serve as implicit guidelines for how to behave. As discussed in Chapter 7, this function addresses the ways in which nonverbal cues dictate what behavioral programs are expected, what roles people are playing, how formal the interaction is to be, what topics are proscribed, and so forth.

Once people come together, nonverbal cues enable us to determine who the actors are. Twin functions are operative here, one on the encoding side and one on the decoding side. *Identification and identity management* (see Chapter 8) refers to senders' use of nonverbal cues to project self-identity. Part of this process arises from conforming to social norms for one's culture, race, and sex. Stereotypic identities—for example, as a white Anglo-Saxon female, an Arab male, or a black Jew—set expectations that influence greatly how people communicate with one another. Personality, age, and other individual differences likewise are often revealed through nonverbal cues. How receivers make sense of these identities comes under the function of *impression formation* (discussed in Chapter 9). Here the emphasis is on the ways in which receivers use different nonverbal codes and cues to judge other people and the accuracy or inaccuracy of those judgments. This function is sometimes referred to as person perception or first impressions.

Nonverbal cues also form the content of messages. Two functions for which nonverbal communication is especially responsible are *emotional expression and management* (see Chapter 10) and *relational communication and relationship management* (see Chapter 11). We rely heavily on nonverbal cues to express our feelings and emotional states. Sometimes these expressions are controlled or managed; other times, not. The cues that are responsible for these expressions and the accuracy with which emotional messages are sent and received are part of the emotion function. Relational communication encompasses those nonverbal cues people use to define the nature of their interpersonal relationships. Relational messages may convey such things as how much people like each other, how much trust they place in one another, who is dominant and who is submissive, how comfortable they are with each other, and how involved they are in the relationship. As senders, we rely on nonverbal cues to create and maintain the kinds of relationships we desire; as receivers, we rely on them to interpret how others are relating to us.

Nonverbal cues also control the communication process itself by *managing conversations* (discussed in Chapter 12). Nonverbal rituals are used to initiate and terminate interaction. Nonverbal behaviors also regulate turn taking by signaling who has the floor and who wants it, and they are largely responsible for producing smooth, coordinated, rhythmic interactions or awkward ones.

Finally, nonverbal cues are enlisted to achieve important communication outcomes. One outcome we may desire is a favorable image. This function, which focuses on how senders actively alter the image they are projecting, is variously referred to as self-presentation or *impression management.* As discussed in Chapter 13, this function emphasizes how communicators can strategically alter their nonverbal performances to appear credible, attractive, and so forth. The principles of successful and unsuccessful performances that fall under this function are also relevant to another outcome-related function, achieving *social influence* (see Chapter 14). This function includes the ways in which nonverbal behaviors aid or inhibit learning, persuasion, and behavioral change. The last function, *deception* (see Chapter 15), represents a culmination of emotional expression, relational communication, impression management, and social influence principles. Although we typically expect people's communication to be the "truth, the whole truth, and nothing but the truth," much communication falls short of that standard. In this last chapter, we consider how actual deception and suspicion of deception are manifested nonverbally, how receivers use nonverbal cues to make truth and credibility judgments, how accurate those judgments are, and how deceptive interactions are likely to be played out.

Although we have selected the above functions for analysis here, we want to emphasize that these do not represent an exhaustive or even mutually exclusive list. For example, other authors (e.g., Patterson, 1990) propose as two functions *providing information* and *facilitating task and service goals.* The former refers to nonverbal indicative behavior (as opposed to communication). Because such behaviors sometimes become communicative, we do actually address them under the other functional categories. The latter refers to behaviors that might be used in the process of completing some task or service activity—such as the use of touch during physical examinations or golf instruction. Because these are not truly communication, we leave these to other authors to analyze.

ISSUES IN STUDYING NONVERBAL COMMUNICATION

Before closing this introductory chapter, we need to consider a few final issues that affect how we study nonverbal communication. One concerns the various disciplinary perspectives that can inform us. A second is the role of context and circumstance in altering nonverbal patterns. The issue is whether cultural differences and the wide variability of situations in which people find themselves make generalizations impossible. A third issue is the nature of individual differences in the use and interpretation of nonverbal behavior and the extent to which such differences also undermine the ability to generate universal principles. A final related issue is the distinction between what is designated ideal or competent behavior and the behaviors people actually perform. In the age of increasing emphasis on communicator competence, we need to be clear on the use of these terms and their importance in the study of nonverbal communication.

Disciplines and Approaches

Nonverbal communication is not the special purview of the communication field. Several disciplines have examined it, each with its own unique assumptions about human behavior and methods for studying it. Ethology and biology deal with signals common to different species and their contribution to survival value. Physiology and systems analysis examine the physical properties of the encoder, decoder, and channel in facilitating or impeding the transmission and reception of communication signals. Anthropology focuses on the normative and routine nonverbal behaviors exhibited in a culture and how they reveal that culture. Linguistics considers the structure of nonverbal codes and their relationship to verbal language. Psychiatry and psychoanalysis are interested in deviant nonverbal behaviors and how they reveal personality or mental health problems. Sociology addresses how nonverbal patterns reveal something about group and organizational dynamics. And psychology investigates the role of nonverbal cues as cause or effect in the larger study of human behavior.

If nonverbal behavior can be viewed as a crystal, each of these disciplines looks at a different facet of it, and it is through the totality of these perspectives that we can gain the fullest understanding of nonverbal phenomena. These various approaches are discussed in detail in *The Unspoken Dialogue* (Burgoon & Saine, 1978). The important point to recognize here is that the principles to be identified in this text draw at different times on all of these perspectives and their various methods for studying nonverbal behavior. We believe that an eclectic approach will bring the most rapid strides in our knowledge about the processes and products of nonverbal communication.

Although we do attempt to incorporate as much useful information as we can from these different fields, our approach to communication study has the most in common with social psychology, sociology, and linguistics. We subscribe to what Burgoon and Saine (1978) outlined as the functional perspective, which is to say that we are guided by the following assumptions:

1 *The nature of the specific communication function determines the nonverbal behaviors to be observed.* Some nonverbal codes may be irrelevant for some functions (e.g., hairstyle is an unlikely clue to deception).
2 *Every function has situational characteristics.* Certain contexts tend to be associated with certain functions and have associated verbal and nonverbal behaviors. Relational expressions of love, for instance, most often occur in dyadic rather than group situations, and kinesic behaviors are salient to a face-to-face interaction but not to a radio broadcast.
3 *Communication is an ongoing, dynamic process.* A given function rarely begins or ends in a single occasion. Although it is convenient to study episodes that cover a finite period of time, a particular purpose may be influenced by previous events and may have consequences beyond the specific interchange. Moreover, any episode may involve several functions that affect one another and evolve as the transaction unfolds.
4 *A single nonverbal cue may serve multiple functions.* Direct gaze, for example, may express relational involvement while facilitating learning and behavioral change.
5 *A single function may be accomplished through multiple nonverbal cues.* Fear may be expressed vocally, facially, posturally, proxemically, haptically, or through any combination of these channels.
6 *A single function typically requires the coordination of verbal and nonverbal behaviors.* Communication is usually a cooperative venture among several nonverbal channels and the verbal channel. To understand how communication goals are enacted, it is necessary to study how the various codes work together to attain their aim.

7 *Immediate causes of nonverbal behaviors are of greater interest than original causes.* Although causes and effects of a given function transcend a particular time period, the immediate situational features and the behaviors of other participants that might elicit one's own nonverbal behavior are considered more revealing about communication than are initial causes, such as a traumatic childhood.

Contexts and Cultures

For anyone who has traveled abroad, it becomes apparent immediately that many subtle and not-so-subtle differences exist in the ways people communicate in other cultures. Likewise, it is intuitively obvious that the kind of nonverbal communication mandated in the boardroom is inappropriate in the bedroom, and vice versa. Context and culture do make a difference.

The question is, just how large a difference do they make, and do they preclude stating any universal principles? The evidence to date suggests that there are indeed some signals that all members of the human species use and understand. Some of these are reviewed in more detail in Chapters 5 and 10. However, even some of these can be modified by culture (see Figure 1-2). Cultures formulate display rules that dictate when, how, and with what consequences these nonverbal expressions will be exhibited. This

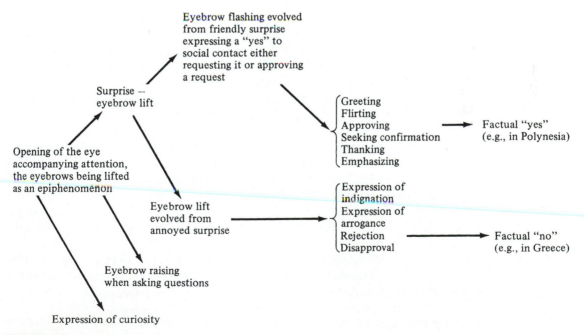

Issues in Studying Nonverbal Communication

FIGURE 1-2
The eyebrow flash appears to be universal, but cultures differ in the meanings they apply to it.

means that even though people the world over might use the same expression for grief in private, their public display may vary greatly. Thus even innate behaviors may appear with differing frequency, interpretations, and degree of social approval across cultures. This does not deny the universality of the behaviors, but it does reduce the ability to make pancultural generalizations about nonverbal communication.

To the extent that cultures hold different social, religious, moral, and political values and patterns for organizing social behavior, their communication patterns may manifest these differences. Gudykunst and Kim (1992), for example, summarized a number of dimensions of cultural variability that will influence nonverbal behavior. Among these, cultures may differ along a *collectivism-individualism* continuum, with some cultures emphasizing the group over the individual and others emphasizing the individual over the group. Cultures may also differ along a *low-context to high-context communication* dimension, with low-context cultures carrying much more of a message's "information" in the coded message itself and those in high-context cultures relying much more on contextual cues and internalized knowledge to make sense of messages. Other differences include such things as degree of *uncertainty avoidance, power distance, masculinity or femininity, orientation toward relationships,* reliance on *diffuse or particularistic judgments* of others, and *instrumental versus expressive interactions.*

These differences are discussed more fully in Chapter 8. What is important to note at the outset of this text is that nonverbal repertoires in one culture may include behaviors not present in another. Mediterranean peoples exhibit far more gestures, for instance, than North Americans. Traditional cultures may use colors and objects in more symbolic ways than technological societies.

Furthermore, cultures may use different behaviors to convey the same meaning (e.g., insult gestures) or use the same gestures to convey different meanings. A prime example is when then vice president Richard Nixon undertook a goodwill tour to Latin America. Photographers at his first airport stop flashed pictures of Nixon holding up both hands in the "A-OK" gesture. Unfortunately, that gesture in many Latin American countries means "Screw you!" Those irretrievable pictures, splashed across the newspapers of several countries, did not do much for international relations.

Despite the apparent diversity, there are many commonalities across cultures in the basic messages, if not the specific forms, of nonverbal communication. What on the surface appear to be fundamental differences may in reality be only superficial variations on the same underlying theme. For example, all cultures have gestures symbolizing death, but each culture may use a different set that reflects the most common means of committing suicide in that culture. To determine commonalities, it is therefore necessary to look more closely at the behaviors in question to see if they are variants from the same class of behaviors.

While the specific nonverbal lexicon may vary from place to place, larger patterns may be consistent across cultures. Acquaintanceship processes, for instance, should all progress through increasing degrees of intimacy, even though the specific intimacy cues used may differ somewhat.

Equally important, many of the differences that can be noted are what Berger (1977) referred to as *irrelevant variety.* There are many interesting differences that actually don't matter as far as communication goes. It doesn't matter, for example, that Euro-

This gesture has meanings ranging from "money" and "OK" to "worthless" to "screw you!"

peans hold their fork one way and North Americans hold theirs another. Before becoming carried away with all the evident variability across cultures, we need to discern what underlying principles operate in each situation and analyze whether these are the same or different for each cultural context.

All of this suggests that nonverbal behaviors cannot be neatly dichotomized as either universal or culture-bound. LaFrance and Mayo (1978a) contended that there are essentially three layers of behavior that range from complete commonality to great dissimilarity:

> The innermost core represents nonverbal behaviors considered to be universal and innate; facial expressions of some emotional states belong to this core. Next come the nonverbal behaviors that show both uniformity and diversity; members of all cultures display affect, express intimacy, and deal with status but the particular signs of doing so are variable. Finally, there are culture-bound nonverbal behaviors which manifest great dissimilarity across cultures—language-related acts such as emblems, illustrators, and regulators show this diversity most clearly. (p. 73)

Beyond the cultural facet of context are other specific features of the situation. These will almost certainly make a difference, but such differences should be systematic and predictable. A task or business setting evokes one set of routines or "scripts" and carries with it a set of assumptions about what is appropriate or inappropriate behavior. A social setting calls forth a different set of appropriate and tolerated behaviors. As long as we can specify the salient features of the situation (e.g., formal or informal, social or task, acquainted or unacquainted, intimate or nonintimate), we should be able to specify regularities in nonverbal behaviors that occur or are expected to occur. For example, even though the greeting ritual with an intimate friend differs from that used with a new business associate, we can predict that each interaction will open with a ritual and that the ritual will fall within certain bounds (e.g., a hug, kiss, or warm handclasp with the friend, a more reserved handshake and no prolonged touching with the business associate).

In sum, the importance of the context in which communication occurs cannot be overstated. Culture and other situational features can alter significantly the patterns of behavior that are observed. However, some of the observed differences are merely superficial and do not represent fundamental differences in function or meaning. And where real differences exist, these are often systematic and predictable. This makes it possible for us to derive quite a few generalizations about nonverbal communication, some of which are discussed in the next section.

Individual Differences

Just as some people believe that situational and cultural diversity makes the study of nonverbal communication impossibly complex, so do they believe that individual differences are too great to make any sense out of it all. It is true that no two individuals are entirely alike in their nonverbal patterns and that the same individual may be changeable from one moment to the next. Moreover, when two or more people are paired together, their joint interaction pattern takes on additional uniqueness. Yet a moment's reflection will reassure us that there must be some consistency in behavior across and within people or we could never carry on a conversation; each encounter would be a new and foreign event.

Our expectations that people will commit certain behaviors and omit others are grounded in the normative or typical behavior patterns for a given class of people. While it may be difficult to say exactly how person A will respond to person B in situation X, it is possible to develop some predictions about how people *like* person A typically respond to people *like* person B in contexts *like* situation X. These predictions are based on the average response pattern of similar people under a given circumstance. If person A is an extrovert and extroverts usually reciprocate direct eye contact, we can anticipate that person A will do the same when person B gazes at A. Our predictions will obviously not be error-free, but imperfect knowledge is better than none and allows us to gain greater control of our environment.

In the past, it has been common to rely on personality traits to explain and predict individual differences. But it may be more productive to shift from the imprecision and poor predictive power of personality variables to an emphasis on skills. As Friedman (1979a) noted, "The concept of nonverbal skill directs attention away from what people are to what they can do interpersonally" (p. 16). Not only can skills be measured more objectively (e.g., a person can be given a percentage correct score on a judgment test), but they also provide a more direct link to actual communication behavior.

The concept of communicator skill appears under many guises—as communicator competence, social competence, social skill, communicator style, expressiveness, empathy, sensitivity, interpersonal orientation, self-monitoring, rapport, and charisma. Typically, three different approaches have been used to assess nonverbal skills: standardized performance measures, individualized performance measures, and self-reports (Riggio, Widaman, & Friedman, 1985). Standardized performance tests present audio and video stimuli about which respondents must make judgments, such as the perceived emotional state, the interpersonal relationship, or the presence of deception. Examples include the Profile of Nonverbal Sensitivity (Rosenthal, Hall, DiMatteo, Rogers, & Archer, 1979), FAST (Ekman, Friesen, & Tomkins, 1971), the Communication of Affect Receiving Ability Test (Buck, 1976, 1979b), and the Interpersonal Perception Task (Archer & Costanzo, 1988; Costanzo & Archer, 1989). In individualized performance tests, respondents usually are videotaped while enacting various emotions, engaging in deceptions, or conducting live interaction; these samples are then assessed by other participants or judges. Sending accuracy scores are obtained for the senders; decoding accuracy scores are obtained for the judges. In self-reports, individuals assess their own nonverbal abilities. Sample measures include the Affect Communication Test (Friedman, Prince, Riggio, & DiMatteo, 1980), the Interpersonal Orientation Measure (Swap & Rubin, 1983), the Communicator Style Measure (Norton, 1983), the Communicator Competency Assessment Instrument (Rubin, 1982), and the Social Skills Inventory (Riggio, 1986). In all, over 100 such measures have been identified (see Spitzberg & Cupach, 1989). Although many of the measures overlap conceptually and empirically (see, e.g., O'Sullivan, 1983; Riggio, 1986; Riggio & Friedman, 1982; Riggio, Messamer, & Throckmorton, 1991), the objective measures that test people's actual ability to send or receive nonverbal cues are not highly correlated with subjective self-report measures (Riggio et al., 1985). Nevertheless, both types of measures have been successful in predicting other behaviors, interpretations, and communication outcomes, so it appears that both can be used to determine communication skills.

Riggio (1992) proposed dividing nonverbal skills into three categories: *expressivity* (or encoding skill), *sensitivity* (decoding skill), and *control* (ability to regulate nonverbal displays). Encoding skills include the ability to send "readable" nonverbal cues of affect, orientation, and intention to others; to integrate and coordinate verbal and nonverbal signals appropriately; and to select and implement communicative acts in a socially appropriate manner. Decoding skills include accurately interpreting nonverbally expressed emotions, interpersonal orientations, and intentions; integrating verbal and nonverbal meanings to detect verbal meanings, sarcasm, joking, and discrepancies; and understanding social contexts and roles (Hall, 1979). Verbal skills can also be divided into parallel dimensions of social expressiveness, social sensitivity, and social control. The three nonverbal dimensions and three verbal dimensions together form the construct "social skill."

Just how important are these social skills? The brief synopsis in Box 1-4 gives some indication. Social skills affect everything from people's ability to make themselves understood to their ability to get along with and influence others. Given this crucial importance in successful nonverbal communication, we will return to the role of nonverbal skills in later chapters. For the moment, however, we can develop a few generalizations about the role of social skills, based on over 100 studies summarized in Buck (1979b), DePaulo and Rosenthal (1979a), Hall (1979, 1984), Knapp (1978), and Rosenthal and DePaulo (1979b):

BOX 1-4

APPLICATIONS: THE SUCCESSFUL COMMUNICATOR

How can you tell if you have the makings of a skilled communicator? Research shows that, in addition to gender, encoding and decoding ability are related to personality, self-esteem, social predispositions, occupation, age, training, verbal elements of academic intelligence, familiarity, and nonverbal style (DePaulo & Rosenthal, 1979a; Friedman, Riggio, & Casella, 1988; Gallaher, 1992; Riggio & Friedman, 1982; Riggio, Throckmorton, & DePaola, 1990; Riggio, Watring, & Throckmorton, 1993; Stinson & Ickes, 1992; Sullins, 1989).

People who are more skilled at nonverbal encoding tend to be extroverted, nonreticent, and physically attractive. They have higher self-esteem, hold a more complex view of human nature, and are less dogmatic. They also are socially participative, have a large social network, and are less lonely. In terms of communication, they are more expressive, animated, and coordinated; their nonverbal behaviors are more novel, intense, complex, changeable, and noticeable; they personalize emo-

tional experiences more often, engage in more self-monitoring, and are more persuasive. They also may be more socially anxious and more likely to seek help.

Decoding skills increase with gregariousness, sociability, experience, age, and training. They decrease as people become more dogmatic. Interestingly, those who see themselves as persuasive may be good at sending nonverbal messages but are not particularly skilled at receiving them, suggesting that more careful listening and observation of others may be warranted.

If you see yourself among the categories of less skilled communicators, take heart. Training and instruction do improve ability. The contents of this book offer much practical information on how you can send the messages you mean to send and how you can more accurately interpret the nonverbal messages of others. If you see yourself among the categories of more skilled communicators, we congratulate you but hope you, too, realize that you can improve your success with more education and experience.

---

1 *There is significant individual variability in encoding and decoding ability.* Some people are very expressive and easily read; others are "opaque." Some people are excellent at accurately interpreting the expressions of others; others are very poor interpreters.

2 *Those who are better encoders tend to be better decoders, and vice versa.* However, the relationship is a modest one. Good encoders are not necessarily good decoders. Although it is often reported that encoding and decoding skills go hand in hand, research findings have actually shown a relatively weak positive correlation (DePaulo & Rosenthal, 1979a).

3 *The various encoding skills are related, as are the various decoding skills.* People who are better at encoding facially tend to be better at encoding vocally, for example, and people who are good at decoding messages of liking and disliking also tend to be more accurate at judging ambivalent messages.

4 *Women are more skilled than men at nonverbal communication.* Women are better encoders of visual cues (especially facial cues) and may be better at sending vocal cues. This difference between men and women is not very pronounced in early childhood but becomes more so past preschool. Women are also better decoders of nonverbal cues, regardless of age and sex of sender. This decoding superiority is greatest for facial expressions, followed by body movements, vocal cues, and brief visual cues. Women are less likely to be more skilled at identifying discrepant or deceptive messages.

Various theories have been advanced for why women are generally more skilled at nonverbal communication. One is that women may be more "accommodating" than men, causing them to attend to the intentional nonverbal messages of others and to not eavesdrop on unintentionally leaked cues. Other plausible explanations are that women's expressiveness is a function of their adherence to learned gender roles; that their social positions give them greater practice than men in observing nonverbal communication because they are more often in passive or submissive roles and because they learn to adopt friendly expressions that appease those in positions of power; that they have an innate advantage; that they have different cognitive styles, possibly including a greater ability to match affects with verbal labels; and that brain lateralization may differ for men and women (e.g., Eagly, 1987; Hall, 1979, 1984; Tucker & Friedman, 1991).

Although women do show a clear and consistent advantage over men in the sending and receiving of visual and auditory cues, the advantage is small (Hall, 1979). Many other factors are important in predicting who will be a skilled communicator. We consider these factors in later chapters.

People's personalities tend to produce parallel encoding and decoding styles (see, e.g., Mehrabian, 1981). Which comes first, skills or personality, is a question yet to be answered. But the answer of which is more useful to us in accounting for individual differences—skills or personality—*is* clear. Focusing on skills replaces the need to look at a multiplicity of personality and demographic variables; it is much simpler and more direct to determine if person A is a skilled encoder or not than to try to assess whether he or she is introverted, anxious, reticent, dogmatic, and so forth, and from those attributes, to infer how the person will communicate.

Of course, identification of communication skills doesn't account for all differences. People also differ in their preferences, goals, and level of motivation, which results in considerable variability from one interaction to the next. As the study of nonverbal communication advances, we should gain greater understanding of how some of these other factors explain individual differences in behavior.

Competence versus Performance

In considering the question of cultural, contextual, and individual differences, a helpful distinction is between the ideal or prescribed behavior, which becomes the standard for competent communication, and people's actual behaviors. If you were to ask people in the United States to describe the basic pattern for turn taking, for example, they would tell you that people speak one at a time; to speak simultaneously is a breach of the "taking your turn" rule. However, if you actually watch people talk, you see lots of interruptions and simultaneous speech.

This is a good illustration of the competence-performance dichotomy. The rule of one turn at a time represents what this culture considers competent behavior. It is the appropriate or preferred way of behaving and is analogous to using grammatical speech. By comparison, people's actual behavior in normal day-to-day interaction may fall short of the ideal because they use colloquialisms and less formal speech. This is not to say that people are incompetent communicators. They may be fully aware of the proper forms of behavior and may be able to produce them on request. But their typical performance deviates from the standard.

This introduces two important considerations. One is that in describing cultural and situational differences, we need to distinguish between the preferred behavior pattern and the normative performance pattern. For example, even though people are expected to avoid certain kinds of personal behaviors, such as twisting hair or rubbing the face during a job interview, they may actually perform these to the same degree that they do in a more private, informal setting. The standards for competent communication differ between the two types of settings, but the actual practice is the same. Conversely, two cultures may both require that subordinates maintain relatively erect posture while listening to a speech by a superior, but one culture may be more lax than the other in adhering to this standard, leading to observed differences in actual performance. Unless it is clear at what level a comparison is being made, this distinction can obscure real similarities and real differences.

The other consideration is that before an individual is classified as lacking communication skills because of a substandard performance, we need to ascertain whether the person knows the proper behavior. It is possible that situational factors are preventing the person from presenting a competent performance or are undermining the person's motivation to do so. Poor performance need not signal incompetence if competence is defined as cognitive knowledge rather than actual practice. If, however, competence is defined as executing the expected behavior at the appropriate time and in the ideal manner, the competence-performance issue is moot. We will try to reserve the term *competence* for cognitive knowledge of the appropriate behavior and to use the expression *competent performance* when the actual performance matches the standard.

SUMMARY

This chapter lays the groundwork for studying the codes, processes, and functions of nonverbal communication. Nonverbal behaviors are an essential part of the communication process. They contribute significantly to the meaning that is extracted from communicative episodes, and they influence communication outcomes. Possible reasons for this impact include nonverbal cues' being omnipresent; forming a sort of universal language system; adding to misunderstanding as well as understanding; expressing what verbal communication cannot or should not; having phylogenetic, ontogenetic, and interaction primacy; and being a trusted system of communication.

Before launching into a detailed study of nonverbal communication, it is necessary to clarify what it entails. A wide range of definitions is possible, some of which use the concepts of information, behavior, and communication interchangeably. In this text, we distinguish among these three. It is also possible to generate different definitions depending on whether one approaches it from a source, receiver, or message orientation. In this text, emphasis is on the third approach, which regards as communication the behaviors that are used with regularity by a social community, are typically encoded with intent, and are typically decoded as intentional. In analyzing these perspectives, we have addressed a number of issues related to intention, awareness, propositionality, and meaning, including whether nonverbal behaviors are signs or symbols. The position advanced here is that the total nonverbal communication system includes a mix of signs and symbols with varying degrees of awareness, volition, and propositionality.

Contributing to that mix of signals are seven nonverbal codes that work together to serve a wide range of communication functions. To gain the fullest understanding of how these codes coordinate with one another and with the verbal code to achieve desired outcomes, the student of nonverbal communication should take into account cultural, contextual, and individual differences. This is the approach that will be followed throughout this text.

SUGGESTED READINGS

Argyle, M. (1967). *The psychology of interpersonal behavior.* Baltimore: Penguin.

Burgoon, J. K. (1980). Nonverbal communication in the 1970s: An overview. In D. Nimmo (Ed.), *Communication yearbook 4* (pp. 179–197). New Brunswick, NJ: Transaction.

Ekman, P., & Friesen, W. V. (1969). The repertoire of nonverbal behavior: Categories, origins, usage, and coding. *Semiotica, 1,* 49–98.

Harper, R. G., Wiens, A. N., & Matarazzo, J. D. (1978). *Nonverbal communication: The state of the art.* New York: Wiley.

Harrison, R. (1974). *Beyond words.* Englewood Cliffs, NJ: Prentice-Hall.

Katz, A. M., & Katz, V. T. (1983). Introduction to nonverbal communication. In A. M. Katz & V. T. Katz (Eds.), *Foundations of nonverbal communication: Readings, exercises and commentary* (pp. xv–xvii). Carbondale: Southern Illinois Press.

Knapp, M. L., & Hall, J. (1992). *Nonverbal communication in human interaction.* New York: Holt, Rinehart and Winston.

Knapp, M. L., Wiemann, J. M., & Daly, J. A. (1978). Nonverbal communication issues and appraisal. *Human Communication Research, 4,* 271–279.

Morris, D. (1985). *Bodywatching.* New York: Crown.

Motley, M. T. (1990). On whether one can(not) communicate: An examination via traditional communication postulates. *Western Journal of Speech Communication, 54,* 1–20.

Ruesch, J., & Kees, W. (1956). *Nonverbal communication: Notes on the visual perception of human relations.* Berkeley: University of California Press.

Scheflen, A. E., & Scheflen, A. (1972). *Body language and social control.* Englewood Cliffs, NJ: Prentice-Hall.

Sebeok, T. A., Hayes, A. S., & Bateson, M. C. (Eds.). (1964). *Approaches to semiotics.* The Hague: Mouton.

Wiener, M., Devoe, S., Rubinow, S., & Geller, J. (1972). Nonverbal behavior and nonverbal communication. *Psychological Review, 79,* 185–214.

VISUAL AND AUDITORY CODES: KINESICS, PHYSICAL APPEARANCE, AND VOCALICS

The dominant organ of sensory and social orientation in pre-alphabet societies was the ear—"Hearing was believing." The phonetic alphabet forced the magic world of the eye. Man was given an eye for an ear. . . . The rational man in our Western culture is a visual man.

Marshall McLuhan and Quentin Fiore

Chapters 2 through 4 introduce the seven basic codes of nonverbal behavior. In this chapter, three codes will be examined: kinesics, physical appearance, and vocalics. Sometimes called performance codes, these three have the greatest impact on visual and auditory senses and are often what people initially think of as nonverbal communication. In Chapter 3, approach-avoidance codes—proxemics and haptics—will be considered, and in Chapter 4 you will see how time, artifacts, and environments can be used to send messages and influence communication. The origin and acquisition of each code, its structural features or code elements, its potential for communication, and norms and standards for its use will be discussed.

Although nonverbal communication is broken into seven distinct codes, codes typically do not operate alone. Discussing them as separate entities is a matter of convenience and tradition, as well as a way of providing a foundation for understanding the processes and functions of nonverbal communication.

KINESICS

The eyes of men converse as much as their tongues, with the advantage that the ocular dialect needs no dictionary, but is understood the world over.

Ralph Waldo Emerson

The term *kinesics* derives from the Greek word for "movement" and refers to all forms of body movement, excluding physical contact with another's body. The popular expression *body language* is almost exclusively concerned with this code. Kinesics is one of the richest of the nonverbal codes, due in part to the large number of possible human body actions:

1 An estimated 700,000 different physical signs can be produced by humans (Pei, 1965).
2 Birdwhistell (1970) estimated that the face is capable of producing 250,000 expressions.
3 Physiologists have estimated that the facial musculature is capable of displaying 20,000 different expressions (Birdwhistell, 1970) (not as large as the previous estimate but nonetheless impressive).
4 Krout (1935, 1954a, 1954b) observed 7,777 distinct gestures in classroom behavior and 5,000 hand gestures in clinical situations.
5 Hewes (1957) reported that 1,000 steady human postures are possible.

This list highlights the large encoding potential of kinesics. When one considers that a person displays more than a single behavior at any instance in an interaction, the many different messages that can be sent by this code are truly enormous. For example, how many ways can you think of to show someone you approve of something he or she has just done? You might engage in a very brief, almost imperceptible head nod or nod your head vigorously. You might smile or combine head nodding and smiling. You might even choose to be more enthusiastic by using arm movements, such as shaking both arms with your hands clenched in fists. All these actions can signal approval to the other person, although each transmits a slight variation on that meaning.

The human capacity to receive kinesic messages is also large. Observers can distinguish movements as short as 1/50 of a second. However, the multiplicity of meanings associated with kinesic behaviors often results in confusion. Box 2-1 provides an amusing example of this.

Origins and Acquisition of Kinesics

When discussing the origin and acquisition of a nonverbal code, it is necessary to consider both the evolution of the act in humans and the development of the behavior in children. The famous biologist Charles Darwin was one of the first scholars to become interested in the evolutionary origin of kinesic behavior. In his book *The Expression of the Emotions in Man and Animal,* Darwin (1965) noted similarities between emotional expressions of humans and those of primates and other lower animal forms. It was his belief that in the development of humans, facial expressions were programmed into the brain due to their importance to survival. For example, closing the eyes, flaring the nostrils, expelling breath, and extending the tongue in the disgust expression were useful in protecting early humans from harmful things in the environment such as rotten food.

Another kinesic behavior that has innate origins is tongue showing (Smith, Chase, & Lieblich, 1974). When people are intensely involved in activities requiring concen-

---

BOX 2-1

A ZEN PARABLE

In a temple in the northern part of Japan two brother monks were dwelling together. The elder one was learned, but the younger one was stupid and had but one eye.

A wandering monk came and asked for lodging, properly challenging them to a debate about the sublime teaching. The elder brother, tired that day from much studying, told the younger one to take his place. "Go and request the dialogue in silence," he cautioned.

So the young monk and the stranger went to the shrine and sat down.

Shortly afterward the traveler rose and went in to the elder brother and said: "Your young brother is a wonderful fellow. He defeated me."

"Relate the dialogue to me," said the elder one.

"Well," explained the traveler, "first I held up one finger, representing Buddha, the enlightened one. So he held up two fingers, signifying Buddha and his teachings. I held up three fingers, representing Buddha, his teachings and his followers, living the harmonious life.

Then he shook his clenched fist in my face, indicating that all three come from one realization. Thus he won. . . ." With this, the traveler left.

"Where is that fellow?" asked the younger one, running in to his elder brother.

"I understand you won the debate."

"Won nothing. I'm going to beat him up."

"Tell me the subject of the debate," asked the elder one.

"Why, the minute he saw me he held up one finger, insulting me by insinuating that I have only one eye. Since he was a stranger I thought I would be polite to him, so I held up two fingers, congratulating him that he has two eyes. Then the impolite wretch held up three fingers, suggesting that between us we only have three eyes. So I got mad and started to punch him, but he ran out and that ended it!"

Source: Sohl & Carr, 1970, pp. 3–4.

---

tration, when the interaction contains negative characteristics such as a reprimand, or when communicators feel a loss of physical control or stress, they tend to display their tongue. Smith et al. reported that other primates such as gorillas and orangutans show their tongues under similar conditions.

Studies of infants provide evidence for innate development of kinesic behavior. Newborns display many kinesic reflexes. Among the most important are innate, genetic facial expressions (Andersen, Andersen, & Landgraf, 1985; Barrett, 1993; Buck, 1981; Camras, 1980a, 1982; Camras, Sullivan, & Michel, 1993; Ekman, 1978; Ekman & Friesen, 1969b; Izard, 1979; Johnson, Ekman, & Friesen, 1975; Saarni, 1982; Shennum & Bugental, 1982; Trevarthen, 1984). These expressions are similar to adult expressions and are linked directly to emotional states. Two important expressions in this newborn period relate to distress or anger and positive feelings (Camras et al., 1993; Emde, 1984). The infant very quickly learns to emit these expressions in response to other people and to use these expressions to control others' behaviors (Argyle & Cook, 1976; Cappella, 1981; Denham & Grout, 1993; Saarni, 1982; Stern, 1980; Trevarthen, 1984).

Another important reflex is the imitation of face and head movements by newborns in the first months of life. This imitation is innate and requires little cognitive function (Bjorklund, 1987). Imitation of facial gestures helps newborns to maintain social interaction with adults, in the period before their abilities to control gaze, head, and mouth movements develop. Once these other kinesic movements arise, the imitation reflex is no longer useful and declines. This reflex also may help newborns learn to integrate information from different senses; this is referred to as intermodal matching (Bjorklund, 1987; Meltzoff & Moore, 1989). That is, newborns practice matching the visual information gained from seeing adult gestures with the internal feelings received from the movement of face and head muscles as the newborns imitate these perceived gestures.

Gestures originate at a very early age (Davidson, 1950; Wood, 1981). The pointing gesture is an important early behavior, usually emerging in the first year. It provides the child with a bridge between prespeech and one-word utterances. In fact, adults are less likely to respond to this pointing gesture as the child acquires more language skills (Hannan, 1992). Children use pointing to name or express interest in an object. The normal behavioral pattern is for the child to first look at the receiver and then point, as if the child is first checking to see that the receiver is paying attention (Hannan, 1992).

Symbolic gestures that are used to communicate seem to develop with language (Bates, Thal, Fenson, Whitesell, & Oakes, 1989). Gestures develop about a month earlier than language production, because they are more visible to the child, easier for adults to guide, and arise from more well-rehearsed sensorimotor behaviors than language (Goodwin & Acredolo, 1993). Blake and her colleagues (Blake & Dolgoy, 1993; Blake, McConnell, Horton, & Benson, 1992) reported that during the transition to language, comment and request gestures increased while emotive and reach-request gestures decreased.

Gestures continue to develop in the first 5 years of life. Age 4 appears to be an important developmental period. Prior to this time, children use more body-part gestures, like describing toothbrushing by extending the forefinger and rubbing it back and forth along the front teeth. After age 4, children switch to imagery-object gestures, such as clenching the hand to the side of the mouth and moving it back and forth as if it is holding a toothbrush (Boyatzis & Watson, 1993).

Table 2-1 summarizes some of the key encoding and decoding abilities that emerge in the first year.

Eye contact, too, has innate properties. Within a few days of birth, infants engage in eye contact and appear to fixate on the caregiver's eyes (Argyle & Cook, 1976; Roedell & Slaby, 1977). Interestingly, the distance at which newborns focus best is the distance from the infant to the mother's eyes when breast-feeding. At this very young age, it is likely that the child's gaze is more a signal of attention than any more complex social message (Stechler & Latz, 1966). Further, eye gaze from others innately arouses infants. Argyle and Cook reported that in the weeks immediately after birth, simply seeing the eyes of a caregiver is sufficient to produce a smiling reaction. Finally, eye contact is necessary for proper maturation of infants. The lack of mutual gaze harms infant interaction and perceptual and social development (Andersen et al., 1985; Robson, 1967).

Not all kinesic behaviors displayed by adults and children are innate. Many are learned through environmental and social experiences. Ekman and Friesen (1969b; also Ekman, 1976; Ekman & Friesen, 1972; Johnson et al., 1975) have suggested that some behaviors, though not innate, arise from experiences that all humans acquire through interacting with any environment. They provide two examples: all humans eat with their hands, and all humans have witnessed death. Thus almost all people possess kinesic behaviors representing eating and dying.

However, many of these behaviors show differences across cultures that reflect experiences that vary from culture to culture. For example, Hewes (1957) documented dif-

TABLE 2-1
DEVELOPMENT OF KINESIC AND VOCALIC ENCODING AND DECODING ABILITIES

First Week	1 to 3 Months	4 to 6 Months	7 to 9 Months	10 to 12 Months
Kinesics				
Reflexively opens and closes eyes. Grasp reflex. Reflexively responds to sudden noise. Smiles spontaneously to soft sounds or other sensory stimuli.	Smiles, stares at faces and voices. Smiles and grunts differently to mother than others. Visually follows a moving person. Shows distress, delight, excitement. Makes eye contact. Calmed by a face. Moves arms and legs.	Discriminates faces from other patterns. Differentiates among faces. Expresses emotions of fear, disgust, anger. Tries to imitate facial expressions. Smiles, tries to pat other children.	Begins imitating human behaviors. Begins to point with index finger. Develops manual coordination, ability to stand.	Imitates facial expressions, gestures, and movements of adults and other children. May stand and wave. Displays moods and preferences, emotions of anger, happiness, sadness, discomfort. Recognizes emotions in others.
Vocalics				
Cries often. Makes animal-like sounds. Distinguishes pitch and loudness. Prefers high-pitched voices. Tries to focus on voices, aware of their location.	Attentive to voices. Recognizes parent's voice. Can distinguish speech sounds. Develops cooing and vowel-like sounds. Vocalizes frequently. Calmed by voices. Expresses excitement. Crying begins to diminish.	Begins to babble (syllable-like sounds). Squeals and coos when talked to. Laughs, giggles. Expresses pleasure and displeasure. Imitates different tones. Vocalizes to initiate socializing. May use vocalizations to interrupt conversations.	Imitates sounds, sound sequences, and intonations. Listens to own vocalizations. Alert to repetitive sounds. Shouts for attention.	Imitates vocal rhythms and inflections better than speech sounds. Controls intonations.

Source: Adapted from Caplan, 1973.

ferences across cultures in common sitting and standing postures that he said are a product of the conditions and tools present in a culture (e.g., the chair-sitting posture in the United States differs from the deep squat common in parts of Asia and Africa, indicating the lesser importance of chairs in the latter regions; see Figure 2-1). Other behaviors that appear to be culture-specific include forms of greeting and parting rituals, occasions for and degree of facial expression usage, and kinesic turn-taking behaviors, to name only a few. Many behaviors are specifically taught by older members of the culture to infants and children. Others are learned through conscious or unconscious imita-

FIGURE 2-1

Posture types from the classification scheme of Hewes. The figures numbered 301 through 306 (top row) are common resting positions; the arm-on-shoulder postures of the next four figures are found mainly among western American Indians. In the next row are variations of the one-legged Nilotic stances, found in the Sudan, Venezuela, and elsewhere. Chair sitting (third row) spread from the ancient Middle East, but the Arabs there have replaced it with floor sitting.

tion. Either way, by school age, children appear to possess a rich repertoire of kinesic behaviors.

Acquisition of nonverbal behaviors continues into the elementary school years as children learn to use the behaviors in socially acceptable ways. Improvements in the performance of facial expressions continue into late elementary school age, when ability stabilizes (Barrett, 1993; Buck, 1977; Denham & Grout, 1993; Ekman, Roper, & Hager, 1980; Odom & Lemond, 1972). At the same time, children learn display rules for the use of these expressions and the ability to mask or inhibit facial expressions (Barrett, 1993; Saarni, 1979, 1982; Shennum & Bugental, 1982), as well as how to use a facial expression symbolically to transmit an emotion that is not felt (Morency & Krauss, 1982; Moyer, 1975). Mothers are children's "expert" tutors in emotional expressions. The affective environment created by mothers, their role as models of expressive behavior, and their responsiveness, especially to children's expressions of distress, are particularly important influences on the socialization of emotional expressions (Denham & Grout, 1993). Finally, many kinesic turn-taking behaviors improve during this period (Andersen et al., 1985).

Thus kinesic behavior is acquired in three ways:

1 From innate neurological processes passed on genetically and developed through evolution.
2 From experiences common to all humans as they interact with the environment.
3 Through culture-specific tasks and social interactions that produce experiences that vary across cultures, subcultures, and individuals.

Before leaving this discussion of origins and acquisition, we must comment on the other side of the process: recognition of kinesic behavior. The ability to recognize kinesic behavior is partly innate and develops rapidly during the first year of life. Orienting gaze toward others appears very early in a newborn's life (Argyle & Cook, 1976). Infants as young as 72 hours imitate adults' tongue protrusions and head movements (Meltzoff & Moore, 1989), imitate facial gestures as early as 2 months (Bjorklund, 1987), and between the ages of 6 weeks and 3 months begin smiling in response to other faces (Stern, 1980), suggesting an ability to decode face and head cues during this period. By 3 months infants recognize familiar faces. Recognition of affect displays also comes quickly (Andersen et al., 1985; Odom & Lemond, 1972). In general, the ability to decode kinesic cues increases with age, peaking during the teens (Buck, 1981; Camras, 1977, 1980b; Hamilton, 1973; Honkavaara, 1961; Hoots, McAndrews, & Francois, 1989; Morency & Krauss, 1982; Odom & Lemond, 1972; Pendleton & Snyder, 1982; Rosenthal et al., 1979; Zabel, 1979).

Classifying Kinesics

In response to the vast number of kinesic behaviors, classification methods have been developed to make the study of kinesics more manageable. Two ways of classifying behaviors have been used, focusing on structure or function.

Birdwhistell's Structural Approach   The system developed by Birdwhistell (1970) is by far the most elaborate and famous example of a structural approach. In his system,

Birdwhistell sought to identify discrete, universal kinesic behaviors that are combined to produce nonverbal communication. He referred to it as the linguistic-kinesic analogy because it is modeled after the linguistic classification system that distinguishes discrete units of language behavior like phonemes and morphemes. Phonemes are units of sound in human speech, and morphemes are combinations of phonemes, like words and sentences, that carry meaning. Birdwhistell reasoned that since kinesics appear to be tied to speech, they should exhibit similar structures as language.

In Birdwhistell's extensive system, the smallest meaningful unit of behavior is a *kineme*. Birdwhistell identified 50 to 60 kinemes that he considered culturally universal. That is, cultural differences in kinesic behavior come from variations within kinemes, not from the use of different kinemes. Birdwhistell divided the body into eight regions: total head; face; trunk; shoulders, arms, and wrists; hand and finger activity; hips, legs, and ankles; foot activity (including walking); and neck. Figure 2-2 shows his notation system for expressions in the face region alone.

Kinemes actually comprise behaviors that are recognizable in a culture but do not possess unique meaning. These are known as *kines*. Variations in the intensity, duration, or extent of these behaviors are called *allokines* or *kine variants*. For example, although trained observers have noted as many as 23 different eyelid positions (Birdwhistell himself claimed to observe 15), only four positions appear to change the meaning. Thus muscular adjustments of the eyelid around these four kineme positions are considered allokinic. Other groups of allokines are based on the side of the body used to display the kines. Winks by the left and right eye can be considered allokines, as can movements by left and right forefingers. The test is whether it makes a difference which side of the body displays the kine. If it does not, the kines are allokines.

When used, kinemes are combined into *kinemorphs,* which are similar to words in the linguistic system. Kinemorphs are grouped by classes and often occur in concert with other kinemorphs to produce complex kinemorphic constructions similar to sentences. It is at the level of kinemorphic constructions that the meaning of kinesic behavior becomes fully understandable. For instance, if you want to comfort a distraught friend, you might lower your head, lower your eyelids slightly, and lean your body in her direction. These behaviors singly and separately may not communicate sympathy, but displayed together, they indicate your compassion and understanding.

Additional behaviors classified by Birdwhistell include kinesic *markers, stress,* and *juncture.* Kinesic markers are movements that occur with or stand for syntactic arrangements in speech. Markers can stand for pronouns, indicate pluralizations, mark verbs, designate area, and indicate the manner of events. Kinesic stress includes movements that occur regularly, marking special linguistic combinations such as clauses, phrases, and adjectives with nouns. Four levels of stress are *primary stress* (strong movements), *secondary stress* (weak movements), *unstressed* (normal flow with speech), and *destress* (reduction of kinesic behavior below normal). Finally, kinesic junctures are behaviors that serve to connect or separate kinesic phenomena, such as a slight lengthening of movement at the end of a complex kinemorphic stream.

Functional Approaches to Classifying Facial Expressions and Gestures   An alternative approach, originally introduced by Ekman and Friesen (1969b) and now favored

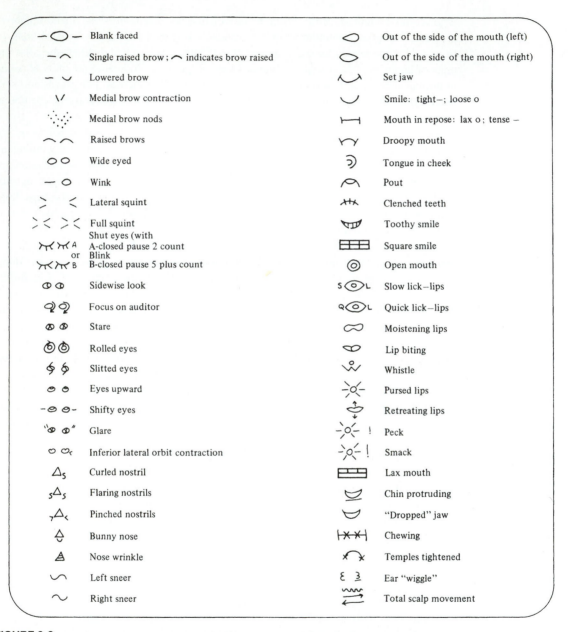

FIGURE 2-2
Birdwhistell's notation symbols for facial kinemes.

by many nonverbal researchers, is to focus instead on the functions of kinesic behaviors. This approach considers what the behaviors *do*. Ekman and Friesen's system divides kinesics into five categories—emblems, illustrators, regulators, affect displays, and adaptors—each performing different functions or displaying different meanings. These categories are not mutually exclusive. A single gesture, for example, may do more than one thing at the same time.

Emblems are kinesic behaviors that meet the following criteria (Ekman, 1976; Ekman & Friesen, 1969b):

1 They have a direct verbal translation and can be substituted for the words they represent without affecting the meaning.
2 Their precise meaning is known by most or all members of a social group.
3 They are most often used intentionally to transmit a message.
4 They are recognized by receivers as meaningful and intentionally sent.
5 The sender takes responsibility for them.
6 They have clear meaning even when displayed out of context.

As noted in Box 2-2, the form and meanings of particular emblems differ from culture to culture, but emblems serve the same functions in all cultures.

Common American emblems include palms turned up and lifted shoulders meaning "I don't know," running an extended forefinger across the front of the neck meaning "Stop what you are doing," and outstretched arm with waving hand meaning "Hello."

Illustrators (also called gesticulations) are kinesic acts accompanying speech that are used to aid in the description of what is being said, trace the direction of speech, set the rhythm of speech, and gain and hold a listener's attention. They may accent, complement, repeat, or contradict what is being said. Ekman and Friesen isolated eight types of illustrators: *batons* emphasize a phrase or word, *ideographs* draw the direction or path of thought, *deictic movements* point to an object, *spatial movements* show a spatial relationship, *kinetographs* display a bodily action, *pictographs* sketch a picture of the refer-

---

BOX 2-2

APPLICATIONS: EMBLEMS AND THE SAVVY TRAVELER

When visiting another culture, you may be struck by the fact that some emblems help you bridge communication difficulties while others add confusion. Paul Ekman and his colleagues (Ekman, 1976; Ekman & Friesen, 1969b, 1972; Friesen, Ekman, & Wallbott, 1979; Johnson et al., 1975) reported that emblems are common in every culture. Some cultures, like middle-class U.S. culture, have less than 100 emblems, while others, like Israeli student culture, have over 250 emblems. Luckily for you, some emblems carry cross-cultural meaning. Ekman reported that emblems perform six functions in all cultures: (a) insulting others, (b) giving interpersonal directions ("come here" or "be quiet"), (c) greeting others, (d) signaling departure, (e) replying positively or negatively to requests, and (f) commenting on physical or emotional states. Further, all cultures seem to use emblems in similar places in conversations—at the beginning or end of a turn, in filled pauses, and preceding or accompanying the words they repeat. Emblems such as those deriving from facial affect displays carry common meaning across cultures. Other emblems, such as eating and drinking emblems, bear some cross-cultural similarity because they arise from common experiences with the environment. However, most have unique meanings in each culture.

If you like, turn to Figure 8-1 and see if you know what each emblem means. If you want to avoid embarrassment when traveling abroad, you should learn in advance what that culture's emblems mean and what emblems might be misread as insults.

ent, *rhythmic movements* show timing or rhythm of an event, and *emblematic movements* repeat or substitute for words in illustrating the spoken words. Some researchers (e.g., Hadar, 1989) distinguish between those illustrators that are tied to the rhythm of speech and those that are tied to its content. The former may be referred to as motor movements and the latter as lexical movements.

Regulators are kinesic behaviors designed to maintain or regulate turn taking between two or more interactants. They are the "traffic cops" of conversation. Rather than comment on the verbal stream, they coordinate and pace the flow of conversation. These behaviors are learned at a very early age, displayed at a low level of awareness, and produced almost automatically. We discuss these cues at great length in Chapter 12.

Affect displays reveal emotions. In their extensive work in this area, Ekman and Friesen identified a number of universal emotions that are tied to neurological processes. Emotional expressions may be intentional or unintentional, accompany speech or stand alone, and transmit true emotions or be used symbolically, like emblems. These affect displays are discussed more fully in Chapter 10.

Adaptors are behaviors that satisfy physical or psychological needs. They have their origins early in life. Adaptors satisfy personal needs (e.g., need for comfort), respond to internal states (e.g., anxiety, relaxation, perceptions of crowding, feelings of submissiveness or defensiveness), perform bodily functions, structure the body's external aspect, shield the individual from interfering stimuli, manage emotions (e.g., discomfort, guilt), maintain interpersonal contact and personal image, and complete instrumental activities (D'Alessio & Zazzatta, 1986; McBrayer, Johnson, & Purvis, 1992). Because they are designed to help the individual adapt to stresses and needs, adaptors are habits that usually are not intended to communicate. However, they can be quite informative about the sender's internal state and occasionally are used with intent as an insult or message of disrespect.

There are three types of adaptors—*self-adaptors, alter-directed adaptors,* and *object adaptors*—distinguished by the target of the behavior. Scratching your arm, playing with your hair, or picking your nose are self-adaptors. Alter-directed adaptors are movements related to interpersonal contacts. When nervous about talking with someone, you might cross your arms on your chest to protect against the other communicator or release anger by swiping at someone. Finally, object adaptors involve the manipulation of objects in the environment, such as tapping a pencil or smoking a cigarette.

A more recent functional approach introduced by Bavelas and colleagues (Bavelas, 1994; Bavelas, Chovil, Lawrie, & Wade, 1992; Bavelas, Hagen, Lane, & Lawrie, 1989) focuses specifically on symbolic gestures used during conversation. As shown in Table 2-1, *conversational gestures* can be divided into *topic gestures*—ones that relate to the content itself—and *interactive gestures*—ones that function to distinguish true dyadic interaction from monologues. Speakers use interactive gestures within their speaking turn to refer to receivers, so they feel included in the dialogue, without speakers giving up their turn. They may use them to ask receivers to fill in an unstated part of the message, figuratively hand over the speaking turn, indicate that a receiver's question is being answered, refer to a previous topic, signal a word search, request agreement from the receiver, or mark a rhetorical question. Interactive gestures occur more frequently in face-to-face interaction than when the receiver is not visually available or when people

Adaptors are behaviors that satisfy the same physiological and psychological needs. Which kinds of adaptors are present on the left and on the right? What needs do they satisfy?

are alone, evidence that they are more oriented to the receiver than to the content of the message.

The relationship of these gestures to the Ekman-Friesen system is identified in Table 2-1.

Approaches to Classifying Eye Behavior   Eye behavior is one of the most important facets of kinesic behavior. The eyes are used to perform many of the same functions as other kinesic behaviors, including expressing interpersonal attitudes or emotions, regulating interactions, signaling attention, and producing anxiety or arousal in another person (Argyle & Cook, 1976). Eye behavior does have a special function—to gather information from others (Argyle & Cook, 1976; Rutter, Pennington, Dewey, & Swain, 1984; Rutter & Stephenson, 1979; Rutter, Stephenson, Ayling, & White, 1978).

While eye behavior has been the subject of a good deal of research, very few systems identifying the units of eye behavior exist. Von Cranach and Ellgring (1973) proposed a structural system based on the length, direction, duration, and reciprocation of gaze. For these authors, a *one-sided look* is a gaze in the direction of the partner's face

TABLE 2-1
THE BAVELAS (1994) FUNCTIONAL APPROACH TO CLASSIFYING GESTURES

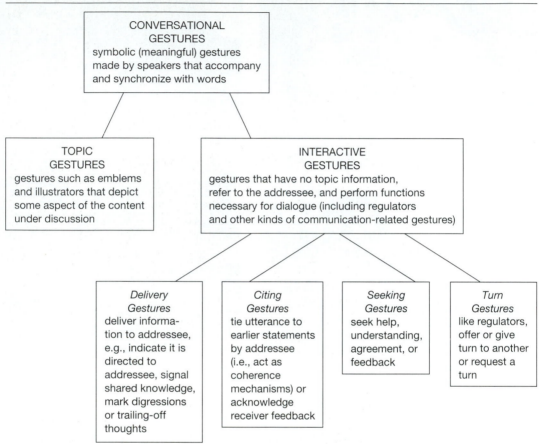

that is not reciprocated by the partner. There are two types of one-sided looks: *face gaze* (unreciprocated gaze at the partner's face) and *eye gaze* (unreciprocated gaze at the partner's eyes). Gaze by both partners directed at each other's faces is considered a *mutual look,* whereas gaze by both partners directed at each other's eyes that both partners are aware of is *eye contact.* Finally, *gaze avoidance* occurs when one partner intentionally avoids the other partner's eyes, and *gaze omission* happens when a partner fails to look at the other person without intent to avoid eye contact.

Rutter and his colleagues (Rutter et al., 1984; Rutter & Stephenson, 1979; Rutter, Stephenson, Ayling, & White, 1978) distinguished *looking* and *eye contact* on the basis of their functional nature. Looking is face gaze or mutual gaze intended to discover how the partner is reacting to the communication. Eye contact is mutual gaze with no need for information. As yet, Rutter's distinctions have not been adopted extensively by other scholars; however, his research suggests that this distinction is useful for classifying eye behavior (Rutter et al., 1984).

Kinesic Norms and Expectations

Although individual variability exists, kinesic behaviors are highly normative at the cultural and subcultural level. To identify norms of behavior, it is essential to understand the background against which the behavior is performed—characteristics of the persons involved, their relationship, and the context. Allport and Vernon (1937) identified 11 personal characteristics that influenced the selection and frequency of behaviors: personality, sex, race and culture, age, body deformities, health, metabolic or structural peculiarities, body type, strain or fatigue, transitional emotional states or moods, and special habits from unique training (athletic or dramatic training). Individual goals should also be added to this list. You can no doubt come up with many examples of how these variables might influence the choice of kinesic behaviors and the perceptions of kinesic norms. Chapter 8 is devoted to a discussion of cultural, racial, gender, and personality characteristics because of their impact on how we communicate nonverbally.

The relationship between the communicators has a major effect on kinesic norms and usage. How well two people like each other and the degree to which they have equal or unequal status will affect what kinesic patterns are normative and preferred. In newer relationships, interactants are more likely to misinterpret the meaning of a kinesic cue, especially if it is used in an unusual way by the relational partner. The longer people are in a relationship, the more likely they are to negotiate a definition specific to that relationship (Miller & Steinberg, 1975), thus the less likely outside persons or groups are to determine the norms.

Another consideration is the purpose of the interaction. Interactions can be distinguished loosely as task-oriented or social-oriented and as formal or informal. Each calls for a different set of kinesic behaviors. Many behaviors are determined by the norms of a culture or social group; these can be labeled conventions.

Finally, environmental features place constraints on what kinesic patterns emerge. For instance, emblems are more likely to be displayed when noise or distance blocks verbal communication (Ekman, 1976). A more extended discussion of this is presented in Chapter 7.

The people characteristics, relationship variables, and context factors combine to produce variability in the use and interpretation of kinesic cues. This is not to say that predictable, consistent patterns are always evident, but the interrelationship of these factors produces a complex system where no behavior exists in isolation. With this qualification in mind, let us examine the norms and standards for each of Ekman and Friesen's kinesic categories.

Emblems   We noted earlier that emblems serve the same functions in all cultures. Unfortunately, many emblems have meaning only for members of a particular culture. Generally, this simply means that the person to whom you are communicating may not understand your meaning when you use an emblem from your home culture. Among the more complete catalogues of emblems used in a wide variety of cultures are Morris, Collett, Marsh, and O'Shaugnessy's *Gestures* (1979) and Morris's *Bodytalk* (1995).

Many groups, like businesses and professions, also develop their own emblems that improve communication among their members. These emblems carry meaning only among members of these groups and knowing these emblems identifies you as a group member. For example, Davidson (1950) documented emblems used by grain traders on the floor of the Chicago Board of Trade. The noise and chaos made verbal communication almost impossible, so traders indicated their intentions through emblems: palm of hand held up and inward ("buy"), palm of hand held outward ("sell"), fingers held vertically to indicate quantities traded (5,000 bushels per finger), fingers held horizontally to indicate price (1/8 cent per finger). Emblems were also used to identify the brokerage house.

Illustrators   Norms of illustrator usage have not been well documented, although it is evident that some cultures and subcultures are more "illustrative" than others. Exaggerated and stylized gestures used to be more common among actors and public speakers. At the turn of the century, the Del Sartre School of Oratory believed that particular forms and loci of gestures would dictate particular meanings. In more recent years, public speakers have gained more flexibility in the illustrators they use. Guerrero (1994) reported that illustrators and overall animation were higher in conversations between same-sex friends than between opposite-sex friends or romantic couples. Both same-sex and opposite-sex friends nodded more than romantic couples.

Regulators   Regulator behaviors are the most rule-governed of all kinesic behaviors and are usually displayed automatically in interactions. One regulator for which norms have been investigated is eye behavior. The following facts have been established (Ellsworth & Ludwig, 1972; Kendon, 1967, 1978):

1 The normal amount of gaze in an interaction ranges from 28 percent to 70 percent of the time.
2 Under stress conditions, the range broadens to from 8 percent to 73 percent of the time.
3 Eye contact increases when listening (30 percent to 80 percent of the time) and decreases when speaking (25 percent to 65 percent of the time).
4 Individuals are consistent in their looking patterns.
5 Interactants coordinate their looking patterns.
6 Gaze aversion is more frequent when discussing difficult topics, when uncertain, or when ashamed.
7 Sex, race, and personality affect the amount of eye contact.

Not all gaze serves a regulatory function; gaze also performs surveillance, information-gathering, attention-signaling, and relational functions. Rutter suggested that looking increases when information is needed from another person and that the amount of looking is influenced by the interpersonal relationship. The need to monitor behavior and to be seen by the other person influences the frequency of gaze (Rutter et al., 1984; Rutter & Stephenson, 1979; Rutter et al., 1978). Not surprisingly, romantic couples engage in more eye contact than same-sex and opposite-sex friends (Guerrero, 1994).

Affect Displays   At a basic level, all cultures share a limited set of facial affect displays (Ekman, Sorenson, & Friesen, 1969); however, cultures have unique rules governing when affect displays are appropriate and when they are inappropriate (Ekman & Friesen, 1969b). For example, U.S. culture encourages boys to mask negative emotions such as sadness or grief and not to display an overabundance of tenderness, affection, or emotionality. Conversely, women are allowed to show more emotions than men, but they have been trained to maintain a pleasant front. A more extended discussion of gender differences in affect displays appears in Chapters 8 and 10.

Adaptors   The primary norm governing adaptor display is to avoid using adaptors in public. This is especially true of self-adaptors, which are permitted only in the privacy of one's own home and in the presence of very intimate relational partners. The comedian Bill Cosby has noted that at home, only fathers are allowed to have "gas." Alter-oriented and object adaptors are more permissible in public. Cigarette smoking remains acceptable in many social situations, especially outside the United States. Gum chewing is less acceptable in many social situations and is considered déclassé behavior in many countries, such as Germany. Often object adaptors are used to signal membership in a particular group. In some academic circles, pipe smoking by professors and their protégés is quite common. Beyond the public versus nonpublic and group-specific rules, few other norms for adaptor behavior exist.

Communication Potential of Kinesics

When considering a code's communication potential, it is important to examine how well it lends itself to use by a sender—its encoding potential—and to perception by a receiver—its decoding potential. Several characteristics make kinesics one of the most powerful codes in the nonverbal communication system, perhaps the most powerful.

Encoding Potential   The enormous number of kinesic behaviors at a sender's disposal has already been mentioned. This code easily exceeds any other in the sheer number of possible cues. In addition, a single sender can perform many of these cues at the same time. This produces a multichanneled message capable of many shades of meaning. A sender can perform multiple functions simultaneously. At a given point in a conversation, kinesic cues can signal an emotion, coordinate the switch between speaker and listener, comment on the relationship of the source and receiver, and maintain a desired front. Only the vocalic code rivals kinesics in its ability to transmit multiple meanings and perform multiple functions simultaneously. Finally, the innate basis of many of the kinesic cues makes it almost an unconscious choice to transmit many messages. Although some cues are unintentional, children learn very early in life to manipulate kinesic cues to affect the people around them.

Decoding Potential   Humans have a strong bias to attend to kinesic cues, as a result of the innate tendency to orient to others visually, the overtly noticeable and attention-getting characteristics of kinesics, and the many functions kinesic cues serve.

There is, however, a downside to the communication potential of kinesics. First, the large number of cues and their many combinations are often ambiguous or confusing, leading to misunderstandings and conflict. Also, the intrinsic relationship between many kinesic cues and communicators' feelings and emotions often leads to unintentional displays. Since receivers are likely to consider kinesic cues as intentional and truthful, communicators are sometimes faced with unexpected or undesirable reactions due to unwitting displays. Finally, people learn to mask or substitute kinesic cues, which makes accurate decoding more difficult. This is especially true for facial expressions and thus does not bode well for communicators biased toward attending to facial cues. All in all, though, the many advantages of kinesics outweigh these few disadvantages, leading to the conclusion that kinesics is a powerful nonverbal channel for communication.

PHYSICAL APPEARANCE

Being well groomed is an asset.

Dry cleaner's slogan

Physical appearance has been an important issue for humans since prehistoric times. Natural features and body adornments are overt, attention-getting, and diverse. They are especially important in impression formation and management. In encounters with others, we frequently make judgments of others based only on physical appearance cues. These are essential to the communication process because they allow us to interact successfully with strangers, about whom we have little information. As communicators, each of us manipulates these physical appearance cues. According to Cash (1988), 82 percent of American men and 93 percent of American women are actively oriented toward developing and maintaining an attractive appearance.

Origins and Acquisition of the Appearance Code

Most natural features are genetic and have developed through the evolution of the human species. Differences in facial structure, skin color, hair texture, eye color, and the like stem from independent evolutionary development. Natural features are passed from generation to generation because natural characteristics have survival value for the species (Darwin, 1965; Freedman, 1969).

Beyond natural features, cultures and subcultures determine a person's conception of what is attractive, how natural features should be styled, and how the body should be adorned. Excavations of human burial sites from Neanderthal times have found evidence of natural pigments used to paint the body. Drawings, carvings, and writings from the earliest civilizations reveal that ancient peoples painted the skin, constructed elaborate jewelry, created clothing and uniforms, and applied perfumes and oils, all in an effort to enhance the body's appearance. Here are some examples:

1 Face painting by Asians, Africans, and American Indians is thought to be a forerunner of today's cosmetics. (See Cordwell, 1976, for a historical overview of cosmetics and body decoration.)
2 There are many biblical accounts of perfumes, oils, essences, and lotions used to anoint the body.

3 In Roman and medieval societies, purple robes were symbols of authority.

4 Body disfigurations such as tattoos, foot binding, circumcision, and flesh piercing have occurred at various times in history.

For more on the historical roots of physical attractiveness, see Box 2-3.

For many of us, physical appearance needs rank alongside food and shelter needs. In today's society, beauty and fashion are multibillion-dollar industries. We purchase enormous quantities of cosmetics, perfumes, deodorants, soaps, clothing, jewelry, and shoes. Many people are employed in service industries related to physical appearance, including fashion consultants and retailers, hairdressers and barbers, manicurists, orthodontists and dentists, and plastic surgeons. Some of these industries are among the most financially stable even in the worst economic times. Many fads revolve around physical appearance. Each day many people rearrange work, leisure, and sleep habits to sweat, hurt, and moan in the name of beauty. Although there are many health benefits to jogging, aerobics, weight training, and other participatory sports, a major purpose of these physical fitness programs is improving the body's attractiveness (Hayes & Ross, 1987). Moreover, people strive to look good while exercising. Grubby sweatsuits have been replaced by stylish designer outfits.

Notions of attractiveness develop early. Infants get a sense of their own body and those of others through touch, sight, and smell. Parents, other adults, and peers instill in the child the appearance norms of the culture and subculture. Babies learn accepted clothing norms through the clothes they wear and see on others. Children are taught to wear clothing appropriately; keeping pants and dresses on in public is an important norm that must be learned. By nursery school age, children's notions of beauty are surpris-

---

BOX 2-3

GLAMOUR AND BEAUTY THROUGH THE AGES

Women of the Italian Renaissance and Victorian England . . . used to take belladonna (a poisonous plant in the nightshade family whose name means "beautiful woman") to enlarge their pupils before they went out on a date.

Throughout the ages, people have emphasized their facial features with makeup. Archaeologists have found evidence of Egyptian perfumeries and beauty parlors dating to 4000 B.C. and makeup paraphernalia that dates to 6000 B.C. The ancient Egyptians preferred green eye shadow, which was topped with a glitter made from crushing the iridescent carapaces of certain beetles, kohl eyeliner and mascara, blue-black lipstick, red rogue, and fingers and feet stained red with henna. They shaved their eyebrows and drew false ones.

Roman men adored cosmetics; field commanders had their hair coiffed and perfumed and their nails lacquered before they went into battle. A second-century Roman physician invented cold cream, whose formula has changed little since then.

We may remember from the Old Testament that it was Queen Jezebel who "painted her face" before embarking on her wicked ways, a fashion she learned from the high-toned Phoenicians around 850 B.C. In the 18th century, women were willing to eat Arsenic Complexion Wafers to make their skin whiter, which worked by poisoning the hemoglobin in the blood so that they developed a fragile, lunar whiteness. Rouges often contained such dangerous metals as lead and mercury.

Source: Ackerman, 1990.

ingly similar to adult perceptions, and like many adults, as they get older, children prefer attractive friends (Berscheid & Walster, 1972, 1974).

One way adults reinforce appearance norms for children is through their reactions to children's appearances. Brody (1963) found that the ways in which black mothers dealt with blacks and whites affected their children's concept of being black. Berscheid and Walster (1972, 1974) and Dion (1972) conducted a series of studies on teacher perceptions of attractive and unattractive students. Their results showed that teachers hold more favorable impressions of attractive students, which could lead to special treatment, cuing other children that beauty is preferred. Dion's experiment is particularly interesting because it focused on teacher reactions to physical aggression by children. Unattractive students were regarded as engaging in more chronic antisocial behavior and severe transgressions, as more likely to transgress in the future, and as more dishonest and unpleasant overall than attractive children, even though the transgressions were identical. Box 2-4 exemplifies the effect of parental reactions on children's notions of physical attractiveness.

Another important source of attractiveness and appearance norms is the media. Actors and actresses in most programs and advertisements are "beautiful people," conforming closely to cultural stereotypes of appearance. Even "hidden camera" commercials of "real" people show at least moderately attractive people. The effect of pop stars' taste in clothing on the dress styles of young people is testament to the media's ability to shape appearance norms and fads.

BOX 2-4

PARENTS' PREFERENCES FOR BEAUTY CAN HARM KIDS

In a letter to Ann Landers, a woman wrote that parents' concern about how a child looks "comes through as 'rejection' and can ruin a child's life." She recounted how her mother's reactions to her looks affected her. The woman writes, "My mother focused on my homeliness as far back as I can remember. If it wasn't my hair, it was my teeth, my height, or my posture." The woman says that her mother's criticism made her so "self-conscious and miserable" that she avoided mirrors and photographs (*Landers,* May 21, 1981, D2).

A recent study reported by the Associated Press (*Arizona Daily Star,* May 20, 1995) found that parents' reactions start at a young age. "Mothers of cute newborns showed more affection toward their infants than mothers of homely babies did." They held them closer and patted and cooed to them more than mothers of homely babies. Mothers of homely babies gave more attention to other people and checked diapers more frequently than mothers of cute babies. The researcher,

Jean Ritter, assistant professor of psychology at California State University, Fresno, was not sure how these subtle differences would affect the child's development. She noted that all mothers behaved positively toward their babies and evaluated the babies positively. But therapists are only too aware how lasting an impact parents' views can have on their children.

The Ann Landers letter-writer was more fortunate than many. She overcame the unfavorable attention her mother gave to her homeliness. A love affair boosted her self-confidence and self-esteem, because her lover thought she was beautiful. Ann Landers observed that "in our culture, too much emphasis is placed on good looks, not only by mothers but society." She also cautions that being beautiful has pitfalls. Beautiful people may feel that they don't need to reach out to others or develop skills because the world will admire them simply for their beauty.

Classifying Physical Appearance

Natural Features   Unlike kinesics, little effort has been directed at classifying units or cues of physical appearance. However, a few researchers have been interested in body shape or somatotype, the most prominent natural feature. Somatotype relates to the general shape of the body. Because body shape is for the most part genetic, it is usually not considered part of the nonverbal communication system. However, somatotypes can be altered by diet, exercise, and surgery, to a limited extent, and may be communicative if a person intentionally alters it to manipulate impressions. Although intentional encoding of body shape is restricted, we sometimes treat it as an indication of personality traits (Cortes & Gatti, 1965).

Cortes and Gatti (1965) identified three somatotypes: endomorph, mesomorph, and ectomorph (see Figure 2-3). The *endomorph* is round, short, plump, and soft. Rush Limbaugh and Roseanne Barr are endomorphs. The *mesomorph* is athletic, trim, muscular, average in height, and V-shaped, with wide shoulders and a body that tapers to a thin waist. Denzel Washington and Steffi Graf are mesomorphs. The *ectomorph* is tall, thin, and frail. Tom Hanks and supermodel Elle MacPherson are ectomorphs.

A second prominent natural feature is *physiognomy,* which is one's hereditary facial structure, skin color, hair texture (and to some extent color), eye shape, and eye color. There are three general classes of physiognomies. *Negroid* characteristics include generally large round brown eyes, flat nose with flared nostrils, very full lips, brown skin pigmentation, and thick, tightly curled dark brown or black hair. *Caucasoid* characteristics generally include medium round brown or blue eyes, large thin nose, thin to medium-full lips, white skin, and straight or slightly curly blond to dark brown hair. *Mongoloid* features entail thin to medium slanted brown or black eyes, small and slightly flat nose, thin lips, light yellow or red skin, and straight dark brown or black hair. An

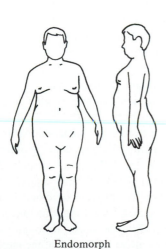
Endomorph

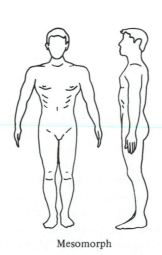
Mesomorph

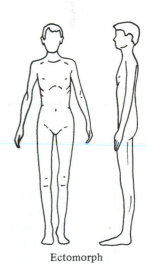
Ectomorph

FIGURE 2-3
The three somatotypes.

individual may closely fit the central characteristics of one of these groups or may show a blend of features. Consequently, physiognomy is not a very dependable predictor of racial or ethnic background. Moreover, because these features are involuntary and remain relatively stable throughout a person's life, they should not be considered part of a communication code.

Similarly, because *skin color* is inherited and largely a static cue, it has limited communication capacity, although it can be manipulated slightly through makeup and tanning. As a source of information, skin color may identify cultural and subcultural boundaries. In turn, some subcultures have preferences for, and reactions to, skin color that determine who will or can communicate with whom.

Hair, including *body, facial,* and *cranial hair,* is a highly variable natural feature. It can be stiffened, frizzed, curled, braided, perfumed, tinted, cropped short, grown out, shaved off completely, and covered with a wig. For body hair, amount and location are the main considerations. Facial hair shows more variation, with amount, location, color, and style being most important. Cranial hair is by far the most varied in amount, location, color, texture, and style. A whole industry has developed around the maintenance of cranial hair.

Adornments   Clothing, jewelry, accessories, and cosmetics are adornment features, so called because they are worn on the body. Adornment features are more communicative than natural features due to perceptions of intentional choice and placement on the body. Clothing, often thought to be an extension of the skin (Frank, 1971), has the most variability and the largest number of cues of any adornment feature. Color, style, location, amount, fabric texture, pattern and design, neatness, and fashionableness can all be varied. People also decode or interpret clothing on numerous dimensions. These include fashionability, color, pattern, decoration, comfort, interest, conformity, conventionality, and economy (Aiken, 1963; Bickman, 1974a; Birren, 1952; Compton, 1962; Gibbons & Gwynn, 1975; Pinaire-Reed, 1979). Many times, however, selection is based on personal preference or moods (Compton, 1962; Rosenfeld & Plax, 1977) and is less communicative. Nevertheless, the effect of dress on impressions of one's physical, socioeconomic, and personality characteristics makes clothing cues very important to the communication process.

Jewelry, accessories, and *cosmetics* also are highly variable in color, style, location, amount, construction, materials, pattern and design, and fashionableness. As with clothing, though, selection is not always communicative.

Attributes that can be both a natural and an adornment feature are *scents and odors.* People's bodies generate their own natural olfactic signature, recognizable to others (Lord & Kasprzak, 1989; Porter, Cernoch, & Balogh, 1985; Porter, Cernoch, & McLaughlin, 1983; Porter & Moore, 1981; Russell, 1976). There are also changes in body odors associated with hormonal cycles. Women who live or work together often report that their menstrual cycles synchronize. Recent research shows that this may be caused by a chemical secreted in perspiration and sensed by the nose (although the chemical has no recognizable smell). Male odors also may affect the length of the menstrual cycle (Cutler, Preti, Krieger, Huggins, Garcia, & Lawley, 1986; McClintock, 1971; Russell, 1976).

Like many natural features, odors generated by the body have limited communication value, although they may be quite indicative. While we can imagine sending a message to people we dislike by not bathing prior to meeting with them, most bodily odors are based on biological processes over which we have limited control. The use of scented cosmetics, oils, and perfumes may be more communicative, like other forms of adornment. For example, they can be used to set a mood or trigger memories of past encounters (Knapp & Hall, 1992).

Appearance Norms and Expectations

Generally in the North American culture, the preferred body types are mesomorphic males and ectomorphic females. This does not correspond to the average body type of the population, since most people are slightly overweight relative to the preferred body shape. This departure from stereotypic shape is especially evident for women. Huon, Morris, and Brown (1990) reported that the body size preferred by women was thinner than their ideal healthy size, their actual size, the size women thought men would prefer, and the size men actually preferred. It should not be surprising, then, that women often distort the size of their own body. Galgan, Mable, Ouellete, and Balance (1989) reported that in their study, women's actual weight was 1.8 percent below the midpoint of their healthy weight range, but women perceived themselves to be 11.8 percent above their appropriate weight. Moreover, women who were more preoccupied with their weight had a more distorted overweight view of themselves than women who were less preoccupied. Preoccupation with weight and perceptual distortions may be at the root of some eating disorders in women (Galgan et al., 1989; Hayes & Ross, 1987).

Physical appearance appears to be much more important to and for women than men (Rosenwasser, Adams, & Tansil, 1983; Tseëlon, 1992). Women may be more conscious of their appearance and spend more time evaluating their own and other women's appearance than do men. Rosenwasser et al. (1983) found that women spent more time looking at pictures of other women than at pictures of men. Men spent more time looking at pictures of women, probably because of opposite-sex attraction. Lest you get the impression that women are unattracted to the male physique, women in this study spent the second most amount of time looking at pictures of men in bathing suits.

Stereotypes of female attractiveness are better documented than stereotypes of male attractiveness. Iliffe (1960) and Huon et al. (1990) reported a high degree of consistency in preferences for feminine beauty. Singer and Lamb (1966) also reported a consistent norm of feminine beauty—height: 5 feet, 5 inches; weight: 120 pounds; bust: 35 inches; waist: 22.5 inches; hips: 35 inches; neck: 11.3 inches; wrist: 5.7 inches; ankles: 7.22 inches. Preferences for height, weight, bust, waist, and hip measurements were more consistent across respondents, suggesting that people do not have stereotypes for neck, wrist, and ankle sizes. As for male attractiveness, one study reported that women prefer V-shaped over pear-shaped body types. That is, they like broad arms and upper trunk and thin lower trunk and legs (Lavrakas, 1975).

Two additional stereotypes about body size deserve note. Obesity is definitely a stigma in this culture (Cahnman, 1968). Obese people are avoided by others. One study showed that people were less eager to work with an obese person than a normal-weight person and obese women were preferred even less than obese men. Further, obese people were considered lazy, lacking in self-discipline, and insecure (and if male, unkempt, sloppy, and ill-dressed; Jasper & Klassen, 1990). Unfortunately, obesity is not always controllable; sometimes it is genetically or physiologically determined. In some cultures, though, obesity is favored: "Where affluence is attainable only by a privileged few, obesity, especially in women, is likely to be regarded as prestigious and therefore attractive" (Cahnman, 1968, p. 287).

Although being heavy is not universally prized, being tall appears to be. Kitahara (1985) suggested that this preference is rooted in the evolutionary advantage of larger size. In the history of primate evolution, the clear tendency has been to increase body size in order to better control the environment and its resources. Socially, there has been a long-standing desire for larger sizes in all objects.

There may be a general preference for Caucasoid features in North American culture. Hispanics with fair skin tones and Caucasoid features, as opposed to Hispanics with Mongoloid features acquired from intermarrying with Native Americans, are socially privileged; they tend to have more education, more prestigious occupations, and higher incomes, and receive less discrimination from others (Arce, Murguia, & Frisbie, 1987). Historically, African Americans with lighter skin color and Caucasian features also have had social advantages (Keith & Herring, 1991; Neal & Wilson, 1989). Martin (1964) found that beauty standards among African American respondents favored black women with Caucasoid features over women with Negroid features. (This was not true for a Nigerian sample, which rated Negroid features as equally attractive.) Keith and Herring (1991) found in a sample from the late 1970s that lighter-skinned African Americans had greater educational attainment, more prestigious occupations, and higher incomes than darker-skinned African Americans. Porter's sample (1991) of African American children in 1985 also confirmed these preferences. Thus, despite the "black is beautiful" movement of the 1970s and the more recent social and political moves toward cultural diversity, the standard still prevails. Beyond the scientific evidence, consider as anecdotal evidence the fact that the singer Vanessa Williams, the first African American Miss America, and the pop star Michael Jackson have lighter skin and more Caucasoid features. There are also several hair and cosmetic products used by many African American women to bleach their skin and straighten their hair.

By contrast, Caucasians often darken the skin through tanning, something that became popular only in this century. Before the 1900s, white skin was prized, because a tan indicated poverty or outdoor labor. Now, people with tanned skin are considered to be more attractive, socially active, popular, sexy, and healthy (Broadstock, Borland, & Gason, 1992; Miller, Ashton, McHoskey, & Gimbel, 1990). Tanning is especially prevalent among adolescents (Johnson & Lookingbill, 1984). The increased concern over wrinkling and skin cancer caused by too much sun exposure may be reversing this trend.

Currently, among males, shorter cranial hair and little facial hair is normative, and beards are less popular now than in the past (Pellegrini, 1989). Facial hairstyles for men have changed greatly throughout history. At times, beards may have been disfavored because they gave opponents a handhold during hand-to-hand military combat (Basow, 1991).

Women's cranial hairstyles are more varied and changeable. The vast majority of women in American culture remove their body hair. In Roman times, women removed body hair with hot tar and razor-sharp shells. The 20th-century hair removal norm developed as clothing styles exposed more of women's bodies and lack of body hair came to mean sexual attractiveness and youthfulness (Basow, 1991; Hope, 1982). The standard was promoted by the "Great Underarm Campaign" of the Gillette Safety Razor Co. between 1915 and 1919. At that time, the practice was referred to as "smoothing," not shaving. By 1945 the majority of women in the United States removed underarm and leg hair. In Basow's recent survey of professional women, most started removing body hair by age 14, mainly for appearance's sake, although the greater the growth rate of body hair, the more likely women were to shave. It is interesting to note that prior to 1915, a glimpse of a woman's body hair was considered sexually attractive. We talk more about this norm in Chapter 8.

There are, of course, subcultural and individual differences in what is considered attractive. The cliché that beauty is in the eye of the beholder is indeed valid. Physical appearance preferences fluctuate across age groups, socioeconomic levels, occupations, regions, and races, as well as across time (see Figure 2-4 for different eras in hemlines). Fashions seem to originate in metropolitan areas on the east and west coasts of the

Skirts Up—The Roaring Twenties   Skirts Down—The Great Depression

Skirts Up—Active Wartime Economy   Skirts Down—Post-War Austerity

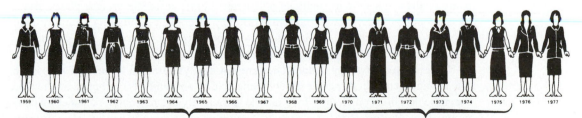

Skirts Up—The Swinging Sixties   Skirts Down—The New Recession

FIGURE 2-4
One interesting clothing norm is skirt length. In this century, skirt length norms have correlated with economic conditions. When economic conditions are poor, skirt lengths tend to go down; when the economy improves, skirt lengths go up.

United States, then move into suburban and rural areas. People in colder climates tend to wear darker colors, while people in warmer climates wear brighter and lighter colors. People in equatorial locations often wear less clothing than those in colder climates. The use of a veil to cover a woman's face is still seen in a few middle eastern countries. Covering of the genital region is nearly a universal norm, and in many cultures women cover their breasts. Athletic teams specify uniforms to be worn on the field, and sometimes they specify the attire to be worn off the field (Harris, Ramsey, Sims, & Stevenson, 1974). Other groups do not specify uniforms but have implicit or explicit dress codes. You and your friends probably dress similarly. This similarity can be considered an implicit dress code. Businesses frequently have explicit dress codes.

In one of the few studies on dress norms, Ramsey (1976) was able to identify groups in a prison population by the clothes and other adornments they wore. For instance, black Muslims were characterized by neat, pressed clothes; short, trimmed hair; and similar hats. "Tough" guards wore neat, pressed uniforms, while "easy" guards wore wrinkled uniforms.

So far, we have considered only natural features and adornments when discussing physical attractiveness. But people also rely on facial cues and tone of voice when judging physical attractiveness. A smiling person is considered more physically attractive than a nonsmiling person (Reis et al., 1990). Zuckerman, Miyake, and Hodgins (1991) showed that ratings of physical attractiveness are influenced by the attractiveness of a speaker's voice, whether or not the speaker is physically visible. Thus the entire nonverbal demeanor, not just natural features and adornment cues, can influence perceptions of attractiveness.

Box 2-5 provides powerful evidence of norms for attractiveness, in the context of dating and marriage.

Communication Potential of Appearance

Encoding Potential   In number of cues and visual impact, physical appearance has great communication potential. Some natural and most adornment features lend themselves to variation in amount, location, color, texture, style, pattern and design, and fashionableness, allowing a communicator to construct a complex appearance. Because such cues stimulate the tactile and olfactory senses as well as the visual ones, these cues have high potential for arousal, attracting immediate attention from the decoder. Further, many of these cues are available at a distance, before interaction takes place, giving physical appearance cues a significant primacy effect in establishing an impression. They also play a limited role in emotional expression (to the extent that selection is based on moods), social influence, and relational communication.

However, physical appearance cues are not always selected to encode a message. The ambiguity of whether a cue is communicative or not limits its communication value. Purchase decisions on clothes, for example, commonly occur without considering communication. Preferences for a particular style or color and decisions to conform to appearance norms are influenced by personality, desire to be accepted by peers, desire to be liked, interest in fashion, exhibitionist tendencies, degree of practicality and comfort, femininity or masculinity, and interest in fashion design (Compton, 1962; Gibbons &

BOX 2-5

APPLICATIONS: PHYSICAL ATTRACTIVENESS ON A DATE

Apart from academic progress, students are concerned about their social life, and in this social life, physical appearance plays an important role.

Using an ingenious method, Berscheid and Walster (1974) arranged dates for college dances through computer matching. Dance attendees completed a predance questionnaire concerning characteristics they desired in a date. They were also rated on their physical attractiveness. Unknown to the participants, dates were matched on the basis of physical attractiveness only. At intermission, attendees completed a questionnaire assessing liking for the dates, attendees' perceptions of how much their dates liked them, attitude similarity of dates, and desire to date the same people in the future.

The results showed that for first impressions, beauty is best. Both males and females expressed a desire for physically attractive dates; however, physical beauty was much more important for males. Females, meanwhile, had stronger preferences for intelligent, considerate, and outgoing dates and frequently placed more weight than males on these perceptions (Berscheid, Dion, Walster, & Walster, 1971; Berscheid & Walster, 1969, 1972, 1974; Brislin & Lewis, 1968; Coombs & Kenkel, 1966; Walter, Aronson, Abrahams, & Rottman, 1966).

Congruence in physical attractiveness between partners, however, may be more important than absolute attractiveness, which offers hope for the less attractive.

Both predance desires and postdance reports showed a matching affect. That is, more attractive individuals desired more attractive dates and had a better time with more attractive dates, while less attractive participants desired less attractive dates and had a better time with them (Berscheid & Walster, 1969, 1972, 1974; Berscheid et al., 1971; Brislin & Lewis, 1968; Coombs & Kenkel, 1966; Walster et al., 1966). Congruence in physical attractiveness also seems to be expected by others. Bar-Tal and Saxe (1976) found that matched spouses were thought to be happier in their marriage. In unmatched couples, unattractive men married to attractive women were rated higher on income, occupational status, and professional success than attractive males. It seems observers felt that these positive characteristics of the unattractive males balanced the attractiveness of their female partners.

The conclusions of this research are clear. Physical attractiveness is an advantage in social interactions with others. However, physical attractiveness is much more important to males. Females judge dates on other dimensions, such as intelligence, social skill, and etiquette. Further, people seem to gravitate to partners at the same level of attractiveness and to judge others partly on the attractiveness of their partners. This supports two clichés: "Beauty is in the eye of the beholder" and "There is someone for everyone."

Gwynn, 1975; Iliffe, 1960; Rosenfeld & Plax, 1977; Taylor & Compton, 1968). Because intent is often not clear, appearance cues become ambiguous as to their message value. This is exacerbated by the fact that an appearance choice may be an intentional statement one day and not the next. You may purchase a particular blouse or shirt because you think it looks "sexy," yet you do not always wear it with the intent of sending a message of sexual receptivity. For these reasons, appearance cues are not always communicative; however, decoders do make inferences about them and feel that at some level choice is intentional.

A second communication limitation of physical appearance is the lack of variability within a single interaction. This is especially true of natural features. They can only be changed by special methods (plastic surgery, hairstyling, tanning booths). Adornment features are relatively more changeable. Yet after initial selection and arrangement, we generally do not manipulate them for a large part of the day, except for occasional straightening or reapplication. Consequently, in a single interaction, physical appearance cues are static. We do not quickly modify their meaning or use them to transmit specific messages. A few exceptions do come to mind. A male supervisor can communicate relaxation by loosening his tie late on a Friday afternoon. Lovers can communicate sexual interest by removing their clothes. However, to carry on the equivalent of a conversation with only physical appearance cues would be nearly impossible.

Over time, there is more opportunity to communicate through appearance. An employer may communicate that task-oriented norms are being followed by wearing a suit to the office; however, the same boss communicates that social-oriented norms are in effect by wearing jeans and a t-shirt to the company picnic. A boyfriend or girlfriend who becomes increasingly slovenly in appearance for dates may signal less concern for the relationship.

Decoding Potential   From a decoding perspective, physical appearance has only moderate communication potential. On the plus side, many physical appearance cues are symbolic, so they are easily and readily understood. Second, humans have an excellent ability to make fine discriminations between cues. Third, although much of the information transmitted by physical appearance cues is stereotypic, it is often accurate. Fourth, the high potential for arousal by this channel is likely to increase attention to these cues.

There are a few decoding disadvantages that limit the communication potential of physical appearance cues. The interpretation of cues is often ambiguous, as is the degree to which cues are intentionally manipulated. Finally, there are fewer communication functions to which the cues can be applied, limiting both its decoding and encoding potential.

In sum, the communication potential of physical appearance is only moderate. There are many cues, and they have great attention-getting and arousal value. Decoders notice these cues and make consistent inferences about the source. At the same time, ambiguity of meaning, unintentional cue selection, and limited manipulability reduce the communication potential of physical appearance.

VOCALICS

most people are perfectly afraid of silence.

e.e. cummings

The voice is a rich channel in the nonverbal communication system. It contains many behaviors besides the spoken word that are used to complement, accent, emphasize, and contradict what is said, as well as to send additional messages. Pitch, loudness, silences, pauses, laughs, sighs, coughs, and sneezes are a few examples of cues in the code. Vocalic cues are among the most powerful in the nonverbal repertoire. They rival kinesics in number and variety, ability to use them, and tendency to attend to them. Cultures have dominant vocalic patterns, with numerous subcultural variations.

The vocal aspect of nonverbal communication has been alternately labeled paralanguage ("along-with language") and noncontent speech behaviors. We consider the former label too broad because it frequently encompasses kinesic behaviors. The latter, generally confined to pitch, loudness, tempo, pauses, utterance duration, and the like, is too narrow. The label *vocalics* is preferable and encompasses any vocal-auditory behavior except the spoken word.

Origins and Acquisition of Vocalics

Vocalics are by no means exclusive to the human species. Many living beings depend on vocalics for communication with other members of their species. Vocal-auditory communication has been observed in crickets, grasshoppers, finches, thrushes, doves, mynahs, whales, and porpoises, as well as humans (Thorpe, 1972). Vocal behavior in primates is strikingly similar to that of humans. Van Hooff (1972) documented numerous examples of laughlike behavior in primates, consisting of a relaxed open-mouthed facial expression accompanied by screeches and squeals. In fact, during play involving children and chimpanzees, children engage in laughter, while chimps engage in the relaxed open-mouthed facial expression with squealing. Moreover, pitch levels and contours appear to be used for the same purposes by humans and other vertebrates. Vocalic threats and dominance displays invariably entail deep-pitched, harsh vocal patterns, while nonthreatening, nurturing contexts, such as mothers cooing to infants, show high-pitched, softer patterns.

An important process in language acquisition is auditory feedback. Children listen to their own voices as they pronounce words. This feedback helps them adjust vocal sounds to conform to adult standards. It also reinforces attention to the voices of others. The importance of auditory feedback is highlighted by the retarded speech development of deaf infants. At age 3 months, crying subsides in normal infants and is replaced by noncrying speech sounds. In deaf infants, crying subsides but is not replaced by speech sounds, because the infant cannot hear its own voice (Roberts, 1987). (See Box 2-6 for some interesting aspects of vocalic development and language acquisition in infancy.)

Children continue to learn to use pitch after acquiring language to modify the meaning of their sentences (Menyuk, 1971, 1972). Yes or no questions appear about age 3, and children learn to encode vocalically such concepts as similarity versus difference, expectedness versus unexpectedness, finality versus nonfinality, doubt versus certainty, and subordination versus superordination between ages 3 and 10.

Fundamental pitch changes from birth to puberty. The greatest changes occur between infancy and 2 years and at puberty. The number of pitches a child can encode also expands from five tones at birth to approximately 10 tones by age 7 (McGlone, 1966; Sheppard & Lane, 1968). Use of pausing and hesitations in speech is almost adultlike and highly stable by the time a child enters kindergarten (Levin, Silverman, & Ford, 1967; Wood, 1981). Children display a high degree of conversational congruence (matching pause behavior with conversational partners) by this time, and congruence continues to improve as they progress through elementary school. Tempo and loudness patterns are well established and adultlike by school age (Wood, 1981).

Perception of vocalic cues also undergoes developmental changes. Infants appear to attend to vocalic cues innately from birth (Harris & Rubenstein, 1975), and the ability to discriminate between intonation patterns improves markedly during the babbling period (Menyuk, 1971, 1972). Discrimination at this stage is between large vocal units such as statements and questions. Attention to smaller, wordlike utterances comes later in the babbling period when the infant begins to acquire words. Improvements in decoding vocalic behaviors continue as the child matures (Pendleton & Snyder, 1982; Rosenthal et al., 1979). For instance, Matsumoto and Kishimoto (1983) tested children's abilities to decode happiness, surprise, sadness, and anger from vocalic cues. Four- and 5-year-old

---

BOX 2-6

APPLICATIONS: BRINGING UP BABY

Newborns have an amazing ability to communicate vocally with parents. Further, infants can change their vocalizations (principally crying) to reflect physiological needs during this *prebabbling period* (Menyuk, 1971, 1972; Wood, 1981). For example, a hunger cry is moderately pitched and very loud, with a regular rhythm and short pauses to breathe; a pain cry is extremely high-pitched, with long squeals. Parents (especially mothers) are able to distinguish between different types of cries and respond to crying in some characteristic ways (Roberts, 1987). The attempt to comfort a crying baby may be an innate response. When a mother hears her baby crying, the milk in her breasts also becomes warmer. Beyond communicating basic needs, crying helps the baby develop the use of pitch, pausing, loudness, and tempo.

Some time beween the third and sixth month, infants enter the *babbling period.* Crying subsides and is replaced by noncrying speech sounds (Roberts, 1987). Originally, it was thought that infants encoded only sounds specific to their own language. More recently, babbling has been shown to consist of other sounds as well. As the infant progresses through the babbling period, vocalic cues specific to the language are rewarded by parents, while other vocalizations become less frequent (Menyuk, 1971, 1972; Wood, 1981).

Babies learn a very important skill during this period, the use of intonation (Lieberman, 1967). Research using intonagrams, which measure the fundamental frequency, duration, and intensity of vocalic cues, has found that by 2 months of age infants produce intonation patterns similar to those of adults. Narration and assertion utterances appear at this time. These involve a gradual rise and fall in intensity and fundamental frequency. Between 6 and 8 months babies begin to imitate intonation patterns in their noncry utterances. Requests appear, followed by calling, responses to calling by another person, and commands. All these patterns involve only vocalic cues; no language has yet emerged.

As infants approach 12 months, their babbling becomes more characteristic of their own language sounds and word lengths. By the 11th or 12th month, most children begin to use single-syllable words, which are quickly followed by multisyllabic utterances.

In the first year, then, there is a rich communication exchange between the infant and its parents. (Review Table 2-1 for a summary of infant encoding and decoding abilities.) This exchange enables the infant to signal its needs and desires. The exchange also helps the parents care effectively for the infant. Finally, in this exchange the infant learns from the parents important basic communication skills that it will continue to use once it develops language.

American children correctly identified only surprise, and Japanese children at the same age identified only surprise and sadness. However, American children could correctly identify all four emotions by age 6, while Japanese children did so by age 7.

Children have a difficult time perceiving messages in which the vocal behavior conflicts with kinesic cues. A common example of such messages is sarcasm. Children generally do not understand sarcasm until reach their teens, although with practice they can learn to interpret sarcasm accurately at a younger age (Bugental, 1974; Bugental, Kaswan, & Love, 1970). It is therefore unwise to tell your 5-year-old niece sarcastically that you are "happy" she knocked over your favorite houseplant if you want the others to remain untouched.

Classifying Vocalics

Next to kinesics, vocalics possess the largest number of nonverbal cues. The earliest systems for classifying vocal behavior, developed in the late 1950s, are similar to the structure-centered approaches to classifying kinesics. In fact, many of the researchers interested in vocalics worked or corresponded with those examining kinesics.

The best example of these early approaches is Trager's classification system (1958, 1961). Actually, Trager's system encompasses both speech and body movement. He believed that vocalic behavior was only one facet of speech, intimately related to language, kinesics, and background characteristics of the speaker.

Analysis begins with *voice set,* which consists of the mental, physiological, and physical characteristics of a speaker, against which all vocalic and speech behaviors are judged. Sex, age, state of health, body build, rhythm state, position in a group, mood, bodily condition, and geographic location all influence the voice set. For instance, women generally encode higher fundamental pitch than men.

The next level of analysis is *speech.* Trager saw speech as a combination of language and paralanguage. *Paralanguage* includes voice qualities and vocalizations. *Voice qualities* are vocalic behavior related to speech, such as *pitch range, articulation control, resonance,* and *tempo.* Each of these characteristics represents a vocalic continuum. For example, pitch range varies from spread to narrowed, articulation control from precise to slurred, resonance from resonant to thin, and tempo from fast to slow. *Vocalizations,* by contrast, are specific vocal sounds or noises separate from language. These include *vocal characterizers*—sounds such as laughing, crying, yelling, whispering, moaning, groaning, whining, breaking, belching, and yawning—*vocal qualifiers*—the features of intensity, pitch height, and extent that "qualify" large or small stretches of language material—and *vocal segregates*—sounds such as pauses, clicks, snorts, and vocalic emblems like "uh-uh" for no, "uh-huh" for yes, "uh" for hesitation, and "sh" for quiet.

Birdwhistell (1970) related a delightful story that illustrates the communicative power of this last category of noises:

> My mother's thin-lipped smile, which could be confined to her mouth, when accompanied by an audible input of air through her tightened nostrils required no words—Christian or otherwise—to reveal her attitude. My mother was a sniffer, a great sniffer. She could be heard for three rooms across the house. And, to paraphrase Mark Twain, her sniff had power; she could sniff a fly off the wall at 30 feet. I might even say she was an irresponsible sniffer, for she always denied her sniffing. When we'd say, "Well, you don't have to sniff about it," she'd respond firmly, "I have something in my passages—and a lady doesn't blow her nose." "Mark my words," she'd say and sniff again. (pp. 52–53)

Other attempts to classify vocalic cues include Crystal's distinction (1969) between prosodic features (sounds linked directly to speech, similar to vocal qualities), paralinguistic features (sounds linked loosely to speech, like vocal characterizers), and nonlinguistic features (sounds not linked to speech, like vocal segregates). Street (1990) also distinguished between prosody (discrete coded behaviors such as stress, peak or primary stress, juncture, pitch direction, pitch height, and pitch range) and paralanguage (continuously coded behaviors such as vocal intensity, fundamental frequency, silence, speech duration, and speech rate). Harris and Rubenstein (1975) grouped all vocalic behavior into nonsegmental features, distinguishing them from segmental features (vowel and consonant sounds).

Many famous people are known by their voices. Can you recall the distinctive vocal characteristics of each of these public figures?

Poyatos (1991, 1993) offered the most elaborate system. *Primary qualities* are always present in the human voice and include timbre, resonance, loudness, tempo, pitch (level, range, registers, intervals), intonation range, syllabic duration, and rhythm. *Voice qualifiers* modify syllables and longer speech segments and other vocalic sounds. They include *breathing control, laryngeal control* (e.g., breathy, strident, hoarse, or shrill voice), *esophageal control, pharyngeal control* (e.g., husky, muffled, or hollow voice), *velopharyngeal control* (e.g., nasal, denasal, or twangy voice), *lingual control, labial control, mandibular control, articulatory control* (e.g., lisping, overarticulated voice), *articulatory-tension control,* and *objectual control* (objects in the mouth, such as pipes, gum, or food). These are determined by biological, physiological, and sociocultural factors.

Paralinguistic differentiators are equivalent to Trager's vocal characterizers: *laughter, crying, shouting, sighing and gasping, panting, yawning, coughing and throat clearing, spitting, belching, hiccuping,* and *sneezing.* Finally, *paralinguistic alternants* are wordlike constructions such as *aah, pooh,* and *brrr.*

One of the problems with these classification systems is the failure to distinguish between acoustic parameters (the actual physical signals made by the voice) and perceptual parameters (the way the sounds are heard by the ear). In Table 2-2, we distinguish between acoustic and perceptual vocal cues. The background against which these are judged remains the voice set. The vocal behaviors themselves are separated into three large categories. *Segmentals* include the linguistic sounds in the voice: phonemes, morphemes, and phonemic clauses that are heard as vowels, consonants, syllables, words, and discrete vocalizations such as sighs and belches. Vocalic cues are divided into *nonsegmentals* (including cues related to *time, fundamental frequency, formants* [frequency of the vocal sound that gives it a characteristic quality], and *intensity or energy*) and *suprasegmentals* (which contain many of the cues referred to by others as paralanguage and prosody).

One vocalic behavior that has been specified further is pausing or silences. Silences during interactions can give a communicator time to think, inflict harm, respond to personal anxiety, prevent verbal communication, prevent others from saying the wrong thing or appearing foolish, express emotions, and signal that the person has nothing to say (DeVito, 1989).

Wood (1981) distinguished between *unfilled* and *filled* pauses. The former are silences in a period of speech not filled by any vocal activity. Unfilled pauses frequently occur at the ends of sentences and at points of decision, such as a difficult word choice. Filled pauses are periods between language containing excess vocalizations: elongated vowels *(ah, eh, uh),* repeated syllables, words or word groups, and false starts. Filled pauses are often used to maintain a speaking turn.

Jaffe and Feldstein (1970) offered a more complex system for classifying pauses. They distinguished between *pauses* (intervals of joint silence bounded by vocalizations by the same speaker) and *switch pauses* (intervals of joint silence bounded at one end by vocalization by one speaker and at the other end by vocalization by another speaker). Three additional concepts are important in this system. *Vocalizations* are periods of uninterrupted vocal sound (usually speech) by a speaker, *speaking turns* are back-and-forth sharing of the speaker role, and *simultaneous speech* is overlapping speech, often indicating the absence of a switch pause.

TABLE 2-2
STRUCTURE OF VOCALICS

A. Voice set	background (characteristics of speakers and context)	
B. Segmentals	*Acoustic Parameters*	*Linguistic Features*
	phonemes, morphemes	vowels, consonants, syllables, words
	phonemic clauses	phrases, discrete vocalizations (e.g., sighs, belches)
C. Nonsegmentals	*Acoustic Parameters*	*Perceptual Features*
Time:	total duration	message length
	number of sound portions	tempo
	number of silent portions and relationship to average duration of sounds	fluency (e.g., stutters, repetitions, filled pauses, hesitations, omissions)
	average duration of silences	pauses
	speaking-turn	turn switches, response latencies
Fundamental frequency:	mean	pitch level (key, register)
	range	pitch range
	variance	variety
Formants:	frequency and structure	unique voice qualities (e.g., breathy, flat, nasal, denasal, throaty)
		vocal clarity (articulation, enunciation)
		pleasantness
Intensity or energy:	total energy of sound unit	loudness
	range	loudness range
	variance	loudness variety
	energy at fundamental frequency	emphasis, stress
	energy at formant frequency	quality (e.g., resonance)
D. Suprasegmentals		*Prosodic/Paralinguistic Features*
		intonation
		pitch height
		stress
		terminal junctures
		extent (duration)
		rhythm
		accent
		vocal characterizers (e.g., moaning, whispering, laughing)

Vocalic Norms and Expectations

All cultures have a preferred or standard vocalic pattern accompanying the "received" language for that culture. American English, British English, European French, Castillian Spanish, and classical Arabic are preferred languages in the United States, Britain, Quebec, Spain, and Egypt, respectively (d'Angeljan & Tucker, 1973; Giles, 1973a; Giles

& Powesland, 1975; Lambert, Hodgson, Gardner, & Fillenbaum, 1960; Ryan, 1979). Generally, these preferred vocalic and language patterns are considered more prestigious by members of these cultures (Thakerar & Giles, 1981). Even speakers of nonpreferred dialects rate the preferred pattern more favorably.

An interesting example of the preference for a particular vocal style comes from Britain. Earlier in this century, accent training became an unofficial requisite of the British educational system. To promote the elitism of the educated class, students from London to Liverpool were subtly encouraged to adopt the accent of their Oxford masters. This "official" accent connoted intelligence and distinction. Many newscasters for the British Broadcasting Corp. adopted this vocal style; hence it acquired the nickname BBC English.

However, not every member of a culture follows the language and vocalic norms of the preferred pronunciation. Rather, subcultural variations persist in every culture. For instance, southern, Appalachian, New England, Brooklyn, west Texan, Mexican American, and Black English variations exist in our culture. These are generally rated lower on prestige but higher on benevolence and group solidarity dimensions (Giles, 1973a; Ryan, 1979; Thakerar & Giles, 1981). That is, if you encounter someone who speaks with an accent similar to your own, you will view them as friendlier, more similar to you, a member of your subculture, and more attractive. Positive relational perceptions and the maintenance of group identity promote the continuance of these nonpreferred patterns in a culture (Ryan, 1979).

Speakers can exploit this by intentionally adjusting their accent patterns within and across interactions. Giles referred to this as accommodation and developed the *communication accommodation theory* to explain how the nature of the interaction (formal or informal) and the perceived characteristics of the interactional partner (high or low status) cause speakers to either shift their accent toward the partner's accent, maintain their own regional accent, or shift toward a more pronounced regional accent (Giles, 1973a, 1980; Giles, Bourhis, & Taylor, 1977; Giles & Powesland, 1975; Giles & Smith, 1979; Street & Giles, 1982; Thakerar, Giles, & Cheshire, 1982). Beyond accent, the theory explains reactions to shifts in speech rate (Buller & Aune, 1988, 1992; Buller, LePoire, Aune, & Eloy, 1992; Putnam & Street, 1984; Smith, Brown, Strong, & Rencher, 1975; Street & Brady, 1982), utterance duration (Street & Giles, 1982), response latency (Street, 1982), pause duration (Jaffe & Feldstein, 1970; Welkowitz & Feldstein, 1969), and interaction length (Stang, 1973). We discuss the role of accommodation in relational communication and social influence in Chapters 11 and 14.

In later chapters, vocalic norms related to regulation of conversations and communication of affect are described. Before leaving this section, however, let's consider the type of vocalic pattern considered most desirable, appropriate, or pleasant. Heinberg (1964) described the *good* voice as maintaining sufficient muscle tone in the vocal folds to produce a highly complex vocal tone at a desired frequency and intensity, positioning the glottis at the correct vertical level, having proper horizontal positioning of the tongue for articulation and audibility, making proper use of the nasal cavity, and creating the right amount of sympathetic resonance. Confused? An easier way of understanding what constitutes a good voice is to consider what defines deviant ones. Among the voices Heinberg considered deviant are breathy voices (too much air escaping through the larynx because of insufficient muscle tone in the vocal folds and poor posture), husky voices (too little air expelled through vocal folds, causing a series of impulses), nasal voices (too much resonance in nasal passages), flat voices (low monotone occurring when glottis blocks out some tone qualities), and throaty voices (moving the tongue upward and toward the back of the mouth to produce a muffled quality).

Zuckerman and Miyake (1993) recently examined the vocal cues that contribute to perceived attractiveness of the voice. More attractive voices had higher articulation and resonance, low to moderate shrillness, moderate pitch, small to medium pitch range, and low nasality. In turn, attractive voices were associated with more positive evaluations of the speaker's personality (see also Zuckerman & Driver, 1989). Less monotonic and more and less squeaky voices with intermediate pausing also received positive personality evaluations in this study.

The interpersonal relationship can determine vocalic patterns. Guerrero (1994) showed that conversations between opposite-sex and same-sex friends were characterized by more fluency, shorter response latencies, fewer silences, and more vocal interest than conversations between romantic partners.

Communication Potential of Vocalics

Encoding Potential   Because of their primacy, frequency of manipulation, number of cues, and range of information and functions, vocalic behaviors possess great communication potential from the encoder's perspective. Research on the origins and acquisition of vocalics clearly shows that they are primary in human development. An infant begins to communicate with vocal cues long before words appear, and reliance on vocalics as a communication channel continues throughout life. Vocalic behaviors are encoded during every conversation. In addition, there are many vocal cues from which to choose in any given conversation. We actively manipulate them simultaneously to produce a variety of meanings. The range of information transmitted by vocal cues and the functions that they serve in human communication are as large as kinesics. Vocal cues communicate emotional reactions, comment on relationships, indicate social attitudes, and regulate the back-and-forth exchange in conversations.

As with other codes, intentionality is not always certain, but vocalics seems to be used intentionally more often than many other codes, probably because of the intimate connection to language, which is almost always encoded deliberately. However, the awareness of vocalic cues is probably less than the awareness of the words they accompany, and nonlinguistic expressions, such as emotional cues, may be far less intentional or conscious.

Decoding Potential   On the decoding side, the vocalic channel also possesses characteristics that make it an important nonverbal communication vehicle. Along with reliance on vocalic cues to communicate messages, an infant decodes meaning from the vocalic behavior of others. In fact, decoding ability develops before encoding ability. As adults, the focus on vocalic cues remains strong, due in part to attention to the spoken word. As people listen to words, they cannot help but process vocalic meaning, giving vocalic cues a perceptual advantage over other nonverbal channels. Finally, humans are capable of making very fine discriminations among vocal cues.

One qualification to this glowing appraisal of decoding ability must be made. Given their nature, some ambiguity exists in vocalic cues. Few vocal behaviors are tied to specific meanings. Further, multiple vocal dimensions, such as pitch, tempo, and rhythm, generally are encoded at the same time. Thus mistakes in decoding are common.

This qualification notwithstanding, vocalic behaviors are very important and powerful in the nonverbal communication system, ranking second only to kinesics in overall impact.

SUMMARY

This chapter examines the visual and auditory codes: kinesics, physical appearance, and vocalics. Kinesics and vocalics are the two most powerful nonverbal codes, and exceed physical appearance in their encoding and decoding potential. All three codes, and the codes discussed in Chapters 3 and 4, are acquired by three means: they are inherited genetically; they arise from common experiences with the environment; and they emerge from culture-specific tasks and social interactions. All three codes share a high attention-getting and arousal value that increases their communication potential. In addition, all three codes contain many elements that can be varied to send messages. Kinesics and vocalics, though, possess more code elements than physical appearance because it is difficult to vary most natural appearance features (with the exception of hair and skin), and adornment features are relatively static. All three codes are governed strongly by cultural and subcultural norms that are learned at an early age, while kinesics and vocalics also include significant innate components. Together, these three visual and auditory codes play a major role in accomplishing the communication functions we discuss in Part Two.

SUGGESTED READINGS

Basow, S. A. (1991). The hairless ideal: Women and their body hair. *Psychology of Women Quarterly, 15,* 83–96.

Berscheid, E., & Walster, E. (1972, March). Beauty and the best. *Psychology Today, 5,* 42–46.

Birdwhistell, R. L. (1970). *Kinesics and context.* Philadelphia: University of Pennsylvania Press.

Buck, R. (1981). The evolution and development of emotion expression and communication. In S. S. Brehm, S. M. Kassin, & F. X. Gibbons (Eds.), *Developmental social psychology* (pp. 127–151). New York: Oxford University Press.

Huon, G. F., Morris, S. E., & Brown, L. B. (1990). Differences between male and female preferences for female body size. *Australian Psychologist, 25,* 314–317.

Krauss, R. M., Morrel-Samuels, P., & Colasante, C. (1991). Do conversational hand gestures communicate? *Journal of Personality and Social Psychology, 61,* 743–754.

McNeill, D. (1985). So you think gestures are nonverbal? *Psychological Review, 92,* 350–371.

Morris, D. (1995). *Bodytalk.* New York: Abrams.

Poyatos, F. (1993). *Paralanguage: A linguistic and interdisciplinary approach to interactive speech and sounds.* Amsterdam: Benjamins.

Rutter, D. R., & Stephenson, G. M. (1979). The functions of looking: Effects of friendship on gaze. *British Journal of Social and Clinical Psychology, 18,* 203–205.

Street, R. L., Jr. (1990). The communicative functions of paralanguage and prosody. In H. Giles & W. P. Robinson (Eds.), *Handbook of language and social psychology* (pp. 121–140). Chichester: Wiley.

Trager, G. L. (1961). The typology of paralanguage. *Anthropological Linguistics, 3,* 17–21.

Woods, B. S. (1981). *Children and communication: Verbal and nonverbal language development* (2d ed.). Englewood Cliffs, NJ: Prentice-Hall.

3

CONTACT CODES: HAPTICS AND PROXEMICS

Touch is the basic mammalian mode of communication, one warm-blooded creature's way of saying to another, "You're not alone. I'm here."

Anne Gottlieb

The flow and shift of distance between people as they interact with each other is part and parcel of the communication process.

Edward T. Hall

The very existence of conversation is contingent upon the recognition of distance.

Z. D. Gurevitch

One of the fundamental dimensions of human relationships is that of coming together and coming apart, of union and separation, of closeness and distance. We are constantly in a state of approaching or avoiding others, a basic tension well illustrated in a famous German fable:

> Once upon a wintry night, the porcupines gathered together for a little socializing. Because of the chill night air, they tried to move close together to gain a little warmth. But every time they did, they would prick each other with their quills. So they moved farther apart, but once again became cold. They continued to rearrange themselves until they found a distance at which they could be both warm and comfortable. Henceforth, that distance became known as good manners.

Like the porcupines (and many other members of the animal kingdom), we attempt in our day-to-day social relations to strike a proper balance or equilibrium between desires for closeness and affiliation and desires for separation and privacy. On the one hand, the drives for propagation and for protection from predators create pressures toward approach. On the other hand, the need for individual access to food, water, and shelter and the need for insulation from physical threats from other group members lead to pressures toward separation and the establishment of individual territories.

Regardless of whether the human species is governed by similar biological forces or is responding more to psychological needs for intimacy and privacy, humans display the same approach-avoidance patterns. When we choose to live in cities rather than the country, to plan social get-togethers with friends and family, and to congregate in crowds at political rallies, we are manifesting approach tendencies. When we seek solitude or attempt to limit the amount of sensory input we are receiving, we are manifesting avoidance tendencies. Have you ever noticed how quickly you attempt to escape the crowd after a football game or how annoyed you are by someone accidentally brushing against you on a subway or bus? Although we are more likely to display avoidance tendencies toward strangers and approach tendencies toward significant and familiar others (friends, family, coworkers), we sometimes need distance and time alone from even our closest friends. Thus our daily encounters entail continual choices about approaching and avoiding others.

These forces give rise to two different communication codes: haptics and proxemics. *Haptics* refers to the *perception and use of touch as communication,* and *proxemics* refers to the *perception, use, and structuring of space as communication.* Because these two codes are intimately linked, we will not treat them separately but rather examine them together in this chapter. We will first take a biosocial perspective, examining how these two codes originate out of powerful and pervasive biological needs for touch, distancing, and territory and how social learning further shapes their acquisition and use. We will then explore their structure and interrelationships with other nonverbal codes; what the norms, standards, and expectations are for their use; and what potential they have as communication vehicles.

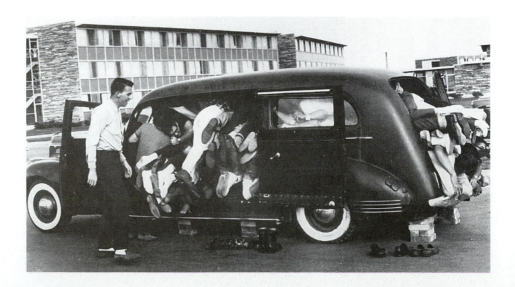

ORIGINS AND ACQUISITION OF THE CONTACT CODES

We are a touch-starved society.

Desmond Morris

Frequent, loving physical contact with other human beings: cuddling, snuggling, stroking, hugging, holding hands, walking arm-in-arm, arms around each other's shoulders, arms around each other's waists. All of us need it. And most of us probably don't get enough of it.

Anne Gottlieb, 1980, p. 80

The Need for Touch

It is well documented that touch is essential to the physical, emotional, and psychological well-being of human infants and to their intellectual, social, and communication development (Fisher, Rytting, & Heslin, 1976; Frank, 1971, 1972; Montagu, 1978; Morris, 1967, 1971).

Physical Impact   The physical importance of tactile stimulation is grounded in the need for comfort and protection and begins before birth. The first sensory experience of the fetus is through the skin. At about 2 months, the skin develops sensitivity around the nose and mouth, and by 14 weeks, the entire body is responsive to its environment in the womb. From 17 weeks until birth, touch reactions to stimuli are largely the same as those shown after birth (Hooker, 1952).

In the womb, the developing fetus is well protected by the warm, fluid environment of the uterus that both cushions it from sharp or jarring movements and provides a controlled temperature. It is pleasantly stimulated by the heartbeat and rhythms of the mother and coordinates its own rhythms to hers (Meerloo, 1955). Birth, therefore, provides the newborn with a radical change in tactile experiences. Besides the trauma of labor contractions and passage through the birth canal, the infant is thrust into an alien environment that includes light, changes in temperature and atmospheric pressure, and contact with humans and foreign objects. Even the experiences of the infant's own respiratory system taking control are novel.

This is a time of great vulnerability and dependence for the newborn. Physical contact with others, particularly the mother, produces an essential element of security. Physical contact buffers the infant from impact, shelters it from hostile stimuli, alleviates fear, and provides needed warmth. Holding, rocking, and patting restore the familiar, soothing rhythms of the womb and can quickly calm a crying baby. Furthermore, the synchrony of rhythm developed between mother and child may regulate the infant's own cardiac, respiratory, and digestive systems.

The warm, protective touch that normally accompanies feeding forges a link between pleasurable human contact and satisfaction of basic human needs. Pediatricians stress that frequent holding and cuddling are as important as the form of feeding itself (breast or bottle). This belief in the value of touch is reinforced by the famous Harlow monkey studies (Harlow, 1958; Harlow, Harlow, & Hansen, 1963; Harlow & Zimmerman, 1958), which raised infant monkeys in isolation from their mothers. When given a choice between a wire mesh surrogate "mother" that supplied food and a terrycloth contraption equipped with a light bulb for warmth, the infant monkeys chose to spend up to 18 hours a day clinging to the cloth mother, only visiting the wire mother briefly for nourishment. Harlow concluded that this deep attachment toward cloth mothers indicated the overriding importance of *contact comfort* and intimacy to the development of the organism.

Other evidence of tactile deprivation among humans further confirms the critical importance of touch to human physical well-being (Montagu, 1978). During the 19th century and the early part of the 20th, the mortality rate among infants in orphanages and children's hospitals was a staggering 90 percent to 100 percent from a disease called *marasmus,* which means "wasting away." Even in institutions providing the best care, babies progressively showed signs of becoming listless, unresponsive to stimuli, depressed, and hysterical. They would engage in autistic rocking, self-biting, and head banging. Eventually, many would develop serious illnesses and die. Those who survived were often seriously retarded or maladjusted for life. What caused this tragic pattern of death and debilitation was the absence of adequate stimulation, including touch. Because the addition of a modicum of caressing and holding significantly reduced the death rate, tactile experiences were regarded as essential:

> These are the reassuringly basic experiences the infant must enjoy if it is to survive in some semblance of health. Extreme sensory deprivation in other respects, such as light and sound, can be survived, as long as the sensory experiences at the skin are maintained. (Montagu, 1978, p. 79)

Less extreme forms of tactile deprivation, such as those experienced by premature babies placed in incubators, have also been associated with health problems later in life, including allergies, eczema, and vulnerability to illness (Montagu, 1978). It has even been argued that infants delivered by cesarean section, who fail to experience the normal birth process, may be prone to more ailments.

The health benefits of touch are not limited to the first years of life. Physical contact appears to have positive effects on adults as well. Petting an animal, for example, is reported to reduce blood pressure in nursing home patients.

Perceptual and Intellectual Impact   Touch not only affects physical development but also contributes to the proper development of mental abilities. Physical contact with the mother in just the first 2 days of life produces a more adaptive infant (Hill & Smith, 1984). The infant's initial rooting and grasping behaviors provide its first awareness of objects in the environment. These early tactile experiences help the infant begin to integrate a number of sensory stimuli into complex patterns. Tactile explorations with the tongue, lips, and hands promote the perceptual discrimination of size, shape, weight, and texture. They facilitate recognition of spatial and temporal relationships, abilities that are essential to mental growth. By contrast, inadequate tactile stimulation leads to limited abstract thinking and conceptualizing and has been associated with learning disabilities and speech difficulties in later years (Despert, 1941; Frank, 1957, 1971; Montagu, 1978).

Emotional and Psychological Impact   As the developing infant explores its environment and its own body through touch, it begins to acquire a sense of self as separate from the world. The child's body becomes a source of great fascination and preoccupation. The quality of these early self-explorations shapes the child's self-identity and body image. Frank (1971) wrote:

> The baby begins to communicate with himself by feeling his own body, exploring its shapes and textures, discovering its orifices and thereby begins to establish his body image which, of course, is reinforced or negated by pleasurable or painful tactile experiences with other human beings. (p. 37)

Children who are discouraged from touching their own or others' bodies or punished for doing so may develop negative body images and guilt feelings about self-touch. Monkey studies suggest that deprivation of physical contact with others may lead to limited self-awareness (Mitchell, 1975).

Other-touch and a certain amount of self-touch also appear necessary for healthy emotional development (see Box 3-1 for an example). Touch brings comfort and reassurance, pleasure and self-gratification. Its palliative effects are evident in the positive response of emotionally disturbed children to stroking and rhythmic slapping. Studies show that infant monkeys raised in isolation resort to self-clinging and rocking to satisfy their need for tactile comfort (Mitchell, 1975). Human infants display the same need for pleasurable contact in their attachment to blankets or stuffed animals and in thumb sucking.

The absence of adequate touch can have serious consequences on mental health. A study of children who were later diagnosed as psychotic found that home movies of their interaction patterns with their mothers differed from those of normal infants. Over

---

BOX 3-1

KIDS WHO GOT HUGS FOUND TO BE HAPPY ADULTS

If you want to help your children have a happy adult life, cuddle them while they are young.

A new study has found that having warm, loving parents in early childhood was more important than other factors like being from a well-to-do or poor family, or even having parents who were divorced or alcoholic, in determining whether, at the age of 41, people had satisfying marriages and close friends and enjoyed their work.

The study is believed to be the first to measure affection between parents and young children, and then examine the children's adjustment once they reached midlife.

Adults whose mothers and fathers were warm and affectionate were able to sustain long and relatively happy marriages, raise children, have close friends and like their work.

"They also showed psychological well-being, a sense of zest and satisfaction with themselves and with their lives," Franz said. "Parental warmth is very good for you as an adult. If you had warm parents, you're likely to be doing better in many realms of life."

While the notion that good parents are warm is now conventional wisdom, it was not when the children in the study were young.

Dr. Carol Franz, a psychologist at Boston University who led the study, said, "In the 1950s, Dr. Spock's advice to be more permissive and loving seemed shocking to many parents."

She added that the study was the first "to show the benefits of parental warmth this late in life."

Source: Excerpted from Goleman, 1991, pp. 1C, 3C.

a 6-month period, mothers of disturbed children reduced reciprocal touch with their infants and increasingly avoided them (Massie, 1978).

Social and Communicative Impact   Most important to our interests in nonverbal communication, adequate touch experiences are essential to the social and communication development of humans. Instinctively, the newborn seeks physical contact and responds to human touch. Its sucking and grasping at the mother's breast express its primal needs for sustenance and protection. In turn, the mother fondles, kisses, pats, rocks, and gently cleans the infant, establishing the roots of intimacy and sealing the bond between child and parent (Morris, 1971). This pattern of infant actions and maternal reactions sets up a feedback system that results in mutual modification of behavior. The more contact between infant and mother, the more synchronization of behavior cycles and the more coordination of communication (Hill & Smith, 1984). Thus the infant's rudimentary communication system originates through touch.

Early tactile experiences in turn set the stage for satisfactory relationships in later life. Children experiencing tactile deprivation show greater difficulty developing attachments to others; they are more prone to introversion and alienation. As Montagu (1978) wrote:

> The body-feeling image we have of ourselves as sensitive or insensitive, sensuous or unfeeling, relaxed or tense, warm or cold, is largely based on our tactual experiences in childhood. The skin of those who have been tactually deprived is "turned off" to those experiences which the tactually satisfied enjoy. (p. 206)

Other aspects of social behavior also depend on adequate touch experience as a prerequisite to healthy development. Animal studies provide inferential evidence. Mice that are allowed physical contact with littermates show more positive behavior than those separated by wire mesh (Porter, Matochik, & Makin, 1983). Monkeys raised in isolation fail to learn appropriate play and courtship rituals, become increasingly aggressive, exhibit sexual dysfunction and inadequate mothering, fail to develop normal gaze avoidance behaviors exhibited by mature monkeys, cannot decipher the dominance hierarchy, and cannot combine unlearned behaviors such as postures, gestures, and vocalizations into meaningful communication patterns (Harlow, 1959; Harlow & Harlow, 1962; Mitchell, 1975). In short, they lack social and communicative competency.

Anthropological research on human behavior shows similar aberrant behavior associated with the absence of touch. Prescott (1975), summarizing a study of 49 primitive cultures, reported that limited physical contact in infancy and adolescence was strongly correlated with high levels of adult violence. In 36 of the societies, high degrees of affection and physical contact corresponded to low degrees of adult violence, while low amounts of infant affection corresponded to high incidences of violence, including killing, torturing, and mutilating enemies. Of the remaining 13 societies, those that were repressive regarding premarital sex also showed high violence, while those that were permissive sexually showed low violence, despite low levels of infant contact. In other words, opportunities for pleasurable body experiences during adolescence compensated for any detrimental effects from deficient physical affection in infancy.

Even though Prescott (1975) concluded, "The deprivation of physical pleasure is a major ingredient in the expression of physical violence" (p. 65), his anthropological studies along with the animal studies do not establish direct causation between the absence of pleasurable tactile stimulation and antisocial behavior. They do imply that touch is a necessary ingredient in the healthy development of individuals and societies, but what is not clear is how much touch is needed, when, and by whom. It has been argued that the need for touch diminishes as people mature into adulthood (Frank, 1957; Morris, 1971).

> To some extent, physical contact is supplanted as a means of communication and self-gratification because we learn other ways of communicating messages that we could originally transmit only through touch. Mothers talk and sing to their children while they hold them, comfort them and reassure them. Slowly the child learns to associate the mother's voice with comfort and security, and eventually learns the words. At the same time, the child is learning his or her own verbal and gestural language systems with which to communicate needs and wants. Thus, touch is slowly replaced by other kinds of communicative signals. The pleasure gained from contact is also partially replaced by other kinds of stimuli that indirectly impinge upon the sense of touch—things like clothing and the rhythm of music. These socially acceptable forms are slowly substituted for self-touching and touching others. (Burgoon & Saine, 1978, p. 78)

Nevertheless, the desire for touching remains. Morris (1971) suggested that we go through cycles of seeking and avoiding touch throughout our life span. The frequent contact of infancy gives way to reduced contact with parents as the child begins to assert independence and to shed "babyish" ways. In adolescence, child-parent contact is at a minimum but is offset by the desire for intimate and sexual contact with others. Intimate touch again becomes extensive and, as young people establish pair bonds, is supplemented by intimate touch with new offspring. The cycle then repeats itself within the new family unit. Research by Mosby (1978) implicitly supports these patterns. She reported that people aged 18 to 25 and 30 to 40 engaged in the most touching, and, regardless of how much touching they actually experience, people at all ages would like more. This discrepancy between actual and ideal touch testifies to the continued desire for touch beyond early childhood. What changes, then, is not the desire for pleasurable contact with others but the contexts in which it occurs. A child may hug a stranger without compunction; adults are far more selective. The important point to realize is that relatively infrequent touch in a given culture is not an accurate barometer of the need or desire for it.

The Need for Territory and Personal Space

> *The history of man's past is largely an account of his efforts to wrest space from others and to defend space from outsiders. . . . To have a territory is one of the essential components of life; to lack one is one of the most precarious of all conditions.*

> Edward T. Hall, 1973, p. 45

A counterpoint to affiliation and contact needs are needs for privacy and distance. These are satisfied by establishing territories and maintaining personal space, behaviors that can act as potent nonverbal messages.

Definitions   Before considering the extent to which such needs exist, we should distinguish between the concepts of territory and personal space. A territory is a *fixed geo-*

graphic area that is occupied, controlled, and defended by a person or group as their exclusive domain (Altman, 1975; Altman & Haythorn, 1967; Goffman, 1963; Hall, 1959; Hediger, 1961; Lyman & Scott, 1967; Pastalan, 1970; Sommer, 1966, 1969; Stea, 1965). Typically, territories function to regulate access to scarce resources such as food, water, and shelter; to guard accumulated resources; to protect the family unit from disease and physical harm; to provide privacy for mating and child rearing; to permit protracted action or thought without disruption; and to create solidarity within a social unit. Thus they are strongly associated with species survival and physical needs. The existence of a territory is revealed through the territorial behavior of its occupants. Key elements of territoriality include (a) marking boundaries and personalizing a space to declare ownership, (b) using warning signs or displays to alert intruders that they are trespassing, (c) patrolling perimeters or creating barriers to access, and (d) defending the territory from intrusion (Altman, 1975; Bakker & Bakker-Rabdau, 1985; Vine, 1975).

Personal space, by contrast, is an *invisible, portable, adjustable bubble of space surrounding an individual that is actively maintained to protect the person from physical and emotional threats* (Burgoon & Jones, 1976; Ciolek, 1983; Dosey & Meisels, 1969; Hall, 1966; Hayduk, 1978; Horowitz, Duff, & Stratton, 1964; Sommer, 1959). As originally conceived by Katz (1937), it is a person's perceived self-boundary and has been referred to as a *body-buffer zone* (Horowitz et al., 1964). A. L. Scott (1988, 1992) has defined "personal space boundaries" as more than just a physical space issue. She has conceptualized them as invisible boundaries that separate a person's internal self (body, mind, and spirit) from the external environment. Because they are grounded in individual needs, preferences, idiosyncrasies, and situational factors, personal space boundaries are permeable and flexible, expanding or contracting depending on the circumstance. They can also be viewed as both a trait and a state. As a trait, people may tend to develop open or closed boundaries and rigid or flexible boundaries. As a state, the degree of openness or flexibility may be influenced by a host of listener, environmental, and momentary individual factors. To illustrate, a hospitalized patient who has fixed, closed boundaries typically may be distant from others, unwilling to touch or be touched, and nondisclosive. But she may drop her invisible shield if her health is in crisis and a female nurse approaches her gradually.

Although territories and personal space are similar in their self-protection roles, they differ in several ways. Territories are usually fixed geographic areas with visibly marked boundaries; personal space is tied to the person and has invisible, changeable boundaries. Territories are also stationary (an automobile being an exception), whereas personal space is mobile (Sommer, 1959). Intrusions on one's territory or personal space are both likely to create discomfort, but territoriality invasions are more likely to provoke a fight or aggressive response, whereas personal space invasions may provoke a flight or avoidance response.

Innateness of Territoriality   Although the extent to which territoriality and personal spacing patterns are inborn or learned is the subject of considerable controversy (e.g., Altman, 1975; Ardrey, 1966, 1970; Bakker & Bakker-Rabdau, 1985; Vine, 1975), that humans show strong spatial needs seems indisputable. Evidence of innateness comes from a variety of perspectives, including ethological, anthropological, biological, sociological, psychological, and communication observations and experiments.

Evidence from anthropology, ethology, and biology   The case for human territoriality begins with a biological perspective that humans are subject to the same evolutionary processes as other species and share some of the same underlying survival response patterns as other vertebrates (Hediger, 1961). Often observations of territorial behavior in other mammals are used to bolster the claim that territoriality is a necessity for many species including humans and that failure to secure adequate territory has serious consequences.

Two of the most famous studies are Christian's of Sika deer (Christian, Flyer, & Davis, 1961) and Calhoun's of rats (1962, 1966), both of which demonstrate the detrimental effects of overcrowding. In the 1950s, Sika deer were thriving on James Island in Chesapeake Bay, an ideal habitat that was free of natural predators and had ample supplies of food and water. Suddenly, the deer population began to die in large numbers until the population had dropped from 300 to 80. The autopsies conducted on the deer

Human territoriality has been compared to that of other species.

were compared to earlier samples and revealed that the deer did not die from disease. Their only abnormality was greatly enlarged adrenal glands. Because the adrenal cortex responds to stress by producing larger quantities of adrenaline, which, over time, can be fatal, Christian concluded that the lack of adequate living space had created such stress for the deer that it literally caused their deaths. He further argued that mice, dogs, guinea pigs, monkeys, and even humans would be prone to respond to density-induced stress in the same way.

Calhoun studied the deleterious effects of excess population density and inadequate space by observing rats in a controlled laboratory setting. He built a pen that had ample water, food, air, nesting material, and opportunities for social contacts. All was well until the rats began to propagate. Soon there were too many rats for the small space, and bizarre behaviors began to appear, including a change in female nesting and nursing habits, premature births and aborted fetuses, sexual dysfunction, cannibalism, homo-sexuality, hyperactivity, vicious attacks by some males and cringing withdrawal by oth-ers, and increased illness. Calhoun labeled this deterioration of behavior in the face of excess population density a "behavioral sink."

These studies, among others, are used as illustrations of the harmful consequences of animals having inadequate territory. The inference drawn is that humans will respond in a similar fashion. A chief proponent of this position was Ardrey (1966, 1970), who argued that Homo sapiens are territorial creatures whose territoriality is partly a function of biological heredity and partly a function of culturally learned patterns of behavior. He cited examples of modern-day warfare as evidence that territorial and aggressive instincts have not been extinguished. His position is an intuitively appealing one because it relies on familiar incidents of individuals, groups, and countries creating and defend-ing territories.

However, many scholars (e.g., Altman, 1975; Boulding, 1968; Edney, 1976; Gorer, 1968; Leach, 1968; Montagu, 1968; Schneirla, 1968; Vine, 1975) did not share Ardrey's conviction that territorial behavior is innate and criticized his position as overly sim-plistic and anecdotal. They cautioned that humans cannot be compared directly to other species. Such factors as complex social organization, the existence of cultural norms, nomadic patterns or high mobility among some cultures, unique human motives, and cognitions regarding territory and space challenge the comparability of circumstances between humans and other mammals. Vine (1975) noted that many lower primates, who are humans' closest relatives, are themselves not strongly territorial. Edney (1976) also pointed out that humans invite people into their territories for visits and often take flight rather than engage in aggressive defense of a territory. Nevertheless, both researchers believed that human individuals and societies do display territorial proclivities.

A different form of biological evidence comes from work on brain processes (Esser, 1971, 1972), which indicates that the more primitive areas of the brain (i.e., the R-com-plex and the limbic system) govern territorial and fight-or-flight behavior. These parts of the brain, which are oldest in an evolutionary sense, are most closely tied to instinctive and innate response patterns. This suggests that territorial defense is an inborn reflex.

Equally important to territoriality is the need to maintain a certain amount of per-sonal space, which may in fact be the more fundamental drive. Many experts on animal spacing (e.g., Leyhausen, 1971; McBride, 1971; Schneirla, 1965; Vine, 1975) have contended that members of the same group characteristically adopt a distance between themselves and others that reconciles approach and withdrawal forces. Because personal space is mobile, it is possible simultaneously to preserve spatial insulation and to avoid aggressive encounters by simply moving out of range of another individual or group. This makes defense of a fixed territory less essential. Many species also permit overlapping territorial boundaries without conflict, and "time sharing" of the same location may even occur to regulate use of prime spaces. Because needs for territory and space intermingle, the distinction between territoriality and personal space motives is often blurred. When aggressive or withdrawal behaviors are observed, it is unclear whether they are reactions to a territorial intrusion, a violation of personal space, or both. It may well be that a main purpose for establishing territories is to ensure adequate personal space.

Evidence from sociology, psychology, and communication   Most of the research by social scientists falls into one of four categories: naturalistic observations of territorial definition and defense, observational studies of overcrowding, experimental (controlled laboratory) studies of overcrowding, and experimental studies of personal space invasion. The inference to be drawn from this large body of research is that if humans carve out territories or experience ill effects from inadequate territory or space, they must have a basic need for it.

Personal experience alone attests to people's strong habit of establishing territories. At school, you may choose a particular seat in class and return to that seat repeatedly. If someone else then sits in it, you may feel vaguely violated. At home, the person who does most of the cooking may treat the kitchen as his or her territory and may resent interference from well-meaning relatives or friends. Videotaped observations of home patterns (Scheflen, 1971) and questionnaire data (Altman, Nelson, & Lett, 1972) confirm that most U.S. households have clearly defined territories. Observations of other types of residences (e.g., mental institutions, delinquent residences, and dormitories) and of workplaces likewise reveal strong inclinations for people to claim territories and for others to respect those territories (Goffman, 1971; Lipman, 1970; Roos, 1968; Sommer, 1969; Vinsel, Brown, Altman, & Foss, 1980).

Where home territories are inadequate or nonexistent, individuals may band together to create a group-controlled space. Sociological observations of adolescent street gangs and urban criminal gangs reveal that such groups use a wide variety of means to block entry to their "turf" and often resort to violence to expel intruders (R. N. Johnson, 1972; Whyte, 1943). This proclivity to declare and defend a territory is especially pronounced in areas where poverty and overcrowding are the norm and is an adaptation to stressful circumstances. Census data and observations of congested areas, ranging from midtown Manhattan to inner-city Paris, show that as population density increases, so do such serious health and mental problems as crime, tuberculosis, respiratory ailments, mental illness, infant mortality, suicide, and juvenile delinquency (e.g., Davis, 1971; Dubos, 1965; Newman, 1972; Stokols, 1972). Illness complaints in prisons are likewise systematically related to crowding-induced psychological stress (McCain, Cox, & Paulus, 1976), and crowding has been cited as a major contributor to prison riots. Conversely, where residents of urban areas have "defensible spaces" and clearly recognizable territorial boundaries, conflict, crime, and social disruption are less frequent (Newman, 1972).

Even in a college dormitory setting, those who use diverse means to regulate privacy in their dorm room are more likely to stay in school; those who fail to develop such territorial control mechanisms during their first year are more likely to drop out (Vinsel et al., 1980). Although the connection between congestion and these problems is only correlational and not causal, it does suggest that inadequate territory or territorial control leaves people more susceptible to physical, emotional, and health dangers.

Territorial violations occur when there is unauthorized use, unwanted surveillance, direct intrusions, or contamination from trash others leave behind (Lyman & Scott, 1967). One way people take preventive or restorative action is to use *markers*. These may include boundary markers (such as hedges, fences, and "No Trespassing" signs), which identify the perimeter of the space, or central markers, which locate the middle of a locale. The homeless may lay claim to part of a public park just by erecting a cardboard box with their meager belongings in it. A simple bottle of suntan oil can reserve your favorite spot on a public beach. Sociological and experimental evidence reveals that where space is at a premium or where occupancy is long-term, territorial marking increases and typically deters encroachments by others (Altman, 1975; Becker, 1973; Edney, 1972; Edney & Jordan-Edney, 1974; Sommer & Becker, 1969).

Another way that people prevent contamination and repel intrusions is through *barriers to entry*, such as walls, door locks, guard dogs, and security guards. One of the main attractions to having one's own secretary or receptionist at work is the gatekeeping function the person serves, limiting others' access to one's office territory. Finally, *occupancy* itself will often prevent violations by others because it represents the potential for forcible resistance. Rightfully or not, occupancy is usually taken as a sign of ownership of a space and is sufficient to keep others from intruding. That may explain why law enforcement people are so reluctant to evict squatters.

Impact of Violations   All these defensive maneuvers imply that people are distressed by violations, intrusions, or contamination of their territory. Experimental research by psychologists and communicologists confirms that deprivation or intrusion upon territory or space elicits the characteristic features of stress. These fit under what is called the general adaptation syndrome (GAS), which consists of behavioral and physiological indicators of alarm, resistance, and exhaustion (Evans & Eichelman, 1976; Selye, 1956). Specifically, research on personal space invasion, excess density (too many people in a locale), and overcrowding (perceived deficient supply of space relative to demand) reveals six effects; Box 3-2 is one example.

1 *Physiological responses.* Consistent with the GAS, laboratory experiments have found increased blood pressure and heart rate, increased skin conductance, and heightened EEG activity with personal space violations and crowding (Aiello, DeRisi, Epstein, & Karlin, 1977; Aiello, Epstein, & Karlin, 1975; Epstein, Woolfolk, & Lehrer, 1981; Evans & Eichelman, 1976; Gales, Spratt, Chapman, & Smallbone, 1975; McBride, King, & James, 1965).

2 *Anxiety cues.* A number of ingenious experiments, such as having an accomplice join a stranger at a library table or invade the personal space of a salesperson, have demonstrated anxiety reactions to territorial or personal space invasion. The nonverbal responses to such intrusions include avoiding gaze (sometimes preceded by a threat stare), body blocking, building barriers with possessions, leaning away, adopting an

---

BOX 3-2

THESE CONS WEREN'T SURPRISED: THEY EXPECTED RIOT

Residents at the Michigan Parole Camp stood at the edge of the camp property Tuesday and watched as flames shot up from temporary inmate housing units across the street. They watched as a thousand prisoners in the north complex at Jackson Prison swarmed around the yard, armed with sticks and clubs, flinging rocks and sticks through windows.

Later, as the prison tried to pull itself back together, there were no outward signs of emotion as the parole camp residents related what they had seen—just a resigned acceptance.

"You have to do time over there to know what it's like," said 43-year-old camp cook Joe Weems, convicted of armed robbery and a veteran of the Michigan prison system. "There's more tension inside those walls than you can find anywhere else in the world.

". . . They [prison officials] brag about the school and the recreation facilities, but it's not geared to the number of people they put in there. [The north complex] was designed for about 750 inmates. Then they bring in these [temporary housing] modules and cram 1000 people in there.

". . . It's just like packing sardines in a can. If you keep stuffing them in there, the pressure builds up inside and pretty soon the top's going to blow."

Source: Walker-Tyson, 1981, pp. 1B, 4B.

---

indirect body orientation, and increasing postural tension, nervous gestures, self-touching, and random hand and foot movements (Argyle & Dean, 1965; Baxter & Deanovitch, 1970; Burgoon & Aho, 1982; Daley, 1973; Epstein et al., 1981; Felipe & Sommer, 1966; Garfinkel, 1964; Garner, 1972; Goldberg, Kiesler, & Collins, 1969; Patterson, Mullens, & Romano, 1971; Patterson & Sechrest, 1970; Sommer, 1959, 1969; Sundstrom, 1975).

Another coping strategy is to develop a nonperson orientation. This is exactly what people do when confronted with strangers in an elevator—they pretend others are not there by treating the strangers as objects rather than persons. Experiments have shown that people are far less anxious when approaching or being approached by an object such as a picture or a hat rack than by another person (Horowitz et al., 1964; McBride et al., 1965). Sommer (1969) noted, "A nonperson cannot invade someone's space any more than a tree or chair can. It is common under certain conditions for one person to react to another as an object or part of the background" (p. 24). He pointed out that we often treat maids, janitors, and hospital patients the same way. By ignoring them, their presence no longer constitutes a spatial intrusion.

3 *Interaction avoidance, withdrawal, and flight.* Although people may respond to invasions of their home territory with physical defenses, verbal aggression, arguments, or pleading, surprisingly, in other social situations people rarely use verbal means to get an intruder to depart. Rather, most people respond by reducing or avoiding interaction and ultimately, if the intrusion continues, taking flight (Ahmed, 1980; Baum & Greenberg, 1975; Baum, Harpin, & Valins, 1975; Baum, Riess, & O'Hara, 1974; Felipe & Sommer, 1966; Greenberg & Firestone, 1977; Griffitt & Veitch, 1971; Knowles, 1972; Konecni, Libuser, Morton, & Ebbesen, 1975; Milgram, 1970; Smith & Knowles, 1979; Stokols, 1976; Valins & Baum, 1973). This pattern was demonstrated in a series of experiments designed to study the effects of extended confine-

ment in a small space such as a submarine or a bomb shelter (Altman, 1971; Altman & Haythorn, 1967; Altman, Taylor, & Wheeler, 1971; Smith & Haythorn, 1972). Pairs of sailors were placed in isolation together for 8 to 20 days. The most striking finding was that a majority of the subjects in one study were unable to complete the experiment. They found the experience too stressful and literally bailed out. Moreover, both aborters and incompatible pairs who completed the experiments showed increased territoriality over time, while compatible pairs showed a high degree of territoriality early on. The designation of separate territories and withdrawal from interaction, labeled *cocooning* behavior, was interpreted as attempts to adapt to a perceived stressful situation.

4 *Decreased task performance.* People subjected to crowding in the form of personal space invasion perform worse on cognitive tasks than people who are not crowded (Aiello et al., 1977; Evans & Howard, 1973; Heller, Groff, & Solomon, 1977; Paulus, Annis, Seta, Schkade, & Matthews, 1976; Worchel & Teddlie, 1976; Worchel & Yohai, 1979); see Box 3-3 for implications in designing work spaces. Even shoppers do worse completing shopping tasks when under crowded conditions (Langer & Saegert, 1977).

5 *Perceived discomfort and crowding.* When people are placed in a high-density environment, are surrounded by a lot of people in a small space, or have their personal space invaded, they report more uneasiness, discomfort, and feelings of crowding (Baum et al., 1975; Epstein et al., 1981; Evans & Howard, 1973; Greenberg & Firestone, 1977; Rodin, Solomon, & Metcalf, 1978; Stokols, Rall, Pinner, & Schopler, 1973; Sundstrom, 1975; Valins & Baum, 1973; Walden, Nelson, & Smith, 1981; Webb, 1978; Worchel & Teddlie, 1976; Worchel & Yohai, 1979). The sensation of crowding is especially pronounced when the person has little or no control over the situation.

6 *More verbal aggressiveness, less affiliativeness, or both.* The discomfort of crowding also causes victims to express more verbal hostility, show less friendliness nonverbally, or become less disclosive than those in uncrowded circumstances (Baum et al., 1975; Sundstrom, 1975). Just the expectation of crowding causes people to dislike

---

BOX 3-3

APPLICATIONS: ELBOWROOM IN THE WORKPLACE

The research on personal space and territory has implications for how workspace should be designed to accommodate employees' needs. To give employees some sense of physical integrity and separation, their work area should allow for distance and insulation from others. The lack of such distance is one reason employees dislike open-pit or "bull pen" office arrangements, that is, arrangements where several people have desks in the same open space. Even small cubicles are preferable to open area arrangements because they provide a buffer against personal space invasions and permit employees to mark their own territory with personal possessions and the like.

Supervisors can show greater sensitivity to spatial and territorial needs by not invading an employee's territory without permission. The manager who walks into an employee's office without knocking or, worse yet, rifles through an employee's desk and mail is intruding on a fundamental need. Such intrusions may trigger all the reactions described in the GAS. A sensitive supervisor or employer recognizes such signals from an employee as a possible plea for more distance or space.

others in the environment (Baum & Greenberg, 1975). Citing the stimulus overload that confronts people in large metropolitan areas like New York City, Milgram (1970) noted that "a city dweller blocks inputs by assuming an unfriendly countenance, which discourages others from initiating contact" (p. 1462).

Of course, as with other human behavior, territoriality and personal space defense are complex processes that do not operate in the same way for all people. Men tend to show more stress, aggressiveness, and poor task performance in crowded situations than women; sometimes women are actually more affiliative and effective when crowded (Aiello et al., 1977; Epstein & Karlin, 1975; Evans & Howard, 1973; Freedman, 1975; Freedman, Levy, Buchanan, & Price, 1972; Griffitt & Veitch, 1971; Leibman, 1970; Stokols et al., 1973). Men and women also react differently to side-by-side versus face-to-face approaches (Fisher & Byrne, 1975). Age alters reactions. Younger people find close proximity stressful and debilitating, while older people, who have less opportunity for affiliative contact, find it pleasant and facilitative of performance (Smith, Reinheimer, & Gabbard-Alley, 1981). Furthermore, the nature of the task, the cognitive experience of crowding, personality factors, and interference with goal attainment make a difference (e.g., Ahmed, 1980; Aiello et al., 1977; Freedman, 1975; Langer & Saegert, 1977; McCallum, Rusbult, Hong, Walden, & Schopler, 1979; Rodin et al., 1978; Stokols, 1972; Thalhofer, 1980; Worchel & Yohai, 1979). Nonetheless, the evidence is substantial that human affiliative drives are matched by powerful drives toward territoriality and spatial insulation. These strong needs underlie the potency of haptics and proxemics as communication codes.

Development of Haptics and Proxemics

The ability to send and interpret haptic and proxemic messages begins with an infant's first human contacts after birth. As Table 3-1 illustrates, the first year of life is a crucial period in the infant's acquisition of tactile abilities and, particularly, the use of touch as a means of expressing needs and affection. At the same time, the newborn develops the spatial and depth perception necessary for understanding proxemic messages and in the latter half of the first year shows signs of having established a personal space zone. Research indicates that by the end of their first year, children who initiate approaches toward strangers typically get no closer than 4 or 5 feet, while approaches initiated by strangers typically evoke apprehension in the child (Horner, 1983).

Although the earliest touch and proxemic behaviors of infants are undoubtedly grounded in innate response patterns, very early in their development, infants and children begin to acquire the patterns of behavior that are appropriate for their culture, subculture, and gender (Hall, 1966). They also learn the norms for different social contexts (Andersen & Sull, 1985). These patterns develop because of the different experiences to which children are exposed and because of active modeling and reinforcement by adults. One of the norms children learn is to exercise restraint in how closely they approach others (Aiello & Aiello, 1974). Photographs of people walking with companions and observations of parents walking with children reveal, for instance, that average distance increases from preschool age through the teen years and into adulthood (Burgess, 1983; Sigelman & Adams, 1990).

TABLE 3-1
DEVELOPMENT OF HAPTIC AND PROXEMIC ENCODING AND DECODING ABILITIES

1–3 Months	4–6 Months	7–9 Months	10–12 Months
Haptics			
Becomes quiet when held. May start or stop crying, depending on who is holding baby. Adjusts posture to body of person holding baby. Grasps, clasps people. Roots and sucks at breast. Voluntary grasp develops. Most significant stimulation is haptic and oral.	Responds to and enjoys handling. Wants to touch, hold, turn, shake, mouth objects. Shows anticipation, waves and raises arms to be picked up. Tries to get close to person near crib. Clings when held.	Explores body with mouth and hands. Pushes away unwanted objects.	Gives affection to humans and to objects like toys.
Proxemics			
Clearly discriminates proximity and object size. Distinguishes near and far objects in space. Experiments with changes in proximity by extending and contracting arm. Orients and signals distinctively to each of several people.	Aware of differences in depth and distance.	Approaches and follows mother. Rejects confinement. Aware of vertical space. Recognizes dimensions of objects. Fears heights.	Ranges distant space into regions of different depths. Senses self as distinct from others. Perceives objects as detached and separate and related in time and space. Reacts to approach of strangers.

Source: Adapted from Caplan, 1973.

In the case of touch, boy and girl infants have different touch experiences in their first year of life. Prior to 6 months of age, boys apparently receive more touching, rocking, holding, and kissing, while after 6 months, girls receive more (Lewis, 1972; Lewis & Goldberg, 1969). At preschool age and into adolescence, boys and girls engage in more same-sex touch than opposite-sex touch, but girls have more contacts, especially reciprocal ones, than boys (Berman & Smith, 1984; Williams & Willis, 1978; Willis & Hoffman, 1975; Willis, Reeves, & Buchanan, 1976). Boys are also more likely to touch a male teacher, while girls touch male and female teachers equally. Teachers reinforce the pattern by engaging in more same-sex touch than opposite-sex touch with children and by using different types of touch by gender (Perdue & Connor, 1978). Overall, use of touch decreases among all children as they age, with white children reducing their touch rates faster than black children (Willis & Hoffman, 1975; Willis & Reeves, 1976; Willis et al., 1976).

The use of touch for communication purposes is also linked to language development. A study of language-impaired and normal-speaking children found that children with language difficulties used far more touch than their nonimpaired peers and were equivalent in touch use to younger children at the same level of language development. Among normal-speaking children, touch use declined with age (Rom, 1979). Thus touch appears to be a compensation for lack of ability to communicate effectively through language. This conforms to the argument that touch is a more primitive form of communication that eventually gives way to more sophisticated, precise forms of expression (such as language).

In the case of interpersonal distance, children soon learn adult patterns of behavior. The older they get, the farther away they tend to position themselves from others (Aiello & Aiello, 1974; Andersen, Andersen, Wendt, & Murphy, 1981). Whereas a 3-year-old may sit close enough to touch a playmate while working on a task, 5- and 7-year-olds space themselves farther apart (Lomranz, Shapira, Choresh, & Gilat, 1975). Between the ages of 5 and 10, children begin to show the same distance patterns as adults. This means that they learn to vary their distance according to circumstances (Hutt & Vaizey, 1967). Guardo and Meisels (Guardo, 1969; Guardo & Meisels, 1971; Meisels & Guardo, 1969) conducted a series of studies on what kinds of spatial differentiations are made and when. They found that by third grade, children have well-established schemas that associate proximity with interpersonal closeness (i.e., they decrease distance with people they like). By sixth or seventh grade, they also make discriminations on the basis of such contextual factors as familiarity and gender, with girls showing a more refined schema earlier than boys (a pattern consistent with their earlier acquisition of language skills).

Other observational research supports that children adapt their distancing behavior to sex, ethnicity, and social roles (Aiello & Jones, 1971; Berman & Smith, 1984; Jones & Aiello, 1973; Pedersen, 1973). By fifth grade, boys adopt greater distances and more indirect body orientation than girls. Some evidence for opposite-sex attraction appears in that children generally adopt the least distance from opposite-sex peers, followed by opposite-sex adults. Racial or ethnic differences may also be a factor, but the research evidence is inconclusive. Finally, the nature of the social relationship makes a difference: the distance between children at play correlates with the number of friendly or unfriendly acts committed by a playmate (King, 1966). Thus children acquire haptic and proxemic norms by the time they complete elementary school. This development is clearly gender-linked, with girls developing more adultlike management of distance sooner than boys (Altman, 1975).

Two other aspects of proxemic development that have received less attention are the use of territory and the acquisition of the concept of privacy. Although all children become more aggressive in response to increased density (Loo, 1972), which would suggest that they are predisposed to maintain some degree of territory or spatial integrity, this need appears to differ by sex. One study found that boys maintain more space, spend more time outdoors, and enter more areas than girls (Harper & Sanders, 1975). This tendency for boys to "claim more territories" for themselves is consistent with the findings that males require more personal space and respond to crowding with more aggression, hostility, and discomfort than females. This should in turn result in their communicating territorial needs under different levels of crowding and possibly responding to territorial encroachments in different ways.

As might be expected, the concept of privacy becomes increasingly complex with age, although children have a good understanding of it by age 9 (Wolfe & Laufer, 1974).

The increasing need for independence, solitude, and secrecy is evident in the expressions of privacy that develop. As children grow, they use more privacy markers (e.g., closing doors) and follow more privacy rules (e.g., knocking on doors), with these expressions of privacy becoming especially prevalent in adolescence and in cross-sex relationships such as father-daughter or brother-sister (Parke & Sawin, 1979).

The combined haptics and proxemics literature reveals mature patterns of touch and spacing behavior long before children leave adolescence.

CLASSIFYING THE CONTACT CODES

Haptics

Until recently, touch was not even recognized as a communication code. Many nonverbal texts subsumed tactile expressions under kinesics or proxemics. However, evidence of its significant impact on human relations has kindled a growing interest in its role as a communication vehicle.

The approaches taken to determining the code elements of haptics can be divided roughly into structural and functional categories.

Structural Approaches   Structural approaches patterned after linguistics focus on the basic forms and features that make up the haptic code and its semantic content. Kauffman (1971) and Harrison (1974) suggested that types of touch comparable to the kineme and kinemorph can be identified. These basic building blocks, called either *tacs* and *tacemorphs* or *haptons* and *haptemes*, presumably consist of the types of movements listed below (many of which come from Argyle, 1975, and Morris, 1977):

hit	slap	pat	hug	pinch
kiss	tug	caress	brush	stroke
kick	punch	shake	poke	grasp
rock	hold	pull	tap	lick
embrace	tickle	guide	groom	tackle
jab	grab	tweak	push	restrain
bite	shove	nibble	rub	nuzzle

As yet, no systematic work has deciphered which of these (or similar types of touch designations) are regarded as separate units and which are merely variations on the same type of touch. For example, is a tap actually different from a pat?

A different structural approach considers the *dimensions* or physical properties that distinguish one type of touch from another. Immediately apparent dimensions are (a) the intensity or amount of pressure used (soft to hard), (b) the duration of touch (brief to prolonged), (c) the location of the touch on the body (e.g., shoulders, face, hands), (d) the body part delivering the touch (e.g., hand, foot, upper torso, lips), and (e) the frequency of contact (single to multiple contacts). To illustrate, a pat is a soft, relatively brief, often repetitive movement delivered by the hand to various body locations but usually occurring in the upper body region. Because a pat to the derriere may signify something quite different from a pat on the head, the dimensional approach, by including location as one distinguishing feature, adds some descriptive specificity missing from the simple labeling of types of touch.

Of course, the ultimate goal of a structural approach is to identify meaningful semantic units or dimensions. In pursuit of this goal, Nguyen, Heslin, and Nguyen (1975; 1976; Heslin, Nguyen, & Nguyen, 1983) conducted a series of studies to identify the meanings associated with various types of touches and locations of touches. They found that different types of touch do convey different meanings. Among a pat, a stroke, a squeeze, and a brush, a pat was seen as the most playful and friendly; a stroke as the most loving, pleasant, and sexual; a squeeze as relatively playful, warm, and pleasant; and a brush as nonsexual. (Some of these meanings differ by gender.) Interestingly, different body locations also carry different meanings. A touch to the leg is playful. A touch on the hands is loving, friendly, and pleasant. And a touch to the genital area conveys sexual desire. Finally, the researchers found that certain meanings, such as loving, pleasant, friendly, and playful, are highly related to one another.

Functional Approaches   Functional approaches also have to do with the meanings associated with touch but focus instead on the purposes of touch rather than their form and on the contextual or relationship factors that constrain meaning. Heslin (1974; Heslin & Alper, 1983) proposed five different types of situations or relationships under which various touches can be classified:

1 *Functional, professional.* This is the least intimate category and consists of one-sided, instrumental touches (those needed to complete some task such as a physician's examination or a golf pro's lesson). Edwards (1981) proposed some forms of touch that also fit this category: (a) information pickup touch (e.g., taking a pulse), (b) movement facilitation touch (giving someone a boost or carrying someone to safety), (c) prompting (providing manual guidance in learning), and (d) ludic touch (touch as part of games, such as holding hands during ring-around-a-rosy).
2 *Social, polite.* These touches are relatively formal and governed by social norms. Included are touches that are social amenities such as handshakes and other kinds of contact during greeting and parting rituals.
3 *Friendship, warmth.* These are moderately intimate touches, usually exchanged between well-acquainted individuals. Congratulatory, comforting, or nurturing touches fit here. Because such forms of touch may be easily confused with more intimate, sexual touches, they are more likely to occur in public than in private.
4 *Love, intimacy.* This highly intimate contact is usually regarded as pleasant and welcome in close relationships and a source of discomfort if committed by a nonintimate.
5 *Sexual arousal.* The most intense and most intimate class of contacts.

To see how various touches relate to one another, Edwards (1984) asked counseling subjects to report their own touching and their receipt of touch during a cocounseling course. Nurturant, celebratory, ludic, and cathartic touches were found to be highly interrelated. Caring touch and sexually arousing touch were seen as separate, as were the perception of touch as threatening and one's own ability to threaten others with touch. The inclusion of aggressive and threatening touches adds an important antisocial dimension of touch that is missing in the Heslin-Alper classification.

An even more elaborate classification comes from Jones and Yarbrough (1985), who arrived at their categories on the basis of participant logs of over 1,000 actual contacts. They found that touches could be classified as one or more of the following types, depending on the context:

1 *Positive affect touches.* Communicate unambiguous positive emotions, including support (nurturing, reassuring, promising protection), appreciation (expressing gratitude), inclusion (enhancing togetherness and psychological closeness), sexual intent or interest (expressing physical attraction), and affection (expressing generalized positive regard).
2 *Playful touches.* Designed to lighten an interaction and possibly give double meaning to a verbal message, including playful affection and playful aggression.
3 *Control touches.* Direct the behavior, attitude, or feeling state of another, including compliance, attention giving, and announcing a response (emphasizing the feeling state of the initiator).
4 *Ritualistic touches.* Involved in greetings and departures.
5 *Hybrid touches.* Combine other types, including greeting-affection and departure-affection.
6 *Task-related touches.* Associated with the performance of a task (such as the functional-professional touches of the previous system).

Except for the omission of negative affect and aggressive touches, which are less likely to be reported by participants, this taxonomy appears complete. Grounded as it is in actual observations of touch across a wide range of circumstances, it represents an excellent compendium of the meanings and purposes for which touch is employed. What is needed next is to cross the structural approach with the functional approach to determine more precisely which types of touch convey which meanings independently or in combination with other cues. For example, what types of touch qualify as playful aggression, and what specific accompanying nonverbal and verbal behaviors signal that a punch is playful aggression rather than serious hostility?

Proxemics

Less progress has been made in establishing the basic code elements of proxemics. Although the literature makes distinctions among home range, living space, true territory, social distance, individual distance, personal spheres, and personal fields for animals (e.g., Hediger, 1950, 1961; McBride, 1971), the three categories that have received the most attention for humans are territory, personal space, and conversational distance.

Territories   Altman (1975) distinguished among primary, secondary, and public territories. Primary territories are those that are most central to the daily lives of the individuals or groups within them. They are occupied or owned on a consistent, exclusive, and usually permanent or semipermanent basis, enough so that others identify the space as belonging to the owner or occupant. Homes, offices, bedrooms—even a patient's bed in a hospital—qualify as primary territories. These territories represent physical and psychological retreats and are so significant that people's identities are often connected to them. To violate such a territory is a serious affront.

Secondary territories, by contrast, are more peripheral to day-to-day functioning, may involve more temporary and nonexclusive use, and generally have more permeable boundaries. They are "semipublic" territories and as such have less definite rules about their use and what constitutes encroachment. A country club or a neighborhood bar are examples of secondary territories. Formal or implicit membership in the group often determines who has access to the territory.

Public territories are those to which almost anyone has free access and no occupancy privileges. Use of such spaces is also more transitory by any one individual or group. Playgrounds, beaches, sidewalks, and the like are available for use by the public at large and are regulated only by the society's laws and customs.

Another similar system for classifying territories comes from Lyman and Scott (1967), who defined four types: *body, home, interactional,* and *public.* Body territory, as the label implies, is one's own person and the space immediately surrounding it (which corresponds to what we have called personal space). Usually the individual has complete autonomy over who has access to it, and touching is allowed only with permission. In the American culture, as with other western cultures, the body territory is the most private and inviolate. We are outraged by rapes, assaults, and murders precisely because they are the ultimate violations. Opponents of capital punishment view executions the same way.

Home territory, similar to primary territory, is any geographic locale, whether grass hut, tent, or private estate, that a person or group regards as an exclusive and private domain. Residents have ultimate control of such space and are justified in using force to expel intruders. Offices, desks, and automobiles also qualify as home territories.

Interactional territory, like secondary territory, is semipublic, with loosely defined rules and customs over who is entitled to access. Movie theaters and classrooms are interactional territories. You are supposed to enter only if you buy a ticket or pay tuition. In practice, encroachments are far more common in interactional territories because social sanctions are not always enforced against intruders.

Public territory in Lyman and Scott's system coincides with Altman's category of the same name.

It is probably true that competent communicators in this culture can distinguish conceptually among these various types of territories. However, in actual performance there appears to be considerable confusion about the use and misuse of these territories. For example, when school cafeterias are extremely busy, there are often disputes between studiers and diners about who has rights to the tables. Leaving your possessions at a table may not guarantee that the table will be vacant when you return with your food. By the same token, if you ask to join someone else's table in a crowded dining room, the person may feel reluctant to refuse you. The reason is that it is not clear whether such territories qualify as interactional or public areas. If they are interactional, then diners who are conforming to the legitimate activity for the territory—eating—have more claim to tables than do studiers. And people who mark their space with possessions or occupy it first have the right to treat it as their own. But if areas are public territories, then no one's rights prevail over anyone else's, so long as no one is violating any law.

This confusion over definitions of territories can take a humorous turn, as in the story of a penniless couple who, due to a broken-down car, took up residence in the basement of a college office building. Because the building had at one time been the president's home, it was equipped with servants' quarters that had been converted into a faculty office. The squatter couple soon discovered that a faculty office with a couch, carpet, bathroom, and refrigerator was far more accommodating than their makeshift arrangement of a wicker basket for food and sleeping bags on the concrete floor. So they gradually began shifting their living activities into the faculty office. The faculty member returned one evening to find laundry hanging from the ceiling pipes, a trail of clothes leading to the bathroom, and the sounds of giggles and splashes wafting through the bathroom door. What he presumed to be his home territory had now become theirs! Moreover, as others learned about the couple's activities, they, too, began taking liberties with the office, turning it into a lounge—an interactional territory. The confusion over what kind of territory it was eventually got resolved through a time-sharing arrangement: the professor reclaimed his office as his own territory during the day and early evening but relinquished it to the couple at bedtime.

Personal Space and Conversational Distance   These two concepts refer to dynamic, mobile (nonfixed) space. Although writers have traditionally referred to the spacing patterns between two or more individuals as personal space, personal space as originally conceived refers to the minimum amount of spatial insulation a person requires. Yet people may space themselves at much greater distances than their protective needs dictate. The concept of interpersonal or conversational distance reflects the normal distances that people maintain between themselves and others. We will use the latter label because we are most interested in communication contexts.

The prevailing system for classifying dynamic spacing patterns remains the one originally proposed by anthropologist Edward Hall (1959, 1966). His four perceptual categories of distance represent simultaneously an actual range of physical distance, a degree of psychosensory involvement, and a designation of the level of intimacy and formality of an interaction (see Figure 3-1). Each category has a close and a far phase, for a total of eight distance ranges.

1 *Intimate distance (0 to 18 inches).* This range is reserved for the most private and intimate of interactions. At this distance, people's kinesthetic receptors are highly aware of the presence of another. You can feel another's breath, smell body odors, perhaps even sense body heat. The other person dominates your visual field, your detail vision is blurred, and the person's facial features look distorted and enlarged. You can easily touch his or her trunk region, and accidental touch is likely. The other person literally fills up your senses. At such close range, you are also likely to speak in soft, barely audible whispers about secret or highly confidential topics.

2 *Personal-casual distance (1 1/2 to 4 feet).* This category's close phase (1 1/2 to 2 1/2 feet) is noticeably different from its far phase (2 1/2 to 4 feet). The close phase is commonly used with family, friends, and close acquaintances and is likely to be used for self-disclosive, private conversations. The far phase is more common for casual acquaintances and less personal topics. In the close phase, it is easy to hold hands

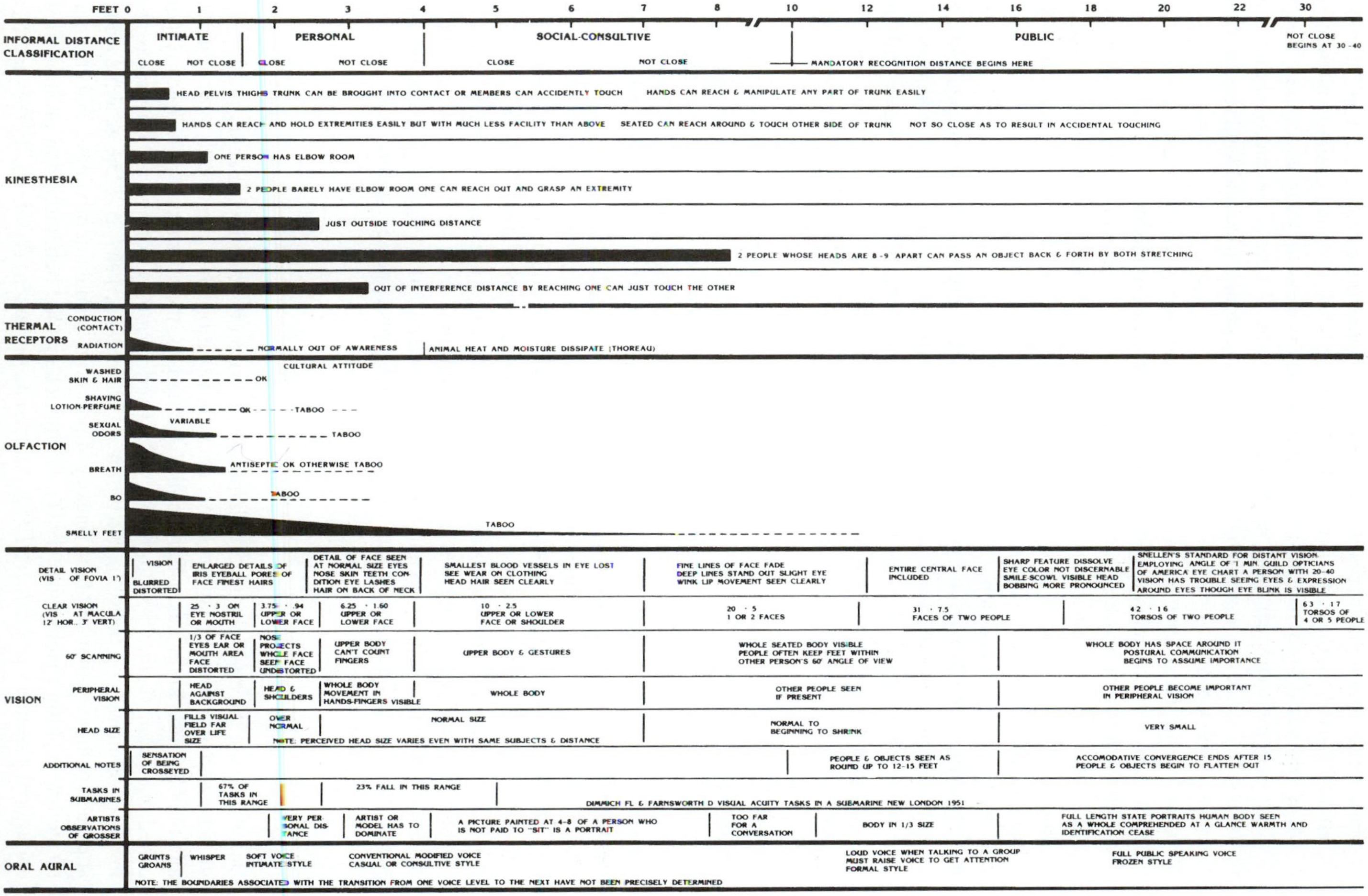

FIGURE 3-1

Chart showing the interrelationships among sensory channels in each distance zone.

but not easy to touch other body parts; in the far phase, the other person is "at arm's length." As you increase distance in this category, it becomes increasingly difficult to sense odors and body heat from the other person (unless they are excessive). Facial features begin to appear more normal in your vision. At the close end, you may still use a softer voice; as you move to the far phase, speaking tone and loudness become more conventional.

3 *Social-consultive distance (4 to 10 feet).* This distance is used for activities ranging from impersonal social conversations in the close phase to business transactions in the far phase. Sensory involvement is significantly reduced compared to the two previous categories, and the other person moves out of touching range. In the far, consultive phase, other people become visible in one's peripheral vision, communication styles become more formal, voices begin to get louder, and the distance is less conducive to carrying on a conversation.

4 *Public distance (10 feet and beyond).* This distance is typical between speakers and their audience, dignitaries and their admirers, or high-ranking military leaders and their subordinates. At this distance, other people and objects easily compete with the communicator for attention, and sensory involvement is greatly reduced. This distance forces people to speak louder and usually elicits a more formal, frozen communication style.

Although Hall (1959) cautioned that he derived his categories from observations of predominantly white, middle-class North Americans, many students and scholars of proxemic behavior have embraced his four distance ranges as precise and widely generalizable. Based on our own research, we feel that they should be viewed only as rough approximations. For example, "intimate" distances may occur under nonintimate circumstances, such as in side-by-side seating in a classroom (Heston & Garner, 1972). This makes the "intimate" range inaccurate or the label inappropriate. Research by Altman and Vinsel (1977) also reveals that most people conduct standing interactions at personal or intimate distances and conduct seated interactions at personal or social distances. These combined results suggest that distance categories may be better captured by the following three zones: (a) a very narrow intimate zone of 0 to 12 inches that is reserved for the most private and intimate encounters, (b) a very large personal and social zone of 1 to 7 feet that is the "normal contact" zone, and (c) a public zone of 7 feet and beyond that is used for more formal encounters.

Haptics, Proxemics, and Immediacy

Before leaving the code elements of haptics and proxemics, another category needs to be introduced. Nonverbal behaviors rarely occur in isolation; they are usually part of a system of behaviors. In the case of proxemics and haptics, they form part of a larger system called *immediacy behaviors.* Immediacy has been variously defined as "directness and intensity of interaction between two entities" (Mehrabian, 1967, p. 325); as abbreviated approach behaviors that heighten sensory stimulation, signal attentiveness, and communicate one's liking (Mehrabian, 1981); as multichanneled behaviors that promote psychological closeness (Andersen, 1979; Andersen, Andersen, & Jensen, 1979); and as a combination of affection, inclusion, and intensity of involvement messages (Burgoon & Hale, 1984). In short, immediacy behaviors express approach or avoidance and, in the process, affect the level of sensory involvement of the participants. Moreover, it is assumed that people approach things they like and avoid things they dislike, so immediacy behaviors also communicate positive or negative evaluations of the interaction partner. All the definitions of immediacy stress that it involves a combination of nonverbal and verbal behaviors working together as a system to increase or decrease the degree of physical, temporal, and psychological closeness between individuals. Mehrabian (1981) argued that this closeness-distance dimension is so important that immediacy is one of the three main metaphors governing interpersonal relations.

The nonverbal cues most often associated with immediacy and its opposite, nonimmediacy, are interpersonal distance, touch, gaze, body lean, head orientation (facing), and body orientation (Andersen, 1979; J. Andersen et al., 1979; Argyle & Cook, 1976; Burgoon et al., 1984; Mehrabian, 1967, 1981; Patterson, 1973a, 1973b). Increases in one of these behaviors may be accompanied by decreases in one or more other behaviors so that the total level of sensory involvement remains relatively stable (Argyle & Cook, 1976; Argyle & Dean, 1965; Firestone, 1977; Hale & Burgoon, 1984; Knowles, 1980; Patterson, 1973a, 1976; Schaeffer & Patterson, 1980). For example, an increase in proximity may be offset by a decrease in gaze. This pattern of compensation occurs both within the person, to maintain a comfortable level of approach or avoidance, and at the interpersonal level, to create the appropriate level of intimacy for the relationship at any given time.

The fact that nonverbal immediacy behaviors compensate for one another (and for the verbal level of immediacy) underscores their interrelatedness. It is not sensible to talk about what meanings are being expressed by touch or distance alone without taking into account what is happening with the other immediacy components such as eye contact. It is possible, for example, to signal a close relationship, even if touch is inhibited, by adopting a close conversational distance and increasing gaze. By the same token, adding several cues together can intensify a particular meaning. In a study of five immediacy behaviors, Burgoon et al. (1984) found that even when a conflicting cue was present, two cues conveying the same level of involvement were sufficient to nullify the meaning of an opposite third cue. Thus touch and distance must be viewed as part of a larger system of immediacy behaviors, and any interpretations that are drawn must consider the co-occurring immediacy behaviors.

NORMS AND EXPECTATIONS

Because Chapter 8 examines in detail the role that culture, race, sex, and personality play in haptic and proxemic identity displays, we cover those factors here only briefly, focusing instead on a general profile of what appears to be typical, expected, and preferred in North America and similar cultures. We then consider other prominent factors that lead to variability within cultures. (The interested reader will find additional useful summaries on proxemic and haptic norms and expectations in Aiello, 1987; Burgoon, 1978b, 1992c; Knapp & Hall, 1992; Morris, 1971; and Thayer, 1986.)

Differences between Cultures

Earlier, we presented evidence that humans appear to have deep and abiding needs for both physical contact and protection from such contact that give rise to the haptic, territoriality, and distancing patterns observed during interactions. This evidence, which reflects an ethological or biological theory of proxemic and haptic behavior, implies that such behaviors are innate or genetic and therefore universal. At one level, all cultures do share a basic understanding of the meanings of touch and distance because these behaviors form the bedrock for such innate displays as association, bonding, caregiving, fight, and flight. For example, all societies recognize the underlying messages of approach and avoidance in distance behavior and rely on distance to signify who is included or excluded from the group. Physical contact is also an essential ingredient in the protection of newborns, in play behavior, and in mating. However, within these broad parameters, cultural differences abound, not only in what distance and touch behaviors prevail but also in what behaviors are permissible or prohibited and what meanings and evaluations are assigned to them. Something else must account for the differences.

Explaining Cultural Differences   As an alternative to the *ethological-sociobiological* view, Gillespie and Leffler (1983) identified three other theoretical explanations for variability in proxemic behaviors (and implicitly, haptics). One, the *enculturation-socialization* theory, is that differences are due to culture or to learning processes. What is regarded as appropriate use of distance, space, touch, and immediacy is partly grounded in a culture's expectations and standards for conduct (although what people actually do often may depart from these ideals.) The expectations and standards themselves arise from different social and religious values, status hierarchies, child-rearing practices, long-standing cultural traditions, and possibly even economic factors (Burgoon & Saine, 1978). The sociocultural perspective implies that there should be a fair degree of homogeneity within cultures or subgroups. Yet this is not uniformly the case.

A third, *situational resources* position holds that different social characteristics such as status accord people different access to spatial resources. A final, *internal states* perspective holds that variability is due to individual differences in personality, mood, and so forth. In what follows, we will see that many of these sociological and individual difference factors are involved in norms and expectations above and beyond what is dictated by culture.

Contact and Noncontact Cultures   It has been popular to designate cultures as "contact" or "noncontact" (Hall, 1966; Montagu, 1978). Those in the former category supposedly are more prone to frequent physical contact, close interaction distance, direct body orientation, and direct gaze—in other words, more immediate and involving interaction styles—than those in the latter category. "Contact" thus implies not only touch but the other related immediacy behaviors. Arab, Indian, Mediterranean, and Latin cultures are often classified as contact cultures, while North American and northern European cultures are often classified as noncontact ones. Although the contact-noncontact distinction has been criticized as overly simplistic, it serves as a useful starting point for examining variability in the use and evaluation of haptics and proxemics. Those cultures near the noncontact end of the continuum not only should be less inclined to use a lot of touch, they should also be less likely to interact at intimate distances, more likely to compensate for an increase in one immediacy behavior with a reduction in another, and more likely to find frequent touch, close proximity, and high immediacy disconcerting or discomfiting.

Research tends to bear out part but not all of this distinction. Cultures do vary widely on actual frequency and form of physical contact. People from Arab, Latin, and southern European cultures, for example, have been observed engaging in closer interaction distances and touching one another more frequently (Watson, 1970; Watson & Graves, 1966). In contrast to the restrictive and somewhat punitive view toward self- and other-touch in the United States, many cultures are far more permissive toward familial contact, premarital and extramarital sexual contact, and self-exploration. In some primitive societies, painful touch experiences in the form of scarification rituals or pain endurance tests may be a central ingredient in sacred ceremonies. Meanings also differ. Among Americans, a handshake is encouraged as a cordial greeting; among the French, the same handshake between an unacquainted man and an unmarried woman is discouraged because it conveys a "pact of friendship" that is presumptuous and improper (Morris, 1971).

However, as we will see in Chapter 8, the contact-noncontact distinction often fails to match reality. Some observational studies, for example, have failed to find that seated and standing distances, touch, and body orientation conform to the contact-noncontact designations of various cultures (Remland, Jones, & Brinkman, 1991). And cultures may be more similar than dissimilar in their desire for physical contact. The survey by Mosby (1978) cited earlier found that no matter how much touching people receive, they generally want more, especially in satisfying relationships. Morris (1971) even

Can you distinguish the contact culture from the noncontact culture?

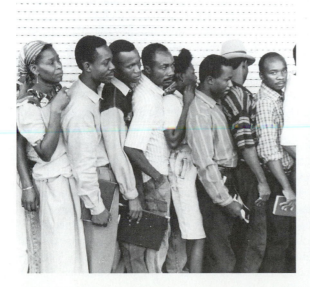

claimed that the discrepancy between actual and desired touch leads to the use of "licensed touchers"—people such as hairdressers, manicurists, and masseuses who are paid to supply touch.

Noncontact cultures also may be similar to contact ones in the degree of immediacy they exhibit when interacting with others. During conversation, people in western cultures expect and prefer moderately high displays of immediacy and involvement, even with strangers (Burgoon & Le Poire, 1993; Burgoon & Walther, 1990; Honeycutt, 1991). This level of engagement appears to be an intrinsic part of politeness and so may be fairly common across cultures, although cultures can vary in where the upper "comfort threshold" lies.

In short, then, the contact-noncontact distinction may blur when it comes to the communicative use of touch, distance, and immediacy.

Differences within Cultures: Factors Affecting Norms

It may be that variability is greater *within* cultures than *across* cultures. We thus turn our attention to the numerous factors within cultures that also influence haptic and proxemic norms, expectations, and preferences. These can be divided into characteristics of *communicators, relationships, messages,* and *context.*

Characteristics of Communicators   Many features that individual communicators bring to interactions influence the behaviors they expect and desire from others and the behaviors they themselves display. We consider some of the most prominent characteristics here.

Sex   As is discussed in Chapter 8, men and women truly differ in their proxemic and haptic patterns. But the differences partly hinge on whether they are interacting with someone of the same or opposite sex. In same-sex interactions, men expect, prefer, and adopt greater conversational distance than women. They routinely sit and stand at greater distances and tend to become more uncomfortable when approached closely by another male. They also adopt more indirect body orientations, although they may partially offset the greater distance by leaning forward more than women. Opposite-sex distancing depends on how intimate the relationship is: male same-sex dyads adopt the greatest distances, female same-sex dyads and romantic opposite-sex dyads adopt the least, and nonintimate opposite-sex dyads adopt intermediate distances (Aiello, 1987; Evans & Howard, 1973; Guerrero, 1994; Hall, 1984; Hayduk, 1978; Sussman & Rosenfeld, 1982).

Sex differences related to touch are far less clear-cut. It has been claimed that touch initiation is asymmetrical, with men touching women more than women touch men (Henley, 1977), but the actual research findings are quite mixed on this issue. Touch initiation may depend not on sex alone but also on the intentionality of the touch, the age and relationship of the participants, and the setting in which the touch occurs. Some evidence suggests that women engage in more same-sex touch than do men, especially if they are elderly, and many studies have shown that the amount of same-sex touch exceeds opposite-sex touch (Dean, Willis, & Rinck, 1978; Hall, 1984; Hall & Vecchia, 1992; Major, Schmidlin, & Williams, 1990; Stier & Hall, 1984; Willis & Rinck, 1983).

But few studies have distinguished romantically involved couples from platonic ones. An exception: dating couples engage in far more touch than opposite-sex or same-sex friends during conversations (Guerrero, 1994).

As for evaluations of touch, women generally find it more pleasant than men do. They evaluate touchers and the contexts in which touch occurs more favorably than men do, and people regard touch from women as more desirable than touch from men (Burgoon & Walther, 1990; Fisher et al., 1976; Hall, 1984; Heslin, 1978; Maier & Ernest, 1978; Major & Heslin, 1982; Stier & Hall, 1984). There are exceptions, however (see Box 3-4 and Figure 3-2).

Age   We have already noted that interpersonal distance generally increases as one moves from childhood into adulthood. But once into adulthood, distance may not differ across people of different ages (Remland et al., 1991), although people generally adopt closer distances with peers than with younger or older people.

In childhood, most touch is with parents, peers, and teachers of the same sex. By college age, this pattern has reversed so that opposite-sex touch is more common and more body parts are accessible to touch from opposite-sex others (Henley, 1973; Jones, 1984, 1986; Jourard, 1966a; Lomranz & Shapira, 1974; Major, 1981; Mosby, 1978). Compared to younger and middle-age people, the elderly may be deprived of pleasurable physical contact. This may explain why older people touch younger people more than vice versa.

Race and ethnicity   Research in the area of race and ethnicity is sporadic and inconclusive. Some studies in the United States have found that people of Hispanic origin adopt closer interaction distances than do Anglos or blacks, but the research has been

---

BOX 3-4

APPLICATIONS: TO TOUCH OR NOT TO TOUCH

Whether on a date or in a business meeting, the question of when to touch is a puzzling one. Part of the answer lies in how pleasurable people find touch and who is doing the touching. Although women generally like touch more than men do, reactions depend on the toucher's status and familiarity. Men and women both respond favorably to touch from someone who is of a higher status than themselves. Women also respond favorably if the person's status is equal to their own or unknown, but men respond more negatively to such touch (Major, 1981). If the touch is from a stranger, the situation reverses: women don't like it; men do (Heslin, 1978; Heslin, Nguyen, & Nguyen, 1983). Curiously, single women and married men have more negative reactions to touch with sexual connotations than do married women and single men, and men generally read more sexual connotations into any kind of touch than women do (Heslin & Alper,

1983). Also, men are more likely to initiate touch in public settings when the couple is courting, whereas women are more likely to initiate it when the couple is already married (Willis & Briggs, 1992).

These findings speak to the advisability of initiating touch in potentially romantic relationships. If the object of your romantic intentions is female, she is likely to object to touch if you are a stranger or if the touch has sexual overtones but may like it if you are a friend, are of a higher status, or the touches are playful, nurturing, or affectionate. And if you marry her, she should find touch increasingly pleasant and be more likely to initiate it in public. If the object of your romantic intentions is male and single, he is likely to interpret any touch as sexual and to find it especially appealing if you are a stranger. But don't expect as much initiation of public touch after the honeymoon.

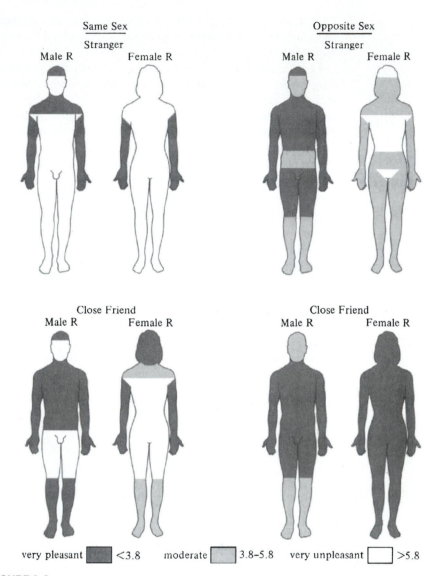

FIGURE 3-2
Perceived pleasantness of touch from same-sex and opposite-sex strangers and close friends for males and females.

very limited. People with Latin ancestry supposedly hail from contact cultures and therefore should be receptive to more intimate interaction distances and more touch (Watson, 1970), but we have already noted that the contact-noncontact distinction does not always hold up. Some studies also have found that blacks prefer and report less touch and maintain greater distances among themselves while conversing than do whites; other studies have found the reverse; and still others have found no racial differences in distancing or touch (see, e.g., Norwood, 1979; Smith, Willis, & Gier, 1980; Willis, Rinck, & Dean, 1978).

Geographic region   Touch and distancing patterns may also differ geographically. In the United States, for example, regional differences have been observed (see Box 3-5), although the differences appear to be modest at best (Andersen, Andersen, & Lustig, 1987).

Personality   Numerous personality factors, many of which are discussed in more detail in Chapter 8, are associated with haptic and proxemic expectations, evaluations, and usage. In general, people who are extroverted, gregarious, assertive, and self-confident prefer close distances and intimate touch, while those who are more introverted and nonsocial prefer greater interaction distances and avoid touch, especially in opposite-sex interactions (Andersen et al., 1987; Andersen & Leibowitz, 1978; Fromme et al., 1989; Guerrero & Andersen, 1991; Scott, 1988). Other factors, such as conservatism, self-image, and body image, may also strongly influence attitudes toward touch (Norwood, 1979).

Characteristics of Relationships

Familiarity and liking   Compared with sex, liking and intimacy may be far better predictors of distancing and touch patterns (Aiello, 1987; Burgoon, 1978b; Crane, Dollahite, Griffin, & Taylor, 1987; Guerrero, 1994; Mehrabian, 1968c, 1969). People move closer to those they like. Females in particular appear to differentiate their use of space according to degree of acquaintance: women adopt increasingly closer proximity as the relationship changes from stranger to acquaintance to friend. Happily married couples choose closer distances for conversation than do unhappily married ones. As with other immediacy cues, the likelihood of touch increases as a relationship becomes more famil-

---

BOX 3-5

EMBRACEABLE USA—BY REGION

Southerners do it more than Northerners. Women are more willing to do it than men. And older people do it less but need it more.

"It" is touching.

Whether you're comfortable touching other people in social situations may depend on where you live, your age, and your sex.

A survey of 20,000 people in 25 states by Greg Risberg of Northwestern University Medical School found [that] families influence touching.

"No-touch doesn't mean no love," he said. "But low-touch families do not express affection physically. They save that for special occasions. High-touch families will hug or caress for all kinds of reasons, or no reason at all."

Among his findings:

- In the South—80 percent come from medium- to high-touch backgrounds, 15 percent from low-touch and 5 percent from no-touch.
- North—90 percent are from low- to medium-touch, 5 percent each from high-touch and no-touch.
- Midwest—80 percent are from low- to medium touch, 10 percent each from high-touch and no-touch.
- Westerners—85 percent from medium- to high-touch, 10 percent low-touch, 5 percent no-touch.
- Only 5 percent felt touched enough; 98 percent wanted more; 89 percent held back their inclinations to touch.
- Women are much more comfortable touching, Risberg said; the elderly are more reluctant because they expect to be touched less.

Source: Howard, 1985, p. A1.

iar and intimate. People do not expect contact from strangers; they do expect and like it from friends (as long as it is not prolonged) and from romantic partners. Their expectations, however, will also be shaped by their family experiences.

Status   People are more likely to approach those of equal status than those of unequal status. They also expect others of equal or higher status to approach them more closely than those of lower status and find close proximity more desirable from those of equal or higher status (Burgoon & Walther, 1990; Gifford, 1982; Hall, 1984).

Characteristics of Messages and Contexts

Furniture   Perceived comfort of furniture is likely to be the first determinant of where people sit. Everyone has had the experience of trying politely to avoid an antique ladder-back chair or stiff-looking sofa in a formal living room. Where early entrants choose to sit in turn influences the choices of later arrivals. Interior designers say that the "arc" for comfortable conversation is about 6 to 8 feet. Research by Sommer (1959, 1962) confirmed that people prefer to sit across from one another—say, on facing couches—unless the distance across is uncomfortable for conversation and exceeds that of side-by-side seating. People typically shift to side-by-side seating at about 5 1/2 feet.

Space and sensory stimulation   We have already noted how crowding and over-stimulation from an environment can affect a variety of response patterns. They also affect distancing. Men—and sometimes women—in noisy, crowded situations and smaller spaces sit and stand farther apart than in larger and less occupied spaces (Bell & Barnard, 1984; Worchel, 1986). Although this may be partly a function of noise and the poorer acoustics in larger spaces, it may also be a reaction to a sense of crowding. If people feel "trapped," they are likely to develop greater personal space bubbles as insulation. This would also explain why people tolerate closer distances in outdoor environments—their movements are less constrained and they have ready access to escape routes—than indoor ones (Cochran, Hale, & Hissam, 1984).

Purpose   As might be expected, people adopt closer distances for informal and intimate conversations than for formal and task-oriented ones (Hall, 1974; Little, 1965). Preferred seating arrangements also depend on the kind of task or interaction taking place. People engaged in social conversation or activities typically choose adjacent or directly opposite seating because it combines physical closeness with good opportunities for eye contact, both of which facilitate conversation. Similarly, students in classrooms and discussion groups prefer semicircular or U-shaped arrangements over straight-row seating for the same reasons. People engaged in cooperative tasks typically select side-by-side or adjacent seating because it maximizes their ability to focus on the task at hand. Those engaged in competitive activities prefer opposite or even diagonal seating that permits some surveillance while keeping an opponent at a distance (Burgoon, 1992d; Knapp & Hall, 1992).

Some occasions, such as greetings and departures, call for touch. One need only observe greetings and good-byes at airports to confirm that people engage in a lot of intimate contact during these rituals—a solid hug, a kiss on the mouth or cheek, a touch to the upper body or head, an arm around the waist, handholding, and handshakes (Greenbaum & Rosenfeld, 1980; Heslin & Boss, 1980). The more intimate the relationship, the more intimate the greeting. Dancing, sporting events, and play are also acceptable occasions for touch. Competitive sports afford men a rare opportunity for friendly physical contact with other men. The congratulatory embrace, what Morris (1971) called the "sportsman's triumph," is commonplace. And the amount of contact may be quite high. One study of bowlers, for instance, found an average of 16.2 contacts per hour, with blacks showing more frequent touch than whites (Smith et al., 1980). Roughhousing may also be one of the few ways for men to touch male friends and fathers to touch sons. Morris (1971) observed that when a man feels the urge to touch another man's head, he may resort to mock aggression, such as grasping the other's head in the crook of his arm or ruffling his hair.

Henley (1977) offered a list of the communication situations during which one is likely to touch or be touched (see Table 3-2). Touch is likely to be initiated for more dominant functions, such as giving instructions or trying to persuade, while receipt of touch is more associated with submissive communication functions, such as asking advice. This is congruent with the finding that in unequal-status relationships, the person of higher status is usually the one to initiate contact.

Meanings of behavior   Frequency of and desire for touch also depend on its type, location, and meaning. For example, Morris (1971) claimed that the partial shoulder embrace is six times more likely than the full frontal embrace because the former is, by convention, considered nonsexual. Among strangers or business acquaintances in the United States, handshakes are expected and preferred far more than intimate touches such as an arm around the waist or an arm around the shoulder (Burgoon & Walther, 1990).

The previously mentioned study of touch by Jones and Yarbrough (1985) offers a summary of touch norms. Participants in that study recorded not only the kinds of touch they experienced in daily interactions but also the relationship between interactants, the characteristics of individual communicators, the meanings of touches, and the constraints on touching. The results, shown in Table 3-3, provide an excellent depiction of touch practices in mainstream American culture.

TABLE 3-2
TYPES OF TOUCH SITUATIONS AND LIKELIHOOD OF TOUCHING OR BEING TOUCHED

Situation	Others More Likely to Touch When . . .	Others Less Likely to Touch When . . .
Information	Giving	Asking
Advice	Giving	Asking
Giving Orders	They're	You're
Favors	Asking	Agreeing to do
Trying to Persuade	They're	You're
Feeing Worried	You're	They're
Feeling Excited	They're	You're
Conversation	In deep	In casual
Place	At a party	At work

Source: Adapted from Henley, 1977, p. 105.

TABLE 3-3
CHARACTERISTICS OF MEANING CATEGORIES FOR INDIVIDUAL TOUCHES

Category, definition, and types	Key features
A. Positive Affect Touches	
1. Support Serves to nurture, reassure, or promise protection; mainly holding (47%), although prolonged holding is rare; also spot touches, pats, and squeezes (41%), with a few caresses (10%)	a. Situation calls for comfort or reassurance b. Initiated by person who gives support c. Verbalization common (82%), usually demands/commands or inquiries about welfare, but may be redundant when situation is clear d. Almost any relationship among acquainted but mainly close relationships (72%) and cross-sex (72%)
2. Appreciation Expresses gratitude; mainly holding (69%), but also brief touches (spot pat, squeeze, or handshake)	a. Situation: receiver has performed service for toucher (100%) b. Touch initiator verbalizes appreciation, usually some kind of "thanks" (88%) during or after, not before, the touch c. Mainly close relationships (75%) and cross-sex (69%), although female-female and male-male touches occur
3. Inclusion Draws attention to act of being together; suggests physical closeness; sustained touch, mainly holding (72%), especially holding/pressing against, with some prolonged spot touches and repeated brushes	a. Situation is usually involvement in a common task, rather than just conversation, but both occur b. Verbalization usually occurs but is seldom related to the act of being together c. Close relationship (91%), mainly sexual intimates and close friends
4. Sexual Expresses physical attraction or sexual interest; mainly holding and caressing (100%) and some mutual hugs (38%)	a. Mainly when people are alone, occasionally in crowds or focuses small groups b. Mainly cross-sex relationships among sexual intimates
5. Affection A residual category that expresses generalized positive regard beyond mere acknowledgment; holding and some caresses (64%), but some spot touches and pats	a. Primarily close relationships (86%) and cross-sex relationships (75%) but some female-female touches; male-male touches rare
B. Playful Touches	
1. Playful Affection Serves to lighten interaction; serious affection is qualified; includes spot touches, holding, but also wrestling, tickling, punching, pinching, bumping, patting	a. Combines affectionate or sexual message with play signal b. Mainly close relationships (77%) and cross-sex relationships (81%) but some male-male touches (19%)
2. Playful Aggression Serves to lighten interaction; serious aggression is qualified; includes mock strangling, mock wrestling, punching, pinching, slapping, grabbing, and standing on toes	a. Combines aggressive message with play signal b. Verbalization usually occurs; instances of silent aggression appear to be relationship-specific c. Mainly male-male (39%) and cross-sex (50%) touches

TABLE 3-3
CHARACTERISTICS OF MEANING CATEGORIES FOR INDIVIDUAL TOUCHES (*Continued*)

Category, definition, and types	Key features
C. Control Touches	
1. Compliance Attempts to direct behavior and oftentimes also attitudes or feelings of another; primarily hand to body part contact, including holding, spot touches, and pats	a. Initiated by person attempting influence b. Verbalization usually occurs (91%) and takes form of direct or implied demands/commands or requests for information and action; situation may make touch clear in itself, so words only reinforce or are absent c. Close relationships most common but can occur in any acquainted relationship d. Both sexes initiate to same and opposite sex, although female-to-male touches are more common than male-to-female
2. Attention-getting Serves to direct recipient's perceptual focus to an object or event or to the verbalization itself; primarily brief touches (spot, pat, brush) directed to 1–2 body parts	a. Initiator verbalizes (clarifies purpose) b. Any kind of relationship, including strangers c. Both sexes initiate to same and opposite sex, although most touches are female-initiated (76%)
3. Announcing a Response Calls attention to and emphasizes a feeling state of initiator; implicitly request affect response from another; primarily hand to 1–3 body parts	a. Initiated by person verbally announcing feeling directly or indirectly b. Mutual touches, while rare, always express congratulations c. Primarily close relationships (80%) and mainly female-initiated (67%)
D. Ritualistic Touches	
1. Greeting Serves as part of acknowledging another at the opening of an encounter; usually involves minimal form of contact (handshake, spot touch, pat or squeeze)	a. Situation is beginning of an interaction b. Verbalization of standard greeting phrase occurs before or during but not after the touch c. All kinds of relationships and sex composition types
2. Departure Serves as part of the act of closing an encounter; mainly pats and spot touches but also holding, caresses (not handshakes)	a. Situation is end of an encounter b. Verbalization of standard greeting phrase occurs before or during but not after the touch c. Rarely occurs between family members or intimates; primarily close and not-close friends d. Mainly same-sex touches (80%)
E. Hybrid Touches	
1. Greeting/Affection Expresses affection and acknowledgement at the initiation of an encounter; includes some "borderline" touches that resemble pure greetings but most touches involve hugs and/or kisses (71%)	a. Situation is beginning of an interaction b. Verbalization occurs in form of standard greeting phrases and expressions of endearment c. Mainly close relationships (86%) and cross-sex touches (76%), with some female-female contact

TABLE 3-3
CHARACTERISTICS OF MEANING CATEGORIES FOR INDIVIDUAL TOUCHES (*Continued*)

Category, definition, and types	Key features
2. Departure/Affection Expresses affection and serves to close an encounter; principally hugs and/or kisses (85%)	a. Situation is end of interaction b. Verbalization occurs in form of departure phrases; some direct expressions of affection c. Mainly close relationships (94%) and cross-sex touches (82%), with some female-female contacts

F. Task-Related Touches
  1. References to Appearance
  A touch which points out or inspects a body part or artifact referred to in a verbal comment about appearance; in form of a spot touch by a hand (100%)
	a. Words accompany and justify the touch
	b. All female-initiated (100%)
	c. Mainly close relationships (90%) such as close friends
	d. Some translations suggest a secondary meaning of affection or flirtation

2. Instrumental Ancillary A touch which occurs as an unnecessary part of the accomplishment of a task; takes form of hand-to-hand contacts (91%)	a. Although touch is usually self-explanatory, verbalization usually occurs b. Variety of relationships, including acquainted persons who are not close c. Most are cross-sex (54%) or female-female (39%) contacts d. Some touches carry apparent secondary meanings (flirtation, compliance, inclusion, affection)
3. Instrumental Intrinsic Touch which accomplishes task in and of itself	a. Verbalization usually occurs despite fact that touch is self-explanatory b. Mostly occurs in close relationships but all kinds of relationships represented c. Most are cross-sex (54%) or female-female (42%) contacts d. Some translations carry secondary message of flirtation, inclusion, or affection
G. Accidental Touches Touches which are perceived as unintentional and therefore meaningless; consist of single, momentary contacts, principally brushes or spot touches	a. Words seldom occur and are unrelated to the touch b. Accepted, unrepaired touches occur principally among the acquainted c. Touches between strangers are rejected and/or repaired d. All sex-composition types, although cross-sex touches are most common e. Some touches may be motivated since some persons who seldom initiate other types of touches have many accidental touches

Source: Abbreviated from Jones & Yarbrough, 1985, pp. 28–35.

COMMUNICATION POTENTIAL

As communication systems, haptics and proxemics share a number of strengths and weaknesses. Their innate importance to the developing human foretells their significance in the encoding and decoding of nonverbal messages.

Encoding Potential

Physical contact, tactile stimulation, and spatial perception are essential to human protection, growth, and development. This gives haptic and nonverbal behaviors a primacy unequaled by other codes.

As part of our biological heritage, haptic and proxemic behaviors have high arousal value. They have the capacity to arrest a receiver's attention:

> Cutaneous sensations, especially if aroused in unusual patterns, are highly attention-demanding. It is possible, therefore, that the simplest and most straightforward of all messages—warnings and alerts—should be delivered cutaneously. (Geldhard, 1960, pp. 1583–1584)

One limitation of the haptics and proxemics codes from a sender's standpoint is that they can be highly ambiguous. This reduces their viability as primary message vehicles. Consider, for example, trying to convey a need for assistance through touch or distance alone. You can imagine how tapping another person on the shoulder or moving into close proximity could easily be misinterpreted without the benefit of other accompanying nonverbal cues.

Perhaps because of this ambiguity, another limitation is that touch and distance messages are less integral to some communication functions than are other codes. For example, although it is possible to express an emotional state through touch or distance, people are more likely to rely on kinesic and vocalic cues to convey how they are feeling. Similarly, people are less likely to rely on these codes to signal their personal identity (even though how close a person stands to others can be revealing). Because these codes often are relegated to the supporting cast for certain communication purposes, they cannot be considered as powerful as kinesics and vocalics. Nevertheless, they play a significant role in nonverbal communication. And, in the case of some of the most elemental messages such as affection or threat, they are the central actors.

Decoding Potential

The high arousal value of touch and proximity are also likely to affect receivers' comprehension of messages. When touch or proximity stand alone or duplicate a verbal message such as a warning, they doubtless strengthen its impact. However, when they accompany another sort of verbal message, they may either reinforce it or distract from it. These competing effects on comprehension are covered in later chapters.

In terms of physical ability to discriminate among coding elements, haptics and proxemics appear to be somewhat limited relative to other codes. Proxemically, although humans have the visual and kinesthetic capacity to make fairly fine spatial discriminations, in practice we do not distinguish, say, between a 3-foot and a 3 1/2-foot conver-

How can you tell that this apparently aggressive touch is merely play?

sational distance. As noted earlier, we tend to recognize distances of 4 to 8 feet. Haptically, humans are capable of making discriminations along multiple dimensions, which could give haptics greater communication potential. The skin is able to detect location differences (although some of the distinctions are crude ones), to make temporal distinctions based on the frequency of contact (e.g., a single tap versus incessant tapping), to detect up to 25 different durations, and to recognize around 15 distinctions in pressure (Geldhard, 1960). Still, this ability to discriminate pales in comparison to what is possible kinesically or auditorily. The eye and ear have far greater physical capacity to handle a wide array of stimuli than the skin.

In terms of accuracy, there is good potential for accurate recognition through touch (Goldberg & Bajsy, 1984), and haptic discriminations tend to be more accurate than visual ones, which are subject to perceptual distortions. However, perceptual biases involved in visual distortions also plague proxemic discriminations, which explains why personal space perceptions do not always match reality.

A further source of inaccuracy stems from the aforementioned ambiguity associated with haptics and proxemics. Just as this multiplicity of interpretations can (or should) discourage senders from relying on these codes to send important messages, so it interferes with receivers' accurate decoding of haptic and proxemic behavior. Touches and distances are fraught with ambiguities about what they mean or even whether they mean anything at all. For instance, if a potential dating partner sits across from you rather than next to you at a restaurant, what does it mean? (Probably nothing, if that is the convention in your culture.) If a person brushes against you while passing you in a hallway, should that be interpreted as an aggressive act or written off as an accident? These examples highlight a major decoding limitation of these two codes.

This ambiguity is compounded by cultural variability in use, which not only limits experience with such codes in noncontact cultures but also restricts the generalizability of some of their meanings. Close distance or handholding in one place may have a very different interpretation in another. Consequently, communicators, especially those who have little practice encoding and decoding haptic and proxemic messages, will be disinclined to rely on these codes as sole carriers of messages.

SUMMARY

The interrelated codes of haptics and proxemics appear to have developed from competing drives for approaching and avoiding others and reflect strong personal preferences and social norms. People share fundamental needs for contact, for territoriality, and for personal space, needs that are central to their healthy development and functioning. The detrimental effects of inadequate tactile stimulation and space, and reactions to territorial or personal space invasion, such as the general adaptation syndrome, offer compelling evidence of how fundamental tactile and proxemic patterns are to human existence. Consequently, haptic and proxemic behaviors become potent means of expressing those needs and establishing satisfactory relationships with others. At the same time, cultural and group norms shape how these behaviors are transformed into acceptable or unacceptable communication patterns and what meanings are associated with the behaviors.

As a communication code, touch can be classified according to (a) the forms of touch, (b) the dimensions that produce a given touch, or (c) the functions and meanings associated with touch. Proxemic behaviors can be categorized according to type of territory or degree of conversational distance. Another concept, immediacy, incorporates proxemic and haptic behaviors with kinesic and vocalic cues to signal approach or avoidance. Immediacy underscores the importance of examining nonverbal codes as systems rather than as isolated behaviors.

Although all people experience needs for touch and needs for distance at various times, such factors as gender, race, age, personality, and culture shape what communication patterns become normative and expected. Patterns become fairly well established in childhood and undergo little modification into adulthood.

Because cultures vary dramatically in whether they are contact or noncontact, the potential for haptics and proxemics to serve as communication vehicles also differs dramatically. Beyond the possible primacy of these two codes stemming from their innate importance, haptics and proxemics also have significant potential to arouse the receiver, thereby gaining attention. Human beings also are able to make relatively accurate but not widely ranging discriminations of tactile stimuli, which limits the haptic code. The proxemic code has an infinitely large range of possible distance and spatial behaviors that could be encoded, but it is likely that people recognize only a few gross distinctions, and the proxemic code is plagued by the same biases in visual perception as kinesics. Cultural differences in frequency of use and meaning, ambiguities in meaning within the same culture, and the inapplicability of haptics and proxemics to some communication functions are further limitations on their communication potential. Nevertheless, they can act as very subtle and potent forms of communication.

SUGGESTED READINGS

Aiello, J. R. (1987). Human spatial behavior. In D. Stokols & I. Altman (Eds.), *Handbook of environmental psychology* (Vol. 1, pp. 389–504). New York: Wiley.

Altman, I. (1975). *The environment and social behavior.* Monterey, CA: Brooks/Cole.

Ardrey, R. (1979). *African genesis.* New York: Dell.

Bakker, C. B., & Bakker-Rabdau, M. K. (1985). *No trespassing! Explorations in human territoriality.* San Francisco: Chandler & Sharp.

Burgoon, J. K. (1992). Spatial relationships in small groups. In R. S. Cathcart & L. A. Samovar (Eds.), *Small group communication: A reader* (6th ed., pp. 287–300). Dubuque, IA: Brown.

Burgoon, J. K., & Walther, J. W. (1990). Nonverbal expectancies and the evaluative consequences of violations. *Human Communication Research, 17,* 232–265.

Frank, L. K. (1971). Tactile communication. In H. A. Bosmajian (Ed.), *The rhetoric of nonverbal communication.* Glenview, IL: Scott, Foresman.

Gillespie, D. L., & Leffler, A. (1983). Theories of nonverbal behavior: A critical review of proxemics research. In R. Collins (Ed.), *Sociological theory* (pp. 120–153). San Francisco: Jossey-Bass.

Hall, E. T. (1959). *The silent language.* Garden City, NY: Doubleday.

Hall, E. T. (1966). *The hidden dimension* (2d ed.). Garden City, NY: Anchor Press/Doubleday.

Hayduk, L. A. (1978). Personal space: An evaluative and orienting overview. *Psychological Bulletin, 85,* 117–134.

Hediger, H. P. (1961). The evolution of territorial behavior. In S. L. Washburn (Ed.), *Social life of early man* (pp. 34–57). Chicago: Aldine.

LaFrance, M., & Mayo, C. (1978). *Moving bodies.* Monterey, CA: Brooks/Cole.

Major, B. (1981). Gender patterns in touching behavior. In C. Mayo & N. M. Henley (Eds.), *Gender and nonverbal behavior* (pp. 15–37). New York: Springer-Verlag.

Montagu, A. (1978). *Touching: The human significance of the skin* (2d ed.). New York: Harper & Row.

Morris, D. (1971). *Intimate behavior.* New York: Random House.

Morris, D. (1977). *Manwatching: A field guide to human behavior.* New York: Abrams.

Sommer, R. (1969). *Personal space: The behavioral basis of design.* Englewood Cliffs, NJ: Prentice-Hall.

4

PLACE AND TIME CODES: ENVIRONMENT, ARTIFACTS, AND CHRONEMICS

No species can exist without an environment, no species can exist in an environment of its exclusive creation, no species can survive, save as a nondisruptive member of an ecological community. Every member must adjust to other members of the community and to the environment in order to survive. Man is not excluded from this test.

Ian McHarg

The two codes we will examine in this chapter are often overlooked as forms of communication. Yet these codes—place and time—can have a profound impact both because they convey messages in their own right and because they influence the meaning and impact of other nonverbal and verbal messages.

ENVIRONMENT AND ARTIFACTS

It is typically human to affect and change the environment. Humans are affected by their physical surroundings as well. As a nonverbal code, environment and artifacts includes a very diverse set of elements. We can define the environment and artifacts code as *the physical objects and environmental attributes that communicate directly, define the communication context, or guide social behavior in some way.* The research that we will concentrate on comes from a broad multidisciplinary area, including architecture, urban planning, environmental psychology, cultural anthropology, and communication.

Origins and Acquisition: Reactions to the Environment

Unlike other nonverbal communication codes, the environmental code is not really "acquired" in any direct sense. Rather, we acquire *reactions* to the environment; that is, we learn (a) to interpret meaning from the environment, (b) that certain contexts prompt different kinds of interaction, and (c) that certain environmental cues imply sets of rules and guides for behavior. Our reactions to the environment are learned through socialization and involve a mix of classical, operant, and modeling learning strategies. The meanings interpreted from the environment are heavily influenced by our cultural background. For example, westerners may not draw much meaning from a formal Japanese rock garden, whereas the Japanese interpret quite important meanings from it. Similarly, most westerners find the formal Japanese teahouse ceremony simply a quaint way to enjoy tea in a serene setting. However, for the Japanese, the teahouse and ceremony constitute a rich context, full of cues and prompts for appropriate behavior.

Anthropologist Edward Hall has spent much of his career investigating the cultural aspects of the environmental code (see Hall, 1959, 1966, 1981). One distinction Hall has made is between *high-context* and *low-context* cultures:

> A high-context communication (HC) or message is one in which most of the information is either in the physical context or internalized in the person, while very little is in the coded, explicit, transmitted part of the message. A low-context (LC) communication is just the opposite; i.e., the mass of the information is vested in the explicit code. (1981, p. 91)

High-context cultures use messages with implicit meanings that the communicators are presumed to know or meanings that are obvious in the context of the interaction. In such cultures, context and environment assume a very important communicative role.

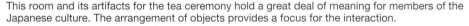

This room and its artifacts for the tea ceremony hold a great deal of meaning for members of the Japanese culture. The arrangement of objects provides a focus for the interaction.

Low-context cultures use explicit verbal messages that depend very little on the context as a carrier of meaning. Hall has often used the Japanese culture as a prime example of a high-context culture. As you might guess, American culture is classified as low context (along with others such as the German and the Swiss). This distinction does not mean that environments and artifacts are meaningless for low-context cultures, simply that they are less important than for high-context cultures. The distinction between high- and low-context cultures indicates that one's culture determines how much attention is paid to the environmental context and how much communicative meaning is invested in it. Rules and expectations are also inculcated at an early age. Parents teach children how to behave in different environments (such as when to use "inside" voices versus "outside" voices). When a child unknowingly breaks a rule, a parent's usual immediate response is to get the child to conform.

Are there any innate features to this code? Yes, at least in one basic sense. Humans have always altered the environment for their purposes, interpreted meaning from it, and relied on environmental cues for guides to behavior. These are all adaptations to the environment that have survival value. For example, the way a culture works out the issues of crowding, privacy, and allocation of space allows the culture to mediate conflict about these issues and thus has survival value. Further, we can say that simply solving the problem of shelter for members of a culture has survival value. Clearly, different cultures have evolved different forms of adapting to the environment, but all cultures have had to adapt. In sum, most of what we consider to be pertinent to the environmental code is learned and culture-bound; however, the basic factor of making some kind of adaptation to the environment has had survival value and may be innately based.

Classifying Environments and Artifacts

Potentially, a large number of structural features of artifacts and the environment can play a role in communication. Research in architecture, urban design, and other areas focuses on the relevant features to consider. These may vary from culture to culture, and even across subcultures. Hall (1966) provided very useful distinctions for categorizing environmental features: *fixed-feature elements, semifixed-feature elements, and nonfixed-feature elements.* The last category—which Hall called "informal elements"—largely coincides with proxemics and so is covered in Chapter 3.

Fixed-Feature Elements   The category of fixed-feature elements consists of everything that is relatively permanent or slow to change. Standard architectural elements, such as floors, ceilings, and walls, fall into this category.

As Rapoport (1990) indicated, the *spatial organization* of such basic elements may communicate something about the people who inhabit an environment or those who designed it. The ways in which urban and suburban areas are spatially organized vary greatly, even within one culture. The spatial organization of a New England town differs quite dramatically from that of an Indian pueblo or a large city like Los Angeles. These spatial organizations have a very basic effect on the communication networks people develop. Cross-culturally, even greater differences exist in the degree to which space is highly segmented functionally and partitioned physically (Kent, 1991).

Another fixed-feature element is *size or volume of space*. We have all been in rooms and other spaces that we considered too big or too small for the activity taking place in them. Too many students in a small classroom can be distracting, for instance. A public event, such as a political rally, can be erroneously perceived as a failure if the space makes a substantial turnout appear small. How smoothly and successfully an event unfolds can often depend on how appropriate the amount of space is.

The volume of space and size of architectural features in an environment can have other effects as well. Large, high-ceilinged rooms, a huge pipe organ, or a long staircase may create feelings of expansiveness and grandeur, leaving a person feeling insignificant.

Linear perspective is another fixed-feature element. The linear perspective of an environment has to do with the lines created by walls and objects and the relationship of these lines to each other. Work in landscape architecture (Simonds, 1961) suggests that various kinds of lines in an environment can create different impressions. In American culture, there is a heavy and almost exclusive use of right angles and straight lines, which may reflect a culture in a modern and technologically oriented stage of development (although Romans also favored a grid system because it facilitated military maneuvers and defense against intruders). Many traditional cultures tend to use curved lines in their designs and architecture, which may reflect closer ties to the natural environment. Europeans also favor street layouts that create picturesque views at every turn. Thus linear perspective may reflect a culture's positions on traditional versus technological and efficiency versus leisure continua. Another possibility is that contemporary straight-line architecture reflects the standardization of building materials that we have at our disposal to construct environments, even though the work of Buckminster Fuller showed that straight-line architecture is not always the most desirable or efficient. The impact of straight-line architecture on communication is, for the moment, an open question. However, curved lines in a space create more lines of convergence and perhaps more opportunity for eye contact and communication between individuals.

Materials used in the environment—permanent materials used in the walls and floors and changeable items such as wall hangings and carpet—have both fixed and semi-fixed aspects. Ruesch and Kees (1970) described the effects of this element in the following way:

> Wood, metal, brick, and textiles produce a variety of anticipation of touch sensations. Wood against wood, metal against brick, a stiffened fabric against a soft and pliable one— all set up "chords" of tactile images that often produce sharp and immediate physical and emotional reactions. Metal may be highly polished or finished with a dull patina; containers may be opaque, translucent, or transparent. Surfaces—whether raised, carved, rough, or smooth—when exposed to light reflections, are likely not only to express the moods of those who shaped them, but also to suggest such subtle and abstract manners as interpenetration or merely the simple adjoining of boundaries. (p. 146)

As Ruesch and Kees suggested, materials have much to do with setting up how the context "feels." Soft, plush, and textured materials may create a relaxed atmosphere that is more inviting for conversation, while hard surfaces and bright, angular objects may create feelings of energy or anxiousness. Materials may also have symbolic values, reflecting everything from one's social class to one's interpersonal style and need for creative expression (Sadalla & Sheets, 1993). All of the previous elements combine to form a final fixed feature, *architectural style.* Greco-Roman architecture differs from contemporary styles, for example, not only in its aesthetic and functional properties but also in the kinds of interaction it promotes or inhibits. Even contemporary styles vary dramatically. For example, traditional modern homes create more pleasant, familiar, informal, and nonarousing perceptions than do postmodern and deconstructivist homes (Buslig, 1991). Homes, like other forms of architecture, also carry significant symbolic meaning (Nasar, 1989; Sadalla, Vershure, & Burroughs, 1987).

Semifixed-Feature Elements   The category of semifixed-feature elements comprises relatively mobile and changeable features of an environment. One such element is *arrangement of objects and artifacts.* The placement of furniture, paintings, rugs, and so forth can affect the kind of interaction that takes place and whether any particular object in the environment will be perceived as significant. Several studies have shown that the placement of chairs in a room can encourage or discourage interaction. For example, people who wish to discourage conversation in their office place their desk so that their back is to others. The arrangement of seating has an effect on other nonverbal codes, particularly kinesics and proxemics, and may affect other communicative functions such as role definition (leader-follower emergence), mode of interaction (cooperative versus competitive), and status. These functions are discussed in detail in later chapters. Arrangement of objects may also provide a focal point for interactants in the environment. For example, judges in courtrooms often sit behind a large dais in the front of the room, elevated above everyone else. The environment clearly states who is most important in the room. The focal point in an environment may also be occupied by an object, such as an expensive piece of art that is placed in a prominent location to signal the owner's values or status.

A second semifixed-feature element is *selection of objects and artifacts* used in the environment. Beyond their arrangement, the objects and artifacts themselves can provide strong and distinct messages about an environment and the people who inhabit it. Objects and personal possessions may be used to "personalize" an environment. For example, one of our relatives has a large wall display of telephone memorabilia. This display not only provides a focus for conversation but also reveals that the owner is a telecommunications history buff. Even something as simple as one's choice of Christmas decoration can signal sociability (Werner, Peterson-Lewis, & Brown, 1989).

Light and shade in an environment are a third semifixed feature. A number of studies have investigated the effects of amount of light on work performance, but relatively few have explored the effects of lighting level on communication. Lighting may influence whether a setting is seen as social or task-oriented. All other factors being equal, lower levels of light are conducive to social conversation, while higher levels of light set a task tone. Sometimes lighting is set inappropriately, as, for example, in a bar where the lights are too bright for social and intimate conversation. Similarly, many of us have found ourselves in a classroom with inadequate lighting. Academic performance often suffers under such situations.

A fourth semifixed feature, *color,* can significantly affect human behavior (Birren, 1950; see also Box 4-1). The available evidence suggests that color is associated with people's mood states (Mehrabian & Russell, 1974; Wexner, 1954) and level of arousal (Acking & Kuller, 1972; Wilson, 1966). Specifically, blue and green tones have been found to be relaxing, yellows and oranges to be arousing and energizing, reds and blacks to be sensuous, and grays and browns to be depressing. One reason that these colors set such moods is that colors also have symbolic meanings. Some of the more common moods and symbolic meanings associated with colors in our culture are presented in Table 4-1.

Color also affects our perceptions of other dimensions of the environment, such as temperature. One study (Lewinski, 1938) that examined reactions to different colors of light found that blue and green were associated with feelings of coolness, while red created a feeling of being hot. In fact, in one case, cafeteria customers complained that a particular room was always too cold. The problem was eliminated by changing the color of the walls. Note that symbolic reactions to color are culture-bound. Our reactions to color in the environment, in terms of mood state, mode of interaction, and other variables, will differ from those of members of other cultures.

The actual *temperature in the environment* is a fifth semifixed feature. People report feeling most comfortable at 79°F and feeling only "slightly cool" to "slightly warm" across a range of temperatures from a low of 68°F to a high of 80°F (Rohles, 1971). Other factors, such as humidity level, physical activity level, air movement, and amount of clothing worn, also affect how comfortable a temperature feels (McCormick, 1976).

Temperature probably affects communication much in the way that color does—by affecting interactants' moods and prompting certain modes of interaction. Although no research has directly addressed the effect of temperature on communication, extended exposure to uncomfortable temperatures may induce fatigue, boredom, and irritability

---

BOX 4-1

PINK JAILS AND INMATE VIOLENCE

One controversial example of the use of color to affect behavior occurred in the corrections institutions in this country. Several jails and penal institutions around the country painted some of their inmate cells pink (actually, a very specific shade of pink—hot pink; Johnston, 1981; Pellegrini, Schauss, & Miller, 1978). On the advice of Alex Schauss, a corrections consultant, jails in New Orleans; Mecklenburg County, NC; San Bernardino, CA; San Jose, CA; and elsewhere integrated pink holding cells for inmates. According to Schauss, the specific shade of pink he advocated drastically reduced inmates' violent behavior by weakening human muscles, thus calming the inmates. This reasoning is based on the possibility that visual processing of light may affect neu-rological and endocrine functions and that shades of pink and orange can result in loss of strength. Anecdotal reports by some jail directors supported Schauss's claims. However, one empirical study (Pellegrini et al., 1978) of the pink jail failed to show any long-term effects due to the color, and a number of environmental design researchers expressed skepticism. Although the "pink clink" controversy has yet to be resolved, it appears that changing environmental colors from the usual industrial green to another color (even pink) does have some effect on inmates, even if it is only to make them think that corrections officials are more responsive to their environmental needs.

TABLE 4-1
COLOR IN THE ENVIRONMENT: MOODS CREATED AND SYMBOLIC MEANINGS

Color	Moods	Symbolic meanings
Red	Hot, affectionate, angry, defiant, contrary, hostile, full of vitality, excitement, love	Happiness, lust, intimacy, love, restlessness, agitation, royalty, rage, sin, blood
Blue	Cool, pleasant, leisurely, distant, infinite, secure, transcendent, calm, tender	Dignity, sadness, tenderness, truth
Yellow	Unpleasant, exciting, hostile, cheerful, joyful, jovial	Superficial glamor, sun, light, wisdom, masculinity, royalty (in China), age (in Greece), prostitution (in Italy), famine (in Egypt)
Orange	Unpleasant, exciting, disturbed, distressed, upset, defiant, contrary, hostile, stimulating	Sun, fruitfulness, harvest, thoughtfulness
Purple	Depressed, sad, dignified, stately	Wisdom, victory, pomp, wealth, humility, tragedy
Green	Cool, pleasant, leisurely, in control	Security, peace, jealousy, hate, aggressiveness, calm
Black	Sad, intense, anxiety, fear, despondent, dejected, melancholy, unhappy	Darkness, power, mastery, protection, decay, mystery, wisdom, death, atonement
Brown	Sad, not tender, despondent, dejected, melancholy, unhappy, neutral	Melancholy, protection, autumn, decay, humility, atonement
White	Joy, lightness, neutral, cold	Solemnity, purity, chastity, femininity, humility, joy, light, innocence, fidelity, cowardice

Source: Burgoon & Saine, 1978, p. 110.

(Holahan, 1982). We would expect communication to become more difficult and less effective under those circumstances. We might also expect temperature to be related to context perception within the thermal comfort range, warm temperatures being associated with social interaction and cooler temperatures with task interaction. Cold and hot temperatures outside the comfort range have been shown to have detrimental effects on task performance, although the evidence suggests these relationships are complex (see Holahan, 1982, pp. 137–138, for a review). However, the specific relationship between heat and aggressive behavior has received a good deal of research attention (for a review, see Anderson, 1989). This research suggests that as temperatures rise beyond a comfortable zone, so does one's temper. As one interesting example, Reifman, Larrick, and Fein (1991) examined archival data from major league baseball games during the 1986 through 1988 seasons. They found a strong and positive linear relationship between temperature and the number of batters hit by a pitch during these games. As temperatures rose, major league pitchers apparently became more aggressive, hitting batters more often. Phrases like "hot under the collar" and "steamed" may be more than just idle descriptions.

A sixth semifixed element is *noise*. This factor has been heavily investigated in recent years, probably because of government regulations on noise levels. But what precisely is noise? Holahan (1982) suggested that noise is any sound that a listener doesn't want to hear. It is also important to note that noise is not dependent on simple physical characteristics. Instead, noise is *psychologically defined*. Loud sounds are not necessarily noise to some people, while soft sounds may be. Someone whispering next to you can be as noisy and distracting as a fire engine passing outside.

Primarily, we expect noise to have negative and detrimental effects on communicative processes. We have all tried to carry on a conversation in a noisy room, felt too distracted to do so, and given up. Most research on noise has examined its effects on performance of simple mental and psychomotor tasks or more complex experimental tasks that require attention and vigilance. A review of this research (Cohen & Weinstein, 1981) indicated that noise produced in laboratory settings does not adversely affect performance on simple tasks. However, it does adversely affect performance on complex tasks (Boggs & Simon, 1968), tasks that require a high level of concentration (Jerison, 1959; Woodhead, 1964), and tasks that require handling a large amount of information (Glass & Singer, 1972; Woodhead, 1966). Most communication fits a complex task description in that it requires the handling of large amounts of information and a high level of concentration.

Research has also shown that noise characteristics and timing can affect performance. Intermittent noise is more annoying than continuous or aperiodic (irregular) noise (Eschenbrenner, 1971; Theologus, Wheaton, & Fleishman, 1974). Interestingly, Acton (1970) showed that intelligible speech is the most disruptive of several types of noise. Moreover, longer exposure to noise produces more negative performance effects (Hartley & Adams, 1974), and performance continues to suffer even after one leaves a noisy situation (Glass, Singer, & Friedman, 1969).

A seventh semifixed element is *overall level of sensory stimulation* in the environment. It is a composite of fixed and semifixed elements, such as lighting, windows, color, materials, odors, and noise, all of which contribute to the level of stimulation present. A certain amount of stimulation in an environment is necessary for people to feel comfortable and be productive. Too much or too little is undesirable. In fact, studies indicate that total lack of sensory stimulation over a period of time can be uncomfortable and frightening.

Moderate rather than extreme stimulation appears to be the ideal. Sensory stimulation affects the inhabitants' level of arousal, which in turn affects performance. The Yerkes-Dodson Law (Yerkes & Dodson, 1908), developed in early experimental psychology, posits an inverted U-shaped function between level of arousal and performance: moderate levels of arousal are optimum for good performance, while low or high levels of arousal are detrimental. Thus environments that provide a moderate level of stimulation, and hence a moderate level of arousal, should be optimal for communication.

However, two factors qualify the stimulation-performance relationship. Research on task complexity suggests that more complicated tasks (which probably includes communication processes) achieve an optimum level of performance at somewhat lower levels of arousal, although the function still has an inverted U shape. Further, people seem to adapt to different levels of stimulation, some liking less and others liking more.

How can we explain these idiosyncratic differences? Helson's adaptation-level theory (1964) suggests that people adapt to and become habituated to different levels of stimulation over time. As a result, idiosyncratic preference levels for stimulation may develop. It may be, for example, that family experience sets an initial norm for environmental stimulation. After that, stimulation preferences may change gradually over time.

Norms, Expectations, and Standards for the Environmental Code

Norms and expectations for the environmental code in any given culture are reflected in how environmental elements are used for communicative purposes. These become part of the culture's schema for environmental perceptions and affective reactions (Purcell, 1986).

Semifixed Features and Norms   According to Rapoport (1982), in our culture semifixed elements are likely to be used for communication:

> Thus in our own culture, both in domestic and non-domestic situations, semi-fixed feature elements tend to be used much—and are much more under the control of *users;* hence they tend to be used to communicate meanings. Yet they have been ignored by both designers and analysts who have stressed fixed-feature elements. (p. 92)

As a result of the different points of view of creators and users, environments often do not fulfill the functions and purposes for which they were designed. Sommer (1974b) described architecture that does not respond to the needs of the user as "hard architecture," while "soft architecture" is design that takes user needs into account.

In some cases, users are denied the ability to modify semifixed elements to meet their needs. When CBS designed its headquarters in New York City, an aesthetician was placed in charge of choosing art, colors, plants, furniture, and all other environmental elements so that the semifixed elements would be consistent with the overall building design (Rapoport, 1982). The designers prohibited the use of any personal objects (calendars, pictures, plants, etc.) by the workers in order to preserve the aesthetic ideal of the building.

As you might guess, the users of the building disagreed with the designers and attempted to bring in personal effects anyway. Some of the workers even brought suit against the company. To the users of the environment, the prohibition against modifying the semifixed elements of their workspace was going too far. Similarly, in the past on many college campuses, students have been prohibited from decorating the walls of their dorm rooms because the maintenance costs of painting every year are too great (Sommer, 1974b). These prohibitions violate inhabitants' needs to personalize the environment and to give it meaning, and can have negative effects on motivation and productivity. Incidentally, CBS eventually relented and allowed the workers to personalize their offices, but not before a very open and public quarrel.

We might wonder whether this state of affairs is found in other cultures. The answer seems to be: not always. As Rapoport (1990) indicated, in cultures that are less technologically standardized and specialized, decisions about both fixed and semifixed features of the environment are still often left to the user. The culture may prescribe a range of choices, but it is the user who makes those choices. One broad overall norm, then, has to do with the environment and artifacts elements that are considered pertinent to environmental meaning in a culture. Developed and specialized cultures appear to place the most emphasis on semifixed elements, whereas more traditional cultures emphasize both fixed and semifixed elements. For example, in Navajo culture, both the dwelling's structure (the hogan) and the settlement pattern (very dispersed) are meaning-laden and reflect historical values of the culture.

Fixed Features and Norms   Within a culture, there are more specific norms and standards to consider. Perhaps the best way to examine those norms is to analyze specific environments and the effect these norms have on the communication processes that occur in these environments. Two such environments are homes and schools.

Homes   Residences are among the most important environments for members of a culture. As noted in Chapter 3, they are primary territories that provide the most environmentally direct expressions of crowding and privacy functions in a culture, and in our culture, they allow the highest degree of personalization and communication of identity (Wright, 1981). Such elements as the styles of furniture, colors, levels of lighting, objects in the environment, and materials and textures do not always communicate (unless used symbolically), but they clearly provide a great deal of personal information about the inhabitants of a residential space. (See Box 4-2, for an example.)

Schools   Another significant environment in which most of us spend a great deal of time is the classroom. The standard classroom features the teacher at the front and

---

BOX 4-2

APPLICATIONS: COMMUNICATION AND THE AMERICAN HOME

A striking aspect of the American home is its compartmentalization. Instead of the open floor plans common in many other cultures (Polynesia, for example), Americans erect permanent walls to create lots of separate rooms, each with specialized functions (Kent, 1991). These spatial arrangements reflect notions of privacy. For instance, intimate conversation may become associated with the bedroom or bathroom. Because the amount of space allocated to a room typically reflects its importance in daily routines, it can also influence the kinds of communication that take place. The kitchen—once one of the largest rooms in the house—was the hub of family interaction, especially for rural and farm families. But today, with far less time devoted to food preparation, the family room or den has taken over. A completely different set of activities is associated with it (television watching being a primary one) and with it, a different pattern of family interaction. For a cultural contrast, consider that in many countries, the total living space is equal to that of an average American living room.

External features of a residence also often communicate something about its inhabitants. The size and style of house, as well as its location in a neighborhood, reveal information about the inhabitants' status, social standing, wealth, and even friendliness. Landscaping and gardens create the "front," the most visible and easily evaluated aspect of the residence (see Rapoport, 1990, Chap. 5, for a review).

Sometimes exteriors must meet neighborhood restrictions, but residents often come to prefer them that way. Rapoport presents a number of examples where a house of an unusual and innovative design was built in an established neighborhood. Residents complained that the new house "didn't fit in" and turned the neighborhood into an "eyesore." Apparently homogeneity is prized over uniqueness when it comes to a home "identity."

These home exteriors suggest different things about the inhabitants.

students arranged in a rectangle of columns and rows. Little use of color (other than industrial green and tan) is evident, and often there is little variation on other semifixed features. The overall effect is to produce a very somber, almost boring environment that hampers communication among students and limits the possibilities for communication between students and teacher.

One alternative classroom design, the *open-space* classroom, has been employed in some schools. This design is literally a school without walls where large open spaces are partitioned into smaller usable spaces for as many as five classes. The aims of this classroom design are to create more flexibility in the use of space for educational processes and to encourage more interaction among teachers and between teachers and students (Educational Facilities Laboratories, 1965).

Few studies have evaluated the effectiveness of open-classroom design, and their limited results are not clear-cut. One study found that open-space design leads to the use of more spaces in the classroom for educational activities (Gump & Good, 1976). Others (Azrentzen & Evans, 1984; Brunetti, 1972; Burns, 1972) determined that the open-space design results in a greater level of visual and auditory distraction. Another investigation (Rivlin & Rothenberg, 1976) discovered that the use of space in an open classroom was very unevenly distributed, with students and teachers spending most of their time in one area of the room. Further, students spent most of their time engaged in individual activities instead of the group-focused activities open classrooms are designed to encourage. However, when open-space classroom design was modified with sound-absorbing partitions to correct for some of the noise, distraction, and privacy problems, students asked more work-related questions and the rate of verbal and nonverbal inter-ruptions in the classroom dropped off sharply (Evans & Lovell, 1979).

Box 4-3 describes another alternative school design.

Communication Potential of the Environmental Code

Encoding Potential   Now let us consider the degree to which the structural elements we have discussed actually meet the criteria for a nonverbal code in the strict sense of the term. The elements we have considered often play a contextual and situational role and are not part of the communicative act itself, but sometimes they clearly do play a communicative role—as when they communicate symbolically or by signs or prompt the use of certain rules for interaction.

As we have said earlier, one key criterion for deciding if something is communication is whether it has consensually recognized meaning. It is clear that we all have per-ceptions of the environment and its elements, some of which are very detailed and elaborate (for a review of work on environmental perception and cognition, see Holahan, 1982, chaps. 2–3; or Ittelson, 1973). Those that have symbolic value, such as archi-tectural forms for churches, colors, and certain artifacts, will be interpreted consensu-ally. The environment and its artifacts may also communicate on a sign level. A very common example is international signs. These signs often employ icons (visual ima-ges), such as the shape of males and females on rest room doors, to communicate content.

Additionally, environment and artifacts have great communication potential by virtue of the behavioral routines that they cue. Rapoport (1982) described the "mnemonic function" of the environment: the environmental cues elicit appropriate emotions, behaviors, interpretations, and transactions. These environmental cues remind people of what is expected of them. Goffman (1963) referred to "occasioned places" as environments that contain regulative indications of how to behave. Such environmentally based prescriptions to behave confirm that we all share perceptions of indicators in the environment.

Decoding Potential   The communication potential of environment and artifacts can be demonstrated on other grounds as well. First, there are structural elements to be con-

BOX 4-3

USER PARTICIPATION IN ENVIRONMENTAL DESIGN

Many environmental designers and architects have taken the view that user needs and preferences should be included in environmental design. In one example (Institute for Environmental Education, 1978), a Navajo school in northwestern New Mexico was designed so that the school would (a) be a departure from standard building design, (b) reflect Navajo values and culture, and (c) focus on the ways that design would prompt traditional forms of communication in the Navajo culture. Surveys and focus group discussions were used to assess the Navajo users' views of the design. Results indicated a wish for design features that included use of openings instead of doorways throughout the building, incorporation of natural materials from the environment and use of natural landscaping, use of earth colors to blend the building in with the environment, use of natural light via skylights, sloping floors and different floor levels to create spaces for cultural activities, and inclusion of sizable common areas that would accommodate traditional forms of communication among users. Many of these features resemble hogans, a traditional dwelling for Navajo. In this case, the users saw these features as ones that would enhance their communication and be consistent with their values.

In another interesting example, one of your authors recently participated in the preliminary design process for new space in his church. The consulting architect emphasized the importance of getting the views of the congregation, and making sure that all of the users' needs and preferences were taken into account throughout the design process. This can be a lengthy process for multi-user and multifunctional space. Similar to the Navajo school project, surveys and focus group techniques were used to solicit user views of what the space should be. The final design will eventually evolve from a collaboration of users and the architect. While this seems like a logical way to proceed, the design of spiritual space has rarely relied on user views. Rather, churches have often relied on denominational views of what a church "should look like," and sometimes "divine inspiration." Whether a design is concerned with the creation of educational space that reflects cultural values or a space for spiritual reflection that incorporates congregation members' views, taking account of the user's views is an increasing trend, and one that leads to greater user satisfaction with the spaces they inhabit.

sidered. As we have already discovered, the potential combinations of those elements to produce different communication messages and effects are numerous. Second, humans have the visual and tactile capacity to decode subtle variations in artifactual patterns. Third, most of the senses—sight, sound, touch, and smell—can be stimulated by the structural elements we have been discussing. Since most of the senses are stimulated by the structural elements, the decoding potential is bolstered. Fourth, our reactions to environment and artifacts cues are not only cognitive and perceptual but also emotional and attitudinal, which indicates a strong coding potential. Reactions to the environment are often not simply a matter of taste but a function of the attitudes we have about environmental elements. Seeing a home decorated with lime green carpet, art deco clocks and lamps, and floral-print furniture, we know immediately whether we like it or not, an opinion that reflects our attitudes about living spaces. Finally, environmental and artifactual elements, because of their static nature, serve as a constant statement in any communicative setting and may serve as a framework for interpreting the interactions that take place.

However, many environmental and artifactual elements may be mistaken for communication when they are merely information. Moreover, their static nature means that they can make only one statement at a time and are incapable of adapting to the ongoing interaction. Finally, although environmental and artifactual elements are relevant to several social functions, there are some for which they are irrelevant (e.g., expressive communication, relational communication). Compared with codes such as kinesics and vocalics, then, they may be somewhat more limited in their communication potential.

CHRONEMICS

You may delay, but time will not.

Benjamin Franklin

Time talks. It speaks more plainly than words. The message it conveys comes through loud and clear. . . . It can shout the truth where words lie.

Edward T. Hall, 1959, p. 15

Philosophers, biologists, physicists, and even songwriters have been intrigued by the concept of time. Our interest is in its biological, psychological, and cultural implications for communicators. As Fisher (1978) noted, "Time is, without a doubt, one of the most crucial, yet most neglected, variables of communication" (pp. 79–80). The very concept of communication as process implies that it is a time-bound activity. The way time is structured may in itself also send messages to others. Chronemics, then, is *how humans perceive, structure, and use time as communication.*

Consider a few examples of how time affects our daily communication. Our work and school activities revolve around schedules and deadlines. Waiting too long for an appointment may make us impatient or angry. We regard the amount of time a friend spends with us when we are in need as a statement about the importance of our relationship. Parents today are urged to spend "quality time" with their children.

Origins and Acquisition of Chronemics

Infants have no sense of time other than their awareness of their own biological cycles. Young children likewise have limited understanding of the passage of time and future events. They may be disturbed, for example, when a parent goes away on a brief business trip. Yet by age 6, children have learned such formal time categories as the days of the week, and by age 12, they have mastered the key elements of a given culture's time system.

Piaget (1981) suggested that children's sense of time depends on their operational stage of development. Cognitive maturation is partly a biological process: a child cannot develop a mature sense of time until the higher stages of cognitive development are reached, at around age 12. Nevertheless, ideas, expectations, and rules about the chronemic code are likely to be learned through socialization. Thus the great cultural diversity that exists in chronemic behavior is best explained through social learning.

Classifying Chronemic Patterns

Perception of time is partly due to the perception of patterns of events—their starting, stopping, cycling, frequency, and duration (Bruneau, 1980; Doob, 1971). Those patterns, which can be linked to our biological, psychological, and cultural levels of experience, form the structure of the chronemic code. We will review the biological and psychological levels here; cultural patterns will be considered in the section on norms and expectations.

Biological Cycles   Although the exact relationship between biology and time as a vehicle of communication remains unknown, there is little doubt that our sense of time is affected by biological cycles. Biologists believe that most species, including humans, have some kind of internal *biological clock* (Cloudsley-Thompson, 1981; Hamner, 1981) that governs such diverse phenomena as plant flowering, migration, navigation, and sleep rhythms. When you experience jet lag after a long plane trip, you are actually experiencing a lag between your biological clock time and the clock time in the local environment. Recent research on work schedules at manufacturing plants shows that rotating shift schedules adversely affect worker health, alertness, and productivity. Giving workers more time to adjust their biological clocks to a new work schedule can overcome these negative effects.

One of the best-known biological cycles affecting behavior is the *circadian rhythm* (*circadian* meaning "about day"), an approximately 24-hour cycle exhibited by almost all organisms (Hamner, 1981). This rhythm tends to persist despite environmental changes. For example, one study took participants to a northern latitude where the sun shines continuously and subjected them to daily cycles of varying lengths (21 hours, 27 hours, etc.) by speeding or slowing the clocks. Although participants changed their activities to match the new clock times, basic physiological cycles such as secretion of urine and salts remained in circadian rhythm (Hamner, 1981). Further evidence of the persistence of such biological rhythms comes from the discovery of seasonal affect disorder (SAD), which occurs in people who are particularly sensitive to light and darkness cycles. As days shorten in the fall and winter, individuals with SAD become increasingly depressed. It is thought that the shortening light cycles throw the hormone melatonin out of balance. Exposure to artificial light in the morning hours helps SAD sufferers reduce their depression.

It is possible that other biological cycles such as biorhythms affect our communication behavior. Biorhythms have physical, sensitivity, and intellectual cycles. The physical cycle involves endurance and energy levels, the sensitivity cycle involves fluctuations in emotional states, and the intellectual cycle reflects changes in mental alertness and accomplishments. When "critical days" occur—days when the cycles change from positive to negative or vice versa—behavior is supposedly most vulnerable to impairment. Although empirical evidence of the impact of biorhythms is lacking, many industries plan work schedules around biorhythms for employees in risk-related occupations. Even if we view biorhythms with some healthy skepticism, it should be evident that biological rhythms provide the most fundamental time framework we have.

Psychological Time Orientations   Our ideas and expectations about time form four basic psychological time orientations (Reinert, 1971). Individuals with a *past* orientation dwell on events in the past, relive old times, and take a sentimental view toward time. Such people often see events as recurrent and time as circular. ("Those who fail to learn from the past are condemned to repeat it.") Individuals with a *time-line* orientation literally see time as a continuum integrating past, present, and future, a linear and systematic progression of events. These people often view time analytically and scientifically. Individuals with a *present* orientation are focused on the here and now. They pay little attention to the past or future and tend to deal with events, activities, and problems spontaneously. Finally, individuals with a *future* orientation are focused on anticipating and planning for future events and relating them to the present. As Boxes 4-4 and 4-5 indicate, these orientations have some practical implications.

More recent research (Gonzales & Zimbardo, 1985) suggests some refinements to these orientations. Past orientation was found to be rare among respondents (1 percent of the sample; this is consistent with previous research), and present orientation was also infrequent (9 percent). Fully 57 percent of the respondents indicated a time-line orientation and 33 percent a future orientation. Gonzales and Zimbardo analyzed the responses to the Stanford Time Perspective Inventory with factor analysis, a statistical technique that identifies underlying patterns in the responses to the Inventory. This analysis identified seven different time perspectives (see Table 4-2). Four are future-oriented, two are present-oriented, and one reflects an emotional reaction to time pressure. These results suggest that time orientation is more complex than earlier work indi-

---

BOX 4-4

APPLICATIONS: TIME ORIENTATIONS AND YOUR CAREER

Has it ever occurred to you that the way you deal with time could affect the occupational choices you make? A *Psychology Today* survey report (Gonzales & Zimbardo, 1985) suggested that time orientation may be related to income, gender, and occupational choice. Although the results, which came from *Psychology Today* readers, may not be representative of the population at large, they do indicate some patterns.

If your time orientation is associated with an occupation that you currently hold or plan to hold in the future, the news is good. Gonzales and Zimbardo showed that people gravitate to jobs with matching time orientations, and job success and satisfaction depend on intensifying that time orientation. Moreover, one's time orientation may depend on one's socioeconomic background and upbringing: children with skilled and professional parents may acquire the kind of time orien-

tation that allows them to succeed in skilled and professional occupations; children raised by unskilled parents may develop a present orientation that predisposes them to unskilled and semiskilled occupations. The researchers recommended remedial time training for those from unskilled backgrounds who aspire to professional-level jobs. Finally, they suggested that we would all be better off if we could be flexible enough to shift time orientations when the situation called for it. At work, a future orientation is best for productivity and success. But when it is time to socialize, relax, and enjoy friends, a present, hedonistic orientation is more appropriate. Given the number of workaholics that many of us encounter on a daily basis, this sounds like good advice. More research in this area may support the maxim "Work hard, play hard."

cated and that it is a function of several things, including work motivation, perseverance, goal seeking, and planning. These factors relate to age, income, and occupation. Both men and women became more future-oriented as they aged. Sensitivity to time pressures also increased with age in this sample. Those with higher incomes tended to be more future-oriented, whereas lower incomes were more associated with a present orientation. Finally, job choice was related to time orientation. For example, the most characteristic occupation for factor 1 was white-collar manager; for factor 4, professional or teacher; and for factor 5, retired manager.

These time orientations can affect communication in many ways. The content of conversation may be affected: those with a past orientation may spend time retelling old stories, while those with a future orientation may talk about predictions for the future. The urgency of communication may be affected: those who are present-oriented may be far less concerned about achieving closure on decisions or plans, while those who are time-line and future-oriented may be insistent upon it. The structure of communication likewise may be affected: people with past or present orientations may see little need for punctuality or adherence to others' time pressures, while those with a time-line or future orientation may see schedules, calendars, and deadlines as necessities.

Even though much of what we have said about time orientation suggests that it is a somewhat permanent and traitlike concept, our perception of time is changeable. Some authors have ventured that our perception of time passing slowly or quickly may depend on communication factors. For example, Bruneau (1980) suggested that the novelty of events results in time being perceived as passing quickly. Brodey (1969) advanced sim-

---

BOX 4-5

PSYCHOLOGICAL TIME AND FAVORITE TELEVISION CHARACTERS

As people watch television for longer periods of time, they may begin to form parasocial relationships with television characters similar to themselves. In other words, they may come to especially favor TV characters who are similar to them, and one important point of similarity may be psychological time orientation.

One recent study by Furno-Lamude (1991) found support for this idea. In this study, viewers with a future time orientation favored science fiction characters. Captain Jean-Luc Picard *(Star Trek: The Next Generation)* was a favorite character of this group. Viewers with a past time orientation favored characters that had difficulty severing ties with the past and dealing with new situations. Hawkeye *(M*A*S*H),* Murphy Brown *(Murphy Brown),* and Kevin *(The Wonder Years)* were often mentioned by this group. The relationship between present time orientation viewers and their favorite TV characters was less clear in this study, but characters that were often mentioned included those on *Married with Children, Roseanne,* and *The Simpsons.* In a sense, characters on these shows do portray lives led in the present, even if the portrayals have a sarcastic edge to them.

Have we really gotten to the point where we love our sitcom characters more than those around us in the real world? Hopefully not, but we might become concerned if advertisers start to employ these findings in the way products are marketed: old-fashioned oatmeal for those who watch the past shows, instant microwave oatmeal for the futurists, and for the present time orientation viewers, as Homer Simpson would have it, donuts, man!

TABLE 4-2
TIME-ORIENTATION FACTORS AND ITEMS

Factor 1: Future, work motivation, perseverance

    A. Meeting tomorrow's deadlines and doing other necessary work comes before tonight's partying.

    B. I meet my obligations to friends and authorities on time.

    C. I complete projects on time by making steady progress.

    D. I am able to resist temptations when I know there is work to be done.

    E. I keep working at a difficult, uninteresting task if it will help me get ahead.

Factor 1 embodies a positive work motivation and a work ethic of finishing a task despite difficulties and temptations.

Factor 2: Present, fatalistic, worry-free, avoid planning

    A. If things don't get done on time, I don't worry about it.

    B. I think that it's useless to plan too far ahead because things hardly ever come out the way you planned anyway.

    C. I try to live one day at a time.

    D. I live to make better what is rather than to be concerned about what will be.

    E. It seems to me that it doesn't make sense to worry about the future, since fate determines that whatever will be, will be.

People with this orientation live one day at a time, not to enjoy it fully but to avoid planning for the next day and to minimize anxiety about a future they perceive as being determined by fate rather than by their efforts.

Factor 3: Present, hedonistic

    A. I believe that getting together with friends to party is one of life's important pleasures.

    B. I do things impulsively, making decisions on the spur of the moment.

    C. I take risks to put excitement in my life.

    D. I get drunk at parties.

    E. It's fun to gamble.

In contrast with the present-oriented people described by factor 2, hedonists fill their days with pleasure seeking, partying, taking risks, drinking, and impulsive action of all kinds. Gambling is often an important element.

Factor 4: Future, goal seeking, planning

    A. Thinking about the future is pleasant to me.

    B. When I want to achieve something, I set subgoals and consider specific means for reaching those goals.

    C. It seems to me that my career path is pretty well laid out.

Compared to factor 1, the items here center less on work per se and more on the pleasure that comes from planning and achieving goals.

Factor 5: Time pressure

    A. It upsets me to be late for appointments.

    B. I meet my obligations to friends and authorities on time.

    C. I get irritated at people who keep me waiting when we've agreed to meet at a given time.

This factor doesn't fall neatly into a present or future orientation (although it does correlate positively with the future factors). It centers on a person's sensitivity to the role time plays in social obligations and how it can be used as a weapon in struggles for status.

TABLE 4-2
TIME-ORIENTATION FACTORS AND ITEMS (*Continued*)

Factor 6: Future, pragmatic action for later gain
    A. It makes sense to invest a substantial part of my income in insurance premiums.
    B. I believe that "a stitch in time saves nine."
    C. I believe that "a bird in the hand is worth two in the bush."
    D. I believe it is important to save for a rainy day.

    These people act now to achieve desirable future consequences. The researchers thought that item C would be characteristic of present orientation. Instead, the respondents saw it as advice to do or have something concrete now rather than gambling on an uncertain outcome. Thus it is a conservative strategy to safeguard future options.

Factor 7: Future, specific, daily planning
    A. I believe a person's day should be planned each morning.
    B. I make lists of things I must do.
    C. When I want to achieve something, I set subgoals and consider specific means for reaching those goals.
    D. I believe that "a stitch in time saves nine."

    This factor describes individuals obsessed with the nitty-gritty of getting ahead. They adopt a somewhat compulsive attitude toward daily planning, make lists of things to do, set subgoals, and pay attention to details.

Source: Gonzales & Zimbardo, 1985, pp. 20–26.

ilar arguments. This "time-binding" aspect of the chronemic code is an important feature to consider.

Norms and Expectations for Chronemics: Cultural Time Orientations

We turn now to the cultural level of the chronemic code. Perhaps the best way to understand the parts of the chronemic code that are most relevant to daily life is to examine time at the cultural level. Elements at this level are those we are most often aware of on a day-to-day basis; they reflect a culture's view of time and include its norms and standards for time.

It is often difficult for us to realize that there is any time orientation other than our own. Yet in many cases, the chronemic code in other cultures has little in common with our own. Hall's work in *The Silent Language* (1959) still stands as one of the best accounts of how cultures vary in terms of chronemic behavior. For a better grasp of how other cultures deal with chronemics, we need first to examine our own culture's view of time.

That our culture is obsessed with time is an understatement. Time in the United States is infused with a strong sense of urgency. We play an endless game of beat the clock. Time is seen as a precious resource, a valuable and tangible commodity. We spend time, save it, make it, fill it, and waste it. It is seen almost as a container with defined boundaries. This tangible view of time is also reflected in how we mark its passage. It is highly divisible: we break it into years, months, weeks, days, hours, minutes, seconds, tenths of seconds, even nanoseconds. The average American thinks of time in 5-minute blocks, which are very small chunks of time. The way we schedule events also reflects the urgent and precise way we deal with time. We expect classes to start on time (within a minute or so), and when they don't, we wait only so long (20 minutes at the most) before leaving. Imagine how restless students would become if professors lectured to the end of their train of thought before dismissing class.

Few aspects of our culture do not reflect the fast pace of our lives, from fast food to fast banking to instantaneous Dow Jones quotations. For many of us, the workday is strongly governed by the clock. We must arrive at work at an appointed time (certainly within a minute or two), typically take only an hour for lunch, and leave at an appointed time (although working "late" is sometimes acceptable). The more we consider the way our culture deals with time, the clearer our obsession with it becomes. Hall (1959) claimed that Americans are surpassed only by the Germans and the Swiss in having an urgent, precise, and fast-paced orientation to time. The Japanese may share that orientation now.

Keep in mind that various groups within our culture deviate significantly from this general time orientation. Subcultures, ethnic groups, even the population of entire regions can have a different orientation to time than that of the mainstream culture. For example, the Sioux have no words for *late* or *waiting* in their language. Pueblo Indians start many of their ceremonies "when the time is right," not at some scheduled time. For the traditional Navajo, time and space are very much the same; only the here and now is real, and the future is a foreign concept (see Hall, 1959, for a more thorough discussion of these subcultural differences). It is well known that the pace of life is slower in rural regions than in urban areas. Native Hawaiians operate under two time systems. *Haole time* reflects the influence of the early missionaries in the islands and is very much like the mainstream culture's time system. *Hawaiian time,* on the other hand, is very lax. When you meet someone in Hawaii and plan to meet again at a given time, it is important to know under which time system. If the islander says to you, "See you at three," you can expect to meet at that time. However, if the islander says, "See you at three Hawaiian time," that really means that you will see each other whenever you both happen to arrive.

Hall (1959) suggested that three distinct time systems operate in any culture: technical time, formal time, and informal time. *Technical* time is probably the least relevant to the chronemic code. It is concerned with the scientific and precise measurement of time. Examples include the setting of a standard time (such as Greenwich mean time) via an atomic clock and the distinguishing among solar, sidereal, and anomalistic years.

Formal time is the traditional way a culture views time. It is the conscious, formally taught system for measuring time. In our culture, we are regulated by a calendar comprised of many cyclical and hierarchical units. Other cultures do not always use this system. Some cultures use phases of the moon, summer and winter solstices, or the fall and spring equinoxes as formal time systems. For example, the ancient Southwest Indian culture, the Anasazi, probably used the spring and fall equinoxes to mark important cultural events and rites. It was recently discovered at Chaco Canyon National Historical Park that features of the pueblo buildings line up with the angle of the sun so that the sun strikes these architectural features (often portals in a kiva wall) on the equinox. By closely examining the architectural arrangements and sun position, researchers now think that the Anasazi could know on what day an important ceremony (and the equinox) would fall and could anticipate the arrival of that day (see Zeilek, 1985a, 1985b).

Other elements of this system that we learn formally are how our culture orders events, the kinds of cycles it recognizes, the values it places on time, what duration means for the culture, and the degree of depth and tangibility that culture assigns to time. Thus North Americans see the days of the week following a fixed order; we are highly aware of weekly, monthly, and seasonal cycles; we place a monetary value on time; we judge duration by the clock rather than by natural events; we attribute some depth to time as we often profess to be interested in our own history; and there is no doubt that we see time as something concrete.

Other cultures treat these elements quite differently. Many cultures mark the order of time on the basis of natural events and not by clock or calendar time as we do. A striking example of this contrast is that some North African cultures view the clock as the "devil's mill" (Levine & Wolff, 1985). We view the clock as indispensable and a source of order, whereas they associate it with something evil. Further, cycles in time are often marked differently. Hall (1959) noted that the Tiv of Nigeria name days according to what is to be sold at market each day.

The different values that cultures place on time is also evident in the treatment of waiting time. In our culture, waiting is considered a waste of time and often provokes anger. Possibly the most striking example of our impatience with waiting comes from many computer users who complain that their PC is too slow, and that they have to "wait too long" for the computer to perform a task—when in fact it takes the computer only a few seconds to do something that would once have taken several minutes or even hours. Obviously, we want our technology to perform at high speed. In other cultures, such as Japan, India, and many of the Arabic cultures, waiting is not seen as unproductive. The duration of an event is for us a matter of clock time, but it may be "as long as it takes" for people in other cultures.

Cultures also vary in the level of depth and tangibility they attribute to time. Arabs view time as an endless process and the individual as an insignificant speck in its huge expanse (Hall, 1959). For many other cultures, time just is; it is not something to be spent, controlled, or wasted.

Our formal time system, because it is deeply rooted in traditions, has the power to evoke strong emotions. Old ways are valued and new ones are viewed with suspicion. This was no more clear than when daylight saving time was first instituted. A Kansas farmer wrote to the state legislature to protest, saying that the extra hour of sunlight would burn up his tomatoes.

Informal time is probably the most interesting and least understood time system of the three. Informal time elements are loosely defined, are not explicitly taught, and typically operate outside consciousness. They most often take the form of rules and expectations we learn from our culture, but it is not clear when or if we all learn these rules.

Punctuality is one of the most prominent concepts in the informal time system. Arriving for an appointment or an event at the appropriate time is often a very important part of having a successful interaction with others. What constitutes being "on time," however, varies across different types of situations. Being on time for a business appointment most often means literally arriving at the appointed time. Arriving more than 5 minutes late is a violation of this rule and often requires an apology or an explanation. We can classify these kinds of situations as formal and task-oriented. Social situations that can be characterized as informal imply a different rule. If you are invited to a party by friends that starts at 8:00 P.M., arriving "on time" may mean showing up at 8:30 or 9:00, possibly later. No explanation for lateness is given because you are not perceived to be "late." But some situations can be described as both formal and social. For example, if you are invited to dinner at a friend's house at 7:00 P.M., most often the expectation is that you will arrive either at 7:00 or shortly thereafter. The formality of this situation is introduced by the effort your friend goes through to prepare dinner. It is expected that you will respect that effort by arriving promptly so that the food does not spoil.

To complicate matters, different regions of the country often have different versions of these informal rules. In New York City, going to a party that starts at 9:00 P.M. often means arriving at 10:30 and staying until the event is over. Being invited to dinner in a Mormon community often means that you are expected to arrive early, as Mormons tend to be quite punctual. Imagine, however, that you followed this rule in another part of the country. You might arrive to find your hosts madly rushing about, attempting to clean house and prepare food at the same time. Needless to say, this would not be a good way to start the evening. Since these kinds of rules are rarely communicated explicitly, people who move from one region of the country to another are likely to follow the wrong rules and be perceived negatively.

There are also individual differences in the way that people follow these informal time rules. Some adopt a *displaced-point* time pattern. Some view an appointment time as an end point, arriving either at or before the appointed time, but rarely after. For example, the wife who is to pick up her husband at 6:00 P.M. at a given place will arrive shortly before or at 6:00 P.M. Others adopt a *diffused-point* pattern, viewing appointed times as approximate. Such people arrive somewhere around the appointed time, either early or late, within an acceptable deviation. Interesting things happen when people of different patterns have an appointment. If the displaced-point wife arrives at 6:00 P.M. and the diffused-point husband shows up at 6:20, a conflict most likely will ensue. Knowing that each operates on a different time pattern may help in such situations. However, given that waiting is often an onerous experience, knowing about someone else's time pattern may not help much.

Rules for punctuality in other cultures are quite different, as Levine and Wolff (1985) report. Levine, a professor of psychology, discovered when teaching at a university in Brazil that students arriving as late as 11:00 for a class held from 10:00 to 12:00 showed few signs of concern for their "lateness." Equally disconcerting was that, unlike American students, when the end of class arrived, only a few students left. Even 15 minutes after the end of class, many of the Brazilian students were still there, asking questions. At 12:30, Levine himself ended class, as it appeared that some of the remaining stu-

dents were settling in for an even longer stay! Such behavior in an American university class is unheard of. In an informal survey, Levine found that Brazilian students feel less personally responsible for lateness, they express less regret for their lateness, and blame others less when they are late. This work is consistent with earlier observations made by Hall (1959). Clearly, the informal time sense for punctuality is very different in Brazil from our own culture.

Despite cultural differences in what is meant by being punctual, the timing of one's arrival can have strong message value in each culture. A related chronemic message is *waiting time.* Here again, misunderstanding is common because the informal rules are not known. A common problem for North American business people traveling to Latin America, for instance, is adapting to the local time system. Corporate executives may find themselves waiting up to an hour and a half to meet their Latin American counterpart, and they may find that several appointments have been scheduled at once, so that there is no clear sequence for seeing visitors. North Americans, who have no tolerance for waiting or going out of turn, find this system incomprehensible and often take such treatment as a personal insult when no insult is intended.

However, it is also possible to use such behaviors as punctuality and waiting time to send an intentional message. The story is told about Harry Truman, who, shortly after becoming president, was visited by a newspaper editor. After waiting 45 minutes in the outer office, the editor asked an aide to tell the president he was becoming annoyed by the long wait. Truman replied, "When I was a junior senator from Missouri, that same editor kept me cooling my heels for an hour and a half. As far as I'm concerned, the son of a bitch has 45 minutes to go!"

Other informal time system elements that have message potential are duration, urgency, monochronism, activity, and variety. Hall (1959) suggested eight informal levels of *duration* in our culture: immediate, very short, short, neutral, long, very long, terribly long, and forever. When someone says, "I'll do that immediately," does it mean 1 minute, 5 minutes, or 3 weeks? It probably depends on whether the person is promising to turn on the television or process your loan application. *Urgency* similarly concerns the immediacy and importance of events. The amount of lead time between the assignment of a task and its due date can be used to communicate urgency. The less lead time, the greater the urgency. The timing of an event can have the same effect. A knock at the front door at 3:00 A.M. connotes far more urgency than one at 3:00 P.M.

Contrast these patterns with the Truk Islanders, who treat the past as if it were the present and who have no past tense in their language (Hall, 1959). Events are indefinite in duration and old conflicts never lose their immediacy because they are treated as if "they happened just yesterday."

Monochronism, or doing one thing at a time, can be contrasted with *polychronism,* or doing several things at once. In a culture where monochronism is the norm, doing several things at once can carry a potent message. Imagine, for example, you are meeting with a professor about a serious grade problem and the professor proceeds to riffle through files on his desk while listening to you. Or imagine that you are trying to clinch an important sale and the client accepts several telephone calls during your meeting. When someone gives us their divided rather than their undivided attention, we may take offense. Elsewhere it may be quite common for people to conduct several activities simultaneously, and consequently, polychronism doesn't take on communicative import.

Finally, *activity* and *variety* refer to the degree to which time is filled with activity or not and whether such activities are varied or repetitive. For westerners, to be inactive is to be lazy, unambitious, and wasteful. Novelty and variety are stimulating and prevent boredom. In eastern cultures, too much peripatetic activity and variety may be a sign of inadequate thought, reflection, and maturity.

In sum, the informal time system consists of at least six elements: punctuality, duration, urgency, monochronism, activity, and variety. Further, within these elements are some specific chronemic patterns that may reflect intentional use, as in the waiting time pattern and the punctuality element. Informal time systems provide us with some of the most striking differences in chronemic behavior across cultures. They also cause many difficulties when members of different cultures communicate.

Communication Potential of the Chronemic Code

Encoding Potential   The communication potential of time is somewhat limited. On the encoding side of the equation, many chronemic cues are manipulated unintentionally. They reflect a person's response to internal cycles or to cultural norms, rather than an intentional message. Moreover, this code is often part of the situational framework in which interaction takes place and thus may serve as either information or communication. Such diverse chronemic actions as following a schedule, being early or late for an appointment, and filling time with activity are certainly examples of informative behavior. But the behavior does not qualify as communication if it is unintentional and is not used regularly by members of a social community to mean something in particular.

When communicators intend to send messages with the chronemic code, they can find the code's encoding potential limited because the number of identified elements in the code is relatively low. It is not clear which forms of time manipulation qualify as messages in a given culture. Moreover, little is known about the possible relevance of chronemic codes to such primary communication functions as emotional expression and message processing. All these factors, then, limit the encoding potential of chronemics.

Decoding Potential   Given the fact that some chronemic cues are unintentional, there is a great deal of ambiguity in particular behaviors. Also, chronemic cues are often subtle. On the other hand, such cues do have an ability to evoke strong emotional reactions.

Accuracy in the perception of chronemic cues also varies. The formal and technical elements of this code tend to be perceived quite accurately, but the informal time system, which contains the elements most likely to affect behavior, tends to be perceived less accurately. Subcultural and ethnic background, region of the country, and some individual difference factors complicate our perceptions of the informal elements so that in our culture there is often less than consensual agreement on what a given informal element may be taken to mean. Further, since these elements are often not explicitly taught, there may be additional room for misperception.

All these problems reduce the decoding potential of chronemics. Since there are also limitations in its encoding potential, the chronemic code emerges as lower in overall communication potential than the nonverbal codes discussed in Chapters 2 and 3.

SUMMARY

Both the environmental code and the chronemic code play very important roles in communication. Elements from these codes are often used in a communicative fashion and may also provide a great deal of situational and contextual information. Environmental code elements act as communication cues by communicating meaning directly in symbolic form, providing a context for interaction, or by guiding behavior by prompting rules for interaction. The elements of the environment and artifacts code can be classified as fixed-feature elements, which are relatively permanent and slow to change, and semi-fixed elements, which are mobile and easily changed. In general, people in our culture have a much greater degree of control over semi-fixed than fixed features. Other cultures have a greater degree of control over features in both categories. Finally, some recent analysis indicates that some cultures are more oriented toward the use of elements of this code for communicative purposes (high-context cultures), while other cultures are less likely to do so (low-context cultures). Although the American culture qualifies as a low-context culture, this chapter has shown that we still make extensive use of these code elements as part of communication.

We are still discovering the importance of the chronemic code elements, but it is already apparent that they are very relevant to all cultures. The elements of this code exist on three levels: biological, psychological, and cultural. The biological elements appear to provide a fundamental framework for the experience of time. The psychological elements indicate the kinds of expectations we hold for time and the activity and behavior that people wish to engage in. The cultural elements indicate how each culture perceives time and uses it as a means of sending messages. Given that the elements of this code are often learned on an implicit basis and that there is great cultural and subcultural variation in their use and meaning, many communication difficulties can be explained by an analysis of chronemic elements. Much is yet to be learned about this interesting and subtle code, especially in interpersonal and relational contexts.

SUGGESTED READINGS

Anderson, C. A. (1989). Temperature and aggression: Ubiquitous effects of heat on occurrence of human violence. *Psychological Bulletin, 106,* 1161–1173.

Doob, L. W. (1971). *Patterning of time.* New Haven, CT: Yale University Press.

Hall, E. T. (1959). *The silent language.* Garden City, NY: Doubleday.

Hall, E. T. (1966). *The hidden dimension* (2d ed.). Garden City, NY: Anchor Press/Doubleday.

Holahan, C. J. (1982). *Environmental psychology.* New York: Random House.

Ittelson, W. H., Proshansky, H. M., Rivlin, L. G., & Winkel, G. H. (1974). *An introduction to environmental psychology.* New York: Holt, Rinehart and Winston.

Lauer, R. H. (1981). *Temporal man.* New York: Praeger.

Levine, R., with Wolff, E. (1990). Social time: The heartbeat of culture. In J. A. DeVito & M. L. Hecht (Eds.), *The nonverbal communication reader* (pp. 322–328). Prospect Heights, IL: Waveland.

Meerloo, J. A. M. (1970). *Along the fourth dimension.* New York: Harper & Row.

Mehrabian, A. (1976). *Public places and private spaces.* New York: Basic.

Rapoport, A. (1982). *The meaning of the built environment: A nonverbal communication approach.* Beverly Hills, CA: Sage.

Reifman, A. S., Larrick, R. P., & Fein, S. (1991). Temper and temperature on the diamond: The heat-aggression relationship in major league baseball. *Personality and Social Psychology Bulletin, 17,* 580–585.

5

RELATIONSHIPS BETWEEN VERBAL AND NONVERBAL COMMUNICATION

While verbal and nonverbal communication may be different, they are not separate. There is a dynamic tension, an inseparable bond between them.

A. M. Katz and V. T. Katz

"I can never bring you to realize the importance of sleeves, the suggestiveness of thumb-nails, or the great issues that may hang from a bootlace."

Sherlock Holmes to Dr. Watson

Like strands in a tapestry, verbal and nonverbal codes are inextricably intertwined. This view, shared by many other nonverbal scholars (e.g., Argyle, 1972a; Bavelas, 1994; Kendon, 1994; Knapp, 1978; Patterson, 1983; Poyatos, 1983), means that "it is impossible to study either verbal or nonverbal communication as isolated structures. Rather, these systems should be regarded as a unified communication construct" (Higginbotham & Yoder, 1982, p. 4). Some have gone so far as to suggest that some nonverbal behaviors such as gestures be treated as verbal rather than nonverbal (McNeill, 1985, 1987). In this chapter, the interconnectedness of verbal and nonverbal communication should become increasingly apparent as we compare verbal and nonverbal cues in terms of impact, origins, structure, and functions.

RELATIVE IMPACT OF NONVERBAL AND VERBAL CODES: CHANNEL RELIANCE

What I hide by language my body utters.

John Barthes

The issue of channel reliance answers the question: Do people depend more on non-verbal or verbal channels when deciding what something means? Research has investigated this question in a variety of ways. It has looked at the relative impact of nonverbal and verbal cues when people judge others' credibility or dominance, size up their personality, infer their emotions and attitudes, or determine the "objective meaning" of utterances. Sometimes investigators have conducted experiments in which they manipulated some combination of verbal and nonverbal cues and measured what interpretation receivers assign to the cue combination. For example, three versions of a verbal message—positive, neutral, and negative—might be paired with three levels each of facial expression (positive, neutral, and negative) and vocal tone (positive, neutral, and negative), for a total of 27 different verbal-facial-vocal combinations. Receivers are asked to judge the meaning of a given combination on a positive-to-negative continuum. In cases where the cues are not consistent with each other—say, the facial cue is negative and the other two are positive—it is possible to determine if the facial cue carries more weight than the verbal and vocal cues by seeing if the meaning is negatively skewed or is judged as positive.

Other investigations have looked at naturally occurring conversation or monologues, measured the nonverbal and verbal behaviors that appeared, then determined statistically which ones most influenced the outcomes. For example, observers might watch videotaped segments from a job interview and rate the applicant on intelligence, personality, and hirability. The nonverbal and verbal behaviors appearing on the tapes could then be coded and correlated with the observer evaluations of the applicants.

The experimental approach allows examination of all possible combinations of a particular subset of cues so that congruent and incongruent combinations can be studied. It also ensures that each cue can be presented with equal frequency and strength. It usually means looking at a very limited number of cues, however. The natural observation approach permits studying the full range of verbal and nonverbal behaviors that normally occur, but those cues may not arise with equal frequency, extremity, or consistency. Also, cues typically do not appear in all possible combinations; incongruent patterns are especially rare. The second approach is therefore much more informative about consistent cue patterns than about contradictory ones.

Six Principles of Channel Reliance

Fortunately, enough research has used both approaches to permit making some generalizations. On the basis of close to 100 studies, a number of conclusions can be drawn. These kinds of generalizations, or principles, are often called *propositions*.

(1) *On average, adults rely more on nonverbal cues than on verbal cues in determining social meaning.* The figure most often cited to support this claim is the estimate that 93 percent of all meaning in a social situation comes from nonverbal information, while only 7 percent comes from verbal information. This estimate has found its way into almost every popular article on nonverbal communication.

Unfortunately, it is erroneous. It is based on extrapolation from two studies, one comparing vocal cues to facial cues (Mehrabian & Ferris, 1967) and one comparing vocal tone to single words (Mehrabian & Wiener, 1967), rather than a study comparing all three. In the vocal-verbal study, only single words were used, which provides a very limited test of the impact of verbal information. In the vocal-facial study, the verbal component was held constant—the word *maybe* was used in all cue combinations—so it never had a chance to make a difference to receivers' interpretations. The two studies also dealt only with attitude inference, not the full range of meanings available in a social encounter. Hence the verbal component was not given a fair test. These and other faults have led many scholars to treat Mehrabian and Ferris's proposed weighting as highly suspect and exaggerated (see, e.g., Hegstrom, 1979).

Nevertheless, other, more temperate estimates have given priority to nonverbal cues (e.g., Danziger, 1976). Birdwhistell (1955), for example, asserted that 60 percent to 65 percent of the meaning in a social context is conveyed nonverbally. A summary of much of the channel reliance literature provided statistical support for Birdwhistell's claim (Philpott, 1983). It showed that approximately 35 percent of social meaning is derived from verbal behaviors, leaving the remaining 65 percent to be accounted for by nonverbal behaviors or their interplay with verbal information. Typical of the kinds of investigations that have confirmed the general superiority of nonverbal over verbal cues is a series of experiments by Argyle and associates (Argyle, Alkema, & Gilmour, 1971; Argyle, Salter, Nicholson, Williams, & Burgess, 1970). In one version, subjects saw videotaped segments of speakers reading friendly, neutral, or hostile passages accompanied by friendly, neutral, or hostile kinesic-vocalic nonverbal presentations. In another version, the segments displayed verbal and nonverbal combinations of superior, neutral, and inferior attitudes. Subjects were asked to determine what meanings were being expressed. Results showed that if the verbal and nonverbal cues were relatively equal in strength when judged separately, the nonverbal cue dominated the verbal one when they were paired together. The nonverbal elements were actually 12.5 times as powerful as the verbal message in one experiment. Even when the verbal message was subsequently strengthened to give it a better chance to influence meaning, it still lost out to the nonverbal channel when the two channels were presented together.

Among the circumstances under which nonverbal cues prevail over verbal ones are (a) judging a communicator's leadership ability and credibility, (b) accurately judging interpersonal styles, (c) completing comprehension and behavioral tasks, (d) answering interpretive questions, and (e) assessing true attitudes, feelings, and ideas from inconsistent expressions (Archer & Akert, 1977; Fujimoto, 1971; Gitter, Black, & Fishman, 1975; Mehrabian & Wiener, 1967; Perlmutter, Paddock, & Duke, 1985; Wahlers, 1976). Box 5-1 presents a vivid illustration of this in patient-provider relationships.

All of this research points to the superiority of nonverbal over verbal behaviors in contributing to meaning. Although this is indeed the general trend, a number of circumstances alter the pattern. Thus this generalization needs to be qualified by the specific conclusions that follow.

(2) *Children rely more on verbal cues than adults do.* In fact, most of the research suggests that children believe words more than they do facial expressions or intonations (Bugental, Kaswan, Love, & Fox, 1970; Reilly & Muzekari, 1979; Solomon & Yeager, 1969a; Wass, 1973; Woolfolk & Woolfolk, 1974). For example, if you tell your 3-year-

BOX 5-1

APPLICATIONS: WATCH WHAT I DO, NOT WHAT I SAY—NONVERBAL CUES IN THE CLINIC

Several studies have found that patients give more weight to a therapist's or doctor's nonverbal behavior than to what is said. In the counseling realm, nonverbal cues are far more important than verbal ones in judging a therapist's empathy, genuineness, and respect for the client (Haase & Tepper, 1972; Seay & Altekruse, 1979; Tepper, 1972; Tepper & Haase, 1978). For example, forward trunk lean, direct eye contact, a concerned voice, and a concerned facial expression are better at conveying empathy than words are. When positive verbal statements are accompanied by contradictory negative kinesic and vocal behaviors rather than positive nonverbals, counselors are rated as less effective and as having less regard for their clients (Reade & Smouse, 1980).

Nonverbal cues may also be more sensitive in distinguishing distressed from nondistressed couples (Rubin, 1977).

Likewise, the nonverbal stream, especially vocal intonation, is more significant than the verbal stream in physician-patient interactions and becomes increasingly important with more visits (Friedman, 1979c; Hall, Roter, & Rand, 1981; Waitzkin, 1984).

The photograph of the hospital patient Ron is illustrative. Although the poster greeting is nice, the nonverbal expressions of caring, affection, and concern from the nurses doubtless meant a lot more to this young cancer patient.

Which conveys more affection and caring for this cancer patient—the nurses' facial expressions, postures, and proximity or the verbal birthday greeting posted over his bed?

old nephew in an affectionate, teasing voice that he is "really strange," he will think you really don't like him. A teacher who tempers criticism with a smile will still be regarded as critical, not helpful. Philpott (1983) estimated that children are five times as likely to believe the words as the nonverbal behaviors. However, one study (James, 1969) found that children were much like adults in relying more heavily on nonverbal than verbal cues; they just didn't discount the verbal content as much as adults did when the verbal and nonverbal channels were in conflict.

Whether children are truly more literal is hard to say. It is also not clear at what age they make the transition to greater reliance on the nonverbal channel. But it would be safest not to use sarcasm with a young child if you want the true intent of your message to be understood.

(3) *Adults rely more on nonverbal cues when verbal and nonverbal channels conflict than when these channels are congruent.* Communicators frequently encounter "mixed" messages in which the combination of nonverbal and verbal cues do not provide a clear, unambiguous message. Sometimes these mixed messages are deliberate. Jokes and sarcasm rely on mixed messages for their effect. Other times, mixed messages are indicative of internal confusion. Uncertainty, indifference, and ambivalence (e.g., simultaneously liking and disliking another person) produce mixed messages. Further, deceptive communicators inadvertently display mixed messages that can clue others in on their duplicity.

Mixed messages are difficult to decode. One must sort out the conflicting cues and make an interpretation based on less certain information than in pure messages. Receivers, though, can and do decode mixed messages (DePaulo & Rosenthal, 1979a; Johnson, McCarty, & Allen, 1976).

That people rely on nonverbal cues in sorting out mixed messages is demonstrated by two sample studies. McMahan (1976) had people respond to four different combinations of dominant and submissive verbal and nonverbal presentations. When respondents rated interpretations of the statements and the speaker's intent, the presence of incongruent nonverbal cues significantly altered their ratings compared to the congruent conditions, indicating that conflicting nonverbal cues influenced their judgments. Zahn (1973) combined verbal and vocal elements on a friendly-to-hostile continuum. He found that nonverbal cues generally affected interpretations more than verbal cues, especially when they were in conflict (e.g., one positive and one negative). However, when the verbal and vocal cues were consistent with each other, the verbal component carried more weight.

Other research also shows that the verbal content equals or exceeds the nonverbal content in importance when the two channels are not completely contradictory. For example, two studies on impressions and hiring of job interviewees (Hollandsworth, Kazelskis, Stevens, & Dressel, 1979; Sigelman & Davis, 1978) showed that verbal and nonverbal cues were nearly equal in their impact on impressions, and verbal content appropriateness was the biggest predictor of hiring likelihood. Because ratings were made on naturally occurring interview behaviors, it can be assumed that the interviewees attempted to coordinate their verbal and nonverbal behavior and did not engage in blatant contradictions. Similarly, people making evaluative judgments based on excerpts from vice presidential debates or on interviewees' replies to positive, negative, and neutral questions based more of their judgments on the verbal information than the nonverbal cues (Krauss, Apple, Morency, Wenzel, & Winton, 1981).

Overall, the research evidence indicates that people are especially inclined to turn to nonverbal cues when they are receiving mixed messages. They rely on the nonverbal cues to resolve the conflict in meaning. When the verbal and nonverbal channels are relatively consistent, the verbal information is more readily accepted.

(4) *Channel reliance depends on the communication function at stake.* Verbal content is more important for factual, cognitive, abstract, and persuasive interpretations, while nonverbal content is more important for judging emotional and attitudinal expressions, relational communication, and impression formation. In McMahan's study involving judgments of communicator dominance (1976), respondents were asked to determine the factual content of the speaker's statements and to form evaluations of the speaker. When they were asked to reconstruct the overt statements, they relied most on the verbal information. When they had to volunteer impressions of the speaker, they relied more on nonverbal cues. Friedman (1978) likewise found that judgments of what grade a teacher might give a student were influenced more by verbal information, while judgments of a teacher's friendliness toward a student were influenced most by facial cues. Similarly, Solomon and Yeager (1969b) found that verbal content prevails when one is assessing "objective meaning" and intonation prevails when one is inferring a speaker's liking for a listener. In a deception context, verbal content is also better when detecting factual lying, while nonverbal cues are more helpful when detecting emotional deception (Hocking, Bauchner, Kaminski, & Miller, 1979; Kraut, 1978; Maier & Thurber, 1968).

In fact, most of the research cited to support the general superiority of nonverbal cues (proposition 1) comes from studies involving relational, affective, or impression-leaving outcomes, while those showing increasing impact for verbal content (proposition 3) come from studies involving interpretations or reconstructions of verbal meanings. In his synthesis of research, Philpott (1983) attempted to divide research along functional lines. He concluded that for symbolic or persuasive communication, verbal information accounts for far more of the meaning than nonverbal information does. For emotive, relational, or attributional (impression formation) outcomes, nonverbal cues account for varying but greater amounts of the meaning than verbal ones. This is consistent with Noller's conclusion (1985) that "the importance of the verbal channel increases with the amount of information contained in the words and is greater for more cognitive (rather than affective) tasks" (p. 44).

(5) *When the content in different channels is congruent, the meanings of the cues tend to be averaged together equally; when content is incongruent, there is greater variability in how information is integrated.* Scholars who are interested in information processing are intrigued by the issue of how people combine information from different channels. Does each channel get counted equally? Do some channels consistently carry more weight than others? Are some cues ignored when they are inconsistent with other cues? Although these questions have yet to be answered definitively, it appears that

when the information in the various channels is not totally at odds, people tend to add up their individual meanings and arrive at an average meaning based on all the contributing channels (Apple, 1979; Philpott, 1983; Zahn, 1973). For example, in judging a speaker's nervousness, audiences will tend to add together the separate bits of information presented by the kinesic and vocal cues of anxiety.

However, when mixed messages are being sent, different people may handle such conflicting information differently (Zahn, 1973). In some cases, people may use a discounting strategy, that is, ignoring one noncongruent cue when two others are consistent with each other (Anderson & Jacobson, 1965). In a study of immediacy cues, Burgoon et al. (1984) found that is what people did when judging the relational meaning of a set of five cues: if two were consistent, a third inconsistent one was usually unable to reverse or neutralize the interpretation drawn from the other two. Other research has shown that people believe whichever cue is the most extreme or most negative (e.g., Bugental, 1974; Bugental, Kaswan, & Love, 1970; Friedman, 1979b; Hegstrom, 1979).

But this is not always the case. The bulk of evidence reviewed so far would suggest that visual cues tend to be counted more strongly than vocal cues, which in turn are counted more heavily than verbal ones. Fujimoto's finding (1971) that vocal cues carried more weight even when the verbal cue was extreme and the vocal cue was neutral tends to support this interpretation. But firm conclusions await further research.

How people combine information channels has a number of interesting implications. If people are most biased toward visual information, this may help explain the immense popularity of television. It may also suggest some instructional strategies for improving classroom learning (e.g., more films, videotapes, and slides). If, however, people place great faith in the voice, it may explain why so often people have their most intimate conversations over the telephone rather than in person. The relative weight each channel carries may also account for why people are easily deceived in some situations and not in others. Finally, it may help us decide as communicators the best vehicle for sending important messages to others—letters, telephone, electronic mail, or face-to-face conversation.

However, before you decide that there is one best way to send information, you should be aware of the next conclusion, which places further limitations on our generalizations about channel reliance.

(6) *Individuals have biases in their channel dependence.* Some people consistently rely on certain nonverbal channels, some usually rely on verbal content, and some are situationally adaptable. One study showed that people are consistent in relying on either facial cues or language when judging incongruent emotional expressions (Shapiro, 1968). Another showed that people making judgments of a speaker's level of stress can be divided into three groups: those who are verbal-reliant, those who are nonverbal-reliant, and those who shift back and forth in their channel preference, depending on the context or type of judgment being made (Vande Creek & Watkins, 1972).

No doubt people's channel preferences are related to which channel they have the greatest ability to encode and decode accurately. Since people differ in their skill at sending and interpreting linguistic, facial, or auditory information and in decoding pure or mixed messages (Berman, Shulman, & Marwit, 1976; Krauss et al., 1981; Levy, 1964; Rosenthal, Hall, DiMatteo, Rogers, & Archer, 1979; Thompson & Meltzer, 1964), it makes sense that they might come to rely on those channels that they are best able to use and "read." This is just speculation at this point. However, research has at least established that the ability to decode visual mixed messages differs from the ability to decode vocal ones and varies according to such factors as the degree of cue discrepancy and the decoder's sex and age.

The Primacy of Visual Cues

Throughout this research, an important conclusion that has emerged is that visual cues carry the day for both adults and children. In attempts to resolve the inconsistency in mixed messages, receivers rely heavily on information communicated by visual cues (i.e., kinesic cues) (DePaulo & Rosenthal, 1979a; DePaulo, Rosenthal, Eisenstat, Rogers, & Finkelstein, 1978; Hegstrom, 1979; Philpott, 1983; Tepper & Haase, 1978). For example, the classic study by Mehrabian and Ferris (1967) found that people rely most on visual cues, less on vocal cues, and least on verbal cues when decoding inconsistent messages. Bugental, Kaswan, and Love (1970) also found a visual primacy among both adult and child subjects. Research on nonsocial visual (e.g., lights) and auditory (e.g., tones) cues, in which subjects indicate whether a light flashes or a tone sounds on their right or left, similarly found that perceivers displayed a strong visual bias (Posner, Nissen, & Klein, 1976).

At least four explanations have been offered for this visual bias (Keeley-Dyreson, Bailey, & Burgoon, 1988). First, when it comes to decoding emotional information, visual cues provide more information and possess more meaning than vocal cues (Berman, Shulman, & Morwit, 1976; Buck, 1980). Visual cues are more semantically distinctive and more efficient transmitters, providing more units of meaning per time unit (DePaulo & Rosenthal, 1979a). Second, Posner et al. (1976) argued that humans attend deliberately to the visual channel because, unlike auditory cues, it is not automatically alerting. This deliberate attention reduces the input from auditory cues, giving visual cues more impact. Third, encoders have greater control over the face, thereby giving decoders more intentional information. Fourth, Berman et al. (1976) speculated that people rely more on visual cues because they can quickly scan the face and then concentrate on the most informative facial cues, whereas with the voice, decoders can only process the cues sequentially and fleetingly. Thus the amount of emotional information in the visual channel, its lower alerting capacity, its greater intentionality potential, and the longer duration of facial cues cause people to rely more on visual cues when decoding mixed messages (DePaulo & Rosenthal, 1979a).

Visual cue primacy is greater when mixed messages involve the face rather than the body (DePaulo & Rosenthal, 1979a; DePaulo et al., 1978). The face has long been recognized as a rich source of emotional content (Ekman & Friesen, 1967), so it is not surprising that receivers place more weight on facial cues when resolving inconsistencies.

Visual cue primacy also is stronger when decoding emotions related to positivity (agreeableness, conscientiousness, positive or negative attitude), especially when visual cues include the face. Conversely, body and vocalic cues become more important when decoding dominance, assertiveness, and anxiety (Burns & Beier, 1973; DePaulo & Rosenthal, 1979a; DePaulo et al., 1978; Scherer, Scherer, Hall, & Rosenthal, 1977; Zuckerman, Amidon, Bishop, & Pomerantz, 1982). The face is particularly important in judging positivity because receivers associate the smile with positivity, a link that has no analogue in the body and voice. Dominance, by contrast, is communicated very well by intense, emphatic body movements and vocal loudness, leading to greater reliance on these two channels when judging mixed messages of dominance, assertiveness, and anxiety (DePaulo & Rosenthal, 1979a; DePaulo et al., 1978).

In the nonsocial research on visual primacy, as the discrepancy between visual and auditory cues increased, the ability to distinguish between the differences in the two channels increased and auditory cues had more impact (Posner et al., 1976). This effect seems to apply to mixed nonverbal messages as well. DePaulo (DePaulo & Rosenthal, 1979a; DePaulo et al., 1978) reported that as the discrepancy between visual and vocalic cues increases, visual cue primacy decreases and receivers increase their reliance on vocalic cues.

Women are more likely to display visual cue primacy, especially when the visual cues involve the face and judgments of positivity (DePaulo & Rosenthal, 1979a; DePaulo et al., 1978). This may be due to greater visual interaction by females. Women engage in more eye contact than men in interpersonal interactions and are uncomfortable when they cannot see their conversational partner. Further, women have been observed to increase their visual interaction in positively valenced interactions (Argyle, Lalljee, & Cook, 1968; Exline, Gray, & Schuette, 1965; Exline & Winters, 1965). The attention to visual cues may also be the result of a learned tendency for women to be "polite" communicators by paying less attention to vocalic channels likely to "leak" information the source did not intend to send (Rosenthal & DePaulo, 1979b).

Finally, children encountering mixed messages use decoding processes somewhat different from those of adults. DePaulo and Rosenthal (1979a) found that younger children can detect mixed messages communicating positivity but have difficulty decoding those communicating dominance. Further, when decoding positivity, children seem to discount positive visual cues when they are paired with negative vocalic cues, especially when the positive cue is a smile by a woman. Younger children appear to assume the worst, placing more weight on the negative meaning in these mixed messages, whereas adults counterbalance negative vocalic cues with positive visual cues. In sum, the ability to decode mixed messages increases with age, and the ability to decode mixed messages containing positive emotions develops earlier than the ability to read mixed messages containing dominance cues (Bugental, Kaswan, & Love, 1970; Bugental, Love, Kaswan, & April, 1971).

Explanations of and Speculations about Channel Reliance

As important as who relies most on nonverbal versus verbal channels and when, is why the nonverbal stream so often dominates people's determinations of meaning. A number of intriguing conjectures have been advanced.

Argyle et al. (1971) offered three possibilities. One is that we are innately programmed to signal affective states through nonverbal displays and are likewise programmed to recognize such signals. As support for this position, they noted that many nonverbal behaviors are universal and unlearned. To the extent that all humans come equipped to send and recognize nonverbal cues, this would give nonverbal behaviors an edge over verbal expressions, which must be learned.

A second possibility is that because of an efficient division of labor, verbal communication handles more abstract, nonsocial tasks such as problem solving while nonverbal communication handles more social, interpersonal matters. Because verbal and nonverbal communication patterns occur simultaneously, the nonverbal channels can silently handle monitoring, feedback, and relational definition functions that are crucial to interpreting what is happening in the verbal stream. The nonverbal cues thus become the frame of reference against which verbal interpretations are checked. Scherer (1982b) made the same point when he noted:

> Through speech, humans can at the same time communicate symbolic meaning via language, with all the advantages that the design features of language command, and reveal information about their biological and social identity, transitory states, and relationship to the listener via a nonverbal vocal signalling system. (p. 138)

This distinction between the content and relational facets of communication recurs in Chapter 11.

A third, related possibility is that, because of their ambiguity, subtlety, and deniability, the nonverbal channels may be especially well suited to expressing sensitive and risky interpersonal information. As we note in Chapter 1, nonverbal codes can express what the verbal code cannot or should not. If you offer verbal criticism of a friend's behavior and it is rebuffed, you may find yourself very embarrassed, with little ability to retract your statement. But if you express the same concern through looks, touches, and vocal tones rather than words, this gentle approach may be more effective. If not, you can always disclaim any unkind intentions.

Some other possible reasons for the power of nonverbal cues are cited in Chapter 1. The primacy of nonverbal communication as a means of expression for the species and for infants may predispose us to rely more on nonverbal behaviors as dependable and familiar sources of information. The temporary shift in early childhood to greater reliance on words may be due to the novelty and challenge of learning the verbal communication system. We may return to relying on nonverbal cues because we believe they are more spontaneous, uncontrolled expressions of "true" feelings.

One other possible explanation concerns the structure of verbal and nonverbal coding systems and how the brain is able to handle such information. It may be that the more continuous, nonsegmented nature of many nonverbal signals makes them especially well designed for right-hemispheric processing, where more holistic, impressionistic, and affective judgments are made. That is, the structural properties of the code system may determine how and where such information is processed and, consequently, what types of interpretations are made. We consider this possibility in more detail later.

ORIGINS OF NONVERBAL AND VERBAL CODES: NATURE VERSUS NURTURE

Is there a signalling code—a language without words—common to all men?

I. Eibl-Eibesfeldt, 1972, p. 297

A major controversy regarding human communication—as with human behavior in general—is nature versus nurture. Are behavioral patterns biologically and genetically determined, or are they shaped by environmental and cultural influences?

Are Nonverbal Codes Innate?

As noted in previous chapters, to the extent that nonverbal signals are innate or part of a pattern of experience common to all humans, they will form a universal communication system. This would make nonverbal codes unlike verbal languages, which are largely learned, culture-bound systems.

The evidence on the innateness or universality of nonverbal behaviors is highly mixed, with staunch proponents at both ends of the nature-nurture spectrum. Those who take the inborn position rely on three types of evidence: (a) comparative studies between humans and other mammals, particularly primates, which imply a genetic heritage; (b) cross-cultural similarities, which may produce evidence of inborn or at least universal behavior patterns; and (c) studies of child development, particularly of handicapped children, which reveal patterns common to all developing humans.

Ethologists have observed a number of similarities between human behavior and that of lower primates. For example, the broad smile and wide-mouth laugh in humans resemble closely the silent bared-teeth and relaxed open-mouth displays in primates (see Figure 5-1; van Hooff, 1972). Analogues between humans and other mammals include alarm vocalizations, alert responses such as eye widening, and play behaviors such as mock aggressive touch (e.g., see Andrew, 1972; Smith, 1974; Thorpe, 1972).

Underlying these comparisons is a belief that commonalities across species demonstrate the evolutionary character of behavior. Consistent with Darwin's theory of natural selection, it is assumed that behaviors retained in the human repertoire over the millennia have *survival value;* that is, they have served the species well in surviving dangers and adapting to environmental changes. According to the theory, behaviors that are useful become part of the permanent signal system of the species, while those that are nonfunctional eventually disappear, leaving a largely universal communication system.

As noted in Chapter 2, observations by Darwin (1965) in 1872, which predated "sci-

FIGURE 5-1
Note the similarity between the wide-mouth laugh of the boy and the relaxed, open-mouth display of the chimpanzee.

entific" study of human behavior by many decades, documented some hereditary and apparently universal communication patterns. Especially interesting were his cross-generational comparisons. He found children using the same finger-rubbing gesture, for instance, as a grandparent whom they had never met. He noticed that British adults don't display the shoulder shrug, but British children do. This led him to conclude that many behaviors are mistakenly assumed to be culture-specific because adults have learned *not* to exhibit them when in reality they originate as universal behaviors. Darwin's speculations about the commonality of many emotional expressions across cultures have since been confirmed by contemporary research (for summaries, see Chapter 10; Ekman, 1973; Knapp & Hall, 1992).

Anthropologists have produced further examples. One is the eyebrow flash—a quick, almost imperceptible raising of the eyebrows, common in friendly greetings in a number of widely different cultures.

Another form of evidence for the innate position comes from developmental studies revealing that all infants display the same reflexes and emotional expressions, regardless of culture, and uniformly engage in both vocal and manual babbling as a precursor to acquiring language (Petitto & Marentette, 1991). It might be argued that children learn these expressions from their caretakers. But this possibility is disputed by observations of blind, deaf, and limbless children, who display the same smiling and grief expressions as sighted and hearing children (e.g., see Eibl-Eibesfeldt, 1973). Deaf and blind children could not have learned these behaviors through auditory or visual imitation, and institutionalized limbless babies (born to mothers who took thalidomide during pregnancy) were especially limited in their ability to learn nonverbal signals from adult models because they lacked opportunities for tactile exploration or frequent reinforcement from contact with caretakers. That they presented many of the same vocal and kinesic expressions as normal babies is taken as evidence that there are some basic behavior patterns endemic to all members of the human species.

All this research suggests an innate basis for a variety of nonverbal cues, and recent work shows that links between nonverbal and verbal cues are also in part innate. Several studies in developmental psychology have shown systematic links between language development and hand gesture use and generally indicate that young children's ability to use gestures parallels their capacity for spoken language (cf. Hoots et al., 1989). In a study of very young children, ages 9 to 14 months, the emergence and use of gestures were linked to the stages of cognitive development and language acquisition, and similar patterns of use were found in both Parisian-French and English-Canadian infants (Blake & Dolgoy, 1993).

A study of slightly older children, ages 14 to 28 months, who were one-word speakers (Morford & Goldin-Meadow, 1992), found that all children produced gestures in combination with speech, and that gestures that occurred with speech were understood both when the gestures were redundant and when the gestures substituted for language. The authors concluded that, even at a young age, gestures and speech form an integrated communicative unit.

Finally, Thal and Tobias (1992) studied gestural use in a group of children with delayed onset of expressive language (termed late talkers) and compared their gestural use to a group of children exhibiting normal language use. Results showed that late talkers used significantly more communicative gestures and a greater variety of gestures than did nor-

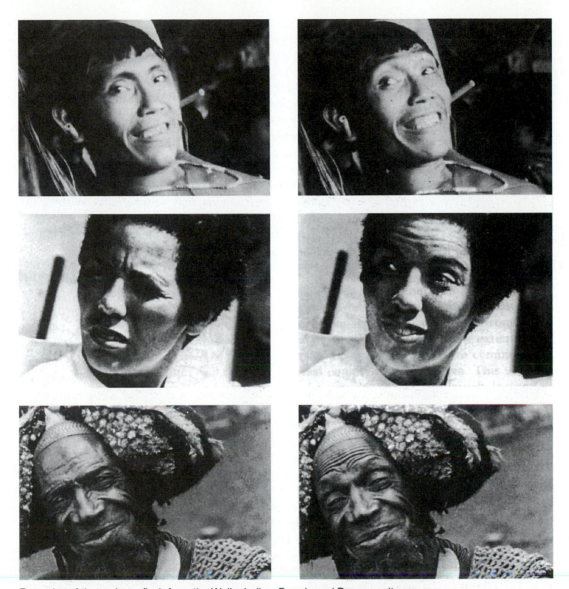

Examples of the eyebrow flash from the Waika Indian, French, and Papuan cultures.

mal language children. A one-year follow-up of these children found that there were actually two subgroups of late talkers: talkers who remained delayed (truly delayed late talkers)
and talkers who had developed normal language use (late bloomers). A reanalysis of the
initial data showed that late bloomers used a greater variety of gestures to compensate for
a limited oral expressive vocabulary, while truly delayed late talkers did not.

These studies show that cognitive development, language acquisition, and gestural
use and variety progress systematically, may develop similarly across cultures, and
reflect the integrated development of the overall communication message system. As

such, the evidence supports the view that the overall development of both verbal and nonverbal channels is, in part, innately based.

At the opposite end of the nature-nurture continuum are theorists who take an acculturation-socialization point of view. They believe that all behavior is learned and culture-specific (e.g., Birdwhistell, 1970; LaBarre, 1947). They also contend that surface similarities in the structure of behavior across cultures or species mask real differences in function and meaning. Further, they maintain that the rules for usage and interpretations of behaviors are culture- and context-specific and therefore must be learned.

For example, even though various cultures display the eyebrow flash, its usage and meanings vary considerably. In North American cultures, it is a very common gesture that may express everything from pleasure at greeting to attentiveness to approval. By contrast, in some eastern cultures it is an inappropriately demonstrative behavior that may be regarded as rude. (A professor learned this, much to her embarrassment, after nearly a week of "flashing" a group of Chinese students whom she was teaching, ironically, about nonverbal communication.)

Other examples of cultural differences abound. Belching after dinner is polite in some countries, rude in others such as ours. Americans and Europeans point with the forefinger; many Africans and Asians point with their lips or head. As noted previously, emblem gestures may look the same but have entirely different meanings across cultures, or different-appearing behaviors may have the same meaning. And patterns of behavior may appear in one culture that are totally absent in another. This tremendous variety in form and function of nonverbal signals across cultures is taken as evidence that there is no universality to nonverbal communication and therefore no innateness.

A third position is a blend of these two extremes. It holds that a common core of expressions shared by all humans is grounded in our genetic and neurological heritage but that these expressions are also embedded in a matrix of learned cultural rules and environmental influences (see, e.g., Buck, 1984; Eibl-Eibesfeldt, 1972; Ekman, Friesen, & Ellsworth, 1972). Such things as facial expressions, glances, spacing behavior, touch, and the link between language and gesture may have biological roots, but their use and interpretation have been modified and adapted by each culture to meet its own needs and values. Further, several behaviors, such as emblems and vocal inflections, are strictly learned and unique to a given culture. Even Darwin acknowledged that many behaviors require instruction and practice before they are performed in a useful or socially acceptable manner. The end result is great diversity in the kinds of nonverbal displays and meanings that appear but a universal ability to understand some basic displays such as the smile or territorial defense postures.

We subscribe to this third position. It seems likely that some behaviors do have an evolutionary base but may have to conform to cultural or contextual rules, while others originate within a particular culture and are idiosyncratic to it. Given this middle-of-the-road nature-nurture position, how do nonverbal codes compare to verbal ones?

Is Language Innate?

Intuitively, it seems as if verbal languages are totally acquired. After all, one cannot travel to Moscow or Nairobi and automatically speak the local dialect. Children do not inherit language; they must be taught vocabulary and the rules of grammar. And words themselves are largely arbitrary human creations that may or may not survive even to the next generation.

This is not to say, however, that nature plays no role in language. It has been argued that humans may be inherently predisposed to develop language. Eisenberg and Smith (1971) wrote:

> We know that the capacity for language is innate, for all human beings display a predis-position to use a language composed of discrete sounds linked together by syntactical rules. Regardless of the culture in which he is raised, a child learns to use language in the same chronological sequence as all other children. For instance, he will utter sentences at the same age in all cultures. (p. 42)

Beyond this developmental evidence of the inherency of language, prominent lin-guists believe that language may be patterned after the way the brain organizes infor-mation, lending a further innate dimension to language. Add to this some nonarbitrary elements of the lexicon such as onomatopoeia (words that sound like the thing they rep-resent) and the consistent use across different languages of sounds that evoke the colors associated with the words in which they appear (Marks, 1975), and it becomes apparent that language is also not strictly a learned system.

Clearly, one cannot put nonverbal communication at the nature end of the continuum and verbal communication at the nurture end. The situation is far more complex than that. Moreover, many vocal and kinesic behaviors are part and parcel of speech, so that wherever they are placed on the continuum, they must be placed together with language. Probably the most accurate conclusion to be drawn is that both verbal and nonverbal communication share some biologically governed properties, including an inherent incli-nation of humans to develop a *communication* system, and both share many learned fea-tures. But of the two, nonverbal has a more innate base than verbal communication. This foreshadows some differences in the structure of each system.

COMPARING NONVERBAL AND VERBAL CODES: STRUCTURAL FEATURES

Analogic and Digital Coding

Nonverbal codes commonly have been characterized as *analogic,* to distinguish them from verbal communication, which is said to be *digital.* The distinguishing features of an analogic code are that it is comprised of an infinite, continuous range of naturally occur-ring values. The color spectrum and the natural number system are good examples of analogic systems. By contrast, a digital code consists of a finite set of discrete and arbi-trarily defined units. An A-to-E grading system is a good example: it has only five finite categories, each is mutually exclusive and distinguishable from the next (i.e., discrete), and the number of grade levels is an arbitrary, human decision. There could as easily be 10 grade levels or 100.

Although there is no quarrel with labeling language a digital system, to call all non-verbal codes analogic is overly simplistic and inaccurate. True, many nonverbal signals have intrinsic, or naturally arising, meaning (e.g., crying to signal pain or unhappiness) and may take on an infinite range of values. But many others must be regarded as digital, either because they are arbitrarily concocted (e.g., the A-OK sign) or because they are discrete (e.g., the greeting kiss). Dittmann (1978) presented a compelling case that many other apparently continuous behaviors become essentially discrete units for communication purposes. Examples of behaviors that we regard as single or stand-alone units include the smile, the nod, eye contact (present or absent), postural shifts, hairstyles, vocal characterizers such as a shriek, emblems, and various gestures such as the ear tug. Moreover, most of the classification schemes for nonverbal codes (e.g., kinemes or tacemes) reduce behaviors to discrete categories on the assumption that they represent what is meaningful.

Hence the nonverbal codes (and it should be emphasized that we are talking in the plural) include a mix of analogic and digital elements. It may be that the more we treat a given nonverbal behavior or pattern as communicative, the more we treat it as digital. That is, we may mentally transform a continuous, naturally arising behavior into a more manageable, digital form to make sense of it.

Design Properties of Verbal Language

The most complete analysis of formal design features of verbal human language can be found in Hockett (1960). Other structural and organizing features of language in use are discussed in Ellis (1982). Applications to nonverbal and animal communication can be found in Burgoon (1985b), Lyons (1972), and Thorpe (1972), among others.

Here is a baker's dozen of the most obvious and most important properties:

1 *Discreteness.* As already noted, language is composed of recognizable, separable units. In spoken language, there is actually a dual system of sound units (phonemes, phones, allophones, etc.) and symbol units (letters) that are combined to form semantically meaningful components called morphemes (words, prefixes, etc.). Units are combined in increasingly complex hierarchies, but at each level, the separate units are distinguishable.

2 *Syntax rules.* Language has rules for combining and sequencing elements, for example, rules for what letters or sounds can follow each other, rules for noun-verb order in sentences, and rules for the positioning of prepositions.

3 *Semantic rules.* Language follows rules for associating words with their referents and assigning literal meanings to utterances. Dictionaries tell us what a given word denotes at a particular point in time. Other rules exist for extracting meaning from the ordering of elements in sentences (e.g., a noun-verb-noun sequence is to be interpreted as agent-action-object).

4 *Polysemy.* Words may have multiple denotations. The word *run,* for instance, may denote rapid locomotion, a score in a baseball game, a batch of goods in a factory, or a snag in hosiery.

5 *Arbitrariness.* A major feature of symbolic communication is that meanings are assigned by convention. There is no necessary connection between a referent and the symbol selected to stand for it.

6 *Culture- and context-bound meaning.* A corollary of the arbitrariness principle is that words in one language do not carry over to another language. Meanings are

therefore tied to a specific language community, and even cultures that use the same language may assign different meanings to the shared lexicon. A corollary of the polysemy principle is that contextual information is often necessary to determine which meaning to select. The net result of these two properties is that no verbal language qualifies as universal.

7 *Displacement.* Language can refer to things removed in space and time, to the "not here" and the "not now." For example, changes in tense allow us to talk about the past or the future, rather than just the present. The use of the negative allows us to talk about things that are absent or nonexistent.

8 *Reflexivity.* Language has the special property that it can be used to talk about itself. In other words, it can reflect on itself—theoretically, an infinite number of times. The sentence "My last statement was nonsensical" is an example of self-reflexivity.

9 *Prevarication.* Language need not be truthful. It can be used to lie and intentionally mislead.

10 *Transformation.* A given meaning can be transformed into a number of alternative expressions. This refers to the linguistic distinction between deep structure and surface structure. The same underlying meaning can give rise to several actual sentence forms. For example, "The man gave the girl a balloon" is equivalent in meaning to "The girl was given a balloon by the man." The surface differences are superficial.

11 *Productivity.* The language system is open in that words and sentences can be put together in novel ways to create an infinite variety of new messages that are readily understood. Although the initial pool of elements is relatively small, the number of new utterances that can be created is limitless. Language is therefore "productive."

12 *Coherence mechanisms.* Language includes devices such as prepositions and question-answer sequences that allow speakers and listeners to draw connections between a series of utterances in a larger discourse.

13 *Pragmatic rules.* Just as there are rules for how to construct language and assign meaning to it, so there are rules for its use in actual practice. These are socially dictated prescriptions for when and how to use various language forms.

Linguistic Properties of Nonverbal Codes

We now come to the heart of the issue of how intertwined and similar verbal and nonverbal codes are and, indeed, whether nonverbal cues even qualify as part of a coding system. The extent to which nonverbal cues share "linguistic properties" and take on digital form, they strongly resemble verbal languages. But, are they truly an independent symbolic system or merely an inadvertent by-product of producing speech? A lively controversy surrounds this issue.

On one side of the issue is the position that nonverbal cues such as gestures, facial expressions, and vocalizations accompanying speech serve primarily an intrapersonal rather than interpersonal function such as assisting a speaker in retrieving a word from memory or signalling when a person is having difficulty putting thoughts into words (see, e.g., Chawla & Krauss, 1994; Feyereisen, 1987; Krauss, Morrel-Samuels, & Colasante, 1991; Rimé & Schiaratura, 1991). In this view, these nonverbal acts are not truly communication, that is, they are not intended to convey meaning to another but rather are "spill-over" from the speech production process.

On the other side of the issue is the position that such nonverbal cues are used deliberately to communicate and are part and parcel of the total message. Scherer (1980), for example, classified codes into four categories, all of which apply to nonverbal cues: (a) the *semantic code,* which includes all symbolic forms that convey relationships between signs and their referents, (b) the *syntactic code,* which applies to relationships between signs, specifically, their order and patterning, (c) the *pragmatic code,* which covers relationships between signs and their users and is concerned with expressing social identity, and (d) the *dialogic code,* which includes relationships between signs and interacting sign users as a system. As discussed shortly, nonverbal cues such as emblems have symbolic features and so are linked to the semantic code. A variety of other cues, from vocal properties to rhythmic hand gestures and body movements, also serve to structure, pattern, and punctuate the stream of communicative behavior and thus are linked to syntactic features. Yet other cues function to express identity, from dress and apparel to proxemic behavior to specialized gestures, and as such fit into the pragmatic code. These are covered in detail in Chapter 8. Other cues serve expressly as relational messages (see Chapter 11) or regulate the flow of conversation (see Chapter 12) and so fit the dialogic code. These cues also can be divided according to whether they are part of rehearsed, highly ordered discourse or more spontaneous, improvisational communication (see Ellis, 1992).

McNeill (1985, 1987; McNeill, Cassell, & McCullough, 1994) has carried the argument further, claiming that gestures during speech, particularly iconic, metaphoric, pointing, and beat gestures as opposed to emblems or more lexicalized hand movements, should be considered verbal, not nonverbal. His contention that gestures and speech are part of a single system for expressing human thought is based on the following forms of evidence:

1 Gestures occur only during speech.
2 Gestures and speech have parallel semantic and pragmatic functions.
3 Gestures synchronize with parallel linguistic units.
4 Gestures and speech dissolve in parallel ways in aphasia (a brain injury).
5 Gestures and speech develop in tandem in children.
6 Gestures, although analogically encoded, are used for abstract expression.
7 Gestural information that doesn't match accompanying speech becomes incorporated into new versions of retold stories.

Other scholars (e.g., Bavelas, 1994; Kendon, 1994; Streeck, 1994) point to the highly collaborative nature of gestures when used in face-to-face conversation as evidence of their communicative role. For example, speakers may look at their own gestures while using words that "point" to the gesture so that listeners attend to them. The analysis that follows addresses more specifically the extent to which nonverbal cues constitute language by considering how each of the linguistic properties we have identified applies to nonverbal cues.

Discreteness and Arbitrariness   We have already said that many nonverbal cues are discrete or are treated as such in communication. All of the nonverbal codes have some discrete elements: gestures in kinesics, vocalized pauses in vocalics, symbolic colors for clothing in physical appearance, formal seating arrangements in proxemics, categories of touch such as a slap in haptics, appointment time in chronemics, and status symbols in artifacts. Some of these, such as emblems or status symbols, are created by convention and are therefore arbitrary. Others, such as the laugh or the slap, are natural behaviors rather than linguistic inventions. Thus nonverbal codes meet these criteria partly but not completely.

Syntactic and Semantic Rules   It has been popular to claim that nonverbal communication is not rule-governed. Yet closer inspection shows that we follow rules both in the construction of nonverbal expressions and in their interpretation. At the syntactic level, there are rules of combination and rules of ordering. For example, a smile and a scowl do not appear together because they would create a bizarre expression. Certain parakinesic and paralinguistic behaviors are consistently used to punctuate spoken language. Illustrator gestures accompany speaking, not listening. Greeting rituals follow the order of eye contact before handshake, not vice versa. At the semantic level, individual cues and sets of cues have consistently recognized meanings. Laughter may express happiness, anxiety, or contempt; it never means "I want a turn at talk." Close proximity may have several meanings, but when combined with smiles, caresses, and constant gaze, it becomes restricted to meanings of intimacy or physical attraction. Meanings are also derivable from larger cue patterns and sequences, as in the departure ritual (see Exline and Fehr, 1978, and Kendon, 1983, for additional examples). Thus nonverbal codes used in a communicative sense are indeed rule-governed. The best evidence of this is our ability to recognize "ungrammatical" expressions—unorthodox combinations of signals and uninterpretable sequences.

Polysemy and Culture- and Context-Bound Meaning   The fact that a nonverbal cue such as gaze has no single meaning is often cited as evidence against nonverbal behavior forming a language. Yet this is no different from the property of polysemy in verbal language. It merely means that one must rely on context and culture to decide which interpretation to select. Many nonverbal behaviors depend on simultaneously occurring verbal and nonverbal information for their interpretation. Similarly, one may need to know the culture before choosing an interpretation. Downcast eyes may mean sadness in the United States, for example, but respect for elders in an African village. Much nonverbal communication, then, is like verbal language in being context- and culture-bound.

Displacement   Some parakinesic and paralinguistic behaviors act as verb tense and place markers (e.g., Birdwhistell, 1970). Otherwise, nonverbal codes tend to be tied to the here and now. Although one might display anxiety cues in anticipation of an uncomfortable situation or long after an unpleasant occasion has passed, the time referent of the anxiety, in the absence of further information, would be unclear to an observer. Pantomime narratives occasionally attempt flashes backward or forward in time, but they are usually accompanied by some verbal explanation. By contrast, verbal languages explicitly index tense through morphemic, phonological, or paralinguistic changes.

Reflexivity   It is difficult to envision an example of nonverbal behavior that can reflect on itself indefinitely. A smile might comment on a preceding smile or a laugh on a previous laugh, but it is hard to imagine this going beyond one iteration. Nonverbal codes are therefore probably best regarded as not self-reflexive.

Prevarication   Can one dissemble nonverbally? Can one misrepresent or misdirect nonverbally? The obvious answer is yes. People are continually masking true emotions and constructing self-presentations that are more favorable than reality. And it is easy to deceive others through the omission of some nonverbal information or the addition of false information. The defendant in a child molestation case, for instance, shaved his beard, cut his hair, dressed in conservative clothing, and wore a cross so as to seem a moral and upstanding person on the witness stand.

Transformation   Nonverbal codes display transformation just as verbal codes do. There are alternate ways to signal that you want to relinquish a turn, numerous ways to initiate a courtship ritual, and different cue combinations that express surprise.

Productivity   The feature of transformation in itself ensures that a code has productivity. This means that nonverbal codes are capable of endless varieties of utterances and that they are open and evolving systems.

Coherence Mechanisms   Birdwhistell (1970) identified a number of kinesic behaviors analogous to paralinguistic cues that serve many of the same coherence functions as markers in verbal language. They cross-reference what is going on verbally, work at a syntactic level to connect larger sequences of utterances, may distinguish different personal pronouns, and may identify tense. All these features help a listener make sense of discourse. Similarly, familiar nonverbal sequences allow a person to interpret a proffered hand in a greeting context not as a request for money but as a desire to shake hands. The extent of coherence mechanisms in nonverbal communication is only beginning to be understood.

Pragmatic Rules   The concept of display rules provides evidence that there are rules for the management of nonverbal behaviors in public. Each culture can easily articulate what behaviors are considered appropriate or inappropriate for use in various contexts.

Based on the features compared so far, it is clear that nonverbal codes include many of the same properties as verbal languages. However, some additional code properties are unique to nonverbal systems.

Unique Properties of Nonverbal Codes

Analogic Coding   We have said that nonverbal codes include some digital and some analogic elements. Some behaviors are truly analogic in that they form a natural continuum. These include conversational distance (although we may reduce it to a few simple categories), sociopetal-sociofugal furniture arrangement, length of eye gaze, touch intensity and frequency, colors used in clothing and artifacts, and most vocal features. Because of the infinite range and intensity of values that are possible, analogic codes permit subtle shadings of meaning.

Iconicity   Behaviors are iconic to the degree that they resemble directly what they refer to and preserve a one-to-one correspondence in size. A hologram or life-size statue of a person would be the most iconic form of representation; a photograph is less iconic, although it preserves the proportionality of the physical features that are visible; a stick figure would be less iconic; and a verbal description would have no iconicity.

Many emblems are iconic because they attempt to mimic what they represent. For example, the death emblem of the finger drawn across the throat imitates slashing the throat with a knife. Facial emotion expressions, some illustrators, and some artifacts are iconic. Iconicity gives nonverbal behaviors a vividness that is missing from verbal versions of the same referent.

Universality   Only the nonverbal codes can claim some universally used and understood behaviors, such as smiling or crying.

Simultaneity   The nonverbal codes have the potential for simultaneous multiple message transmission. Within each nonverbal code, several features can be manipulated at the same time. In kinesics, for instance, gaze and facial expression together may send one message while posture sends another and gestures send a third. With touch, one can tickle another in a playful manner with one hand while holding the victim in a not so playful, viselike grip with the other. If one considers all the nonverbal codes as an interdependent system, the opportunity for cross-modality multiple messages increases dramatically. Because of this capacity for simultaneous message encoding, nonverbal codes may be used in combination, all sending the same message—thereby greatly increasing message redundancy and the likelihood of accurate reception—or they may modify and complement each other to produce a complex and possibly incongruent message. A variety of thoughts and feelings can be conveyed much faster this way than through the sequential transmission required with verbal expression.

Sensory Directness   Because nonverbal behaviors can impinge directly on the senses, they may produce more rapid, automatic, and emotional responding in receivers. By contrast, verbal descriptions require an intermediate cognitive translation step before the individual can respond. The maxim "A picture is worth a thousand words" takes some of its truth from this principle that direct stimulation of the visual senses has far more impact than the most elaborate verbal description of the same phenomenon. (See Box 5-2.)

Spontaneity   Just as the reaction to nonverbal cues may be more rapid because of the direct link to the senses, much nonverbal encoding may be rapid and relatively uncontrolled, especially behaviors that are intrinsic biological signals and those that are overlearned, habitual expressions. A by-product of the ease of such encoding is that receivers come to believe nonverbal communication is more spontaneous and therefore more "truthful." As noted in Chapter 1, this may partly account for the power of nonverbal

BOX 5-2

APPLICATIONS: A PICTURE IS WORTH A THOUSAND WORDS

A vivid example of the directness of sensory stimulation comes from the period of the war in Vietnam. While many people watched TV during the dinner hour one night, much to their horror, they witnessed a South Vietnamese officer parade a prisoner before the camera, put a pistol to his head without warning, and summarily execute him. Viewers not only saw the man's body crumple to the ground, his blood spattering on the street, but they also heard the gun firing and the shocked vocal responses of the onlookers. Seeing this event produced powerful visceral responses in the viewers that could not be captured by the next day's newspaper account of it. You can partially re-create the experience by viewing the accompanying photos here. Compare the pho-

tograph of the moment prior to the shooting to the written account. Similarly, look at the other photograph. Which is more compelling, this stark photograph of the innocent victims of war or newspaper accounts of starving families in Africa?

There are other examples of the impact of direct sensory stimulation from television. The few minutes of videotape of the beating of Rodney King set off strong reactions that are ongoing in the United States. Imagine if we had all learned of Rodney King's beating by written newspaper accounts. Would there have been the riots, social protest, community anger, and extended legal battles if we had all only read about the incident instead of seeing it?

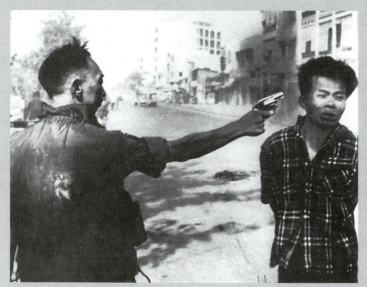

Saigon police chief Nguyen Ngoc Loan summarily executes a Viet Cong suspect at the height of the Tet offensive, 1968.

A starving child in Rwanda tries to help his stricken mother.

behavior in communication. Although in reality many nonverbal behaviors are controlled and manipulated deliberately, the faith placed in their verisimilitude gives nonverbal codes yet one more unique property.

It should be clear from these unique features that verbal communication and nonverbal communication do not have identical linguistic and message properties. But they do share enough similarities to regard nonverbal acts as integral to the functioning of language. Early on, Leach (1972) concluded that nonspeech behavior (nonverbal communication) does form a sort of language and noted some of the same comparisons we have been making:

> It does not consist of isolated sets of trigger signals . . . but of gestures and symbols which are related to one another as a total system after the fashion of a language. Such nonspeech "languages" are both simpler and more complex than "normal" spoken or written language. They are simpler because the syntactic rules are fewer in number and more explicit—the difference between right and wrong nonverbal behaviour is more clear-cut than the difference between right and wrong speech forms—but they are more complex because non-speech is a multi-channel phenomenon. . . . The receiver of a message is likely to be subjected to communicative signals through several different sense channels simultaneously. Sound, sight, smell, taste, touch and rhythm may all be "relevant," not only singly but in combination. (p. 318)

The verbal and nonverbal codes are also so inseparable in producing a total communication system that the more relevant question for future analysis may be what *code* properties are significant in achieving human goals and social organization rather than what *linguistic* ones are important (see Table 5-1).

TABLE 5-1

COMPARISON OF VERBAL AND NONVERBAL CODES ON LINGUISTIC CODING PROPERTIES

Linguistic properties	Present in verbal code?	Present in nonverbal codes?
Discreteness	yes	yes (but not in all)
Syntax rules	yes	yes
Semantic rules	yes	yes
Polysemy	yes	yes
Arbitrariness	yes	yes for many behaviors and codes
Culture- and context-bound meaning	yes	yes for many behaviors and codes
Displacement	yes	to a limited extent
Reflexivity	yes	to a limited extent if at all
Prevarication	yes	yes
Transformation	yes	yes
Productivity	yes	yes
Coherence mechanisms	yes	yes
Pragmatic rules	yes	yes
Analogic coding	no	yes for many behaviors and codes
Iconicity	no	yes for some
Universality	no	yes for some
Simultaneity	no	yes
Sensory directness	no	yes
Spontaneity	no	yes

LINKS BETWEEN NONVERBAL AND VERBAL COMMUNICATION: SOCIAL FUNCTIONS

The functions of any given communication behavior are not realized in isolation from the other communication components but are dependent on the organization of the entire system for the expression of meaning.

D. J. Higginbotham & D. E. Yoder, 1982, p. 5

The interrelatedness of verbal and nonverbal codes in producing a total communication system becomes most evident when we analyze communication according to the functions it serves. It has been popular to use Ekman and Friesen's five basic functions of nonverbal behavior (1969b) as the basis for such analysis. Those five functions are:

1 *Repeat what is said verbally.* Nodding one's head while saying yes is one example of repetition. Typically, much of what people do nonverbally is somewhat redundant with the verbal message. In that way, accuracy of communication is improved.
2 *Substitute for portions of the verbal message.* Visual symbols may replace words. A simple smile may replace the need to say yes. A loud laugh may signal that a joke is understood.
3 *Complement or clarify the verbal message.* Nonverbal cues may add to the meaning expressed by words. Verbal hesitancy in the midst of a heated conflict may be accompanied by nonverbal avoidance cues that amplify the person's desire to escape the battle.
4 *Contradict the verbal statement.* This produces a mixed or ambiguous message in some cases, sarcasm or irony in others. The statement "How nice of you to come," expressed in a flat voice, becomes condescending and insincere.
5 *Emphasize the words.* Pointing, pounding a table, and yelling are examples of ways to underscore what is being said.

This analysis, however, consistently treats nonverbal behavior as subordinate or supplementary to verbal communication—an approach that is at odds with our concept of nonverbal communication as serving multiple functions. Our view is that nonverbal behaviors need to be analyzed in conjunction with verbal behavior, and that the overall nonverbal and verbal message system accomplishes a variety of social functions.

In Part Two, we examine a variety of important social functions and their link to nonverbal communication. Those social functions include the following.

Producing and Processing Messages

The most basic function of communication is to transmit information and create meaning. With regard to this function we examine in Chapter 6 how nonverbal cues affect the creation, processing, and comprehension of overall messages. We will discover that the effective transmission of information requires nonverbal as well as verbal cues.

Structuring Interaction

Researchers in communication and psychology have long recognized that the context and situation in which interaction occurs is exceedingly important. In this regard, we consider in Chapter 7 how nonverbal cues are used to structure situations for interaction, and how such situational factors affect communicators.

Creating and Managing Identities

A core objective for interpersonal communicators is to establish and manage a sense of identity and self. The literature on self-image and identity increasingly acknowledges that personal identity is partly a social construction; that is, it is shaped and negotiated through interactions with others. Furthermore, according to *social identity theory* (Tajfel, 1981) the self is defined not only by personality but also social, cultural, and demographic factors. Cultural, social, demographic, and personal characteristics serve as "identity badges," allowing individuals to project their own sense of self and identity and at the same time enabling others to recognize them instantly by these characteristics. As we learn in Chapter 8, numerous interrelated nonverbal cues serve this function.

Forming Impressions

Identification and identity management take the encoder's perspective and are concerned with communicator projections of "who they are" through nonverbal cues. Impression formation, by contrast, takes the decoder's perspective and examines how receivers use the same cues to answer the question, "who is that?" That is, impression formation has to do with how receivers perceive others. We discover in Chapter 9 that various factors affect our judgments of others, and that several principles of impression formation help us to understand how we form impressions.

Communicating Emotions

Communication of emotions is possibly the largest area of research in nonverbal communication, and certainly the area with the longest history. Relatively speaking, nonverbal rather than verbal channels predominate in this function. Researchers are concerned with the nature of the emotional expression, the nonverbal channels and cues involved, the cross-cultural meaning of emotional expression, and the accuracy of encoding and decoding emotional expression. Affect management is a less recognized feature of this overall function; in this regard, researchers examine the role of nonverbal cues in regulating one's own experience of strong affect. By voluntarily controlling nonverbal immediacy and expressive behaviors, people can intensify or diminish a felt emotion. Thus, overt nonverbal behavior is used to regulate internal emotional experiences. Nonverbal emotional communication is discussed in Chapter 10.

Defining and Managing Relationships

Defining and managing relationships (discussed in Chapter 11) includes two interrelated topics: (1) how nonverbal behavior defines interpersonal relationships; and (2) in so doing, how it moves relationships toward greater or lesser intimacy, commitment, and satisfaction. Many communication scholars have noted that every communication message has both a content or report aspect and a relational or command aspect. Non-verbal communication predominates in the relational or command aspect of communication messages and therefore plays a major role in defining the nature of relationships. While relational messages are not exclusively nonverbal, the division of labor between the verbal and nonverbal channels is such that the nonverbal channels do most of the relational "work."

Over the long term, nonverbal cues also signal stages of relationships: development, maintenance, and dissolution. This function constitutes a growing area of research in tracking relationship paths over time to determine how both verbal and nonverbal channels communicate points along these paths.

Regulating Conversations

The function of regulating conversations (discussed in Chapter 12) shows how closely verbal and nonverbal channels are integrated. Nonverbal cues set the stage for a verbal interaction, start the interaction, manage who will speak when, determine when and how topics are changed, shut down the interaction, and more. As Burgoon (1994) has suggested, nonverbal cues are a lubricant: they keep the conversational machine well oiled. Many features of this function seem to be taken for granted: that is, they are unnoticed until something goes awry, and we are made painfully aware of how much we rely on nonverbal cues in this context.

Managing Impressions

In considering impression management, we return to the encoder's perspective, examining how communicators strategically craft nonverbal performances to create desired images, that is, who they want to be. Impression management (discussed in Chapter 13) is analyzed in terms of interrelated sets of nonverbal and verbal cues, and these cues are related to a variety of rules and principles that determine how we present ourselves to others.

Influencing Others

The function of social influence has to do with how nonverbal and verbal channels may persuade, change attitudes, and modify behavior. Nonverbal cues in conjunction with verbal cues achieve social influence in several ways (Burgoon, 1994, details at least eight). While research in this area has progressed steadily, more work is needed to examine how verbal and nonverbal cues together make social influence possible. Social influence is discussed in Chapter 14.

Deceiving Others

Deception (discussed in Chapter 15) may span several other communication functions. With regard to this function, we examine how people send messages designed to foster beliefs contrary to what they themselves believe. Deception may take many forms—

falsehoods, white lies, equivocations, evasions, hyperbole, and omissions. Although there is an impressive body of research on this function, researchers have only begun to examine nonverbal deception in truly interactive contexts. In general, research has focused on (a) how accurately receivers can detect deception from verbal, nonverbal, and combined channels; (b) what kinds of verbal and nonverbal behaviors people exhibit while lying; (c) what verbal and nonverbal strategies people might attempt when perpetrating deception; and (d) how deceivers and targets of deception adjust to one another's messages and are both responsible for the outcome of deceptive communication.

Taken together, all these social functions reflect strong links between verbal and nonverbal channels, and, at the same time, show how powerful the role of nonverbal behavior is in fulfilling them. It is likely that there are additional communication functions or sub-functions; but we are confident that these too would show the integration of verbal and nonverbal codes and reflect the strength of nonverbal behavior.

SUMMARY

We have reiterated throughout this chapter that nonverbal and verbal codes are part of an indivisible communication system. Although nonverbal information prevails over verbal information for much of our interpretation of the meaning of social situations, the verbal stream carries important and sometimes overriding information for many functions and receivers. We have discussed possible reasons for the nonverbal dominance effect. One explanation resides in the relative differences in origin between the verbal and nonverbal codes. Nonverbal behavior appears to have more innate features than the verbal code. Another area of difference is the structural properties of the respective verbal and nonverbal codes. Although nonverbal codes share many linguistic features with the verbal system, there are a few differences, and nonverbal codes include many coding features not present in verbal language. Despite these differences, verbal and nonverbal codes are closely coordinated to produce messages, and they are well integrated for achieving a variety of communicative functions. To treat them as independent systems is therefore an artificial and counterproductive distinction.

SUGGESTED READINGS

Burgoon, J. K. (1985). Nonverbal signals. In M. L. Knapp & G. R. Miller (Eds.), *Handbook of interpersonal communication* (pp. 344–390). Beverly Hills, CA: Sage.

Burgoon, J. K. (1985). The relationship of verbal and nonverbal codes. In B. Dervin & M. L. Voight (Eds.), *Progress in communication sciences* (Vol. 6, pp. 263–298). Norwood, NJ: Ablex.

Key, M. R. (1980). *The relationship of verbal and nonverbal communication*. The Hague: Mouton.

Leach, E. (1972). The influence of cultural context on nonverbal communication in man. In R. A. Hinde (Ed.), *Non-verbal communication* (pp. 315–344). Cambridge: Cambridge University Press.

Lyons, J. (1972). Human language. In R. A. Hinde (Ed.), *Non-verbal communication* (pp. 49–85). Cambridge: Cambridge University Press.

McNeill, D. (1992). *Hand and mind: What gestures reveal about thought.* Chicago: University of Chicago Press.

Noller, P. (1985). Video primacy—A further look. *Journal of Nonverbal Behavior, 9,* 28–47.

Poyatos, F. (1992). Audible-visual approach to speech. In F. Poyatos (Ed.), *Advances in nonverbal communication* (pp. 41–57). Amsterdam: Johns Benjamins.

Rimé, B., & Schiaratura, L. (1991). Gesture and speech. In R. S. Feldman & B. Rimé (Eds.), *Fundamentals of nonverbal behavior* (pp. 239–281). Cambridge: Cambridge University Press.

Thorpe, W. H. (1972). The comparison of vocal communication in animals and man. In R. A. Hinde (Ed.), *Non-verbal communication* (pp. 27–47). Cambridge: Cambridge University Press.

TWO

FUNCTIONS OF NONVERBAL COMMUNICATION

6

PRODUCING AND PROCESSING MESSAGES

The communicator's problem . . . is not to get stimuli across, or even to package his stimuli so they can be understood and absorbed. Rather, he must deeply understand the kinds of information and experiences stored in his audience, the patterning of this information, and the interactive resonance process whereby stimuli evoke this stored information.

Tony Schwartz

If messages are the heart of the interpersonal communication enterprise, then nonverbal cues are the arteries through which the linguistic lifeblood courses.

Judee K. Burgoon (1994)

To understand a man, you must know his memories.

Old Chinese proverb

Our ability to understand one another is at the very heart of communication. Until recently, many scholars thought that nonverbal cues had little to do with human understanding and thinking processes, that they were more relevant to the affective or emotional side of human behavior. Now, however, research is beginning to show that nonverbal cues are involved in a variety of processes that lead to understanding. These processes, which focus on how information embedded in messages is processed, can be divided into (1) production or encoding and (2) comprehension or decoding.

We noted in Chapter 5 that some scholars dispute the communicative nature of nonverbal cues in the production of messages. They contend that nonverbal cues are merely a by-product of encoding speech. As we shall see, others view nonverbal behaviors as key in generating verbal utterances and as integral to the total message. The crux of the matter seems to rest with the issue of intent—do senders intend to produce the nonverbal cues that accompany verbal utterances and do receivers regard such cues as part of the communication system? Or are they instead background features of communication, attendant to it but not part of it? We are persuaded that nonverbal cues are indeed inherent features of the message and essential to receiver understanding, but even for those who take the alternate view, the material covered in this chapter demonstrates the importance of nonverbal elements in message processing.

Human information processing is concerned with how humans acquire, store, retrieve, produce, and use information (see Anderson, 1980; Craig, 1978; Reed, 1982; also see Roloff & Berger, 1982, for work relevant to communication). Often, information-processing models describe a series of processing stages or sequences such as attention, short-term memory storage, conceptual knowledge activation, inference making, long-term memory storage, and long-term memory retrieval. These stages can be used in both the production or encoding and comprehension or decoding of messages. Regardless of the particular model, it is clear that, in one way or another, people do "process" information and that both verbal and nonverbal information are processed in some way. How, then, do nonverbal cues affect the production and comprehension of the overall communication message? Do they play a supportive role for verbal processing? Are they sometimes the focus of message production and comprehension efforts? These questions, and others, are the central concerns of this chapter.

NEUROPHYSIOLOGICAL PROCESSING

A starting point for examining message production and processing is to review what we know about the neurophysiological aspects of verbal and nonverbal behavior, that is, how the brain handles verbal and nonverbal information in sending and receiving messages. A computer is a useful metaphor here: these neurophysiological aspects are the "hardware" of message processing, whereas the processes themselves are the "software."

One possibility is that nonverbal codes have different structural features from verbal codes because they are processed differently by the brain. The crux of this argument lies in the designation of the left hemisphere of the brain as the "verbal" side and the right hemisphere as the "nonverbal" side. There is some basis for this distinction. Many verbally related activities such as word and symbol recognition occur in the left hemisphere, and the left side of the brain is typically dominant for rational, logical, and analytic tasks (which themselves involve verbal abilities). Conversely, the right hemisphere is said to be dominant for spatial, pictorial, musical, geometric, and emotional stimuli, including such nonverbally related activities as voice recognition and depth perception (see Campbell, 1982; Restak, 1979; Springer & Deutsch, 1981). This lateralization of many functions led Andersen, Garrison, and Andersen (1979) to propose that nonverbal and verbal communication can be distinguished from one another by where they are processed in the brain.

This view is too simplistic, however. Most of the literature applies only to where stimuli are initially *perceived.* It does not address where the stimuli are *interpreted* as communication signals. It is possible, for example, that the right hemisphere initially apprehends that a person is 6 feet away but the left hemisphere takes over in determining what message is implied by that choice of conversational distance. The lateralization literature also applies largely to the decoding but not the encoding of stimuli. If you choose to stand 6 feet from someone as a message of detachment, where does that communicative decision take place?

Contemporary work on information processing suggests a far more complex, synchronized relationship between the two hemispheres in the perception, comprehension, retrieval, and encoding of social information. (Box 6-1 presents one striking illustration.)

For example, both hemispheres are involved in speech production. The left hemisphere governs vocabulary, rhythmic patterns, and free movements that accompany speech, while the right hemisphere processes social gestural speech and automatic speech. Interpretation responsibilities are also shared. Right hemispheric involvement is necessary to understand jokes, metaphors, stories with a moral, and emotions. People who have had the right hemisphere damaged give inaccurate, disjointed, or overly literal versions of these. Where interpretation takes place may also shift, depending on how familiar the person is with the code. Most people initially process music in the right hemisphere; they respond to it as an analogic code. However, once musicians become familiar with a particular piece of music, they process it in the left hemisphere, treating it like a digital code. It is a reasonable hypothesis that communicative stimuli that are treated in a holistic, gestalt fashion are processed as analogic information and therefore

---

BOX 6-1

THE PRESIDENT'S SPEECH

What was going on? A roar of laughter from the aphasia ward, just as the President's speech was coming on, and they had all been so eager to hear the President speaking. . . .

There he was, the old Charmer, the Actor, with his practised rhetoric, his histrionisms, his emotional appeal—and all the patients were convulsed with laughter. . . . The President was, as always, moving—but he was moving them, apparently, mainly to laughter. What could they be thinking? Were they failing to understand him? Or did they, perhaps understand him all too well?

It was said of these patients, who though intelligent had the severest receptive or global aphasia, rendering them incapable of understanding words as such, that they none the less understood most of what was said to them. . . . [Why?] Because speech—natural speech—does *not* consist of words alone. . . . It consists of *utterance*—an uttering-forth of one's whole meaning with one's whole being—the understanding of which involves infinitely more than mere word-recognition. And this was the clue to aphasiacs' understanding, even when they might be wholly uncomprehending of words as such. For though the words, the verbal constructions, *per se,* might convey nothing, spoken language is normally suffused with 'tone,' embedded in an expressiveness which transcends the verbal—and it is precisely this expressiveness, so deep, so various, so complex, so subtle, which is perfectly preserved in aphasia, though understanding of words be destroyed. . . .

In this, then, lies their power of understanding—understanding, without words, what is authentic or inauthentic. Thus it was the grimaces, the histrionisms, the false gestures and, above all, the false tones and cadences of the voice, which rang false for these wordless but immensely sensitive patients. It was to these (for them) most glaring, even grotesque, incongruities and improprieties that my aphasic patients responded, undeceived and undeceivable by words.

This is why they laughed at the President's speech.

Source: Sacks, 1985, pp. 76–79.

handled by the right hemisphere, while those that are segmented into finer, discrete categories are processed as digital information by the left hemisphere. This conclusion is consistent with Campbell's contention (1982) that the left brain is better for deductive, convergent, discrete, intellectual, objective, literal, and denotative tasks, while the right brain is better for imaginative, divergent, continuous, sensuous, subjective, metaphorical, and connotative tasks. As Campbell put it:

> The right brain is not a linguistic idiot. It has its own codes, its own rules, and these are worth examining. It does have some comprehension of spoken language, and it is good at detecting pitch, intonation, stress, cadence, loudness, and softness. It knows whether a sentence is asking a question, giving an order, expressing a condition, or making a statement. . . . It can recognize the ridiculous and inappropriate, and be aware that words are embedded in a wide matrix of relationships. (pp. 244–245)

Recent neurophysiological research casts further doubt on the simple nonverbal right–verbal left distinction. The brain can also be viewed as tripartite, consisting of the *R-complex,* the most primitive brain, located at the end of the brain stem; the *paleomammalian brain,* composed of the limbic system surrounding the R-complex; and the *neomammalian brain,* which is the cortex itself. Each brain controls different aspects of communication and nonverbal behavior. The R-complex controls instinctive behavioral and aggressive displays (e.g., territorial defense). The paleomammalian brain controls emotional expression and experience, as well as bodily functions. The neomammalian brain controls higher order thought processes and symbolic activity, presumably including such nonverbal symbols as emblems. Stacks (1982) argued that one can better understand the interrelationships between verbal and nonverbal communication by analyzing the interplay among these three levels of the brain and which is in control during a particular nonverbal or verbal expression. Thus some communicative activities, such as threatening others, may be primarily controlled by the R-complex. Other activities, such as emotional expressions, may require the careful coordination of both verbal and nonverbal channels but rely more heavily on the spontaneously generated nonverbal signals of the limbic system.

Recent findings suggest a complex interplay among different subsystems of the brain. Several left-hemisphere sites, both cortical and subcortical, have been shown to be involved in the production of symbolic gestures, and the comprehension of pantomimic gestures and nonverbal sounds has been linked to the left hemisphere (Feyereisen, 1991). The facial musculature is under the direct control of facial nuclei located in the brain stem, and those neurons receive signals from basal ganglia and the motor cortex (Rinn, 1984, 1991). Feyereisen pointed out that if behavioral categories are large and cover global terms like gesture production or emotional processing, it is unlikely that corresponding brain functions will be precisely located. Since it is just these kinds of behavioral categories that we are interested in, one conjecture is that we will eventually find nonverbal communication behavior to be a function of several areas and features of the brain. However, as Feyereisen noted, research is needed to settle these issues. Recent advances in magnetic resonance imaging (MRI) and other forms of neurophysical measurement and observation should lead to more interesting discoveries.

NONVERBAL CUES IN MESSAGE PRODUCTION

How we construct utterances in communication situations is remarkable yet often taken for granted. The speed with which we can produce novel utterances, the amount of information embedded in utterances, and the depth and clarity that utterances can have for other communicators are all qualities that distinguish humans as a species concerned with communication.

Nonverbal cues are involved in message production in three ways. First, nonverbal cues provide the structural frame for utterances—that is, they mark the units in which utterances are produced. Second, nonverbal cues facilitate language encoding by helping the speaker activate and recall words, thoughts, images, and ideas that become part of the utterance. Third, some nonverbal cues are indicators of difficulty in encoding and constructing utterances.

Marking Encoding Units: The Phonemic Clause

One characteristic of conversational utterances is that they occur in "chunks." *Phonemic clauses* constitute the chunks of speech that make up the overall stream of spontaneous conversational verbalization. Conversational speech is not made up of sentences and paragraphs like written language. But there are discernible units in speech, the turn (discussed in Chapter 12) being one. Within turns, there are noticeable segments of speech, and these segments are for the most part phonemic clauses. Boomer (1978, pp. 246–247) gave the following example to illustrate phonemic clauses. Imagine hearing someone say the following:

The man who called me yesterday just telephoned again.

How do you hear this phrase being uttered in your mind? Research on phonemic clauses suggests that you hear this in two chunks:

The man who called me yesterday / just telephoned again.

The slash indicates where most people are likely to put a break point in the phrase, separating it into two chunks, or phonemic clauses (Boomer, 1965; Boomer & Dittmann, 1962).

Boomer (1978) indicated that three vocal cues identify a phonemic clause: *pitch, rhythm,* and *loudness.* The pitch contour or intonation pattern accompanying our sample phrase should have a characteristic pattern, with the pitch being relatively level over *The man who called me,* abruptly rising over the *yes* in *yesterday,* and gliding back down over *-terday.* A similar though not identical pattern should be found over *just telephoned again.* A change in the rhythm of the utterance typically coincides with the pitch change just described. Specifically, *The man who called me* and *just telephoned a-* parts of the phrases should be heard with relatively even rhythm. *Yesterday* and *-gain* should be heard as slightly longer and stretched out, the same points at which the pitch changes occur. Finally, Boomer indicated that the *yes-* and *-gain* parts of the utterance should be slightly louder than the rest of the segment. The simultaneous changes in pitch, rhythm, and loudness produce what is called *primary stress* and mark the whole phrase into two segments. In phonemic clauses, primary stress occurs at or near the end of the clause. Pitch, rhythm, and loudness fall off and assume previous levels, a feature called a *terminal juncture*. A phonemic clause, then, is defined by one primary stress and a terminal juncture.

Thus spoken language is segmented into noticeable units, but instead of those units being sentences marked by grammatical rules, the units are rhythmic and marked by vocal properties. Research supports the importance of the phonemic clause as a production unit for speakers and a decoding unit for listeners. One study (Dittmann & Llewellyn, 1967) linked the phonemic clause to *listeners'* reactions. Listener responses such as nods and brief interjections like *um-hmm*—what we refer to elsewhere as backchannel responses—were found to occur primarily at the end of phonemic clauses, immediately after terminal junctures. This suggests that listeners recognize phonemic clause units and coordinate their responses to the units so that they don't "step on" the speaker's lines. Dittmann (1972a) found similar patterns for other kinesic cues. Boomer (1978) reported evidence that phonemic clause units may be found in a number of languages, including Russian, French, and Dutch. These units provide a frame for conversational utterances and thus play an important role in language production.

Facilitating Message Production

When people produce speech, three processes are involved (Levelt, 1989). First is *message generation.* Speakers must formulate preverbal ideas and plans into intentions to send a message. These ideas then must be translated into words. This is *semantic encoding.* When the message is to be conveyed in oral rather than written form, it must also undergo *phonological encoding*—putting the right sounds with the words. Nonverbal cues are intimately involved in all three of these processes.

Some nonverbal cues are an integral part of messages and may convey the semantic meaning of a total utterance. This is partly evident in that gestures and language emerge simultaneously early in childhood and both are tied to linguistic and cognitive development and expressiveness (Blake & Dolgoy, 1993; Morford & Goldin-Meadow, 1992; Thal & Tobias, 1992). Gestures also typically coincide with or even precede the words they accompany, leading many scholars to conclude that gestures and speech originate together as part of the same communicative plan (Birdwhistell, 1970; Freedman & Steingart, 1975; Kendon, 1980, 1983; McNeill, 1985, 1992; McNeill & Levy, 1982; Poyatos, 1983, 1992; Rimé & Schiaratura, 1991). Such a view is also consistent with cognitive theories that posit dual coding of mental representation, that is, that information is stored in both a semantic and imagistic form. Gestures may facilitate activation of words, concepts, ideas, and images that can be used in message construction (Collins & Loftus, 1975; Paivio, 1971; for examples of how these models can be applied to nonverbal and verbal communication, see Kendon, 1983, and Motley, Camden, and Baars, 1981).

You can confirm this for yourself by observing that when people give complex directions to others or try to make fine verbal discriminations, they use lots of gestures to fill in meaning (Baxter, Winters, & Hammer, 1968; Cohen, 1977). If they are prevented from gesturing, they pause a lot more and replace the missing gestures with more verbiage (Graham & Heywood, 1975).

Even when we can't be seen, we use gestures to facilitate our own encoding.

Some nonverbal cues also facilitate the encoding of language—priming the pump, so to speak. You may have noticed that people talking on the telephone continue to use facial expressions and gestures, even though their listeners cannot see them. It may look foolish, but researchers are learning that it serves a useful purpose because gestures accompanying speech may assist speakers in retrieving lexical items (words, phrases) from memory (Chawla & Krauss, 1994; Krauss et al., 1991). Kinesic and vocalic expressiveness are such a natural part of the encoding process that even when they serve no benefit to the listener, they help us translate our meanings into words.

Finally, nonverbal cues may assist phonological encoding by supplying necessary vocal and kinesic punctuation. Rhythmic illustrator gestures that are synchronized to the vocal-verbal stream, parakinesic behaviors like head nods, self-touching, and other adaptor behaviors may be especially helpful in this respect (Birdwhistell, 1970; Ekman & Friesen, 1972; Freedman, 1972; Hadar, 1989; Harrigan, 1985).

Of course, we also adapt to the auditor and situation. For example, people giving directions or presenting a narrative use more illustrator and interactive gestures in a face-to-face situation than when speaking over an intercom, through a partition, or to a tape-recorder or videocamera (Bavelas et al., 1992; Bavelas et al., 1989; Cohen, 1977; Cohen & Harrison, 1973). This demonstrates that communicators are cognizant of their listeners' needs and abilities when trying to fashion their messages.

Indicating Difficulty and Complexity of Encoding

Can you tell when someone is thinking, or whether they are having difficulty putting their thoughts into words? Many scholars, believing you can, have gone in search of reliable external indicators of what is variously referred to as *cognitive effort* or *cognitive load*. Describing this search, Scherer (1992) explains:

> . . . while we cannot look inside the head, we can look at it, particularly at the face, and . . . we can use facial expressions to infer some ongoing cognitive processes. (p. 141)

The same goes for vocal cues, which are especially good prospects for revealing cognitive effort because they are intimately tied to verbal expression. Ideally, such cues can signal when communicators are engaged in activities thought to be cognitively demanding—activities such as speaking (rather than listening), expressing new and unrehearsed ideas, becoming more self-conscious, experiencing social anxiety, or even deceiving (Cappella & Palmer, 1990).

To date, a collection of facial, eye, gestural, and vocal behaviors have been identified as reliable indicators of encoding effort and difficulty (Beattie, 1981; Chawla & Krauss, 1994; Goldman-Eisler, 1961a, 1961b, 1968; Siegman, 1976, 1978; Siegman & Pope, 1965).

One set of cues involves the eyes. Several muscles in the eye and forehead region combine to produce knit eyebrows, which are typically associated with deep concentration, reflection, or determination. People also typically avert gaze. The avoidance of gaze, coupled with the eye and brow muscle movements, may serve to regulate visual input while sharpening the acuity of other senses.

Another set of cues includes gestures. Illustrators and self-adaptors increase as verbal complexity or difficulty increases.

A third set of cues includes fluency and pauses. Hesitation (silent) pauses occur more frequently when people are speaking spontaneously and at junctures where it is difficult to anticipate the next word. More difficult tasks requiring greater cognitive planning to encode an utterance also result in longer pauses. Other kinds of vocalic phenomena, including filled pauses and nonfluencies, are also associated with greater cognitive planning.

NONVERBAL CUES IN MESSAGE PROCESSING

Message processing has been and continues to be a major subject of study for communication, psychology, and other social science disciplines. Most previous efforts to explain message processing have focused on language and its features. Now, however, it is evident that nonverbal as well as verbal cues must be taken into account. Moreover, the theoretical models used to explain message processing have shifted over the past two decades from an emphasis on operant and classical conditioning principles to information-processing principles, which provide a more elaborate view of comprehension than previous conceptions.

The term *comprehension* may be an overly simplistic misnomer. Comprehension is not a process in and of itself but a series of stages through which information is processed in order to gain an understanding of a message. We first examine the properties of each stage and then consider the nonverbal cues associated with them.

Stage 1: Attention

Traditionally, attention is the first stage in most information-processing models. You cannot understand something unless you have attended to it.

Properties of Attention   Although there are several views of attention, most researchers agree on a number of its attributes (Reed, 1982).

First, *attention is selective.* When humans attend, they take in some part of the total possible stimulus field and screen out the rest. The implication for nonverbal cues is that some nonverbal cues are included in the focus of attention, while others are not. Nonverbal cues that meet the definitional criteria outlined in Chapter 1 are especially likely to receive attention.

Second, *attention requires mental concentration.* One well-known illustration is the cocktail party situation (see Cherry, 1964). It takes serious concentration to focus on a conversation with the host or to eavesdrop on a nearby conversation in the midst of a crowded room. Such concentration inevitably entails paying attention to both verbal and nonverbal cues.

Third, *attention is a limited-capacity stage.* At some point, when attention is divided by different kinds of tasks and stimuli, humans become less efficient. For example, suppose you are trying to listen carefully to a speech given by another person while at the same time being intrigued by the speaker's striking physical attractiveness. In this situation, you probably will pay little attention to what is being said. Although there must be some upper limit on how much nonverbal and verbal information a communicator can take in, just what that limit is has yet to be established. In a classic work, Miller (1956) identified one limit to attention and short-term memory capacity: humans can process roughly seven bits of information, plus or minus two bits, at a time. However, Miller and other researchers identified strategies that humans can use to exceed this limit: *chunking,* or combining units of information into larger units, and *rehearsal,* repeating information and keeping it active in short-term memory. Some of the rhythmic properties of nonverbal cues may aid in chunking or rehearsing, thus expanding the capacity of attention and short-term memory. Research by Newtson and his colleagues (Newtson, 1973; Newtson & Engquist, 1976; Newtson, Engquist, & Bois, 1977) suggested that features of nonverbal behavior are used to segment the stream of interaction into perceptual chunks.

Fourth, *attention can be either automatic or effortful.* Automatic processing occurs when attending requires very little effort or capacity, as when dressing or eating, because the activity is habitual and routine. Effortful processing occurs when attention requires much or most of one's mental capacity, such as when learning to utter a phrase in a new language. Most nonverbal cues may be attended to automatically when a person communicates with a familiar other because that person is accustomed to the recipient's nonverbal displays. However, behavior from an unfamiliar other, as in an employment interview situation, may prompt effortful processing to form a distinct impression of the job applicant. Similarly, deviant or unexpected behavior may prompt more focused attention (Burgoon & Hale, 1988).

Fifth, *attention can be either bottom-up or top-down.* Bottom-up processing occurs when features of the stimulus field determine where attention is focused. Thus when certain features of the stimulus field catch our eye, bottom-up processing may be said to occur. Some research (e.g., Nisbett & Ross, 1980) suggests that vivid and novel stimuli attract attention. Nonverbal cues that are vivid or novel, such as hand gestures that point at objects or rhythmically reinforce phrases, may promote a bottom-up attention mode. Stacks and Burgoon (1981) proposed that extremes in physical attractiveness and extreme conversational distances distract attention from what is being said and draw it to the speaker.

Top-down processing occurs when units of knowledge (i.e., what we already know) determine the focus of attention. We pay more attention to a familiar other compared to a stranger, for example. Nonverbal cues may be involved with a top-down attention mode in at least two ways. First, they may help to activate semantic concepts that are then used to guide attention. For example, assume that one communicator tells another about a recent fishing trip and uses a hand gesture to indicate the size of the one that got away. Use of such a gesture may prompt the listener to recall a variety of details about similar fishing trips (not to mention the stories told about them) and may affect what the listener pays attention to subsequently. Second, top-down attention to nonverbal cues may result from a communicator's observational goal. A communicator may be suspicious of deceit on the part of another communicator and thus pay a great deal of attention to nonverbal cues for leakage.

Many of these features of attention have yet to be investigated empirically by nonverbal researchers, in part because some of these distinctions are relatively recent. However, the research that we discuss later suggests that nonverbal cues do facilitate attention levels.

Vocal Cues Affecting Attention   Vocal variety and tempo are two variables that have been linked to increased attention. Usually increased attention is inferred from evidence that nonverbal behaviors lead to increased comprehension. For example, vocal variety, which includes variations in pitch, tempo, intensity, and tonal quality, has been shown to result in increased comprehension (Beighley, 1952, 1954; Glasgow, 1952; Woolbert, 1920). The explanation for these effects is that variations in these vocal parameters serve to increase the listener's attentiveness, and as a result, comprehension is facilitated. Further, listeners have reported that they prefer more varied pitch presentation (Diehl, White, & Satz, 1961).

A key vocal behavior thought to increase attention is tempo. Research on the speed of vocalization has established that the normal rate of speech ranges from roughly 125 to 195 words per minute (wpm). Investigators have found that, contrary to what might be expected, listeners can comprehend verbal messages presented at faster tempos than the normal rate. Researchers have used a variety of techniques to speed up the rate of presentation of recorded speech artificially. One technique, called the *speed-changing method,* increases the rate of speech by reproducing a message at a higher playback speed. However, when this is done, vocal pitch is also raised, which results in an unwanted confounding effect. Another technique, termed the *sampling method* or *time compressed speech,* accelerates speech by removing most periods of silence from recorded speech (Foulke & Sticht, 1969). This method increases speech rate without increasing vocal pitch and can be accomplished by computerized devices that sample the verbal stream for periods of silence to eliminate. Most researchers now agree that the sampling method is the best technique for compressing speech.

These compression techniques have allowed researchers to investigate the effects of accelerated speech on attention and comprehension. Early research showed that speech could be speeded up significantly without serious loss of comprehension until it reached 325 wpm (Orr, 1968). For example, one study (Fairbanks, Guttman, & Miron, 1957) found that at 282 wpm (close to double the normal rate of speaking), listener comprehension was 90 percent of what it was at normal rates of presentation; at 353 wpm, comprehension dropped to 50 percent. More recent research (e.g., Duker, 1974; LaBarbera & MacLachlan, 1979; MacLachlan, 1981; MacLachlan & LaBarbera, 1978; MacLachlan & Siegel, 1980) showed that accelerated speech not only does not jeopardize comprehension but may actually aid it. For example, radio commercials that were speeded up by 25 percent were 50 percent better remembered and also better liked (LaBarbera & MacLachlan, 1979). Psychology students who heard either a compressed or normal speed version of a *60 Minutes* segment had much higher recall two days later if they heard the compressed speech version (MacLachlan & Siegel, 1980). Commercials produced for industry yield higher recall and motivation when they have a 10 percent to 15 percent speed-up, which is almost imperceptible, and the preferred rate of speech is about 30 percent faster than normal (200 wpm; see MacLachlan, 1981).

A plausible explanation for these findings is that faster-paced speaking requires more effort from listeners. They must attend more carefully and exert more effort to keep up with what the speaker is saying. At the same time, moderately accelerated speech does not exceed a listener's information capacity, yet it can prevent attention gaps. The net result is that a faster pace may be most desirable if attention and comprehension are the goal.

Of course, time-compression techniques can be used successfully in mass media contexts but not in interpersonal ones. The application of rapid speech to interpersonal settings may be limited by several factors. First, some people may be unable to vocalize as fast as or faster than 200 wpm. Second, verbal variables such as the complexity of the information being presented may interact with tempo, making a rapid rate less effective with difficult verbal material. Finally, listeners' interest and motivation in paying attention can affect whether a faster rate facilitates attention. Speaking faster may aid attention when you are talking to a friend about a topic of mutual interest but may harm it when you are talking to a stranger on a boring topic. Nevertheless, a moderately quickened pace usually should increase attention, comprehension, and receiver pleasure.

Environmental Cues Affecting Attention   Environmental features have the potential to stimulate the senses, making it easier to comprehend and retain information or to distract. Noble (cited in Proshansky, Ittelson, & Rivlin, 1970) explained it this way:

> Normal consciousness, perception and thought can be maintained only in a constantly changing environment; when there is no change a state of "sensory deprivation" occurs. Experiment has shown that a homogeneous and unvarying environment produces boredom, restlessness, lack of concentration and reduction in intelligence. . . . Office blocks in which each floor has the same layout, color, materials and climate are just asking for trouble. . . . The sort of variation that we often demand instinctively on aesthetic grounds has a sound physiological and psychological basis. A change in environment stimulates our built-in devices to perceive and respond rapidly to significant events and efficiency is thereby increased. (p. 464)

One environment where paying attention is especially crucial is the classroom. Yet many classrooms are poorly designed and may actually be distracting. The windowless classroom, an innovation intended to reduce the distractions from outdoors (and to reduce heating costs), has failed to improve learning and has resulted in less pleasant student moods (Karmel, 1965). Open classroom designs, also intended to aid learning, have likewise harmed attention by not providing enough privacy for groups of students and by allowing too much noise to occur in the environment (Rivlin & Rothenberg, 1976). It has been argued that learning environments should tend toward simplicity, as too many stimuli can prove distracting (see Fisher, Bell, & Baum, 1984). One study

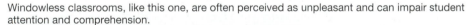

Windowless classrooms, like this one, are often perceived as unpleasant and can impair student attention and comprehension.

confirmed that greater learning occurs in less complex settings (Porteous, 1972). Ideally, one would like to strike a balance between environments that are too complex and distracting and environments that are so simple and bland as to be boring. It is possible that the type of learning (rote versus experiential versus semantic-based) and the complexity of the material to be learned may determine the level of attention and environmental stimulation needed.

Finally, color and intensity of lighting may affect attention and comprehension. Experimenters found that placing children in brightly colored playrooms increased their IQ by 12 points, while those placed in white, black, or brown rooms lost 14 IQ points (cited in Silden, 1973). Presumably, the environment affected their general level of alertness and mental quickness. In another investigation (Sadesky, 1974), subjects received the highest scores on a multiple-choice test after interacting in a room with either low-intensity red lighting or medium-intensity blue lighting. Test scores were lowest when high-intensity white light was used. If an attention effect was at work in this study, high-intensity white light might be distracting. Such an effect seems plausible, as there are many reflective surfaces (white paper, floor tile) off which white light may bounce, creating distraction in typical classrooms.

Other environmental elements such as obstructions to view or inefficient climate control also can affect student attention.

Kinesic and Haptic Cues Affecting Attention   Smiles and touch from teachers have been found to increase students' attentiveness in the classroom (Kazdin & Klock, 1973). Emphatic hand gestures that accompany the verbal stream and underscore high information segments should also promote attention. A varied overall nonverbal style may operate much like vocal variety, enhancing a decoder's attention because the nonverbal part of the message is intrinsically more interesting. Some work has suggested that nonverbal cues may refocus a communicator's attention by shifting it away from the verbal portion of the message and toward the nonverbal part (see Woodall & Burgoon, 1981). In a review of this research, Buller (1986) concluded that some nonverbal cues, particularly nonverbal violations of expectations, shift the communicator's attention away from verbal message components and toward nonverbal source characteristics. Two in particular that may draw attention away from the verbal message are physical attractiveness and distance changes (Stacks & Burgoon, 1981).

One qualification should be made about much of the research just cited. As you may have noticed, *comprehension* is often used as a measure of attention. The attention stage of information processing is difficult to assess directly. Strictly speaking, this presents us with a somewhat confounded situation. Some researchers have argued that since various factors can affect attention and comprehension, using comprehension as a criterion to measure attention can be potentially misleading. Other options do exist. For example, reaction time techniques, whereby researchers measure the time it takes for a decoder to identify some target stimulus, can be used as a more direct way to assess attention. However, comprehension does indicate *something* about what was attended to and can be used—carefully—as a rough guide.

To sum up, nonverbal communication is often the first mode to occur between interactants. For this reason alone, nonverbal cues can affect and direct attention. It is increasingly clear that nonverbal communication and the attention stage of information processing are related in many ways.

Stage 2: Comprehension

Distinguishing Understanding from Recall   Ortony (1978) argued that two fundamental and important cognitive capacities make up an adequate model of human cognition: the capacity to understand and the capacity to remember. The processes involved in understanding information are different from those involved in recalling it. This distinction between understanding and memory is a break from previous work that either lumped such capacities together or treated them as one and the same (see Folger & Woodall, 1982; Woodall, Davis, & Sahin, 1983). It reinforces the fact that these two capacities are often independent of each other in our day-to-day experience; that is, we often understand something but later cannot remember it, and we may also remember something that we did not understand very well.

Nonverbal Cues Affecting Semantic Understanding   Space is inadequate to cover all the models that have been offered to explain how understanding occurs (for a review, see Anderson, 1980; Reed, 1982). Ortony (1978) used semantic network models of long-term memory (e.g., Collins & Loftus, 1975) to explain the understanding process. These models conceive of human long-term memory as a network of associated nodes that represent the storehouse of knowledge that a person holds. Each node in the network could be a concept or proposition, and the nodes are connected by different types of relationships. For example, the node *professor* would be linked to the node *professional* by a class relationship, allowing the proposition "a professor is a professional" to be generated. *Professor* could be linked to other nodes, such as *hardworking, intelligent, insightful,* and *underpaid.*

Understanding, according to Ortony (1978), occurs as information stored in a semantic network is used to make inferences about information just received (verbal and nonverbal cues that make up a message). The input information activates some relevant set of concepts in memory. Hewes and Planalp (1982) pointed out that both *integration* and *inference making* are components of the understanding process. Integration is the process of combining new data with prior knowledge; inference making refers to deductions based on existing and newly integrated information. In slightly more simple terms, we understand because what we already know is related to the message and allows us to make inferences.

Many factors determine the nature of understanding. First, understanding rests partly on how far activation "spreads" in the network, or how many concepts are activated at input. Two factors affect the *spread of activation*: (1) *contextual information* and (2) *depth of processing.* Contextual information—cues that surround and accompany language—can enhance the number of concepts activated when new information (a message) is encountered. Depth of processing has to do with the degree of semantic involvement during the processing of a message (Craik & Lockhart, 1972; Folger & Woodall, 1982). Nonverbal cues can affect understanding by providing contextual information that prompts greater spread of activation of concepts, greater integration of input information, more inference making, and thus deeper processing.

Some nonverbal cues such as hand gestures have semantic features that provide a basis for the spread of activation and integration. Freedman (1972) described two categories of gestures. *Speech primacy gestures,* which include any gesture that has no clear representational or semantic properties, occur as an "overflow from the emphatic aspects of speech" (p. 158) and are tied to the rhythm of speech. *Motor primacy gestures* include gestures that are representational and carry some semantic information and relationship to concurrent language. Similar classifications have been offered by Ekman and Friesen (1969b, *illustrators* versus *emblems*) and McNeill and Levy (1982, *iconic gestures* versus *beats*). All these classifications distinguish between gestures that have semantic content and those that do not.

Motor primacy or emblematic gestures have the potential to result in greater activation and integration because they offer some form of semantic representation. Further, they may do so in a way not embodied in language; that is, they provide semantic information in a visual mode. Stimuli that are visual may be more concrete and vivid (Paivio, 1971) and can affect both integration and inference making (Nisbett & Ross, 1980). Support for hand gestures affecting processing in this way has been found in two studies. In one investigation (Woodall & Folger, 1981), a series of random sentences was paired with either an emphasizing gesture or a semantically related gesture. Participants viewed a videotape in which an actor spoke the sentences and performed one gesture or the other. Later, participants shown the videotape (without sound) were better able to recall the sentences when they were accompanied by semantically related gestures. Here, higher levels of recall indicate greater concept activation, integration, and inference making.

As noted earlier, some scholars question whether gestures actually add substantial semantic information or are merely a physical by-product of the verbal message (see Krauss et al., 1991; Rimé & Schiaratura, 1991). But there is ample evidence that receivers attempt to incorporate both the gestural and verbal meaning when the two are mismatched; that receivers often begin to respond to the nonverbal meaning even before the words are fully uttered; and that receivers better understand messages accompanied by gestures than those that are not (Bavelas, 1994; Kendon, 1994; McNeill et al., 1994). Receivers themselves signal that they are attending to these gestures by shifting their gaze toward them and by filling in their own verbal interpretation of them, and senders in turn monitor this feedback, using it to adapt their message further to facilitate receivers' understanding (Streeck, 1994). Gestures thus become an important means of securing comprehension.

Other visual cues such as head nods, eye movements, and lip and facial movements have also been shown to improve message comprehension (Rogers, 1978). It may be that artifacts and adornments such as flags, uniforms, insignias, and symbolic colors that have semantic properties similarly prompt greater activation and integration of concepts.

Nonverbal cues such as speech primacy gestures that do not have semantic features can also prompt deeper information processing. When messages are ambiguous or have multiple meanings (e.g., metaphors, double entendres, and ironic statements), nonverbal cues may serve to clarify the communicator's intended meaning by highlighting that the message is not to be taken at face value (Folger & Woodall, 1982). Exaggerated voices or facial expressions are examples of such nonverbal cues. When some form of incongruity exists between language and nonverbal cues, the nonverbal cues also may permit inferences that enable understanding of the total message. Sarcasm, jokes, and deception provide complementary or contradictory information that can cause the receiver to go beyond the literal meaning of the utterance. Finally, nonverbal cues that are out of sync with the verbal stream may either distract receivers, reducing their comprehension (Woodall & Burgoon, 1981), or elicit greater cognitive effort that focuses greater attention on the verbal content.

Nonverbal Cues Affecting Social Understanding   So far, we have concentrated on how nonverbal cues might affect semantic understanding. A second kind of understanding relates more generally to receivers' information processing about other people. Social cognition theorists (e.g., Hastie & Carlston, 1980) have pointed out that humans have a social memory domain that includes stereotypes, implicit personality traits, and information about social events, processes, and persons.

In any communicative situation, inferences about what is said as well as who said it can be made and can determine the nature of one's overall understanding. From an information processing point of view, impression formation relies on inference making that uses both message information and social information stored in social memory. Burgoon (1980) indicated three general types of social judgments that rely on nonverbal cues: (1) sociological and personality judgments, (2) judgments of credibility and attraction, and (3) judgments of veracity and deception. In these cases, nonverbal cues trigger inferences about others and determine the concepts activated in social memory. Social understanding—a grasp of who the other communicators are, why they act as they do, and what their intentions and motivations are—is based on information-processing principles.

Does our social understanding of people affect our semantic understanding of their messages? One investigation (McMahan, 1976) has suggested a limited yes as an answer. Participants viewed one of four different videotapes in which nonverbal cues displayed either dominance or submissiveness consistent with or in contrast to dominant or submissive verbal statements. After viewing a tape, participants were asked to give written impressions of the speaker and to recall the message. Impressions of the speaker were dominated by references to nonverbal cues, while reconstruction of the verbal message was dominated by references to verbal information. Moreover, in the inconsistent conditions, participants rated the intent of the speakers as less sincere than the sincerity of their statements. According to McMahan, the result "lends support to the theory that perceivers discriminate between statement and intention, and they attribute intentions to the person which are used to reinterpret the verbal message when the incongruent verbal and nonverbal cues are received" (p. 202). At least in incongruent message conditions (what we referred to earlier as an ambiguous encoding condition), inferences about the person may affect inferences about the semantic meaning of the message.

To sum up, nonverbal cues affect the understanding stage of information processing by having an impact on concept activation, integration of message information with what is already stored, and inference making. Nonverbal cues may have these effects by providing a context that offers semantic features or features that can clarify ambiguous encoding situations, by providing social information that can be used to reinterpret the verbal message, and by affecting the topic management process (please see Box 6-2 for some examples).

Stage 3: Memory

According to Ortony (1978), memory "involves the retrieval, recognition and in some cases even the regeneration of representations of knowledge" (p. 57). Memory, then, has to do with the storage and retrieval of information. There are three issues to explore here. First, what can be said about the storage and retrieval of nonverbal cues themselves? Second, do nonverbal cues aid in the storage and retrieval of other information about the communication interaction? Third, what role do nonverbal cues play in our memory of other people, often called *person memory?*

Storage and Retrieval of Nonverbal Cues   With a little reflection, you will probably realize that nonverbal cues themselves are often an important part of memory. The clearest example of this is facial recognition. A number of studies have supported what most of us have no doubt experienced personally—that it is easier for people (at least in our culture) to recognize a person's face than it is to recall the person's name (see Watkins, Ho, & Tulving, 1976). This is primarily applicable to people with whom one is only somewhat acquainted (e.g., the students in a class with you).

BOX 6-2

APPLICATIONS: TRACKING CONVERSATIONS

Because nonverbal regulative cues are used to manage the content of what is talked about, they may affect our understanding of dialogue. This is clearest when the topic regulation process breaks down and affects understanding in a negative way. For example, if a communicator does not use nonverbal cues in clear and skillful ways to mark a change in topic, other communicators are likely to lose track of what is being talked about. In information-processing terms, losing track of the conversational topic could have several implications. First, concept activation, integration of message information, and inference making are likely to suffer because the communicator is no longer sure of the overall theme of information being discussed. A second possibility is that misunderstandings develop because one communicator assumes that topic A is being discussed and the other, topic B. This is most likely to occur when a subtle shift has been made to a closely related topic and when a topic change is implicitly sig-

naled but not explicitly noted by the person changing topics.

The importance of topic shifting in a clear and comprehensible way has probably occurred to you before, although you may not have recognized the issue as such. More than likely, you have found yourself lost in a conversation, unsure of what the other person is talking about. This can be an uncomfortable situation, to say the least. Do you stop the other person to clarify the topic? This could be embarrassing, as an admission of inattention. Open criticism of the other person for having lost you in the conversation is rude and can be construed as an accusation of incompetence as a communicator. Clearly, the skillful use of nonverbal cues to demarcate topic shifts is important for keeping interactants on track in their understanding of each other and for promoting positive perceptions of a communicator's skill.

The ability to decode, store, and retrieve facial features develops early in humans. At 6 months, infants are able to discriminate familiar faces from unfamiliar faces, and stranger anxiety emerges as a result. Although facial recognition may have a number of functional bases, its early appearance means that it can be considered from an ethological point of view. An infant's ability to discriminate parent from stranger could have had survival value at some point in human history. Thus, as noted in Chapter 2, the ability to recognize faces may have an innate basis.

The ability to recognize a face suggests something about how nonverbal information is coded in memory. Of the many possible views on the coding of information in memory, the one that makes the most sense for our purposes is the *dual-coding position* (see Paivio, 1971). This position holds that information can be coded in two ways for storage: by a semantic code (as in a semantic network) or by an imagistic code that stores information pictorially. Facial recognition probably uses an imagistic code, the features of a familiar face being stored as an image. It is thus likely that other nonverbal cues are stored imagistically as well. Box 6-3 considers how these nonverbal cues affect memory for conversation.

Both recognition and recall are ways of retrieving information from storage. *Recognition* occurs when the information to be remembered is presented and the person must determine whether it has been encountered before. *Recall* occurs when retrieval of information is made through some association other than the information to be remembered.

BOX 6-3

CONVERSATIONAL AMNESIA: DIDN'T I TALK TO YOU YESTERDAY?

People often claim that they remember who they have conversed with during the recent past. How accurate is that claim? Not very accurate, according to studies by Russell Bernard, an anthropologist at the University of Florida. Russell has conducted a number of studies in which he surveyed, at random intervals, a variety of people about the conversations they were having at that moment (members of a consulting firm, a university office, and a fraternity have been used in these studies). A week later, Bernard would again ask these individuals to look at lists of people in their organization and indicate how often they had spoken with each. Results showed that the respondents remembered talking to individuals that they had in fact never spoken to, denied speaking with individuals to whom they had spoken, and were accurate about the amount of contact they had with others less than 50 percent of the time.

On the face of it, these results aren't very encouraging for one's ability to recall conversations. However, they do fit with the research we have been discussing.

First, it seems to be the case that we are better at recalling some nonverbal visual features of conversation, primarily other interactants' faces, than their names. So it is not surprising that interactants would have difficulty recalling who they had spoken to a week earlier. Second, it may very well be the case that the difficulty in recall is due to the inability of respondents to retrieve information, and not due to forgetting the information. Information-processing principles that govern the storage and retrieval of conversational event information suggest that some kind of contextual cue is necessary for retrieval. Simply asking the respondents who they had spoken to may not have given them enough context to retrieve the names of the other interactants. Although what individuals can recall from conversations is still being studied, Bernard's studies do indicate that we should treat such recalled information with care and some skepticism.

Source: Adapted from Cory, 1983, p. 22.

Memory for nonverbal cues may employ either retrieval strategy. In the case of face recognition, a recognition retrieval process is used; in other cases to be discussed shortly, a recall retrieval process is used.

Other kinesic cues are also likely to be recognizable and stored in memory. For example, emblematic gestures such as the A-OK sign and the greeting wave are immediately recognized not only because the meaning associated with them is well understood but also because we know what the gestures look like. When an emblematic gesture is recognized, the information stored in both imagistic and semantic domains is used to help make the discrimination.

Cues from other nonverbal codes are processed in much the same way. Researchers in environmental psychology (Fisher et al., 1984) have pointed out that rather elaborate cognitive "maps" of environments are stored as part of memory. Such map information allows a person to discriminate familiar environments from unfamiliar ones. In addition to allowing humans to adapt and function in a given environment, such maps may also provide procedural information (in the form of scripts) and situational information that affects how communication proceeds between interactants. Similarly, when one is concerned with one's territory, determining that an area is territory partly rests on the ability to recognize familiar environmental and proxemic features. The recognition retrieval process is used to make such discriminations. Finally, unique vocal characteristics may be part of recognition memory. The ability to recognize familiar voices suggests that we have features of that voice stored in memory.

Nonverbal Cues Affecting Storage and Retrieval of Messages   Nonverbal cues are related to memory processing in a second way: some nonverbal cues are decoded and stored as context for other features of communication events, primarily verbal behavior. As stored context, nonverbal cues may be used to recall features of a communication event. Thus nonverbal cues may help one to remember what another person said. Tulving and colleagues (Tulving & Thomson, 1973; Watkins et al., 1976; Watkins & Tulving, 1975) explored how we store and recall information for events. For example, suppose that you and a friend are at a social gathering, discussing the music being played on the stereo. You are unfamiliar with the group's music, and your friend casually mentions the name of the group. Later, you try to recall the name of the band because you want to purchase one of their CDs. How do you recall such information? Tulving's research suggests that the most likely way to recall such incidentally learned information is to try to think of the context in which you encountered the information to be remembered. The contextual cues will aid recall if they were stored in memory at the same time as the target information. In this case, you could try to recall what the party was like, who was there, what your friend was wearing, what else he or she said, or what the music sounded like. Thinking of these contextual nonverbal cues should help you to recall the name of the group.

Several investigations have tested this possibility. One experiment (Woodall & Folger, 1981) determined if different types of hand gestures could act as context for concurrent utterances. Participants saw a series of videotaped segments, each containing a short verbal utterance (e.g., "We just seem to go around and around in circles") and an accompanying gesture. There were two hand gesture conditions: an emphasizing condition, in which an emphasizing gesture accompanied the verbal utterance, and an emblematic condition, in which a gesture that was semantically linked to the utterance was included in the segment (for example, a gesture of drawing circles in the air accompanying the "around in circles" phrase). After viewing the videotaped segments, participants were given a recognition test for the verbal utterances. Contextually cued recall was then tested by playing the videotaped segments back to the participants without the sound.

Results showed that by using hand gestures that accompanied the utterances, participants were able to recall utterances that they were previously unable to recognize. This occurred in both gesture conditions, indicating that nonverbal cues can play a contextual role for accompanying language.

The results also indicated much higher cued recall for emblematic than for emphasizing gestures (see Figure 6-1). Since emblematic cues have more semantic features, they provide a more elaborate and richer context for the verbal utterances. This results in deeper processing of both context and target information, a more elaborate form of storage, and better retrieval after storage. Riseborough (1981) reported somewhat similar results for iconographic and kinetographic gestures and single words. These gestures, which depict shape, size, and movement of objects (and thus have semantic features), showed a facilitating effect on recall of single words when paired with those words.

Two other investigations (Woodall & Folger, 1985) extended these patterns to natural conversations and explored whether nonverbal cues are used over longer periods of time as effective retrieval cues. To simulate conversational conditions, the researchers developed a script for a conversation between two interactants (actually actors) who learned the script and were then videotaped under one of three conditions: (1) a no-gesture condition, in which the actors used no gestures during dialogue; (2) an emphasizing-gesture condition, in which only emphasizing gestures were used during dialogue; and

(a)   (b)

FIGURE 6-1
These gestures might accompany the statement "The discussion kept going around in circles."
The emblematic gesture (a) aids recall of the accompanying phrase more than the emphasizing gesture (b).

(3) an emblematic-gesture condition, in which only emblematic gestures were used during dialogue. After viewing one version of the videotaped conversation, participants saw a series of video-only gesture-utterance segments to help them recall the utterances. Participants recalled 5 percent of the utterances in the no-cues condition, 11 percent in the emphasizing cues condition, and 34 percent in the emblematic cues condition, thus providing support for contextual cuing in more naturalistic social contexts. Similarly, Riseborough (1981) found that iconographic and kinetographic gestures enhanced recall when embedded in a short conversational text.

Woodall and Folger (1985) also examined the durability of these nonverbal behaviors as retrieval cues over a greater period of time. In their study, cued recall tests were given immediately and then repeated a week later. The researchers theorized that, although recall should be less after a week's interval, the differences in recall across the type of cue should persist if these cues still provide access to the concurrent utterances. Their results conformed to these expectations: participants were able to recall 37 percent of the utterances in the emblematic condition after a week, whereas 7 percent of the utterances were recalled in both no-cues and emphasizing-cues conditions after a week's time. This suggests that nonverbal cues with semantic features can act as effective retrieval cues even after some passage of time. Although conversants generally are poor at recalling conversational content (Stafford & Daly, 1984), nonverbal cues may enhance their recall.

Other nonverbal behaviors such as facial and head cues may act as retrieval cues for concurrent language. Although such cues are likely to have fewer semantic features than hand gestures, they may still provide access and retrieval. Vocalic cues also may play a contextual role (Geiselman & Bellezza, 1976, 1977; Geiselman & Crawley, 1983). In one set of studies, Geiselman and colleagues found that subjects could identify which of two speakers had uttered a given sentence from a list of sentences about 70 percent of the time. This occurred even when subjects were not told to remember who said what—that is, they stored and recalled characteristics of the speaker's voice incidentally. The researchers explained these findings by way of a voice connotation hypothesis: a speaker's voice sometimes is remembered because the connotation of the voice influences the perceived meaning of what is said. Box 6-4 offers evidence of how age affects use of vocal cues in message recall.

Nonverbal Cues Affecting Person Memory   A third way in which nonverbal cues may relate to memory is by enhancing *person memory* (see Hastie et al., 1980)—how humans store and retrieve information about others.

In Chapter 9 we examine a wide variety of nonverbal cues that can affect the impressions we form of others. Another way to view impressions is to conceptualize them as person memory. Nonverbal cues often contribute to impressions by being linked to a social stereotype or a set of implicit personality traits (an example would be the color of a person's hair indicating something about his or her personality). Such memories of people are formed during early acquaintanceship stages in relationships when stereotypes are more likely to be employed.

Nonverbal cues may prompt recollection of idiosyncratic and unique qualities of individuals. Trager (1958) suggested that vocal characterizers impart information about the

BOX 6-4

MEMORY, AGING, AND VOCAL CUES

Although we all rely on vocal cues to clarify the meaning of the messages that we receive and process, evidence indicates that older people rely on vocal cues for information processing more than younger people do. A study by Stine and Wingfield compared older adults and college graduates in the ability to recall recorded messages. A variety of messages were used, including actual sentences, strings of nonsense words, sentences read with normal intonation, others without, and sentences read at both normal and speeded up rates.

Differences in recall between elderly and college-age participants occurred when sentences were read without intonation, particularly at high speed. Under these conditions, elderly participants recalled only half the words correctly, while college students made very few mistakes.

The authors explained the findings by suggesting that, with age, people lose mental speed in processing information. In order to compensate, elderly individuals tune into and rely more on vocal intonation, emphasis, and timing in order to clarify what others say to them. Interestingly, as we grow older, vocal cues take on added importance for our understanding of messages.

Source: Adapted from Chollar, 1988, p. 10.

person through vocal properties. Such information, if central to the impression of a particular individual, could be an important part of one's memory of that person. For example, no one who was listening some 50 years ago will ever forget the sound of Edward R. Murrow's voice on the radio as he broadcast from London's rooftops during the blitzkrieg, opening each broadcast with the familiar "This . . . is London." Similarly, small nonverbal mannerisms that were earlier termed adaptive behaviors sometimes become part of person memory for a particular individual. Many people in our culture, instantly recognize a certain adjustment of the tie as belonging to Rodney Dangerfield.

One final point must be emphasized. At the beginning of this chapter, we pointed out that understanding and the other information-processing stages are a fundamental part of a basic aim of communication—to know. But how many times have you left important situations *not knowing*? Whether it was an interaction with a doctor, a lawyer, an educator, or a financial adviser, the consequences of not understanding in these situations were usually negative. This chapter could be relevant to these situations. Application of what is being discovered about information processing and nonverbal behavior could help to achieve knowledge and understanding where little existed before. And that is what communication is about.

SUMMARY

Human information processing can be said to occur in a series of stages that involve both message production and message decoding. Nonverbal cues of various types play roles in all these stages. For message production, several nonverbal cues are associated with complexity and difficulty in message encoding. Nonverbal cues also provide the frame for verbal utterances by supplying vocal cues that define phonemic clauses.

Message decoding also involves a number of information-processing stages. Nonverbal cues have been shown to affect the attention a communicator pays to a message. A rapid tempo, for example, may enhance comprehension by increasing a listener's attentiveness. Other cues may serve as distractors. Understanding of a message likewise can be affected by concomitant nonverbal cues. Nonverbal behaviors that have close ties to the accompanying language, through either semantic links or rhythmic and proximity links, appear to be most efficient in prompting retrieval of event information. When nonverbal cues provide the context for verbal behavior in communication situations, they can aid retrieval of message information at a later point. Nonverbal cues responsible for impression formation may also facilitate person memory.

SUGGESTED READINGS

Anderson, J. R. (1980). *Cognitive psychology and its implications*. New York: Freeman.

Boomer, D. S. (1978). The phonemic clause: Speech unit in human communication. In A. W. Siegman & S. Feldstein (Eds.), *Nonverbal behavior and communication* (pp. 245–262). Hillsdale, NJ: Erlbaum.

Cappella, J. N., & Palmer, M. T. (1990). The structure and organization of verbal and nonverbal behavior: Data for models of production. In H. Giles & W. P. Robinson (Eds.), *Handbook of Language and Social Psychology* (pp. 141–161). Chichester: Wiley.

Craig, R. T. (1978). Cognitive science: A new approach to cognition, language, and communication. *Quarterly Journal of Speech, 64,* 439–467.

Craik, F. I. M., & Lockhart, R. S. (1972). Levels of processing: A framework for memory research. *Journal of Verbal Learning and Verbal Behavior, 11,* 671–684.

Dittmann, A. T. (1978). The role of body movement in communication. In A. W. Siegman & S. Feldstein (Eds.), *Nonverbal behavior and communication* (pp. 69–95). Hillsdale, NJ: Erlbaum.

Folger, J. P., & Woodall, W. G. (1982). Nonverbal cues as linguistic context: An information processing view. In M. Burgoon (Ed.), *Communication Yearbook 6* (pp. 63–91). Beverly Hills, CA: Sage.

Hastie, R., Ostrom, T. R., Ebbesen, E. B., Wyer, R. S., Hamilton, D. L., & Carlston, D. E. (1980). *Person memory: The cognitive basis of social perception*. Hillsdale, NJ: Erlbaum.

Hewes, D. E., & Planalp, S. (1982). "There is nothing as useful as a good theory . . ." The influence of social knowledge on interpersonal communication. In C. Berger & M. Roloff (Eds.), *Social cognition and communication* (pp. 107–150). Beverly Hills, CA: Sage.

Kendon, A. (1983). Gesture and speech: How they interact. In J. M. Wiemann & R. P. Harrison (Eds.), *Nonverbal interaction* (pp. 13–45). Beverly Hills, CA: Sage.

Woodall, W. G., & Folger, J. P. (1985). Nonverbal cue context and episodic memory: On the availability and endurance of nonverbal behaviors as retrieval cues. *Communication Monographs, 52,* 319–333.

7

STRUCTURING
INTERACTIONS

Often, it is not so much the kind of person a man is as the kind of situation in which he finds himself [that] determines how he will act.

Stanley Milgram

It is by the reading of these less perceptible signs that one person is able to respond to the sentiment of another. In a face-to-face group changes in facial expression, slight gestures, and the like, although largely in the field of unverbalized reactions, enable an individual to sense a situation instantly. Thus, they define the situation and promote rapport.

F. M. Thrasher

A significant self-revelation for many people is that we behave differently in different situations. Depending on the situation in which we find ourselves, we may adjust how, with whom, and what we communicate. Many of these adjustments are due to the influences of nonverbal cues that structure our behavior. This chapter is devoted to exploring some of the ways in which nonverbal cues frame and control our interactions with others.

NONVERBAL CUES AND THE STRUCTURING OF INTERACTIONS

In many situations, we merely respond to contingencies that are presented to us. We enter a doctor's office and passively accept the solitary wait, the uncomfortable seating on an examining table, the impersonal probing of our body by the physician. In other situations, however, we create and manage various aspects of the social context to achieve our own goals. When we invite guests for dinner, we may make decisions about such nonverbal features as what time our guests should arrive, where they should congregate before the meal, whether the meal is to be formal or informal, what seating arrangement at the dinner table will enhance conversation, and what attire guests should be told is appropriate. These decisions are not trivial, for they can affect how enjoyable the evening turns out to be. Failure to provide sufficient structure may result in immense discomfort for the friend who arrives promptly, dressed in suit and tie for a formal dinner party, only to find the other guests arriving an hour later, dressed in jeans for a casual outdoor barbecue.

The nonverbal features we discuss in this chapter are largely cues that elicit behavior without people's being consciously aware of their influence. That is, people respond to them in relatively passive, unconscious ways. Although most of these nonverbal features can also be used deliberately to structure a situation to accomplish some instrumental goal, we will focus more extensively on their strategic use in Chapter 14. For the moment, our interest lies primarily in the elusive yet obvious background elements of which we are at once consciously unaware and yet unconsciously, profoundly aware. Such features, like a puppet's strings, appear to control our actions invisibly but are readily detectable if we choose to look closely.

Nonverbal code elements function to structure our behavior in at least three ways. First, some nonverbal elements *control the occurrence of interaction.* They affect with whom we interact, when, and how often. They can control whether interaction even takes place.

Second, nonverbal cues *set expectations* for situations yet to be encountered. They often "telegraph" upcoming interactions by suggesting what a given situation will be like. Environmental designs, for example, evolve out of a culture's customs and expectations and therefore evoke anticipations of what behaviors will be exhibited in a previously unencountered setting. Our ability to prepare for new interactions and situations is strongly based on nonverbal codes.

Third, nonverbal elements *set the stage* for current interactions. As an episode unfolds, nonverbal elements embedded in the situation provide elaboration of its definition. They may prompt certain kinds of behavior, identify or clarify role relationships among interactants, and imply rules for behavior (Goffman, 1967, 1974; Scheflen, 1974). In so doing, the totality of situational features, including the nonverbal cues that are present, create a *frame of reference* or lens through which to see and understand a situation and provide structure for the interaction that occurs. Moreover, once people arrive at an understanding of a situation, they typically conform in a habitual and relatively mindless fashion to the behavioral routines associated with it. This further reinforces the prevailing definition of the situation.

Erickson and Shultz (1982) referred to this process of cuing the appropriate behavioral programs as *telling the context:*

> People of varying ages and cultural backgrounds all seem to be actively engaged while they interact, in telling one another what is happening as it is happening. . . . The particular ways this telling is done—what signals are used and how the signals are employed and interpreted by the interactional partners—may vary developmentally across the life cycle and may also vary from one culture to another. But some ways of telling the context seem to be present in all instances of face-to-face interaction among humans. People seem

to use these ways to keep one another on the track, to maintain in the conduct of interaction what musicians call "ensemble" in the playing of music. (p. 71)

NONVERBAL SIGNALS AS PRECURSORS TO INTERACTION

One of the chief ways that nonverbal behaviors structure interaction is to determine if interaction will occur at all. Three nonverbal signals are posited to be especially influential in determining if and how much people will interact: propinquity, gaze, and physical attractiveness.

Propinquity

One of the intriguing discoveries of social scientists is just how much pressure propinquity, or geographic proximity, exerts on people to interact (see Box 7-1). Propinquity controls the opportunities for interaction. Mehrabian and Diamond (1971) noted that environments can facilitate communication by providing an excuse for people in relatively close proximity to engage in similar activities. Moreover, proximity encourages

---

BOX 7-1

APPLICATIONS: BUILDING RAPPORT THROUGH PROPINQUITY

Several studies in the 1950s and 1960s (e.g., Blake, Rhead, Wedge, & Mouton, 1956; Byrne, 1961; Deutsch & Collins, 1951; Festinger, Schachter, & Back, 1950; Maisonneuve, Palmade, & Fourment, 1952; Mann, 1959; Priest & Sawyer, 1967) revealed that people in residences or classrooms are much more likely to interact and develop friendships with those who are physically closest to them. In a housing project, for example, those whose houses are closest together or who see each other frequently while checking mailboxes or sitting in the yard are more likely to develop friendships. In an apartment building, those who live adjacent to one another, reside on the same hall, or share the same elevator or stairwell are far more likely to become acquainted than those who live on different floors. The likelihood of interacting is directly proportional to the physical and psychological distance between dwellings. Early on, it was even observed that a disproportionate number of marriages occurred among people who lived within 20 blocks of each other (Kennedy, 1943).

A study of Maryland police trainees (cited in Wegner & Vallacher, 1977) confirmed that propinquity fosters interaction and friendship. The trainees were assigned classroom seats and living quarters alphabetically, so that those whose names were closest together in the alphabet sat and lived together. After 6 weeks of training, "the Andersons and Bakers preferred each other to the Youngs and Zimmermans" (p. 201). A similar study of naval apprentice trainees showed that those whose bunks were closest talked to each other the most (Sykes, 1983), leading to the conjecture that proximity leads to talk which leads to attraction.

Mann (1959) attempted to determine if increased contact between people could decrease racial prejudice. Black and white students were placed in leaderless groups (which gave everyone equal status) and interacted with one another for a 3-week period. Afterward, students were asked to rank who they would like to have as continuing friends. Their sociometric choices indicated that interracial exposure reduced their tendency to use race as a criterion for choosing friends. In other words, the sheer force of physical proximity and the interaction it fostered broke down some racial prejudices. This has obvious implications for avoiding segregated schools and neighborhoods. Such findings have caused scientists (e.g., Deutsch & Collins, 1951; Festinger, 1951) to encourage architects and planners to take greater account of propinquity when planning and anticipating the social consequences of various housing developments and residential designs.

interaction. You may have noticed your own urge to exchange pleasantries with someone who shares a bus seat or sauna with you. Goffman (1963) reported that when workers in businesses and medical offices are seated within 12 feet of each other, they seek interaction. The happenstance of propinquity often leads to communication.

One reason that proximity promotes interaction is that it connotes belonging: "Our expectancies about proximity—called *spatial schemata*—are closely related to our belonging schemas" (Wegner & Vallacher, 1977, p. 191). We use spatial relationships to infer with whom we are affiliated and to signal to others our expectancies of belonging. The result is that we tend to feel we belong with those close to us and use communication to express that bond.

Of course, the probability of interacting with others need not be a chance occurrence. By intentionally increasing or decreasing physical distance, people can control their own or others' interaction availability. The use of such privacy-gaining mechanisms as fences, walls, and hedges can override the power of propinquity. Conversely, the absence of territorial markers or an open-door policy in an office may promote the kinds of accidental contacts that open communication channels. Men and women who are successful at picking someone up in a singles bar rely in part on their quarry feeling the obligation to speak to them when at close ranges. In these ways, it is possible to structure the communication situation actively rather than passively react to it.

Gaze

In most unfocused social situations, where there is no intention of carrying on a conversation, the rule is to engage in *civil inattention*. It is impolite to stare at strangers in a restaurant or a department store. Although it is often unavoidable to look briefly at a passerby on the street, this usually occurs while at a distance and is followed by "casting the eyes down as the other passes—a kind of dimming of lights" (Goffman, 1963, p. 84). The mere act of making eye contact, then, serves as an invitation to interact.

Its potency in establishing a social bond is evident in the words of the famous sociologist Georg Simmel, who wrote in his *Soziologie* about the union that is brought about by mutual gaze (cited in Parks & Burgess, 1924):

> Of the special sense-organs, the eye has a uniquely sociological function. The union and interaction of individuals is based on mutual glances. This is perhaps the most direct and purest reciprocity that exists anywhere. . . . The totality of social relations of human beings, their self-assertion and self-abnegation, their intimacies and estrangements, would be changed in unpredictable ways if there occurred no glance of eye to eye. This mutual glance between persons, in distinction from the simple sight or observation of the other, signified a wholly new and unique union between them. (p. 358)

Physical Attractiveness

We have noted that beauty may be only skin-deep, but the attractiveness of the veneer often determines whom we choose to approach or avoid. The fact that attractive people are often viewed as more curious, complex, outspoken, assertive, flexible, candid, amiable, happy, active, confident, and perceptive than unattractive people (Miller, 1970) suggests we may be more willing to interact with attractive strangers because we attribute appealing characteristics to them.

More direct evidence comes from the computer-dating studies cited in Chapter 2 and a similar "Coke date" study (Byrne, Ervin, & Lamberth, 1970). Experimenters paired subjects with members of the opposite sex and asked them to spend 30 minutes getting acquainted over a Coke at the student union. Afterward, students evaluated their dates. Results showed that students were much more attracted to their date if the date was physically attractive (both as rated by the partner and by the experimenters). A follow-up study at the end of the semester also revealed that students were more inclined to see their Coke date partner again if the date was handsome or pretty. Thus physical attractiveness may affect not only with whom we interact but also the likelihood and amount of subsequent contact.

The importance of physical attractiveness in approach or avoidance decisions is strongly linked to sexual attraction and the mating process. It is natural for men and women to size up potential partners on physical appeal. It may be, however, that the sizing-up process works overtime, extending to social interactions that do not have sexual undercurrents. It would be interesting to study whether physical attractiveness governs same-sex interactions to the same extent that it does opposite-sex relations.

NONVERBAL INDICATORS OF INTERACTIONAL SITUATIONS

Because the situation is such an important feature of social behavior, situational concepts have been given prominence in a wide variety of communication and social behavior theories. Kurt Lewin, the founder of what we now know as social psychology, laid the basis for much research in social science by proposing the well-known equation $B = f(P,S)$. This asserts that behavior (B) is a function (f) of two main factors, the person (P) and the situation (S) (Lewin, 1935). Subsequent theories as diverse as attribution theory (see Jones & Nisbett, 1972), various personality theories (see Mischel, 1968, 1979), and cognitive schema theories (see Schank & Abelson, 1977) have given situational factors a significant role. Communication researchers have turned their attention toward an analysis of situations as an important part of understanding interpersonal communication (see Cody & McLaughlin, 1985). The impact of the situational definition on how people communicate and behave cannot be overstated.

The Nature of Situations

Distinguishing Situations, Settings, and Episodes   The term *situation* probably has some intuitive meaning for you, but what does it really mean? Not surprisingly, it has a number of interpretations. Magnusson (1978) found in reviewing the literature on situations that definitions could range from the microscopic (including specific stimuli or small sequences of events known as episodes) to the macroscopic (including both physical settings not tied to any particular occasion and environments, which include social as well as physical factors).

Most scholars, however, see situations as some intermediate combination of physical, temporal, and psychological frames of reference tied to particular occasions. Furnham and Argyle (1981) offered a relatively concrete definition that captures most of what we consider relevant. A situation is made up of the following components:

1 *Elements of behavior.* These are the specific verbal utterances and nonverbal behaviors accompanying the situation.
2 *Goals or motivations of the participants.* For example, is this a learning, selling, or socializing situation?
3 *Rules of behavior.* The rules for carrying on a dinner party differ from those for a classroom lecture.
4 *Roles different people must play.* A committee chair plays a different role and follows different rules from those of the secretary.
5 *Physical setting and equipment.* A classroom, with its chalkboard or overhead projector and straight-row seating, creates a different situation from a living room with overstuffed chairs and a coffee table.
6 *Cognitive concepts.* Dominance may be a salient consideration in some situations, supportiveness in others.
7 *Relevant social skills.* A decision-making context implies that certain skills will be needed to achieve the goal.

Situation, then, refers to an overall gestalt that is the sum of all these factors.

From this perspective, a *setting* is one defining feature of a situation. As we will see, many nonverbal environmental features are useful in symbolizing this aspect of a situation. An *episode,* by contrast, is any sequence of events that "has some principle of unity" (Harré & Secord, 1972, p. 154). An interview can be divided into four episodes: an opening, a period during which the interviewer asks questions, a time when the candidate asks questions, and a closing. A situation can often be defined by the nonverbal episodes within it or elicited by it. The style of an episode—an effusive, intimate greeting versus a polite handshake—may distinguish one type of situation from another.

The various features that differentiate settings and episodes, distinguish skillful performances, and are associated with adherence to rules and roles and violations of rules and roles are often nonverbal. Hence nonverbal cues are prominent in defining situations and in structuring interpersonal interactions. Typically, these nonverbal elements work together to create an overall gestalt. That is, we respond to the totality of the cue pattern rather than to individual cues. Because so much redundancy is built in across codes, we are able, instantly and effortlessly, to determine the kind of situation that is presenting itself and our corresponding behavioral obligations. An example of a gestalt perspective on situations is Simonds' sample environmental designs (1961), which, through a combination of volume of space, linear perspective, materials, artifacts, lighting, color, and sound, create radically different moods and types of interaction (see Figure 7-1).

It is possible that our recognition ability is also aided by reducing judgments of situations to a few categories or continua that underlie our cognitive perceptions of them.

Situational Dimensions   Interactants tend to perceive social situations along some stable *dimensions.* Such dimensions help distinguish, for instance, a business negotiation from a matrimonial proposal.

Researchers have proposed various sets of dimensions that can be used to represent

Fright

Gaiety

Free spaces. Smooth, flowing forms and patterns. Looping, tumbling, swirling motion accommodated. Movement and rhythm expressed in structure. Lack of restrictions. Forms, colors, and symbols that appeal to the emotions rather than the intellect. Temporal. Casual. Lack of restraint. Pretense is acceptable. The fanciful is applauded. Often the light, bright, and spontaneous in contrast to the ponderous, dark, and timeless. Warm, bright colors. Wafting, sparkling, shimmering, shooting, or glowing light. Exuberant or lilting sound.

Sensed confinement. A quality of compression and bearing. An apparent trap. No points of orientation. No means by which to judge position or scale. Hidden areas and spaces. Possibilities for surprise. Sloping, twisted, or broken planes. Illogical, unstable forms. Slippery, hazardous base plane. Danger. Unprotected voids. Sharp, intruding elements. Contorted spaces. The unfamiliar. The shocking. The startling. The wierd. The uncanny. Symbols connoting horror, pain, torture, or applied force. The dim, the dark, the eerie. Pale and quavering or, conversely, blinding garish light. Cold blues, cold greens. Abnormal monochromatic color.

Sublime spiritual awe

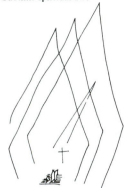

Overwhelming scale that transcends normal human experience and submerges one in a vast well of space. Soaring forms in contrast with low horizontal forms. A volume so contrived as to hold man transfixed on a broad base plane and lift his eye and mind high along the vertical. Orientation upward to or beyond some symbol of the infinite. Complete compositional order—often symmetry. Highly developed sequences. Use of costly and permanent materials. Connotation of the eternal. Use of chaste white. If color is used, the cool detached colors, such as blue-greens, greens, and violet. Diffused glow with shafts of light. Deep, full, swelling music with lofting passages.

Pleasure*

Spaces, forms, textures, colors, symbols, sounds, light quality, and odors all manifestly suitable to the use of the space—whatever it may be. Satisfaction of anticipations, requirements, or desires. Sequences developed and fulfilled. Harmonious relationships. Unity with variety. A resultant quality of beauty.

Displeasure*

Frustrating sequences of possible movement or revelation. Areas and spaces unsuitable to anticipated use. Obstacles. Excesses. Undue friction. Discomfort. Annoying textures. Improper use of materials. The illogical. The false. The insecure. The tedious. The blatant. The dull. The disorderly. Clashing colors. Discordant sounds. Disagreeable temperature or humidity. Unpleasant light quality. That which is ugly.

* It is to be noted that "displeasure" and "pleasure" are general categories, whereas "tension," "relaxation," "fright," and the others mentioned are more specific. With these more specific responses, we can list in more specific detail the characteristics of the volumes designed to induce them. The degree of "pleasure" or its opposite, "displeasure," would seem to depend on the degree of sensed fitness of the volume for its use, and a unified and harmonious development of the plan elements to serve this function. It can be seen that one could therefore experience pleasure and fright simultaneously (as in a fun house) or pleasure and sublime spiritual awe simultaneously (as in a cathedral), and so forth.

FIGURE 7-1
Sampling of environmental features that can create various moods.

Tension

Unstable forms. Split composition. Illogical complexities. Wide range of values. Clash of colors. Intense colors without relief. Visual imbalance about a line or point. No point at which the eye can rest. Hard, rough or jagged surfaces. Unfamiliar elements. Harsh, blinding, or quavering light. Uncomfortable temperatures in any range. Piercing, jangling, jittery sound.

Relaxation

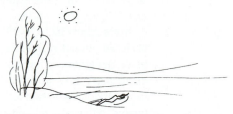

Simplicity. Volume may vary in size from the intimate to the infinite. Fitness. Familiar objects and materials. Flowing lines. Curvilinear forms and spaces. Evident structural stability. Horizontality. Agreeable textures. Pleasant and comfortable shapes. Soft light. Soothing sound. Volume infused with quiet colors—whites, greys, blues, greens. *"Think round thoughts."*

Dynamic action

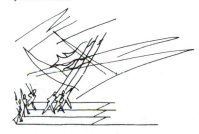

Bold forms. Heavy structural cadence. Angular planes. Diagonals. Solid materials as stone, concrete, wood, or steel. Rough natural textures. The pitched vertical. Directional compositional focus. Concentration of interest on focal point of action—as to rostrum, rallying point, or exit gate through which the entire volume impels one. Motion induced by sweeping lines, shooting lights, and by climactic sequences of form, pattern, and sound. Strong primitive colors— crimson, scarlet, and yellow-orange. Waving flags. Burnished standards. Martial music. Rush of sound. Ringing crescendos. Crash of brass. Roll and boom of drums.

Contemplation

Scale is not important since the subject will withdraw into his own sensed well of consciousness. The total space may be mild and unpretentious or immense and richly ornate— so long as the structural forms are not insistent. No insinuating elements. No distractions of sharp contrast. Symbols, if used, must relate to subject of contemplation. Space must provide a sense of isolation, privacy, detachment, security, and peace. Soft, diffused light. Tranquil and recessive colors. If sound, a low muted stream of sound to be perceived subconsciously.

Sensuous love

Complete privacy. Inward orientation of room. Subject the focal point. Intimate scale. Low ceiling. Horizontal planes. Fluid lines. Soft, rounded forms. Juxtaposition of angles and curves. Delicate fabrics. Voluptuous and yielding surfaces. Exotic elements and scent. Soft rosy pink to golden light. Pulsating, titillating music.

and understand a situation. Forgas (1976) found that homemakers judge social episodes according to the dimensions of *perceived intimacy* (is the situation intimate or nonintimate?) and *self-confidence* (would they feel self-assured or not in that situation?).

Mehrabian (1972, 1976) advocated three very general dimensions that represent the basic emotional responses to environmental stimuli. (They also parallel Mehrabian's three metaphors of human interaction as discussed in Chapter 11.) These are *pleasure-displeasure, dominance-submissiveness,* and *arousal-nonarousal.* Relationships, situations, and environments can all be judged according to how much they make us feel happy, satisfied, and contented or annoyed, melancholic, and distressed (the pleasure dimension); the extent to which they make us feel dominant, important, and in control or restricted, weak, and impotent (the dominance dimension); and the degree to which they make us feel active, stimulated, alert, and responsive to external stimuli or unaroused, relaxed, sluggish, or inattentive (the arousal dimension).

Environments and situations can also be scaled along a general *sociofugal-sociopetal* continuum (Osmond, 1957). Sociofugal environments thrust people apart, whereas sociopetal ones bring them together and encourage interaction. We prefer to cast this dimension in terms of *publicness-privacy,* which is much broader and entails more than whether or not the environment encourages people to interact.

Studies of dyadic and group interaction (Wish, 1979; Wish, Deutsch, & Kaplan, 1976) have discovered four or five dimensions underlying people's perceptions of interpersonal relations that can also describe situations: *friendly-cooperative versus competitive-hostile, dominant versus equal, intense versus superficial, socioemotional versus task-oriented,* and *impersonal-formal versus personal-informal.* A birthday party is an example of a friendly, equal, socioemotional, informal, and somewhat intense occasion. Interestingly, Wish (1979) also found that these dimensional perceptions differed by communication channel. Verbal and nonverbal audio information contributed most to perceptions of cooperativeness, task orientation, and formality. The visual channel, by contrast, contributed most to perceptions of intensity and dominance. These results reveal that certain nonverbal channels and cues may be more important to some situational dimensions than to others.

Though not an exhaustive list, these dimensions provide a starting point for analyzing how nonverbal features structure interaction. Moreover, it appears that situational dimensions remain stable and consistent over time (Magnusson, 1971), which permits us to draw some valid cross-situational generalizations. We turn now to specific nonverbal cues and patterns that are associated with some of the most important dimensions.

Cuing the Private-Public Dimension

The alternative to privacy is the ant heap.

P. Kelvin, 1973, p. 260

One of the first features of a situation we are likely to apprehend is the degree to which it is public or private. Public situations invoke entirely different roles, rules, and behavioral repertoires than do private ones.

The Concept of Privacy   *Privacy* is a complex concept. Consider just a few possible definitions:

1 Ability to exert control over self, objects, spaces, information, and behavior and to deny access to others (Warren & Laslett, 1977; Wolfe & Laufer, 1974).
2 Being protected from unwanted access from others, including physical access, personal information, or attention (Bok, 1982).
3 An interpersonal boundary process whereby a person or group regulates interaction with others (Altman, 1975; Derlega & Chaikin, 1977).
4 Freedom of choice in a particular situation to control what, how, and to whom the person communicates information about the self (Proshansky et al., 1970).
5 Individual independence and reduced vulnerability to the power and influence of others (Kelvin, 1973).

These definitions reveal that privacy may pertain to an individual, dyad, or group; that it can be defined according to what is desired or what is actually achieved; and that it implies some degree of freedom and control.

Embedded in the various conceptualizations of privacy are four major types or *dimensions of privacy:* physical, social, psychological, and informational (Burgoon, 1982). *Physical privacy* refers to the degree to which an individual, dyad, or group is physically inaccessible to others. It involves freedom from intrusion on one's "body buffer zone," from the discomfort of overcrowding, from surveillance, and from excessive sensory stimulation. The number of nonverbal sensory channels through which people are accessible or inaccessible to others (sight, sound, touch, smell) provides one barometer of the degree of physical privacy that a situation affords (Kira, 1966). The more channels through which one is accessible to others, presumably the less privacy.

Social privacy refers to the ability to control the degree of social contacts at the individual, dyadic, or group level. It includes the capacity to control the who, when, and where of communication. A fundamental facet of privacy is the ability to withdraw from social intercourse and to limit approaches from others to a manageable number. This is necessary so that gratifications from such relationships can be maximized and annoyances and conflicts minimized (Calhoun, 1970; Desor, 1972; Milgram, 1970). When the number of social contacts becomes excessive, the amount of stimulation "overloads" the system, creating stress and a desire to withdraw. At the dyadic or small-group level, social privacy becomes a means for facilitating intimacy within the relationship while inhibiting social overtures from others. A dating couple, for example, may engage in courtship behaviors that are designed to foster togetherness while simultaneously alerting others that their company is unwelcome. Such behaviors accomplish social privacy.

Psychological privacy refers to an individual's ability to control affective and cognitive inputs and outputs. On the input side, psychological privacy means a person is free to think, formulate attitudes, hold beliefs and values, develop an individual identity, engage in emotional catharsis, assimilate new experiences, and make plans without interference, undue influence, criticism, or distraction from others. On the output side, it means determining with whom and under what circumstances one will share thoughts and feelings, disclose intimate or secret information about oneself, offer emotional support, and seek advice (Burgoon, 1982; Goffman, 1959; Kira, 1970; Westin, 1967). The concept and its importance were well put by Simmel (1950):

> Just as material property is, so to speak, an extention of the ego, and any interference with our property is, for this reason, felt to be a violation of the person, there is also an intellectual private property whose violation effects a lesion of the ego in its very center. (p. 322)

Finally, *informational privacy* refers to the right to determine how, when, and to what extent personal data are released to others (Carroll, 1975). It is grounded in legalistic concerns such as protections over the gathering, computerization, and dissemination of information about private citizens. Because demographic, financial, legal, military, consumer, lifestyle, and even personality data about individuals or groups can be compiled and shared without their knowledge or permission, informational privacy differs from psychological privacy in that it is less under personal control.

These four dimensions of privacy represent four continua, from private to public, along which any situation can be evaluated. The nonverbal features responsible for signaling the degree of privacy desired or present in a situation can be divided into five categories: (1) environmental and artifactual, (2) spatial and haptic, (3) temporal, (4) kinesic and vocalic, and (5) physical appearance. It should be recognized that verbal behaviors may also play a significant role in establishing or restoring privacy. (For a discussion of these, see Burgoon, 1982.)

Environment and Artifacts   Included in environment and artifacts are the features of fixed- and semifixed-feature space, plus specific artifacts, that define a setting as public or private.

Architectural design fosters physical privacy by creating barriers (walls, fences, partitions, gated parking lots) and insulation that protect the individual from visual, auditory, olfactory, and bodily intrusions (Altman, 1975; Derlega & Chaikin, 1977; Marshall, 1972; Sommer, 1974b). Through the imposition of distance and gatekeepers, architectural design can also make access to the occupants of a locale difficult. Corporate executives often have offices in largely impenetrable spaces. They may be buffered by several stories, winding corridors, private elevators, multiple secretarial offices or desks, and personal receptionists that separate them from the public and subordinates. (See Box 7-2 for some interesting findings.)

Doors are a particularly significant barrier in our everyday experience. Schwartz (1968) referred to doors as "a human event of significance equal to the discovery of fire" because they can be used deliberately and selectively to regulate physical and social intrusion and because they contribute to psychological self-definition:

> Doors provide boundaries between ourselves (i.e., property, behavior, and appearance) and others. Violations of such boundaries imply a violation of selfhood. Trespassing or housebreaking, for example, is unbearable for some not only because of the property damage that might result but also because they represent proof that the self has lost control of its audience. (p. 747)

The importance of doors for privacy is evident in a study of first-year college students, 92 percent of whom reported they shut their door as a way of reducing contact with others (Vinsel et al., 1980). It is further evidenced by a remark from one of Hall's informants (1966): "If there hadn't been doors, I would always have been in reach of my mother" (p. 127).

BOX 7-2

APPLICATIONS: NO TRESPASSING! ACHIEVING SECURITY THROUGH ARTIFACTS AND ENVIRONMENTAL DESIGN

Defining a territory with markers elicits behaviors from others that are more respectful and deferential toward the owner or occupant. In turn, identifiable territories provide a sense of personal security, comfort, and permanence. Patterson (1978) found that when elderly people use such territorial markers as No Trespassing signs, welcome mats, and electronic surveillance devices, they have less fear of assault and property loss. Conversely, students who use fewer decorations such as posters, pictures, and mementos to personalize a dorm room are less likely to remain in school (Vinsel et al., 1980). This suggests that territorial markers are indicative of one's sense of belonging to and security in an environment.

On a broader scale, Newman (1972) identified general environmental design features that increase the security of high-density living spaces such as low-income apartment buildings in urban areas. In an extensive study of low-income public housing in New York City and other major urban areas, Newman labeled four environmental design features that reduce vandalism and crime and increase the occupants' sense of security, well-being, and control over their environment:

1 Providing a territorial definition of space that reflects the areas of influence of the inhabitants. This is done by dividing the areas surrounding the building into small zones that encourage residents to adopt proprietary attitudes.
2 Positioning apartment windows so that residents can survey the exterior and interior of public areas of their living environment.
3 Using building forms that do not prompt perceptions of vulnerability and isolation of the inhabitants, achieved primarily through use of low-rise and medium-density buildings.
4 Enhancing safety by locating residential developments in areas that are not adjacent to activities that provide continued sources of threat.

In comparing developments that have employed these design considerations to those that have not, Newman (1972) found that "poorly designed buildings and projects have crime rates as much as three times higher than those of adjacent projects housing socially identical residents at similar densities" (p. 7).

Architecture and artifacts may symbolically designate a setting as private by creating a "forbidding" appearance. People are more inclined to behave formally and with restraint when surrounded by expensive interior decor. By invoking status and power connotations, massive exteriors, expansive properties, and exclusive locations tend to deter approach from all but vandals, thereby defining a locale as socially and physically private. Or, as Newman suggested, architectural features that prompt surveillance and proprietary attitudes may catalyze residents to be more self-reliant and responsible for their own space, thus cutting down on crime and vandalism. It is not by accident, then, that most property crimes and muggings occur in squalid, rundown neighborhoods where inhabitants are socially isolated by building design and there are no physical symbols to inhibit approach and intrusion. These problems are much less likely to occur in exclusive, well-protected areas or neighborhoods where a sense of community and social contact is encouraged by residential design. Ironically, the massiveness of many public buildings such as libraries and government offices may also discourage people from entering them because people view the structures as either semiprivate settings reserved for an elite group of users or as so large and impersonal as to be overwhelming.

Architectural design also signals implicitly whether spaces are private or semipublic by the number of enclosures and the degree of functional differentiation associated with them. The design of most American homes, for example, creates separate spaces for sleeping, bathing, elimination and personal hygiene, cooking, and so forth. The more spatial divisions in a setting and the smaller the volume of space in each, the greater the sense of physical and psychological privacy and social intimacy (Kira, 1966, 1970; Marshall, 1972; Simonds, 1961). Large, open spaces create a feeling of vulnerability and

Compare these two environments. What kind of privacy messages do you get from each? What nonverbal cues are responsible for these messages?

tend to define a situation as more public. Greater differentiation of the functions of each space also results in some spaces such as bedrooms and bathrooms being defined as highly private, intimate locales (Edney, 1976; Goffman, 1963).

Furnishings and artifacts supplement fixed architectural features by providing additional barriers and insulation in such forms as drapes, blinds, lamps, room dividers, bookshelves, and white noise from air conditioners or radios. These can carve settings into smaller spaces, block visual and auditory access, and cushion noise. Filing cabinets in small offices and book stacks in libraries serve such purposes (Sommer, 1970; Stea, 1970).

Architectural features and personal artifacts together may demarcate a particular place as someone's territory. Numerous scholars (Altman & Chemers, 1980; Edney, 1976; Edney & Buda, 1976; Goffman, 1961a; Stea, 1970) have noted the value of territories in ensuring physical protection, regulating social interaction, creating a sense of personal identity, and promoting group identity and bonding:

> Among many animal species there is broad recognition of a territory holder's "rights"— his claim to privacy and relative immunity to arbitrary challenge and interruption when he is on home ground. The complementary restrictions on a visitor on another organism's territory—his circumspection, inhibition, and restraint—seem to be tacit recognition of those rights. . . . The geographic separation of individuals into personal territories gives those individuals physical distinctiveness, but the effects of this spatial distinctiveness also appear on a psychological level. . . . [Territory] is also likely to facilitate social bonding through a cognitive sense of similarity, and it may also help to preserve bonds because a person has to lose his territorial identity if he leaves the group. (Edney, 1976, pp. 37–40)

Arrangements of furniture and artifacts may also create sociofugal or sociopetal environments (Osmond, 1957). Institutional arrangements of benches along a wall, church pews, and rows of rigid, connected seats in airports inhibit interaction, while small conversational groupings of chairs facing each other in a home or hotel lobby encourage it. The arrangement therefore signals whether social encounters are permissible and expected (see Figure 7-2).

Proxemics and Haptics   How people space themselves in an environment and the degree to which touch occurs can likewise be interpreted as defining a situation as private or public. Recall that Hall's distance categories (1974) range from intimate (0 to 18 inches) to public (12 feet and beyond). Intimate distances tend to correspond to situations that are regarded as private. As conversational distance increases, so does the perception of the situation as more public. By the same token, frequent touch and touch to more intimate body regions are more likely to occur in private contexts and therefore define those situations as private (Evans & Howard, 1973; Jourard & Friedman, 1970; Rosenfeld, Kartus, & Ray, 1976). For instance, we are often surprised and offended by a couple's prolonged fondling and kissing in public precisely because such behavior seems out of place in nonprivate settings.

A number of other proxemic behaviors may color a situation as one of physical, social, or psychological privacy. In libraries and other public settings, people desiring privacy select seating positions at tables that are farther from others, permit greater surveillance of the entrances, and reduce their own vulnerability to surveillance (Sommer, 1970). When we enter a library or museum, we recognize the relatively private quality of what is otherwise a public setting and respond with appropriately quiet, unobtrusive, and nonintrusive behavior. Indirect body orientation and extreme sideways or backward

FIGURE 7-2
Which arrangements are sociofugal? Which are sociopetal?

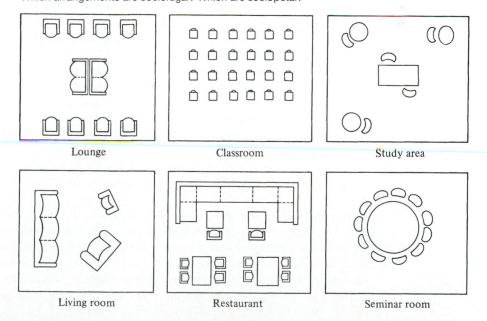

leaning connote the desire for individual privacy, whereas direct body orientation, moderate degrees of leaning and reclining, and side-by-side or adjacent seating connote a situation of dyadic intimacy and privacy (Bond & Shiraishi, 1974; Cooper & Bowles, 1973; Morris, 1971).

Proxemic and haptic codes also signal privacy loss. When people feel threatened physically or psychologically or when the amount of social involvement is excessive, they may attempt to compensate by increasing the behaviors just cited—greater distance, indirect orientation, leaning away, and gaze aversion (which increases psychological distance)—and may erect body and artifact barriers (Argyle & Dean, 1965; Baum & Greenberg, 1975; Felipe & Sommer, 1966; Hayduk, 1978; Knowles, 1972; Patterson, 1973a; Patterson et al., 1971; Patterson & Sechrest, 1970; Stokols, 1976; Sundstrom & Sundstrom, 1977). In short, they respond with displays of nonimmediacy. If these fail, they may resort to flight or, rarely, fight (Baum et al., 1974; Elman, Schulte, & Bukoff, 1977; Felipe & Sommer, 1966; Ginsburg, Pollman, Wauson, & Hope, 1977; Hayduk, 1978; Konečni et al., 1975; Loo & Smetana, 1978; Matthews, Paulus, & Baron, 1979; Smith & Knowles, 1979; Stokols, 1976; Sundstrom & Sundstrom, 1977).

The expression of privacy through proxemic and haptic behavior extends to other behavior patterns and individual differences as well. Table 8-3 (p. 246) summarizes research from several sources (cf. J. F. Andersen et al., 1987; P. A. Andersen & Liebowitz, 1978; P. A. Anderson & Sull; Guerrero & Anderson, 1991; Landis, 1970; Scott, 1988) that provides a link between individuals with open and flexible personal space boundaries and high touch comfort, and those with closed and rigid personal space boundaries and high touch avoidance. As you can see from the table, those with open boundaries and high touch comfort have personality characteristics that are in the socially affinitive direction and behavior that is generally expressive. Those with closed boundaries and high touch avoidance have personality characteristics that are more reserved and cautious, and behavior that is reticent, wary, and somewhat withdrawn. Clearly, these characteristics and behaviors would lead one to view a person as either a more "private" or "public" individual.

Finally, people may use a proxemic shift (Erickson, 1975) to signal their desire to end an episode within an encounter. If, for example, people find a discussion becoming embarrassing or too invasive of their psychological and informational privacy, they may use the proxemic adjustment as a cue that they are ready to change the subject.

In sum, the dynamic proxemic and touch behaviors participants use cue each other and onlookers as to whether they view the situation as private or public and whether they wish to alter that definition. The use of these and artifactual elements as privacy statements is nowhere more evident than in prison, as Box 7-3 shows.

Chronemics   Use of time is another way of defining the degree of privacy of a situation. Time can be manipulated to regulate privacy in at least three ways. One is to segregate use of a particular setting by time. In the animal kingdom, different species may have territories that overlap but use the commonly held space at different times (Leyhausen, 1971). With humans, this may take the form of maximizing privacy in an otherwise heavily trafficked area by using it at times when one expects other people to be

---

BOX 7-3

PRISON CODES

Within the prison setting, where verbal communication is tightly controlled, an awareness and sensitivity to all types of nonverbal messages is vital to successful functioning. . . .

One may communicate invasion of privacy and rudeness by looking into another's cell without invitation. This is especially true if it occurs on a range other than one's own.

When in the yard or other open space, someone crossing the eight-to-ten-foot barrier is perceived as trespassing. In closed quarters, depending on the need for privacy, the distance is reduced to two or three feet. The outer limits become important when approached from the rear or when an approach is combined with direct constant eye contact. Conversational distance between two inmates is approximately two feet; between an inmate and a guard it increases to three feet. Invasion of boundaries communicates disrespect and violation of one's person. . . .

While one's cell is the only claim to privacy available, some inmates or groups of inmates stake out rights to seats in the auditorium and cafeteria. New inmates learn very quickly that violation of such space is strongly dealt with. When the auditorium is filled, there is usually a seat between every two men. An inmate would rather stand in the back than sit down right beside a stranger. . . .

Although most of the time spent in the cell is behind locked doors, the individual cell is perceived as an extension of one's self. It is the only place where an inmate may even begin to relax. Locked doors keep one inside, but they also keep others out. Any uninvited intrusion into the cell is considered a direct assault. Only guards have continual access and as long as their visits fall into expected patterns, the feeling of relaxation is not disturbed.

Source: Ramsey, 1976, pp. 39, 43–44.

---

absent. A prime example is coordinating the use of a solitary bathroom in a large household or when guests come to visit.

A second way that people declare a situation as private is by using interactional or public territories during nonpeak hours. A person who truly wants solitude may seek out a church sanctuary during the week, when it is not in use. A dating couple may seek out a secluded corner of a public park late at night when there is little traffic. Early risers or late-night workers may consciously alter their work schedule to avoid rush-hour traffic. And students in dormitories report avoiding use of the bathrooms when they are most crowded (Vinsel et al., 1980).

Finally, a setting may be assigned different functions by time. In many parts of the world and in lower socioeconomic households, what is the living room during the daytime may become a bedroom at night. In dormitories, fraternities, and sororities, a common room may be designated as a study room during certain hours and a place for entertaining guests during other hours. Thus the kinds of social interactions that are permissible vary by time. When the time-space pattern for a setting affords inadequate privacy, people may cope by changing schedules or making more explicit rules about what functions are acceptable at what time. We know of a graduate student who became so annoyed by his officemate's public displays of affection with a girlfriend that he began coming to his office late in the day and working until the middle of the night. Both students saw the office as a private place, but the use of it for intimate behavior by one intruded on the felt privacy of the other. The radical change in schedule should have been a tip-off to the officemate that something was awry.

Kinesics and Vocalics   A wide variety of facial, body, and vocal behaviors can be used to judge how private or public the participants consider the situation. Most of these behaviors have already been discussed as relational messages, but they may also serve the function of establishing a situation as one of physical, social, or psychological privacy.

Especially important are turf defense and exclusion cues. These include (a) threat displays such as staring or tongue showing, (b) dominance displays such as expansive postures and loud voices, (c) body blocks and face covering, (d) emblems such as "go away" that express unapproachability, (e) dyadic postures and orientations that create a closed unit, (f) silences, (g) gaze aversion or reduced facial regard, and (h) other forms of reduced immediacy (Burgoon, 1982; Burgoon, Parrott, LePoire, Kelley, Walther, & Perry, 1988).

As a signal that a situation is affording inadequate privacy, people may also display anxiety and negative affect cues. Many of these were reviewed in Chapter 3 in the context of personal space invasions. Reduced smiling and increases in such behaviors as self- and object-adaptors, postural shifting, restless trunk and limb movements, negative facial affects, and vocal tension all frequently accompany situations that provide inadequate physical, social, or psychological privacy (Baum & Greenberg, 1975; Greenberg & Firestone, 1977; Hayduk, 1978; Maines, 1977; McCauley, Coleman, & DeFusco, 1978; Patterson, 1973a; Patterson et al., 1971; Sundstrom, 1975, 1978; Westin, 1967).

At a more general level, a key indicator of the privacy of a situation is the extent to which participants engage in rule- and role-conforming or rule- and role-violating behaviors. Goffman (1959), in his self-presentational approach to human interaction (see Chapter 13), distinguishes between frontstage behavior, which is the set of behaviors appropriate to a given role that one is performing, and backstage behavior, which includes behaviors that occur when one "lets down the mask." To engage in backstage behavior is to view a situation as private. Backstage, one is free to commit behaviors that violate general social norms, to engage in emotional release (Westin, 1967), "to escape from the compulsion of one's social role" (Chapin, 1951, p. 164), and even to denigrate that role. The ameliorative value of defining a situation as backstage was expressed by Burgoon (1982):

> The privacy associated with the backstage region enables one to recuperate from the traffic of day-to-day living and to regenerate energy and initiative. The metaphor of the backstage thus gives social privacy a spatial and temporal dimension. It is seen as a place—a "behind-the-scenes" hideaway where people go to escape from the demands of daily social transactions, to heal after stressful encounters, to rehearse and prepare for future contacts—and also a duration of time—a "grace" period during which the normal rules of conduct can be suspended. (p. 219)

Beyond violating or digressing from general social norms and the behavioral repertoire of a given role, some specific behaviors that may be associated with the backstage include use of more adaptor behaviors, more emotional expression (especially of negative emotions), more postural and vocal relaxation, and more profane language (a verbal behavior).

Finally, because people may attempt to achieve psychological privacy by being "enigmatic" (Jourard, 1966b, 1971), they may suppress their felt emotional expressions and adopt impassive, "polite" ones. The "inscrutability" attributed to many Asians may be just because of this use of inexpressiveness to achieve psychological privacy in their culture.

Physical Appearance   Physical appearance may signal individual or group definitions of privacy. At the individual level, one may use clothing as a form of physical insulation that carries psychological connotations: in psychiatric settings, it has been recognized that more layers of clothing symbolize a closing-off of self from others and a greater desire for psychological privacy. Clothing may also establish *anonymity,* which minimizes self-identity but contributes to individual psychological privacy. Goffman (1961a) observed that institutions strip people of individual identities by issuing regulation hospital garb, giving standard haircuts and forbidding facial hair, and enforcing restrictions on other aspects of personal grooming. The military and prisons rely on the same kinds of uniformity in appearance to create mass rather than individual identities. Groups like the Neo-Nazis and skinheads also achieve individual anonymity and hence privacy through the use of similar clothing and hairstyles.

Conversely, clothing may establish one's identity and specifically one's status level, which affects how much social and physical privacy one is accorded (Altman, 1975). Occupational uniforms and other role-related dress denote levels of social status. As status increases, approachability decreases. Military uniforms, police uniforms, business suits, or surgical scrubs are far less likely to invite approach than are jeans or factory overalls. Other clothing may directly signal approachability. Veils worn by women in the middle east cue strangers that they are not to be spoken to, while the near nudity of beach attire in the west invites conversation and possibly even physical contact.

Finally, the clothing worn by an assemblage of people can directly define roles and the interactional context. If everyone is dressed in skiwear, the context can safely be assumed to be recreational and hence more public than private. If, however, people at the head of a congregation are wearing ceremonial robes, one may conclude that a religious or other special ritual is in progress and may only be accessible to a select group. Thus appearance is one of the primary signals of the collective definition of a situation and, by implication, the amount of privacy associated with it.

Cuing the Informal-Formal Dimension

Closely related to privacy is the dimension of *formality.* The more informal a situation is, the more it tends to be viewed as private, and vice versa. But it is also easy to think of situations that are both private and formal (e.g., a boss "dressing down" a subordinate behind closed doors), so formality must be regarded as separate from privacy. Another set of terms often used in association with *informal-formal* is *personal-impersonal.* We will use *formal* to refer to situations that are also relatively impersonal and proper in nature and *informal* to refer to those that are relatively personal, casual, and relaxed.

Environment and Artifacts   Physical setting is an obvious influence on how comfortable and relaxed or restrained and formal we feel in a situation. Some environments put us at ease immediately; others make us feel that we must be on our best behavior. Volume of space is one influence. Simonds (1961) noted that the size of a room affects the kinds of activities and communication that occur in it. Large spaces produce formal activities like conversing, holding a banquet, or discussing serious topics. Small spaces correspond to far more informal activity, such as chatting, arguing, or singing (see Figure 7-3).

Artifacts can set a formal tone for interaction. Objects that are meant to impress others primarily by their costliness can create a formal setting. Knowing that the office you have just entered has a real Monet or Van Gogh hanging on the wall may elicit formal behavior. Furniture and decorations that are traditional in style and design can have a similar effect. Other artifacts, such as family pictures on a desk, can set an informal and friendly tone. Interior designs that emphasize comfort also set an informal and personal pattern of interaction. It is difficult to imagine, for example, carrying on a formal discussion in a room where people are seated in recliners.

Lighting may contribute to formality or informality. Lighting that is moderately bright to bright lends a formal and impersonal character to a situation. Softer and lower levels of light emphasize informality and relaxation (as well as intimacy).

Proxemics and Haptics   Seating arrangements express the informal or formal character of situations. Work by Mehrabian (1981) and Sommer (1969) has shown that office

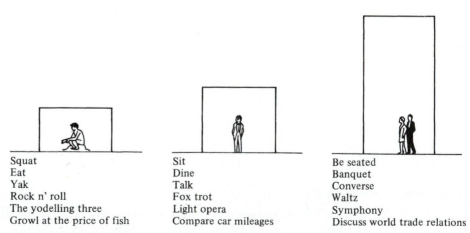

Squat	Sit	Be seated
Eat	Dine	Banquet
Yak	Talk	Converse
Rock n' roll	Fox trot	Waltz
The yodelling three	Light opera	Symphony
Growl at the price of fish	Compare car mileages	Discuss world trade relations

FIGURE 7-3
The amount of space that is available is likely to affect the kind of communication that goes on. Activities appropriate for a small space are far more informal than those appropriate for a large space, as the sample activities listed under each space suggest.

furniture arrangements that create barriers and distance between interactants stress formality in a situation. Groupings that reduce distance and provide few or no barriers set up a more informal interaction style. This argues for not leaving office arrangements to chance or personal preference. If a professional's goal is to put clients at ease and develop rapport (in a therapeutic situation, for instance), furniture arrangements that create obstructions and distance make it all the more difficult to accomplish that goal.

As conversational distance increases, so does formality (Aiello & Cooper, 1972; Byrne, Baskett, & Hodges, 1971; Mehrabian, 1967; Sundstrom & Altman, 1976; Willis, 1966). Hall's distance categories (1973) are described in part according to the degree of formality of communication associated with each. Presumably, absence of touch is common in formal settings where distances tend to be greater, and frequency of touch coincides with more personal, informal communication at close distances.

Chronemics   Emphasis on punctuality marks the formality or informality of an occasion. It may not be rude to arrive 30 minutes late for a potluck supper, for instance, but it definitely is to arrive that late for a formal dinner party. Generally, adherence to schedules and a careful management of chronemic elements reflect formal situations, while a flexible and socially negotiated approach to chronemic elements reflects informality. A displaced point pattern of dealing with appointments is characteristic of the former; a diffused point pattern is characteristic of the latter.

Physical Appearance   As with privacy, physical appearance cues provide constants that help to define a situation in terms of culturally accepted levels of formality and informality. In our culture, phrases like "formal wear" and "black tie affair" denote occasions that require not only formal costumes but formal demeanor as well. Overdressing or underdressing for an occasion is a common social fear. If the dress requirements are unclear in advance, we usually inquire to be sure that our attire matches the formality of the situation.

Unfortunately, we do not always receive accurate advice. In self-presentational terms, we sometimes receive "inadequate dramaturgic direction" (see Chapter 13). Recently, one of your authors and spouse decided to try a new restaurant. Calling ahead, we were assured that informal dress (jeans) was fine. However, when we arrived our waiter appeared dressed in a black tie and white dress shirt. As other well-dressed patrons began arriving, we were soon the most casually dressed people in the whole restaurant. Our embarrassment at being inappropriately dressed spoiled what should have been an enjoyable meal.

Cuing the Task-Social Dimension

A major feature that can distinguish one situation from another is whether it is task-related or social. Researchers in small-group behavior, organizational behavior, and communication have found that the task-nontask dimension runs through virtually all interactions (Fisher, 1980; Goldhaber, 1983; Shaw, 1981). The features that characterize a task-oriented situation closely parallel those for a formal situation, whereas a socially oriented situation tends to be more informal.

Environment and Artifacts   Most contemporary adult life is spent in work settings. We might consider these settings to be task microenvironments that are designed (with greater or lesser efficiency) to prompt task behavior. Such work microenvironments are a composite of diverse environmental elements that can indicate the type of task to be completed as well as the degree of task orientation required.

Lighting, color, temperature, and noise jointly set the scene for task behavior. Bright lights typify a task setting, dim lighting, a more social environment. Although there is no one color that people in our culture associate with task behavior, colors that provide moderate sensory stimulation, are easy on the eyes, and are nondistracting—greens, blues, earth tones—are most common in work settings. Imagine how nerve-racking it would be to work all day in a bright red cubicle! Moderate temperatures also correspond to task-oriented situations. Within the comfort range identified in Chapter 4 (68° to 80°F), cooler temperatures promote more of a work orientation. Noise operates in a similar fashion. White noise is commonly used to maintain a modest degree of sensory stimulation while masking distracting, irregular sound patterns. High levels of noise are avoided in environments requiring complex mental tasks. Loud music therefore becomes a cue (intentional or otherwise) that a situation is not devoted to task accomplishment. In some cases, such as the library, we have explicit rules to ensure that the environment is conducive to the task at hand. Such quiet environments in turn set expectations for the kinds of behavior that are appropriate.

The overall layout of a microenvironment and the artifacts in it give interactants very specific clues about the orientation to expect. Office environments, full of the implements of work (computers, desks, workstations, etc.), give direct and obvious signals about the activities that occur there. Moreover, the layout of the workspace can clarify whether tasks are to be collaborative or independent. Common spaces in which workers can gather for task activity imply cooperative activities; layouts that isolate individuals, by contrast, point to individual effort. Unfortunately, the people responsible for the design of an environment are not always aware of its strong effect on interaction. Supervisors can find it difficult to get employees to work together cooperatively when the physical layout hampers such activity.

Proxemics   A study by Batchelor and Goethals (1972) found, not surprisingly, that closer interpersonal distances occur among people engaged in task interaction than those not working together. Likewise, small-group research has confirmed that the nature of the topic influences the direction of interaction patterns (Hare & Bales, 1963; Steinzor, 1950; Strodtbeck & Hook, 1961). In task discussions, people direct more comments to those seated across from them in a circle or at a table, whereas in social discussions, they are more likely to talk to the person seated next to them. The presence of a directive leader may also encourage more talking to those in adjacent seats.

Seating position in turn can affect group leadership in task-oriented groups. Not only do people who are of higher status or power gravitate toward seats that afford them access to the other group members, but people who sit at the head of a table or opposite others, either by choice or assignment, tend to become more participative and dominant during ensuing discussions and to be perceived as leaders (Hare & Bales,

1963; Howells & Becker, 1962; Russo, 1967; Strodtbeck & Hook, 1961; Sommer, 1961; Ward, 1968). Thus leadership and "central" seating positions are directly related.

Seating arrangements can make a situation more social by encouraging interaction, or less social by discouraging it. We have noted that sociofugal arrangements tend to discourage interaction. Sommer (1969) found that state hospitals often arranged their lounges with chairs lining the walls so as to ease the work of custodians and orderlies. He found that by simply rearranging the chairs into sociopetal patterns, previously non-communicative and depressed patients significantly increased their communication with others and concomitantly showed improvement in their mental health and ability to relate to others.

A two-part study was conducted to determine which seating arrangements are most conducive to participation in a classroom (Heston & Garner, 1972). In the first part, while the classroom was empty, all the chairs were piled in the center of the room. This forced entering students to create their own arrangement of chairs and to choose their own preferred distance from one another. It was assumed that they would place the seats in a pattern that was most comfortable and desirable for classroom interaction. The unexpected result was that students voluntarily placed themselves 17 inches apart, within the intimate zone. This was greater than the 13 inches found between seats in undisturbed classrooms but still closer than expected, revealing that people prefer proximity for situations involving interaction.

In the second part of the study, students were each given a floor grid and asked to draw the seating arrangement they considered most conducive to attention, comfort, learning, and participation. The preferred seating pattern was a circle or semicircle.

This preference seems to be based on two considerations: proximity and visual access to others. It is consistent with other research showing that as proximity or visual access increases, so does classroom participation (Sommer, 1969). For example, when a classroom has straight-row seating, most participation comes from the front and center seats, creating a triangle of participation. These seats maximize visual contact between student and teacher. Similarly, the most active participants in a seminar seating arrangement are the people sitting opposite the teacher, and those sitting closest to the instructor may be shut out of a highly directed discussion. A laboratory seating arrangement (everyone seated around lab tables) produces the most total participation, probably because when people face so many others, they are more inclined to talk.

A final feature distinguishing task from social situations is territoriality, which is especially prominent in the workplace. Workers usually feel the need to identify an area as their own work space. Further, territories are often established and marked in terms of a given group's function. For example, at CBS headquarters in New York City, most upper-level managers have their offices on the 20th floor. Staffers are aware that this is the locus of decision making. When projects are proposed for broadcast, they have to be "cleared by the 20th floor" (Halberstam, 1979).

Chronemics   In a culture as obsessed with time as ours, it should come as no surprise that chronemic elements are significant definers of a task orientation. Preoccupation with the duration of tasks, punctuality, timing of events, deadlines, schedules, and the compartmentalization of time characterize a task-oriented situation. Contrast that with the more flexible approach to time in social situations. Although there may be a social agenda, punctuality is usually a minor issue, and there are no set schedules or deadlines to adhere to. Superimposing a task time orientation on a social situation can transform an enjoyable leisure activity like a hike into a chore, particularly when someone is bent on plotting out every minute's activities and insisting that everyone follow a schedule.

Physical Appearance   As with privacy and formality, uniforms and other occupational insignia declare one's task role in an environment. In a large company, slight differences in style of clothing or personal artifacts may even distinguish members of one department from another. Salespeople may carry home valises large enough to hold sample merchandise, while supervisors carry thin attaché cases and upper managers carry nothing (the notion being that executives have complete freedom during their off-work hours). Engineers are stereotypically depicted as having a plastic sheath full of colored pens and pencils in their shirt pocket, something salespeople "wouldn't be caught dead wearing." Uniforms may also be useful in reducing ambiguity about role responsibilities. In a hospital, the doctors' and nurses' uniforms are distinct from one another and from those of lab technicians or orderlies. This enables patients and visitors as well as the staff themselves to know who is who. Consider how willing you would be to allow someone *not* dressed in a nurse's uniform to draw blood from your arm. Our guess is not very willing. (See Box 7-4 for some findings about situational factors in hospitals.)

This use of uniforms to designate role or status is culture-specific. It is common in some Asian businesses for the company president to wear the same uniform as an assembly line worker. This lack of role differentiation through clothing can cause consternation or embarrassment for Westerners, who are accustomed to relying on such cues to govern how they carry on international business dealings.

Cuing the Cooperative-Competitive Dimension

Embedded in a task situation is the degree to which cooperative or competitive behavior is expected. Deutsch (1973) defined competition as a state of affairs in which opposition in the goals of interdependent parties is such that the probability of goal attainment for one decreases as the probability for the other increases. Competing with coworkers for a promotion at work or competing with siblings for a parent's affection are examples. Cooperation, by contrast, involves mutual activity by both parties toward the attainment of a mutually beneficial goal.

Nonverbal elements play a role in the *perception* of a situation as cooperative or competitive. Sometimes individuals misperceive a situation, reading it as competitive when in fact it is cooperative, or vice versa. It is these perceptions, not actuality, that are relevant here.

BOX 7-4

APPLICATIONS: APPLYING NONVERBAL FEATURES OF SITUATIONS TO HEALTH CARE

Different hospitals and mental health institutions may have different aims, but they share one situational goal: to provide patients with a therapeutic context that encourages recovery. Do current health care contexts meet this goal? Do they actually help patients get well?

The answer seems to be no. Many experts are increasingly convinced that there is an important link between communication and regaining health. To become well, patients need to participate actively in the healing process. However, becoming a patient often means adopting a passive role and assuming that others will "fix" the problem (Mechanic, 1972). Situational factors in health care facilities encourage this passivity. Olsen (1978) suggested that the symbolic function of the health care environment often communicates to patients that they are ill and dependent and should behave passively, even though this is not in their best interest. Other researchers suggest that environmental factors in many health care facilities serve to dehumanize and deindividuate the patient (Leventhal, Nerenz, & Leventhal, 1982). Important to us are three aspects of dehumanization these authors cite: a sense of isolation, a sense of inability to communicate, and planlessness and loss of competency.

What environment and artifact elements contribute to dependency, inactivity, and dehumanization? Work by Sommer (1974b) provided some indications. His description of the "hard" architecture found in mental institutions closely matches the conditions found in many health care institutions: long straight halls, cold tile, mostly white paint, chairs bolted to the floor in long rows, and small rectangular rooms. These conditions are better suited to a prison than a therapeutic context. Corridor arrangements of rooms along halls, sociofugal seating patterns in lounges, and a lack of areas for patients to congregate serve to lower social contact and isolate patients. The sterile atmosphere of health care facilities (lack of color, cool temperatures, few interesting artifacts) provides limited sensory stimulation, further reinforcing passivity. Moreover, patients lose social control over the environment. They cannot control who enters their space, nor do they have much ability to personalize their surroundings. This lack of environmental control can undermine their sense of well-being.

The technology and equipment that treatment sometimes involves can also contribute to a sense of helplessness and dehumanization. Patients may feel—as a result of radiation therapy, chemotherapy, or other invasive treatments—that they have lost the ability to care for themselves. They are likely to lose the motivation to communicate or may feel that they can no longer communicate competently. The effect on the process of healing is not positive—as is clear in Norman Cousins's *Anatomy of an Illness* (1979), an anecdotal account of the author's struggle against these and other problems in health care settings. As the excerpt from his book reveals, only by taking an active role in his own healing—in this case, prescribing laughter therapy for himself and making arrangements to move to a hotel room—did Cousins begin to feel that he would recover (something which did in fact occur and which he attributed to his gaining more control over the medical situation):

There was, however, one negative side-effect of the laughter from the standpoint of the hospital. I was disturbing other patients. But that objection didn't last long, for the arrangements were now complete for me to move my act to a hotel room. One of the incidental advantages of the hotel room, I was delighted to find, was that it cost only about one-third as much as the hospital. The other benefits were incalculable. I would not be awakened for a bed bath or for meals or for medication or for a change of bed sheets or for tests or for examinations by hospital interns. The sense of serenity was delicious and would, I felt certain, contribute to a general improvement. (p. 40)

A review of research on hospital design and human behavior (Reizenstein, 1982) provides some surprising insights. First, there is surprisingly little empirical research on hospital design and behavior, despite the prompting of researchers like Sommer (1974b) and Goffman (1961a). Second, of the available literature, over half is not empirically based and is often the "show-and-tell" type that simply describes a new medical facility without evaluating design effectiveness. When recommendations are made about how to design health care facilities, they are often poorly substantiated. Third, user groups such as patients, visitors, and nonmedical staff have received far less research attention than the medical staff. Finally, those who make design decisions about health care facilities tend *not* to use the research that is available. The overall picture is rather disappointing. It confirms that health care environments,

Box 7-4 (continued)

instead of being systematically designed to help patients take an active role in becoming healthy, increase patient passivity and dehumanization.

Chronemic elements in health care situations play much the same role. It is immediately obvious to patients that they have lost control over the scheduling of events. Patients control neither *who* enters their space nor *when*. Patients may be visited only during certain hours, must eat during certain times, take medication on a prescribed schedule, and undergo examination at times convenient for the medical staff. Admittedly, some aspects of this kind of scheduling have to do with large-scale institutional health care and are unavoidable. However, waking patients in the middle of the night for routine exams and tests is avoidable (see Cousins, 1979, for some vivid examples). All these scheduling practices contribute to patients' sense of loss of control and planlessness.

Finally, physical appearance often reinforces the passive patient role. Patients are usually given hospital garb that may consist of a surgical gown or pajamas. Other clothes, including the patient's own sleepwear, are often prohibited. Since these clothes are not of the patient's choosing, the patient is deprived of yet another choice, and one more element of institutional control is imposed. In critical-care situations, such practices are often necessary, but it is difficult to believe that in noncritical situations clothing cannot be chosen by the patient.

You might begin to wonder at this point how anyone ever gets well in a hospital. Of course, most hospital patients do get well. But it is worth speculating whether more patients might get well and get well sooner if nonverbal situational elements were different. Recent concern over the cost of medical care adds fuel to the fire. If patients took less time to recover and more of them recovered quickly, that could significantly lower medical costs. Such considerations argue for more careful examination of how nonverbal situational elements structure interaction and behavior in health contexts and other institutional settings. Research that has begun to explore nonverbal communication in the medical context (Blanck, Buck, & Rosenthal, 1986; Buller & Buller, 1987; Burgoon, Pfau, Parrott, Birk, Coker, & Burgoon, 1987) should provide some answers.

Environment and Artifacts   Just as layout can determine whether a task is to be a joint or individual effort, so too can it determine whether it will be a cooperative or competitive endeavor. Highly compartmentalized work spaces tend to minimize cooperation, while open ones promote it. In fact, one of the main arguments for the use of open work environments is that they should foster more interaction and hence more cooperative spirit. The same principle applies to traditional versus open classrooms. The latter, by permitting students to work together in common areas and by physically facilitating group projects, reinforces the concept of collaborative effort.

Proxemics   At the most basic level, cooperative tasks require closer proximity than competitive or parallel (coaction) tasks. Thus closer interpersonal distances may signal a cooperative situation, farther distances, a competitive one. The designation of territories also implies competition, since territories are designed to create separate identities and to regulate access to scarce resources.

Seating arrangement also reveals the cooperative or competitive nature of task behavior. Several studies (Cook, 1970; Haase, 1970; Mabry & Kaufman, 1973; Norum, Russo, & Sommer, 1967; Sommer, 1965) have shown that children, British and American university students, and other adults prefer side-by-side or cross-corner seating for cooperative tasks, opposite seating for competition, and catercorner seating for coaction. Sitting across from someone for competition is probably preferred because it allows one to watch the opponent while still being able to minimize surveillance of one's own work through body blocks.

We have now covered a variety of situational dimensions and have linked them to a number of nonverbal elements. It is useful to remind ourselves, however, that on a day-to-day basis, it is the totality of these elements that make the situation such a powerful determinant of behavior. It is also useful to remind ourselves that the relationships outlined here are likely to be quite different across cultures. As potent and complex as situational elements seem in our culture, other cultures stress them even more. Hall's notion of context sensitivity (1959, 1981) has particular importance for this point. High-context cultures place strong emphasis on context and situation. Much information is embedded in the environment and ritualized behaviors, and interpretations of communication events depend on understanding the culture's contextual language. Consequently, such cultures are no doubt more attentive to the structuring of situations than are low-context cultures such as ours, which rely more on the content of the verbal messages that are exchanged to draw accurate interpretations. Even so, context may play a crucial role in low-context cultures when it comes to choosing among alternative interpretations of an event. To gain a clearer picture of how situational factors affect communication in daily interactions, "typical" or "standard" situations can be analyzed. Such case analysis can identify situational factors and gauge their combined strength.

SUMMARY

Nonverbal patterns play a significant role in defining and structuring communicative situations. Situational definitions and constraints in turn have a strong effect on how we communicate and behave. Nonverbal situational features can affect communication by setting expectations for interaction, prompting the use of different social rules, and clarifying roles for interaction. As communicators, we sometimes have the ability to structure situations and therefore can influence the outcomes of interaction. At other times, we are passive respondents to situational factors. Among the most important continua along which situations are judged are public-private, formal-informal, competitive-cooperative, task-social, and dominant-equal. Most of the nonverbal elements that help to structure situations can be seen to do so by relating to these dimensions.

Four nonverbal codes—environment and artifacts, proxemics, physical appearance, and chronemics—are especially important in structuring situational definitions and behavioral patterns. These codes are most likely to play situational roles because they are relatively stable during and across encounters and therefore remain an unchanging frame of reference. As case analysis suggests, these codes combine in an overall situational whole to provide strong influences on how interactants communicate.

SUGGESTED READINGS

Baum, A., & Singer, J. E. (1982). *Advances in environmental psychology: Vol. 4. Environment and health.* Hillsdale, NJ: Erlbaum.

Bossley, M. I. (1976). Privacy and crowding: A multidisciplinary analysis. *Man-Environment Systems, 6,* 8–19.

Burgoon, J. K. (1988). Spatial relations in small groups. In R. S. Cathcart & L. A. Samovar (Eds.), *Small group communication: A reader* (5th ed., pp. 351–366). Dubuque, IA: Brown.

Forgas, J. P. (1979). *Social episodes: The study of interaction routines.* London: Academic.

Furnham, A., & Argyle, M. (1981). *The psychology of social situations: Selected readings.* Elmsford, NY: Pergamon.

Goffman, E. (1959). *The presentation of self in everyday life.* Garden City, NY: Anchor/Doubleday.

Goffman, E. (1967). *Interaction ritual: Essays on face-to-face behavior.* Garden City, NY: Doubleday.

Korda, M. (1975). *Power! How to get it, how to use it.* New York: Ballantine.

Mehrabian, A. (1971). *Silent messages: Implicit communication of emotions and attitudes* (2d ed.). Belmont, CA: Wadsworth.

Mehrabian, A. (1976). *Public places and private spaces: The psychology of work, play, and living environments.* New York: Basic.

Secord, P. (1982). *Explaining human behavior.* Beverly Hills, CA: Sage.

Sommer, R. (1974a). Studies of small group ecology. In R. S. Cathcart & L. A. Somovar (Eds.), *Small group communication: A reader* (2d ed., pp. 283–293). Dubuque, IA: Brown.

8

CREATING AND MANAGING IDENTITIES

The language of behavior is extraordinarily subtle. Most people are lucky to have one sub-cultural system under control—the one that reflects their own sex, class, generation, and geographic region within the country. . . . [Nonverbal communication] systems are interwoven with the fabric of the personality and into society itself, even rooted in how one experiences oneself as a man or a woman.

Edward T. Hall

IDENTITY AND NONVERBAL CUES

Irish, Polynesian, Lebanese, Brazilian, Jewish, African American, Native American, female, male, elderly, young, introvert, extrovert—what pictures do such labels bring to mind? How would you know a member of one of these groups if you encountered one? What labels do you use to describe yourself? Do you think your own personal identity is immediately evident to others?

As the opening quotation from Hall (1981) suggests, our sense of self is deeply connected to our cultural, racial or ethnic, sociodemographic, and personal identity, and our identity is reflected in the language of nonverbal behavior. We use our nonverbal demeanor to signify to the world who we are or think we are. Similarly, we identify others. We rely on their nonverbal cues—as we rely on "name badges"—to discern what groups they belong to and whether they appear similar or dissimilar to us. This process of identification is at the heart of our self-concept and is a driving force behind our feelings of belonging to valued or stigmatized groups. It is the means by which we come to identify, and identify with, ingroups and outgroups in our society.

In this chapter, we consider some ways nonverbal cues are used to manage identities, to signify people's identification with their own culture and racial or ethnic sub-

215

cultures, and to "declare" their age, gender, and personality. Because self-identity is a complex interplay of genetic, biological, and social influences and develops from earliest childhood, many manifestations of identity are deeply ingrained and habitual. In that respect, they may not seem so much "managed" as unintentionally expressive and revealing (what elsewhere in this text has been called *indicative* rather than *communicative* behavior). However, people can choose to adhere to norms or violate them, to emphasize or downplay their ethnic and racial heritage through their appearance and demeanor, to adopt androgynous or nondifferentiated roles instead of masculine or feminine styles, to act "old" or "young," and so forth. Thus nonverbal signals of identity are subject to deliberate management. By the same token, although much processing of social information about others is subconscious, receivers may consciously attend to nonverbal signs when pigeonholing others into cultural, sociodemographic, and personality classifications.

How, then, do nonverbal cues serve an identification function?

> Manifest indications of one's cultural, social, demographic, and personal characteristics serve as "identity badges," enabling individuals to project their own identification with various personal and social categories while simultaneously enabling observers to use the same cues as an instant means of classification. Thus, not only may individuals rely on their own nonverbal behaviors as affirmation or self-verification of their own identities . . . , but others may also treat such information as outward reflections of the inner self. (Burgoon, 1994, p. 245)

A host of identity-related factors could be considered here. We focus on five classes that routinely attract the attention of laypeople and scholars: culture; race and ethnicity; age; gender; personality. Because each of these is open to stereotyping and distortion, it is useful to place any generalizations in context, lest they be misused to foster further stereotyping and prejudice rather than accurate communication and understanding (Jensen, 1985). Among the risks associated with interpreting findings related to these factors are:

1 *Overgeneralization.* Variations within entire cultures, subcultures, age groups, genders, or personality types are enormous, and differences are often glossed over or simplified because of their complexity.
2 *Mythical "average person."* The discussion that follows refers to the average person. But this is a hypothetical concept, and it is likely that no such person actually exists. It must be remembered that group norms represent an amalgamation of characteristics possessed by individuals.
3 *Equality of cues.* Not all cues occur with equal frequency or effect.
4 *Exaggeration of differences.* Because the emphasis is on similarities among members of a given group, the few differences that are highlighted may seem more frequent or pronounced than they actually are. And in many cases, their effect on communication may be negligible.
5 *Distortion of primary causes.* Differences in nonverbal patterns between groups are often taken to be the source of communication problems. But such problems can and frequently do arise from other factors, such as individual personalities.

6 *Ethnocentrism.* People exposed for the first time to cross-cultural differences may fall into the trap of viewing them through the eyes of their own culture and thus regarding "foreign" behavioral patterns as odd or inferior. It should be recognized that what counts as appropriate or inappropriate varies by society, and one's own cultural practices may seem equally peculiar to those from different backgrounds.

7 *Viewing norms as static.* Just as people constantly change over a lifetime, norms associated with various classes of people are also dynamic. Thus nonverbal identity markers are subject to change.

Consequently, what we present in this chapter is, at best, an incomplete atlas of nonverbal cues in identification and identity management. However, this sampling should heighten your sensitivity to the innumerable ways in which people nonverbally pronounce self-identity and group identifications, and to cues upon which onlookers rely when judging who people are.

Identification and identity management are most relevant when we are considering intergroup relationships, the interface between two or more cultural, ethnic, gender, age, or personality groups. In intergroup relationships, communicators orient their identities to both members of their own social group (i.e., ingroup members) and people outside their group (i.e., outgroup members). Communication accommodation theory (Giles, Coupland, & Coupland, 1991) proposes that individuals typically manage their identities to match the behavior of other ingroup members, while they often enhance the behavioral differences between themselves and outgroup members. This pattern of accommodation promotes social attraction and cohesion between ingroup members, and marks boundaries between cultural, ethnic, gender, age, and personality groups. Of course, if an outgroup member is attractive to a communicator, matching can promote a positive intergroup relationship as well.

IDENTIFIERS OF CULTURE

Cross-cultural communication is more frequent than one might imagine, and its frequency is increasing as distances shrink because of advances in transportation and telecommunications. Cultures that just a few decades ago led an isolated existence now find themselves thrust onto the world stage and into the global economy. Individuals who might have had little contact with other cultures if they had lived only a generation ago are now confronted with live audiovisual images of people worldwide on the nightly news and through micromultimedia such as CD-ROM computers, computer networks, and videoconferencing. These cross-cultural interactions can have long-term consequences, because cultural identities can be altered by such contact. (To take just one example, consider how young people in eastern Europe have adopted the appearance norms of western teenagers in just the last few years.) Thus it becomes important to recognize what behaviors in each nonverbal channel act as cultural identifiers and set cultures apart. These nonverbal cues are often the primary means by which people signal their identification with cultural or subcultural ingroups and distinguish those regarded as outgroups.

Kinesics

Emblems   Emblems exist in every culture, but their form varies greatly between cultures (Ekman, 1976). Figure 8-1 shows emblems identified in various cultures for greeting, parting, replying to questions, beckoning to others, and commenting on others.

There are several considerations in using emblems for cultural identification. First, the unique emblems in a given culture make it possible to recognize people from, say, a Mediterranean culture or a northern European one. At the same time, there is some commonality across cultures: all cultures use gestures for the same functions, but the same meanings may be expressed through different gestural forms. Rubbing noses; pressing lips to hand, cheek, arm, or lips of another; juxtaposing noses and inhaling; and smelling heads all signal affection. Many emblems, though, possess contradictory meaning when displayed cross-culturally. For example, the head throw for no displayed by Greeks, southern Italians, Bulgarians, and Turks could be mistaken for yes in cultures where nodding signifies affirmation. The Bulgarian turn of the head for yes may appear to be shaking the head, a sign of negation in many cultures. Beckoning gestures are also a source of misunderstandings. The palm-down fluttering-fingers beckoning gesture observed in Asian and Latin American cultures may be interpreted as "go away" by North Americans. In sum, although emblematic differences allow us to identify cultural group membership, they can also create cross-cultural misunderstandings and unfavorable attributions.

Lest you think these emblematic contradictions are trivial, contradictory meanings have produced geopolitical embarrassment (Harrison, 1974). We noted earlier the example of Richard Nixon's displaying the A-OK emblem, which is considered obscene in Latin America, denoting the female genitalia. Nearly 15 years later, when the Soviet premier Leonid Brezhnev visited the United States to meet with President Nixon, he exited his plane with his hands clenched over his head. This Russian emblem signifies gracious receipt of a tribute, and Brezhnev was acknowledging the welcoming ceremony he was receiving. But this emblem was inappropriate in the host culture, because in North America this emblem denotes superiority and victory. Needless to say, neither man's emblematic mistake did much to promote international goodwill.

Emblems can vary between groups within a culture. Social and occupational groups develop special emblems to identify group membership (such as a fraternity handshake) and to facilitate accurate task communication (drawing an extended finger across the neck to indicate "stop the program" in radio broadcasting). Sometimes emblems originating in social or occupational groups enter into general usage and become identifiers of culture. The peace emblem (fist with index and second fingers raised in a V) came into general usage in the United States in the early and mid-1970s. A similar emblem was adopted by the British during World War II, but it had an altogether different meaning: victory!

Illustrators   Differences in illustrators have not been identified as frequently as differences in emblems. There is a stereotype of Italians, Jews, and certain others from Mediterranean countries as using illustrators more frequently and more expansively than northern Europeans and North Americans. Efron (1972), examining first-generation Ital-

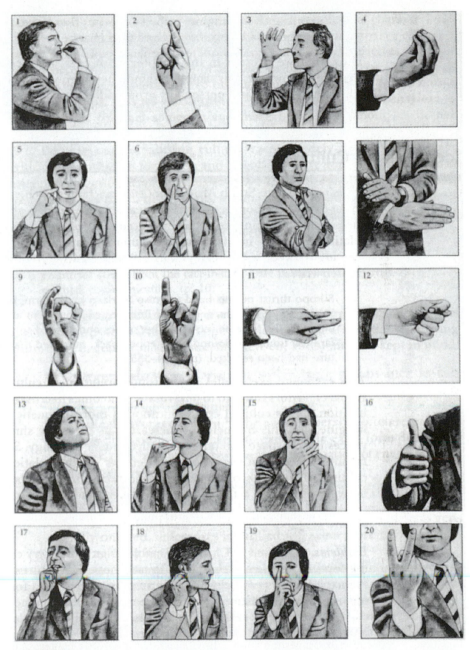

FIGURE 8-1
These 20 common emblems have different meanings in different cultures. How many meanings can you identify for each?

Nonverbal behaviors can identify social group membership. Here the chanting, dancing, artifacts, and costumes identify members of the Hare Krishna.

ians in the United States, found that they tended to use broad, full-arm gestures. By comparison, he found that first-generation Jews gestured close to the body, and their gestures appeared to trace the flow of their speech. Shuter (1979) found that cultural differences in illustrators faded in second-generation Italians and Jews. Thus the stereotype may be valid only in Italy, Israel, and insular Italian and Jewish communities in the United States.

Another illustrator that shows some culture specificity is the facial cutoff gesture. Used by Japanese women, particularly those adhering to traditional sex roles (see Figure 8-2), the gesture communicates shy femininity, caution, coyness, and self-consciousness (Morsbach, 1973; Ramsey, 1981). Less frequent and less varied cutoff gestures have been observed in European, African, South American Indian, and Indonesian flirting behavior (Eibl-Eibesfeldt, 1972). Americans and Europeans use cutoff gestures when under stress, to reduce or block reception of environmental stimuli rather than to block transmission of a facial cue (Morris, 1977).

Gestural forms also differ. Where North Americans generally point with the index finger, Germans point with the little finger (Michael & Willis, 1969). Davies (1990) described a gesture among the Chinese that involves a genteel guillotine slice or karate chop coupled with a large, ingenuous smile. This is a confrontational gesture used to reject the influence of others who are considered inferior to the actor or the society. Ricci Bitti (1993) described four unique Italian gestures, two involving the hand purse (rocking hand up and down at wrist, with fingers pointing upwards, tips together) and two others involving a waving gesture where the hand is waved up and down in front of the body

FIGURE 8-2
Facial cutoff gestures used by Japanese women.

with the palm pointed toward the body with hand extended. The meaning of these two gestures is altered by the accompanying facial expression. The hand purse accompanied by a questioning expression indicates that the communicator is asking a real question, while the same illustrator with a skeptical expression signifies a rhetorical question with an ironic, critical component. Likewise, a waving gesture, when accompanied by a lowering of the corners of the mouth and raising of the chin, communicates "much" or "too much." If a communicator puffs out the cheeks while performing the waving gesture, she means "too much" or "how boring."

Gesturing can be more important in some cultures than in others. In some Arabic cultures, for example, illustrators compensate for the absence of facial expression when women and sometimes men wear veils covering the face. In these cultures, gestures can be more elaborate and many are made over the veil and include adjustments to the veil.

To summarize, illustrators may differ across cultures in the space they occupy, their function and importance, and their form, with some illustrators, like some emblems, being unique to a culture.

Gaze   The major distinguishing features in the cross-cultural use of eye contact are the frequency of gaze and the focus of the listener's eyes (Noesjirwan, 1978; Watson & Graves, 1966). For example, Arabs generally engage in more eye contact than do North Americans. In North America and England, listeners are socialized to gaze in the direction of the speaker's face, particularly the eye region. English listeners gaze more continuously at a speaker, while North American listeners look away more often (Hall, 1959). By contrast, African listeners are taught to avoid eye contact when listening, especially with a person of higher status (Byers & Byers, 1972).

Posture   Cultures may vary in the directness of body orientation interactants assume. Indonesians have been observed to use less direct body orientations than Australians (Noesjirwan, 1978), and Arabs use more direct body orientations than Americans (Watson & Graves, 1966).

Differences in sitting or resting postures display large cultural variability. Hewes (1957) documented over 1,000 such postures (see Figure 2-1 in Chapter 2). As he pointed out, many of these postures result from the types of furniture and other environmental features present in a culture. However, Smutkupt and Barna (1976) showed that cultural beliefs can dictate posture. For example, Thais consider feet to be the lowest, most objectionable part of the body and deem it insulting to have a foot pointed at them. Thus Thai communicators may be embarrassed by an American with crossed legs who points a foot in their direction or who places his or her feet on a table or desk.

Posture can also be used to inhibit interactions with other cultures. Davies (1990) reported that Chinese visitors to nonsocialist cities in eastern Asia often adopt a walking posture with hands clasped behind the back. He proposed that this is a defensive, insecure posture that avoids contact between the socialist Chinese and their capitalist neighbors.

Facial Expression   Facial expressions possess many universal characteristics (see Chapter 10). Cross-cultural differences do occur, however, because cultures possess unique display rules dictating what facial expression can and cannot be displayed and what object or event elicits an emotion (Cuceloglu, 1970; Ekman & Friesen, 1975). For instance, the Japanese seem to have a unique display rule pertaining to eyelid position for expressing the intensity of anger (Matsumoto, 1989). The Japanese communicate less intense anger if they include raised eyelids, whereas American men and women signal more intense anger when their expressions include raised eyelids. The same display rule appears to exist for expressions of fear by Japanese men, but Japanese women follow the rule pertaining to Americans—higher eyelid position communicates more intense fear (Matsumoto, 1989). Likewise, the United States and Israel have different rules for responding to a smile from a stranger. It is expected that Americans will respond with a smile, and failing to do so is considered socially incompetent. By contrast, there is no norm for returning the smile among Israelis (Alexander & Babad, 1981).

According to Matsumoto (1991), cultural differences in expressiveness can be explained partly by the collectivism and power distance in a culture. Collectivistic cultures like the Japanese foster emotional displays that maintain and facilitate group cohesion, cooperation, and harmony more than individualistic cultures like the United States. Collectivistic cultures, however, place less value on relationships with outgroups (e.g., strangers, casual acquaintances) than do individualistic cultures, so members of collectivistic cultures encode less positive emotions with outgroup individuals than do members of individualistic cultures. Further, collectivistic cultures are less tolerant of variation in behavior than are individualistic cultures; hence, they permit a narrower variety of emotional displays. Power distance can determine how status affects display rules. Cultures with high power distances, that is, those that emphasize power differentials between people, promote emotions that preserve status differences, so individuals in these cultures should display positive emotions to higher-status others and negative emotions to lower-status others. By contrast, cultures with low power distance behave in ways that minimize status differences, so they show the opposite emotional pattern, directing positive emotions to lower-status individuals and negative emotions to higher-status individuals.

Some cultures even have facial expressions whose meanings are unrecognizable to outsiders. The New Guinean blend of a sad brow and angry mouth, the North American "smug" expression, and the British wry smile (one corner of the mouth up in a partial smile and the other down in a signal of doubt) are decoded accurately only by members of these cultures (Brannigan & Humphries, 1972; LaFrance & Mayo, 1978b).

Communicators can learn display rules from another culture in the process of cultural assimilation. Matsumoto and Assar (1992) showed that bilingual (Hindi and English) Hindi living in India recognized anger, fear, and sadness more accurately when the test was conducted in English as opposed to Hindi. Male judges were more accurate determining all expressions when tested in English rather than Hindi. Also, more intensity was attributed to females expressing sadness in the English test but more intensity was assigned to females expressing anger in the Hindi test. Matsumoto and Assar (1992) proposed that the close connection between culture and language suggests that as individuals become more fluent in a language, they also become more acculturated, understanding and adopting the social and cultural rules of a culture. Thus it is not surprising that as bilinguals move from one language to another, they also alter the display rules they use to interpret emotional expressions. The authors acknowledged that some of the differences arising from language use may be due to the fact that the English language contains more labels for emotions and these terms are more specific than in several other languages.

Proxemics and Haptics

The amount of contact (proxemic and haptic) between interactants in various cultures has received extensive attention. Hall (1966) argued that cultures can be distinguished by the distances at which members interact and how frequently members touch. He proposed that some cultures—which he called *contact* cultures—are characterized by tactile and olfactory (smell) modes of communication; others—*noncontact* cultures—are based on visual communication. In his preliminary analysis, Hall suggested that Latin Americans, French, and Arabs, among others, live in contact cultures, whereas Germans and North Americans live in noncontact cultures (Hall, 1966).

Early studies of proxemic patterns and preferences (e.g., Little, 1968; Watson, 1970; Watson & Graves, 1966) tended to confirm this distinction. So have reports of touch norms. Desmond Morris (1971, 1977), one of the most prodigious observers of nonverbal behavior, stated that people of Anglo-Saxon cultures engage in far less frequent contact in daily encounters than do, say, people from Mediterranean and Latin countries and are far less intimate in what public contact does occur. To illustrate, the friendly full embrace between males is far more acceptable among Latin men than among British or American men. Likewise, the arm link between two men is much more common in Latin countries than in non-Latin western ones. Jourard (1966a) observed that couples in San Juan, Puerto Rico, averaged 180 contacts per hour, those in Paris averaged 110, those in Florida averaged only 2, and those in London made zero contacts in a public circumstance (i.e., a café). Henley (1973) found similarly low levels of public touch in Maryland.

More recently, it has become apparent that the contact-noncontact distinction is too simplistic. Cultures that are geographically contiguous and similar in values have developed different norms. A comparison of Central and South American cultures (Shuter, 1976), which have often been grouped together as "Latin," reveal that they, too, differ in the amount of touch that occurs and the distances typically adopted for conversation. Costa Ricans interact at closer distances and engage in more touch than Panamanians and Colombians. In western Europe differences appear as well: Frenchmen kiss each other on the cheek in greeting; British men rarely do (Morris, 1971).

Cultures may be high contact for certain behaviors or certain contexts and noncontact for others (see Box 8-1). A number of cultures also display gender differences in their spacing and touching. Italian culture is characterized by tactile males and nontactile females, for example, whereas German and American cultures contain tactile females and nontactile males (Shuter, 1977).

Observed similarities may also mask real differences due to context, status, and degree of acquaintance. For example, a laboratory setting may minimize actual differences between people of different cultures. Although all cultures generally adopt closer distances as familiarity increases, absolute preferred distances for interactions with friends, acquaintances, and family members may differ markedly across cultures (see LaFrance & Mayo, 1978a, for a summary of such mitigating factors).

Nevertheless, some broad trends are evident. North American, northern European, and Australian communicators are similar in that they adopt greater interaction distances and use less touch than people from many Latin and South American, southern and eastern European, middle eastern, and Asian cultures (Barnlund, 1975; Elzinga, 1975; Hall & Whyte, 1966; Klopf, Thompson, Ishii, & Sallinen-Kuparinen, 1991; Little, 1968; Montagu, 1971; Noesjirwan, 1978; Sechrest, 1969; Shuter, 1977; Sommer, 1968; Sussman & Rosenfeld, 1982; Watson & Graves, 1966). For example, Russians, Italians, and

BOX 8-1

APPLICATIONS: EAST MEETS WEST

Increasingly, people from the United States and western Europe are coming into contact with Pacific Rim countries, most prominently Japan. Westerners faced with this prospect need to be prepared for important but subtle differences in nonverbal communication.

Many nonverbal cues are intended to convey social position. One is bowing, a key element in greeting rituals. Depending on its initiation, depth, and duration, a bow can convey different meanings and different status. The deeper the bow, the more respect shown, and it is the higher-status person who terminates the ritual (Morsbach, 1973). People of higher status also tend to use more erect postures with feet planted on the ground, compared to the more relaxed postures of westerners of higher social rank (Morsbach, 1973).

One of the trademarks of Japanese culture is the use of attire and accessories to signify social position (Morsbach, 1973; Ramsey, 1983). Japanese people frequently wear badges or uniforms characteristic of their place of employment, sports group, or city—behavior that often leads westerners to stereotype them as always dressing alike. Yet an accessory Americans are fond of wearing—sunglasses—found little acceptance in Japanese markets in the 1970s because the Japanese equated them with gangsters. It seems that dress stereotypes work both ways!

Another notable difference is that Japanese people often mask negative emotions with smiles and laughter and display less facial expression overall, leading to the common stereotype of the inscrutable Asian (Friesen, 1972). This appears contrary to the premium Asian cultures place on nonverbal communication over verbal communication. Some trace this behavior to the time of the samurai, when exhibiting any expression that offended an authority figure could result in immediate execution, and to the influence of Zen Buddhist teachings that place high value on the unspoken side of interpersonal communication (Ishii, 1973; Kunihiro, 1976; Morsbach, 1973; Ramsey & Birk, 1983). Others (e.g., Miller, 1982) challenge this as just a myth propagated by the ruling class. Regardless of its origins, the Japanese appear to be one of the least expressive cultural groups.

This extends to gesturing as well: extremely frequent gesturing is considered childish (Ramsey, 1983). But there are still a host of unique Japanese emblems. Beckoning is done by holding the palm down and fluttering the fingers. (The American "handscoop" beckoning gesture is reserved for children and is insulting when used with adults.) Extending the little finger upward is the emblem for a female; extending the thumb upward indicates a male. And an invitation to have a drink is done by miming drinking from a small sake cup with index finger and thumb extended.

The Japanese are somewhat similar to westerners in their public use of space. Like other noncontact cultures, they maximize conversational distance, especially with authority figures, and avoid touch or other public displays of affection. But the pattern in private is altogether different. People converse at closer distance, parents and children often sleep together in the same room, and infants and babies are held and comforted with touch much more so than infants in other noncontact cultures (Condon & Kurata, 1974; Engebretson & Fullman, 1972). Thus proxemic patterns reflect a mix of extremes—distance and restraint in public but closeness and nonrestraint in private.

Two further differences that can cause communication difficulties in east-west interchanges are eye contact and conversational backchanneling. Contrary to the western pattern of looking people in the eye, the Japanese are taught to avoid eye contact when listening by focusing on the speaker's neck (Bond & Komai, 1976; Byers & Byers, 1972). As a result, westerners may consider Japanese listeners inattentive and Japanese speakers may consider western listeners rude. Japanese listeners also commonly signal attentiveness during conversation by the word *hai,* which literally means *yes* but is meant to convey only that the person is listening (much like the American *uh-huh*). Ignorance of these differences can result in the same kind of mistake one American businessman made when he interpreted his Japanese counterpart's nonverbal cues as an agreement to deliver services. Too late he learned that that the Japanese businessman was merely being polite; he had actually rejected the request (Morsbach, 1973).

Venezuelans live in high-contact, high-immediacy cultures, whereas Danes and Germans are even less immediate than Australians or Britons.

However, a culture can be immediate on some behaviors and nonimmediate on others, reflecting differences in degree of affiliation (signaled by closeness, touching, and smiling) and degree of dominance (signaled by body orientation and gaze). For instance, Indonesians tend to display higher levels of both affiliative and dominance cues than Australians, resulting in a mix of immediacy behaviors.

These immediacy patterns may be linked to language (Matsumoto & Assar, 1992; Montagu, 1971; Prosser, 1978). It has been suggested that Germanic-language cultures tend to be noncontact, while Romance-language cultures tend to be contact. Nonliterate cultures may also tend more toward contact, in keeping with Hall's contention (1966) that contact cultures rely less on visual and more on tactile and olfactory communication. In support of the link to language, one study found that Japanese and Venezuelan participants adopted their culture's normative interaction distance when they interacted in their native language but gravitated toward American norms when they shifted to English (Sussman & Rosenfeld, 1982).

Vocalics

Although researchers have paid less attention to documenting cross-cultural differences in the vocalic channel, a few interesting differences have been reported. Loudness shows the most cultural dissimilarity. Arab cultures are characterized by loud speech: loudness connotes strength and sincerity to Arabs, while softness communicates weakness and deviousness (Hall & Whyte, 1966; Watson & Graves, 1966). Britons and other Europeans use softer volumes relative to Americans (Hall, 1966). It is not unreasonable to speculate that Americans are likely to be seen as brash by Britons and Europeans, and Arabs are considered pushy and rude by non-Arabs.

Vocalic backchanneling also displays cultural differences. British listeners may use less vocal backchanneling than Americans, substituting eye blinks (Hall, 1959).

Chronemics

Cultures have characteristic tempos that reflect the dominant time orientation (Bruneau, 1979). One of the most prominent differences is the extent to which a culture is clock-bound. North American culture and northern and western European cultures are clock-bound: time is based on an arbitrary, objective system (a mechanical clock). Members of these cultures see time as linear, one event following another in an orderly progression. Not surprisingly, these cultures are distinguished by a monochronic use of time (see Chapter 4).

African, Latin American, and some Asian cultures are not clock-bound. Time is based on subjective, personal, and often natural systems (daylight cycle, seasons, etc.). Members of these cultures view time holistically, from a point perspective. Events occur in a less orderly fashion than in clock-bound cultures. The present may or may not have a relationship with the past or the future. Polychronic time usage is the norm. It is quite common to schedule many events at the same time, a practice that clock-bound people find exasperating. In non-clock-bound cultures, emphasis is placed on activities, not time units (Hall, 1981; Morsbach, 1973).

Sensitivity to Cultural Identifiers

It should be apparent by now that cultures have distinct ways of using nonverbal communication and that insensitivity to these differences can cause communication problems. Simple exposure to another culture does not seem to guarantee more accurate nonverbal communication (Michael & Willis, 1969); training in culture-specific cues is necessary.

Collett (1971), for example, trained British communicators to behave nonverbally like Arab communicators. Arab communicators subsequently evaluated the trained British communicators more favorably than untrained British communicators, showing that use of, and sensitivity to, culture-specific nonverbal communication can go a long way toward achieving good cross-cultural relationships. However, communicators may at times prefer a nonverbal style to match the cultural context in which the exchange

Cultures can also be readily identified by dress and adornment features.

takes place. Dew and Ward (1993) reported that both Palagi (white New Zealand) women and Samoan women interviewed in New Zealand preferred female interviewers who displayed a nonverbal style congruent with the New Zealand culture (Palagi) as opposed to a style congruent with the Samoan culture.

IDENTIFIERS OF RACE AND ETHNICITY

Cultures are far from homogeneous. Groups within cultures, known as *subcultures,* often display nonverbal cues in unique ways. As with culture, differences in nonverbal behavior can and often are used to distinguish members of one subculture from another. Although most cultures possess more than one racial or ethnic subculture, the number varies considerably. Due in large part to colonization and mass immigrations, cultures in the western hemisphere contain many racial and ethnic subcultures. A few cultures (Japan is a good example) remain very homogeneous, having had few immigrants over the centuries (Morsbach, 1973).

The limited research on racial or ethnic differences in nonverbal communication, especially in the United States, focuses largely on normative differences among blacks (usually urban black groups), whites, and Hispanics, because these are the predominant racial and ethnic groups. Moreover, most research centers on black-white comparisons. The limitations listed at the beginning of this chapter are especially applicable to this research.

Kinesics

Gaze   People in different racial subcultures learn different norms for appropriate eye behavior with adults in authority. Blacks tend to engage in less eye contact than whites and may consider frequent eye contact impolite, arrogant, disrespectful, and disdainful (Byers & Byers, 1972; Ickes, 1984; Vrij & Winkel, 1991; Winkel & Vrij, 1990). This pattern of eye behavior among blacks may be a carryover from eye contact norms in Africa, where it is impermissible for a child to look an adult in the eye. This caused problems for at least one Peace Corps teacher in an African town. The teacher required her students to look her in the eye when she reprimanded them. This was such a violation of social norms that the elders of the tribe had the teacher sent elsewhere. (See also Box 8-2.) Puerto Ricans may have a similar norm for eye contact. Byers and Byers related many problems encountered by white teachers who expect Puerto Rican students to look at them during conversations.

Posture   Some research indicates that racial subcultures use different postures. Jones (1971) found that black and Chinese males adopted more indirect body orientations when interacting with other males of their racial subgroups. However, in a second study, Jones found no difference in body orientation.

Johnson (1972) described two postures characteristic of blacks. The "rapping stance" is used by black males as a masculinity display when interacting with a black female. The male adopts an indirect body orientation, with his head tilted toward the female, eyes partially closed, one hand limp at the side, and the other hand in the front pocket. A

BOX 8-2

APPLICATIONS: EYEING RACE RELATIONS

Eye behavior during conversations shows distinct differences between white and black communicators. When speaking, whites look away from listeners continuously and look at listeners only intermittently, particularly at "listener response–relevant moments" (LRRMs—points in a conversation at which the speaker expects a response from the listener and nonverbally signals this expectation to the listener). White listeners are expected to look at the speaker continuously, and looking away is interpreted as a sign of inattention (Erickson, 1979; Fugita, Wexley, & Hillery, 1974; Hall, 1974; Kendon, 1967; LaFrance & Mayo, 1976). Among blacks, conversely, speakers maintain constant gaze, while listeners are expected to look at the speaker only intermittently. Black listeners frequently use speaker-directed gaze as a "listener response" (LR) to LRRM cues from speakers.

You may think that these differences are trivial, but they can create profound problems when whites and blacks interact (Erickson, 1979). Whites may consider black listeners to be inattentive and uninterested in the conversation, since whites expect constant eye contact from black listeners but receive intermittent eye contact instead. White speakers may also fail to see LRs by blacks listeners. Blacks use nods *or* vocal backchanneling *or* eye contact as LRs; white listeners give a combination of head nods *and* vocal backchannels *and* eye contact. Thus black LRs are often insufficient for white speakers, causing white speakers to repeat their previous statements. Black listeners may believe that these repetitions signal that white speakers consider them incompetent or stupid. Blacks also may perceive white interactants to be hostile or overbearing, since whites engage in continuous eye contact when listening, less eye contact when speaking, and multicue LRs.

Thus a subtle difference in eye contact norms can have dramatic and undesirable effects on interracial interactions. Smoother race relations may ensue when whites and blacks become more cognizant of this and other nonverbal differences and strive to modify their behaviors when interacting with one another.

---

posture used by black females when communicating hostility is performed by placing the hands on the hips with the weight on the heels and the buttocks extended. While Johnson's observations are over 20 years old and may be a bit dated, Halberstadt and Saitta (1987) later reported that in media portrayals at least, blacks still adopted postures with more head canting and body canting than whites, consistent with the head and trunk position in the two postures described by Johnson.

Illustrators   Research by Vrij and Winkel (1991, 1992) identified unique nonverbal styles for black and white citizens in the Netherlands. Kinesically, blacks in these studies smiled and gestured more than whites and were more animated (they used more trunk movement, nonindicative hand and arm movements, and body adaptors). Research from the United States presents a mixed picture on smiling. In comparison to whites, Ickes (1984) found less smiling by blacks in conversations and Halberstadt and Saitta (1987) reported more smiling by blacks in media portrayals. However, Halberstadt and Saitta's observations (1987) in natural settings revealed no differences in smiling between blacks and whites.

Proxemics

Proxemic norms of ethnic subcultures have been examined, with mixed results. Some studies suggest that blacks prefer closer interaction distances than do whites (Aiello &

Jones, 1971; Bauer, 1973; Hall, 1966; Jones & Aiello, 1973). Others have found that blacks use greater distances than whites (Baxter, 1970; Willis, 1966). Research with Hispanic communicators is also mixed. One researcher found no ethnic differences when comparing blacks, Puerto Ricans, and Italians (Jones, 1971). Baxter (1970) reported that Hispanic communicators used less distance than blacks but the same distance as whites. Aiello and Jones (1971) found that blacks and Hispanics adopted the same distances, both closer than whites. Moore and Porter (1988) found that male Hispanics used more vertical space (by displaying more upward body movements) and were more likely to physically intrude on others than male Anglos, whereas female Hispanics used less vertical and horizontal space and were less likely to physically intrude on another than female Anglos.

For distancing norms, socioeconomic status is probably more important than race. Two studies (Aiello & Jones, 1971; Scherer, 1974) found that middle-class interactants preferred farther distances than did lower-class interactants. Also, gender affects distancing norms within ethnic groups. For example, when black and white males and females are compared, black males require the greatest distance during an interview, while black females require the least, with white males and females adopting intermediate distances. Black females also exhibit more synchronous leaning than do black males or white females (A. Smith, 1983). Finally, it is possible that blacks use distance more fluidly than other subgroups, moving in and out of proximity as the conversation unfolds. If so, results that attempt to state a stable interaction distance for blacks can be highly misleading.

Haptics

Research comparing haptic behavior of black and white interactants is more consistent. Blacks engage in more touching than whites (D. E. Smith et al., 1980; Willis et al., 1976). Also, from kindergarten to sixth grade, touching among white children appears to decline significantly, but touching among black children does not (Willis & Hoffman, 1975).

A tentative conclusion is that the black subculture is more contact-oriented than the white subculture, particularly with regard to haptics. However, the mixed results of research on proxemic behavior and the possible influence of socioeconomic status (yet to be applied to haptic research) may temper this conclusion. The research is presently insufficient to form any strong conclusions about space and tactile norms in other racial subcultures.

Vocalics

Vocalic differences between racial subcultures, though not as pronounced as gaze and other kinesic differences, do exist and can cause difficulties in interracial interactions. In Chapter 2, it was noted that subcultural dialects, such as Mexican American and Black English, are less preferred and less prestigious than the "received" General American dialect. Ethnic group membership is often identified by the vocalic pattern associated with each dialect. Further, people have learned to manipulate vocalic differences either to accentuate or minimize ethnic group membership.

Specifically, white and black children are taught to pause at different points in verbal conversation (French & von Raffler-Engel, 1973). White children pause at the beginning of clauses or before conjunctions, whereas black children pause whenever a significant change in pitch occurs. Sometimes these pauses by black children are within clauses, causing white children to perceive black children's speech as less grammatical than the speech of other white children.

Erickson (1979) identified racial differences in nonverbal cues that white and black speakers use to mark LRRMs. White speakers typically mark LRRMs by simple junctures or pauses. Black speakers mark such LRRMs by sharply falling intonation. These differences are likely to be confusing in interracial interactions, producing inappropriate or nonexistent LRs.

Beyond these differences, Vrij and Winkel (1991) reported that in the Netherlands, blacks had more speech disturbances, spoke more slowly, and used higher pitch for exclamations. Loveday (1981) observed that blacks raise their pitch and have a greater pitch range than whites.

Finally, Gallois and Markel (1975) found that Hispanic interactants use longer *switch pauses* (silences between one person's turn and another's turn) than white interactants. Moore and Porter (1988) found that Hispanic women were less likely than Anglo women to interrupt another communicator (this interethnic difference did not appear among men).

On the surface, these differences can cause communication problems, but members of minority racial and ethnic subcultures (blacks and Hispanics in the United States) display a learned ability to code-switch. Black and Hispanic communicators frequently adopt white communication behaviors when interacting with whites, thereby avoiding many potential problems (Erickson, 1979; Gallois & Markel, 1975; Wylie & Stafford, 1977). Such code switching does not occur as frequently among white interactants.

Physical Appearance

The most prominent physical appearance identifier of race is physiognomy (see Chapter 2) and accompanying differences in skin color. Beyond this, there are differences in dress and adornment, although these are likely to be influenced by other factors such as urban versus rural locale, socioeconomic status, and gender.

Sensitivity to Racial-Ethnic Identifiers

Garratt, Baxter, and Rozelle (1981) found that as with culture cues, it is possible to train members of one subculture to encode cues indicative of another racial subculture with positive results. They trained white police officers to use nonverbal behavior typical of black interactants (larger distances, less direct body orientation, and less eye contact when speaking) during interviews with black subjects. The black interviewees rated the trained white officers more favorably on personal, social, and professional competence than untrained white officers.

IDENTIFIERS OF GENDER

You may think that differences between men and women are too obvious to require discussion. After all, there are genetic, as well as physical, differences in the human body. Birdwhistell (1970) called genetic differences *primary* gender differences and physical differences *secondary* gender differences. However, as he pointed out, there are also many *tertiary,* or behavioral, gender differences in nonverbal communication by men and women which are not the result of chromosomal or anatomical differences and by which they signal gender.

One origin of communication differences between men and women is the sex-role expectations taught by our society (LaFrance & Mayo, 1979). Some scholars argue that women are trained to be affiliative, to create close relationships characterized by equality, to criticize others in acceptable ways, to be sensitive to others, and to interpret accurately the behavior of others. By contrast, men are socialized to assert their position of dominance, to be proactive, and to attract and maintain an audience (LaFrance & Mayo, 1978b, 1979; Mulac, Studley, Wiemann, & Bradac, 1987; Noller, 1993; Weitz, 1976). Some scholars contend that women and men inhabit different cultures, with different rules for taking part in conversation and interpreting conversational behavior. Men desire independence, while women desire involvement (Bem, 1981; Eagly, 1987; Noller, 1993). Another argument is that some sex differences represent attempts by men to exert power over women, while other differences—like men's insensitivity to nonverbal cues—are an outgrowth of their greater social power, which requires less adeptness at communication (Henley & Kramarae, 1991).

Research on sex differences suggests that while the distinctions based on differences in culture and power may have some merit (Noller, 1993), these explanations may oversimplify gender differences. In particular, several studies have challenged the notion that sex differences should be attributed to dominance (see, e.g., Hall & Halberstadt, 1986; Marche & Peterson, 1993; Staley & Cohen, 1988; Stier & Hall, 1984). For example, Mulac (1989) suggested that gender differences in talk are consistent with the appearance of power but not necessarily that actual implementation of it. More damaging is Halberstadt and Saitta's failure (1987) to find differences in nonverbal behavior consistent with the power-dominance explanation. Power cues appear to be moderated by whether or not a task is linked to gender. Men display more nonverbal power-related behavior than women on masculine and non-gender-linked tasks. By contrast, women display more nonverbal power-related behavior than men on feminine tasks (Dovidio, Brown, Heltman, Ellyson, & Keating, 1988). Brown, Dovidio, and Ellyson (1990) found that this difference in power-related behavior was linked to the familiarity of men and women with the task: greater familiarity led to more power-related behavior. In fact, when Brown et al. (1990) trained their experimental participants and equalized their familiarity with task, sex differences in power-related behavior were eliminated. Social skills and personality also appear to moderate sex differences. Highly skilled, charismatic females in one study were friendlier and more dominant than less skilled and non-charismatic females (Tucker & Friedman, 1993). These same women were seen as having aggressive-hostile personalities. Thus gender differences may result from factors such as familiarity, communication skill, and personality that have little to do with a desire by one sex to control the other.

Recently, La France, Hecht, and Noyes (1994) have introduced *expressivity demand theory* to account for sex differences. Based on reviews and meta-analyses of an enormous amount of research, they concluded that the combination of sex, relationship, and situational features call forth different levels of expressivity. Women are expected to be more expressive and will often meet those expectations. When caregiving social roles are salient, women will also smile more than men. This is especially likely when people are equal in status or power. But when status and power differ, men are like women: Both smile more when in the low power position and smile less when in the higher position. And when the situation calls for it, both men and women will be expressive and smile.

One must keep in mind that (1) gender differences are most apparent in children and young adults (older adults display fewer differences); (2) context frequently overrides gender differences; (3) gender differences vary by culture and subculture; and (4) people differ in their acceptance of sex roles (Epstein, 1986; LaFrance & Mayo, 1979). These last two qualifications deserve additional comment. Variance in gender-related communication norms between cultures and subcultures is very common. In some groups, adherence to very traditional feminine and masculine roles is dictated. Other groups are less strict, allowing women to display masculine traits and men to display feminine traits. Further, sex-role expectations are constantly in flux. North American culture, where much of the research reported in this section was conducted, has experienced significant changes in sex-role expectations in the past 25 years. It has become more

What appearance cues are used here to signal gender identities?

acceptable for women to assume roles previously reserved for men (especially in the work environment) and for men to assume roles previously reserved for women (especially in the home environment). This adaptation has led to increased androgyny (Bem, 1974), the display of both feminine and masculine traits. Thus one must be careful not to pigeonhole another person solely on overt biological sex differences. A competent communicator, instead, bases notions of sex-role acceptance on the behaviors and opinions expressed by the interactant.

Kinesics

Emblems   Limited evidence suggests that social norms may permit women to use emblems more frequently than men, and women have been observed to use more emblems than men. Baglan and Nelson (1982) found that both men and women thought it was more appropriate for women to use beckoning gestures than men. Poling (1978) observed that women use more emblems of all kinds than men. This is especially true for physically attractive women, suggesting a norm for usage by this group. Contrary to the social-power explanation, use of emblems is greater for dominant than submissive female communicators, especially in cross-sex interactions.

Illustrators   Research on gender differences in illustrators is mixed. Ickes and Barnes (1977) and Rosenfeld (1966a) found women use more illustrators overall than men, but Duncan and Fiske (1977) and Kennedy and Camden (1983) observed no differences between women and men. It may be that differences exist in the types of gestures used rather than overall frequency. One study found that women use more palms-up gestures and men use more pointing gestures. Palms-up gestures frequently accompany the shrug emblem (Friesen et al., 1979), signifying uncertainty or hesitancy. Pointing gestures, conversely, can be interpreted as more dominant. Thus these findings may support the social-power explanation of gender differences.

Adaptors   One study found that women use more adaptors than men (Peterson, 1976); however, this difference may be a matter of type, not frequency. Kennedy and Camden (1983) found no differences in overall frequency. Women, though, used more self-adaptors and men used more object-adaptors.

Gaze   Female dyads engage in more eye contact than do male dyads (Dabbs, Evans, Hopper, & Purvis, 1980; Exline, 1963; Exline et al., 1965; Libby, 1970; Mulac et al., 1987). The same gender difference has been observed by Wada (1990) in Japan. The greater amount of gaze occurs while speaking, while listening, and during silence (see Table 8-1). This is consistent with the finding that women are more sensitive communicators (Rosenthal et al., 1979). Keeley-Dyreson et al. (1991) confirmed women's superior sensitivity to nonverbal cues, although they also found that males' sensitivity improved with practice. Increased visual surveillance is likely to improve sensitivity to nonverbal cues. Mulac et al. (1987) speculated that there may be less mutual awareness in dyads that include a male because of more one-sided gazing in these dyads. Further, there may be a norm or expectation in the North American culture that women engage in

TABLE 8-1
TIME ENGAGED IN EYE CONTACT, PERCENT

	Mutual	Listening	Speaking	Total
Males	3.0	29.8	25.6	23.2
Females	7.5	42.4	36.9	37.3

Source: Exline, 1963, p. 11.

more eye contact during conversations than men. Kennedy and Camden (1983) found that women who did not engage in eye contact were more likely to be interrupted by men in small-group interactions. They surmised that lack of eye contact by a woman is considered a cue of inattention or disinterest, making her more vulnerable to interruption. This interpretation did not occur when men failed to engage in eye contact.

Posture   Mehrabian (1981), in his early analysis of posture, observed that men assumed more potent, more dominant, less affiliative, and less intimate postures than women. In other studies, men have been observed to use less direct body orientations and more backward leaning than females in interpersonal conversations (Jones, 1971; Mehrabian & Friar, 1969; Shuter, 1976, 1977); however, Wada (1990) found that in Japan men adopt more direct head orientation than women. Further, it may be more appropriate for men to lean backward and to display more postural relaxation than women (Baglan & Nelson, 1982). By contrast, in small-group interactions, men were observed to lean forward while women leaned backward. Backward leaning by women may indicate less involvement and lead to more interruptions by men (Kennedy & Camden, 1983). Another study found that men tilt their heads forward, while women cock their heads to the side (Kendon & Ferber, 1973). Willson and Lloyd (1990) observed more head canting by men than women and Dovidio et al. (1988) recorded more chin thrusts by men.

Facial Expression   A prevalent sex-role stereotype is that women are more expressive communicators than men. This stereotype is, in general, upheld by research on facial expressions. Women are more expressive facially than men (Eakins & Eakins, 1978; LaFrance & Mayo, 1979) and display warmer cues than men (Weitz, 1976). Women appear to be better encoders than men (Buck, Miller, & Caul, 1974); however, this varies on the type of emotion expressed. In a study by Zaidel and Mehrabian (1969), women were more accurate senders of negative emotions and men were more accurate senders of positive emotions. Androgynous males (those with both masculine and feminine traits) may also be better senders than traditionally masculine males (Weitz, 1976).

One explanation for why encoding ability varies by the type of emotion is that baseline or at-rest facial expressions are different for women and men. That is, women generally have a positive baseline facial expression; therefore, negative emotions are more distinctly displayed by women. Conversely, men generally have a neutral or negative facial expression; thus their positive facial expressions become more noticeable.

Consistent with this speculation is the general finding that women smile more than men, regardless of the emotion they feel at the moment (Dovidio et al., 1988; Eakins & Eakins, 1978; Halberstadt, Hayes, & Pike, 1988; Halberstadt & Saitta, 1987; Hecht, LaFrance, & Haertl, 1993; Henley, 1977; Kennedy & Camden, 1983; LaFrance & Mayo, 1979; Mackey, 1976; Rosenfeld, 1966a). In some of these same studies, women encoded more positive head nodding than men. Moreover, communicators expect women to smile more frequently than men and this expectation is resistant to information to the contrary (Briton & Hall, 1995). This expectation also may be applied to young children. Haviland (1977) showed a group of people pictures of infants and asked them to identify the sex of the infant. Infants with positive facial expressions were more likely to be judged females, and those with negative facial expressions were more likely to be judged males. Hecht et al. (1993) reported that the smiling norm was stronger in whites and college-aged women than blacks and high-school-aged women.

For a woman, smiling is an interactional phenomenon, whereas for a man it is an emotional expression (LaFrance & Mayo, 1979). Communicators seem to recognize this distinction. Bugental, Love, and Gianetto (1971) found that children attributed greater friendliness to their fathers who smiled than to their mothers who smiled. Another study found that women, who smiled more than men even when alone, increased their rate of smiling when paired with another woman more than men paired with men did. Women were also more likely than men to respond to a smile of greeting with a smile of their own. Beekman (1975) found that a woman's smile was associated with her feelings of social anxiety, discomfort, deference, and abasement, whereas a man's smile was correlated with his desire to be affiliative and sociable. It appears, then, that women are socialized to use the smile as an interactional tool. Men, by contrast, are taught to reserve it for times when they feel genuinely happy or friendly.

Proxemics

Compared with men, women are approached more closely, tolerate more spatial intrusions, give way more readily to others, and adopt closer sitting and standing distances in interpersonal and small-group interactions (Aiello & Jones, 1971; Giesen & McClaren, 1976; Hartnett, Bailey, & Gibson, 1970; Mehrabian & Diamond, 1971; Patterson & Schaeffer, 1977; Pelligrini & Empey, 1970; Silveira, 1972; Willis, 1966). Advertisements often depict women as taking up less space than men, and women have been known to use the armrests in airplanes less often than men (Goffman, 1976; Hai, Khairullah, & Coulmas, 1982; Mehrabian, 1981). These lesser spaces apparently are not distressing, as women behave more cooperatively and less aggressively than men under conditions of high density (Freedman et al., 1972).

In cross-sex interactions, men are also more likely to dictate spacing and distancing patterns and more likely to violate female territorial markers than vice versa (Shaffer & Sadowski, 1975). Typically, male-female interactions are characterized by closer distances than male-male interactions and, sometimes, female-male interactions (Baxter, 1970; Evans & Howard, 1973; Shuter, 1976, 1977).

Gender differences can appear even in mundane circumstances like selecting a seat in a taxi: Australian women opt for a back seat opposite the driver; men opt for a front seat next to the driver, even when traveling with a female companion (Kenner & Katsimaglis, 1993).

Haptics

Paralleling proxemic patterns, women give and receive more touch than men (except when initiating courtship) and appear to seek more physical contact (Elzinga, 1975; Fisher et al., 1976; Jones, 1984; Jourard, 1966a; Rosenfeld et al., 1976). Moreover, female dyads are characterized by more touching than male dyads or cross-sex dyads, and women in cross-sex dyads receive more touch than the men (Andersen & Leibowitz, 1978; Stier & Hall, 1984; Willis & Hoffman, 1975; but see Guerrero & Andersen, 1991, for an exception and the possible moderating effect of relationship).

Henley (1977) hypothesized that men initiate more touch than women as part of a general pattern of dominant behavior by males and submissive behavior by females, but more recent research (e.g., Jones, 1984; Stier & Hall, 1984) finds women equaling or exceeding men in initiation of touch. Women also reciprocate others' touch and have their own touch reciprocated more often than men do (Major & Williams, 1980). The results of one observational study of 799 instances of intentional touch (Major & Williams, 1980), shown in Table 8-2, are illustrative.

Jones (1984) proposed that the greater total amount of touch and reciprocation of touch for women occurs because touch is a feminine-appropriate role behavior and a masculine-inappropriate one. Indeed, respondents in one study considered touch by females to be more desirable than touch by males (Burgoon & Walther, 1990). Thus girls and women are encouraged to touch and be touched as part of their feminine, nurturing role. Males are discouraged from touching because touch becomes synonymous with feminine rather than masculine behavior. As further evidence of this, Jones reported that males who are verbally aggressive are least likely to initiate touch. Major (1981) contended that women are expected to be more passive, affiliative, and emotional than men and that the patterns of touch between men and women reflect these stereotypes.

These gender-specific space and touch differences are believed to originate in mother-child interactions (Frank, 1957). Mothers have been observed to touch female infants more than male infants (Goldberg & Lewis, 1969), and female children seek and offer more nonaggressive touch than male children (Whiting & Edwards, 1973). It seems that women are taught to have a different attitude toward touch than men (Heslin, 1978;

TABLE 8-2
RESPONSES TO INTENTIONAL TOUCH, PERCENT

	Reciprocated	Unreciprocated	Total
Male to female	21	15	36
Male to male	6	9	15
Female to male	14	13	27
Female to female	11	11	22

Source: Adapted from Major & Williams, 1980.

Major & Heslin, 1982; Stier & Hall, 1984). In a study by Fisher et al. (1976), women reacted positively to touch, while men reacted ambivalently. Similarly, Whitcher and Fisher (1979) found that touch by nurses in a therapeutic setting resulted in positive evaluations and increased reciprocal touching by female patients. Male patients, however, gave more negative evaluations of touching nurses and were less likely to reciprocate the nurses' touch.

Vocalics

The most obvious gender difference in vocalic behavior is that adult males have a lower fundamental frequency, or pitch, than adult females. This is partly because men have larger larynxes and longer, thicker vocal cords as a result of physiological changes at puberty (LaFrance & Mayo, 1978b, 1979; Sachs, Lieberman, & Erickson, 1973; Schwartz & Rine, 1968). Men also have lower resonances due to larger supralaryngeal vocal tracts.

Gender-linked pitch differences are not entirely due to physiological differences. Boys and girls are socialized into different speaking styles at a very early age (Siegman, 1978). Sachs et al. (1973) found that boys and girls who had not yet reached puberty could be distinguished by voice alone. They offered as a further explanation girls', and subsequently women's, tendency to smile more than boys and men. Smiling changes the vocal cords by shortening them, thereby increasing overall pitch (Mattingly, 1966; McConnell-Ginet, 1974; Meditch, 1975).

Women also seem to encode vocalic patterns containing a more varied range of tone changes than men (Brend, 1975; McConnell-Ginet, 1974). One pattern is the "high-low down-glide" frequently used to indicate surprise ("Oh, how awful!"). Another is a "request confirmation pattern" ("You do?"). Still others are a "hesitation pattern" ("Well, I studied . . .") and a "polite cheerful pattern" ("Are you coming?"). Finally, women often answer questions with declarative statements that end in rising pitch, an intonation pattern characteristic of a question. This can make women appear uncertain or hesitant when making statements (Lakoff, 1973).

Women's vocalic patterns, then, are not due just to physical differences in their vocal tract. Social norms prescribe different vocalic patterns for men and women, and children learn to encode these patterns at a very young age (LaFrance & Mayo, 1979).

When it comes to overall time talking, it is quite clear that men talk and women listen, contrary to the stereotype of the "chatty" female. Men dominate the talking time in mixed-sex dyads; they talk more when interacting with women than with other men; and they talk with greater intensity than women (Argyle et al., 1968; Hilpert, Kramer, & Clark, 1975; Markel, Prebor, & Brandt, 1972; Mulac, 1989; Soskin & John, 1963; Strodt & Mann, 1956; Strodtbeck, 1951). All three differences conform with the social-power explanation of sex differences, although they also fit the cultural explanation that men are socialized to seek and hold an audience.

Several studies with adults show that men also interrupt women more than women interrupt men, another possible indication that men tend to dominate conversations with women (Argyle et al., 1968; McCarrick, Manderscheid, & Silbergeld, 1981; McMillian, Clifton, McGrath, & Gale, 1977; Natale, Entin, & Jaffe, 1979; Octigan & Niederman,

1979; West, 1979; West & Zimmerman, 1983; Willis & Williams, 1976; Zimmerman & West, 1975). However, interruptions are sometimes invited by women's display of low involvement, such as backward leaning and less eye contact, or facial pleasantness, like smiling (Kennedy & Camden, 1981, 1983).

The sex differences in interruption behavior are far from consistent. Beattie (1981b) failed to observe a sex difference in interruptions, as did Dindia (1987). McCarrick et al. (1981) reported that women interrupted the interrupter. Most recently, Marche and Peterson (1993) in a study of children and adults did not find that males interrupted females any more than females interrupt males. Further, many of the sex differences reflected the behavior of ninth-grade females, who interrupted their partner. Even though interruption behavior was frequently asymmetrical in the dyad (i.e., one partner interrupted the other more frequently than vice versa), interruption frequency was similar in same- and opposite-sex dyads and sex of the partners did not predict who was likely to interrupt more. Marche and Peterson concluded that it is unwarranted to believe that men interrupt women more than women interrupt men and unwarranted to believe that this asymmetrical behavior occurs because men consider women to be interruptible, believe that what women have to say is less important than what men have to say, or attempt to exert more power or status by interrupting women.

Finally, there may be a sex difference in pausing during speech. Fitzpatrick, Mulac, and Dindia (1994) reported that male speech contained more pausing and in particular more vocalized or filled pauses than female speech. These authors also showed that women were more likely to converge toward the speech of men than men were likely to converge toward the speech of women. This implies that women are more likely to code-switch than men; however, Fitzpatrick et al. also noted that the greatest amount of convergence was witnessed in husbands toward their wives' communication style. So, men are not incapable of code switching and may be motivated to accommodate to the style of intimate female partners.

Box 8-3 gives an overview of some effects of gender differences in nonverbal communication, noting that these can be very significant.

IDENTIFIERS OF AGE

Age produces subcultures with different nonverbal communication styles. In outlining the origins and acquisitions of each of the nonverbal codes, we noted numerous differences in nonverbal behavior between children and adults. However, there are also differences among adults, especially between young adults and elderly to middle-age people.

Physical Appearance

Probably the most obvious identifiers are the overt changes in physical appearance that take place as we age. Skin and muscle lose their elasticity, wrinkles appear, the hair grays, and posture becomes more stooped. However, there are other age-related changes in the brain, sensory apparatus, and respiratory and phonatory systems that change the nonverbal communication of older adults (O'Hair, Allman, & Gibson, 1991).

BOX 8-3

APPLICATIONS: NONVERBAL BATTLE OF THE SEXES

Gender differences are interesting and often humorous, but in actual practice, they can cause tension in male-female conversations.

The first place where tension may exist is in the eye behavior of men and women. As noted, women are expected to engage in more eye contact. Moreover, when females fail to make eye contact, they are more likely to be interrupted by males, especially in group situations. Lack of eye contact by women may be interpreted as inattention or disinterest, making them more vulnerable to interruptive attempts. Men, however, do not seem to fall victim to a similar interpretation.

Eye contact and interruption differences may contribute to perceptions of women as submissive and men as dominant. Women may also accede control to men by occupying less space, assuming less relaxed postures, and occupying less conversational time. Women are more accommodating than men toward the gaze and speech patterns of opposite-sex partners, consistent with other evidence that women code-switch more than men (Noller, 1993).

The sex role adopted by parties in an interaction may be more important to communication between males and females than biological sex differences. Ickes, Schermer, and Steeno (1979) showed that interaction patterns changed when the interactants were either sex-typed (i.e., masculine or feminine) or androgynous. An interaction between two traditional males or two traditional females is characterized by less nonverbal involvement than an interaction between two androgynous individuals. Androgynous communicators may have more skills, being both instrumental (masculine) and expressive (feminine), that they can use to maintain an appropriate level of involvement. Androgynous individuals may compensate for the interaction

skills of sex-typed, opposite-sex partners but not sex-typed, same-sex partners. In turn, people are more satisfied when at least one member of the dyad is androgynous.

Other differences in nonverbal behavior can create relational stress between males and females and reduce relational satisfaction. The avoidance of close interactions and touch by men and the desire for more contact by women may produce dissatisfaction. Women may also be uncomfortable with men's common association of touch with sexual intentions, while men may be confused by women's need for touch that does not culminate in sexual intercourse.

Finally, stress between the sexes can arise in group interactions. Women may experience more difficulty than men when placed in leadership positions, because they receive more negative nonverbal emotional responses and fewer positive responses than men in leadership positions when offering the same arguments and suggestions (Butler & Geis, 1990). By comparison, men receive at least as many positive nonverbal emotional reactions as negative ones from other group members. Negative responses to women can devalue their leadership relative to male leadership.

Thus gender differences are far from trivial. They have the potential to create tension, conflict, and dissatisfaction between men and women. This may be increasingly true as more women move into male-dominated areas in business and politics. In these areas, power and influence are important considerations, and to the extent that women's behaviors handicap their abilities to exercise control, their success may be limited. On the social front as well, these differences may bode ill for male-female relationships as men's and women's communication styles come into conflict.

Kinesics

Neuronal loss in the frontal lobes of the brain can reduce motor control and coordination. This can impair or ultimately eliminate gesturing (O'Hair et al., 1991).

Sensory deficits in vision can impair the encoding and decoding of kinesic behavior (as well as proxemic and physical appearance cues that also rely on visual acuity). Sensory abilities can start to decline as early as age 40 but do not seem to impair behavior until age 60 (Kalymun, 1989). Older adults can still compensate for some of the sensory difficulties, so that substantial changes in conversational abilities often do not occur until age 70 or 80 (O'Hair et al., 1991).

On the encoding end, sensory deficits may produce slower conversational styles, including slower body movements (Corso, 1977; Eisedorfer & Wilkie, 1972). On the decoding side, reduction in visual capacity may decrease the accuracy with which kinesic cues, especially facial expressions, are interpreted. Moreover, losses in memory abilities can make it difficult to recognize familiar faces (Ferris, Crook, Clark, McCarthy, & Rae, 1980; O'Hair et al., 1991). Research by Stine, Wingfield, and Myers (1990) showed that decoding difficulties associated with age are particularly acute when older adults must decode two nonverbal channels (i.e., facial expressions and voice tone) simultaneously. However, decoding impairments may be most evident when interpreting the communication of young adults. Parham, Feldman, Oster, and Popoola (1981) observed that older adults were more accurate when judging facial expressions from other older adults than from younger adults. Experience with one's age cohort may make an individual more attuned to subtle nuances in kinesic behavior that helps overcome processing deficits (O'Hair et al., 1991). Another interpretation is that the slowing of muscle movement reduces the number of cues emitted (and the speed with which they are encoded), making it easier for older adults to recognize communicative expressions.

Proxemics

Adults who experience hearing loss often compensate by relying more on sight to interpret communicative behavior. This compensation often results in the adoption of closer conversational distances to help them detect visual cues. Thus hearing loss associated with age may cause older adults to stand closer to conversational partners (Lawton & Nahemoir, 1973; Nussbaum, Thompson, & Robinson, 1989).

Vocalics

Humans experience structural changes in the respiratory and phonatory systems as they age, which alters their vocalic style (Leaf, 1973). Reduced lung capacity may produce speech with inadequate loudness and vocal variation and may make it more difficult to maintain sound production for sufficient periods without pausing. These changes can produce rough, breathy, or hoarse voices, monotone voices, slurred speech, slower speech, or uneven vocal rhythm among older communicators (Kent & Burkhard, 1981; O'Hair et al., 1991). One study (Smith, Wasowicz, & Preston, 1987) showed that the voices of older adults contained longer sounds (i.e., sentences, syllables, consonants, and vowels). Changes in sensory abilities linked to age also can alter vocal style. Hearing loss can produce louder or badly articulated speech (O'Hair et al., 1991; Whitbourne, 1985).

Hearing impairment also reduces vocalic decoding skills. Even a slight hearing loss can require a louder and slower conversational style of the partner in order to ensure accurate interpretation (Corso, 1977; Eisedorfer & Wilkie, 1972). Emotional expressions communicated by the voice seem to be particularly problematic to hearing-impaired individuals (Hooyman & Kiyak, 1988). Hearing aids often do not solve the decoding problems because they also amplify background noise that further interferes with the decoding process (Corso, 1977). These changes in older people's communication style can alter the way younger people communicate with them, as Box 8-4 shows, and not always for the better.

IDENTIFIERS OF PERSONALITY

At the core of our identities are our individual personalities—those unique traits and characteristics that distinguish us from other members of our same cultural, ethnic, gender, or age cohort. Nonverbal cues are a primary means by which we make public "who we are." That these nonverbal cues capture essential aspects of personality is illustrated in Figure 8-3. It shows samples taken from a recently developed nonverbal assessment of personality (Paunonen, Jackson, & Keinonen, 1990). Unfortunately, the descriptions associated with different personality types are ambiguous and lacking specifics (e.g., impulsivity is indicated by emotional volatility; sentience is characterized by high sensitivity to smells, sounds, sights, tastes, and textures). We must therefore turn to other research for clues to personality.

BOX 8-4

APPLICATIONS: THE COMMUNICATION PREDICAMENT

Many of the differences in nonverbal communication highlighted in this section produce difficulties for older adults. Many of these difficulties arise not simply from mental, sensory, and motor deficits of older adults but from the inferences and behaviors of their conversational partners (Ryan, 1994; Ryan, Bourhis, & Knops, 1991; Ryan & Cole, 1990). Younger adults often stereotype older adults as less competent communicators. Consequently, younger adults adopt a communication style with older adults designed to make it simpler for older adults to understand what is being communicated to them.

Specifically, Ryan and colleagues (1994; Ryan et al., 1991; Ryan & Cole, 1990) observed that younger adults talk more loudly and more slowly to older people. Kemper (1994) found that younger adult caregivers and service providers reduced the length of their utterances, had more utterances per turn and more repetitions, spoke more slowly, and paused longer when speaking to older adults. In another study, Kemper, Vandeputte, Rice, and Cheung (in press) reported that younger speakers again used more utterances, encoded shorter utterances, and spoke more slowly to older listeners; however, older speakers did not alter their communication style when speaking to older as opposed to younger adults.

Notably, this conversational style with older adults can improve older people's performance on tasks (Kemper et al., in press). However, it is also very patronizing, reinforces low self-esteem in older adults, and may lead older adults to perform age-linked behaviors, resulting in a self-fulfilling prophecy (Ryan, 1994; Ryan et al., 1991; Ryan & Cole, 1990). The patronizing message of this style may account for why older adults hesitate to compensate for the processing difficulties of other older adults in their communication style.

Thus younger adults should exercise caution when interacting with older adults. They should not automatically assume that older adults are incompetent and need help in understanding a message. Even in situations in which processing deficits are apparent, younger adults need to be sensitive to the relational message sent to older adults when younger adults "simplify" their communication style.

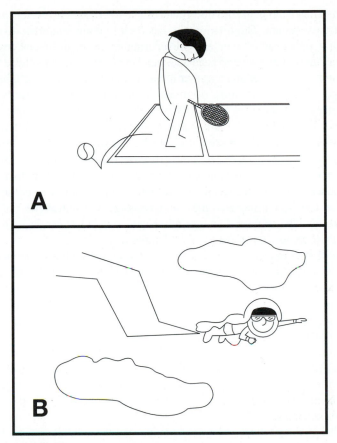

FIGURE 8-3
Sample items from nonverbal personality questionnaire illustrating aggressive behavior (frame A)
and thrill-seeking behavior (frame B) from Paunonen, Jackson, and Keinonen (1990).

Two categories of investigation offer insights: (1) research on personality characteristics such as introversion and need for affiliation and (2) studies of mental disorders
such as schizophrenia and paranoia. What follows is a very selective sampling of the
ways in which nonverbal cues manifest underlying personal traits and states.

Kinesics

Eye gaze and direct facing are intuitively recognizable indicators of people's gregariousness and social tendencies (Exline, 1963; Mobbs, 1969; Gifford, 1991; Simpson,
Gangestad, & Biek, 1993). Extroverts and people with a high need for affiliation use
more eye contact than introverts and those with low need for affiliation. In fact, introverts often resist visual interaction as if fearing involvement. Men high in sociosexual-

ity also make frequent flirtatious glances and avert gaze less often when interacting with attractive women. The relationship between looking and affiliative tendencies makes sense: Eye contact is one means of securing attention and social companionship.

Facing is one of several head and facial cues (e.g., nodding, head tilting, and smiling) that tend to co-occur and together are associated with a host of other personality traits. People who are ambitious, dominant, extroverted, warm, expressive, and generally socially skilled are more likely to display these cues than are people who are aloof, introverted, lazy, submissive, unassuming, or ingenuous (Akert & Panter, 1988; Gifford, 1991; Gilbert, 1991; Simpson et al., 1993; Tucker & Friedman, 1993). As discussed in Chapters 11 and 12, these cues convey liking, openness, approval, and agreement and so may serve as positive feedback to others. It makes sense, then, that people who want to influence others, to get ahead, or just to be around others will put their expressive skills to use. Extroverts may also have an advantage over introverts because they pay more attention to the nonverbal cues of others due to their greater desire for social stimulation and their greater experience in social situations.

Skill at controlling these displays is associated with another personality trait: self-monitoring. High self-monitors are better at inhibiting expressions of triumph over an adversary than are low self-monitors (Friedman & Miller-Herringer, 1991). They may conceal their happiness by biting their lips and distorting their mouths in other ways.

Kinesic anxiety cues tend to be associated with negative personality traits and disorders (Gifford, 1991; Gilbert, 1991). For example, lazy, submissive, unassuming, and ingenuous communicators display more object adaptors than dominant and ambitious ones. Adolescents high in neuroticism show more facial anxiety cues than those low in neuroticism when having blood drawn but not when giving a speech. Curiously, psychotic adolescents show more positive facial expressions during both presumably anxiety-producing activities.

One stable predisposition that is evidenced through all of these kinesic cues is communication reticence (also referred to as unwillingness to communicate and communication apprehension). Originally, this was called stage fright but has come to mean something much more than freezing in front of an audience. Communication reticence can be prompted by almost any situation calling for interpersonal, group, or public communication. In general, reticent communicators look ill-at-ease, apathetic or depressed, unanimated, uninvolved, and possibly submissive. Specifically, their kinesic profile includes negative forms of arousal such as increased bodily tension, more self-adaptors, more uncoordinated or random movements, and more protective behaviors such as body blocking, face covering, and leaning or facing away from their communication partner. Their posture is often more rigid and their behavior more restrained, with little facial or gestural expressiveness, nodding, and smiling. They also engage in less eye contact, as well as reduce immediacy through indirect body orientation (Burgoon & Koper, 1984). These kinesic and proxemic patterns are typically accompanied by vocal indicators of anxiety such as nonfluencies (Harper et al., 1978). Thus, people who are apprehensive about communicating reveal themselves through an inexpressive, anxious, and detached demeanor which ironically may lead others to avoid them and perpetuate their anxieties about interacting.

Proxemics and Haptics

People's willingness to approach and be approached, to touch and be touched, is another reflection of their personality. Scott (1988) proposed that people's orientations toward touch, conversational distance, and other communicative behaviors reflect the kind of *personal boundary* they have. Some people have open, permeable personal boundaries that allow exchange between the person and his or her surroundings (including other people), while others have closed boundaries that restrict such interaction. People also may have flexible boundaries that allow them to adapt from one situation or person to the next or they may have rigid boundaries that lead them to respond the same way across situations and interactions. Scott's conceptualization of boundaries shares much in common with a number of personality traits and attitudes toward contact. As shown in Table 8-3, people who have open, flexible boundaries fit a high contact profile: They enjoy and seek touch and close interaction and they exhibit many other nonverbal and verbal behaviors indicative of being sociable, impulsive, and warm. Conversely, those with closed and rigid boundaries exhibit many behaviors indicative of discomfort with, and avoidance of, interaction. Thus, sets of proxemic and haptic behaviors coincide with a collection of personality characteristics.

Somatotypes

Somatotypes may be related to personality insofar as they indirectly affect one's view of self and others. Stereotypes exist of the jolly, easygoing fat person and the sensitive, high-strung thin person, and many traits stereotypically associated with each of the somatotypes show up when people rate their own temperament (Cortes & Gatti, 1965, 1970). They also show up in parents' and teachers' evaluations of children (Walker, 1963). The most commonly found associations are listed in Table 8-4.

Why are behaviors and personality traits associated with somatotype? Temperament has physiological determinants and the genetic, organic, and metabolic processes that produce a certain somatotype may influence temperament. Alternatively, communicators may respond to children according to their appearance—plump endomorphs and skinny ectomorphs get negative reactions and teasing; mesomorphs receive a lot of positive reinforcement because they are considered more attractive. Research on somatotypes and body attractiveness as they relate to self-esteem seems to support this view (Berscheid, Walster, & Bohrnstedt, 1973; Jourard & Secord, 1955). One should be careful, though, not to overinterpret these associations. There is no direct evidence that possessing a particular somatotype causes one to adopt certain behavioral patterns and personality traits.

Physical Appearance

Clothing and other features of adornment are related to personality. In Chapter 2, we noted that Aiken (1963) classifies clothing and accessories along five dimensions: (1) interest, (2) economy, (3) decoration, (4) conformity, and (5) comfort. Choices on these dimensions were related to personality. For example, those who showed great interest in dress were conventional, conscientious, compliant before authority, stereotyped in think-

TABLE 8-3

CHARACTERISTICS OF COMMUNICATORS WITH OPEN/FLEXIBLE OR CLOSED/RIGID PERSONAL SPACE
BOUNDARIES AND HIGH TOUCH COMFORT OR HIGH TOUCH AVOIDANCE

Individuals with open and flexible personal space boundaries and/or individuals who report being comfortable with touch
tend to have the following characteristics:

Behavior	Personality traits
talkative	impulsive, takes risks
shares self with others	moves rapidly into relationships
enjoys being around people	easily attracted to objects and people
likes to touch and be touched	seeks close relationships
readily shows emotions	overresponsive
admits errors easily	democratic
little control over impulses	easily distracted, short attention span
spontaneous, with infantile dependence	hypersensitive to the environment
assertive	satisfied with self and life
socially acceptable self-presentation	
active interpersonal problem-solving style	

Individuals with closed and rigid boundaries and/or those who are uncomfortable with touch and avoid opposite-sex touch
tend to have the following characteristics:

Behavior	Personality traits
adopts large interpersonal distances	low self-esteem
infrequent touch in new or developing relationships	fears closeness in interpersonal relationships, cautious
apprehensive about communicating	non-risk-taker
reticent, quiet, shy	emotionally detached
nondisclosive	lacking self-confidence
protects secrets and territory	fears not being able to maintain facade
prefers to be alone	passive-aggressive conflict
passive interpersonal style	negative emotional states (e.g., depression)
nonopen communication style	strives for internal and external control
holds grudges	autocratic
highly structured	long attention span
negative views of touch	

Sources: Compiled from Andersen, Andersen, & Lustig (1987), Andersen & Leibowitz (1978), Andersen & Sull (1985), Guerrero & Andersen
(1991), Landis (1970), and Scott (1988).

ing, persistent, suspicious, insecure, and tense. Although the results may now be out-
dated, they support the relationship of personality to clothing and adornment.

Rosenfeld and Plax (1977) conducted a study that was designed to follow up and
extend Aiken's work. Male and female subjects were given a clothing questionnaire and
an extensive set of personality measures. Again, the dimensions of attitudes identified in
the study were related to the personality characteristics of both males and females. Here
are some of the results:

1 *Clothing consciousness.* "The people I know always notice what I wear." Females
strong on this dimension were inhibited, anxious, compliant before authority, kind,
sympathetic, and loyal to friends.

TABLE 8-4
PERSONALITY TRAITS COMMONLY ASSOCIATED WITH SOMATOTYPES

Endomorph	Mesomorph	Ectomorph
Affable	Active	Aloof
Affected	Adventurous	Anxious
Affectionate	Argumentative	Awkward
Calm	Assertive	Cautious
Cheerful	Cheerful	Considerate
Complacent	Competitive	Cool
Cooperative	Confident	Detached
Dependent	Determined	Gentle-tempered
Extroverted	Dominant	Introspective
Forgiving	Efficient	Meticulous
Generous	Energetic	Reflective
Kind	Enterprising	Reticent
Leisurely	Hot-tempered	Sensitive
Placid	Impetuous	Serious
Relaxed	Optimistic	Shy
Soft-hearted	Outgoing	Tactful
Soft-tempered	Reckless	Uncooperative
Warm	Social	Withdrawn
	High need for achievement	Low need for achievement
	Nonconforming	Conforming

Source: Compiled from Cortes & Gatti, 1970, pp. 32–34, 42–44.

2 *Exhibitionism.* "I approve of skimpy bathing suits and wouldn't mind wearing one myself." Males strong on this dimension were aggressive, confident, outgoing, unsympathetic, unaffectionate, moody, and impulsive.

3 *Practicality.* "When buying clothes, I am more interested in practicality than beauty." Females strong on this dimension were clever, enthusiastic, confident, outgoing, and guarded about personal self-revelations.

4 *Designer image.* "I would love to be a clothes designer." Males strong on this dimension were cooperative, sympathetic, warm, helpful, impulsive, irritable, demanding, and conforming.

Color preferences also appear to be related to personality (see, e.g., Lüscher, 1971). The predominant colors in a person's wardrobe can produce stereotypic impressions of personality. Compton (1962) found that assertive, sociable women preferred deep shades and saturated colors, while submissive, passive women preferred lighter tints.

Vocalics

Research on many aspects of the voice has yielded evidence of a significant number of relationships to personality. Early research found that inflection correlated with intelligence and breathiness related to neuroticism, introversion, and submissiveness (Crawford & Michael, 1927; Moore, 1939). In 1934, Allport and Cantril concluded that (1) the voice conveys correct information about inner as well as outer characteristics of personality; (2) although there is no uniformity in expression of personality from the voice (that is, certain personality traits are not consistently evidenced by certain vocal features), many features of personality can be determined from the voice; and (3) the more highly organized and deep-seated traits and dispositions are judged more consistently and more accurately than physique and appearance features.

Subsequent research added more information on the relationship between vocalics and personality. Markel, Phillis, Vargas, and Howard (1972) examined loudness and tempo. They found that *loud, fast* voices correlate with being self-sufficient and resourceful, expecting the worst of people, and blaming oneself for problems. The *loud, slow* voice is associated with being aggressive, competitive, confident, self-secure, radical, self-sufficient, and resourceful; tending toward rebelliousness for its own sake; being low on introspection; and responding to stressful situations with hypochondria. The *soft, fast* voice correlates with being enthusiastic, happy-go-lucky, adventuresome, thick-skinned, confident, self-secure, radical, phlegmatic, composed, optimistic, nonconforming, independent, and composed under stress. Finally, the *soft, slow* voice is associated with being competitive, aggressive, enthusiastic, happy-go-lucky, adventurous, thick-skinned, reckless, and carefree, but withdrawn and introspective under stress. Other investigations that have looked at such vocal features as resonance, loudness, pitch, and tempo have found that vocal profiles correlate with personality profiles (Mallory & Miller, 1958; Markel, 1969). In sum, voices are often good indicators of actual personality traits. You might want to compare your own voice qualities to personality features listed in this section to see if they apply to you.

SUMMARY

In studying nonverbal communication, one must be cognizant of nonverbal "badges" of culture, ethnicity, race, gender, age, and personality that help place a person in psychological space and create self-identity. Cultures can be identified by their expressiveness, amount of contact, and degree to which they are clock-bound. Each culture is also made up of subcultures that make cultural classification less accurate. The most important ethnic-racial identifiers involve gaze and vocalic cues. These differences appear to cause difficulties in interracial interactions. Gender identifiers are also prevalent, especially in kinesic expressivity, degree of immediacy, and use of vocalic cues. Age is most readily apparent from physical features and dress and adornment selections, as well as from posture and body movement at extreme ages. Age also is reflected by how younger people talk to older people, often through vocalic patterns that may patronize the elderly. Nonverbal behavior identifies personality differences among members of these subcultures, especially in kinesic, physical appearance, and vocalic behaviors. Somatotypes, dress and adornment, and vocalic cues are the most reliable identifiers of personality.

Being sensitive to these nonverbal identifiers and encoding appropriate cues can improve the quality of intercultural, interracial, intergender, intergenerational, and interpersonal relationships and the communication that occurs within them.

SUGGESTED READINGS

Burgoon, J. K., & Koper, R. J. (1984). Nonverbal and relational communication associated with reticence. *Human Communication Research, 10,* 601–627.

Collett, P. (1971). On training Englishmen in the non-verbal behavior of Arabs: An experiment in inter-cultural communication. *International Journal of Psychology, 6,* 209–215.

Dovidio, J. F., Brown, C. E., Heltman, K., Ellyson, S. L., & Keating, C. F. (1988). Power displays between women and men in discussions of gender-linked tasks: A multichannel study. *Journal of Personality and Social Psychology, 55,* 580–587.

Eibl-Eibesfeldt, I. (1979). Similarities and differences between cultures in expressive movements. In S. Weitz (Ed.), *Nonverbal communication* (2d ed., pp. 37–48). New York: Oxford University Press.

Erickson, F. (1979). Talking down: Some cultural sources of miscommunication in interracial interviews. In A. Wolfgang (Ed.), *Nonverbal communication: Applications and cultural implications* (pp. 99–126). Orlando, FL: Academic.

Gifford, R. (1991). Mapping nonverbal behavior on the interpersonal circle. *Journal of Personality and Social Psychology, 61,* 279–288.

Hall, E. T. (1981). *Beyond culture.* Garden City, NY: Anchor/Doubleday.

Henley, N. M. (1977). Body politics revisited: What do we know today? In P. J. Kalbfleisch & M. J. Cody (Eds.), *Gender, power, and communication in human relationships* (pp. 27–61). Hillsdale, NJ: Erlbaum.

Henley, N., & Kramarae, C. (1991). Gender, power, and miscommunication. In N. Coupland, H. Giles, & J. M. Wiemann (Eds.), *"Miscommunication" and problematic talk* (pp. 18–43). Newbury Park, CA: Sage.

Ickes, W. (1984). Compositions in black and white: Determinants of interaction in interracial dyads. *Journal of Personality and Social Psychology, 47,* 330–341.

Jourard, S. M. (1966). An exploratory study of body-accessibility. *British Journal of Social and Clinical Psychology, 5,* 221–231.

LaFrance, M., & Mayo, C. (1979). A review of nonverbal behaviors of women and men. *Western Journal of Speech Communication, 43,* 96–107.

Matsumoto, D., & Assar, M. (1992). The effects of language on judgments of universal facial expressions of emotion. *Journal of Nonverbal Behavior, 16,* 85–100.

Morris, D. (1977). *Manwatching: A field guide to human behavior.* New York: Abrams.

Noller, P. (1993). Gender and emotional communication in marriage: Different cultures or differential social power. *Journal of Language and Social Psychology, 12,* 132–152.

O'Hair, D., Allman, J., & Gibson, L. A. (1991). Nonverbal communication and aging. *Southern Communication Journal, 56,* 147–160.

Ryan, E. B., & Cole, R. (1990). Evaluative perceptions of interpersonal communication with elders. In H. Giles, N. Coupland, & J. Weimann (Eds.), *Communication, health, and the elderly* (pp. 172–190). Manchester, U.K.: University of Manchester Press.

Samovar, L. A., & Porter, R. E. (1985). *Intercultural communication: A reader* (2d ed.). Belmont, CA: Wadsworth.

Shuter, R. (1977). A field study of nonverbal communication in Germany, Italy, and the United States. *Communication Monographs, 44,* 298–305.

Stier, D. S., & Hall, J. A. (1984). Gender differences in touch: An empirical and theoretical review. *Journal of Personality and Social Psychology, 47,* 440–459.

Vrij, A., & Winkel, F. W. (1992). Cross-cultural police-citizen interactions: The influence of race, beliefs, and nonverbal communication on impression formation. *Journal of Applied Psychology, 22,* 1546–1559.

9

FORMING IMPRESSIONS

Men trust their ears less than their eyes.

Herodotus

Beware, as long as you live, of judging people by appearances.

Jean de La Fontaine

As to your practice, if a gentleman walks into my rooms smelling of iodoform, with a black mark of nitrate of silver upon his right forefinger, and a bulge on the side of his top hat to show where he has secreted his stethoscope, I must be dull indeed if I do not pronounce him to be an active member of the medical profession.

Sherlock Holmes
in "A Scandal in Bohemia," by Arthur Conan Doyle

Put yourself in the situation of meeting someone for the first time. Would you be able to use as much skill as Sherlock Holmes in forming an impression of that person? Assume that this person is wearing a kind of blue fatigue outfit with the name of a well-known Japanese corporation emblazoned across the back, and his name, John, monogrammed on the front left side. Ah, you think, a worker from the new Japanese microchip factory. After he asks you what you do for a living, you say, "Well, you must work in the new silicon chip plant just down the way here. Are you a foreman on one of the production units?" He gives you a quizzical look and says, "Oh no, I'm vice president for manufacturing." The conversation becomes awkward and stilted because both of you are embarrassed. Not quite a Holmes-like series of judgments, would you say?

What does this little scenario illustrate? (1) We tend to form impressions of others quickly and automatically and to draw inferences about them; (2) we often base our impressions of others on external and nonverbal characteristics, in this case dress and adornment features; and (3) impressions and inferences can be incorrect, especially when we are unfamiliar with the person and the situation, such as the Japanese corporation in this example. Employees of Japanese companies, managers and workers alike, often wear the "company uniform" (Halberstam, 1986; *Newsweek,* February 2, 1987). Since executives in American companies rarely, if ever, wear such uniforms, one might incorrectly presume that someone wearing such a uniform would not be very high up in the company hierarchy. To be fair, it's not quite clear what Holmes would do in this situation.

In this chapter we consider principles and nonverbal cues that allow people to form impressions of others. From this, you should gain a better understanding of how impressions are formed, and how the impressions you form affect the way you interact with others. Whether we wish it or not, impression formation is such a basic part of social perception that it is virtually automatic and habitual for most people. Such perceptions play very important—and in some cases necessary—roles in social life. As Asch (1946) noted,

> This remarkable capacity we possess to understand something of the character of another person, to form a conception of him as a human being . . . with particular characteristics forming a distinct individuality is a precondition of social life. (p. 258)

Impressions are the source of much of our attitudes and intentions toward others and a powerful guide to behavior. At times, impressions can also misguide behavior. In either case, the significance of our views of others, and how we come to them, is great.

Keep in mind that *impression formation* and *impression management,* a related topic to be covered in Chapter 13, are really two sides of the same coin. Impression formation is studied from the decoder's perspective and is concerned with how we form impressions of a communicator on the basis of nonverbal cues. Impression management, on the other hand, takes the encoder's perspective and is concerned with what we, as communicators, can alter and control intentionally to present ourselves to others in desirable ways.

The research on impression formation falls under such headings as social cognition, first impressions, person perception, and interpersonal perception. Among the key issues that this research addresses are: (1) How accurate or biased are first impressions? (2) How much consensus is there across observers in judgments made from nonverbal cues or channels (Kenny, 1991)? (3) Which nonverbal cues are most responsible for the impressions? (4) How long do first impressions last? (5) What other attributions are associated with nonverbal-based impressions?

PRINCIPLES OF IMPRESSION FORMATION

Folk sayings reveal our culture's interest in impression formation. Phrases like "You can't judge a book by its cover" and "Beauty is only skin deep" suggest a cautious and hesitant approach to impression formation. By contrast, "What you see is what you get" suggests that impressions are straightforward and reliable. Like many commonsense views of social behavior, these phrases do not quite hit the mark. The principles that researchers have found to govern the formation of impressions provide a more thorough and systematic view.

People develop evaluations of others from limited external information. By necessity, what we know about someone when we first meet, and even after several encounters, is quite limited. Despite this, we form impressions comprised of an extensive series of judgments. What drives people to make judgments with so little information? Some research (Berger, 1979; Berger & Bradac, 1982; Berger & Calabrese, 1975) indicates that impressions are a product of the uncertainty about the other person (usually a stranger) and the situation. Impressions provide some level of predictability about how the interaction with the person will proceed. Alternatively, people make rapid judgments to estimate whether the relationship is likely to be a rewarding one or not (Sunnafrank, 1986). In either case, making judgments on the basis of limited information is presumed to be psychologically satisfying.

What kind of information do we rely on to make inferences and judgments? As Berger and Calabrese (1975) pointed out, in first impression situations, since most initial conversation is limited to social amenities and standard social topics such as the weather and movies, we are not likely to know a lot about the other person by verbal means. Therefore, nonverbal cues predominate in the impression formation process.

Impressions are based partly on stereotypes. When forming impressions, we rely on what we already know about others in general. Alternately called person schemas, personality stereotypes and attributes, person themes, and person memory, we rely on our "person knowledge" when forming an impression because the amount of external information that is gleaned about an individual is limited. This stereotyping is especially likely to occur when people have little motivation to make individuated judgments and when they are "cognitively busy." Stereotyping becomes a way of arriving at a judgment without investing a lot of cognitive effort (Pendry & Macrae, 1994). Impressions are a combination of the limited information we know about an individual and what we know about people in general. This process reflects a general principle of comprehension and information processing called the *given-new* (Haviland & Clark, 1974) or *fact-inference* (Kintsch, 1974) distinction. This explains how we can go beyond given information to extract an understanding from a variety of new verbal materials and tasks. Interestingly, the way we form impressions of others parallels the way we comprehend things in other information domains.

Can nonverbal cues be linked to the general person knowledge most people have in our culture? The answer is clearly yes. As you will see shortly, there are a variety of nonverbal cues that elicit stereotypes about people. For example, many personality stereotypes are based on physical appearance features: the color of one's hair suggests personality traits (blondes are fun-loving, sexy, and not too bright; redheads are temperamental), as does one's height (tall men are aggressive and domineering). Vocal cues have also been linked to stereotypic judgments, with loud, deep, and resonant voices suggesting ambition and soft and hesitant voices implying shyness.

First impressions are often based on outward appearance. As we saw in the scenario that began this chapter, first impressions rely heavily on physical appearance. There may be a variety of reasons for this, but one reason is that physical appearance is readily available as a source of information during first encounters. Before you know any-

What impressions do you think the older woman has of the younger woman?

thing else about strangers, you know what they look like (presuming a face-to-face encounter). Other nonverbal cues come into play over time. Current research indicates that kinesic and vocalic demeanor and proxemic patterns are the next most available sources of information, but physical appearance cues are quite potent initially.

Several studies have affirmed this principle. As discussed in Chapter 2, physically attractive individuals are seen as more responsive, sensitive, kind, sexy, modest, poised, sociable, extroverted, intelligent, well adjusted, and interesting than unattractive individuals (Berscheid & Walster, 1974; Dion, Berscheid, & Walster, 1972). Taller and thinner men earn higher salaries (see Box 9-1). Finally, some jury simulation studies (Efran, 1974; Jacobson, 1981) have shown that guilty defendants who are physically attractive receive lighter sentences than unattractive ones.

The implications of these studies, and the principle in general, paint a somewhat unflattering picture of general social conduct in our culture. At least in initial encounters, people tend to judge books by their nonverbal covers. Subtle forms of prejudice and discrimination based on physical appearance may affect a number of initial encounter situ-

BOX 9-1

BEING TALL PAYS

Research regularly shows that the thinner and taller the male executive, the fatter the salary. Professors Irene Frieze and Josephine Olson surveyed 1,200 graduates of the University of Pittsburgh's MBA program. They found that tall men earned more than their shorter colleagues, and that men who were at least 20 percent overweight made $4,000 less than their thinner coworkers. A typical 6-foot male professional earned $4,200 more than his 5-foot-5 counterpart. When weight and height were combined, the taller and trimmer man earned about $8,200 more than the shorter and heavier man. Olson explained the survey findings by pointing out that "people imagine a male manager as tall, strong and powerful. And the man who meets that image gets rewarded."

The results for women were not conclusive because of the small number of female respondents who were significantly tall or overweight. However, Frieze indicated that "it's more complex for women than men. If a woman is seen as fairly attractive and she is doing these male-dominated jobs . . . there's a suspicion of how she's gotten there, how much she's used her attractiveness to get there." For tall and thin men, social stereotypes about physical appearance attributes and personal characteristics work advantageously. As for the rest of us, the implications are not so positive.

The connection between tallness and trait judgments of dominance and strength gets made early. One study (Montepare, 1995) examined the impact of variations in height in preschool aged children, and found that children judged taller male and female targets as stronger and more dominant. When given both male and female targets of different heights to judge, taller female targets were judged to be stronger, more dominant, and smarter when paired with shorter male targets. It would appear that, as both children and adults, tallness pays.

Source: Tucson Citizen, March 2, 1987, p. 9A.

ations, such as hiring interviews, court appearances, and even a teacher's initial assessment of a student's academic potential. Lip service is paid to basing judgments in these situations on relevant and meritorious attributes, but this unfortunately may not always be the case.

Initial impressions form a baseline for subsequent impressions and judgments. Initial impressions can have a lasting impact, but their importance diminishes in proportion to the amount of new information gained over time. Some impressions formed at an initial encounter do not change very much because of limited contact with the individual. These impressions can sensibly be called first impressions and are most likely to be affected by the principles already discussed. Other impressions do change because we have subsequent contact and literally get to know the person. These impressions are more detailed, complex, and stable. The longevity of an initial impression thus hinges on the amount of subsequent communication and new information that becomes available between the parties involved. Even so, research indicates that first impressions often serve as a template, guiding the interpretation of subsequent information, so a bias in person perception may persist due to first impression information. For example, consensual judgments observers formed of an individual before interacting (i.e., at "zero acquaintance") persisted after interaction with the individual began (Kenny, Horner, Kashy, & Chu, 1992). Also, communicators led to hold certain expectations about another's communication style continued to hold those views even when the person's actual nonverbal behavior contradicted the expectations. A horrible social blunder you commit during an initial encounter may leave a lasting impression that colors interpretations of your subsequent social competence. Repairing such impressions may require many behavioral counterexamples.

Impressions consist of judgments on at least three levels: physical, sociocultural, and psychological. Judgments on the physical level have to do with a person's age, gender, race, body shape, height, and weight. Sociocultural judgments are concerned with socioeconomic status, education level, occupation, place of residence, ethnic or cultural background, religious identity, political and social group membership, and attitudes that correspond to one's socioeconomic and cultural background. Psychological judgments have to do with psychological makeup, temperament, and moods, including inferences about personality and attributions of causality concerning behavior.

ACCURACY AND CONSISTENCY OF IMPRESSIONS

Many people wonder whether the impressions they form are accurate. After all, if you think of a friend in certain terms, it would be nice to know that your perceptions are accurate. Unfortunately, impression formation isn't that simple. The impressions we form may be *accurate,* in the sense that they reflect a person's "true" characteristics, or merely *consensual,* that is, consistent across several people who form impressions of the same individual but inaccurate. Research is beginning to show that several factors affect both accuracy and consistency.

First, the level of an impression affects the likelihood of its being accurate. Impressions generally are more accurate when made at the physical level, somewhat less accurate at the sociocultural level, and least accurate at the psychological level. In other words, as one moves from making judgments about external and fairly easily verifiable characteristics about a person to characteristics that are more internal and more difficult to verify, the less accurate one becomes. Cook (1979) indicates that overall, "the most striking finding to emerge from the extensive, jumbled literature on 'accuracy of person perception' is how very inaccurate most people are most of the time" (p. 119).

Despite inconsistent results in this area, recent research has shown that "hunches" can also be accurate (Smith, Archer, & Costanzo, 1991). As we have already noted, judgments of characteristics, such as sex, age, and occupation, typically are accurate because the characteristic being judged is external. Judgments of internal characteristics from nonverbal cues, such as attitudes, values, beliefs, and some personality traits, tend to be less accurate because these characteristics are more variable and subject to stereotyping. However, *some* personal and interpersonal characteristics can be judged with accuracy. Berry (1991) found that enduring facial and vocal cues accurately predicted self-ratings of warmth and power. Kenny et al. (1992) reported high accuracy as well as consensus on judgments of extroversion; Ambady and Rosenthal (1993) have shown that observations of nonverbal behavior as brief as 30 seconds predicted supervisors' and students' ratings of teachers' effectiveness.

Berry (1991) offered three possible explanations for the high degree of accuracy for some internal judgments: (1) There may be direct links between some features of personality and behavior (e.g., "approachable" people may use softer, warmer vocal patterns); (2) Self-fulfilling prophecies occur (e.g., obese people are expected to be jolly, are treated as such, and may then internalize jolliness); (3) Repetitive expressions of affect become permanent features of appearance (e.g., frequent scowling produces frown wrinkles, or chronic depression produces slumped posture). In addition, many studies documenting inaccuracies examined single cues or codes rather than the multiple codes that are actually available to interactants. Impressions founded on combinations of cues, especially dynamic cues available during interpersonal interaction, may be more accurate because interrelationships among concurrent cues provide clearer information. Smith et al. (1991) concurred:

> It now appears that multiple, redundant, interpretable cues are "diffused" throughout an interaction. . . . As a result, there are *many* paths to a correct inference, and perceivers will (quite correctly) cite as significant a disconcertingly wide variety of nonverbal cues. (p. 16)

In sum, our ability to judge internal characteristics accurately from nonverbal cues is mixed. Some characteristics, such as extroversion, are readily judged from a variety of nonverbal cues; other internal characteristics, such as an attitude toward incumbent politicians, are much more difficult to assess from nonverbal cues.

Another complication has to do with the term *accuracy* itself. To determine the accuracy of any judgment, some reliable information about the judgment must exist. Reliable information usually exists for the physical and sociocultural judgments we make about people. That is, if we think we know Sally as a white woman weighing about 115 pounds, standing 5 feet 4 inches, from Little Rock, Arkansas, who has a bachelor's degree in education and is a member of the Tri-Delta sorority, information is available to verify all these judgments. However, when we make inferences about Sally's personality and psychological makeup, the reliability and availability of relevant information decreases. If you judge Sally as outgoing, vivacious, flippant, judgmental of others, rigid, and bigoted, what information could verify these judgments? You could cite several examples of Sally's behavior, but you would still be relying on your *perception* of her behavior. Personality tests would not help much, either. The correlation between measured personality traits and behavior has been found to be low (Mischel, 1968), so the results from these tests would probably not be consistent with your impressions.

Thus it may be more useful at a psychological level of impression formation to focus on whether inferences are consensual, that is, similar and consistent across a variety of individuals who are making the judgments. Not surprisingly, many judgments at this level are consensual and consistent: people often agree on the personality traits of a given individual. However, research on what nonverbal cues produce consensual judgments about personality says little about what nonverbal cues provide accurate impressions.

Two more qualifying comments are in order about the research evidence we will review. First, since much of this research has investigated only one or two nonverbal cues at a time, what is known is often the impact of a fragmentary set of cues on impression formation. While researchers have made progress in cementing these nonverbal pieces together into something that corresponds to everyday interaction, much research on large sets of cues has yet to be done. Second, most of the research has not included situational and contextual factors, which may affect impression formation in a variety of ways.

NONVERBAL CUES AND TYPES OF IMPRESSIONS

Physical and Demographic Judgments

Judgments about physical characteristics—a person's age, gender, race, body shape, height, and weight—should be the easiest to make and the most accurate, but they are not infallible. These judgments typically are made on the basis of physical appearance and vocal cues, with other codes such as kinesics, proxemics, haptics, and artifacts playing a secondary role.

Age   At first glance (no pun intended), judging the age of someone unknown to you wouldn't seem very difficult. However, the difficulty of determining age depends in part on how exact the judgment needs to be. We are most successful at making estimates within broad age categories, particularly "infant," "preteen," and "elderly." Physical appearance cues are very likely to influence impressions of age. However, physical appearance cues can be misleading. Since our culture values youth so highly, a wide variety of cosmetics, drugs, preparations, and cosmetic surgery procedures are used to take years off one's physical appearance. As several researchers have pointed out (Burgoon & Saine, 1978; Leathers, 1976), these factors complicate age judgments and increase errors.

Clothing can also make specific and accurate age judgments difficult. Some clothing styles may identify the wearer as someone older, but this is usually because they emphasize comfort over fashionability. As younger people opt for more comfortable attire or "recycle" previously popular styles, the differences between old and young become less evident.

According to a number of studies, vocal cues can lead to fairly accurate judgments of age (Addington, 1968; Nerbonne, 1967; Pear, 1931). The accuracy of these judgments is probably due to changes in a variety of vocal parameters that occur with aging (see Chapter 8). As one grows older, for example, the pitch level of the voice drops, although in the elderly, gender may make a difference in this pattern (McGlone & Hollien, 1963). One study (Mysak, 1959) found that speaking rate drops with age: middle-age and older people speak more slowly than college-age people. However, children increase their speaking rate as they get older, because they pause less and become more articulate (Kowal, O'Connel, & Sabin, 1975). These results indicate that vocal cues change with age in ways we can implicitly recognize. Although these changes may allow some broad judgments to be made about age, Siegman (1978) suggested that more research is needed on vocal changes across the entire developmental time span before relationships between age and vocalics can be fully understood.

The relationship of other nonverbal codes to age judgments is speculative. Burgoon and Saine (1978) suggested that kinesic cues such as general posture, frequency of gestures, speed of movement, and apparent energy level could be related to age judgments. Similarly, proxemic cues—larger or smaller conversational distances—could indirectly indicate differences in age among people in a group.

To sum up, of the cues we have covered, vocal cues appear to provide the most reliable information about age. In fact, convergence of vocal and other nonverbal cues may help the observer to make more accurate and specific age judgments than research has suggested so far.

Gender   Although impressions of gender are relatively accurate, many people have embarrassing stories to relate about being mistaken in such judgments, particularly women with very short haircuts and men with earrings.

Physical appearance cues are often assumed to be clear indicators of gender. However, these cues do not present as clear a picture as it would seem. Clothes can often mask gender-related characteristics, and since it is common for males and females to wear similar styles of casual clothes, judging gender from certain angles can be difficult. Body type can also be an unreliable indicator of gender. People come in all shapes and sizes, regardless of gender. As films such as *Mrs. Doubtfire* and *The Crying Game* have shown, a he can certainly look like a she. Some styles of physical appearance conform more closely than others to our stereotypical view of masculinity and femininity, and the cues that are part of these styles can lead to gender judgments about individuals that are at least consensual, if not accurate.

As with age, vocal cues seem to be reliable indicators of gender (Epstein & Ulrich, 1966; Hollien, Dew, & Philips, 1971; Pear, 1931). In Chapter 8 we note many vocal cues that differ between males and females, and this wide variety of physiological and learned differences is probably what allows observers to distinguish between male and female voices. Other cues from the kinesic, proxemic, and haptic codes confirm our impression that someone is masculine, feminine, or androgynous.

Race and Ethnicity   Another fundamental part of an impression has to do with race and ethnicity. It is important to realize that the inferences people make in this area are based on racial stereotypes, not on judgments of racial or ethnic ancestry per se. The extent and impact of this stereotyping from nonverbal cues is illustrated in Box 9-2.

Physical appearance may allow us to categorize an individual into one of three broad racial groupings, often called Mongoloid, Negroid, and Caucasoid. However, it is often difficult to place people in one of these three broad groupings, much less to make any finer distinctions, on the basis of appearance. North Americans, for example, are not very adept at distinguishing between Koreans, Japanese, Chinese, Vietnamese, and Thais on the basis of facial structure, skin color, and hair. Note also that even within each broad racial category, there is a great deal of individual variation in physiognomy, so that any given individual may be difficult to categorize.

Another feature of physical appearance that may be relevant here is clothing. However, variations in dress are also due to other factors, such as geographic region, socioeconomic status, gender, and rural or urban location. For example, in India, distinct differences in the way Sikhs and Hindus dress are immediately recognizable. In North American culture, however, because of the mass production of clothing, dress is not a reliable indicator of race or ethnicity.

Similarly vocal cues do not provide a good basis for making judgments about race and ethnicity. Although one study (Nerbonne, 1967) suggested that vocal cues allow the discrimination of an individual's race, other studies contradict this finding (Knapp,

1978). This is somewhat surprising because, as we note in Chapter 8, research has identified some vocal differences among racial groups.

Several factors help to explain this seeming contradiction. First, it may be that some vocal differences are too subtle for the untrained ear to hear and cannot be used by most people to discriminate another person's race. For example, the finding that black children pause primarily at pitch changes in utterances, while white children pause at the beginning of clauses or conjunctions (French & von Raffler-Engel, 1973), is probably not noticeable to most people; it would take the trained ear of a sociolinguist and systematic research to pick up on the difference. Second, even though researchers have

---

BOX 9-2

FALSE IMPRESSIONS AND NOT "TELLING IT LIKE IT IS"

Though we might like to think otherwise, our judgments about a communicator's ethnicity can strongly affect how and what we communicate to that person. One recent study shows how judgments of ethnicity based on vocal cues alone can color attitudes expressed in an interaction. In this investigation, reported in the *Washington Post National Weekly Edition* ("How Perceptions of Race Can Affect Poll Results, Morin, June 26–July 25, 1995), researchers Lynn Sanders, Michael Dawson, and Ron Brown conducted the National Black Politics Study, a nationwide survey of 1,204 black respondents phone interviewed between November 1993 and February 1994. In this study, only black interviewers were used to carry out the phone interviews, which queried respondents on their political opinions. Respondents were not told the race of the interviewers, but clearly respondents did infer the race of the interviewer from vocal and verbal cues during the interview. At the end of the interview, respondents were asked to indicate what they thought the race of the interviewer was. Interestingly, results of the answers to this question showed that, as we noted earlier, judgments of ethnicity from vocal cues are not always correct: 76 percent of the respondents got it right, while 14 percent thought their black interviewer was white, and another 10 percent were not sure. Sanders reported that "respondents make racial assessments even when they cannot see the person interviewing them."

When Sanders looked at responses to the key political attitude questions based on whether the respondents thought they were being interviewed by a black or white interviewer, she discovered large differences in the answers given by the respondents. In general, respondents gave much more conservative

answers to these questions when they thought they were talking to a white interviewer than when they thought they were talking to a black interviewer. Some examples: (1) 64 percent of the respondents who thought they were being interviewed by a black interviewer agreed that "black elected officials can best represent the interests of the black community," while 49 percent of the respondents agreed with this statement when they thought they were being interviewed by a white interviewer; (2) 84 percent of the respondents who thought they were being interviewed by a black interviewer agreed that "The American legal system is unfair to blacks," while 72 percent agreed with this statement when they thought they were being interviewed by a white interviewer; (3) 14 percent of the respondents who thought they were being interviewed by a black interviewer agreed that "American society is fair to everyone," while 31 percent agreed with it when they thought they were being interviewed by a white interviewer.

Besides representing a serious challenge to survey researchers, these results tell us a great deal about vocal cues, ethnicity, and attitudes expressed in social interaction. First, we often draw inferences about the ethnicity and racial characteristics of others based on how their voice sounds, and those inferences may not necessarily be accurate (in this case, judgments *within* one's ethnic group were accurate about three-quarters of the time). Second, the attitudes and views we express are strongly affected by the perceived ethnic characteristics of others. Nonverbal cues play a key role in this sequence of events, and show that ethnicity still provides a significant frame of reference for how we act towards others.

identified dialects such as Black English that are tied to race and ethnicity, the use of these dialects is a sociological rather than a racial or ethnic phenomenon. Not all blacks speak Black English; middle-class blacks may either code-switch or not speak Black English at all. Further, Dillard (1972) showed that southern whites often use Black English forms. When a person hears the vocal cues associated with Black English, there is only a moderate probability that the speaker is actually black. One further complicating factor is the current trend of different ethnic groups' copying one another's style in music, urban street talk, and slang. For example, although rap mostly originated in the African-American community, members of other ethnic groups (Anglos and Hispanics) have become successful rap performers, and in doing so, have emulated the vocal style of black rap performers (much the same has happened in rhythm and blues). Similar cases of vocal emulation have occurred between different ethnic groups in street talk usage, all in the effort to sound "hip." With so much borrowing of vocal contours between ethnic groups, it has become difficult indeed to use vocal cues to reliably identify an individual's ethnicity. To sum up, the most reliable information for racial background judgments appears to come from physical appearance elements. Other codes appear to play supplementary roles at best, and none are highly accurate.

Body Traits   Although body characteristics are fairly accurately estimated from physical appearance cues, some evidence suggests that they can be derived from other nonverbal cues as well. Studies have shown that extremes in height and weight can be inferred from vocal cues. However, height and weight in the middle ranges are apparently difficult to estimate from vocal cues (Fay & Middleton, 1940; Lass & Davis, 1976). Knapp (1978) made two important points about these judgments: First, the precision required for the judgment to be considered accurate can affect whether vocal cues are found to be useful guides for these judgments. Interestingly, in the Lass and Davis study, the average difference between actual height and estimated height was only 0.8 inch, and the average discrepancy in weight was only 3.48 pounds. Second, it is still unclear what particular vocal cues are informative for extremes in weight and height judgments. It could be loudness, resonance, intonation, breathiness, or some other vocal cue. This area provides an opportunity for some interesting research.

In sum, judgments in the physical features category are often accurate, but not as accurate as one might guess. Physical appearance cues are usually good indicators of age, gender, and body shape but only moderately accurate indicators of race and ethnicity. Vocal cues provide good indicators of age and gender and somewhat accurate indicators of body characteristics but not very accurate indicators of race. Other codes appear to play a supporting and contextual role for these judgments.

Sociocultural Judgments

Included in the broad category of *sociocultural* impressions are such judgments as socioeconomic status, region of residence, religion, and political leanings. As with physical judgments, physical appearance and vocal cues are most relevant, although cues from other codes play a supporting role.

Socioeconomic Status, Occupation, and Education   Judgments of socioeconomic status, occupation, and educational level are highly correlated. An impression of one of these characteristics can lead to inferences about the others. Therefore, we discuss all three together here.

Imagine the following people on a bus or subway: a woman dressed in a sweater and jeans, a woman in a light-blue business suit, a man in a three-piece pinstripe suit with overcoat in hand, a man in corduroy pants and tweed sports jacket, and a man in jeans and a knit sportshirt. Do these clothing cues prompt you to make assumptions about these people's occupations, socioeconomic status (SES), and education? Your answer is probably yes. You might conclude that the people in jeans are students, the man in the pinstripe suit is a banker, the woman in the business suit is a middle-level corporate manager, and the man in the cords and tweed jacket is a college professor. These judgments may not be accurate, but they are most likely consensual.

Studies by Douty (1963), Rosencranz (1962, 1965), and Fortenberry, Maclean, Morris, and O'Connell (1978) have shown that observers make consistent status distinctions on the basis of clothing cues. Other anecdotal evidence indicates that many groups and corporations stress clothing as a means of indicating status and prestige via dress codes for employees.

Sybers and Roach (1962) noted that clothing is a symbol of status, that people are acutely aware of the status cues that clothing provides, and that people rely on apparel as a means of signaling professional aspirations and personal values. Further, people expect others to recognize their status and socioeconomic aspirations from their clothing. As a result, many individuals believe that if they don't conform to the dress norms for their social level and occupation, advancement up the ladder of success will be slowed, if not blocked. In some sectors of our culture, this is so; many people, rightly or wrongly, take dress seriously. In fact, Sybers and Roach indicated that clothing often communicates not only people's present SES, occupation, and education but also what they aspire to.

Before leaving clothing cues, it's worthwhile to note that one of the most straightforward clothing indicators of SES, education, and occupation is the uniform. Cultures formalize through the symbol of clothing the status of such occupations as police officer, judge, doctor, and clergy. This is further testimony to the need for readily accessible visual information about a communicator's social role.

Vocal cues are informative for some judgments, less so for others. Listeners can accurately identify a speaker's SES from vocal cues (Ellis, 1967; Harms, 1961; Moe, 1972). Although it is unclear from these studies exactly what vocal cues are responsible, pronunciation and pausing patterns are possibilities (Siegman, 1978). Siegman and Pope (1965), for example, found a correlation between silent pausing and SES in an interview study with female nursing students. In this study, lower-class and lower-middle-class subjects showed more pausing than upper-middle-class and upper-class subjects.

Judgment of occupation from vocal cues, however, is less precise. Some investigations (Allport & Cantril, 1934; Pear, 1931) have found limited support for accurate judgments of occupation from vocal cues. Another study that provided subjects with a wider range of occupational categories (Fay & Middleton, 1940) found a great degree of consistency among subjects' occupational judgments but little accuracy. Put in context, these results make a great deal of sense. A person's socioeconomic status is a constant

How do appearance cues and artifacts communicate the different socioeconomic statuses of these groups?

feature of his or her everyday life—people are born into a family at a given social stratum and are socialized by that family. As language researchers have shown, verbal and vocal behavior are affected by socialization at different levels of SES. Occupational choices, by contrast, typically are only made as an adult and thus do not have the powerful socializing effects that a person's socioeconomic background does. Short of very specialized occupations that require some kind of vocal training (such as radio announcer), it is unlikely that occupation has much recognizable effect on vocal cues; therefore, it is not used by listeners to make occupational judgments.

In sum, both physical appearance and vocal cues can be consistent, if not accurate, indicators of education, occupation, and SES. Being able to judge one of these three characteristics accurately greatly increases the odds of accurately judging the other two.

Region of Residence   Both physical appearance and vocalic cues can be indicators of the region in which a person resides. Of course, the communicators must dress and use vocal cues that are typical of their own region. Cowboy hats and western boots are at home in Albuquerque and Tucson but might be out of place in Baltimore and Cincinnati. Similarly, eastern seaboard "preppie" styles of clothing might look appropriate in Boston but less so in Boise. There are two important qualifications to the accuracy of inferences about geographic residence on the basis of clothing. First, because of the increased mass marketing of clothing in this country, a variety of styles are now available in most areas of the country. As a result, distinctive regional clothing styles may be disappearing. Second, often a particular regional clothing style becomes popular and is mass-marketed. That clothing style, then, is no longer a reliable indicator of region of residence. For example, while the "grunge look" originated in Seattle, this clothing style can now be found in just about any community in the United States.

Most of us are aware of the role that regional accent plays as an indicator of geographic residence. Trained and knowledgeable linguists can often accurately determine not only the state a person comes from by features of accent but the county or community as well. Most communicators do not have that precise an ear for accent, and the empirical evidence indicates that listeners can determine only the general region from which a person hails (Nerbonne, 1967; Pear, 1931). These broad regional discriminations may be easiest when a speaker uses a dialect that is not of one's own region. Brooklyn listeners can immediately recognize a speaker's southern accent, and residents of Mobile, Alabama, will know that a person with a Chicago accent is from the north.

Two factors complicate the judgment of regional residence from vocal cues. First, some parts of the country, like Florida and California, have experienced great influxes of people from other regions. As a result, it is difficult to determine what the local and regional dialects and accents are, and very mixed patterns of regional accent may result. Second, researchers have discovered that communicators often accommodate to the surrounding linguistic community's accent patterns. A person from Pennsylvania who moves to Oklahoma will after a while begin to sound like an Oklahoman.

Culture   Cultural judgments can be more difficult than one might think, and to some extent they overlap judgments of race and ethnicity. While features of physiognomy and skin pigmentation can often help define a person's ethnic and cultural ancestry, other physical appearance cues, such as clothing and grooming, are more useful in defining his or her *current* culture. Unfortunately, most observers may not know enough about other cultures to recognize clothing and grooming cues that would indicate ethnicity. For example, most westerners do not know enough about different traditional Asian folk costumes to distinguish between a kimono (traditional Japanese attire for females) and a hanbuk (traditional Korean attire). In our own culture, there are many subcultures whose members would theoretically be identified by clothing cues if traditional forms of clothing were worn. If individuals from Navajo, German, and Italian communities wear traditional costumes, an observer should be able to identify their ethnic backgrounds. However, since traditional forms of dress are infrequent these days, such cues are of little use in practice.

The ability of a typical observer to make ethnic or cultural judgments on the basis of vocal cues also appears to be limited. Different languages do have different vocal patterns and parameters in terms of rhythm, inflection, rate, and other vocal qualities. One study indicated that listeners may be best at identifying vocal patterns of their own language (Cohen & Starkweather, 1961). American subjects who heard filtered samples of Chinese, English, German, and Italian identified the English voice more accurately than any of the others. However, the extent to which a speaker exhibits these vocal cues and the degree to which a listener is familiar with them may be limited.

Group Membership   An individual's membership in social, political, religious, civic, and other groups is often communicated nonverbally, primarily through physical appearance cues. Whether the group is the Kiwanis, a local softball team, or a gangsta rap band, a variety of physical appearance cues will identify an individual as a member. Beyond inferences about group membership, observers will also make inferences about an individual's social, political, moral, and religious views, which are linked to these groups. In one study (Kelley, 1969), subjects were shown drawings of different clothing styles and then asked to indicate whether the wearer was liberal or conservative, supported or opposed the war in Vietnam, was religious or not, and was politically active or apathetic. Results of the study showed that unconventional dress was associated with the political left, greater activity in politics, and use of various drugs. Although this study is somewhat dated, some similar results would probably be obtained if it were replicated today. If this study were repeated using individuals in grunge style clothing as stimuli to be judged, no doubt we would discover that a variety of inferences would be made by observers based on clothing style, and those inferences would be connected to one's overall views of Generation X. So, regardless of what time era we may explore, individuals make judgments about others based, in part, on clothing style and how that clothing style may indicate group membership. On the whole, though, physical appearance cues allow observers a rather straightforward way of making inferences about another person's group membership and related attitudes.

Psychological Judgments and Attributions

People make a whole range of judgments about others' psychological states, personalities, traits, and moods. Many psychological judgments are evaluative in that they represent an attitudinal response to another individual. Also, these judgments tend to rely heavily on stereotypes, scripts, implicit personality theories, and other person-relevant information. As a result, these judgments are often more consensual than accurate. Further, unlike physical and sociocultural judgments, these inferences rely on a broader range of nonverbal cues. In a sense, these inferences are among the most interesting to investigate because they show how willing we are to attribute internal characteristics to an individual on the basis of external cues.

Personality   Perception of a personality trait in another person involves not only relying on one or more nonverbal cues but also linking those cues to a stereotype. Personality traits themselves are stable and enduring internal characteristics that persist across situations. As noted earlier, the accuracy of these judgments is at best difficult to assess. More important is the fact that such inferences and judgments are commonly made by observers about others.

A variety of physical appearance cues can lead to impressions of personality. One of the most basic is body type. Recall that people describe themselves according to a set of stereotypes that are associated with body type or somatotype—endomorph, mesomorph, ectomorph (see Table 8-3 in Chapter 8). These stereotypes are used to perceive not only oneself but other people as well. Walker (1963) showed that these stereotypes are used by parents and teachers to evaluate children. Although the accuracy of these stereotypes can be questioned, the more important point is that as part of the impression formation process, people often invoke such stereotypes based on the somatotype of the person being perceived. Further, if such stereotypes are applied early in life (as Walker suggested), children are consistently responded to and interacted with as if they actually possessed the personality traits associated with their particular body type. As a result, a child's self-concept and personality can be shaped by the expectations that others have on the basis of the child's somatotype. This line of reasoning could help to explain why there is some correspondence between somatotype and self-description in terms of these traits.

Another physical feature that may affect personality attributions is facial and cranial hair (see Box 9-3). Freedman (1969) asked male and female subjects to describe clean-shaven and bearded men. Male subjects (all beardless) described bearded males as more

---

BOX 9-3

APPLICATIONS: WHEN LESS IS BETTER—HAIRINESS AND JOB SUCCESS

Hair length and beardedness (for males) may affect judgments of occupation and even whether one gets a job in the first place. Burgoon and Saine (1978) reported the findings of a survey of 114 college recruiting officers and managers. The respondents in the survey were asked to rate a number of hairstyles and beards in terms of their effect on hiring decisions. The most favorable ratings were given to the moderately short-haired and clean-shaven male model. Although the survey was conducted in 1976 and the popularity of hairstyles and beards has changed somewhat since then, these preferences probably are still in place. It is common for males to get a shorter-than-normal haircut and to shave any facial hair before job interviews. Thus there is still a perception in our culture that short hair and the absence of facial hair makes one *appear* more businesslike and serious and therefore more appropriate for employment.

In many workplaces, long hair and beards are in fact unacceptable for employees, even for those who have been on the job for some time. This may be particularly true in jobs where an individual has to deal with the public, and the organization is concerned with its image. (A notable exception is that if you plan a career in the music industry, longer hair and beards may be perfectly acceptable, even required.) So while some occupations have lessened their restrictions on hair length and beards, many jobs in our culture regulate them, either implicitly or explicitly. Further, it is still the case that some hairstyles (e.g., punk or Rastafarian) rule the wearer out of most careers.

Are women's career concerns affected by hairstyles as well? Little systematic evidence is available on this question, but some authors (e.g., Richmond, McCroskey, & Payne, 1987) suggested that longer hairstyles on women are perceived as sexy and may contribute to perceptions of incompetence from female coworkers and low intelligence from male coworkers.

independent and extroverted, while the female subjects described bearded men as more sophisticated, mature, and masculine. Pellegrini (1973) went so far as to devise a study for which he took photos of men with beards and mustaches, had the confederates shave to goatees, photographed them, had them shave completely, and then photographed them again. These photos were then shown to subjects who were asked to rate them in terms of a series of personality traits. The results consistently showed that the more hair on the face, the higher the ratings on masculinity, maturity, self-confidence, dominance, courage, liberality, nonconformism, industriousness, and good looks.

This finding seems a bit curious in light of our discussion of beardedness and careers in Box 9-2. It may be that while some of the traits cited are desirable for males in careers, others, such as nonconformism, liberality, and dominance, are not. So from a personnel manager's point of view, beardedness presents a mixed picture at best.

As for hair length, while some organizations and companies still have either written or unwritten codes about hair length and beards, attributions about men who have longer hair (or beards) are not as negative as they once were. Personality stereotypes about hair for females exist, especially about length and color. However, these stereotypes have so far received little empirical attention. The larger issue here may be a matter of what is normative in the workplace. Since men and women have varying hair lengths these days, a variety of hairstyles may be tolerated without evoking negative attributions. However, coming to work with your hair dyed in waves of lime green, hot pink, and deep purple might raise many corporate eyebrows.

Finally, there may be a link between clothing and personality stereotypes. Given that people's preferences and attitudes about clothing are linked to their personality traits, it is possible that observers rely on the same dress cues to make personality attributions.

Vocal cues have also been associated with personality. Studies in this area fall into one of three categories: (1) studies that focus on the actual relationship between voice characteristics and personality traits, (2) studies that focus on the accuracy of judges in identifying personality traits, and (3) research that focuses on the perceptions attached to various vocal features. We are concerned with the last category of studies here.

One of the most extensive studies in this area was conducted by Addington (1968). Addington understood that certain vocal cues, in this case voice qualities, are closely linked to impressions of personality. He devised a study in which male and female speakers simulated breathy, thin, tense, flat, throaty, nasal, and orotund voice qualities. Subjects then rated the perceived personality traits. Table 9-1 presents the results of the study. The results indicate that some rather specific personality stereotypes are associated with voice qualities.

Attractiveness   Recent research has begun to examine sets of cues and their impact on a variety of impressions and judgments. Much of this research has focused on judgments of attractiveness, extroversion, maturity (and its opposite, babyishness), and other judgments correlated with these dimensions.

Much attention has been given to cues that foster perceptions of attractiveness. Being

TABLE 9-1
PERSONALITY TRAITS ASSOCIATED WITH VOICE QUALITIES

Voice quality	Personality stereotypes for males	Personality stereotypes for females
Breathy	Young, artistic	Feminine, pretty, petite, effervescent, high strung, and shallow
Thin	No relationships	Social, physical, emotional, and mental immaturity; high sensitivity; sense of humor
Flat	Masculine, sluggish, cold, and withdrawn	Same as for males
Nasal	Unintelligent, short, lazy, immature, fat, boorish, unattractive, sickly, uninteresting—all socially undesirable traits	Same as for males
Tense	Old; unyielding	Young; emotional, feminine, and high-strung; unintelligent
Throaty	Old; realistic, mature, sophisticated, and well-adjusted	Unintelligent, masculine, lazy, boorish, unemotional, ugly, sickly, neurotic, quiet, careless, unartistic, naive, humble, uninteresting, apathetic
Orotund	Energetic, healthy, artistic, sophisticated, proud, interesting, enthusiastic	Lively, gregarious, increased aesthetic sensitivity, proud, humorless

Source: Compiled from Addington, 1968, pp. 492–503.

perceived as attractive carries a great deal of clout in our culture (this is true in other cultures as well, although the specific cues that prompt perceptions of attractiveness are different from what we encounter in the United States). The power of attractiveness is illustrated by a stereotype that some researchers express as "what is beautiful is good." On the basis of this stereotype, attractive people are credited with more positive attributes, such as intelligence, persuasiveness, poise, sociability, warmth, power, and occupational success, than unattractive people (see Hatfield & Sprecher, 1986; Knapp, 1985). Another term for this is the *halo effect:* judgments of attractiveness positively influence judgments in other domains.

Early research in this area demonstrated that a variety of physical appearance cues produce judgments of attractiveness. More recent research (Berry, 1990a, 1992; Zuckerman & Driver, 1989; Zuckerman, Hodgins, & Miyake, 1990; Zuckerman et al., 1991) has shown that a combination of vocal cues can produce a vocally attractive voice, and that this vocal profile produces strong impressions of warmth, likability, honesty, dominance, and likelihood of achievement. Similarly, Berry (1990b, 1991) showed that certain characteristics make up a "facially attractive" impression, leading to a variety of other positive judgments. (See Box 9-4 for some examples.)

Beyond these vocal and facial cues, factors such as nonverbal expressivity, smiling, gaze, nonverbal immediacy and involvement, positivity of facial expressions, and appar-

BOX 9-4

IS BEAUTY BETTER THAN BRAINS?

It has now been nearly three decades since Robert Rosenthal and L. Jacobson published *Pygmalion in the Classroom: Teacher Expectation and Pupils' Intellectual Development* (1968). Rosenthal and Jacobson detailed the effect of teachers' expectations on students' performance and came to the conclusion that the impact was considerable. Subsequent research (see Clifford & Walster, 1973; Elashoff & Snow, 1971) found that students' physical attractiveness was one of the major determinants of teachers' expectations.

This seems unfair to children. A teacher's estimate of a child's abilities should not be so strongly influenced by physical attractiveness; moreover, the child's actual performance will be affected—because of the self-fulfilling prophecy or other such processes. One would hope, then, that these processes would be taken into account by teachers and schools. Ritts, Patterson, and Tubbs (1992) returned to these issues, reviewing 29 studies on expectations and judgments of physically attractive students, and performing a meta-analysis on 17 of these

studies. (A *meta-analysis* is a statistical review and summary of results of several studies). They concluded: "The studies reviewed here clearly show that highly physically attractive students, compared to their unattractive counterparts, are the beneficiaries of more favorable judgments by teachers. This attractiveness effect is reflected in teachers' more positive expectancies of physically attractive students in terms of their intelligence, academic potential, grades, and other attributes" (p. 422).

The significance of this research is hard to miss. Physical attractiveness has an impact early in our lives. It can determine what others, particularly others that figure large in our development, think and expect of us. While it would be overstating the case to indicate that all teachers' expectations are influenced by physical attractiveness, or that other factors don't play much of a role in developing those expectations, physical attractiveness is clearly important, as Rosenthal and Jacobson initially suggested.

ent spontaneity contribute to perceived attractiveness (Burgoon & Hale, 1988; DePaulo, 1992; Friedman et al., 1988; Gallaher, 1992; Kimble & Seidel, 1991; Manusov, 1991; Mueser, Grau, Sussman, & Rosen, 1984; Raines, Hechtman, & Rosenthal, 1990; Reis et al., 1990; Remland & Jones, 1989; Sabatelli & Rubin, 1986). Further, in contrast to previous research, Harrigan, Kues, Steffen, and Rosenthal (1987) found that self-touching confederates were perceived more positively on working relationship, honesty, and outgoing measures than confederates who did not self-touch.

Other Traits   A similar line of research has examined the effect of vocal maturity on perceptions of personality. Voices that have a "mature sound" suggest competence and power (Berry, 1990a, 1991; Montepare & Zebrowitz-McArthur, 1987; Zebrowitz-McArthur & Montepare, 1989). Faces too may have a "mature appearance," and facial maturity results in impressions of competence and power (Berry & McArthur, 1986). Researchers have also examined both vocal and facial cues that contribute to perceptions of childishness or "babyishness," a style of nonverbal behavior that is the opposite of maturity. Specific nonverbal cues involved in both maturity and babyishness include voice (loudness, pitch, pitch variety, tempo, delivery styles, and fluency), height and weight, and facial appearance. People with babyish voices or faces are perceived to be warmer, more honest, less competent, and less powerful than those who sound or look more mature (Berry, 1990a, 1992; Montepare & Zebrowitz-McArthur, 1987; Zebrowitz-

McArthur & Montepare, 1989). This is true of children as well as adults (Berry, Hanse, Landry-Pester, & Meier, 1994).

In sum, a variety of physical appearance cues, vocal cues, and facial cues may prompt impressions of attractiveness, extroversion, maturity, or babyishness. Perceptions of attractiveness have an additional impact: prompting positive impressions on other judgmental dimensions. Many of these judgments are attributions of enduring and stable traits, and as such may be the basis for consistent behavior of others toward the person being judged. It is important, then, to keep in mind that nonverbal cues may lead to these impressions, and that such judgments can have effects on other interpersonal outcomes as well.

SUMMARY

Impressions formed on the basis of nonverbal cues are guided by several principles, including these: (1) Impressions are based on limited information; (2) They incorporate stereotypes; (3) First impressions often make use of physical appearance cues; (4) First impressions often form a baseline for subsequent impressions; (5) First impressions are often consensual and may be accurate. Nonverbal cues from a number of codes have been shown to affect impressions on the physical, sociocultural, and psychological levels. Evidence indicates that impressions are more consensual and less accurate when they are concerned with internal and psychological characteristics than with external and objective characteristics, but recent research suggests that first impressions of some internal characteristics (such as extroversion) can be accurate. Finally, a wide variety of cues affect impression formation on all three levels of judgment, and cues that affect impression formation are widely distributed in the behavioral flow of interaction. "Don't judge a book by its cover" remains a prudent rule for social behavior, but much social life is nevertheless guided by WYSIWYG: "What you see is what you get."

SUGGESTED READINGS

Cook, M. (1979). *Perceiving others: The psychology of interpersonal perception.* London: Methuen.

Gallaher, P. E. (1992). Individual differences in nonverbal behavior: Dimensions of style. *Journal of Personality and Social Psychology, 63,* 133–145.

Harrigan, J. A., Kues, J. R., Steffen, J. J., & Rosenthal, R. (1987). Self-touching and impressions of others. *Personality and Social Psychology Bulletin, 13,* 497–512.

Hatfield, E. E., & Sprecher, S. (1986). *Mirror, mirror . . . the importance of looks in everyday life.* Albany, NY: State University of New York Press.

Kenny, D. (1994). *Interpersonal perception.* New York: Guilford Press.

Kenny, D. A., Horner, C., Kashy, D. A., & Chu, L. (1992). Consensus at zero acquaintance: Replication, behavioral cues, and stability. *Journal of Personality and Social Psychology, 62,* 88–97.

Kimble, C. E., & Seidel, S. D. (1991). Vocal signs of confidence. *Journal of Nonverbal Behavior, 15,* 99–106.

Kleinke, C. L. (1975). *First impressions: The psychology of encountering others.* Englewood Cliffs, NJ: Prentice-Hall.

Knapp, M. L. (1985). The study of physical appearance and cosmetics in Western culture. In J. A. Graham & A. M. Kligman (Eds.), *The psychology of cosmetic treatments* (pp. 45–76). New York: Praeger.

Manusov, V. (1991). Perceiving nonverbal messages: Effects of immediacy and encoded intent on receiver judgments. *Western Journal of Speech Communication, 55,* 235–253.

Montpare, J. M. (1995). The impact of variations in height on young children's impressions of men and women. *Journal of Nonverbal Behavior, 19,* 31–47.

Montepare, J. M., & Zebrowitz-McArthur, L. (1987). Perceptions of adults and children with childlike voices in two cultures. *Journal of Experimental Social Psychology, 23,* 331–349.

Mueser, K. T., Grau, B. W., Sussman, S., & Rosen, A. J. (1984). You're only as pretty as you feel: Facial expression as a determinant of physical attractiveness. *Journal of Personality and Social Psychology, 46,* 469–478.

Raines, R. S., Hechtman, S. B., & Rosenthal, R. (1990). Nonverbal behavior and gender as determinants of physical attractiveness. *Journal of Nonverbal Behavior, 14,* 253–267.

Reis, H. T., Wilson, I. M., Monestere, C., Bernstein, S., Clark, K., Seidl, E., Franco, M., Gioioso, E., Freeman, L., & Radoane, K. (1990). What is smiling is beautiful and good. *European Journal of Social Psychology, 20,* 259–267.

10

COMMUNICATING EMOTIONS

"He is the Napoleon of crime, Watson!" As my friend spun round from his position before the fireplace, the flames behind him and the shrill, unnatural quality of his voice lent his attitude a terrible aspect. I could see his nerves stretched to their highest limits. "He is the organizer of half that is evil and of nearly all that is undetected in this great city and in the annals of contemporary crime. . . ." He spoke in deadly earnest, almost babbling with fear. . . . The tirade did not so much conclude as run down. From shrill statements Holmes gradually subsided into inarticulate mutterings and from thence to whimpers. Accompanying this modulation in speech, his body, which had been striding energetically to and fro, now leaned up against a wall, then flung itself absentmindedly into a chair and, before I realized what had happened, Holmes was asleep.

Dr. J. H. Watson in N. Meyer, *The Seven-Per-Cent Solution*

Emotions and their nonverbal expression are an inescapable part of everyday life. We smile, laugh, frown, cry; we often appear surprised, angry, disgusted, contemptuous, interested, ashamed, happy, fearful. Emotions are a primary motivational force. Emotions are also social phenomena: they are more prevalent when we are in the presence of others. As a basis for understanding emotional expression, we first briefly consider the nature of emotions. Then we examine emotional expression itself, including the link between emotional experiences and emotional expressions. We conclude with a discussion of the the interpretation of emotions.

THE NATURE OF EMOTIONS

For over a century, scholars of human behavior have attempted to explain the phenomenon of emotion. Currently, emotion is viewed as a complex of four processes: (1) adap-

The faces of these rock fans display a wide range of emotions and affect blends.

tation and maintenance of balance in the human system, (2) a social signal system, (3) direct subjective experience of emotion, and (4) external emotional expression (Barrett, 1993; Buck, 1984; Fridlund, 1990).

Adaptation

The first component of emotion is adaptation. At the neurological level, *emotion* is an *innate reaction to a stimulus that motivates the organism to behave adaptively* with respect to the stimulus. Emotion communicates information about a person's internal state. It is the primary motivator that stimulates human cognition and organizes human consciousness so that the individual is ready to respond to events of significance to survival (Darwin, 1965; Izard, 1971, 1972, 1977; Tomkins, 1962, 1963).

Basic emotions are universal; that is, all humans, regardless of culture, possess similar neural mechanisms that produce emotions. This prewired emotion system arose through the natural progression of human evolution (Buck, 1984). Today, emotions emerge innately during maturation. For instance, distress at birth is adaptive because it motivates help from the caregiver. Later, the social smile emerges to motivate continued social stimulation and strengthening of interpersonal bonds. Still later, shame prompts the development of self-awareness and self-identity, and guilt prompts self-regulation (Izard, 1978). Table 10-1 details other emotions and the adaptations they motivate, which are necessary for physical development.

TABLE 10-1
DEVELOPMENT OF EMOTIONS AND THEIR ADAPTATIONS

Emotion	Age at emergence	Adaptation
Distress	Birth	Signals need for help from caregiver.
Startlelike movements[a]	Birth	Withdrawal from stimulus; signals caregiver about a potentially dangerous stimulus.
Disgust	Birth	Removal or rejection of distasteful substance from mouth; signals intolerance of substance and/or need for help in removing substance.
Interest	Birth	Attention; exploration; engages caregiver's interest; later regains and maintains perceptual contact, which stimulates learning.
Social smile	8–10 weeks	Continued social stimulation and strengthening of interpersonal bonds; invites attention from others.
Anger	3–4 months	Dealing with frustrations, restraints, and barriers.
Surprise	3–4 months	Increased surveillance and resetting of cognitive activities.
Fear	5–7 months	Self-regulation by defining limits; escape from harm; self-defense.
Joy	5–7 months	Development and maintenance of emotional attachments.
Shame	4–6 months	Development of self-identity and self-esteem; learn skills to increase self-worth and decrease likelihood of experiencing shame.
Contempt	6–12 months	Actions to overcome frustrations, restraints, and barriers.
Guilt[b]	12–18 months	Self-regulation by defining limits; cognitions about self-initiated actions that cause harm to others; understanding of self-responsibility.

[a]Not considered a basic emotion.
[b]Considered the principal emotional motivation in adult conscience.
Source: Adapted from Izard, 1978, pp. 163–201.

Social Signaling

The second component of emotion is social signaling. Unquestionably, overt emotion displays have a social function. Fridlund (1990) believed that emotional expressions develop as socially motivated behavior forming a communication system (see also Chovil, 1991; Jones, Collins, & Hong, 1991). This idea is consistent with the principle in Chapter 5 that behaviors originating as analogic signals become digitalized when treated as symbolic.

However, there is a controversy over whether what we see as emotional displays really reflect underlying emotional states or are serving other social functions instead. According to Chovil and Fridlund (1991, 1994).

> [F]acial displays almost never signify emotions. Typically, they are messages about attitudes, opinions, affirmations, ruminations, blocked goals, and social conventions. . . . They also act as syntactic markers, greeting signals, or provide listener feedback to speakers. (p. 165)

Further evidence that emotional expressions are not just biological reactions is that people are more likely to display emotions when others are present (see, e.g., Chovil, 1991; Fridlund, Sabini, Hedlund, Schaut, Shenker, & Knauer, 1990). Even children have been shown to express emotions more when their mothers also express emotions. For example, Tremine and Izard (1988) found that infants expressed more joy when mothers expressed more joy. Likewise, infants expressed more anger, sadness, and interest when mothers expressed sadness. Buck, Losow, Murphy, and Costanzo (1992) also found that the expression of emotion depended on the relationship with the other person (i.e., whether the other person was a friend or stranger) and that some emotions were less likely to be expressed with another person present. Emotional expressions are thus "adjustable" to social circumstances.

Some emotions are expressed in private and others are felt but not displayed. Cacioppo, Bush, and Tassinary (1992) observed electrical impulses to facial muscles even when the person did not overtly display an emotion. Buck (1991; Buck et al., 1992) concluded that emotion is an interaction between a biologically based system of spontaneous communication and a learned, culturally patterned system of symbolic communication.

Chovil and Fridlund (1991) countered that Buck's spontaneous-symbolic distinction suggests that some emotional expressions are authentic, while others, including most of the communicative expressions, are inauthentic. They asserted that expressions used to communicate attitudes, opinions, and the like are authentic despite the fact that the speaker does not feel an emotion. Further, Chovil and Fridlund asserted that emotional expressions can be simultaneously spontaneous and symbolic.

At this stage it seems fair to conclude that emotional expressions evolved as part of a signaling system, not merely as adaptations to environmental features (Fridlund, 1990, 1991), and may reflect internal affective states, social cues to others present, or both.

Subjective Experience

The third component of emotion is direct subjective experience—the feeling one gets when an emotion is elicited. Imagine the joy you experience when meeting a close friend or receiving a long-sought award, or your depression and sense of loss when a close friend dies or a goal is not achieved.

Origins of Emotional Experience   There is considerable debate over the source of these feelings. In 1890 William James proposed that subjective emotional experience is the *perception* of changes in facial expressions and physiological arousal, and this speculation has produced two different theories of emotional experience. According to the *differential emotions theory,* emotional feelings result from adaptive actions triggered by emotional reactions, especially facial displays (Buck, 1984; Izard, 1971, 1972, 1978, 1981; Tomkins, 1962, 1963, 1981). According to the *cognitive appraisal theory,* the subjective experience is a product of labeling changes in autonomic arousal. We appraise (1) whether to *attend* to a stimulus, (2) how *certain* we feel in the situation, (3) how much *control* we can exert to cope with the stimulus, (4) how *pleasant* or desirable the stimulus is, (5) whether we perceive the stimulus as an *obstacle,* (6) who or what is *responsible* for the stimulus, (7) whether the outcome is *legitimately deserved,* and (8) *anticipated effort* in dealing with the stimulus (Roseman, 1984; Schacter & Singer, 1962; Scherer, 1982a; Smith & Ellsworth, 1985).

These two theories have not yet been fully tested, and the tests that have been conducted provide confusing results (see Buck, 1984; Ekman, Levinson, & Friesen, 1983). Among the most intriguing issue is the "facial feedback hypothesis," which asserts that expressions registered first by the face feed back to the nervous system and elicit the emotional experience. Laird (1974) and Lanzetta, Cartwright-Smith, and Kleck (1976) found that adopting facial expressions of aggression and pain increased the subjective experience of these emotions, but Tourangeau and Ellsworth (1979) found no evidence of facial feedback in their study. (See also Ekman's view in Box 10-1.) Facial expressions may affect the intensity of the felt emotion or create general emotional feelings such as pleasantness or unpleasantness, but facial expressions may not produce specific emotional experiences such as disgust, anger, and contempt (Buck, 1984; Ekman & Oster, 1979; Winton, 1986).

Buck (1984) rejected these explanations in favor of neurochemical causes. Emotional feelings result when certain regions of the brain are activated, regardless of the person's state of arousal, facial expressions, and adaptive nonverbal and verbal behavior. For example, feelings of interest and surprise result from brain stem activation; feelings of pleasure and displeasure are produced by activating certain regions of the hypothalamus; the amygdala produces fear experiences. Thus Buck held that subjective emotional experience is a by-product of biological processes in the brain because awareness of one's own emotional state is essential for human survival.

An illustration of these three approaches is given in Box 10-2.

Categories versus Dimensions of Emotions Researchers have also debated whether people experience emotions as separate, distinct categorical phenomena or as composites of feelings along several dimensions. On one side of the issue are researchers who have

---

BOX 10-1

FACIAL FEEDBACK: DO WE FEEL HOW WE LOOK?

The mere act of putting on an angry face or a disgusted look can trigger the corresponding emotion deep within the brain, researchers have found.

Part of the brain that controls the facial muscles is connected to the lower parts of the brain where the emotions are thought to reside, said Paul Ekman of the University of California at San Francisco.

"By making a face, you can create [or] generate emotions," Ekman said at a press conference during the annual meeting of the American Association for the Advancement of Science. "These changes seem to be very strong."

Ekman has found that the effect occurs with fear, anger, disgust, and sadness. Strangely enough, it does not seem to occur with smiles and happiness, at least according to research done so far, Ekman said.

"Maybe because we smile so much, it's disconnected from the physiology," he said.

Furthermore, he said, the researchers do not yet know whether facial expressions can be used to turn off one emotion by triggering another—whether putting on an angry face can counteract sadness, for example.

Source: Associated Press, June 3, 1985.

BOX 10-2

APPLICATIONS: THE RUNAWAY TRUCK

Given the indispensability of automobile travel, many of us have had the unfortunate experience of an actual or near accident. This situation presents a useful, albeit unpleasant, illustration of the ways in which people may subjectively experience emotion.

Suppose that you are cruising along a four-lane highway late one evening when suddenly you see a large truck swerve over the median and head directly toward you. You immediately become aroused, display a facial expression consisting of widened eyes and parted, tightened lips, scream "Oh,————!" slam your foot on the brake, violently yank the steering wheel to one direction, and pray. At the same time, you subjectively experience fear. What caused this feeling of fear?

William James would have theorized that your feeling of fear resulted from labeling your heightened autonomic arousal and facial expression. Moreover, if you did not display these reactions—say, if you simply remained calm and adopted a neutral facial expression—you would not have subjectively experienced fear.

Differential emotions theory, as developed by Silvan Tomkins and Carroll Izard, claims that your subjective experience of fear resulted from your overt reactions. However, this theory holds that (1) the total combination of overt adaptive responses, not merely the facial expression, contributed to your feeling of fear; (2) autonomic arousal was not a factor in your feeling of fear;

and (3) it was the observation of the responses, not the labeling of responses, that produced the fearful feeling. The adaptive responses carried meaning, and you interpreted this meaning in much the same way as you would have interpreted these actions performed by another person.

In contrast, cognitive appraisal theory maintains that your fear resulted from applying a label to the sudden change in autonomic arousal you experienced upon observing the truck moving toward you. That label stemmed from the attention you devoted to the truck, the certainty, or perhaps uncertainty, that the truck would harm you, your inability to control the truck's movement, the unpleasant anticipated outcome of a collision, the obstacle the truck presented, your lack of responsibility for the event, your belief that the anticipated harm was not deserved, and the amount of effort required to avoid the collision.

Finally, Ross Buck would argue that your feeling of fear resulted from the chemical changes that occurred when certain regions of your brain were activated by the vision of the truck approaching you. That is, you did not observe your own action, nor did you label your arousal, in order to experience fear. Rather, your feeling of fear was a chemical by-product or residue of brain activity, the brain activity that sensed the truck and activated coping behaviors, facial expression, and autonomic arousal.

---

studied facial displays. Tomkins (1962, 1963), Ekman (1971), and Izard (1977) argued that emotions are categorical. Happiness is experienced as distinct from sadness, distinct from surprise, distinct from contempt. Each of these authors offered a set of basic categories that he considered universal (see Table 10-2).

On the other side of the issue is a great deal of evidence that emotions are experienced along two or perhaps three dimensions. The most consistent dimensions include pleasantness and activity. People appear to have an implicit mental map on which the emotions are arrayed in a circle defined by these two dimensions. Figure 10-1 shows that arousal and sleepiness define the activity dimension, while pleasure and misery define the pleasantness dimension. Distress is a highly active, unpleasant emotion. Excitement incorporates high activity and pleasantness. Contentment combines low activity and pleasantness. Finally, depression is an inactive, unpleasant emotion. A third dimension of intensity has been added to this model; see Figure 10-2 (Abelson & Sermat, 1962; Apple & Hecht, 1982; Bush, 1973; Cliff & Young, 1968; Daly, Lancee, & Polivy, 1983; DePaulo, Rosenthal, Finkelstein, & Eisenstat, 1979; Dittmann, 1972b;

TABLE 10-2
UNIVERSAL CATEGORIES OF EMOTION

Tomkins	Ekman	Izard
Interest	Happiness	Interest
Joy	Sadness	Joy
Surprise	Fear	Surprise
Distress	Surprise	Sadness
Fear	Anger	Anger
Shame	Disgust-contempt	Disgust
Contempt		Contempt
Anger		Fear
		Shame
		Shyness
		Guilt

Sources: Ekman, 1971; Tomkins, 1962, 1963; Izard, 1977.

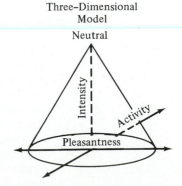

Two–Dimensional
Model

• AROUSAL

• EXCITEMENT

DISTRESS
•

PLEASURE
•

•
MISERY

DEPRESSION •

CONTENTMENT •

• SLEEPINESS

FIGURE 10-1
Universal dimensions of emotions: Two-dimensional model.

Three–Dimensional
Model

Neutral

Intensity

Activity

Pleasantness

FIGURE 10-2
Universal dimensions of emotions: Three-dimensional model.

Neufeld, 1975, 1976; Plutchik, 1962, 1980; Royal & Hays, 1959; Russell, 1978, 1980, 1983; Russell & Bullock, 1985; Russell & Steiger, 1982; Schaefer & Plutchik, 1966; Schlosberg, 1952, 1954; Shepard, 1962).

The two positions are actually complementary. Russell held that the emotional dimensions are innate and universal. Children learn to differentiate their feelings on these dimensions and to label combinations of pleasantness and activity as specific emotions (Russell, 1983; Russell & Bullock, 1985; Russell & Steiger, 1982). Buck (1984) asserted that neurochemical processes in the brain produce both dimensionlike and categorical emotions.

External Expression

The fourth component of emotion is external expression. The function of nonverbal communication in emotional expression is the major focus of this chapter; it is discussed in detail in the following sections.

EXPRESSING EMOTIONS

In considering emotional expression, several questions are important. First, what is the link between emotion and its overt expression? Second, are any expressions—in particular, facial expressions—universal? Third, how are emotions coded nonverbally? Fourth, what factors influence emotional expression?

The Link between Emotional Experience and Expression

The link between emotion and its overt expression has been a source of controversy for over 100 years. Most of this controversy has centered on whether emotional expressions are innate or learned.

The Universalist Position   *Universalists,* including Darwin (1965), Allport (1924), Tomkins (1962, 1963), and Izard (1971, 1977), argued that emotional expressions are innate and inherited. These expressions developed through evolution because they were biologically adaptive in early times:

> Actions, which were at first voluntary, soon become habitual, and at last hereditary, and may then be performed even in opposition to the will. Although they often reveal the state of mind, this result was not at first either intended or expected. Even such words as that "certain movements serve as a means of expression" are apt to mislead, as they imply that this was their primary purpose or object. This, however, seems rarely or never to have been the case: the movements having been at first either of some direct use, or the indirect effect of the excited state of the sensorium. An infant may scream either intentionally or instinctively to show that it wants food; but it has no wish to draw its features into the peculiar form which so plainly indicates misery; yet some of the most characteristic expressions exhibited by man are derived from the act of screaming. . . . (Darwin, 1965, p. 356)

Darwin believed that the primary adaptive purpose of present-day emotional expressions is to signal or communicate internal emotional reactions to others (see also Barrett, 1993).

The universalists have compiled compelling evidence of the cross-cultural, cross-generational, and cross-species consistency of expressions of the basic emotions. (The basic emotions are listed in Table 10-2.) Studies of children born blind and deaf provide additional evidence for this position. These children, who have very little opportunity to learn emotional expressions, encode emotional expressions like laughter, anger, and resentment similarly to sighted and hearing children (Charlesworth & Kreutzer, 1973; Eibl-Eibesfeldt, 1975; Fraiberg, 1971; Fulcher, 1942; Goodenough, 1932). Also, the consistent pattern with which emotional expressions emerge during childhood suggests that they are at least partly innate (Izard, 1978; Oster & Ekman, 1978). The development of emotional expressions will be discussed later.

The Cultural Relativist Position   In opposition to the universalists stand the *cultural relativists* (Birdwhistell, 1970; LaBarre, 1947; Leach, 1972; Mead, 1975). They see emotional expression as specific to a given culture. People learn which expression goes with which emotion in much the same way as they learn language. Cultural relativists argue that even when emotional expressions transcend culture, the rules for emotional expression and the social functions associated with expressions are determined by the cultural context. Cultural relativists have recorded a large number of cross-cultural differences in support of their position.

Neurocultural Theory   Paul Ekman and his colleagues (Ekman, 1971, 1975; Ekman, Sorenson, & Friesen, 1969; Oster & Ekman, 1978) developed a third explanation, *neurocultural theory,* which synthesizes the universalist and cultural relativist positions. Neurocultural theory assumes that emotional expressions are innately prewired in the human brain, but through experience people learn culture-specific rules for their display. The entire expressive process, illustrated in Figure 10-3, involves eliciting events that activate the neurological affect program. This affect program directs overt emotional expressions and other behaviors that cope with the emotion and elicitor. The link between the affect program and overt behavior is moderated by learned display rules. Let us examine each of these components more closely.

According to the theory, the first component of the emotional expression process is *elicitors:* events that stimulate emotion in the human brain. Ekman believed that basic noninterpersonal elicitors, such as hunger, are universal but that many interpersonal elicitors, such as messages from other people, are socially learned and vary from culture to culture. Early in life, noninterpersonal elicitors predominate in the emotional expression process, but by late childhood, learned interpersonal elicitors are more plentiful. Ekman also believed that humans have the capacity to analyze and evaluate elicitors.

In most instances, an elicitor triggers the neurological emotion system, which Ekman labeled the *affect program.* This innate neurological system controls facial and vocal responses, verbal responses, skeletal motor responses, more fully elaborated coping behaviors, autonomic and central nervous system changes, and the subjective experience of emotion. Within this affect system is a set of basic emotions: happiness, sad-

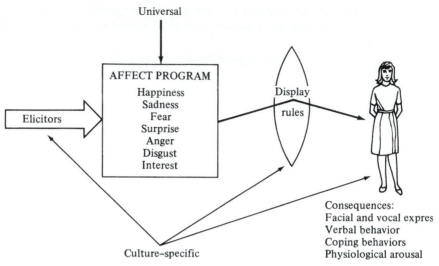

FIGURE 10-3
Process of emotional expression.

ness, fear, surprise, anger, disgust, and interest. The affect program links each primary emotion to a distinctive pattern of adaptive behaviors, including a distinctive facial expression.

These innate emotion-expression links exist because (1) certain facial movements are required to sustain life and (2) it is adaptive to signal emotions and intentions to other humans. Ekman also recognized the role of social learning in the emotion-expression linkage. He believed that as humans mature, they recognize that certain events signal the presence of elicitors. These anticipatory events are learned and linked with facial muscle performance. Through social learning, various objects, ideas, people, and behaviors are associated with the original innate elicitor or anticipatory elicitors and activate the emotion-expression linkage.

Humans do not display simply pure emotional expressions, such as happiness, sadness, or disgust. Rather, the affect program frequently blends pure expressions to create new expressions. People can simultaneously appear surprised and happy, angry and contemptuous, fearful and surprised. These blends are likely to be culture-specific because an elicitor that activates a blended expression is unlikely to be present in another culture. Also, blends often result from culture-specific display rules governing emotional expression. Finally, a common cause of blends is intrapersonal reactions to one's own feelings, which are generally a product of culture (e.g., feeling ashamed of being angry).

Reactions of people around us may be the most potent source of display rules. For instance, mothers regulate angry emotions by their children more than happy ones, which may explain why angry emotional displays are not as socially appropriate (Casey & Fuller, 1994). Children also mimic the emotional expressions of their mothers (Denham & Grout, 1993; Tremine & Izard, 1988).

As we note in Chapter 8, culture dictates many of these rules. Matsumoto (1991) speculated that collectivistic cultures like Japan display emotions in ways that promote group harmony. That is, members of these cultures are less likely to express negative emotions toward fellow members of their social groups but more likely to express negative emotions toward members of other social groups to which they do not belong. Members of more individualistic cultures, like the United States, are less concerned with preserving group harmony, and so are more apt to express negative emotions. Power distance in a culture—the extent to which status differences are preserved—also produces display rules. In cultures with high power distance, like Japan, higher-status individuals are more likely to display negative emotions to lower-status individuals to signal their higher status. In cultures with low power distance, like the United States, higher-status individuals are less likely to express negative emotions to lower-status individuals, to promote equality.

The final step in the expressive process involves the *consequences* of emotional arousal. These are the actual adaptive behaviors directed by the affect program and modified by display rules. These include facial expressions, vocalic responses, verbal behavior, other behaviors that cope with the aroused emotion or elicitor, and physiological arousal.

An important assumption within neurocultural theory is that people are able to control the expressive process. People can alter the activation of the affect program by elicitors, inhibit activation of emotional expressions by the affect program, encode emotional expressions without activation of the affect program, and modify emotional expressions once they begin. This control is possible because a large portion of the emotion process occurs within the somatic neurological system, which is open to active control.

To review neurocultural theory, consider the following example. You are out with a group of friends at a local nightclub. Midway through the evening, one of your friends comes back to the table with a man (the elicitor) she has met dancing. It turns out that you know him from one of your classes, but you consider him a loud, obnoxious type and are annoyed (affect program activated) that she brought him to the table. However, because you are in a social situation and she is a close friend, you do not display an overt expression of dislike or anger, adopting instead a polite but weak smile while talking with the couple (display rules causing a deintensified polite smile to mask anger expression).

The ability to intentionally control the emotion-expression link has led to several interesting speculations. Several researchers have suggested that people can regulate their subjective experience of emotion by voluntarily controlling expressive behavior in a way that promotes or inhibits interaction with other individuals. This process, which Patterson (1987) called the *affect management function,* can intensify or diminish a felt emotion. For instance, when in crisis, people may display sadness in part to obtain comfort from others and thereby alleviate their distress. Expressions of happiness when feeling elated can produce greater involvement with others that intensifies the emotional experience. Embarrassment or shame is expressed in ways that reduce the amount of interaction with others or that elicit sympathy from others. Both strategies seek to lessen this aversive emotional state (see also Cappella, 1991, and DePaulo, 1991, for discussions of this process and Denham and Grout, 1993, for evidence of this process between mothers and children).

Earlier, we introduced the concept of a signal system. The idea that emotions are part of a signal system takes controllability even further. Fridlund (1991, 1994) asserted that in most communication situations, people display emotional expressions that have no correspondence to their internal emotional states. Rather, emotional displays are used as units within the communication code, just like words and gestures. Fridlund took issue with the idea that emotional expressions are elicited only when experiencing an internal emotional reaction and that the actual form of the overt expression is determined by display rules. He particularly disliked the idea that emotional expressions that do not reflect the internal emotional state are inauthentic or false. According to Fridlund, emotional expressions used within the communication code system carry authentic, intentional meaning even though they are not produced by internal emotional reactions.

Scherer (1984, 1994) proposed that the actual form of an emotional expression is the result of a sequential cumulative process of stimulus evaluation checks that each trigger specific facial movements and vocal changes. These checks include registering the novelty and intrinsic pleasantness of the stimulus, its significance for one's goals and needs, one's potential to cope with the stimulus, one's power to respond, and the compatibility of the response with norms and self-behavior patterns. Rather than being unitary expressions, then, emotional displays may comprise indicators of all of these stages of response.

Universality of Facial Expressions

Cross-Cultural Evidence   In developing their neurocultural theory, Ekman and his colleagues explored the universal nature of facial expression (Ekman, 1971, 1975; Ekman & Oster, 1979; Ekman et al., 1969; Oster & Ekman, 1978). Research comparing American, Japanese, Argentinean, Chilean, and Brazilian communicators showed a high degree of cross-cultural similarity in the facial expressions of emotions and the meanings assigned to facial expressions. This research produced evidence of culture-specific display rules, particularly those governing public and private displays of emotions. Independent research by Izard (1971) with Japanese, American, English, Spanish, French, German, Swiss, and Greek communicators also confirmed this cross-cultural consistency in decoding facial expressions (see Box 10-3).

Developmental Evidence   Another area providing evidence for the universality of facial expressions is child development. Both Ekman and Izard reported a universal pattern in the emergence of such expression in children. The neurological emotion system, or affect program, and the facial musculature necessary for expression are fixed at birth (Ekman & Oster, 1979; Oster & Ekman, 1978). Izard's research (1978) shows that the neonate typically displays expressions of distress, disgust, and interest. Smiling begins at this time, although it does not become social until about 8 or 10 weeks later. Expressions of anger and surprise emerge at 3 to 4 months, fear and joy at 5 to 7 months, and shame at 4 to 6 months. Expressions of contempt and guilt appear later, at 6 to 12 months and 12 to 18 months, respectively (review Table 10-1). All children, then—regardless of cultural background—show the same maturation process when it comes

BOX 10-3

APPLICATIONS: THE INSCRUTABLE JAPANESE AND (IL?)LITERATE SOUTH FORE

Ekman and his colleagues traveled extensively to other cultures to demonstrate the universal nature of facial expressions. In one series of studies, they found that Japanese and Americans were accurate judges of pleasant and unpleasant emotional expressions portrayed by communicators from the other's culture. Further, judgments by Japanese and American observers corresponded. When American observers thought the communicator expressed happiness, Japanese observers also thought the communicator expressed happiness. A third study in this series compared actual facial expressions encoded by Japanese and American senders. Once again, broad cross-cultural agreement prevailed.

The research on Japanese communicators also revealed the use of display rules. Japanese and Americans enacted similar disgust and anger expressions, but only when the Japanese were alone and unaware of being observed. When Japanese and American communicators were later interviewed about these reactions, the Japanese masked these expressions with a polite smile, whereas the Americans openly displayed their disgust and anger. Ekman attributed this difference to culture-specific display rules prohibiting public facial expressions of disgust and anger in Japan but permitting them in America. Thus the stereotype of the inscrutable Japanese has a kernel of truth and is partly the result of cultural display rules.

The evidence for universality is open to one criticism. Namely, members of literate cultures might learn to display and judge facial expressions similarly through direct contact with other literate cultures, especially through the mass media. To answer this criticism, Ekman's group traveled to the South Pacific to study the emotional expressions of members of a preliterate culture, the South Fore of New Guinea. This tribe had its own language and very limited contact with literate cultures and advanced technology. Ekman showed facial expressions of happiness, sadness, fear, surprise, anger, and disgust, portrayed by American communicators, to members of the tribe. Many of their emotional judgments were exactly what Ekman had expected. The South Fore were accurate when decoding expressions of happiness, sadness, disgust, and surprise. They did have some problems with expressions of fear and anger, which they mistook for surprise and disgust, respectively.

Next, Ekman videotaped members of the South Fore expressing emotions facially. When his group returned to the United States, they asked American observers to decode the expressions of the South Fore. The American judges were accurate when decoding expressions of happiness, sadness, anger, and disgust. Interestingly, the Americans had difficulty distinguishing fear from surprise, as did the South Fore.

The results of these two experiments rule out the argument that cross-cultural similarities come about by exposure to other cultures and further reinforce the contention of the neurocultural theory that basic emotional displays are universal.

to the basic facial expressions. Once these expressions emerge, though, children begin to learn that they can be controlled voluntarily, displayed without the presence of the emotion, used to achieve certain outcomes, and modified to conform with social rules.

Nonverbal Emotional Cues

Research on emotional expression has tried to identify the nonverbal behavior or clusters of behaviors that transmit each emotional meaning. Facial and vocalic behaviors consistently outperform other nonverbal channels. The body plays a lesser but important role as well (Barrett, 1993).

Facial and vocal expressions of emotion frequently perform the same functions, but they differ in several respects. Facial expressions are only communicative when the recipient is directly oriented to the sender and the distance between them is small. Vocal expressions are omnidirectional—we are likely to hear them even if we are not focusing on them—and can travel farther differences. The face can provide a continuous emotional signal; vocal emotional signals are more intermittent. Because vocal expressions are usually tied to speech, they furnish important context information for the interpretation of speech and in turn may be affected by speech activity. Finally, facial expressions are distinctly adaptive; the adaptive origins of vocal expressions are less obvious (Scherer, 1994).

Facial Cues   Facial behaviors that influence the transmission of emotional meaning can be separated into three groups: static, slow, and rapid (Ekman & Friesen, 1975). *Static signals* are permanent features of the face such as skin color and bone structure. *Slow signals* tend to alter gradually over time, as is the case with skin texture and wrinkles. Static and slow signals can alter or complement the transmission of emotional cues. For instance, you may know people with crow's-feet, small wrinkles emanating from the outside corners of the eyes, who always appear to be expressing pleasant emotions, regardless of their other facial cues. Their negative expressions appear to be blended with at least weak pleasant emotion. Conversely, you may know others whose wrinkles form a permanent scowl.

   Rapid signals are our main concern. They provide the primary cues about emotion, including all kinesic movements usually associated with facial expressions of emotion.

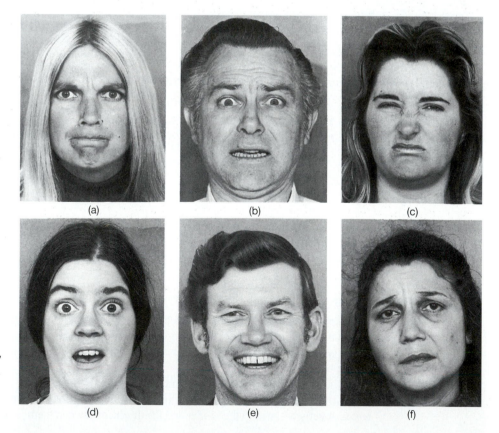

Facial expressions of primary emotions: (a) anger, (b) surprise, (c) disgust, (d) fear, (e) happiness, and (f) sadness.

In analyzing rapid facial movement during emotional expression, Ekman and Friesen found it useful to separate the face into three regions: (1) brows and forehead; (2) eyes, eyelids, and bridge of the nose; and (3) cheeks, nose, mouth, chin, and jaw (Ekman et al., 1971). Each of these areas provides cues that contribute to the emotional meaning of an expression. That doesn't mean that cues from all regions are important to all emotional expressions. Observers may pay close attention to one region, using cues in the other regions only to check their interpretations.

Table 10-3 summarizes the role of each of the three facial regions in expressing various emotions (Boucher & Ekman, 1975; Ekman et al., 1971). It is apparent that disgust is best conveyed by the mouth and cheek region, fear by the eyes and eyelids, sadness by both the eyebrows and forehead and the eyes and eyelids, happiness by both the mouth and cheeks and the eyes and eyelids, anger by both the mouth and cheeks and the eyebrows and forehead, and surprise equally well by all three regions. (See Cuceloglu, 1972, for a similar analysis.)

Forsyth, Kushner, and Forsyth (1981) identified specific facial movements displayed when communicating pleasure, annoyance, interest, certainty, and puzzlement. Pleasure produced an upward mouth curvature accompanied by raised cheeks. This is the classic smile. (Ekman and Friesen, 1982, also reported that the smile is accompanied by a gath-

TABLE 10-3
EMOTIONAL EXPRESSION IN THE THREE FACIAL REGIONS

Emotion	Facial region		
	Eyes and eyelids	Eyebrows and forehead	Mouth and cheeks
Pleasant (happiness, joy)	yes (skin gathered around eye sockets)	no	yes (mouth curved upward, cheeks raised)
Unpleasant (general)	no	yes	yes
Fear	yes	no	no
Sadness	yes	yes	no
Disgust	no	no	yes
Calm	yes	yes	yes
Irritation (general)	yes	yes	no
Anger	no	yes	yes (mouth shortened and opened)
Receptivity (attentive, open)	yes	yes (raised and constricted)	yes (mouth curved, cheeks raised)
Nonreceptivity (indifferent)	yes	yes	no
Certainty	no	no	yes (mouth stretched, cheeks raised)
Uncertainty (puzzled, bewildered)	no	yes (lowered and constricted)	yes (mouth curved down, dropped jaw)

Sources: Adapted from Boucher & Ekman, 1975; and Ekman et al., 1971.

ering of the skin inward around the eye sockets.) Annoyance produced an expression combining a short mouth length and a slightly open mouth. Interest was expressed by curving the mouth slightly upward, raising the cheeks and eyebrows, tilting the head to the side, and constricting the forehead muscles. A combination of higher cheek rise and greater mouth stretch was displayed to communicate certainty. Puzzlement was displayed by curving the mouth downward, lowering the eyebrows and eyelids, dropping the jaw, and constricting the forehead muscles.

Vocal Cues   Along with facial expressions, the voice is a powerful channel for expressing emotion. In fact, people who are accurate expressors in the face tend to be good at expressing emotion in the voice as well (Zuckerman, Larrance, Hall, DeFrank, & Rosenthal, 1979). The primary questions stimulating research on vocal expressions of emotion concern the identification of vocalic qualities associated with each emotion. What this research shows is that the voice is every bit as complex a channel as the face.

In early research on vocal expressions of emotion, Costanzo, Markel, and Costanzo (1969) showed that soft, emphatic emotions, such as grief and love, were expressed through variations in pitch. Harsh, hostile emotions, like anger and contempt, were expressed by changes in loudness. Neutral emotions, including indifference, were expressed through tempo changes. Scherer (1979a; Scherer & Oshinsky, 1977) artificially created voices manipulating five vocalic qualities fundamental to the display of affect: *pitch variation* (moderate, extreme, up contour, down contour), *amplitude variation* (moderate, extreme), *pitch level* (high, low), *amplitude level* (high, low), and *tempo* (fast, slow). The resulting interpretations by judges are shown in Table 10-4. As you might have guessed, an emotion such as happiness involves extreme pitch variation, moderate amplitude variation, and fast tempo. Fear is communicated by voices with high pitch level, up pitch contours, little pitch variation, and fast tempo.

More recently, Banse and Scherer (1994), Frick (1985, 1986), and Pittam and Scherer (1993) reported that anger expressions are characterized by increased fundamental frequency (pitch), intensity, high frequency energy, downward-directed frequency contours, and articulation rate. Anger due to frustration has a higher pitch, but anger due to a threat has a lower pitch. However, both anger expressions contain pitch increases on syllables, exaggerated inflections, and increased loudness. Fearful voices have a high pitch as well. Fear expressions also contain higher fundamental frequency, more high frequency energy, and increased articulation rate. Sadness is expressed vocally by decreased fundamental frequency, intensity, high frequency energy, and articulation rate, and more downward-directed frequency contours, but crying and grief have a higher pitch. Joy (i.e., elation) is expressed through higher fundamental frequency, more intensity, increased high frequency energy, and faster articulation rate. Disgust expressions apparently are not consistently associated with specific acoustical changes. Finally, contempt has a wide downward pitch inflection at the end of a phrase.

Gait   While the face and voice seem to contain the most emotion content, people can express emotions with other nonverbal cues. For instance, Montepare, Goldstein, and

TABLE 10-4
VOCAL CHARACTERISTICS OF EMOTIONAL EXPRESSIONS

Emotional state	Cues[a]
Pleasantness	Fast tempo, few harmonics, large pitch variation, sharp envelope, low pitch level, pitch contour down, small amplitude variation (salient configuration: large pitch variation plus pitch contour up)
Activity	Fast tempo, high pitch level, many harmonics, large pitch variation, sharp envelope, small amplitude variation
Potency	Many harmonics, fast tempo, high pitch level, round envelope, pitch contour up (salient configurations: large amplitude variation plus high pitch level, high pitch level plus many harmonics)
Anger	Many harmonics, fast tempo, high pitch level, small pitch variation, pitch contours up (salient configuration: small pitch variation plus pitch contour up)
Boredom	Slow tempo, low pitch level, few harmonics, pitch contour down, round envelope, small pitch variation
Disgust	Many harmonics, small pitch variation, round envelope, slow tempo (salient configuration: small pitch variation plus pitch contour up)
Fear	Pitch contour up, fast tempo, many harmonics, high pitch level, round envelope, small pitch variation (salient configurations: small pitch variation plus pitch contour up, fast tempo plus many harmonics)
Happiness	Fast tempo, large pitch variation, sharp envelope, few harmonics, moderate amplitude variation (salient configurations: large pitch variation plus pitch contour up, fast tempo plus few harmonics)
Sadness	Slow tempo, low pitch level, few harmonics, round envelope, pitch contour down (salient configuration: low pitch level plus slow tempo)
Surprise	Fast tempo, high pitch level, pitch contour up, sharp envelope, many harmonics, large pitch variation (salient configuration: high pitch level plus fast tempo)

[a]Single acoustic parameters (main effects) and configurations (interaction effects) are listed in order of predictive strength.
Source: Adapted from Scherer & Oshinsky, 1977, p. 340.

Clausen (1987) showed that gait—walking movement—can communicate emotional information. Anger was communicated by a heavy-footed gait and longer strides, pride by longer strides, sadness by less arm swing, and happiness by a faster pace. Pride was the most difficult emotion to decode from gait. Thus people may pay attention to behavior beyond facial and vocal expressions to judge emotional reactions.

Factors Influencing Emotional Expression

Features of Emotions Among the factors affecting emotional expression are specific features of the emotions themselves. For example, several studies show that children and adults are better able to recognize and encode pleasant emotions than unpleasant and socially undesirable ones such as fear (Cuceloglu, 1972; Mayo & LaFrance, 1978;

Plazewski & Allen, 1985; Odom & Lemond, 1972). This may be a result of display rules inhibiting unpleasant and socially undesirable emotional expressions. In a survey of college students, Sommers (1984) found that people who typically express negative emotions are rated most unfavorably and liked least. This is particularly true for women. Conversely, people who are always positive or typically positive are rated as most sociable and popular. People seem to accept and prefer others whose emotional expressions are predominantly positive; thus communicators may learn to repress expressions of negative emotions.

Intensity of the felt emotion may also influence encoding. Zuckerman, Hall, DeFrank, and Rosenthal (1976) found that accuracy of encoding emotional displays increases as the emotion experienced by the encoder becomes more intense. It is probable that more intense emotional experiences trigger spontaneous emotional displays, which are less likely to be modified by display rules.

The foregoing explanation identifies another factor that affects emotional expression: whether the expression is *spontaneous* or *posed.* Spontaneous expressions appear to be similar to posed expressions (Zuckerman et al., 1976; Zuckerman, Larrance, Hall, DeFrank, & Rosenthal, 1979); however, given the intensity of the emotion, spontaneous and posed expressions differ in their ability to communicate emotional meaning. Zuckerman et al. (1976) found that spontaneous expressions are superior emotional cues to posed expressions when extremely pleasant and extremely unpleasant emotions are communicated. In contrast, posed expressions are superior to spontaneous expressions when moderately pleasant or unpleasant emotions were communicated. For extreme emotions, the spontaneous expressions contain sufficient cues to communicate the emotional state of the sender, but for moderate emotions, the spontaneous expressions contain insufficient cues. Posing allows the sender to compensate by displaying either more cues or more stylized cues of emotion. In another study, posed expressions were superior to spontaneous expressions for pleasant emotions in general (Zuckerman, Larrance, Hall, DeFrank, & Rosenthal, 1979). Display rules prescribing positive emotional displays may make communicators more skilled at enacting positive expressions when not experiencing pleasant emotions. A recent study observed that women were better at mimicking facial expressions, but men did so with more intensity (Berenbaum & Rotter, 1992). Finally, children may have difficulty posing emotional expressions in the voice. Plazewski and Allen (1985) showed that the accuracy of children's vocal expressions of positive and negative emotions suffered when the emotional content of the vocal expression did not match the emotional content in the verbal sentence.

Physiology   Perhaps the most interesting physiological factors in emotional expression are *bilateral differences* in facial expressions. In 1978 Sackeim, Gur, and Saucy reported an experiment in which they sliced a series of photographs of facial expressions into left and right halves. They then recombined the halves to create faces that were composites of either the left side or the right side of the face. Observers judged left-side composites as displaying more intense emotions than right-side composites for all emotions except happiness. The authors suggested that the advantage of the left side of the face is a result of its connection to the right brain hemisphere, which appears to play a larger role in processing emotional stimuli. The emotion-dominant right hemisphere exerts more control in facial encoding, which is manifested in a more intense emotional expression in the left side of the face (Borod & Koff, 1990). They also suggested that the superiority of the left side of the face is advantageous from a decoding point of view. An observer's visual field is split bilaterally such that stimuli left of center in the visual field are projected to the right hemisphere and stimuli right of center are projected to the left hemisphere. When observing facial expressions, the superior left side of the face is in the right visual field and is projected to the emotionally inferior left brain hemisphere. Sackeim et al. proposed that the bilateral facial differences may have evolved to compensate for the emotional inferiority of the left hemisphere.

The bilateral differences and Sackeim et al.'s neurophysiological explanations (1978) are intriguing. They fit well with growing evidence for specialization of emotional processes in the brain (Andersen, Garrison, & Andersen, 1979, Buck, 1984). However, this explanation is not immune to criticism. Ekman (1980; Ekman, Hagar, & Friesen, 1981) point out that the bilateral differences occur only in posed or deliberate emotional expressions. Happiness was the only spontaneous expression in the experiment—and the only one that did not show bilateral differences. Positive facial cues are less lateralized than negative facial cues; however, judges still seem to rely more on the left side when decoding the whole emotion (Borod & Koff, 1990; Kleck & Mendolia, 1990).

Personal Characteristics   Characteristics of senders are also factors in emotional expression. For one thing, encoding is related to *age*. Generally speaking, ability to encode emotions increases with age (Mayo & LaFrance, 1978). Young children have difficulty encoding negative or socially undesirable emotions and seem to display positive emotions even in circumstances that elicit negative emotions. Encoding of these negative emotions improves with age, such that by puberty children encode most emotions well (Buck, 1975; Cole, 1986; Custrini & Feldman, 1989; Odom & Lemond, 1972).

Some of these differences may arise from children's understanding of display rules. Halberstadt, Grotjohn, Johnson, Furth, and Greig (1992) observed that fourth-graders (ages 9 and 10) were extremely skilled in masking negative feelings with positive displays and avoided expressing nonverbal negative affect. Cole (1986) also found that female children enacted more positive expressions than male children in a condition that elicited a negative emotion. Female children also encoded positive expressions more than negative expressions when an interviewer was present but not when the interviewer was absent. These findings conform to the preference for positive expressions in this culture, particularly by females.

Several studies have shown that *gender* has a strong effect on emotional expression. Women in most of the studies are more expressive than men (Buck, 1979a, 1979b; Buck et al., 1974; Sabatelli, Buck, & Dreyer, 1980; Wagner, Buck, & Winterbotham, 1993; Wagner, MacDonald, & Manstead, 1986). For example, Wagner et al. (1986) found that women were superior to men in overall encoding. This superiority was particularly pronounced for expressions of surprise and neutrality. Men outperformed women in expressions of sadness.

Female superiority in emotional expression is probably a function of culture-specific display rules. In the American culture, expression of emotion by women is more acceptable than by men. Research has shown that very young children appear to express emotions similarly regardless of gender; however, with age, girls become more accurate and more expressive and boys less accurate and less expressive encoders (Buck, 1975).

Apart from gender, there are two general types of encoders: *externalizers* and *internalizers*. Externalizers are particularly adept at portraying emotion, while internalizers are less skilled in sending cues (Buck, 1979a). Women tend to be externalizers, whereas men tend to be internalizers. These differences in overt expression also appear to be linked to certain personality traits. Externalizers are more extroverted, socially oriented, and higher in self-esteem than internalizers. Externalizing males may also be more self-confident, less self-deprecating, more dominant, and more heterosexually oriented (Buck, 1979a; Buck et al., 1974; Buck, Savin, Miller, & Caul, 1972; Harper, Weins, & Matarazzo, 1979).

Expressiveness also may be affected by *personality and emotional disorders*. Extroverts are more expressive than introverts, for example, and people who suffer from depression are more likely to display furrowed brows, squints, and frowns than happy faces (Segrin & Abramson, 1994; Tucker & Friedman, 1993).

Ekman and Friesen (1975) identified eight idiosyncratic *styles* for displaying emotion in the face. A *withholder* is someone who tends not to be very expressive. Withholders simply do not send the kinds of rapid signals that reveal emotion, and they know it. It is not that they are unemotional; it is just that their faces do not show emotion. *Revealers* are the opposite of withholders. No matter how hard revealers try to control the face to hide emotions, they seem automatically to reveal what they feel. *Unwitting expressors* are much like the revealers, only they do not know just how expressive they are. They are continually amazed that others are able to read their emotions. *Blanked expressors* think they are expressing emotions but are not. For some reason their faces do not display the appropriate cues, appearing expressionless or ambiguous. A *substitute expressor* has a single expression that preempts other expressions. For example, a substitute expressor may encode happiness regardless of his or her actual emotional reaction. Unfortunately, such people are convinced that they are communicating what they feel. *Frozen-affect expressors* also tend to have one predominant facial expression, but it usually results from facial construction. Even when they display other emotions, traces of the primary expression remain. An *ever-ready expressor* is someone who has an initial expression for almost any situation. No matter what the emotion, the initial expression is always the same. As time passes, other expressions may take its place. Last, *flooded-affect expressors* are rare indeed. These people have one or two expressions that continually flood the face. Ekman and Friesen have observed this style only in people undergoing major trauma.

Finally, *training* in emotional expression can improve encoding abilities. Izard (1971) reported that people can improve their accuracy by at least 6 percent and by as much as 51 percent.

INTERPRETING EMOTIONAL EXPRESSIONS

When we consider the decoding of emotional expressions, two questions must be addressed. First, what behaviors, when observed, result in attributions of a particular emotion? Next, how accurately do people decode the overt expression of each emotion? As with encoding, facial and vocal behaviors have received the most attention.

Decoding Facial Expressions

We have already identified the facial behaviors that people display when experiencing or attempting to communicate each emotion. It does not necessarily follow from these experiments, however, that receivers recognize each of these cues and attribute the emotional meaning intended by the sender. Table 10-5 presents the results of one experiment by Wiggers (1982), which directly examined the cues that affect receivers of emotional displays. As this table shows, a combination of two or more facial behaviors contributed to judgments of each emotion. Happiness was inferred when the source displayed a smile accompanied by raised cheeks. Fear judgments resulted when the eyebrows and upper eyelids were raised, lips stretched, and mouth opened. Lowering the eyebrows, raising the upper eyelids, tightening the lips while raising the upper lip and depressing the lower lip, and opening the mouth produced anger interpretations.

While several behaviors had to be combined to produce emotion judgments, Wiggers found that each expression contains one to three cues that are particularly important to the emotion judgment (cues in italics in Table 10-5). These cues are unique to or distinctive of a particular emotion, and their presence is sufficient to cause the emotion interpretation. For example, smiling and raised cheeks are sufficient to cue happiness judgments; raised upper eyelids and stretched lips cue fear; and head moved up with

TABLE 10-5
CUES THAT AFFECT DECODING OF EMOTIONAL DISPLAYS

Emotion	Behaviors[a]	Accuracy, percent
Happiness	*cheeks raised; smiling*	64–100
Fear	eyebrows raised; *upper eyelids raised; lips stretched;* mouth open	64–95
Disgust	*upper lip raised; nose wrinkled;* mouth open, tongue thrust out; chin raised	64–100
Sadness	*inner eyebrow raised;* eyebrows drawn together; lower eyelids raised; *lip corners depressed; lips parted*	67–95
Surprise	*eyebrows raised;* jaw dropped; *upper eyelids slightly to moderately raised;* head moved up; eyes moved down	77–100
Shame	*lip biting;* lips parted; *upper eyelids dropped;* head lowered	87–100
Anger	*eyebrows lowered;* upper eyelids raised; lips slightly tightened; upper lip raised; lower lip depressed; mouth opened	69–100
Contempt	single outer eyebrow corner raised; one or both eyebrows raised; *head moved up; eyes moved down;* one side of upper lip raised; lips parted; one mouth corner pulled inward producing a dimple; chin raised	72–100

[a]Behaviors in italics influence judgments of intensity of emotion.
Source: Adapted from Wiggers, 1982.

eyes moved down cues contempt. The remaining behaviors may be redundant and relied on only to reinforce interpretations based on the primary cues. This may be why in one study people were no less accurate decoding emotions when viewing a profile (i.e., seeing a face from the side) than when viewing a full face (Kleck & Mendolia, 1990).

Table 10-5 also reports the accuracy of observers' judgments in Wiggers's experiment. Shame and surprise were decoded most accurately. Judgments of contempt, anger, disgust, and happiness were slightly less accurate; however, some observers demonstrated high accuracy on these emotions. Fear and sadness were decoded least accurately, with no observer attaining 100 percent accuracy. Still, over two-thirds of these expressions were decoded accurately.

In general, pleasant emotions, particularly happiness, are easiest to decode. Unpleasant emotions, such as anger, disgust, sadness, and fear are more difficult to recognize (Cuceloglu, 1972; Custrini & Feldman, 1989; Feinman & Feldman, 1982; Horatcsu & Ekinci, 1992; Wagner et al., 1986; Zuckerman, Lipets, Koivumaki, & Rosenthal, 1975). Part of this difficulty can be traced to the similarity in facial expressions of different emotions. Although there are particular behaviors that are distinctive to each emotion, there seems to be enough similarity between emotional expressions that observers make consistent mistakes (Schlosberg, 1952, 1954; Wagner et al., 1986; Wiggers, 1982). For example, observers mistake anger for fear because of the eyebrow movement. Fear and surprise are confused because of the brow and eye positions. Surprise is also sometimes confused with happiness. Schlosberg (1952, 1954) asserted that facial expressions can be arrayed along two or three dimensions much like the emotions they represent (refer back to Figures 10-1 and 10-2). Emotions that are similar in pleasantness, activity, and intensity will be similar in expression and more likely to be confused by observers. Thus one is unlikely to confuse happiness with anger or disgust with surprise, but disgust may be confused with anger and happiness with surprise. This confusion increases when one encounters blended facial expressions. Many blends contain similar or related emotions; observers often are uncertain about their interpretations and make mistakes decoding blended expressions.

Not surprisingly, decoding appears to be a skill learned in childhood. Ludemann and Nelson (1988) found that infants could discriminate fear, surprise, and happiness expressions, but infants seemed to rely on familiarity with the expression more than knowledge of particular facial features. Matsumoto and Kishimoto (1983) observed that 4- to 5-year-old American children could accurately identify only surprise; Japanese children at the same age accurately decoded only surprise and sadness. By ages 7 to 9, children in both cultures accurately decoded facial expressions of surprise, sadness, happiness, and anger.

The accuracy of decoding is also influenced by gender. In general, women are better than men at decoding facial expressions (Wagner et al., 1986; Zuckerman, Hall, DeFrank, & Rosenthal, 1976; Zuckerman, Lipets, Koivumaki, & Rosenthal, 1975). However, there are exceptions to this generalization.

Custrini and Feldman (1989), in a study of children, observed that girls with more social competence were better decoders of emotional expressions than girls with less social competence; social competence did not affect decoding abilities of boys. Among adults, extroverted, socially competent women may be better decoders of negative facial expressions, but extroverted, socially competent males seem to be better decoders of positive facial expressions (Zuckerman et al., 1979). Further, males improve their sensitivity to facial expressions as the relationship with the sender intensifies (Zuckerman et al., 1975). Thus males who are socially competent and males in developed relationships may be accurate decoders and no more disadvantaged than women. Increased sensitivity by males in developed relationships, though, may not produce more relational satisfaction. Sabatelli et al. (1980) reported that women in relationships with more sensitive males expressed less love for their partner. This may be a result of cultural rules prohibiting male sensitivity, or it may be that women are uncomfortable when males pay too much attention to their emotional expressions.

Another factor that influences accuracy is whether facial expressions are *spontaneous* or *posed*. Like encoding, skillful decoders of spontaneous facial expressions are more likely to be skillful decoders of posed expressions. People, though, are generally more accurate when judging posed facial expressions than spontaneous ones (Fujita, Harper, & Weins, 1980; Zuckerman, Hall, DeFrank, & Rosenthal, 1976; Zuckerman, Larrance, Hall, DeFrank, & Rosenthal, 1979). The advantage of posed expressions is not surprising in light of the fact that encoders often improve their facial expressions when they are allowed to pose them. Posed facial expressions may be richer in cues and more stylized than spontaneous expressions, especially expressions of less extreme emotions.

Since the beginning of research on facial expressions, there has been a debate over the role of *context* in judgments of emotion. Several researchers have argued that receivers incorporate information from the context into their judgments of facial expressions. These same researchers have expressed concern that much of the research on decoding facial expressions has taken place in contextually sterile environments (e.g., a photograph or videotape of a facial display against a neutral background). As a result of these concerns, experiments have been designed that embed facial expressions in contexts. An immediately apparent conclusion from these experiments is that context is indeed important. Receivers do incorporate contextual information in their judgments of facial expressions, and this information can affect decoding accuracy (Barrett, 1993; Cupchik & Poulos, 1984; Fernandez-Dols, Wallbott, & Sanchez, 1991; Horatcsu & Ekinci, 1992; Knudsen & Muzekari, 1983; McHugo, Lanzetta, & Bush, 1991; Spignesi & Shor, 1981).

The extent to which decoders rely on context varies, though (Spignesi & Shor, 1981). Children apparently have to learn to rely on contextual cues. Older children incorporate contextual cues when judging emotions, but younger children do not. Familiarity with a context also increases communicators' reliance on it when judging emotion. Contextual cues may have a greater influence on interpretations when they are congruent with the emotional expression. When contextual cues are incongruent, people often rationalize discrepancies by devising an explanation for the expression-context pairing, by denying the existence of the emotion, or by seeing the context as implausible. Finally, communicators' existing attitudes may function as contextual cues and influence judgments about facial expressions (Fernandez-Dols et al., 1991; Horatcsu & Ekinci, 1992; Knudsen & Muzekari, 1983; McHugo et al., 1991; Spignesi & Shor, 1981).

Decoding Vocal Expressions

People accurately recognize vocal expressions of emotion about 50 percent of the time (Pittam & Scherer, 1993). The ability to decode vocal emotional expressions varies according to the emotion displayed (see Table 10-6). Sadness, anger, happiness, and nervousness are among the most easily identified emotions in the voice. Sympathy, satisfaction, fear, jealousy, and love are less accurately judged, and disgust and shame are most poorly recognized (Apple & Hecht, 1982; Banse & Scherer, 1994; Costanzo et al., 1969; Davitz & Davitz, 1959; Pittam & Scherer, 1993; Scherer, Banse, Wallbott, & Goldbeck, 1991; Zuckerman et al., 1975). A recent study on children found that happiness was decoded better than anger, while children had the most difficulty decoding a neutral voice (Horatcsu & Ekinci, 1992).

Mistakes in decoding vocal expressions of emotion show the same consistency as mistakes in decoding facial expressions. Receivers often confuse fear with nervousness or sadness, love with sadness or sympathy, pride with satisfaction or happiness, surprise or happiness with sadness, hot anger with cold anger or contempt, and interest with pride or happiness (Apple & Hecht, 1982; Banse & Scherer, 1994; Davitz & Davitz, 1959). Vocal expressions of certain emotions have similar features but differ in intensity, quality, or valence (Banse & Scherer, 1994); (refer back to Table 10-4).

Other factors also affect the ability to decode vocal expressions of emotion. Decoding ability increases with age. Familiarity with the sender also improves the ability to judge vocal expressions, although this improvement may be limited to males. Finally, emotions that are more intensely felt by the encoder are decoded more accurately by receivers (Davitz & Davitz, 1959; Horatcsu & Ekinci, 1992; Hornstein, 1967; Zuckerman et al., 1975).

RELATIONSHIP OF EMOTIONAL ENCODING TO DECODING

Encoding and decoding are, in general, positively correlated. Good encoders of emotions tend to be good decoders as well. Likewise, poor encoders are poor decoders. This is true of one's general skill at encoding and decoding all emotions (Cupchik, 1973; Knower, 1945; Levy, 1964; Zuckerman, Hall, DeFrank, & Rosenthal, 1976; Zucker-

TABLE 10-6
ACCURACY IN DECODING VOCAL
EXPRESSIONS OF EMOTION

Emotion	Accuracy, percent
Anger	65
Nervousness	54
Sadness	49
Happiness	43
Sympathy	39
Satisfaction	31
Fear	25
Jealousy	25
Love	25
Pride	21

Source: Adapted from Davitz & Davitz, 1959.

man, Larrance, Hall, DeFrank, & Rosenthal, 1979; Zuckerman, Lipets, Koivumaki, & Rosenthal, 1975).

However, a person is not always equally good at encoding and decoding the same emotion. That is, people who are skillful encoders of, say, fear are not very accurate decoders of fear, but they generally are accurate decoders of happiness, sadness, anger, and disgust. Two explanations may account for this. First, when display rules do not allow expression of a specific emotion, people do not develop the skills to encode that emotion, but they learn to be particularly sensitive to the prohibited emotion in others. Alternatively, people who find it difficult to decode an emotion may assume that others will have trouble decoding that emotion, and so they may take special care to encode that emotion accurately.

SUMMARY

Emotion is a primary motivator in the adult, controlling adaptive responses to emotion-eliciting stimuli. The structure of the emotion mechanism in our brain is innate and contains a set of basic emotions. It also comprises a social signal system that is used communicatively. The subjective experience of emotion may be a product of three processes: (1) intrapersonal feedback from overt emotional reactions, (2) autonomic arousal causing us to appraise the environment, or (3) neurochemical changes associated with the activation of emotion-producing brain regions. We experience emotions along pleasantness, activity, and intensity dimensions. However, we learn to associate combinations of these three dimensions with categorical labels.

The link between emotion and overt emotional expression is also innate. Ekman's neurocultural theory proposes that noninterpersonal (innate) and interpersonal (learned) elicitors activate the affect program, which controls adaptive responses to the elicitors, including facial and vocal emotional expressions. As we mature, we learn culture-specific display rules for managing emotional expressions. The interaction of these display rules with the affect program determines the emotional expression we encode. We also employ expressions to manage our affect experiences and as part of the code systems we use to communicate.

There is extensive evidence for universal facial expressions of happiness, sadness, fear, surprise, anger, and disgust and for display rules operating to create cultural differences in these primary emotional expressions. Child development research has revealed that infants can encode most of the facial behaviors of adults, and each emotional expression emerges in an innate progression.

An emotional expression is a combination of several cues, some of which are unique to a particular expression. People are more accurate encoders of pleasant and intensely felt emotions. Posing increases the ability to encode moderately felt emotions accurately. For various reasons, facial expressions appear to be more intensely encoded on the left side of the face. Encoding ability also increases with age, among females and externalizing communicators, and with training.

Decoding ability is generally high but varies by emotion. Pleasant facial expressions are easier to decode than unpleasant ones. Nervousness, sadness, happiness, and perhaps anger are most accurately decoded from vocalic cues. Mistakes in decoding result from the similarity between expressions of similar emotions. Decoding ability develops with age. Females are better decoders of facial expressions than males, and posed expressions are easier to decode than spontaneous expressions. When available, decoders integrate contextual information into their judgments of emotional expressions. Finally, good encoders seem to be good decoders of emotional expressions, in general, but good encoders of a particular emotion may not be good decoders of that same emotion.

SUGGESTED READINGS

Barrett, K. C. (1993). The development of nonverbal communication of emotion: A functionalist perspective. *Journal of Nonverbal Behavior, 17,* 145–169.

Boucher, J. D., & Ekman, P. (1975). Facial areas and emotional information. *Journal of Communication, 25*(2), 21–29.

Buck, R. (1984). *The communication of emotions.* New York: Guilford.

Buck, R., Losow, J. I., Murphy, M. M., & Costanzo, P. (1992). Social facilitation and inhibition of emotional expression and communication. *Journal of Personality and Social Psychology, 63,* 962–968.

Davitz, J. R. (1964). *The communication of emotional meaning.* New York: McGraw-Hill.

Ekman, P., & Friesen, W. V. (1975). *Unmasking the face.* Englewood Cliffs, NJ: Prentice-Hall.

Ekman, P., & Oster, H. (1979). Facial expression of emotion. *Annual Review of Psychology, 30,* 527–554.

Frick, R. W. (1985). Communicating emotion: The role of prosadic features. *Psychological Bulletin, 97,* 412–429.

Fridlund, A. J. (1994). *Human facial expression: An evolutionary view.* San Diego: Academic.

Izard, C. E. (1977). *Human emotions.* New York: Plenum.

Russell, J. A. (1983). Pancultural aspects of the human conceptual organization of emotions. *Journal of Personality and Social Psychology, 45,* 1281–1288.

Scherer, K. R. (1992). What does facial expression express? In K. T. Strongman (Ed.), *International Review of Studies on Emotion* (Vol. 2, pp. 139–165). New York: Wiley.

Smith, C. A., & Ellsworth, P. C. (1985). Patterns of cognitive appraisal in emotion. *Journal of Personality and Social Psychology, 48,* 813–838.

Spignesi, A., & Shor, R. E. (1981). The judgment of emotion from facial expressions, contexts, and their combination. *Journal of General Psychology, 104,* 41–58.

Tucker, J. S., & Friedman, H. S. (1993). Sex differences in nonverbal expressiveness: Emotional expression, personality, and impressions. *Journal of Nonverbal Behavior, 17,* 103–117.

Wiggers, M. (1982). Judgments of facial expressions of emotion predicted from facial behavior. *Journal of Nonverbal Behavior, 7,* 101–116.

Winton, W. M. (1986). The role of facial response in self-reports of emotion: A critique of Laird. *Journal of Personality and Social Psychology, 50,* 808–812.

11

DEFINING AND MANAGING RELATIONSHIPS

The unspoken dialogue between two people can never be put right by anything they say.

Dag Hammarskjold

There's a language in her eye, her cheek, her lip;
Nay, her foot speaks. Her wanton spirit looks out
At every joint and motive of her body.

William Shakespeare, *Troilus and Cressida*

The pained look in his eyes told her that he was deeply hurt. She tried to speak, to apologize, but he just shook his head as he turned away. She gently touched his face, turning it toward her, and kissed him tenderly on the cheeks, the eyes, the mouth. The tears in her eyes weakened his resolve as his lips responded to hers. He took her in his arms and held her tightly in silence. . . .

Such is the stuff of which pulp novels are made. But it is also the stuff out of which interpersonal relationships are crafted. Through such nonverbal dialogues, we come to define and redefine the nature of our relationships with other people. That is what relational communication is all about. And through our ongoing exchange of relational messages, we manage our interpersonal relationships, sometimes propelling them to new levels of intimacy, sometimes sparking conflict, and sometimes dragging them into boredom and monotony.

THE NATURE OF RELATIONAL COMMUNICATION

Relational communication addresses the processes and messages whereby people negotiate, express, and interpret their relationships with one another. Through relational messages, people may signal how they regard each other, the relationship itself, or their own identity in the context of the relationship. Expressions of love, noncommitment, power, or irritation are examples of relational messages that reveal the status of a relationship at any given time. The evolution of these relational definitions over time is part of the relationship management process.

Content and Relational Aspects of Messages

It has been said that every communication includes both a *content* and a *relational* component. That is, it includes not only the subject matter under discussion but also a frame of reference for interpreting the content. Because the nature of the relationship may dictate how an exchange is to be understood, relational communication is often referred to as metacommunication. (*Meta-* means *about;* thus these are messages about messages.) A request made by one's boss, for instance, takes on greater force than a request made by a stranger. Much, but not all, relational work is handled by the nonverbal channels, leading many people to equate nonverbal behavior exclusively with an auxiliary metacommunicative role. However, the content is sometimes about the relationship itself. In such cases, nonverbal expressions are themselves part of the central message. Other times, no words may be spoken and yet, the nonverbal messages speak loudly and clearly on their own. So, nonverbal relational messages should not be viewed as only augmenting the verbal stream but as making meaningful statements in their own right.

Dynamics of Relationships: Escalation, Maintenance, and Dissolution

Interpersonal relationships do not materialize instantly; they develop gradually. Some remain stunted, some grow to maturity, some stagnate, and some dissolve.

Research on relational escalation and deescalation, commitment, and satisfaction reveals that the nonverbal tenor of a relationship is often the most important determinant of its success or failure. For example, a single cue—increasingly intimate touch—is a strong indicator of a couple's increasing commitment to each other (Johnson & Edwards, 1991). Extensive research on patterns of marital interaction has confirmed time and again that unhappy couples display disproportionately less positive emotion and exchange far more negatively toned nonverbal cues than happy couples do (Alfred, Harper, Wadham, & Woolley, 1981; Gottman, 1979; Gottman & Levenson, 1992; Huston & Vangelisti, 1991; Markman, Notarius, Stephen, & Smith, 1981). These negative nonverbal exchanges are reciprocated, often becoming part of escalating conflict, where each person's nagging, sarcasm, and the like provoke increasingly heated and hostile exchanges from the partner (Billings, 1979; Burggraf & Sillars, 1987; Harris, Gergen, & Lannamann, 1986; Jacobsen, Follette, & McDonald, 1982; Pike & Sillars, 1985; Sabourin, Infante, & Rudd, 1993; Sillars, Pike, Jones, & Redmon, 1983). Sometimes, physical aggression is the end result. Couples for whom expressions of anger, defensiveness, and disdain are common frequently end up divorcing; and the alternative—completely withdrawing from a partner's demands for attention and problem solving—is no recipe for success (Gottman & Levenson, 1992).

However, behaving pleasantly full time also is no recipe for success. Couples who develop a rigid "positive" communication pattern that glosses over differences are as

This couple's nonverbal cues speak volumes to each other—and to observers—about the current state of their relationship.

likely to fail as those who are caught up in a negative spiral (Julien, Markman, & Lindahl, 1989). Given that aggravations, antagonisms, and arguments are a fact of life in a relationship, it becomes important to know how to navigate "darker" relational waters as well as smoother currents, to prevent relationships from crashing on the shoals of everyday distractions, disruptions, and difficulties.

Because relationships evolve over time, relational communication should be studied from a developmental and processual perspective. Issues that are important in the early stages of a relationship—such as emphasizing similarity—may be far less so in later stages, and behaviors may take on new or different meanings as relationships change. Reliable interpretation of relational communication therefore requires knowing the current stage of a relationship.

Several typologies are available for stages of relational development. Knapp's approach (1984a) is particularly useful because in specifying several gradations during the escalating and deescalating phases, it calls attention to the changing communication concerns that occur at different stages of development. Table 11-1 presents the 10 proposed stages and a brief description of some nonverbal and verbal communication patterns associated with each.

Contemporary scholars, however, point out that relationships do not move smoothly or inexorably through these relational stages. Intimacy waxes and wanes in cycles over the course of a relationship, as does "togetherness" or separateness (Baxter, 1988; Dillman, 1994). Detachment at a given point in time does not mean that a relationship is

TABLE 11-1
STAGES OF RELATIONAL ESCALATION AND DISSOLUTION

Coming together	
Initiating	Behaviors involved in first encounters, including determining if person is cleared for interaction, presenting self as attractive and likable, use of conventional greetings.
Experimenting	Trying to discover the unknown. Often involves small talk, casual and uncritical interaction.
Intensifying	Becoming "close friends," greater awareness of relationship, more active participation. Involves more self-disclosure, informality, direct expressions of commitment.
Integrating	Becoming a couple, fusing two identities into a single relational identity through synchronized routines, exchanges of intimate gifts, increased similarity in dress and manner, increased expressions of intimacy.
Bonding	Formalized public commitment of the relationship, including engagement and marriage, with public evidence of bond, such as wedding rings.

Coming apart	
Differentiating	Process of disengaging, making differences more important than similarities. More emphasis on *I* than *we,* less disclosure, increasing conflict over differences.
Circumscribing	Constriction of communication and information through reduced depth, breadth, and amount of interaction.
Stagnating	Marking time. Communication is at a standstill. Avoidance of many topics, especially the relationship itself.
Avoiding	Eliminating any form of face-to-face or voice-to-voice interaction, increased antagonism, brief encounters, nonperson orientation.
Terminating	Complete dissolution of the relationship. Typical communication behavior varies with the length and level of commitment of the relationship and degree of acrimony over its termination.

Source: Adapted from Knapp, 1984, pp. 32–44.

inevitably headed for termination; it may just be part of the natural dynamics of relational evolution. Some relationships also stagnate and then become rejuvenated. The implication for studying nonverbal relational messages is that nonverbal cues serve as an excellent barometer for the current state of affairs but should not be expected to remain static any more than the relationship remains static. Today's cues may not be a reliable indicator of tomorrow's relational state.

One important feature of treating relational definitions as evolving and dynamic rather than static is the identification of *critical events* that change the nature of the relationship. Rare but significant acts of commission and omission are often more critical markers of a relationship than frequently occurring behaviors (Knapp, 1983a). The first kiss may propel a friendship into courtship; an act of physical aggression may be the most telling sign of a marriage in trouble; the conspicuous absence of an expected handshake may signal that a business relationship has gone sour. In studying relational communication, it is difficult to catch glimpses of these critical behaviors, both because of their rarity and because many are behaviors that appear only in private circumstances. Yet personal experience confirms that these definition-altering behaviors are often the most vivid in memory and have the most impact on how a relationship progresses.

Constraints on Relational Communication

Culture   A number of things may constrain the what, when, and how of relational communication. One is culture. As noted earlier, cultures differ along a number of dimensions, one being the degree to which they stress relational harmony (Gudykunst & Ting-Toomey, 1988). In cultures in which amicable group relations take precedence over individual expression, many negative relational messages such as displeasure or distrust may be suppressed. In their stead may be far more messages signaling cooperation and group solidarity. Cultures that value individual autonomy may have richer repertoires for expressing privacy and may permit more aggressive responses to privacy invasions. High-context cultures with pronounced status hierarchies will rely much more on nonverbal means to signal power and status inequalities than more egalitarian or low-context cultures (Hall, 1976). And cultures that encourage facial and gestural expressivity may have more "readable" relational messages (Halberstadt, 1991; Ricci Bitti & Poggi, 1991). Cultural norms may also limit the relational message repertoire by prohibiting some behaviors and requiring others. This removes any relational content from such behaviors, making them useful only for social or cultural identification. For example, dress in a nonegalitarian (hierarchical) culture may be so controlled by cultural dictates that no personal statements are possible through changes in costume. In other cases, it may be difficult to differentiate relational statements from conformity to normative or expected behavior. When men routinely held doors for women, the gesture could not be taken as a sign of special respect for a particular recipient. Today, the act may take on special meaning because it is uncommon.

Context   Similarly, context may prescribe some behaviors and proscribe others. A hushed whisper may connote intimacy in the midst of a social gathering but not during a church service. One key to whether a behavior has the potential to carry relational meaning is whether it is obligatory or voluntary in the given situation. Voluntary acts are more likely to be seen as messages. So are violations of norms and expectations. A midnight serenade and "dressing up" to meet your date's parents may have greater relational import because of their novelty.

Code Structure   Code structure may limit which behaviors are salient for which types of messages. A distinction introduced earlier is among *static, slow,* and *dynamic signals.* Static behaviors do not vary during the course of an interaction; physical appearance is an example. Slow signals show only infrequent changes; postural shifts or changes in proximity are slow signals. Dynamic signals involve moment-to-moment changes; most vocal behaviors and facial expressions are dynamic. Static signals may be responsible for cuing basic role relations such as high or low status, while slow and dynamic signals express subtle nuances in the tone of the relationship.

Channel Primacy   Channel primacy likewise may influence which codes and behaviors have the most relational significance. The consistent finding that visual information has primacy over auditory information gives preference to kinesics, physical appearance, proxemics, haptics, and artifacts as primary vehicles for conveying relational messages. However, there is some evidence that for dominance messages, auditory cues have primacy (Rosenthal & DePaulo, 1979a; Zuckerman, Amidon, Bishop, & Pomerantz, 1982).

Communication Skills   Another constraint is the communication skills of the participants. As noted earlier, some people are far better than others at encoding and decoding nonverbal communication. This applies to relational communication as well. People with learning disabilities, among others, have difficulty decoding relational messages (Wood, 1985). The accuracy of relational message exchange can only be as good as the least skilled participant.

Multiple Functions   Finally, the multifunctional nature of nonverbal behaviors makes it difficult at times to determine whether a given behavior has relational meaning, is serving some other communication function, or both. A case in point is eye contact. Gazing at another may convey such relational meanings as involvement, affiliation, and dominance; it may be used to request a turn at talk; or it may be part of an effort to persuade someone. Deciphering which of these interpretations to assign to gaze can be a challenge. This illustrates that not all nonverbal behaviors are intended or interpretable as relational signals.

All these factors place limitations on what constitutes relational communication, when and how it will take place, and how likely it is to succeed.

Themes in Relational Messages

So far we have discussed relational communication without specifying the content of such exchanges. We turn next to the basic themes that are possible and the nonverbal behaviors that express them. Here, we examine how these themes, when expressed dyadically, produce different interaction patterns, and we review theories offered for how interaction patterns come about.

The concept of relational communication can be traced to anthropological observations by Bateson (1935, 1958) of symmetrical and complementary relationships among New Guinea tribesmen. In symmetrical relationships, the participants emphasized equality. In complementary relationships, they maximized differences, usually in the form of dominant behavior by one person being followed by submissive behavior from the other. This sparked interest in symmetrical and complementary interaction patterns, later applied to psychiatric contexts by Watzlawick et al. (1967). Issues of dominance versus submission and relational control became a focus of investigators of healthy and distressed interpersonal relationships.

Other work in the psychiatric realm on interpersonal needs and interpersonal behavior (Leary, 1957; Schutz, 1958) added two more interpersonal dimensions: inclusion (the need to establish associations with a satisfactory number of other people) and love or affection (the need to achieve intimacy with others and have it returned). These early directions gave significant impetus to the study of relational communication.

But relational definitions entail far more facets of meaning than just these three. On the basis of a synthesis of ethological, anthropological, sociological, psychological, and communication literature, Burgoon and Hale (1984, 1987b) concluded that there are as many as 12 different *topoi* (basic generic themes) possible in relational communication. These interdependent but distinctive themes represent the underlying continua along which people send and interpret relational messages and ultimately define their interpersonal relationships. (See Box 11-1 for an application of the relational themes to student-teacher interaction.)

Research investigating these themes (e.g., Burgoon, 1991; Burgoon & Hale, 1987; Burgoon & Dillman, 1995; Le Poire & Burgoon, 1994a) has found that many of them are indeed highly interrelated and for convenience can be reduced to the following clusters:

1 *Dominance.* Such messages reflect the degree to which one member of the relationship is dominant, powerful, controlling, assertive, and persuasive and the other is sub-

---

BOX 11-1

APPLICATIONS: MANAGING RELATIONAL MESSAGES IN THE CLASSROOM

You can verify that you use Burgoon and Hale's relational themes to interpret the communication of others by thinking of two professors you have who differ significantly in the way they relate to their classes. Try rating each of them on the following set of relational communication scales (from Burgoon & Hale, 1987b) to see if they appear to be sending their students different relational messages. (Note that some items measure composite themes.) For each statement, 5 = strongly agree; 4 = agree somewhat; 3 = neither agree nor disagree; 2 = disagree somewhat; 1 = strongly disagree.

1 Attempts to persuade the students.
   (dominance)   1 2 3 4 5
2 Dominates class discussions.
   (dominance)   1 2 3 4 5
3 Is calm and poised around students.
   (composure/arousal)   1 2 3 4 5

4 Seems irritated with students.
   (composure/arousal)   1 2 3 4 5
5 Tries to establish common ground with
   students. (similarity/depth)   1 2 3 4 5
6 Wants to keep the relationship at an
   impersonal level. (similarity/depth)   1 2 3 4 5
7 Makes class interactions formal.
   (formality)   1 2 3 4 5
8 Is more interested in a social conversation
   than the task at hand. (task-social
   orientation)   1 2 3 4 5
9 Communicates coldness rather
   than warmth. (affection)   1 2 3 4 5
10 Is interested in what students
   have to say. (involvement)   1 2 3 4 5
11 Is sincere in communicating with
   students. (receptivity/trust)   1 2 3 4 5
12 Wants students' trust. (receptivity/trust)   1 2 3 4 5

missive, passive, unassertive, and so forth. Relationships need not be asymmetrical; partners may each express a sense of equality toward the other.

2 *Intimacy.* This is actually a large collection of interrelated themes, including *affection-hostility* (messages of liking and positive or negative regard), *inclusion-exclusion* (messages of openness, rapport, empathy, and affiliation or nonreceptivity and privateness), *involvement* (messages of approach and engagement or avoidance and distance, often equated with immediacy), *depth* (signals of familiarity and personalism or superficiality), *trust* (messages of sincerity, honesty, and mutual regard or their opposites), and *similarity* (displays underscoring commonalities or differences). The more that each of these subcomponents is present, the more intimate the message or relationship.

3 *Composure/arousal.* Separate from their individual personalities, people in relationships may vary in the degree to which they are relaxed, calm, poised, and self-assured within a relationship; are agitated and irritable; or are excited and stimulated by the other's presence. All these elements relate to degree of emotional and behavioral activation as specifically occasioned by the relationship.

4 *Formality.* Just as environments may be informal or formal, so may relationships. It is the relational message cues that signify just how casual or businesslike a given conversation or relationship will be.

5 *Task versus social orientation.* In work-related situations, an additional relational message is the degree to which one wishes to focus on the task alone or to also interject some "social" elements such as personal conversation or humor. Although this dimension is strongly influenced by verbal content and language style, the nonverbal codes can reinforce the degree of focus on the task or on social relations.

Research Methods for Relational Communication

The literature on relational communication generally falls into related clusters of these themes. Before looking at the nonverbal patterns associated with each, a note about research methods is needed. Some of the research to be reviewed uses an *encoder approach.* Communicators are induced to behave in a certain way (e.g., to be friendly), and the nonverbal behaviors they enact are then studied. Sometimes these actors are told explicitly what meanings to project; in other cases, the possible meanings are inferred from their actions. Other research uses a *decoder approach.* Participants or observers see manipulated or spontaneous nonverbal behaviors and rate the meanings of the behaviors (e.g., rapport). Participants and observers do not always see eye to eye on their interpretations, but, fortunately for our ability to draw conclusions, there is a high degree of consensus in their interpretations (Burgoon & Newton, 1991; Le Poire & Burgoon, 1994a). Finally, some of the research looks at the effects of nonverbal cues on such relational outcomes as attraction and liking. In these cases, the researchers or analysts draw inferences about whether people might use these same behaviors to communicate reciprocal meanings. Seldom is the situation so simple that a given behavior can be taken to have one and only one meaning. More often than not, a combination or sequence of cues is needed before a fairly unambiguous interpretation is possible. We therefore caution you not to assume that you know unequivocally what signals what. People who hold such simplistic and certain views often find themselves bogged down in relational quagmires (see Box 11-2).

NONVERBAL PATTERNS ASSOCIATED WITH RELATIONAL MESSAGES

The history of man's past is largely an account of his efforts to wrest space from others and to defend space from outsiders.

Edward T. Hall

By and by a proud-looking man about fifty-five—and he was a heap the best-dressed man in that town, too—steps out of the store, and the crowd drops back on each side to let him come.

Mark Twain

Messages of Power, Dominance, and Submission

The two primary dimensions that characterize interpersonal relationships are dominance-submission (discussed here) and intimacy (discussed in the next section).

The need to define patterns of inequality and control is no doubt an outgrowth of more primitive survival needs based on identifying friend or foe and establishing a social order. Our instinctive fight-or-flight responses mark the extremes of a continuum of dominance and submission behaviors that are present in varying forms in all species.

BOX 11-2

TESTING YOUR MYTH QUOTIENT

To see how many popular myths you believe about nonverbal communication, first try taking the following true-false test:

_____ **1** People express liking by being completely relaxed.

_____ **2** The person with the most power in a group is the one who looks most often at others.

_____ **3** The longer a couple are together, the more they touch.

_____ **4** To be seen as more dominant, women should increase their eye contact with others.

_____ **5** Leaning forward is interpreted as being overly eager and submissive.

_____ **6** Close proximity and direct gaze always signal attraction.

_____ **7** Slow, deliberate speaking conveys power.

_____ **8** Extended silence is a sign of breakdown and stress in communication.

Now see how others do on these same questions. Give the quiz to 10 other people and see what the average score is. You may want to add some new questions, based on your reading. What do the results tell you about people's stereotypical views of nonverbal relational communication?

Answers: (1) *False.* Moderate relaxation is most likely. (2) *False.* High power people receive, not give, the most frequent eye contact. (3) *False.* Married couples engage in less touch than newly formed couples. (4) *False.* Such behavior by women is seen as submissive. (5) *False.* Forward lean is associated with dominance. (6) *False.* Not always—they may also accompany a hostile confrontation. (7) *False.* Faster tempo is more dominant. (8) *False.* Complete agreement and harmony may also be accompanied by extended silences.

Definitionally, the concept of dominance is murky. It is often treated as synonymous with power and status, but although they are interrelated, these concepts can be distinguished from one another. *Status* denotes a position within a hierarchy: socioeconomic status, political status, organizational status, and so on. High status often fosters power and dominance (Patterson, 1985), since one is higher up in the "pecking order," but it is not a guarantee of powerful or dominant behavior. *Power* refers to the ability to influence others, often due to control of resources. *Dominance,* according to Liska (1988), may be of two types: vested dominance, which is based on birth order, kinship, physical strength, or institutionalized power, and social dominance, which refers to behavioral patterns that succeed in influencing others (Burgoon & Dillman, 1995; Ridgeway, 1987). Although some scholars regard dominance as an individual trait (e.g., Weisfeld & Linkey, 1985), it is more commonly regarded as a social and relational phenomenon. That is, dominance is determined by the subservient or submissive responses of others. It is not dominance unless it works. Even in lower primates, there is growing evidence that dominance is more a social skill that emerges through interaction than an individual trait based on aggressiveness (Mitchell & Maple, 1985; Shively, 1985).

Writing in this area often does not distinguish among these concepts. Hence our review includes messages of status, power, dominance, and individual dominance-proneness (what some have called domineeringness). The literature is organized by code because most of the research has looked at one or two isolated behaviors as they correlate with status, dominance, or dominant personality traits. However, the clear communication of dominance usually relies on the presentation of several cues simultaneously. The greater the number of cues present, the less ambiguous and more intense the message (Henley & Harmon, 1985).

Proxemics and Haptics The most elemental signals of fight and flight, of power and powerlessness, are embedded in these two codes. Territory is a key resource: people display status, dominance, and power by owning, controlling, and accessing more, and qualitatively better, territory (Hall, 1966; Henley, 1977; Lott & Sommer, 1967; Sommer, 1969, 1970, 1971; Sundstrom & Altman, 1976). Territorial privilege may be used to reinforce relational dominance. The chief executive officer of a major publishing company is known to have reserved year-round a string of presidential suites around the country for his occasional visit to each city. He insisted that the staff of one hotel completely rearrange his room to suit his tastes. His prerogative to make such demands clearly signaled to subordinates and service personnel who was in control. In diplomatic negotiations, the person to enter a room first is presumed to be the ranking representative of state. In one set of U.S.–Soviet discussions during the cold war, a second doorway had to be cut into the conference room so that diplomats from both countries could enter the room simultaneously.

Illegitimate bids for territory may also indicate one's relative power position, as the following anecdote from Gay Talese's book *The Kingdom and the Power* (1969) reveals:

Where one sits in *The Times'* newsroom is never a casual matter. It is a formal affair on the highest and lowest level. Young reporters of no special status are generally assigned to sit near the back of the room, close to the Sports department; and as the years go by and people die and the young reporter becomes more seasoned and not so young, he is moved up closer to the front. But he must never move on his own initiative. There was one bright reporter who, after being told that he would cover the labor beat, cleaned out his desk near the back of the room and moved up five rows into an empty desk vacated by one of the labor reporters who had quit. The recognition of the new occupant a few days later by an assistant city editor resulted in a reappraisal of the younger reporter's assets, and within a day he was back to his old desk, and within a year or so he was out of the newspaper business altogether. (p. 131)

Power may be reinforced by insisting that interactions occur within one's own territory. People entering someone else's domain automatically become more deferent and submissive (Edney, 1976), while those on their "home court" gain confidence from the familiarity of their surroundings. To allow yourself to be summoned voluntarily to someone else's home turf is a show of weakness. Inexperienced diplomats and politicians often learn this only after having made too many concessions to adversaries or having lost the respect of allies. The recognized territorial advantage is the reason for insisting on a neutral locale for summit meetings and other serious talks.

To intrude on someone else's territory is the boldest of power ploys. One popular book on nonverbal communication advises power seekers to spread their briefcase and possessions on another person's desk so as to gain the upper hand or at least tip the balance of power back toward their favor. A woman executive reports that a salesperson carried this idea to the extreme by sweeping into her office and taking over her desk. She was so unsettled by this violation of her territory that she lost control of the business deal.

Part of the greater territorial control that accompanies power is the right to demand and gain privacy through the use of gatekeepers, barriers, locks, and other protections against visual, auditory, and spatial intrusions. Older children often have their own room, while younger siblings share a bedroom. Employees whose desks are placed in the middle of an open area without benefit of walls or doors symbolically are being told that they have very low status relative to others in the organization. In turn, having to deal with low-status functionaries is a relational statement in itself. A student who had several meetings with her insurance company thought nothing of being turned over to one of the clerks in the "pit" until she noticed older clients being ushered into enclosed offices.

With greater territory comes the use of more territorial markers (Gillespie, 1978). People of prominence may mark property boundaries more explicitly (e.g., fences, hedgerows, "No Trespassing" signs) and may personalize claimed territories with more possessions, as in the case of a celebrity "taking over" a hotel lobby with luggage and a personal retinue. Verbal or gestural references to markers in one's territory may also be used to reinforce awareness of a position of dominance. A study in which subjects alternated playing student and teacher roles found that when they were in the high-status (teacher) role, they pointed more often toward their possessions (Leffler, Gillespie, & Conaty, 1982).

The use of personal space parallels the use of territory. Dominant and high-status people claim and are accorded more personal space and conversational distance, take up more space with expansive postures, and may initiate more intimate or invasive dis-

Territorial markers and status symbols reinforce a position of power and authority.

tances (Altman & Vinsel, 1977; Burgoon, 1978b; Dean, Willis, & Hewitt, 1975; Gillespie, 1978; Leffler et al., 1982; Lott & Sommer, 1967). Both close and far interaction distances have been associated with being perceived as high status and dominant (Burgoon, 1991; Burgoon et al., 1984; Burgoon & Hale, 1988; Goffman, 1971; Henley, 1977; King, 1966; Patterson & Sechrest, 1970; Summer, 1969). This is because dominant individuals are freer to deviate from normative distances than are submissive individuals and may initiate a more formal or intimate interaction pattern, whereas low-status individuals must maintain deferential intermediate distances in conversation. Control over distance is well practiced in the military. One must have approval to approach an officer or anyone of higher rank, and even at social events, no one enters a banquet hall until the highest in command has made an entrance.

Dominance and power may be signaled through vertical uses of space. King (1987, as cited in Jaworski, 1993) wrote, "The bias [toward "heightism"] is deeply embedded in the visual grammar of western civilization. For a speaker, it has functional advantages. The elevation . . . gives him or her a much larger field of vision. Elevation gathers and keeps attention. . . . [I]t may awaken associations of obedience, even veneration, which are as deep as the roots of human community. (p. 14)

Dominance and status are also signaled by centrality of position. Leaders sit or stand in more central positions in a group, such as at the head of a table or wherever visual access to the most people is maximized (Hare & Bales, 1963; Sommer, 1971; Strodtbeck & Hook, 1961; see also Bass & Klubeck, 1952). High-status mental health professionals choose more central seating in dining rooms (Heckel, 1973), and child leaders position themselves in the middle of peer groups (Barner-Barry, 1980). Similarly, proximity to people in authority confers status by association. The closer your home is to "prestigious" neighborhoods or your office is to the company president's, the more status you are presumed to have.

Body orientation may connote power. An indirect body orientation conveys dominance, whereas a direct orientation conveys deference (Mehrabian, 1968b, 1981). Indirect orientation, which is often accompanied by gaze aversion, increases psychological distance.

Finally, dominance may be displayed by approaching others' territory in a more rapid and deliberate fashion (Mehrabian, 1981) and by being less likely to yield space when approached by another. By contrast, submission is communicated by hesitantly approaching others (implying a reluctance to risk a confrontation), giving way to others, or taking flight.

Underlying these nonverbal behavior patterns are principles of *threat, size, initiation, elevation, privileged access, unexpectedness* (violations), and *centrality.*

Touch behaviors function similarly. Dominant individuals initiate touch. They determine the frequency, intensity, and intimacy of touch. Among status unequals, there is a nonreciprocal pattern of touch analogous to forms of address: high-status people have the prerogative and are expected to be more familiar than low-status people (Burgoon, 1991; Goffman, 1967; Henley, 1977; Stier & Hall, 1984). Just as employers and physicians can call you by your first name, so are they permitted to touch you and to use such intimate touches as a shoulder squeeze or a congratulatory hug. You, however, must refer to them by title, must refrain from touching them if they have touched you first, and must limit your contact to more formal varieties.

By contrast, status equals engage in more reciprocal touching, especially if they are intimately acquainted. Henley (1977) contended that the one-way pattern of familiarity from high to low status mirrors the pattern of nonverbal intimacy among equals, not only for touch but for other nonverbal behaviors as well (see Table 11-2). Thus initiating touch may be interpreted as an assertion of dominance or a status reminder. Conversely, reciprocating touch may be taken as an assertion of equality. In cases of uninvited nonreciprocal touch, the use of touch increases the perceived dominance of the toucher and reduces the dominance of the recipient, compared with people who do not touch (Frieze & Ramsey, 1976; Harper, 1985; Henley & Harmon, 1985; Heslin & Alper, 1983; Major & Heslin, 1982; Stier & Hall, 1984; Summerhayes & Suchner, 1978). Consistent with this pattern, nondominant personalities expect to be touched more and to touch others less (Henley, 1973).

Touch, like spatial invasions, may underscore dominance by being a violation of expectations, something only people in positions of power are entitled to do. Powerful people use touch and pointing as well as proxemic encroachments to intrude on others (Leffler et al., 1982). Again, it is a question of who has access to whom.

As further evidence of the dominance connotations of touch, Henley (1973) reported that touch more frequently accompanies communication functions that are dominance-related, such as trying to persuade someone, giving advice, or giving an order. It is also more common in superior-subordinate relationships. Finally, it should be remembered that the ultimate expression of dominance—physical aggression—is a haptic behavior.

TABLE 11-2
GESTURES OF POWER AND PRIVILEGE: EXAMPLES OF SOME NONVERBAL BEHAVIORS WITH USAGE DIFFERING FOR STATUS EQUALS AND NONEQUALS AND FOR WOMEN AND MEN

	Between equals		Between nonequals		Between men and women	
	Intimate	Nonintimate	Used by superior	Used by subordinate	Used by men	Used by women
1 Address	Familiar	Polite	Familiar	Polite	Familiar?[a]	Polite?[a]
2 Demeanor	Informal	Circumspect	Informal	Circumspect	Informal	Circumspect
3 Posture	Relaxed	Tense (less relaxed)	Relaxed	Tense	Relaxed	Tense
4 Personal space	Closeness	Distance	Closeness (option)	Distance	Closeness	Distance
5 Time	Long	Short	Long (option)	Short	Long?[a]	Short?[a]
6 Touching	Touch	Don't touch	Touch (option)	Don't touch	Touch	Don't touch
7 Eye contact	Establish	Avoid	Stare, ignore	Avert eyes, watch	Stare, ignore	Avert eyes, watch
8 Facial expression	Smile?[a]	Don't smile?[a]	Don't smile	Smile	Don't smile	Smile
9 Emotional expression	Show	Hide	Hide	Show	Hide	Show
10 Self-disclosure	Disclose	Don't disclose	Don't disclose	Disclose	Don't disclose	Disclose

[a]Behavior not known.
Source: Henley, 1977, p. 181.

Artifacts   Closely related to territorial control is the use of physical objects and surroundings to symbolize power and status. As already noted, people in power reveal their influence through possession or access to valued resources, which can include not only larger, more spacious, and prized locations but also luxurious furnishings in homes and offices, expensive automobiles, membership in exclusive clubs, ownership of rare art collections, and the like.

Hitler was a master of such symbols and carefully designed his surroundings to reinforce his power. For example, at Berchtesgaden, the window before which he received dignitaries provided a massive backdrop of sky and mountains that dwarfed his visitors, presumably making them feel insignificant in the presence of such grandeur.

In many organizations, entitlement to such symbols of position is closely regulated. In the military, for instance, rank determines size of office, size of desk, number of filing cabinets, even type of wastebasket (metal or wood). The same is true at many universities. Corporate America routinely uses such office accoutrements as well as access to company cars, limousines, and jets as indicators of status. If you can command a company jet, you are obviously in a position of power. If you get to ride occasionally in the jet, you are still part of an inner circle. If you fly commercial airlines but go first class, you have some rank but haven't yet made the big time. And if you fly coach or don't fly at all, you are down somewhere in the lower echelons.

Even when no formal or informal rules of allocation exist, more dominant individuals will lay claim to scarce and desirable resources. This pattern develops early. Dominant children were found to play longer with desired objects (a pair of gerbils) at the expense of their more submissive peers (Camras, 1984).

Status symbols are a fact of life in every culture, no matter how much it strives for a classless society. In China, western-style athletic shoes and stereos have become status symbols. In other third world or emerging countries, ownership of a major appliance or a VCR is a mark of prestige. What is valued in one country, however, may not be in another. Shuter (1984) reported that a business delegation from the American midwest,

> wishing to give Chinese government officials a quintessentially American product as a gift, gave them wheels of cheddar cheese. What they did not realize is that the Chinese consider cheese to be barely edible. Moreover, the Chinese officials display gifts from foreigners as a mark of pride, and a perishable product defeats the whole purpose. (p. F1)

What constitutes a status symbol in a given culture is constantly in flux. As one editorialist lightheartedly observed,

> . . . except in some cases, people who have latched onto some status cannot be sure how to flash the news to the world, and people who are watching cannot be sure who is dramatizing what sort of status with what symbol. Order Gucci loafers and you only risk winding up shod the same way as the boy who delivers them. A Cadillac today signifies nothing about the owner except that he might well pull in at the next Burger King. . . . Those beepers that summon people to unforeseen telephones? Years ago, when they were rare, beepers emanated some prestige, but today, in profusion, they signal little but duty. (Trippett, 1981, p. 90)

The fact that 9 out of 10 people could probably report current status symbols accurately, however, is testimony to their significance.

The key features that seem to distinguish power and status symbols are that they have *scarce availability*, entail *exclusivity*, or are associated with some special *accomplishment or position of prestige*. Displays of wealth usually reflect possession or access to things outside the economic means of the average person. But expense isn't the only indicator of status. Plaques and trophies have small monetary value but are important symbols of achievement. Flaunting such symbols becomes a way of relationally emphasizing one's status. The current popularity of arriving in a limosine for proms or graduation ceremonies is but one example.

Kinesics   The similarity between many human kinesic displays of dominance and submission and those of our primate cousins has led to speculation that such behaviors share a common evolutionary origin. Although the variability and complexity of dominance patterns among monkeys and apes argues against direct comparisons to humans (Keating, 1985; Mitchell & Maple, 1985), there are enough analogues to support a sociobiological interpretation of such behaviors. This is another way of saying that many of the behaviors have universal meaning for humans.

The behavior most common across primate species is gaze. The threat stare is a primary dominance display. Visual access is such that dominant animals freely scrutinize the group, without too much attention to any one member, while subordinates constantly watch the dominant one (Chance, 1967; Dovidio & Ellyson, 1985).

This parallels human behavior. People in positions of power or status are more likely to engage in unwavering, direct looks or stares and to break eye contact last; submissive individuals are more likely to avert gaze or break eye contact first (Exline, Ellyson, & Long, 1975; Fromme & Beam, 1974; Levine, 1972; McDowell, 1973; Modigliani, 1971; Moore & Gilliland, 1921; Rosa & Mazur, 1979; Snyder & Sutker, 1977; Strongman & Champness, 1968; Weisfeld & Linkey, 1985). In this culture we may be taught to show deference to our elders and authority figures by lowering our eyes (Argyle, 1972b), while they are free to look at us. Moreover, we may perceive their extended gazes at us as dominant and their stares as threatening (Burgoon et al., 1984; Ellsworth, Carlsmith, & Henson, 1972; Le Poire & Burgoon, 1994a; Thayer, 1969). The power of the stare is captured in Secretary of State Dean Rusk's metaphor for the Soviet response to President Kennedy's blockade during the Cuban missile crisis: "Eyeball to eyeball, they blinked first."

Although powerful or high-status people may engage in looks of long duration, they tend to look less frequently at specific others, while themselves being the recipients of more frequent gaze and facing (Collins & Guetzkow, 1964; Efran, 1968; Exline, 1963, 1972; LaFrance & Mayo, 1978b; Mehrabian, 1969). In groups, the least amount of eye contact is directed to low-status group members. Interestingly, though, the highest-status person receives less than a person of moderate status (Hearn, 1957). The notion of deference may explain this tapering-off effect. At the most extreme, powerful people may avoid looking at the speaker altogether. Speakers attribute more authority and control to listeners who either subject them to extended unbroken looks or do not look at them at all (Argyle & Kendon, 1967; Mehrabian & Williams, 1969; Thayer, 1969).

The differences in gaze pattern between dominant and nondominant individuals becomes more evident if the speaking role is separated from the listening role. A higher ratio of looking while speaking to looking while listening is both encoded and decoded as dominant. Exline et al. (1975) have labeled this *visual dominance behavior.* Whereas submissive people spend far more time looking at others while listening than while speaking, dominant people look about equal amounts of time while listening and while speaking. Also, increasing the amount of gaze during speaking is perceived as dominant, while increasing it during the listening phase is perceived as submissive. The normal pattern among people equal in status is to look more while listening than while speaking, but the amount of gaze while listening is far more pronounced by submissives. The visual dominance pattern holds true of both men and women and across such definitions of dominance as high status, control orientation, and expert power (Dovidio & Ellyson, 1982, 1985; Ellyson, Dovidio, & Corson, 1981; Ellyson, Dovidio, Corson, & Vinicur, 1980; Exline et al., 1975; Fugita, 1974; Whitehurst & Derlega, 1985). Figure 11-1 shows some typical results from encoding and decoding studies demonstrating these relationships.

The explanation for the difference in looking while speaking and looking while listening makes sense. During speaking, the amount of cognitive load influences how much we look at others: the more difficult the task, the less we look (so as to minimize distractions). This limits the amount of time speakers will look at listeners, regardless of dominance. But during the listening role, the norm of paying attention is a prevailing consideration, and such factors as situational constraints, personality, and relational definition influence the extent to which someone adheres to the norm or violates it. This makes the listening phase more sensitive to differences in dominance level. (It also makes the listening phase more sensitive to gender differences: women spend far more time looking while listening than do men.)

Like gaze, smile and eyebrow position may have universal significance for dominance. Smiling, which is comparable to the primate grimace, and raised eyebrows connote deference, submission, and possibly appeasement; the absence of a smile and lowered eyebrows convey dominance (Henley, 1977; Keating, 1985; Mehrabian & Williams, 1969; Romano & Bellack, 1980). Nonsmiling is recognized as a dominance cue across a variety of cultures and equally among boys and girls. The consistent interpretation of eyebrow lowering is less certain. Keating (1985) says that "most of the evidence targets brow position as a potential universal dominance cue in humans" (p. 91), but her own cross-cultural research reveals that only some cultures clearly differentiate raised and lowered eyebrows. Whether this is the result of cultural display rules overriding a biologically based signal remains to be seen.

Dominant postures and gestures rely on principles of *elevation, precedence or initiation, expansiveness* or *size, threat, strength, privilege, energy or activity,* and *unexpectedness.* (Burgoon, 1994; Dabbs, 1994; Mehrabian, 1968b, 1969, 1972; Morris, 1977; Poling, 1978; Schwartz, Tesser, & Powell, 1982; Spiegel & Machotka, 1974; Weisfeld & Linkey, 1985). Standing rather than sitting, looming over someone's shoulder, positioning oneself higher or in front of someone else, or dictating the degree of expressivity connotes dominance. Followers keep their heads lowered and walk behind leaders. Erect, full-height, open, or asymmetrical postures, raising the head, leg-apart stances, standing with arms akimbo (elbows extended), hands clasped behind the head, hands

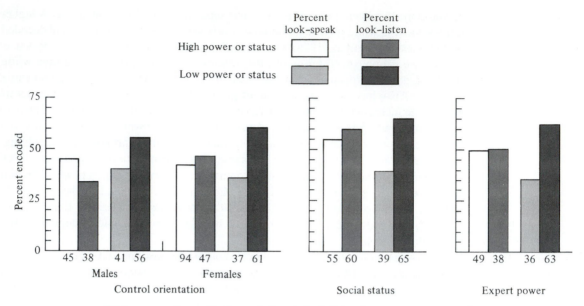

Higher proportions of look–speak time to look–listen time are more commonly encoded by more powerful or dominant communicators.

(a)

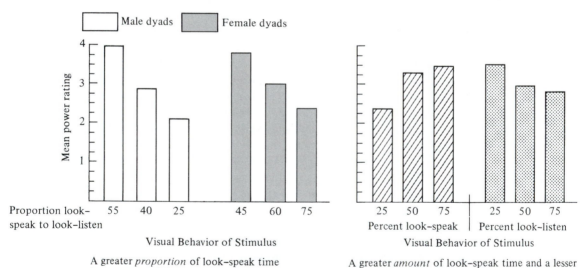

A greater *proportion* of look–speak time is more powerful.

A greater *amount* of look–speak time and a lesser amount of look–listen time is more powerful.

(b)

FIGURE 11-1
Sample results from encoding and decoding studies of visual dominance. (a) Encoding studies: percent looking while listening and looking while speaking for different types of encoders. (b) Decoding studies: attributions of power based on relative and absolute percentages of looking while speaking and looking while listening.

on hips, and "looser" seated postures that take up a lot of space convey power by expanding apparent body size. Large, sweeping gestures also extend the individual's spatial sphere of control and add an air of dynamic energy. Frequent gesturing, use of emblems and pointing gestures, and a confident, rapid gait likewise contribute to the sense of potency. Use of unconventional, idiosyncratic, or sudden emphatic gestures may further underscore a powerful person's uniqueness and status as a "rule maker" rather than a "rule follower." Together these behaviors also imply a defensiveness, a readiness to hold one's ground, that corresponds to a fight response.

In work-related situations, these cues of status and potency may also be interpreted as *task performance cues*—cues that the person will probably make useful contributions to the task at hand. In this way, these cues translate into the ability to influence members of the work group (Ridgeway, Berger, & Smith, 1985).

Conversely, submissive individuals tend to be more circumspect and "tighter" in their behavior. They appear to "shrink in," using closed, symmetrical postures and small gestures or gestures that convey vulnerability such as palm showing, uncrossed arms, and uncrossed legs. A particularly symbolic one is the head tilt, which is reminiscent of the ultimate show of submission in the animal kingdom—exposing the jugular vein to the victor. The head tilt may in fact be a vestige of more primitive forms of human communication.

Another principle underlying status and power is *relaxation* (Goffman, 1961b; Henley, 1977; Mach, 1972; Mehrabian, 1969, 1970a; Weisfeld & Linkey, 1985). In a mixed-status group, people with higher rank exhibit more relaxation, feeling free to slump in chairs or put feet up on a desk. Those of lower rank tend to mirror the postures and level of relaxation of high-status members, but they don't match it fully, maintaining some degree of postural restraint. As similarity of status increases, so do postural congruency and relaxation. This pattern—high-status people adopting more relaxed postures and more informal demeanor while subordinates remain tense and circumspect—again parallels the pattern between intimates and nonintimates of equal status (refer back to Table 11-2). This implies that dominance displays involve some of the same relational messages as intimacy displays. In the absence of other contextual information clarifying the status relationship, there is sometimes confusion about the relational meaning of such displays. Is the person presenting such behavior being aggressive or merely affiliative? When such behaviors are directed by lower-status individuals toward higher-status ones, they may often be regarded as illegitimate challenges to power when they are only intended to be shows of affection (or worse yet, reflect lack of social competence on the part of their exhibitor).

One of the more extreme forms of relaxed behavior is the public display of self-adaptors. Picking one's nose or passing gas in the presence of someone other than a close intimate is taken as a blatant show of disrespect. In fact, prisoners often engage in such displays as spitting to show their disdain for their captors. A female employee reports the experience of being in a mailroom when her supervisor, who was not speaking to her at the time, entered, checked his mail, then paused in the doorway and scratched his derriere before exiting. He had so internalized treating her as a nonperson that he forgot her presence. He would have been sorely embarrassed if caught in the act in a more public situation.

The importance of relaxation and tension cues is documented in an interesting analysis of the 1976 presidential debates between Gerald Ford and Jimmy Carter. Exline (1985) objectively coded such tension-release adaptors as lip licking, postural sway, shifting gaze, eyeblinks, and speech nonfluencies and then had observers rate various segments of the speeches. Observers rated more favorably segments that showed less tension, and Ford—the winner of the first debate—showed fewer of these tension-related adaptors at the outset of his speech. The implication is that power correlates with greater relaxation and poise. To communicate dominance therefore requires minimization of adaptor behaviors unless they are deliberate and recognizable as such.

Finally, it appears that people in lower ranks become most expressive facially when interacting with someone of higher rank, whereas those in higher-status positions have greater flexibility in how expressive they are (Patterson, 1985). This is consistent with the prerogatives of high-status people to adopt highly immediate or nonimmediate interaction patterns.

Vocalics As noted earlier, the voice is more influential than visual cues in determinations of dominance. This may be because it is an innately used and recognized signal. One striking finding from comparative studies is that the same deep-pitched, loud vocal patterns are used across a number of species to signal dominance and threat (Public Broadcasting System, 1984). Common experience tells us that we try to make our voice more imposing when attempting to influence someone or give orders. The louder, deeper voice connotes greater size and implicitly greater physical strength. Conversely, people use soft, high-pitched tones when trying to be nonthreatening. This is the universal vocal pattern mothers use when soothing infants.

Perceptual research also confirms that voices regarded as higher status, dominant, and confident display (1) lower pitch, (2) greater loudness, (3) moderately fast tempo, (4) clearer articulation and enunciation, (5) more intonation, and (6) no accent (Apple, Streeter, & Krauss, 1979; Argyle, 1975; Brooks, 1975; Delia, 1972; Giles, 1973a; Mehrabian & Williams, 1969; Mulac, Hanley, & Prigge, 1974; Packwood, 1974).

Another way in which people may demonstrate dominance is by controlling the conversation (Wiemann, 1985). Dominant people talk more and interrupt others more (Brandt, 1980; Lamb, 1981; Leffler et al., 1982; Markel, Long, & Saine, 1976; Scherer, 1982a; Starkweather, 1964; Stephan, 1952; West, 1979; West & Zimmerman, 1977; Zimmerman & West, 1975). In turn, they are more often perceived as the leader in a group (Kleinke, Lenga, Tully, Meeker, & Staneski, 1976; Sorrentino & Boutillier, 1975; Stang, 1973). This can be seen as another case of the initiation and privileged access principles.

Finally, if silence is regarded as a vocalic cue, one of the more emphatic indicators of dominance is the use of extended silences (Bruneau, 1973; Jaworski, 1993). Silence shows respect for authority. Protocol dictates that subordinates must wait for superiors to break the silence first, and their refusal to do so can be a very potent reminder of the status difference. The ultimate form of silence—failing to acknowledge another's presence with a greeting—is a powerful symbolic message of status inequality, even if unintentional. A person who receives no greeting from a preoccupied equal or superior can easily stew for a week about the perceived snub. Because the "silent treatment" causes frustration, it can provoke behavior that reinforces power:

> Silence can also protect power by aggravating those seeking to destroy or discredit persons in power. This can be done by forcing subordinates into awkward positions whereby they exhibit behaviors detrimental to their own cause—because their frustration is aggravated by silent response to their efforts. Silence as absence of response to or lack of recognition of subordinates may very well be the main source of protection of power in socio-political orders where physical restraint has lost repute. (Bruneau, 1973, p. 39)

Physical Appearance   We have said that proxemic, kinesic, and vocalic behaviors convey dominance in part through implications of physical size and strength. Physical appearance elements that themselves convey these qualities likewise connote dominance. For example, even such uncontrolled features as a square jaw, broad face, smaller eyes, and receding hairline convey dominance, while rounded jaws, large head and eyes, and thicker lips convey weakness and helplessness (Keating, 1985). The reason is that the former features are associated with age and maturity (and hence strength) and the latter with infancy and immaturity (Berry, 1991). Taller people are also assumed to be more powerful, and higher-status people are perceived as taller (Wilson, 1968). The taller of the two candidates typically wins the U.S. presidency. Carter was an exception and was reportedly so concerned by his stature that for a time he stretched his neck in an odd manner to look taller. In more recent elections, candidates have taken to standing on boxes or sitting on stools to minimize the height advantage. Shorter men who attempt to compensate for their stature by being more aggressive and self-promoting are often labeled (pejoratively) as having a "Napoleon complex."

People cannot use such genetically controlled features to encode relational messages, but they can use other appearance elements that emphasize or minimize size and strength. Women may wear young hairstyles, youthful apparel, clothing that makes them look thinner or more petite, and makeup that enlarges the eyes. These efforts can create an impression of helplessness and elicit caretaking behavior on the part of men. (Women who have such nondominant appearances are also judged more attractive; Berry, 1991.) In contrast, men often adopt hairstyles and clothing that make them appear taller, more muscular, and more mature. The initial popularity of "masculine" clothing and hairstyles among professional women reflected a desire to appear more powerful to colleagues and supervisors.

Other obvious appearance indicators include uniforms, more formal attire, and other status symbol accessories. High-status shoppers dress up more, even for shopping trips (Sybers & Roach, 1962). That such dress cues express dominance is evident in the way others respond to them. Passersby are less likely to intrude on a group of people with high-status dress (Knowles, 1973), and anyone who has attempted to purchase a new car has realized that the deference and attention paid to customers is in direct proportion to the formality and expensiveness of their clothing. Because of their high visibility and constancy in an interaction, appearance cues are readily available markers of the dominance hierarchy in any set of interpersonal relationships.

Chronemics   How people use their own time and that of others can be a very subtle but effective signal of dominance. People in power set schedules. They determine the frequency and duration of contact. A senior faculty member may insist on Saturday meetings with research assistants. The corporate executive who routinely schedules mandatory company retreats from 7:30 A.M. until 11:00 P.M. is letting subordinates know who is in control.

Powerful people are free to violate time norms. They may arrive later, stay longer, appear at odd hours, or keep others waiting but are themselves less likely to be violated. One newspaper publisher kept an editor waiting 4 hours while his wife and family packed before driving to an out-of-town meeting. They arrived at the meeting an hour late but made no apologies to the assembled group. Such behavior no doubt enhanced their perceived power. In this culture and others, those who arrive late are seen as higher in status (Levine & Wolff, 1985).

Dominant people also have more access to and demand more of other people's time. They may buy it, request it, or intrude on it. High-status shoppers demand more attention from salespeople and are more patronizing toward them (Sybers & Roach, 1962). An employer may require an employee to give up a weekend or a planned holiday to work on a report. We know of an executive who missed his own 25-year retirement celebration because he was called away for one last service to his employer.

Status is also revealed through greater leisure time and varied activity. The freedom to take a 1 1/2-hour lunch or to plan a spur-of-the-moment ski trip implies a relative position of importance in corporate America.

Finally, dominance and power may be expressed through polychronistic use of time. People in authority are free to give others divided attention. The job interviewer who sifts through a pile of applications while interviewing you is signaling a relative inequality in status, as is the manager who interrupts staff meetings to take telephone calls.

Some popular books advise using these and other chronemic maneuvers as ploys in the power game. But as you will find, some of these behaviors carry negative relational meanings in terms of intimacy and immediacy (see Box 11-3). The cost of successfully communicating dominance may therefore be some other unintended relational statements.

Gender and Power   One of the most provocative questions regarding dominance is whether the fundamental distinction between men's and women's nonverbal displays is one of dominance, with men's displays paralleling those of power and women's those of powerlessness. This issue has generated considerable research and speculation (see, e.g., Aries, 1982; Axelrod, 1980; Burgoon, 1994; Burgoon & Dillman, 1995; Dovidio et al., 1988; Ellyson & Dovidio, 1985; Gillespie, 1978; Greenberg, 1979; Hall & Halberstadt, 1986; Henley, 1977, 1995; Henley & Harmon, 1985; Jones, 1986; LaFrance, 1985b; Leffler et al., 1982; Marche & Peterson, 1993; Noller, 1993; Stier & Hall, 1984). Table 11-2 listed some of the key behaviors cited to support the claim. Although it is true that many behaviors exhibited most frequently by women connote submissiveness and weakness, female displays, as noted in earlier chapters, can also be characterized as affiliative, positive, sensitive, and engaged. Moreover, in same-sex interactions, women are capable of displaying the same dominance behaviors as men, and in opposite-sex interactions,

Richard Nixon shows mastery of polychronistic use of time. What relational messages does his behavior express?

BOX 11-3

APPLICATIONS: RELATIONAL MESSAGES ON THE 'NET

Can you send relational messages when you communicate by computer? Some recent research by Walther and associates (Walther, in press; Walther, Anderson, & Park, 1994; Walther & Burgoon, 1992; Walther & Tidwell, 1994) indicates that you can. Although establishing an interpersonal relationship via electronic mail or teleconferencing takes a little longer, people are quite adept at making up for the absence of some nonverbal cues. They manage to send and receive relational messages despite the channel restrictions. How? Among other things, they use chronemics—such as the timing of messages or how quickly messages are responded to—and visual icons to replace missing relational content and emotional "punctuation."

Such behaviors clearly have relational import. For example, replying quickly to someone else's message conveys greater equality (less dominance) than replying

slowly. Sending a task-related request at night is more dominant than sending the same message during the day. It also conveys less intimacy. (By contrast, a social message sent at night is seen as very intimate.) And writing in all capital letters—the equivalent of shouting—can be both dominant and disrespectful. These few examples presage a need for increasing sensitivity to computer-mediated relational communication as more and more of us become electronically "tethered" to one another. It is possible that we may actually come to prefer the electronic medium to face-to-face communication for some purposes. We may find that the absence of visual and audio cues heightens the sense of relational familiarity, producing "hyperpersonal" interaction (Walther, 1995). Thus, the choice of communication medium—mediated or not—may come to carry relational messages in itself.

women may show greater dominance and power than men when the task is linked to femininity. They may also use subtle behaviors such as touch as a control cue. It is not clear, therefore, that female displays are uniformly nondominant. It may be, as two studies have shown, that women are more likely to monitor their partner's behavior and to accommodate their behavior to their partner's when the partner is male, whereas men maintain a more fixed pattern of behavior (Greenberg, 1979; Mulac et al., 1987). Some women's displays may also be more the result of social nervousness and unease than dominance (Hall & Halberstadt, 1986). Time will tell whether societal change in male and female roles brings a corresponding change in nonverbal dominance displays.

Messages of Intimacy and Nonintimacy

I only said "I want to be alone!"

Greta Garbo

And I have known the eyes already, known them all—
The eyes that fix you in a formulated phrase . . .

T. S. Eliot

Most of the research on intimacy—unlike dominance—has examined combinations and sequences of cues as they relate to a particular outcome, such as liking. Despite differences in labels, most of the research tends to follow the thematic dimensions that Burgoon and Hale (1984, 1987b) found. Involvement and immediacy include cues specifically concerned with approach or avoidance and engagement or detachment. Research invariably includes similarity elements as relationships proceed through the stages of acquaintanceship. Work on attraction and liking corresponds to the affection dimension. Research on such related topics as warmth, responsivity, trust, empathy, rapport, and genuineness fits the combined themes of inclusion, receptivity, and trust, as does work on the opposite end of the inclusion continuum, privacy. A culminating line of work is that on courtship.

Involvement and Immediacy   Involvement behaviors are voluntarily expressed behaviors that signal participation, interest, and occupation with the other person in an interaction. Sometimes involvement is considered synonymous with immediacy, which encompasses behaviors specifically reflecting the degree of psychological distance between participants. However, involvement may also be communicated through expressiveness, good interaction management, altercentrism (focus on the other), and lack of social anxiety (Coker & Burgoon, 1987).

We rely on immediacy behaviors primarily to judge the level of involvement in a specific encounter rather than the status of the entire relationship (Forgas, 1978). The behaviors most often associated with immediacy and warmth are (1) close conversational distance; (2) direct body and facial orientation; (3) forward leaning; (4) increased and direct gaze; (5) positive reinforcers such as smiling, head nods, and pleasant facial expressions; (6) postural openness; (7) frequent gesturing; and (8) touch (Andersen, 1979; Argyle & Cook, 1976; Argyle & Dean, 1965; Beier & Sternberg, 1977; Burgoon, 1991; Burgoon et al., 1984; Cappella, 1983; Cappella & Greene, 1984; Coker & Burgoon, 1987; Edinger & Patterson, 1983; Exline et al., 1965; Henley, 1977; Keiser & Altman, 1976; LaFrance & Ickes, 1981; Le Poire & Burgoon, 1994b; Mehrabian, 1968c, 1971b, 1972, 1981; Mehrabian & Ksionzky, 1972; Mehrabian & Williams, 1969; Patterson, 1973b, 1976; Sobelman, 1973; Thompson & Aiello, 1988). Other kinesic behaviors that people encode to demonstrate expressiveness, good interaction management, and lack of anxiety are more facial animation, more gestural animation and use of illustrators, coordinated movement, use of fewer adaptors, less random movement, and greater postural attentiveness (Coker & Burgoon, 1987). The opposites of these signal detachment and noninvolvement. Although the addition of more cues tends to make a message more pronounced, some cues such as proximity carry more weight than others (Burgoon et al., 1984; Fisher et al., 1976; Henley, 1977). For instance, moving to a far distance may be sufficient to communicate nonimmediacy, regardless of how "warm" the other nonverbal cues are.

Vocal cues have received far less study. Those mentioned as indicative of involvement are speech rate, speech latency, loudness or intensity, speech duration, and interruptions (Cappella, 1983; Patterson, 1983). In a study designed to see what behaviors people actually enact to signal high or low involvement, Coker and Burgoon (1987) found that people expressing higher involvement spoke louder and faster, lowered their pitch, used more pitch variety, had fewer silences or latencies and more coordinated speech, and generally had warmer, more relaxed, resonant, and rhythmic voices with frequent relaxed laughter. Scott (1994) found many of these same behaviors in an ethnographic study of how nurses communicate involvement to patients.

One chronemic element that expresses involvement is monochronistic versus polychronistic use of time. To do more than one thing at once is to show lack of involvement in the interaction. In Box 11-4, Miss Manners provides some lighthearted guidelines on when it is not acceptable to do two things at once.

Physical appearance cues and use of artifacts may also implicitly signal involvement. Table 11-3, which summarizes involvement cues gleaned from several studies, offers some examples.

Although many of these cues are also interpreted as signals of affiliation, taken individually they may indicate only intensity of involvement and should not be viewed as reliable indicators of intimacy (Cappella, 1983). Gaze is a case in point. Two people engaged in a heated and hostile argument may make as much eye contact as two people who are attracted to one another. One study found that decreased gaze indicated disapproval, reduced intimacy, or reduced power, depending on the circumstances (Lochman & Allen, 1981). Thus gaze is primarily an intensifier of affect. Other cues may be similarly ambiguous unless coupled with a sufficient number of other intimacy cues to make the meaning clear.

Depth and Similarity   As members in a relationship progress from strangers to acquaintances to friends to intimates, many of the involvement behaviors become more prevalent. For example, friends gaze more, smile more, show more facial pleasantness, and adopt closer conversational distances than strangers, and such cues are taken as indicative of more familiar relationships (Coutts & Schneider, 1976; Hale & Burgoon, 1984; Keiser & Altman, 1976; Little, 1968; Russo, 1975; Sundstrom & Altman, 1976; Thayer & Schiff, 1974). Subtle nonverbal differences may even distinguish harmonious couples and conflicted couples (those who may be presumed to be in one of the deesca-

BOX 11-4

ADVICE FROM MISS MANNERS

Is it proper to do two things at the same time? . . . It all depends on what two things and where and with whom.

It is proper to drink champagne and make eyes over the top of the glass at the same time. It may not always be wise, but the combination itself is considered socially proper.

However, it was not gallant of dear Gustave Flaubert to smoke a cigar and make love at the same time. Miss Manners dares say he meant it to be improper. . . .

It is never proper to have a television set on when visitors arrive except on election night, but visitors who drop in aren't proper themselves, so they may be told that one is busy just then. Miss Manners thinks it improper to have even so-called background music on when people are talking, but then she thinks such music improper all by itself.

It is proper and even decorative (meaning nicely old-fashioned) for ladies to do needlework in their own homes when company is present on all but the most formal occasions, and on very informal visits to others.

If they are challenged, they may use an old argument left over from Miss Manners' college days about how it is actually easier to pay attention to what someone is saying when one is knitting. The reasoning is that no one can pay constant attention to a lecture anyway, and it is better to have one's hands active than one's thoughts wandering.

This comes with the warning that the professors didn't care for it. It should be kept in mind that the two things anybody who is talking believe that the other person ought to be doing are (1) listening and (2) committing it all to memory.

Source: Martin, 1986.

lation stages). Happy couples sit closer together and touch each other more, while discordant couples touch themselves more and adopt such closed postures as crossed arms (Beier, 1974; Beier & Sternberg, 1977).

An integral part of moving a relationship to a deeper, more familiar level is displays of commonality and similarity. These include adopting similar dress and appearance, vocal patterns, and kinesic mannerisms in addition to modeling each other's language use. Romantic couples universally use appearance to publicly proclaim identification as a duo. They may dress alike, exchange matching rings, or even wear identical hairstyles. The lifelong habit of married couples' mimicking each other's facial expressions often results in their faces looking alike over time.

The use of attire and adornments as a form of shared identity is not confined to romantic relationships. As noted in Chapter 8, cultures and subgroups within cultures rely on nonverbal cues to display their identification with ingroups and to set themselves apart from outgroups. Youth gangs rely on various badges, clothing styles, and colors to proclaim their separateness. Religious cults often enforce a common dress code to promote group identity over individual identity. Law enforcement agencies, private schools, corporations, and renegade groups such as survivalists likewise know the value of a recognizable uniform in fostering group solidarity.

Vocally, affiliated pairs and groups may converge their speech patterns. By matching a partner's speech style, a person may emphasize similarities and enhance attraction. Conversely, a person may signal dissimilarity by diverging from the other's speech pattern. Specific behaviors on which people match or contrast speech include accent, pro-

TABLE 11-3
NONVERBAL CUES OF INVOLVEMENT, AFFILIATION, AND LIKING

Dimension	Associated nonverbal behaviors
1 Immediacy	Close proximity (sitting and standing at close distance, walking side-by-side, approaching the other) High amount of gaze Direct or intent eye contact Forward lean (or backward lean if part of "slouched" posture) Direct face and body orientation Touch (handshakes, instrumental touch to assist someone or while accomplishing a task, incidental touch, soothing contact, pats, hugs, squeezes, kissing) Frequent interaction (e.g., phoning often)
2 Expressivity	Animated facial expressions Frequent use of illustrator and emblem gestures Expansive gesturing Vocal variety (varied tempo, pitch, loudness) Rapid tempo Louder voice
3 Altercentrism	Attentive listening (still posture, eye contact, direct facing) Ignore distractions Serious vocal tone Whispering during intimate or embarrassing topics Absence of interruptions Nodding and other backchannel cues Monochronic use of time Spending large amount of time with person
4 Conversation Management	Fluent speech Few and brief silences Short response latencies and turn switches (some interruptions or talk overs permitted) Brief within-turn pauses Interactional synchrony Self-synchrony (behavioral coordination and verbal-nonverbal coordination) Absence of channel incongruency (mixed messages) Long turns at talk
5 Composure	Moderate vocal arousal (e.g., some nervous vocalizations, high pitch) Moderate kinesic-proxemic arousal (e.g., some use of self- and object-adaptors, some physical movement) but minimal fidgeting, restlessness, or yawning Absence of vocal nonfluencies Moderate postural relaxation (loose, asymmetrical) Relaxed voice
6 Positive Affect	Relaxed laughter Vocal warmth and pleasantness Smiling and facial pleasantness Head tilt Postural mirroring Gift giving, doing favors, sharing or loaning possessions

Source: Compiled from Coker & Burgoon (1987), Fichten, Tagalakis, Judd, Wright, & Amsel (1992), Le Poire & Burgoon (1994a), and Scott (1994).

nunciation, speech rate, loudness, pause length, vocalization length, utterance length, interruptions, and language choice (Feldstein & Welkowitz, 1978; Giles, 1977; Giles & Powesland, 1975; Matarazzo & Weins, 1972; Siegman, 1978; Street, 1982; Street & Giles, 1982).

Kinesically and proxemically, people may show similarities through proximity and postural sharing. People who have similar personalities and attitudes adopt closer interaction distances (Byrne et al., 1970) and echo each other's body positions or adopt mirror-image postures (Morris, 1977; Scheflen, 1964). In turn, people who are induced to share posture perceive themselves to be more similar (Navarre, 1982). Attitudinally and demographically similar dyads also display more affiliative behaviors such as gesturing, self-grooming, and gazing, while dissimilar pairs show more nonaffiliative behaviors such as self-touching and nervous laughter (Gonzales, 1982; Murray & McGinley, 1972). Better adjusted marital couples show more reciprocal gaze (Noller, 1980a, 1980b).

Other indicators of the depth of a relationship are what Morris (1977) called *tie-signs*. These are signals that a couple is to be treated as a bonded pair. Many are haptic gestures, such as linked arms, handholding, arms around waists, hand-to-face touches, and the arm-to-elbow assist. Many other cues exchanged among courting and bonded couples qualify as tie-signs. Interestingly, tie-signs are more prevalent among dating and courting couples than among marrieds. Once a relationship is well established, the need for public displays of affection and oneness are no longer necessary. Thus the stage of the relationship dictates which of these behaviors will be present.

At a more general level, Knapp (1984a) hypothesized that as relationships escalate, styles of communication move from (1) narrow to broad ranges of expressions (such as more facial and vocal blends, fewer dichotomies, and more time together); (2) stylized, conventional forms of communication to more unique, idiosyncratic, and relationally negotiated forms; (3) difficult to more efficient, accurate communication; (4) rigid to flexible patterns of interaction; (5) awkward to smooth, synchronized, convergent communication; (6) public to personal and private revelations (such as previously unknown information and use of adaptors); (7) hesitant to spontaneous, rapid, and relaxed communication; and (8) suspending overt judgment to making such judgments, including negative feedback, explicit. Conversely, as relationships deescalate, they move back toward the narrow, stylized, difficult, rigid, awkward, hesitant, nonjudgmental ends of the stylistic continua.

Affection, Attraction, Liking, and Love   Signals of love and attraction hold a fascination for most of us. They are essential not only to the mating game but also to the development of satisfying friendships, family relations, and work relations. The courtship process is detailed later, so here we consider behaviors that singly or in combination communicate positive or negative affect toward the partner.

The ubiquitous immediacy behaviors are especially significant. People display more immediacy toward someone they like (Coutts, Schneider, & Montgomery, 1980; Mehrabian, 1970a), and people who are induced to show more immediacy come to like the target more (Slane & Leak, 1978). Immediacy cues can even leak unintended evaluations. Tutors who thought they were working with bright children gazed, nodded,

Three variations of body contact tie-signs.

smiled, and leaned forward more than those who thought they were working with dull children (Chaikin, Sigler, & Derlega, 1974).

Of special significance are the eyes. Literary passages abound with references to the power of the eyes to attract and arouse. Consider this one from *The Sleepwalkers:*

> So they smiled frankly at each other and their souls nodded to each other through the windows of their eyes, just for an instant, like two neighbors who have never greeted each other and now happen to lean out of their window at the same moment, pleased and embarrassed by this unforeseen and simultaneous greeting. (Broch, 1964)

Few behaviors have attracted more research attention than gaze and smiling. Research confirms our intuitive observations. People in love do in fact spend more time gazing into each other's eyes, especially at close range (Givens, 1978; Rubin, 1970). More gazing signifies attraction, liking, and friendliness, while averted gaze signals the opposite (Argyle, 1972a; Beebe, 1980; Burgoon, 1991; Burgoon et al., 1984; Exline, 1972; Exline & Winters, 1965; Goldberg et al., 1969; Kleinke, Meeker, & LaFong, 1974; LePoire & Burgoon, 1994a; Lochman & Allen, 1981; McDowell, 1973; Mehrabian, 1968c, 1969; Murray & McGinley, 1972; Palmer & Simmons, 1993; Patterson, Jordan, Hogan, & Frerker, 1981; Reece & Whitman, 1961; Simpson et al., 1993). Encoders select gaze as one of the primary cues to express positive evaluations and decoders interpret it as such. One interesting sex difference is that men are more likely to express liking through gaze while listening, whereas women do so while speaking.

An involuntary eye behavior that also signals attraction is pupil dilation. When people see someone or something they like, their pupils tend to enlarge (Hess, 1975; Hess & Polt, 1960; Janisse & Peavler, 1974). Widened pupils in turn make people look more attractive, a discovery that led women centuries ago to use belladonna to artificially dilate their pupils. Suppose that two people's eyes meet across a crowded room. If the man is attracted to the woman, his pupils automatically will dilate, which makes him appear warmer and more attractive. If the woman's pupils dilate in response, the pair may have the beginnings of a mutual physical attraction. This is one subtle way that people can tell if others are attracted to them.

Facial and bodily expressiveness are also important in communicating liking, friendliness, and attraction. Much of the research on gaze simultaneously has found that smiling, facial pleasantness, and postural mirroring are key indicators of these relational intimacy messages (see also Mach, 1972; Waldron, 1975).

Close proximity and touch likewise are carriers of messages of attraction and liking. People draw nearer to those they like, and proximity is the most important immediacy behavior in decoding liking and attraction (Burgoon et al., 1984; Byrne et al., 1970; Gilbert, Kirkland, & Rappoport, 1977; Kleck, 1969; Lott & Sommer, 1967; Patterson & Sechrest, 1970; Rosenfeld, 1965; Sommer, 1971). Touch is used in the same way to express warmth, love, friendliness, and intimacy, and is interpreted as such, even when it is nonreciprocal (Breed & Ricci, 1973; Burgoon et al., 1984; Burgoon, Walther, & Baesler, 1992; Fisher et al., 1976; Heslin & Alper, 1983; Kleinke et al., 1974; Major & Heslin, 1982; Pisano, Wall, & Foster, 1986). Its potency is captured by Thayer (1986):

> Touch is a signal in the communication process that, above all other communication channels, most directly and immediately escalates the balance of intimacy. . . . To let another touch us is to drop that final and most formidable barrier to intimacy. (p. 8)

Absence of touch may also be a powerful message of repugnance. A study on the frequency of touch in a nursing home found that the staff engaged in much less touching with extremely handicapped patients, even though touch is frequently a necessary part of medical care (Watson, 1975).

Beyond immediacy behaviors, vocal tone may communicate affection. In particular, a louder voice is associated with negative affect (Kimble, Forte, & Yoshikawa, 1981). Conversely, people in love may express their feelings by using oversoft, slurred, drawling, resonant, high-pitched voices (Costanzo et al., 1969; Givens, 1978).

One final indicator of level of affection is the use of silences. Silences may be associated with complete harmony or complete conflict. When people are comfortable in a relationship, there is no need to talk. When relationships are just developing, silences become less common. People who are attracted to each other may use fewer silent pauses (Siegman, 1979). At the other extreme, silences may indicate aversion and disdain:

> Fat persons, dwarfs, very tall persons, crippled persons with mobility problems, blind persons, persons with pronounced speech or hearing disorders, etc., have known nervous silences toward them. Differences in appearance, such as perceived ugliness, dress and color of skin, when different than the situational norm, seem to be greeted by initial silences. (Bruneau, 1973, p. 32)

Equally important to the specific cues of intimacy is their sequencing. A sequence of warm behavior followed by cold is more detrimental to attraction than all cold behavior (Clore, Wiggins, & Itkin, 1975a, 1975b; Thompson & Aiello, 1988). The finding that people place greater importance on the contrast between cold and warm behavior follows gain-loss theory (Aronson & Linder, 1965). Gains or losses in apparent affection are more telling than consistent behavior. This probably explains why we feel we have made more strides with a person who initially seems aloof to us and then warms up to us. We take it as a significant relational statement.

Trust, Receptivity, Warmth, Empathy, and Rapport   Not surprisingly, many of the same kinesic, proxemic, and haptic behaviors that communicate relational depth, similarity, and affection also express trust, empathy, rapport, and other receptive themes. They also function to express comfort to someone in distress (see Bullis & Horn, 1995; Dolin & Booth-Butterfield, 1993). The amount and directness of eye contact increase in response to warm nonverbal cues from a tutor, which suggests greater receptivity; they increase with preferences for intimate relationships (McAdams, Jackson, & Kirshnit, 1984) and are seen as expressing more empathy and warmth (Haase & Tepper, 1972; Ho & Mitchell, 1982; McAdams et al., 1984). However, too much gaze may be counterproductive. One study found that moderate eye contact earned the highest ratings on genuineness and empathy (Reed, 1981).

More smiling, facial pleasantness, head nods, frequent and open gestures, and eyebrow raises have the same effects as more gaze: they accompany a desire for intimacy, are a likely response to an immediate partner, and are interpreted as expressing more empathy, warmth, affiliativeness, and friendliness (Bayes, 1972; Clore et al., 1975b; D'Augelli, 1974; Gutsell & Andersen, 1980; Harrigan & Rosenthal, 1986; Hillison, 1983; Ho & Mitchell, 1982; Janzen, 1984; McAdams et al., 1984; McMullan, 1974; Mehrabian, 1981; Patterson et al., 1981; Sobelman, 1973). Coldness is expressed by such acts as blank stares, gazing away or at the ceiling, and engaging in such adaptor behaviors as knuckle cracking, hair twisting, and smoking.

Postural mirroring or congruence is also a key indicator. Occurring more frequently among cooperative pairs, it is associated with rapport, empathy, and trustworthiness in the short term and over time, and can lead to more liking of the partner when a person is induced to display it (Charney, 1966; Fraenkel, 1983; LaFrance, 1979, 1985a; LaFrance & Broadbent, 1976; Mansfield, 1973; Navarre, 1982; Sandhu, 1984; Trout & Rosenfeld, 1980). However, it is possible that postural sharing is only actually associated with long-term relationships; in brief encounters, it may signal a desire for rapport but be accompanied by discomfort (LaFrance & Ickes, 1981). Facial, postural, and vocal motor mimicry—mimicking someone else's expression of emotion such as pain or leaning in the same direction during a recounting of a near accident—is another form of mirroring that occurs most when it is visible to the sufferer (suggesting that it is an intentional show of sympathy) and is interpreted as knowing and caring how another feels (Bavelas, Black, Chovil, Lemery, & Mullett, 1988; Bavelas, Black, Lemery, & Mullett, 1986).

Close proximity, direct body orientation, forward leaning, and the use of touch also communicate greater empathy, warmth, affiliation, comfort, and rapport, as well as produce perceptions of greater trustworthiness (Breed & Ricci, 1973; Bullis & Horn, 1995; Claiborn, 1979; Fisher et al., 1976; Haase & Tepper, 1972; Hillison, 1983; Kleinke et al., 1974; Major & Heslin, 1982; McMullan, 1974; Patterson, Powell, & Lenihan, 1986; Sobelman, 1973; Trout & Rosenfeld, 1980). However, touch may be a vital relational message of sincerity and intimacy only among friends and family. It may not express the same meanings among strangers, or at least not to the same degree. This was the conclusion of two experiments (Breed & Ricci, 1973; Burley, 1972). In one, actual touch increased more positive feelings among stranger recipients, but empathy was perceived to be even greater when accompanied by no touch or imagined touch. In the other, touch or no touch was coupled with warm or cold behavior. It turned out that the warmth cues made more of a difference than touch. Thus it may be that the affiliative behaviors typically accompanying touch are more responsible for the effects of touch than touch itself. One other interesting observation is that interviewers who are more favorable toward an interviewee touch their foot more (while seated in a foot-on-knee position) (Goldberg & Rosenthal, 1986). This may be a very subtle cue that someone is open to you (see also Box 11-5).

Vocally, more laughter is associated with greater intimacy (McAdams et al., 1984), and more vocal pleasantness with greater affiliation (Mehrabian, 1970a).

Privacy   At the opposite end of the inclusion and receptivity continuum are relational messages expressing the desire for exclusion, nonreceptivity, and privacy. As we noted earlier, people appear to have competing needs for approach and avoidance, even in their most intimate relationships. The nature of privacy and the means through which people express their need for it or a desire to restore lost privacy are not solely relational messages and are discussed in more detail in Chapters 7 and 8. However, it is important to recognize that the relational communication of privacy can be designed either to move a relationship to a more intimate level (when it separates the dyad from others) or to move it, even if temporarily, to a less intimate one. The kinds of behaviors that are most likely to signal a desire for greater individual privacy include a combination of nonimmediacy, nonaffiliation, and dominance behaviors. These are often coupled with manip-

---

BOX 11-5

APPLICATIONS: NONVERBAL RAPPORT AND THE SUCCESSFUL DOCTOR

Good rapport is essential to a successful relationship between physicians and their patients. Without it, patients may not comply with a doctor's recommendations or may even change doctors. We noted in Chapter 5 that empathy and rapport are better expressed through nonverbal than verbal channels. Just what nonverbal cues do physicians use to communicate this to patients?

Immediacy behaviors are very important. Doctors who sit or stand closer to their patients, face them directly, lean forward, nod frequently, and use touch are seen as warmer and more empathic. However, eye contact doesn't work in quite the same way. Doctors who gaze more *toward* their patients but engage in less *mutual* gaze are seen as having the most rapport (Harrigan, Oxman, & Rosenthal, 1985; Harrigan & Rosenthal, 1983, 1986). Whether posture is open or closed is also telling. Symmetrical, open arm positions and hands resting in the lap are associated with greater physician rapport, while crossed arms are seen as the coldest and least empathic expression (Harrigan et al., 1985; Harrigan & Rosenthal, 1986; Smith-Hanen, 1977).

Interestingly, more self-touching by doctors, rather than its absence, is associated with greater warmth and expressiveness. This may be because self-touching often accompanies efforts to encode or decode speech and may be taken as an indication that the doctor is intently interested in what the patient has to say (Harrigan, 1985; Harrigan, Kues, & Weber, 1986; Harrigan, Weber, & Kues, 1986). Gesturing is even more positively evaluated than self-touching, probably because it too expresses high involvement.

Doctors' vocal cues are also strong predictors of whether patients are satisfied with their relationship with the doctor. In particular, a nondominant, anxious, but warm voice leads to physicians' being perceived as warm (Blanck, Rosenthal, & Vannicelli, 1986). A friendly or neutral voice is also perceived as more receptive and trustworthy than an authoritarian voice (Parrott & Le Poire, 1988).

Finally, doctors who are more accurate encoders of their emotional states, whether through audio, visual, or combined channels, have patients who are more affectively satisfied with them (DiMatteo, Prince, & Hays, 1986). In other words, doctors who are more skilled at nonverbal communication are seen as having greater understanding of and rapport with their patients.

---

ulations of the environment, space, and time that afford greater control of accessibility, sensory stimulation, and surveillance (Altman, 1975; Burgoon, 1982).

Conflict   Although we have already noted that the negative ends of the intimacy continua—such as detachment and distrust—are also expressed nonverbally, hostility and conflict are important enough to warrant a section of their own. As Duck (1994) cautions, " . . . real lives are richly entwined with begrudging, vengeful, hostile, conflictive, tensions and struggles (p. 6)," which places a premium on understanding how these conflicts are manifested and managed nonverbally.

Earlier, we observed how nonverbal affective responses are a major determinant of relational satisfaction and commitment. The same is true of satisfactory resolution of disagreements and conflicts (e.g., Alberts, 1989; Gottman, Markman, & Notarius, 1977; Markman & Floyd, 1980; Markman et al., 1981; Newton & Burgoon, 1990). Couples who are able to avoid reciprocating a partner's hostile outbursts typically arrive at more acceptable solutions to problems. Couples who instead reciprocate verbal and nonverbal hostilities find themselves far less satisfied with the communication itself as well as the relationship.

These patterns are learned early. Kahlbaugh and Haviland (1994) found that teenagers signal contempt toward parents through such avoidance behaviors as backward leaning, closed arms, gaze aversion, and self-touching, and parents reciprocate these behaviors.

In an attempt to determine what nonverbal behaviors might accompany constructive and destructive conflict patterns, Newton and Burgoon (1990) coded the nonverbal behaviors accompanying supportive and accusatory verbal disagreement strategies. They found that when couples offered verbal statements validating their partner's claims, they accompanied such statements with a relaxed and "mellow" demeanor—relaxed posture; a soft, slow, deep, monotone voice that included nonfluencies; and frequent self-adaptors. When they made statements affirming the person or the relationship, they displayed a lot of kinesic and vocalic involvement and expressed it in a submissive way. When instead they attacked the other's arguments or personhood, their nonverbal demeanor became highly animated, dominant, strident, and uncomposed. They exhibited increased gesturing; indirect body orientations; sharp, rapid, high-pitched, varied, and fluent voices; and postural tension and random trunk and limb movement. These latter behaviors convey the negative affect that is so often the catalyst for conflict escalation.

So far we have considered the component nonverbal cues that together express messages about the relative intimacy of a relationship, regardless of whether it is a friendship, family relationship, work association, or romantic partnership. Now we turn specifically to the mating game.

Courtship and Quasi-Courtship

Courtship consists in a number of quiet attentions, not so pointed as to alarm, nor so vague as not to be understood.

Lawrence Stern

Courtship runs on messages—on physical signals and displays. Love may be intangible, but love communication is concrete, real.

David Givens

The ways in which courtship is practiced may have varied across history and cultures (Cate & Lloyd, 1992), but the basic signals of romantic interest have not. In fact, they may have a strong evolutionary basis (Givens, 1978; Kenrick, 1994; Simpson et al., 1993). Examinations of commonalities between humans and other species in basic courtship signals and sequences reveal a strong biological base that suggests such signals may be universal.

Courtship cues are intended to express romantic interest and to culminate in an intimate, usually sexual, commitment. They can be distinguished from *quasi-courtship cues* which are flirtatious behaviors intended to express attraction but not to lead to a sexual union. These behaviors, interestingly, were first uncovered by Scheflen (1965, 1974), who found that during family counseling sessions, some women would flirt with the psychotherapist, even with their husband sitting next to them. Under such circumstances, the behaviors were probably not intended to invite a more intimate relationship but rather to invite affirmation of their own sexual attractiveness.

The major distinguishing characteristics of courtship are (1) use of attention-gaining signals, (2) use of submissive behaviors to minimize the possibility that approach will be interpreted as a threat, and (3) reliance on patterns of interaction that parallel parent-child interactions. These various signals unfold through five stages.

The first stage is *attention.* Before anything can happen, the two parties involved must first gain each other's attention. This may be accidental—as in two people catching each other's eye at a bus stop—or intentional—as in an arranged introduction. In fact, Givens (1983) claimed that "all the smiling, firm handshakes, excited greetings, nervous laughter, clown-colorful costumes, and scurrying about you see at parties can be viewed in a detached way as *attention* signals" (p. 11). A key feature of this stage is ambivalence—a mix of tendencies to draw near and to avoid that reflect the tentativeness of this initial period. The two may vacillate between glancing at each other and glancing away or downward, smiling and compressing lips, yawning, stretching, accelerating the tempo of behavior, and engaging in a lot of self-touch as a sign of anxiety (Eibl-Eibesfeldt, 1975; Givens, 1978). They may also display infantile or childlike expressions designed to elicit affectionate responses (Eibl-Eibesfeldt, 1971).

The next stage is *recognition,* or what Scheflen (1965) called *courtship readiness.* If the response of one party to these hesitant approach signals is a stare, blank face, negative facial expression, or orienting away, that ends it. However, if there is some interest, the recipient will display availability signals. These include eyebrow raises and the typical immediacy behaviors of gaze, more direct body orientation, and smiling, but they are tempered by ambivalence signals such as demurely averting gaze downward and engaging in the same adaptor behaviors of yawning, stretching, self-touching, and the like. Sexually oriented men are more likely to smile, laugh, and use frequent flirtatious glances; sexually oriented women may lean forward more and tilt their heads (Simpson et al., 1993).

A common indicator of readiness is increased muscle tone. Posture improves, sagging tummies and derrieres are tightened, bags around the eyes tend to disappear. People appear more alert, eyes seem brighter, and skin may take on a rosier hue due to more blood flooding the capillaries of the face. Accompanying these physiological changes are preening behaviors—such self-grooming acts as smoothing the hair, straightening clothing, tugging at socks (by men), and checking makeup (by women) (see Figure 11-2). You can see a demonstration of these behaviors the next time you are in a public restroom or trying on clothes in a department store. People go through a range of preening behaviors in front of the mirror before presenting themselves in public again.

Anxiety is still evident in this stage and may even result in "freezing." Immobility is especially common after an embarrassing period of mutual gaze. It may serve to reassure the partner that no aggressive intentions exist.

A central characteristic of the displays in this stage, in fact, is their submissive quality. Docile behaviors, by disclaiming dominance, cue the approacher that he or she need not fear hostile responses to the overture. A complex of behaviors that Givens (1978) called the *shoulder-shrug composite* often occurs. This set of submissive behaviors, seen in both children and adults, includes the shoulder shrug itself, eyebrow raising, the head tilt, and an open mouth or pout. In women, physical features reduce apparent aggressiveness even further: "Relative hairlessness, smooth complexion and voice tone [all of] which have a childlike character may contribute to this. They may also dispose the male toward caretaking and protective behaviors" (Kendon, 1975, p. 328).

Some preening behavior of male psychotherapists

A) Tie preen
B) Sock preen
C) Hair preen

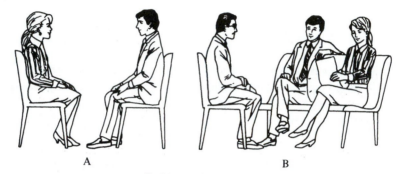

Positioning for courtship

A) With two people
B) With third party present

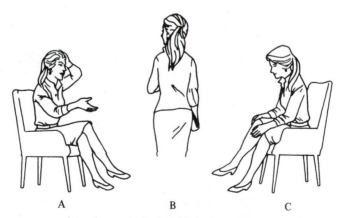

Appealing or invitational behavior of women

A) Presenting the palm with hair press
B) Rolling the hip
C) Presenting and caressing the leg

FIGURE 11-2
Behaviors typical for the second, third, and fourth stages of courtship.

The third stage is *positioning* for courtship and interaction. People place themselves in close face-to-face positions for direct and personal conversation. These positions also serve the function of closing others out. By leaning forward, crossing legs toward each other, orienting the body toward each other, and placing chairs in a way that prevents others from joining them, a couple may become an enclosed unit. If others are present, the upper body may be turned slightly to include them politely while the trunk and lower limbs clearly signal exclusion (Scheflen, 1965) (see Figure 11-2). The topic of conversation is irrelevant to the formation of a bond; it is the manner in which it occurs that is significant. It is highly animated, responsive, immediate, and submissive. Heightened arousal may be evident in an accelerating tempo of activity and in exaggerated behaviors such as emphatic gestures and loud laughter. Responsivity may become evident (to both participants and onlookers) through extended gazes, increased head nodding, postural mirroring, and synchronized movements. Submissiveness is apparent through softer, quieter, higher pitched voices, demure gaze downward (as opposed to away), and continuation of the shoulder shrug composite (Givens, 1978).

The fourth stage is *invitations and sexual arousal*. In this stage come the implicit appeals for a sexual liaison expressed through body language, verbal innuendo, and vocal orchestration. The expressions of affection that appear match those between caregiver and child:

> Barriers to physical closeness have begun to relax in this phase, and tentatively at first, touching, stroking, caressing, massaging, playing with the other's hands, all behaviors that may be observed in the earliest parental responses to the neonate, begin to be exchanged. Paralinguistically, speech continues in a soft and high-pitched manner; semantically, it may be well stocked with childcare metaphors (e.g., "baby," "sugar daddy," "little lady," "babe") and pet names (e.g., "cutie," "dollie," "sweetie"). Even varieties of baby talk may be used. The partners can be expected to give and receive certain activities related to breast-feeding. Nuzzling, licking, sucking, playful biting, kissing, and so on, which appear to have a broad geographical distribution as sexually meaningful signs, can be used to communicate the emotional intimacy that is prerequisite to sexual intercourse. (Givens, 1978, p. 352)

Other behaviors in this stage include grooming the partner (e.g., fixing the hair, adjusting or buttoning clothing), carrying and clutching activities (e.g., handholding, clinging, carrying across a threshold), and sexually provocative behaviors (e.g., rolling or protruding the pelvis, protruding the chest, cocking the head, turning wrists or palms outward to expose more skin, exposing the thigh when crossing legs, stroking the wrist or thigh, unbuttoning clothing) (see Figure 11-2). The tempo might slow somewhat, and the couple might show increased relaxation but extreme attentiveness. Among the behaviors most often "read" as invitations are increased direct eye contact and decreased downward gaze, more eyebrow flashes and flirtatious glances, more smiling, and more head tilts (Simpson et al., 1993). But the overuse of flirtatious looks and gestures can come across as phony.

The final stage is *resolution*. In true courtship, the culminating act is copulation. Here is where courtship differs from quasi-courtship and flirtation. Many of the preceding stages and behaviors may be present when there is no intention to move a relationship to the level of sexual contact. Flirting behavior is common not only in bars but also in the boardroom. The expression of mutual attraction seems to be a rewarding activity in itself because it enhances self-esteem. How, then, does one tell the difference between true courtship and harmless flirtation?

Usually there are clues in the early stages to prevent mere flirtation from advancing to the brink of the resolution stage. One way to let a prospective partner know that this is not an intimate relationship in the making is to abbreviate or omit part of the ritual. Postural involvement may be incomplete, the leg and arm positions open enough to include others. Eye contact may be broken to make contact with others, or voices may be loud enough to be audible to others. Glances and nods in the direction of others serve as reminders that others are present, thereby invoking norms for appropriate conduct. Other cues such as intimate touch or the head tilt may be omitted. Another way is to add cues that conflict with the courtship ritual. Expressing dominance behaviors is at odds with true courtship, even among men (the movie-perpetuated stereotype of the strong male to the contrary). Finally, the context itself, by its inappropriateness, may make evident that true courtship is not taking place. This last indicator may no longer apply. The rise in romantic relationships in the workplace suggests that locale may not be much of an inhibitor.

Before leaving the courtship process, it is worth noting that once a pair has bonded, many of the affectionate cues associated with courtship become infrequent. For example, established couples display far less self-grooming than developing couples (Daly, Hogg, Sacks, Smith, & Zimring, 1983). Flirting behaviors may become redundant and unnecessary to the negotiation of sexual accessibility and consequently eventually disappear. Public displays of affection likewise become minimal. This reduced level of nonverbal activity is often dismaying to married couples and victims of seduction, who find that "courtship seems to be only a *temporary* relationship that occurs between the first meetings and intercourse. After resolution, courting signals become scarce" (Givens, 1978, p. 353).

Messages of Composure and Arousal

Little has been written about the deliberate encoding of messages about degree of physical and emotional responsiveness to a relational partner. How do people signal that they are stimulated or aroused, either pleasantly or unpleasantly, in the other's presence? That they feel composed, calm, and relaxed? That they feel depressed and lethargic? We noted in Chapter 10 that two dimensions are involved. One is the intensity or general degree of activation; the other is the degree of positivity or negativity (Burgoon et al., 1989). Simplified, this produces four combinations: aroused and pleasant, unaroused and pleasant, aroused and unpleasant, unaroused and unpleasant.

Research on the unintentional leakage of anxiety and tension cues and on such affective states as attraction, anger, and embarrassment offers implications for the relational communication of aroused states. Relevant proxemic indicators of anxiety, avoidance, and withdrawal behaviors were reviewed in Chapter 3. Research on other sources of situational arousal and anxiety confirms that as negative arousal increases, so does distance (Brady & Walker, 1978; Nesbitt & Steven, 1974). The exception is that when people are feeling fearful or anxious, they may approach others to gain comfort and reassurance (Kemper, 1984). Kinesic cues encoded during such negative arousal states as embarrassment, anger, and anxiety include both gaze aversion and longer glances, more nervous or forced smiles and facial tics, fewer positive feedback cues such as nodding and facial pleasantness, more indirect head orientation, greater postural rigidity and bodily tension, more postural shifts, more gesturing, and more self-manipulations and extremity movements (although the chronically anxious may display less random movement) (Boice & Monti, 1982; Burgoon & Koper, 1984; Cappella, 1983; Cappella & Greene, 1984; Edelmann & Hampson, 1981a, 1981b; Exline et al., 1965; Jurich & Jurich, 1974; Kimble et al., 1981; Modigliani, 1971; Sainsbury, 1955). Direct gaze increases with both intensely positive and intensely negative emotions (Kimble et al., 1981) and is therefore a good signal of intensity of arousal.

Vocally, negative arousal states produce louder speech, nervous laughter (which may be used to reduce the level of anxiety), more speech disturbances, more silent pauses, faster tempo (although tempo may slow with extreme or chronic anxiety), and higher pitch (Brady & Walker, 1978; Cappella & Greene, 1984; Edelmann & Hampson, 1981a; Kimble et al., 1981; Scherer, 1982b; Siegman, 1985). Anxious communicators engage in fewer interruptions of others (Natale et al., 1979).

If physical attraction can be viewed as a positive form of arousal, increases in positive arousal carry such indicators as closer proximity (Byrne et al., 1970), shorter pauses, shorter response latencies, faster tempo (Siegman, 1978, 1979), and the other attraction cues cited earlier. High levels of social arousal may also be accompanied by natural laughter, which may serve as an arousal release mechanism (Chapman, 1975).

At the opposite end of the arousal continuum are indicators of relaxation and composure or depression and lethargy. Mehrabian (1969; Mehrabian & Ksionzky, 1972) identified a set of interrelated behaviors that he considered relaxation cues. These include asymmetrical leg and arm positions, sideways leaning, arm openness, high rates of gesturing, and less swiveling and leg and foot movement. Burgoon et al. (1984) and Patterson et al. (1981) also found through decoding studies that greater facial pleasantness, smiling, eye contact, and proximity convey messages of calmness, relaxation, and composure. Finally, Mehrabian (1970a) proposed that depressive tendencies and less responsiveness to others are revealed through lower nonverbal activity.

These combined findings suggest that the best way to signal arousal is through heightened physical activity and louder, higher pitched, rapid speech. When coupled with anxiety cues and the absence of positive feedback or affiliative behaviors, such behavior may signal noncomposure and discomfort in a relationship. Because the presence of facial pleasantness, smiling, increased gaze, and proximity may accompany either positive arousal or relaxation, immediacy behaviors by themselves do not reveal level of arousal. If arousal or nonarousal behaviors are evident only in the presence of one relational partner and not others, they can probably be taken as relational messages. Otherwise, they are best treated as indicators of the individual's personality traits or characteristic communication style.

Messages of Formality and Social or Task Orientation

These final two themes of relational communication are related in that what tends to communicate formality also communicates a task orientation and what expresses informality tends to express a social orientation.

As with arousal and composure, very little work has directly considered what non-verbal behaviors express these themes. Common sense would suggest that a more relaxed and asymmetrical posture, pleasant facial expression, smiling, and close conversational distance—in other words, cues of immediacy and relaxation—convey greater casualness and social orientation and that "proper" posture, less expressiveness, and a greater distance communicate a businesslike and formal demeanor. Altman and Vinsel (1977) did find that people stand or sit farther apart in more formal settings.

What has received a little attention is the difference the presence or absence of certain channels makes. The presence of visual information tends to make an interaction more intimate and informal. Thus speaking by telephone is more formal than meeting face to face (Stephenson, Ayling, & Rutter, 1976). This may explain why people don't like to fire someone or deliver bad news in person. The kinesic and proxemic immediacy cues present in face-to-face encounters reduce the sense of distance at a time when the sender wants to increase it. The absence of visual information also aids negotiation and competition (Argyle & Cook, 1976; Morley & Stephenson, 1969), probably because it eliminates the possibility of visual confrontation and the distraction of surveillance. This suggests that you can signal a task orientation by reducing the amount of sensory stimulation you give another and by closing the communication channel through gaze avoidance.

One final indicator of task orientation is undoubtedly monochronistic use of time. Giving only partial attention to the task at hand conveys less serious commitment to it. The receptionist who writes personal letters and paints her nails during work is sending a relational message to her employer of low task involvement.

SUMMARY

In this chapter, we have seen that one of the major functions of nonverbal communication is to define the nature of the relationship between two or more people. Although not all nonverbal behavior has relational import and not all relational meaning is conveyed nonverbally, a wide range of nonverbal signals can carry relational messages. The themes they can convey include not only the central ones of (1) dominance or equality and (2) intimacy, with its multiple facets of depth, similarity, immediacy, inclusion, trust, liking, and attraction; but also (3) composure-arousal, (4) formality, and (5) task or social orientation. The behaviors that convey these themes entail all the nonverbal codes. While many behaviors appear to be biologically based, universal signals with consistent meanings across contexts and relationships, other behaviors carry different meanings depending on whether the relationship is one of equality or inequality and of intimacy or unfamiliarity. The relational definition in turn colors the interpretation of the verbal text. Unlocking the meaning of the relational subtext is therefore crucial to making sense out of any communicative encounter.

SUGGESTED READINGS

Burgoon, J. K. (1994). Nonverbal signals. In M. L. Knapp & G. R. Miller (Eds.), *Handbook of interpersonal communication* (pp. 229–285). Newbury Park, CA: Sage.
Burgoon, J. K., & Dillman, L. (1995). Gender, immediacy, and nonverbal communication. In

P. J. Kalbfleisch & M. J. Cody (Eds.), *Gender, power, and communication in human relationships* (pp 63–81). Hillsdale, NJ: Erlbaum.

Burgoon, J. K., & Hale, J. L. (1984). The fundamental topoi of relational communication. *Communication Monographs, 51,* 193–214.

Cappella, J. N. (1983). Conversational involvement: Approaching and avoiding others. In J. M. Wiemann & R. P. Harrison (Eds.), *Nonverbal interaction* (pp. 113–148). Beverly Hills, CA: Sage.

Cate, R. M., & Lloyd, S. A. (1992). *Courtship.* Newbury Park, CA: Sage.

Ellyson, S. L., & Dovidio, J. F. (Eds.). (1985). *Power, dominance, and nonverbal behavior.* New York: Springer-Verlag.

Givens, D. B. (1983). *Love signals.* New York: Crown.

Goffman, E. (1961). *Encounters: Two studies in the sociology of interaction.* Indianapolis: Bobbs-Merrill.

Harper, R. G., Wiens, A. N., & Matarazzo, J. D. (1978). *Nonverbal communication: The state of the art.* New York: Wiley.

Hendrick, S. S., & Hendrick, C. (1992). *Liking, loving, and relating* (2d ed.). Pacific Grove, CA: Brooks/Cole.

Henley, N. M. (1977). *Body politics: Power, sex, and nonverbal communication.* Englewood Cliffs, NJ: Prentice-Hall.

King, A. (1987). *Power and communication.* Prospect Heights, IL: Waveland.

Le Poire, B. A., & Burgoon, J. K. (1994a). *Participant and observer perceptions of relational messages associated with nonverbal involvement and pleasantness.* Manuscript submitted for publication.

Mehrabian, A. (1981). *Silent messages: Implicit communication of emotions and attitudes* (2d ed.). Belmont, CA: Wadsworth.

Morris, D. (1977). *Manwatching: A field guide to human behavior.* New York: Abrams.

Scheflen, A. (1974). *How behavior means.* Garden City, NY: Anchor/Doubleday.

12

MANAGING
CONVERSATIONS

When people interact, their behaviors intertwine as do the sounds from different instruments in a band.

Frank Bernieri and Robert Rosenthal (1991)

Whenever two or more people engage in conversation, they rely on nonverbal cues to "manage" the interaction. In essence, nonverbal cues are the "traffic cops" of conversation, regulating the initiation, termination, and ongoing sequence of interaction. In this chapter, we consider the various ways in which they enable conversations to take place and to progress smoothly.

THE NATURE OF CONVERSATION MANAGEMENT

The term *conversation management* may seem incongruous. After all, *management* seems to imply a deliberate attempt to control or affect something, and having a conversation with another person may not often seem to take on that quality. But throughout this chapter you will find that conversations are indeed managed in many ways. Participants use a wide variety of nonverbal behaviors to regulate many aspects of interpersonal interactions. Indeed, Cappella (1987) claimed that coordination of interpersonal behavior is the defining feature of interpersonal communication. If the ability to use these cues to regulate conversations were somehow taken away, it would be difficult, perhaps impossible, to have conversations at all.

What kinds of conversational phenomena do we regulate nonverbally? Among other things, we manage how we enter and leave conversations, who speaks when, how we change topics, and throughout, how we coordinate our actions with others. As we will see, nonverbal regulative cues have a profound effect on the whole communication process. We should begin by noting a few basics about this communication function.

First, one reason why it seems odd to think of conversations as managed is that, as we talk, we take much of the regulative process for granted. This makes conversations seem almost automatic and effortless, and in fact, much interaction activity is habitual and routinized. We think about it only when something goes wrong, such as when someone monopolizes the floor and we make strategic choices to regain the floor.

A second basic characteristic of conversation management is that it is often rule-bound. That is, we follow a set of social rules, acquired through modeling and explicit instruction, that tell us how to organize and conduct conversations (Cushman & Whiting, 1972; Pearce, 1976). Among some of the basic, often unstated, rules in many industrialized cultures are:

Conversations are preceded by a greeting.

The conversational "channel" is opened with eye contact.

Only one person at a time may speak; interruptions are discouraged.

Possession of the floor must change from time to time.

Silence is a cue for someone to speak.

Listeners must signal that they are paying attention to the speaker.

Different cultures and subcultures may follow different rules. For example, during storytelling in some African cultures, listeners echo and overlap the speaker's utterances in a musical cadence. Among some Native American tribes, eye contact may be unnecessary to initiate talk and lengthy silences are expected rather than avoided.

Of course, rules are merely guidelines for conversational behavior. As the adage suggests, "Rules are made to be broken," and we do break these rules during conversations. We do so, however, at the risk of negative sanctions from other conversants, although people typically are reluctant to confront others directly about rule violations. Telling someone to pay attention to what you are saying signifies a conversational process already in trouble, and such statements usually are a last resort—an indication that we prefer to regulate conversations nonverbally.

The extent to which we rely on nonverbal cues becomes immediately apparent if you imagine how clumsy dialogue might be without any nonverbal assistance:

Nel: Yes, well, that's very interesting. I'm finished—over to you, Pat.

Pat: The mind boggles, doesn't it? Who knows what possibilities exist! Back to you, Nel.

Nel: I guess it's true that we use only the smallest amount of our mental potential. To you again, Pat.

Pat: Truly remarkable! To think that we could be doing more with our brains. Take it again, Nel. . . .

CB radio conversations are like that. Uncertainty over who has the floor requires inserting expressions like "over" and "come back" to substitute for nonverbal cues present in face-to-face interaction. Clearly, nonverbal regulation is very efficient.

A third basic characteristic of conversation management is that it is linked to other interpersonal functions such as relational communication. That is, how we manage interpersonal interactions with others allows us to coordinate conversations and accomplish other interpersonal objectives as well. Wiemann (1985) summarized evidence showing that, among other things, turn taking is very important in defining power and control in personal relationships, and behaviors that gain the conversational floor may facilitate changing another's attitudes.

Fourth, conversation management is capable of provoking strong emotional reactions. When people break conversational rules, it can be infuriating. Students will complain about an instructor whom they find difficult to follow because they cannot tell when the instructor changes from one topic to another. Workers complain about a boss who interrupts their work, starts a conversation, then leaves just as abruptly. Patients complain of inadequate medical care when doctors don't listen to them and cut off the consultation too soon. These examples illustrate that poor conversation management can lead to relational difficulties.

This brings up a fifth point: conversation management is a fundamental part of competence as a communicator. Exchanging the conversational floor smoothly, shifting topics without losing everyone, and initiating and terminating conversations skillfully are *interaction management skills* (Wiemann, 1977) that—like other nonverbal and verbal social skills—go a long way toward defining a person as a competent communicator. We tend to be most aware of these skills in their absence—in the person who ignores all efforts to terminate a telephone conversation or ends conversations without warning. Such a person may simply lack communication skills, but the behavior may lead to a number of other attributions. Thus effective conversation management has implications for achieving other desired communication outcomes.

BEGINNING AND ENDING CONVERSATIONS

The first task for conversants is knowing how to start and stop interactions. Some conversations begin and end smoothly and effortlessly; others are difficult, uncomfortable, and problematic. Nonverbal cues play a central role in initiating a conversation; the right cues set the stage for effective communication. Ending the conversation in a skillful way makes subsequent interactions more likely. The popularity of etiquette books, self-help manuals, and advice columns on how to start conversations "properly" is an indication of the premium many cultures place on appropriate greeting and leave-taking behavior.

Initiating Interaction

Although most of us are usually unaware of it, nonverbal cues are working long before the first hello is exchanged. These cues signal awareness of the presence of others and willingness to become involved in conversation. (Such cues may also indicate unwillingness to become involved, as illustrated in Box 12-1.) Greeting cues are highly ritualized and habitual, producing what Goffman (1971) called an "access ritual." Morris (1977, p. 77) captured the importance of this ritual:

> Whenever two friends meet after a long separation, . . . they amplify their friendly signals to super-friendly signals. They smile and touch, often embrace and kiss, and generally behave more intimately and expansively than usual. They do this because they have to

BOX 12-1

HANGING OUT YOUR TONGUE AS A "DO NOT DISTURB" SIGN

While there are a variety of cues that indicate approach-ability and a willingness to interact, some indicate just the opposite—in effect saying, "Don't bother me now!" Research at the University of Western Australia identified the protruded tongue as a particularly effective cue for this message. Researchers had participants take a test, the last page of which was indecipherable. Participants had to get another copy of the test from a proctor in order to finish. The proctors had headphones on, kept their eyes closed and tried to appear absorbed, either with tongues showing or not. Participants took significantly longer to disturb proctors with their tongues showing than when they weren't.

To make sure that this wasn't just nervous test-taking behavior, the researchers set up another similar experiment, this time using a campus stall selling cacti manned by two salesclerks. The salesclerks read books and pretended to concentrate on their reading, one with the tongue showing and one not. As before, customers approaching the stall were more likely to disturb the salesclerk whose tongue was not showing. While hanging your tongue out may not be the most pleasant or hygienic way to avoid being disturbed, it does appear to be effective.

Source: Adapted from McCarthy, 1988, p. 16.

make up for lost time—lost friendship time. While they have been apart it has been impossible for them to send the hundreds of small, minute-by-minute friendly signals to each other that their relationship requires, and they have, so to speak, built up a backlog of these signals. This backlog amounts to a gestural debt that must be repaid without delay.

Some researchers, primarily ethologists, have found similarities in human and primate greetings that suggest an evolutionary and biological base for such behavior. For example, eye behavior during greetings is similar for adults, infants, children, blind persons, and nonhuman primates (Pitcairn & Eibl-Eibesfeldt, 1976). The eyebrow flash, a quick raising of the eyebrows held for about one-sixth of a second before lowering, is part of greetings among a wide range of cultures, including Europeans, Balinese, Papuans, Samoans, South American Indians, and Bushmen (Eibl-Eibesfeldt, 1972), and may be universal (Morris, 1977).

Greetings are designed to signal heightened access and determine or reestablish the intimacy level of the relationship. They typically progress through some common stages (Greenbaum & Rosenfeld, 1980; Kendon, 1990; Kendon & Ferber, 1973; Krivonos & Knapp, 1975; Morris, 1977), which may include the following:

1 *Sighting, orientation, and initiation of approach.* After spotting the person to be greeted, one or both parties engage in a *salutation.* The distant salutation begins with smiling and waving or nodding. This is the "official ratification" that the greeting ritual has begun. Emblematic hand gestures such as the thumbs up or raised fist may also appear. One or both parties may then begin the approach.

2 *Head dip.* A movement common at this stage is to lower the head and then slowly raise it, or to toss it back and forth somewhat rapidly. This behavior indicates a shift in activities or psychological orientation. With it comes an averting of gaze so that greeters can escape the awkwardness of maintaining eye contact while traversing the distance between them.

3 *Approach.* Increased gazing and grooming behaviors, such as straightening clothing or patting hair, take place as greeters move toward each other.

4 *Final approach and close salutation.* When interactants are within 10 feet of each other, mutual gazing and smiling resume and verbal salutations are exchanged. Outstretched arms may signal an intention to embrace. Goffman (1963) observed that physical proximity in itself creates pressure to interact. In this final phase, the rituals common to a given culture or subculture for making physical contact also appear, whether in the form of a handshake, cheek kissing, or a full embrace. Handshakes, mutual lip kisses, and face kisses occur before hand-to-upper-body contact.

Common sense tells us, and research confirms, that many factors affect the form and intimacy of these greeting rituals. Our willingness to interact with others may be influenced by how attractive we find them and how similar we judge them to be. Greetings between friends and family may include more intimate touch, such as hugs and shoulder touches, than those among strangers or new acquaintances (Burgoon, 1991; Riggio, Friedman, & DiMatteo, 1981). Perhaps this is why we find overly familiar greetings by salespeople irksome—they mimic a greeting style we usually reserve for people we know well. But people who score higher on nonverbal skills also use warmer, more expressive greeting styles (Riggio et al., 1981), which suggests there may be a fine line between an effective greeting and an overly effusive one.

Gender, social status, and cultural differences in greeting rituals may also exist. Men in many western cultures are inclined to shake hands briefly with other men, while

What behaviors accompany this greeting ritual?

women and those in cross-sex dyads engage in more prolonged and intimate touching (Greenbaum & Rosenfeld, 1980; Riggio et al., 1981). As noted in other chapters, status brings a whole host of rules about how to greet someone of "higher station." Many cultures have rigid prescriptions for how greetings should be handled so as to show proper respect and deference. There was a diplomatic flap during a visit to the United States by Queen Elizabeth, when a "commoner" dared to hug her. The British press was appalled by such a faux pas, because members of the royal family are not to be touched. Indeed, strict rules surround greetings in many cultures and formal situations. Everything from the appropriate amount of gaze or physical contact to the depth of a bow or curtsy is involved. Business travelers ignorant of Japanese customs may confound their Japanese hosts by failing to exchange business cards. Without the critical occupational information supplied by these cards, the Japanese are unable to adopt the greeting pattern and form of address appropriate to the visitor's social rank.

Terminating Interaction

It would be very efficient to end conversations by just walking away. But social norms call for balancing efficiency with appropriateness (Kellermann, Reynolds, & Chen, 1991). Abruptly getting up and saying good-bye is seen as rude, incompetent, or both. If future interaction with the other person is likely and maintaining a decent relationship is important, greater effort must be mustered to conclude interactions acceptably.

Leave-taking rituals in some ways look like greeting rituals in reverse (Knapp, Hart, Friedrich, & Shulman, 1973, O'Leary & Gallois, 1985). First, like initiation rituals, they are designed to signal *supportiveness*. Typically, conversants prefer to leave conversations on a positive note, indicating points of agreement, satisfaction with the encounter, and positive anticipation of the next interaction. This conforms to a "politeness maxim" of avoiding offensive, vulgar, or rude language and projecting mutual support (McLaughlin, 1984). Second, leave-taking may entail *summarization*—summing up what has been said during the conversation—perhaps as a way to achieve psychological closure. Third, rather than signaling heightened accessibility, leave-taking cues are designed to signal impending *inaccessibility*. Usually one can tell that interactants are preparing to bring a conversation to a close before anything is said because their nonverbal cues telegraph that they are closing down their availability for conversation (see Box 12-2).

In an early and now classic experiment, Knapp et al. (1973) explored how verbal and nonverbal leave-taking behaviors accomplish these functions. Participants were paid to conduct information-gathering interviews in the shortest time possible and were told that the shorter the interview, the more money they would make. Unbeknownst to them, the interviewee was actually a confederate instructed to prolong the encounter. Thus the situation was designed to motivate the display of numerous leave-taking cues by interviewers.

Knapp et al. (1973) found that the coded verbal and nonverbal cues fit these functional categories well. The specific nonverbal and verbal termination cues, ranked from most to least frequent and the nonverbal cues within functional categories, are listed in

BOX 12-2

APPLICATIONS: HAPPY ENDINGS

Having trouble ending conversations? Part of the problem may be that polite verbal expressions like "I'll let you go" sound insincere and condescending, while more direct ones like "Are we finished here?" sound unsupportive. It is tricky to signal that you are no longer available for talk without also conveying negativity.

To deal with this problem, try relying on nonverbal cues to wind a conversation down to a close. Kotker (1983) advised:

Cease making eye contact. A person who isn't getting any doesn't feel listened to. This tactic can backfire, however. A famous head of research at Time/Life Books never met her staff members' eyes when they talked to her. In one-to-one meetings, she stared continually over the left shoulder of the speaker. Instead of ending the conversation, the evasion drove some researchers to talk more, describing their sex lives, ratting on peers—anything for attention. (p. 32)

Begin attending to other activities—shuffling papers, clearing dishes from a dinner table, taking phone calls. These polychronic activities may seem rude but are effective.

With the most recalcitrant visitors, use the great movers—proxemics and haptics. Stand, invade their personal space, shake their hand, and if necessary, with a hand on their shoulder, propel them to the door. A final handshake can be a most effective gesture: dismissive but supportive.

Eventually, these cutoff tactics should become automatic. Remember, though, that they won't work with phone conversations. For those, flat pitch and long silences may signal waning interest but may also prompt the other person to reenergize the conversation and fill the void with yet more talk. Effective verbal closings may be essential—for instance, "It's been wonderful talking with you. I hope we can do it again soon." Said with the proper vocal warmth, such closings summarize and support while closing off accessibility.

Table 12-1. All these cues, in one way or another, signal supportiveness, summarization, or inaccessibility. Additional cues include unequal weight stances, breaking eye contact, hand gesturing, and, near the ends of conversations, a general increase in nonverbal activity, with increases in mutual smiling, leaning forward, and leveraging by the departing subjects (Lockard, Allen, Schiele, & Wiemer, 1978; O'Leary & Gallois, 1985). Other cues your authors would add to the list from classroom observations include a general shuffling of feet, shifting of bodies, symmetrical stacking of books in the absolute center of the desk, and longing looks toward the door. Of course, skilled teachers know when to acknowledge these cues and when not to.

There are some differences between friends and strangers in leave-taking; for example, friends exhibit more mutual gaze, more mutual looking away, and more grooming by the departing friend, whereas strangers exhibit more head nodding (O'Leary & Gallois, 1985; Summerfield & Lake, 1977). Doubtless factors such as status inequality and the formality of the situation dictate how conversations are closed. Other researchers (e.g., Albert & Kessler, 1978; Clark & French, 1981; Schegloff & Sacks, 1973) have examined conversational closings in phone conversations but investigated only the verbal side of the sequences.

TAKING TURNS IN CONVERSATIONS

Sandwiched between the hellos and good-byes is the conversation itself, which also must be managed. The task confronting conversants is how to weave the fabric of con-

TABLE 12-1
VERBAL AND NONVERBAL LEAVE-TAKING BEHAVIORS

Rank	Nonverbal variables	Verbal variables
1	Breaking eye contact	Reinforcement
2	Left positioning	Professional inquiry
3	Forward lean	Buffing
4	Nodding	Appreciation
5	Major leg movements	Internal legitimizer
6	Smiling	Tentativeness
7	Sweeping hand movements	External legitimizer
8	Explosive foot movements	Filling
9	Leveraging	Superlatives
10	Major trunk movements	Reference to other
11	Handshake	Personal inquiry
12	Explosive hand contact	Welfare concern
13	———	Continuance
14	———	Terminating

Source: Knapp et al., 1973.

versation without becoming entangled in it. Here again, nonverbal cues help to organize and sequence interactions. Organization occurs on several different levels, ranging
from the microscopic to the macroscopic.

One of the most socially meaningful midlevel organizing units is the turn. It has been
said that a wise person is one who knows when to speak and when to keep silent. This is
also true of the skilled communicator. A key to gaining the conversational floor when
you want it and recognizing when others want a chance to speak is the skillful use of
nonverbal cues.

Definitions

A *conversation* is a series of opportunities to speak and listen. It is made up of *turns*—
times when one speaker has sole possession of the floor. Order, length, and content of
turns can all vary, depending on the occasion and participants (West & Zimmerman,
1982). However, average turn length is a mere 6 seconds (Jaffe & Feldstein, 1970); typically, who speaks first, about what, and for how long are not determined in advance
but are negotiated by the participants.

Although the concept of turns is straightforward, just where turns begin and end is not
so clear. Researchers disagree on how to tell when someone has a turn or not (Feldstein
& Welkowitz, 1978), and their definitions vary according to the extent to which they
rely on vocalic, semantic, and gestural information to mark where a turn begins and
ends (Rosenfeld, 1978). Some definitions are based on the physical change of vocalization from one interactant to another: "A speaking turn begins when one interlocutor
starts solo talking and ends when a different interlocutor starts solo talking" (Markel,
1975, p. 190; see also Jaffe & Feldstein, 1970). Others demarcate turns by relying on

some consensual notion of when a person has finished a verbal contribution or conveyed substantial information (Matarazzo & Wiens, 1972; Yngve, 1970). Sacks, Schegloff, and Jefferson (1974) defined a turn as a period of time during which one has the right or obligation to speak. According to this view, turns are constructed out of *units,* which can include words, phrases, clauses, or sentences. A speaker, on gaining the floor, can produce at least one of these types of units before losing the floor. Finally, some researchers determine when a turn occurs by relying on a reading of speakers' and listeners' intentions, on the basis of gestural and vocalic information: "A speaker is a participant who claims the speaking turn. An auditor is a participant who does not claim the speaking turn at a given moment" (Duncan & Fiske, 1977, p. 177). Knowing when an interactant claims a turn is based on "turn-requesting cues."

Thus knowing when a turn begins and ends is not as simple as it might seem. The difficulties stem in part from three additional features of conversation. One of these is *simultaneous speech.* Although the conversational rule in our culture is one speaker at a time, conversations are actually a little more sloppy than that. There are times when more than one person vocalizes, although we prefer to keep such periods brief. Simultaneous speech can occur by accident, or it can take one of two more deliberate forms. *Noninterruptive simultaneous speech* begins and ends while the participant who has the floor continues to talk. Such listener responses are also called *backchanneling* (backchanneling will be discussed shortly). *Interruptive simultaneous speech* begins when the person who has the floor is talking and ends when the interruptor takes possession of the floor (Feldstein & Welkowitz, 1978). The question then arises as to who has control during these periods of simultaneous vocalization. The answer, as you might guess, depends on which definition of *turn* you adopt. For example, according to Markel's definition (1975), the floor belongs to a conversant until another conversant starts solo talking: if person A is talking and person B interjects a response while A continues speaking, A still maintains control. Other definitions, however, assign periods of simultaneous speech to both or neither of the participants.

A second feature of conversation is the period of silence between turns, called a *switch pause* or *response latency.* Vocalization-based definitions assign these periods of silence to the person who has just stopped talking and include them in that person's turn, but others (e.g., Sacks et al., 1974) view these interspeaker silences as "transition-relevant places" and assign them to no one. Figure 12-1 provides a running time diagram of a conversation sequence, showing what a series of turns would look like using a vocalization-based definition of turn.

A third feature of conversation that is sometimes distinguished is the *listening turn.* This is intended to highlight the active rather than the passive role of the listener—a point often missed by researchers, partly because of the habit of focusing on an individual rather than the dyad or group as the unit of analysis.

All these definitions of turns have their advantages and disadvantages. Vocalization-based definitions have the advantages of operational clarity (researchers and observers have no doubt where a turn begins and ends) and high measurement reliability. However, with such definitions very short utterances—like *uh-huh*—will count as turns, even though they do not seem like turns to conversants or investigators. Definitions that use verbal and gestural criteria have the advantage of relying on multiple cues to mark turns,

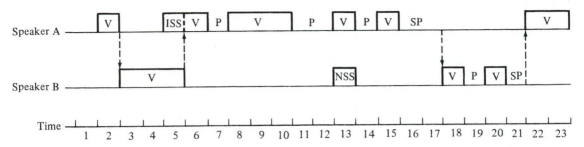

FIGURE 12-1
Diagrammatic representation of a conversational sequence. The numbered line at the bottom represents time in 300-msec units. *V* stands for vocalization, *P* for pause, and *SP* for switching pause (the silence that frequently occurs immediately prior to a change in the speaking turn). The downward arrows mark the end of Speaker A's turns; the upward arrows, the end of Speaker B's. *ISS* and *NSS* stand for interruptive and noninterruptive simultaneous speech, respectively.

thus taking the conversational context into account. But this also makes these definitions more complex and difficult to measure, because they require more inferences and judgment calls. Finally, relying on verbal units alone makes turns very difficult to identify (for proof, just look at transcripts of conversations, which can be quite confusing to follow).

Fortunately, though, definitional differences have little effect on conversants' ability to recognize and exchange turns. We now consider how this is accomplished.

The Turn-Taking Process

It is remarkable how routinely, rapidly, and seamlessly conversants exchange turns. This process is made possible by multiple nonverbal cues, some of which are used by speakers and others by listeners.

Cues Used by Speakers   Speakers' cues fall into two categories: turn-suppressing cues and turn-yielding cues.

Turn-suppressing cues are used to maintain possession of the floor. Early research (Duncan, 1972) identified five turn-suppressing cues: (1) audible inhalation of breath by the speaker; (2) continuation of a gesture; (3) facing away, or diverting gaze away from the listener; (4) sustained intonation, which lets the listener know that more vocalization is yet to come; and (5) fillers (also known as *vocalized pauses*) like *hhmmm* and *uhhh* that fill pauses so that listeners will not use silence as an opportunity to gain the floor. Other possible turn-suppressing cues include increased loudness, light touch (Knapp, 1978), and use of the "stop" hand gesture.

When speakers change their minds, turn-suppressing cues—even a single cue—will be highly effective in discouraging listeners from trying to take the lead in the conversation. This is true regardless of how many turn-yielding cues appear simultaneously.

Turn-yielding cues are used to relinquish the floor. Many turn-yielding cues are simply the opposite of turn-suppressing cues. Termination of gesturing, facing the listener, making eye contact, falling intonation (such as at the end of a declarative statement) or rising intonation (such as at the end of a question), and silences are major turn-yielding cues. Decreased loudness and slowed tempo may also be used to relinquish a turn. In conversations among three or more people, eye contact, gesturing, and head nodding in the direction of a given listener all serve to increase the probability that this person will be the next speaker.

Research has shown that floor exchanges are smoothest when speakers display many turn-yielding cues. The more turn-yielding cues the speaker displays, the more likely listeners are to take the floor (Duncan, 1972).

Cues Used by Listeners   Listeners use three categories of cues: turn-requesting cues, backchannel cues, and turn-denying cues.

Turn-requesting cues are behaviors the listener uses to gain control of the conversation. It is clear that listeners do not sit idly by, waiting for a chance to speak. Rather, they indicate their intention to speak through this type of cue. Wiemann (1973; Wiemann & Knapp, 1975) found that listeners use gaze directed at the speaker, head nods, forward leans, the raised index finger, and an inhalation of breath coupled with a straightened back to signal their intention to speak. Duncan (1974) found that turn-requesting cues occurred primarily at the end of phonemic clause units.

Backchannel cues are behaviors the listener uses to communicate a variety of messages to the speaker without gaining control of the conversational floor (Dittmann, 1972a; Rosenfeld, 1978; Yngve, 1970). These cues can communicate agreement and confirmation or disagreement and disconfirmation, involvement and interest or bore-

This woman's behavior may be a turn-denying cue or simply a failure to give adequate backchanneling. How might her companion interpret and respond to her lack of attentiveness? What affect might it have on smooth turn-switching?

dom and disinterest. Some backchannel cues can also be used to pace the speaker, as when a listener continuously nods at a fast pace to hurry the speaker up. Specific backchannel cues include smiling, frowning, head nodding and shaking, raised eyebrows, short vocalizations *(uh-huh, mm-hmm),* and verbal statements *(yep, right, I see, oh, good).* According to most researchers, these short verbal statements do not constitute turns, especially if they are simultaneous with the speaker's vocalization. Instead, they allow a listener to communicate a variety of meanings without having to take over the conversation. Duncan (1974) found that backchannel cues are distributed fairly evenly throughout a listening turn.

Backchannel responses underscore the dynamic and simultaneous nature of face-to-face interaction. Further, speakers *expect* listeners to display some of these cues, particularly cues indicating involvement. Speakers are disconcerted when listeners fail to signal attentiveness by smiling, leaning toward the speaker, or gazing. In fact, listeners may suppress backchannel cues as a means of signaling that they don't follow what a speaker is saying (Chen, cited in Krauss, Fussell, & Chen, in press). In Chapter 8, we noted ethnic differences in the responses white and black listeners give that can lead to misinterpretations and awkward interchanges. Clearly, backchannel cues play a potent role in conversation.

Turn-denying cues provide a way for a listener to refuse a turn nonverbally. These have been little studied, although Knapp (1978, p. 217) suggested that relaxed posture, silence, and staring away from the speaker are cues that fall into this category.

See Box 12-3 for some practical guidelines regarding turn-request, backchannel, and turn-denying cues.

Ending Turns   How turns are managed varies widely. Jaffe and Feldstein (1970) identified four possible turn endings:

BOX 12-3

APPLICATIONS: GETTING YOUR TURN WHEN YOU WANT IT

Some cues, such as head nods, may be either backchannel cues or turn requests. This can result in some confusion and awkward turn switching if speakers do not "read" these cues as listeners intend. Speakers who monopolize conversations may conveniently fail to recognize turn-request cues, treating them instead as backchannel support. This may occur particularly with women, who use nods more frequently than men simply for social facilitation.

How can speakers and listeners distinguish turn-request cues from backchannel or turn-denial cues? Two points are helpful. First, other cues that occur along with them may clarify their role: for instance, a nod accompanied by other turn-requesting cues will be seen as an intention to speak. Second, the point at which these cues occur may clarify their function. Backchannel cues can appear in a number of places during a turn, though typically not at the beginning. Turn-requesting and turn-denying cues are more likely to occur at turn junctures where the conversational floor could potentially be exchanged.

Good advice for people who have difficulty "getting a word in edgewise" is to use multiple cues when requesting a turn and to minimize cues that also signal supportiveness.

1 *Closed turn ending*—silence between speaking turns (also known as a *switch pause*) is 0.1 second or less.

2 *Open turn ending*—switch pause between turns is 0.1 second to 2.9 seconds.

3 *Overlong turn ending*—switch pause is 3 seconds or longer.

4 *Interruption*—turn ending precipitated by simultaneous speech by the listener, who succeeds in wresting the floor from the speaker.

About half of all turn exchanges are "smooth exchanges" (Kendon, 1967). Typically, we regard an exchange as *smooth* if it results from a closed or open turn ending. If you think about this, it is striking that most turn switches occur in less than 3 seconds and that we regard a delay of 3 seconds or more as too long. Norms for turn exchanges do differ across people and circumstances and are often negotiated by participants during a conversation (Duncan, 1975). That is, communicators develop a norm for how much silence or what degree of interruption is tolerable between adjacent turns. For instance, in highly informal social gatherings or involving task discussions, a fair amount of interrupting may occur, contrary to the "one at a time" rule.

Nevertheless, we tend to regard interruptions as nonnormative behavior and frequently read special significance into them. Early research suggested that men interrupt women far more than vice versa and that interruptions are an expression of social dominance (Henley & Freeman, 1975; Kennedy & Camden, 1981; Zimmerman & West, 1975). Later writers have begun to back away from this conclusion because some interruptions and overlapping speech may signal rapport or understanding of someone else's thoughts rather than dominance—as when people complete each other's sentences (see Drummond, 1989). Also, some interruptions may be "invited" by the speaker's behavior (Kennedy & Camden, 1983). For example, speakers are more likely to be interrupted if they lean away from a group—something women tend to do more often than men. Women's positive facial expressions may invite interruptions by men, while men's positive facial expressions tend to inhibit interruptions by women.

Models of the Turn-Exchange Process   Identifying which cues accomplish turn exchanges doesn't tell us how or why they work. Wiemann and his associates (Wiemann, 1985; Wilson, Wiemann, & Zimmerman, 1984) identified three explanations, or models, of how coordinated turn taking is accomplished.

The first model, called the *signaling* approach, fits Duncan's work. In this model, turn-taking cues are discrete, independent signals that invoke rules or conventions for appropriate responses. These cues have a demand characteristic such that participants are bound by the rules and failure to respond appropriately is supposedly penalized. Interruptions, for example, constitute a rule violation and should incur some sanction or penalty. In reality, however, it is debatable whether those who break conversational rules regularly suffer negative consequences. In some relationships, one partner continually interrupts the other with impunity. The signaling approach offers no explanation for this inconsistency.

A second model, identified by Sacks et al. (1974), is called the *sequential production* approach. This model assumes that turn taking must be managed sequentially, moment to moment. The sequential production model is less restrictive in terms of what participants are required to do; it sees conversation as an open, flexible process. Among the features of this approach are the following:

1 Order, length, and content of turns and conversations are not fixed in advanced and are free to vary.
2 Number of participants may vary, as may the distribution of turns among them.
3 Talk can be continuous or discontinuous.
4 Although one person typically talks at a time, brief simultaneous talk is common.
5 Transitions from one turn to the next occur, for the most part, with little or no gap or overlap.
6 Explicit allocation techniques such as asking a question or making a request may be used.

While many of these features are common to all approaches to turn taking, the sequential production model treats silences and simultaneous speech as expected parts of conversation rather than as breakdowns or violations of rules.

Whereas the signaling model emphasizes the speaker's role in giving the floor to a listener, the sequential production model places much of the responsibility on the listener. At the end of turns, "transition-relevant places" occur, providing opportunities for listeners in multiperson conversations to acquire the floor. There are four options:

1 The current speaker may, but need not, select another person as the next speaker.
2 Should the current speaker not select the next speaker, then another person may select himself or herself as the next speaker. The first person to speak at such a point acquires the turn.
3 If no one takes the floor, then the current speaker may, but need not, continue.
4 If the current speaker does not continue, the option to speak cycles back to the control of item 2.

As these options suggest, listeners potentially can wrest the floor from the speaker at the end of every unit type by treating it as a transition-relevant place. Clearly, though, this does not occur. If it did, conversations would be far more disruptive and turns would be much shorter.

Wilson et al. (1984) developed a third model of turn taking, the *resource* approach. This approach incorporates elements of the other two models and thus has some of their advantages. Specifically, it uses a modified concept of signaling to clarify where transition-relevant places actually occur. At the same time, the floor-exchange options of the sequential production model are retained in order to make clear what can occur at those junctures. As a result, responsibility for turn taking is shared by all participants (both speaker and listeners), and all participants know when the floor can or should be exchanged. An important contribution of the resource model is that turn-taking cues are viewed as *resources* within interactants' behavioral repertoires, to be used when needed. Instead of being seen as signals, which must be responded to in a given way, turn-taking cues become a flexible means toward an end—smooth, efficient turn taking. The model assumes that no turn-taking behavior always means precisely the same thing, but that the meaning and function of cues can vary systematically across different contexts and situations.

There is also a fourth model, advanced by Walker and Trimboli (1984). In this approach, turn taking is a two-stage process whereby intonation and speaking tell the listener when a turn is about to conclude (stage 1), and then the last syllable is accompanied by a set of specific turn-yielding cues (stage 2). Behaviors in stage 1 allow the listener to anticipate when a turn will conclude and prepare to take over almost immediately when the last syllable and the accompanying turn-yielding cues appear in stage 2. This approach (like the signaling model) places the responsibility for smooth turn exchanges on the listener.

Further research should indicate which explanation is most realistic. Meanwhile, these alternative models reveal that what appears to be an effortless and rather easy feat—taking turns in conversations—is actually rather complex. The number of factors that must be taken into account should help us appreciate the human capacity to process information so rapidly and coordinate conversations so deftly.

MANAGING TOPICS OF CONVERSATION

On a broader level, conversations consist of one or more topics. Although much of our maneuvering through topics is the result of following routinized verbal patterns (see Kellermann & Lim, 1990), nonverbal cues may also help to segment and organize topics. They do this by marking the boundaries between episodes and positions.

Episodes are periods within conversations when the discussion focuses on a particular topic (Scheflen, 1974). *Positions* are segments of interaction within an episode in which a person maintains a consistent disposition toward the topic and toward other conversants (Scheflen, 1974). Thus positions reflect interactants' expressed attitudes toward the topic and other interactants. As interest in a given topic wanes, or as attitudes shift, a person's position changes.

Four classes of nonverbal cues serve as *boundary markers. Proxemic shifts*—changes in leaning forward or backward and toward or away from other communicators—have been found to be reliable indicators of changes in episodes and positions (Erickson, 1975). *Extrainteractional activities* include behaviors that are not directly part of the stream of communication, such as lighting a cigarette, reaching for a drink, rearranging personal articles (a jacket, purse, etc.), adjusting a chair cushion, and so on (Pittenger, Hockett, & Danehy, 1960). These cues are more likely to occur at episode and position boundaries—perhaps because if they appeared elsewhere, they might be perceived as inappropriate and indicative of low involvement. *Silences* also clearly function to mark episode and position boundaries, often closing topics participants are no longer interested in pursuing (Schegloff & Sacks, 1973) and allowing participants to relax physically and mentally before pursuing the next segment of interaction. Finally, other *paralinguistic cues,* such as sighs, gasps, and throat clearing, mark episode and position boundaries (Pittenger et al., 1960). Such cues may facilitate changes in speaking style by releasing air from the lungs and relaxing the vocal cords, thereby also allowing loudness, pitch, and tempo to change. Interactants can then "start fresh" vocally with the next topic.

Some research (e.g., Planalp & Tracy, 1980) has suggested that interactants need only verbal information to decide where topic switches are appropriate. This may be true with regard to reading transcripts, but in actual conversation it is likely that non-verbal boundary markers reinforce verbal topic-change signals and also bolster perceptions of communicators' competence in managing conversation. They may also alert participants that the background information required to comprehend an upcoming topic is about to change (Woodall, 1985).

INTERPERSONAL ADAPTATION IN CONVERSATIONS

Conversation is clearly a joint venture requiring intricate coordination by the participants. Nowhere is this more evident than in the larger behavioral patterns through which interactants adapt their behavior to one another.

Have you ever noticed that when two people are talking, their bodies move in similar rhythms, their eyes make and break contact at regular intervals, and their postures and gestures often fall into identical patterns? This conversational "dance" has intrigued scholars for decades, but our knowledge has advanced slowly because researchers have traditionally focused on the individual rather than on interpersonal systems and relationships (Rogers & Millar, 1976). More recent research has made important advances by explicitly examining what interactants do together as a unit and by considering sequential patterns. Additionally, much of the newer research focuses on multiple non-verbal and verbal cues, giving a more comprehensive view of the behavioral stream.

Interactional Adaptation Patterns

Several interactional adaptation patterns have been observed. When two interactants display a similar behavior (or set of behaviors) such as pause lengths, gesturing rates, or lin-

An example of
mirroring.

guistic elaboration, they are said to *match* one another. When matching takes the form of identical visual behavior, such as adopting the same posture, it is called *mirroring* (or sometimes *postural congruence*). Mirroring usually refers to static or slow signals, whereas dynamic signals are usually described as matching. If one person's behavior becomes increasingly like the other's, the pattern is described as *convergence*. If a behavioral change appears to be contingent on, directed toward, or in exchange for the other person's behavior, it is called *reciprocity.* For example, if person A leans forward to show interest and then person B does the same, reciprocity has occurred. One special form of contingent behavior is *motor mimicry,* in which one person displays an empathic response to someone else's actual or imagined circumstance. When a friend recounts accidentally running into a low-hanging tree branch and we wince—that's motor mimicry.

If behavioral similarity is based on interactants' temporal and rhythmic coordination of dynamic behaviors, *interactional synchrony* exists. (In another type of synchrony, *self-synchrony,* individuals coordinate their own kinesic behavior to their own verbal-vocal stream.) Interactional synchrony may occur simultaneously, in which case the listener's behavior synchronizes with the speaker's behavior; or it may occur concatenously, so that the coordination is sequential, from speaker to speaker (for instance, the first person's use of rhythmic emphasizing gestures is echoed by the next speaker's use of the same gestures).

There are opposites of these patterns. In *complementarity,* behaviors are dissimilar or opposite one another, such as one person gazing and the other avoiding gaze. In *divergence,* behaviors become increasingly dissimilar. In *compensation,* one person responds to another's behavior with a behavioral change in the opposite direction. In *dissynchrony,* behaviors fail to mesh and are out of sync.

Of course, interactants may simply fail to adapt to one another, in which case the pattern is described as *nonaccommodation* or *nonadaptation.* (See Bavelas et al., 1988; Bernieri & Rosenthal, 1991; Burgoon, Dillman, & Stern, 1993; Burgoon, Stern, & Dillman, 1995; Cappella, 1981, 1985, 1994; Condon & Sander, 1974; Giles et al., 1991; Street & Giles, 1982, for a more detailed discussion of these patterns.)

Evidence for Interactional Adaptation

Research on these patterns has produced impressive evidence that interactants do influence and adjust to each other's interactional styles. This adaptation occurs at both the microscopic and the macroscopic level and appears to include biologically based, automatic forms of coordination as well as more deliberate, socially learned forms (Burgoon, Stern, & Dillman, 1995; Cappella, 1985, 1991).

At the microscopic level, there is evidence that one person can converge toward or diverge from another person's speech within milliseconds (Street, 1990), and that we may begin at birth (or perhaps even in utero) to synchronize our movements and communication with those of others. Condon and his associates (Condon, 1976; Condon & Ogston, 1966, 1967; Condon & Sander, 1974) recorded interactions with high-speed film, then coded onset, offset, and changes in body movements frame by frame. The behavioral changes were matched with simultaneous verbal changes recorded in a phonetic transcript. Because the film speed ranged from 30 to 48 frames per second, behavior was analyzed down to 1/48 second. This classic work revealed not only that adults entrain their communication with one another but also that neonates synchronize their movements to the mother's voice.

Other research has also shown regularities in how infants and children interact with caretakers and other adults. They reciprocate vocalization durations and pitch, use gaze as a way to escape social interaction (compensatory pattern) or increase it (reciprocal pattern), and synchronize overall involvement (Als, Tronick, & Brazelton, 1979; Bateson, 1975; Bernieri, Reznick, & Rosenthal, 1988; Brazelton, Tronick, Adamson, Als, & Wise, 1975; Gewirtz & Boyd, 1976, 1977; Stern, 1971; Street, 1983; Street & Cappella, 1989; Webster, Steinhardt, & Senter, 1972). Adults and infants go through cycles of high and low involvement over time. For example, when adults are prompted to act unresponsively, infants increase their actions to obtain a response. As Cappella (1985, 1991) noted, the evidence for infant-adult patterns is remarkable and raises interesting questions about the interplay of innate, cognitive, and learning factors. Patterns of interaction in adulthood, as well as the social competencies based on them, appear to be a function of both nature and nurture.

Although some writers have engaged in a lively debate about whether synchrony actually exists (Gatewood & Rosenwein, 1981; McDowall, 1978a, 1978b), the accumulating research findings support extensive meshing and synchronization of activity (Cappella & Planalp, 1981; Hatfield, Cacioppo, & Rapson, 1991; Jaffe & Feldstein, 1970). In fact, the rhythmicity between two people often exceeds that between a speaker's own vocal rate and own heart rate, which suggests a strong predisposition for people to adapt to each other's communication rhythms (Warner, Malloy, Schneider, Knoth, & Wilder, 1987).

Other research at increasingly macroscopic levels shows a strong preponderance of convergence, matching, and reciprocity. This is especially true for noncontent vocal behaviors such as pauses, switch pauses, response latencies, interruptions, tempo, loudness, dialect, and turn duration; for nonverbal intimacy and immediacy behaviors; and for linguistic features such as standardness of speech (Burgoon, Stern, & Dillman, 1995; Cappella, 1981, 1983, 1984, 1985, 1994; Feldstein & Welkowitz, 1978; Giles et al., 1991; Giles & Powesland, 1975; Patterson, 1973, 1976, 1983). Matching and reciprocity do not occur only on positively valenced behaviors; they are also common for negative behaviors. Considerable research has confirmed that hostility and negative affect result in more of the same (Burggraf & Sillars, 1987; Gottman, 1979; Pike & Sillars, 1985).

At the same time, abundant research demonstrates that compensation and complementarity often occur. It is common for increased proximity to provoke a compensatory decrease in gaze or in directness of body orientation. Apart from the natural complementarity of behaviors related to speaker and listener roles, interactants tend to compensate on the combined behaviors of gaze, vocalization, and illustrator gestures. Compensation may also occur in negatively toned situations or situations of dissimilarity and inequality. For example, when you are interacting in a positive situation with friends, you will probably match their eye contact patterns. However, when you are having a disagreement with your employer, you will probably look less if your boss is looking more.

Additionally, interactants may simultaneously reciprocate some behaviors and compensate others. Hale and Burgoon (1984) found that interactants responded to a partner's reduction in nonverbal immediacy with reciprocal decreases in some nonverbal immediacy behaviors but a compensatory increase in verbal immediacy. Burgoon, Le Poire, and Rosenthal (1995) found that when a confederate greatly reduced involvement and pleasantness, this had a reciprocal, depressive effect on the partner's involvement and pleasantness; but partners compensated for the confederate's overly relaxed, blasé demeanor by being more erect and tense. And Iizuka, Mishima, and Matsumoto (1989) found that participants who interacted with a negative (disagreeing) partner compensated increased gaze but reciprocated increased smiling.

Patterns may also depend on the gender composition of the dyad. Women are likely to converge toward male gaze and talk patterns when interacting with men; men are less flexible and more likely to maintain their own style (Mulac, Studley, Wiemann, & Bradac, 1987).

Theories of Interactional Adaptation

The mix of behavioral patterns has led to a variety of theories to explain and predict them. Knowing when each pattern is likely to occur has important implications. Consider: If you are attracted to someone, it is important to know when your intimate overtures may be reciprocated and when they may be rebuffed. Doctors and therapists need to know if adopting an interview style that is too verbal or too dominant will lead patients to become more submissive and reticent—compensatory patterns that may prevent patients from disclosing relevant information. Employment interviewers need to know if behavior they observe in a job applicant indicates an applicant's own style or is simply a reflection of the interviewer's style (i.e., the natural result of reciprocation).

Much of the earliest theorizing focused on biological factors. Research on synchrony and motor mimicry supported the conclusion that human behavior is innately rhythmic and cyclical and that humans are inherently predisposed to synchronize their rhythms and behaviors to one another (Chapple, 1970). The progenitor of many contemporary theories was *affiliative conflict theory,* also called *equilibrium theory* (Argyle & Dean, 1965; Argyle & Cook, 1970). Argyle and Dean proposed that humans have competing drives to approach others and to avoid others, and that we seek to bring these drives into balance. The point at which two interactants are comfortable with their level of immediacy defines an equilibrium point; deviations from that point cause arousal, discomfort, and a resultant compensatory effort to bring the interaction back to its previous level. Thus, if person A moves close to whisper something to person B, then B should compensate by breaking eye contact and adopting an indirect body orientation. (Compensation can also occur within an individual, as when someone moves farther away while talking and simultaneously increases eye contact to offset the physical distance.) Although this theory generated a tremendous amount of research and received some support, a significant shortcoming was its inability to account for patterns of reciprocity. After all, we know that we don't invariably back away whenever someone increases intimacy with us. If we did always back off, no relationship or conversation would ever progress beyond the first polite, distant stage. Sociological evidence indicates that we follow a *norm of reciprocity,* treating others as they treat us and returning good for good (Gouldner, 1960). There is also substantial evidence that verbal self-disclosures produce self-disclosures from a partner (Derlega, Metts, Petronio, & Margulis, 1993). Such findings raised doubts that interactions principally followed a compensatory or complementary pattern.

As an alternative, Patterson (1976) proposed an *arousal-labeling model.* In this model, deviations from a comfortable interaction level still create discomfort and arousal. Arousal is nonspecific and needs to be identified as pleasant or unpleasant; interactants thus examine the situation for cues to label the arousal as "positive" or "negative." The model predicts that positive arousal will produce reciprocity and negative arousal will produce compensation. On the surface, this model is simple and intuitively appealing. A person who labels a situation "pleasant" should reciprocate the partner's behavior; a person who labels it "unpleasant" should compensate. But a moment's reflection raises some questions about this theory. If an unattractive person moves to a far distance, what then? Will that actually be arousing? If so, such detachment normally would be labeled negatively. But that would lead to a prediction of a compensatory increase in proximity. Intuitively, most of us probably would not expect to respond that way. Other problems with the model led Patterson himself to repudiate it and offer a *sequential functional model* and more recently, a *parallel process model* (Patterson, 1983, 1995). These models identify numerous factors (e.g., biology, culture, gender, personality, setting) that influence affective reactions to a partner's involvement changes, assessments of those changes, and cognitive resources available to engage in parallel person perception and behavioral adjustments. These models offer a more realistic picture of the numerous factors affecting interaction adaptation, but they do not specify exactly when compensatory as opposed to reciprocal responses will occur.

Four other theories that have attempted to refine predictions are *discrepancy-arousal theory* (Cappella & Greene, 1982, 1984), *expectancy violations theory* (Burgoon, 1978, 1993; Hale & Burgoon, 1984), *cognitive valence theory* (Andersen, 1985, 1989), and *communication accommodation theory* (Gallois et al., 1995; Giles et al., 1991).

Discrepancy-arousal theory and expectancy violations theory take the same starting point: that interactants have expectations about the communicative styles of others and that behaviors that deviate from or violate these expectations activate behavioral change. According to discrepancy-arousal theory, discrepancies produce changes in arousal, moderate changes produce positive affect, and large changes produce negative affect. Positive affect is variously described as producing reciprocity or approach and negative affect as producing compensation or avoidance. This theory thus relies on the size of changes in arousal and the concomitant affective reactions to predict interaction patterns. It is unclear whether extreme nonimmediacy would generate avoidance (a reciprocal response) or approach (a compensatory response).

According to expectancy violations theory, the valence (evaluation) of the communicator must be factored in as well. For example, increased intimacy by an attractive person is hypothesized to be a positive violation that elicits reciprocated intimacy; the same approach from a repulsive person is hypothesized to be a negative violation that produces a compensatory reduction in intimacy. Some predictions are straightforward but others are less clear, especially when the valence of the communicator is at odds with the valence of the behavior. Suppose, for instance, that someone you like a great deal unexpectedly becomes increasingly detached during a conversation. Will you do the same, or will you try to pull him or her back to a high level of involvement by becoming more involved yourself (a compensatory move)? If someone from an out-group adopts a dialect and tempo similar to your own speech, will this be a positive violation that leads you to match him or her, or will it be a negative violation that leads you to exaggerate the vocalic differences between you?

Cognitive valence theory is less ambitious in scope, being limited to cases where one person increases intimacy behaviors. The theory begins like the arousal-labeling model, arguing that changes in one person's intimacy behaviors prompt arousal changes in the other that must be valenced. The theory identifies six classes of factors that are said to valence behavioral changes: culture, individual predispositions, interpersonal evaluations, relational expectations, situational features, and transitory states. If any one of them is negative, the valence is predicted to be negative. Only when a change in arousal is moderate will the six valencers affect outcomes: positive valence will produce reciprocity and negative valence, compensation. Like discrepancy-arousal theory, cognitive valence theory predicts that large changes in arousal are always aversive and always produce compensation.

Communication accommodation theory is also more limited in scope in that it largely centers on vocalic and linguistic features such as dialect, response latencies, and language style. Adaptation, or accommodation, to someone else is considered a deliberate act that is influenced by social factors such as belonging to an ingroup or an outgroup. Convergence is designed to promote similarity and rapport, usually within an ingroup, whereas divergence is designed to create distance, usually from members of outgroups. This theory has generated a tremendous amount of research and support. However, it does not encompass a wide range of nonverbal cues, and it may not account adequately for highly automatic forms of adaptation.

On the basis of a review of theories and research, Burgoon, Stern, and Dillman (1995) arrived at the following conclusions:

1 *At a biological level, there appears to be an innate pressure to adapt and synchronize interaction patterns but also to make compensatory adjustments when physical safety and comfort are involved.* Adaptations with biological etiologies should be highly automated, unconscious, and rapid. Drive states are dynamic and cyclical rather than constant.

2 *At the social level, the pressure is also toward reciprocity and matching.* Exceptions include role or status relationships (e.g., soldier and superior officer) and differences in competence (e.g., parent and infant) that dictate complementary patterns. Biological and social forces thus jointly predispose people to coordinate interactions through the use of similar behaviors.

3 *At the communication level, both reciprocity and compensation may occur.* Salespeople, for example, may attempt to win over a buyer with a friendly, reciprocal style or an obsequious, ingratiating one that places them in a submissive role relative to the buyer's dominant role. These voluntary forms of adaptation seek to achieve goals such as conveying a desirable image, facilitating information processing, creating a personal relationship, and persuading someone to comply with a request.

4 *Strategic, conscious adaptation may be inhibited or altered by (1) individual consistency in behavioral style, (2) internal causes of adjustments, (3) poor self-monitoring or poor monitoring of a partner, (4) inability to adjust performance, and (5) cultural differences in communication practices and expectations.* People tend to be consistent in their interaction styles. They may also lack the necessary skills to adjust to their partners, or structural features of the situation may prevent adaptation. Thus the degree of adaptation observed may be subtle and should include some stability in people's individual interaction styles.

5 *Biological, psychological, social, and communicative forces set up boundaries within which most interaction patterns will operate, producing mostly matching, synchrony, and reciprocity patterns.* Behavioral changes outside these boundaries will often be met with nonaccommodation, as a means of retarding movement away from the normative range, or with compensation to return interaction to its previous style.

6 *The ability to make predictions about when reciprocity or compensation will occur will be more successful when made at the molar than the molecular level.* This means looking at the functions of sets of cues rather than individual behaviors. It is easier to anticipate how interactants will respond to changes in overall levels of involvement, intimacy, dominance, or formality than to a specific proxemic, haptic, or vocalic cue.

These principles are the foundation for a newly emerging theory, *interaction adaptation theory*. We sketch a few of its key principles here. Burgoon, Stern, and Dillman (1995) have proposed that people bring to interactions a set of needs, expectations, and personal preferences (labeled *required, expected,* and *desired*). For instance, people with strong affiliation needs seek social contact, may expect others to maintain a polite level of involvement and pleasantness during conversation, and may prefer a high degree of nonverbal immediacy when interacting with friends. Their combined required, expected, and desired levels of interaction yield what is called an *interaction position* (IP). The IP refers to the behavior they anticipate the dyad (or group) will adopt. If we are predicting conversational distance, the IP for affiliative people should be moderately close proximity. By contrast, introverts need and prefer more distance from others but also may recognize that the social norm for conversation is moderate distance. Their IP for conversational distance should be in the moderate to slightly far range.

The IP is compared with the partner's *actual behavior* (A) to determine which is more positively valenced. Normally, the IP has a positive valence because it represents what is needed, desired, and expected. If A is different from IP, it is either going to be more or less positive. Suppose, for example, that the partner chooses to interact at a very close distance. For extroverts and those with high affiliation needs, this is positive; for introverts, it is negative.

On the basis of relative valences of the A and IP, interaction adaptation theory makes two simple predictions. If A is more positively valenced than the IP, people should converge toward the partner's desirable behavior (which might even be seen as a positive violation); the result is reciprocity. If, instead, A is more negatively valenced than IP, people should diverge from the partner's behavior or maintain their existing behavior. If they diverge, the result is compensation. If they maintain their existing behavior, their nonadaptation still functions like compensation to retard changes in the dyad's level of a given behavior. Examples of these predictions are presented in Figure 12-2.

Bob has spent the weekend by himself, taking a solitary hiking trip in the mountains. Come Monday morning, what interaction style might we predict between Bob and a coworker?

Bob's *Interaction Position* (IP) will be based on the following:

Required behavior: Bob is feeling lonely and in need of sensory stimulation after his weekend of isolation. Bob should seek out others (be highly involved) to meet his biological needs for affiliation and sensory stimulation.

Expected behavior: Moderate affiliation with coworkers is generally expected as typical and appropriate in a work environment. Greater distance is expected from disliked than liked coworkers.

Desired behavior: Bob believes in separation of work and play. He usually prefers a formal, nonaffiliative interaction style during work hours but likes to engage in small talk with friends over lunch. He is also a shy and private person, which leads him to be reticent with liked coworkers and to avoid disliked coworkers.

Combining these elements, Bob's *IP* should be for moderately high involvement with a coworker, especially at lunch, and moderately low involvement with a disliked coworker (because the required and expected elements take precedence over the desired elements).

This leads to the following patterns, depicted below:

Example 1:   A liked coworker's actual behavior, A, reflects high involvement. This makes A more positively valenced than IP. The model predicts Bob will converge toward and reciprocate that involvement.

converge/match/reciprocate (approach)
------------>

Lower Inv _____Higher Inv
(-)   IP   A   (+)

Example 2:   A liked coworker's behavior instead is somewhat low involvement. This makes the IP more positively valenced than A. The theory predicts Bob will diverge from the coworker's behavior or maintain his own level of involvement in hopes of it eliciting a similar response from the coworker.

compensate or maintain
------------>

Lower Inv _____Higher Inv
(-)   A   IP   (+)

Example 3:   A disliked coworker's A is detached and uninvolved, making A more positively valenced than IP. Bob should again reciprocate but to a lesser degree because of his need for affiliation and sensory stimulation.

match/reciprocate (avoid)
------------>

Higher Inv _____Lower Inv
(-)   IP   A   (+)

Example 4:   A disliked coworker's A is highly involved, making A more negatively valenced than Bob's IP. Bob should compensate for that with a relatively uninvolved interacton style.

compensate or maintain (avoid)
------------>

Higher Inv _____Lower Inv
(-)   A   IP   (+)

FIGURE 12-2
Sample predictions from interaction adaption theory, adapted from Burgoon, Stern, and Dillman (1995)

This cursory introduction to interaction adaptation theory shows how many different elements can be brought together to predict one interactant's response to another's actual or anticipated communicative behavior. The theory can also account for what happens when two people's patterns are at odds. For example, if we predict that one person will approach but the other will avoid the partner, we should expect a compensatory pattern between the two of them. This theory is still in the early development stages and has not yet been tested extensively, but it represents an attempt to integrate other theories while providing a simpler model of interpersonal adaptation. Other recent research pitting various theories against each other (e.g., Andersen, Guerrero, Buller, & Jorgensen, 1995; Burgoon, Ebesu, Koch, White, & Kikuchi, in press; Guerrero & Burgoon, 1994; Le Poire & Burgoon, 1994b) should also shed light on the viability of these theories.

Effects of Interactional Adaptation

Identifying how and when interactants adapt to one another is important in itself. But equally important is how adaptation or nonadaptation affects other interaction outcomes such as attraction, satisfaction, commitment, and persuasion. Coordination of interaction heightens perceptions of rapport (Bernieri & Rosenthal, 1991). Research on romantic and married couples' interactions has shown that reciprocity of nonverbal expressions of negative emotions can lead to severe discord and negative consequences for the relationship. Distressed couples tend to reciprocate more negative affect than nondistressed couples, whereas happy couples are quicker to reciprocate positive expressions (Biglan et al., 1985; Gottman, 1979; Manusov, 1995; Pike & Sillars, 1985). Whether couples' discord is the chicken or the egg (i.e., the cause or the result of limited positive reciprocity) is unclear but may be part of a cycle in which each partner influences the other (Huston & Vangelisti, 1991). For the moment, at least we know a little about what cues are part of expressing positive feelings. In addition to those noted in Chapter 10 (on emotional expression) and Chapter 11 (on relational communication), some research specifically on conflict and reciprocity has discovered that gaze, involvement behaviors generally, submissiveness, and relaxation cues tend to accompany positive expressions of affect (Newton & Burgoon, 1990; Noller, 1984).

Adaptation patterns also affect evaluations of communicators. Convergence on accent, response latencies, and tempo, as well as language, generally earns communicators more favorable evaluations than divergence on perceived warmth, effectiveness, intelligibility, attractiveness, involvement, and competence, as long as this convergence falls within a range of acceptable behavior (Dabbs, 1969; Feldman, 1968; Feldstein & Welkowitz, 1978; Giles, 1977; Giles & Powesland, 1975; Giles & Smith, 1979; LaFrance, 1979; Matarazzo & Weins, 1972; Putman & Street, 1984; Siegman, 1978; Street, 1982, 1984; Street & Brady, 1982; Street, Brady, & Putman, 1983; Welkowitz & Kuc, 1973). Of course, divergence dictated by social norms (such as showing deference to someone of high status) is judged positively unless it is done by an outgroup. Then it may be evaluated as impolite or hostile (Deprez & Persoons, 1984), something that both communication accommodation theory and expectancy violations theory would predict because actions of nonrewarding communicators are judged more harshly than those of rewarding communicators. One other exception to the general desirability of reciprocating is that newly formed pairs may be more attracted to one another when they compensate on floor-holding behaviors (Cappella, 1994); this allows one person to take the lead and another to follow.

Finally, adaptation may influence other interaction behaviors. Kikuchi (1994) wanted to see what would happen in an intercultural interaction if convergence toward another's backchannel behavior occurred; would this facilitate smoother interaction? He found that convergence did indeed increase the tempo of the interaction, while divergence led to a slowing of the tempo and more efforts by the other to check for indications of understanding.

These are just a few examples of how adaptation to the communication patterns of others can have positive or negative consequences.

SUMMARY

Nonverbal behaviors play a key role in managing conversations during all phases and at all levels. They are instrumental in initiating and terminating conversations. Coupled with verbal behaviors, they signal approachability (during greetings) or pending inaccessibility (during terminations), convey supportiveness, and reaffirm the definition of the interpersonal relationship. During leave-taking, they also bolster verbal behaviors that summarize and bring closure to the interaction.

Within the conversation itself, nonverbal cues regulate turn taking. Speakers employ them to signal their intentions to maintain or relinquish control of the conversation. Listeners use them to request or deny a turn and to provide backchannel support to the speaker. The manner in which interactants use these cues determines whether turn exchanges are smooth, overlapped, or interruptive. There are several models of how the turn exchange process works, two of the most promising of which appear to be the resource model and the two-stage model based on rhythmicity.

Nonverbal cues also assist topic switches. Proxemic shifts, extrainteractional activities, silences, and paralinguistic cues are used to signal changes in conversational topics. This is important not only in preparing listeners for the new information to be introduced but also in indicating speaker competence.

Finally, conversations are coordinated through dyadic interactional sequences and patterns. Substantial evidence documents that interactants adapt to one another, producing synchrony, convergence, matching, mirroring, and reciprocity or dissynchrony, divergence, complementarity, and compensation. Many of the patterns appear to be biologically based or acquired early in life as infants and children first interact with caretakers. Several theories have been offered to explain and predict these interaction patterns, among them, affiliative conflict theory, the arousal-labeling model, the sequential functional model, the parallel process model, expectancy violations theory, discrepancy-arousal theory, cognitive valence theory, communication accommodation theory, and interaction adaptation theory. Recent research is now beginning to verify the effects of adaptation on such interaction outcomes as relational satisfaction and evaluations of communicators. It is clear that adaptation patterns have long-term implications for successful human relationships.

SUGGESTED READINGS

Burgoon, J. K., Stern, L. A., & Dillman, L. (1995). *Interpersonal adaptation: Dyadic interaction patterns.* Cambridge: Cambridge University Press.

Cappella, J. N. (1994). The management of conversations. In M. L. Knapp & G. R. Miller (Eds.), *Handbook of interpersonal communication* (pp. 380–418). Newbury Park, CA: Sage.

Giles, H., Coupland, N., & Coupland, J. (1991). Accommodation theory: Communication, context, and consequence. In H. Giles, J. Coupland, & N. Coupland (Eds.), *Contexts of accommodation: Developments in applied sociolinguistics* (pp. 1–68). Cambridge: Cambridge University Press.

Jaffe, J., & Feldstein, S. (1970). *Rhythms of dialogue.* New York: Academic.

Kendon, A. (1990). *Conducting interaction: Patterns of behavior in focused encounters.* Cambridge: Cambridge University Press.

Kendon, A., Harris, R., & Key, M. R. (Eds.) (1975). *Organization of behavior in face-to-face interaction.* The Hague: Mouton.

O'Leary, M. J., & Gallois, C. (1985). The last ten turns: Behavioral sequencing in friends' and strangers' conversational endings. *Journal of Nonverbal Behavior, 9,* 8–27.

Wiemann, J. M. (1985). Interpersonal control and regulation in conversation. In R. L. Street, Jr., & J. N. Cappella (Eds.), *Sequence and pattern in communicative behaviour* (pp. 85–102). London: Arnold.

13

MANAGING IMPRESSIONS

Do we really know anybody? Who does not wear one face to hide another?

Frances Marion, American journalist

In Chapters 6–12, we consider how nonverbal behaviors reveal information about personality and emotions, facilitate the exchange of information itself, define interpersonal relationships, and structure and regulate conversations. These chapters focus largely on what nonverbal cues tell us at the outset of an interaction or how they govern its progress. In chapters 13, 14, and 15, we shift to functions associated more with *outcomes*—to what follows and flows from an interaction. These functions are *impression management, social influence,* and *deception.* They represent end goals to which much communication is directed; and, in contrast to some of the earlier functions, they also involve some of the most deliberate and most strategic use of nonverbal cues.

THE NATURE OF IMPRESSION MANAGEMENT

This chapter centers on how communicators can manage impressions to maximize favorable evaluations, such as liking, attraction, credibility, and power. If identification refers to who we think we are and impression formation to who others think we are, then *impression management* refers to *who we want others to think we are.* The emphasis here is on senders' behaviors—usually behaviors designed to improve others' judgments of us—and the success or failure of those efforts. Box 13-1 provides one illustration of just how important this function of communication can be.

In some respects, impression management resembles relational communication. But there are at least four notable differences between the two functions. First, impression

---

BOX 13-1

CEO IMAGE CAN MAKE OR BREAK FIRM

. . . Call it the charisma enigma or the CEO factor. It's the elusive quality that beams "buy," "sell" or "ignore" signals to investors, an image that screams "trust me" or "beware."

Chief executives can no longer hide behind their gray flannel suits. . . . "The chief executive is the major determinant of the stock price," says Warren Bennis, a University of Southern California management professor and co-author of *Leaders,* a book on business, government, and sports leaders.

Many analysts wouldn't go that far but still believe a CEO's personality is important.

Hugh Zurkuhlen, analyst with Salomon Bros. Inc., says the short-term impact of a chief executive's personality on the stock price is "incredible. . . . A CEO's presentation and personality have a lot to do with how analysts and portfolio managers view a company."

Many analysts say the faces behind the figures can

tell them how a company is run and where it's headed. They look for intelligence, substance, and candor. But if they can also get a touch of pizazz, warmth and humor, they just might fall in love with the company.

That's why impressing analysts is a must for heads of public companies. . . . And that's why public relations firms such as Hill & Knowlton Inc. are busy coaching execs for financial road shows.

Since 1980, about 3,000 executives—a third of them chief executives—asked Hill & Knowlton to help them prepare for non-media appearances, says George Glazer, senior vice president of the New York firm.

"Credibility is more important than projecting image and likeability," says Glazer, but controlling a lip-biting habit or a penchant for gaudy gold jewelry can help. "A misplaced smile can do more damage than a wrong figure."

Source: USA Today, August 18, 1985, pp. A1–A2.

management is more concerned with cause-and-effect relationships (e.g., what nonverbal behaviors foster credibility), whereas relational communication is more concerned with structural properties (e.g., what nonverbal behaviors carry what relational messages).

Second, impression management often takes an observer's perspective, examining judgments others make about a communicator's behavior; relational communication, on the other hand, typically takes the participants' perspective, examining the meanings interactants assign to the behaviors they are exchanging. How communicators succeed in enhancing their attractiveness in the eyes of beholders is a question about impression management; how communicators express their attraction toward one another is a question about relational communication.

Third, techniques of impression management typically are directed toward a generalized audience; relational messages are targeted to a specific partner. This makes impression management more pertinent to public and mass media contexts and relational communication more pertinent to interpersonal contexts (although politicians may attempt to create the impression that they are on an interpersonal basis with their constituents).

Fourth, impression management focuses on a single encoder who is using impression management strategies, whereas relational communication typically focuses on a dyad. For example, when discussing impression management, we might describe a person as using a dominant communication style, a pattern of behaviors creating an impression of power and authority. But in relational communication, behavior is considered dominant only if it elicits a submissive or subordinate response; that is, it is considered dominant only if it functions to exert control and influence within a dyad. Thus relational communication is more concerned with the ongoing dynamics of interaction between two or more people. Nevertheless, many relational message cues can be enlisted to create favorable messages, so the similarities between the functions, rather than their differences, will probably become readily apparent.

At this juncture, some students invariably object that they try to be themselves at all times and never put on a false front. But impression management doesn't imply being insincere or deceptive (although the converse may be true: deception, as discussed in Chapter 15, can be viewed as an extreme form of impression management). Rather, this function of communication recognizes that we are all made up of multiple "selves" and that in social situations, we try to "put our best face forward," adapting our performance to the requirements of the situation so as to minimize actions that might embarrass us or put us in a negative light. This principle underlies the concept of *face*—a concept central to Asian cultures and now becoming increasingly acknowledged in the west (see, e.g., Goffman, 1967; Ting-Toomey, 1994). It is nicely illustrated in an excerpt from Ken Kesey's novel about life in the northwest, *Sometimes a Great Notion* (1964), in which the main character, Lee, describes how—paradoxically, by adopting stereotypic roles— he and a black man were able to develop an uncharacteristically intimate friendship:

> And in our eight months of rooming together and years-long friendship, this homely, lantern-jawed Negro and I established a clear set of limits within which we knew we could comfortably communicate, sagacious and slow-talking Remus to my intellectual dandy. Within this framework, behind our shammed masks, we had been able to approach the most extreme personal truths in our conversations without suffering the embarrassment of such intimacies. (p. 62)

In short, putting on a "front" may make possible greater authenticity in communication, because it frees people from the fear of putting the "naked self" on the line. Sometimes, of course, impressions are managed to create unreal personas. The point, however, is that impression management per se is not to be regarded as deceitful or inappropriate; rather, it is the ends to which it is put that should be evaluated.

A distinguishing quality of impression management is that it involves intentional acts. Increasing scholarly interest in processes of attribution and interpretation has led researchers to tackle the questions of whether senders consciously translate intentions into nonverbal behavior and whether receivers attribute intentionality to nonverbal actions.

Palmer and Simmons (1994) asked students to try to get their partner in a conversation to like them more or less. As we might expect, these intentions showed up nonverbally. Those whose goal was to "increase liking" increased gazing and forward leaning; those whose goal was to "decrease liking" decreased both. Curiously, compared with a control group who received no instructions, both the "increase" group and the "decrease" group also talked and gestured *less;* perhaps those in the "increase" condition wanted to show more attentiveness to the partner and those in the "decrease" condition wanted to reduce involvement. Did these participants know what they were doing? Not entirely. Although they could describe some strategies, few were able to report the specific nonverbal cues they used. This finding reveals that as senders we are capable of engaging in strategic activity without necessarily knowing how we do it.

As receivers, we also attribute intent to many nonverbal cues. According to attribution theory principles, people try to make sense of the behavior of others and typically attribute behavior either to a person's disposition or to the situation (Seibold & Spitzberg, 1981). But they should make dispositional attributions only when they regard the actor's behavior as intentional and controllable. In a clever series of studies designed to test this speculation, Manusov (1990, 1992; Manusov & Rodriguez, 1989) examined whether people make more attributions about negative than positive nonverbal cues. In one case, judgments were made about bank tellers who were either courteous or abrupt. In another case, dating couples played a game during which one partner was a confederate—sometimes acting negatively and sometimes acting positively toward the other. Results showed that unless there are clear extenuating circumstances to explain such behavior (like long lines at a bank accounting for curt service), people are inclined to regard it as intentional and controllable. They make attributions about negative behaviors especially if they are in unhappy relationships, but they also attribute intent to positive nonverbal behaviors if they are in a satisfying relationship.

THEORIES OF IMPRESSION MANAGEMENT

Perhaps more than any other area of nonverbal communication, impression management has generated a significant amount of theorizing and research. In this chapter we review three major theories of impression management and research findings associated with each: self-presentation theory, impression management theory, and expectancy violations theory.

Self-Presentation Theory

The first and most comprehensive of the theories related to impression management is the dramaturgic analysis of the presentation of self introduced by Erving Goffman (1959, 1961b, 1963, 1967, 1969, 1971, 1974). *Self-presentation* is a process whereby we attempt, through nonverbal and verbal communication, to put forward positive images of ourselves for public consumption. Perhaps guided by Shakespeare's oft-quoted line, "All the world's a stage and all the men and women, merely players," Goffman's writings offer an implicit theory of self-presentation that builds on analogies between theater and everyday human interaction. Beyond offering a very broad view of how people manage impressions, his principles and assumptions have shaped numerous other theories.

Dramaturgic Concepts   The dramaturgic approach begins with the notion that, much as actors perform roles, people in daily life present themselves through the roles they adopt and perform. Most of us play a variety of roles on any given day, but our overall goal is to make others view us positively, and this transcends any particular role. In this respect, presentation of self is intrinsically concerned with putting forward a socially acceptable face.

Goffman (1959, 1961b, 1967) used the term *performance* or *line* variously, to refer to the totality of nonverbal and verbal acts that express our view of a given situation and our evaluation of self and others within the situation. For instance, a situation may appear to call for performing the role of "friend and confidant" or "gently chastising parent." Performances occur in the presence of others, who serve as the *audience,* and in particular settings, which are called the *stage.* The *front region* of the stage encompasses the areas the communicator customarily uses to present the performance. Thus people are seen as actors playing roles in the front stage area.

What is put forward is the *front:*

> that part of the individual's performance which regularly functions in a general and fixed fashion to define the situation for those who observe the performance. Front, then, is the expressive equipment of a standard kind intentionally or unwittingly employed by the individual during his performance. (Goffman, 1959, p. 22)

Three elements define the front:

1 *Appearance* includes cues that indicate the performer's social status. As discussed in Chapter 2, physical appearance cues such as clothing may indicate a great deal about a person's status.
2 *Manner* includes cues that indicate the interaction role about to be taken or the performer's attitude toward the role. Various kinesic cues, such as facial expression, posture, and rate of movement, are relevant to this front component.
3 *Setting* includes physical environment cues that assist in defining the dramatic situation for observers. Various elements of the environment and artifacts code discussed in Chapter 4, particularly the changeable semifixed elements, are relevant here.

According to Goffman, all these components should be consistent and act in concert; otherwise observers may begin to doubt the performance. For instance, if you were referred to a well-known, expensive accountant and showed up at his or her office only to find it in a run-down building and the office in a dirty, disorganized, and chaotic state, you might doubt the accountant's performance.

In contrast to the front region where performances occur, Goffman also defined a backstage area. In the *backstage region,* a performer is beyond the sight and sound of the audience and therefore feels free to act and speak in a more informal, less consistent, and more spontaneous way. Actors are allowed to relax, rehearse lines, and prepare for future interactions. A professor's office, for example, can be considered a backstage region from the performance of lecturer. According to Goffman, the backstage region is often used by performers as a place for engaging in behavior that would contradict a performance, such as smoking, swearing, or belching. Further, in this area actors may express dissatisfaction with their roles and derogate the audience—behavior that would be unacceptable in the front region.

The wings in a theater are regions to either side of the stage that hold equipment, props, the prompter, and aids to the performance. Goffman defined *wings* as areas that contain people and equipment used to assist a performer in a role. A kitchen during a party, for example, may be a wings area for the hosts, containing props that are vital to the performance of the role of host.

Finally, Goffman defined supporting roles that can facilitate an individual's performance. Much as a theatrical performer might consult a dialect specialist about certain sounds for a part, everyday actors consult *specialists* to help them prepare for a given performance. There are two types of specialists. A *technical* specialist provides a skill or performs a function required by the performance. For instance, a caterer that you hire for a party may play this supporting role. A *training* specialist instructs the performer in the various actions that make up a performance. An etiquette specialist that you might consult for a formal party would be an example here. Anyone who acts as an adviser, teacher, or counselor can be considered a training specialist. In defining this concept in his dramaturgic analysis, Goffman noted that performances are rarely successful without the support and help of other people.

Principles of Successful Performances   As the next step in his dramaturgic analysis, Goffman identified several principles of successful performances.

1 *A performer must segregate audiences.* Because of the variety and complexity of roles, it is likely that some are inconsistent (or appear to be inconsistent) with each other. As a result, members of one audience should not see the actor performing an inconsistent role for another audience. If an actor fails to segregate audience members, the performances may be compromised or invalidated.

2 *A performer should be aware of and adhere to requirements of decorum that accompany dramatic action.* One must follow a variety of social and interactional rules to be successful at self-presentation. Playing by the rules allows one to be seen in a positive light. Violating social rules may invalidate a performance, allowing the performer to be seen as possessing negative traits. For example, if one inappropriately gains control of the conversation by repeatedly interrupting and not following turn-taking rules, such behavior may lead to an unsuccessful performance. However, as we will see shortly, in certain circumstances violations may be advantageous.

3 *A performer must coordinate verbal and nonverbal codes to create an impression.* We have already discussed how contradictory messages can lead to confusion in interactions. Successful performances must feature consistent verbal and nonverbal cues. Goffman (1959) argued that many nonverbal cues are difficult to control (he termed them ungovernable aspects of behavior), but more recent research has shown that there are individual differences in the ability to control and manipulate a variety of nonverbal behaviors (a point we will return to later). Thus some communicators will be better than others at achieving verbal-nonverbal consistency in self-presentation.

4 *For a performance to be accepted by an audience, the actor must be judged to be sincere.* Messages of sincerity are often conveyed via nonverbal cues. If an actor does not appear to be sincere in a performance, observers will not view the performance as successful. Rather, they may become suspicious and make negative attributions about the performer. It is important, then, that sincerity be effectively portrayed both verbally and nonverbally.

5 *An actor must appear satisfied with the role.* According to Goffman, it is important that a performer appear to like the role and be comfortable with it. Some teaching

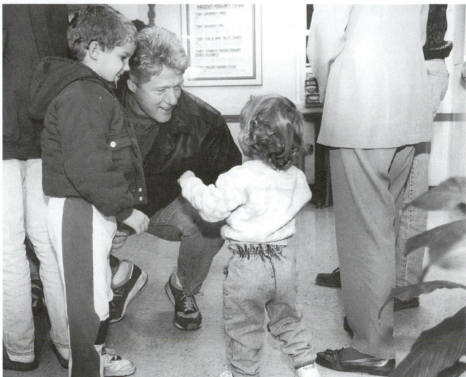

Compare the person in both photos. How are setting and personal front altered to suit two different performances?

assistants at universities appear ill at ease because they are put into a classroom with students who are only slightly younger (and in some cases older) than they are. Their youthfulness alone may prevent them from feeling comfortable with their role. Consequently, their presentations as knowledgeable, poised instructors may suffer.

The ways in which these dramaturgic principles can be put to use is illustrated in Box 13-2.

Violations: Sources of Invalidity in Performances   Just as there are nonverbal factors that foster successful performances, there are important nonverbal sources of *invalidity*—actions that may contradict the impression one wishes to convey to others:

1 *Loss of control.* An actor may accidentally convey incapacity, impropriety, or even disrespect through temporary loss of coordination or muscular control. Belching at a formal dinner, sneezing in the midst of silence at a prayer service, stumbling on the way to a podium to receive an award, hiccupping while trying to propose marriage— these kinds of actions divert attention away from the performance and raise questions about a performer's self-control. That is why Goffman (1967) considered poise extremely important to maintaining a successful line of action.

2 *Too little or too much involvement in a role.* People may jeopardize their performances by appearing overeager or overly concerned—or, conversely, by appearing uninterested. Excessive concern about one's performance, for instance, may be revealed through nervousness, perspiration, halting speech, wrenching of hands, exag-

---

BOX 13-2

APPLICATIONS: THE DOCTOR AS DRAMATIST

How often do people engage in self-presentation performances? In a "My Turn" column in the February 1, 1988, issue of *Newsweek,* Dr. Stephen A. Hoffmann suggested that self-presentation concerns enter into situations and role performances that we might not consider self-presentational. Hoffmann detailed a variety of self-presentation tactics he used on a patient to convince her that he had provided a good diagnosis of her medical problem. When his initial reassurances failed, he resorted to more "dramatic" measures:

And so, I resort to theater. I stage a dazzlingly detailed neurologic exam. There are props: a reflex hammer and an ophthalmoscope, each of which I move about in carefully choreographed patterns.

He described special effects he used to test a patient's vision, accompanied by "hmmms" and "flourishes."

Throughout it all, I'm careful to concentrate on my delivery, timing my words, smiles, and gestures for best effect. . . . It's often said that doctors "play God," but the comment misses the point. Whether or not we're trying to be God's understudies, we always play to our audience. The truth is that people expect it of us.

Whether patients expect such behavior, and whether, as Hoffmann asserted, "Good bedside manner, in fact, is good theater," is debatable. What is interesting to note is Hoffmann's extensive use of nonverbal cues to manage his impressions with the patient.

Many professionals claim that this is part of professional behavior and is expected by clients. Others would say that such behavior represents a less than honest approach to professionalism. What is your reaction?

gerated gestures, and the like—behaviors commonly associated with stage fright. Apathy may be revealed through lax posture, inexpressivity, and careless language—behaviors indicative of poor self-monitoring. In short, performers are expected to demonstrate a certain attitude toward the role, showing that they understand its requirements and are confident of satisfying them. Failure to do so undermines the validity of the performance.

3 *Inadequate dramaturgic direction.* A performer may show unfamiliarity with props and other equipment, with architectural features of the staging area, or with other requirements. This problem can also stem from not consulting "specialists." A former student of one of the authors once showed up for a day of deep-sea fishing in a beautiful silk pants outfit; clearly, she had forgotten to get someone to "clue her in." You may have had a similar experience—showing up for some social occasion and finding yourself obviously overdressed or underdressed. Such public embarrassments may invalidate the rest of the performance.

Team Performances By circumstance or choice, actors may find themselves involved in situations that demand special performances, requiring specific dramaturgic skills and posing new implications for the use of nonverbal cues. Among the special types of performances are those relating to acting as a member of a team, which may be as small as a dyad or as large as an institution.

Team performances are ones in which actors cannot achieve as successful and convincing a performance alone as they can together with others. Goffman (1959) defined a *team* as "a set of individuals whose intimate cooperation is required if a given projected definition of the situation is to be maintained" (p. 104). Sometimes team performances

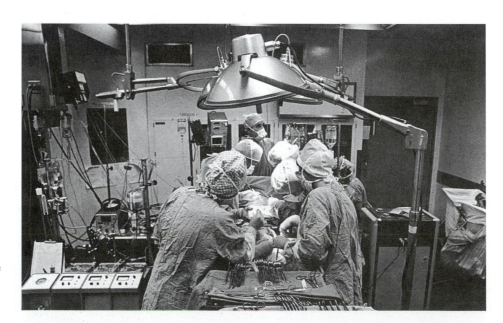

Teams rely on numerous nonverbal cues to create the sense of a team rather than individual performance.

occur because demands are simply too much for a single performer to meet, or because circumstances require coordinated action, as in the case of a surgical team or an attorney-client relationship. In other cases, actors may choose to involve others in order to heighten action, enliven the performance, or create the impression of an authentic encounter. Howard Cosell once recounted how Muhammad Ali took him to a pool hall in Harlem and announced to the assembled habitués, "Here's the white guy who's always giving me trouble on TV." Not until people had crowded around and made Cosell quite uncomfortable did Ali throw his arm around Cosell, saying, "Just kidding." Ali thus conjured up one team (the pool hall regulars) and then switched to another (his friendship with Cosell) to create some drama and rib Cosell.

At other times, the impression to be created is not of an individual but of a larger unit. Husbands and wives, for example, often work to create the outward appearance of a happy couple even when they are experiencing conflict. Likewise, institutions rely on team performances to maintain an identity and to reinforce loyalty. For example, businesses stress that employees are part of the company team and represent the organization to its publics.

Nonverbal behaviors are often enlisted to convince an audience that performers are in fact a team and that their individual performances should be viewed as part of a larger dramatic production. One way nonverbal behaviors serve to sustain this impression is through *symbols of membership* (sometimes called *tie-signs;* see Chapter 11). Apparel and adornments (e.g., similar clothing, insignias, tattoos), artifacts (e.g., similar books, matching hiking equipment), shared gestures (e.g., gang hand signals), and similar vocal patterns (e.g., use of the same dialect or inflection patterns) may help to create an appearance of partnership. Some may also imply possession or subordination: wedding rings serve as symbols of attachment and uniforms signify ranks in a formal hierarchy. Although such symbols sometimes merely reflect adherence to social norms, at other times they are used consciously to signal inclusion in team performances and may even function to reinforce members' identification with, and allegiance to, the team.

Another way nonverbal cues contribute to team performances is by signifying who is in the *leadership* role. Successful team productions depend on one person's acting as a leader or director who cues others' performances, trains new members, and deals with members who violate team "rules." Sometimes this directorial activity can be as subtle as a head nod signaling that a member should take action. Sometimes, however, leaders are easily distinguished by their distinctive dress and manner. Gang leaders, fathers in patriarchal households, and business executives, for example, may adopt a stance and vocal tone that indicate their authority.

One problem facing members of teams and institutions is that the collective performance may require subordinating their own self-presentation to that of the group. Nonverbal indicators of group membership may supplant attire and behavioral patterns indicative of individuality. Military uniforms and prison garb, for instance, promote self-distancing—alienation or disaffection from oneself. The same could be said of religious cults, mental hospitals, and schools that require uniforms, short hair, or shaved heads, and dictate where and how people must sit and stand. Symbols that identify someone as a unique individual are replaced with symbols of the group or institution. Some institutions even confiscate personal property in order to restrict self-presentational behavior.

They may prohibit or seize the props in one's "identity kit"—things like cosmetics, shaving gear, hair spray, cologne, and jewelry that are used to prepare and repair one's personal front (Goffman, 1961a). They may also force members into "disidentifying" roles—patterns of behavior that make individuals accept subservience to the institution and devalue self-worth. Controlling chronemics (requiring people to work long hours, for instance, or to follow disruptive schedules) and proxemics (requiring people to sit at a leader's feet, for example) are two ways in which nonverbal patterns are used to bring self-presentations under institutional control.

In his analysis of asylums, stigmatized performances, and interaction frames, Goffman (1961a, 1964, 1974) identified further ways in which institutions and societies may impose nonverbal patterns on their members and ways in which individuals may attempt to reassert their own identities in the face of these group-oriented performances. What is impressive throughout these analyses is that they resonate with people's day-to-day experiences. They ring true, capturing how people negotiate their own self-presentations in the midst of cross-pressures to adhere to larger team and institutional presentations, and they underscore the centrality of nonverbal elements in creating and sustaining these presentations. Moreover, many of Goffman's claims, which were based on his own astute observations of human behavior, led to more systematic empirical work. Nevertheless, as we will see shortly, not all of Goffman's claims have been supported. In the remaining sections of this chapter, we review theories and lines of research that have been subjected to statistical testing and identify nonverbal strategies and tactics that contribute to successful or unsuccessful impression management.

Impression Management Theory

Impression management theory is concerned explicitly with how people engender positive views of themselves in others while avoiding negative views. Impression management theorists have attempted to uncover strategies and tactics that allow interactants to achieve these goals.

Classifying Techniques of Impression Management   Tedeschi and Norman (1985) synthesized a variety of impression management techniques, including those derived from Jones and Pittman's theory (1982) and Jones's earlier ingratiation theory (1964), into an overall taxonomy of impression management behaviors. Although not all the tactics they cover are relevant for our purposes, some clearly are and others may be.

Tedeschi and Norman's taxonomy rests on two basic distinctions. First, impression management techniques can be described as either defensive or assertive. *Defensive* impression management occurs whenever people experience or anticipate predicaments in which they believe others will attribute negative qualities to them and therefore use impression management techniques to avoid being judged negatively. *Assertive* impression management occurs when people attempt to establish particular attributes in the eyes of others. Someone wishing to be perceived as a skilled computer hacker, for instance, will engage in behaviors designed to enhance that impression.

Second, impression management may be either *strategic* or *tactical*. As Tedeschi and Norman use these terms, strategic impressions have long-term goals and consequences;

tactical impressions have short-term goals and consequences. (This usage parallels military usage. Elsewhere, the term *strategies* often refers to overarching plans, while *tactics* refers to specific behaviors deployed to accomplish those objectives.) Crossing assertive-defensive actions with the strategic-tactical distinction results in a 2-by-2 matrix of possible impression management behaviors, as shown in Table 13-1.

Nonverbal impression management is most closely associated with the assertive-strategic cell in Table 13-1. What follows is a summary of major research findings related to these various strategies. Most of the studies to be reported were not undertaken expressly to test impression management theory. Rather, they represent our analysis of how the empirical studies relate to one another and to the larger communication function of impression management.

Managing Impressions of Attractiveness and Likability   One of the most basic aims of impression management is to get others to be attracted to us and to like us. Elsewhere, this most fundamental of human interaction goals comes under the heading of conveying or promoting affiliativeness, affection, warmth, and immediacy (Mehrabian, 1981). Researchers often measure this impression along such dimensions as sociable-unsociable, friendly-unfriendly, kind-unkind, pleasant-unpleasant, and attractive-unattractive. Despite the variety of labels and measurement formats, these concepts all relate to the same overriding strategy.

Many of the nonverbal cues that promote an attractive image are the same ones we use to communicate to others that we are attracted to them, that is, cues that serve as relational messages of attraction (see Chapter 11). Here we focus on cues that can be used to create generalized impressions of a communicator as attractive, friendly, and likable.

TABLE 13-1
A TAXONOMY OF IMPRESSION MANAGEMENT BEHAVIORS

	Tactical	Strategic

Defensive	Accounts
	  Excuses
	  Justifications
	Disclaimers
	Self-handicapping
	Apologies
	Restitution
	Prosocial behavior
		Alcoholism
		Drug abuse
		Phobias
		Hypochondria
		Mental illness
		Learned helplessness

Assertive	Entitlements Enhancements Ingratiation Intimidation Exemplification Self-promotion Supplication	Attraction Esteem Prestige Status Credibility Trustworthiness

First and perhaps most obvious are behaviors that convey *physical attractiveness.* As noted in Chapter 9, there is a general stereotype that "what is beautiful is good"—people who are physically attractive are more positively evaluated on various other personal attributes. For example, men and women find interactions with the opposite sex more pleasant and like the partner better if the partner is physically attractive (Garcia, Stinson, Ickes, & Bissonnette, 1991). Defendants and plaintiffs in mock sexual harassment cases were rated by "jurors" as more sincere, warm, and intelligent; and the more attractive they were and the less attractive their opponents were, the more verdicts were rendered in their favor (Castellow, Wuensch, & Moore, 1990). The "jurors" were very willing to believe that a beautiful woman had been harassed by an unattractive man but unwilling to believe that an unattractive woman had been harassed by an attractive man. Thus it behooves litigants to maximize their attractiveness. Voting decisions are also strongly influenced by looks:

> Americans pick their candidates, in part, the same way they shop for cars, cosmetics and cantaloupes—by appearance.
>
> In an age of declining party allegiance, . . . voters are judging candidates by the one trait in which they have expertise: looks. . . .
>
> Shawn Rosenberg . . . quantifies how voters react to chins, eyebrows, and the like.
>
> By manipulating appearances using makeup, hair style and camera angles, he discovered he could push ratings up or down five percentage points. In a real election, that would translate into a 10 percent margin—enough to swing a close race. (Krieger, 1994, p. A5).

(See Box 13-3 for an additional example.)

BOX 13-3

APPLICATIONS: ATTRACTIVENESS AND SURVIVAL IN THE ORGANIZATIONAL JUNGLE

We have all heard the adage "Beauty is only skin deep," and we would like to think we are appreciated more for our inner qualities and talents than for our appearance. But in a survey of 662 managers in Fortune 500 firms, personal appearance ranked eighth out of 20 key factors determining survival of the fittest in the "organizational jungle" (Nikodym & Simonetti, 1987).

A review of material from corporate image seminars led Nikodym and Simonetti to propose that those who have the right "corporate image" are more likely to be promoted within their organizations. Key elements to "looking and playing the part" include:

1 *Dress*—conservative in style and color for both men and women: no slacks for women; formality of dress matched to the occasion. (But there now seems to be wider latitude in what is acceptable; see Box 13-4 later in this chapter.)
2 *Hair*—short and neat style for both men and women;

little facial hair for men; clean-shaven legs for women.
3 *Jewelry*—limited and tasteful for both men and women.
4 *Grooming*—pressed clothes, polished shoes, clean and buffed nails for men, manicured nails for women.
5 *Posture and carriage*—proper sitting and standing posture (neither overly relaxed or overly tense); confident but not cocky walk.

It should be evident that all these elements are things everyone can control, regardless of his or her innate physical endowment. Other good news: Even higher on the list of success factors, ranked third, is *communication skills,* including other nonverbal behaviors that promote impressions of credibility and attractiveness. All this means that those who are attentive to nonverbal elements have the prospect of improving their standing in the workplace.

Although physical appearance cues such as apparel, hairstyle, and grooming are obvious factors in achieving an impression of attractiveness, vocalics also play a part. For example, some research has shown that impressions of physical beauty are influenced by vocal cues, and impressions of vocal attractiveness are influenced by physical appearance (Raines, Hechtman, & Rosenthal, 1990a, 1990b; Zuckerman, Hodgins, & Miyake, 1990; Zuckerman, Miyake, & Hodgins, 1991). Interestingly, people who have pleasant voices and faces and who show dominance facially but submissiveness vocally are deemed the most attractive. This is especially true for women.

Without overstating the importance of attractiveness, it should be recognized that in many circumstances, physical appearance is less salient than other nonverbal cues. One study, for example, found that clothing and cleanliness were less important than speech characteristics and demographic factors in predicting interviewers' assessments of job applicants (Parsons & Liden, 1984). And an analysis of cultural differences in the role of physical appearance concluded that collectivist cultures such as China may place less emphasis on physical beauty than individualist cultures like the United States (Dion, Pak, & Dion, 1990).

A second class of nonverbal cues promoting attractiveness and likability consists of cues conveying *warmth and pleasantness* (also known as *positive affect* cues). One investigation examined the separate and combined impact of smiling, head nodding, and eyebrow raising. Participants were shown videotaped segments of an actor verbalizing a standard phrase while using one, two, or all three of these behaviors and rated the actor's social attractiveness. Results showed that the single most powerful cue promoting favorable impressions was the smile, followed by the head nod and then the eyebrow raise; smiling and nodding were the most effective two-cue combination (Woodall, Burgoon, & Markel, 1980). Other research has confirmed the potency of smiles and facial pleasantness in making an actor appear more attractive and likeable (e.g., Bayes, 1970; Burgoon, Birk, & Pfau, 1990; Gutsell & Andersen, 1980; Mehrabian, 1981; Reece & Whitman, 1962; Rosenfeld, 1966a, 1966b).

Like facial pleasantness, vocal pleasantness and warmth are advantageous in creating impressions of friendliness. Personal experience tells us that we rely on vocal cues to judge other people's friendliness over the telephone. A number of features such as rapid tempo, downward pitch contours, pitch variety, tempo variety, and limited variations in loudness are responsible for higher ratings of pleasantness and sociability (Burgoon et al., 1990; Scherer, 1979c; Scherer & Oshinsky, 1977). Additionally, positive backchannel cues like *mm-hmm* are reinforcing and produce positive social perceptions (Matarazzo, Wiens, & Saslow, 1965).

Immediacy cues are a third class of nonverbal behaviors that promote attractiveness and likability. Gaze is especially effective. Wiener and Mehrabian (1968) devised a study in which an interviewer looked more at one interviewee than another. Interviewees receiving more gaze perceived the interviewer to be more favorable toward them than interviewees receiving less gaze did. LaCrosse (1975) had confederates role-play either "affiliative" or "nonaffiliative" counselors, which included 80 percent or 40 percent levels of eye contact, respectively. Participants viewing videotapes of the interactions rated the "affiliative" counselor as more attractive. Similarly, Wiemann (1974) had subjects interview confederates who gazed at them 100 percent, 75 percent, 25 percent, or 0 percent of the time. As predicted, as the confederate's gaze decreased, subjects rated the confederate as less friendly. Other studies, using different methodologies, have arrived at similar conclusions (e.g., Beebe, 1980; Burgoon et al., 1990; Goldberg et al., 1969; Kendon, 1967; Kleinke et al., 1974).

Other immediacy cues that have been linked to attractiveness and likability include increased use of touch, close proximity, gestural activity, open body positions, direct body orientation, and forward leaning (e.g., Andersen, Andersen, & Jensen, 1979; Fisher et al., 1976; Heslin & Boss, 1980; McGinley, McGinley, & Nicholas, 1978; Mehrabian, 1968c, 1969, 1971a; Mehrabian & Ksionzky, 1970; Patterson, 1977). For example, in a study of simulated counseling interactions, counselors who displayed high immediacy were rated as more attractive and facilitative than those who displayed nonimmediacy (Fretz, Corn, Tuemmler, & Bellet, 1979). Another counseling study found that responsive nonverbal behavior, which included positive facial expressions, gestures, head nodding, and forward leaning, yielded significantly higher ratings of attractiveness than nonresponsive nonverbal behavior (Barak, Patkin, & Dell, 1982). Such behavior accounted for 61 percent of the variance (which means that it had a very powerful effect), while attire and verbal jargon accounted for only 4 percent and 17 percent, respectively. Similar findings have been reported in other counseling and interviewing studies (Claiborn, 1979; Imada & Hakel, 1977; Roll, Crowley, & Rappl, 1985; Seay & Altekruse, 1979; Tepper & Haase, 1978; Thompson & Aiello, 1988).

Although the overwhelming conclusion from the evidence is that people can successfully foster attraction and liking by enhancing physical attractiveness and enacting warmth, pleasantness, and immediacy, it is also possible to have "too much of a good thing." An experiment using the context of an employment interview found that inter-

Politicians may rely on immediacy cues to create an impression of warmth and sincerity.

viewers were favorably disposed toward applicants who used these nonverbal cues alone but became more negative when the cues were combined with use of cologne or perfume. Possibly, the interviewers thought that the applicants who wore scent were being manipulative or were trying too hard, speculations reminiscent of Goffman's injunction (1959) to appear sincere in one's performance and Jones's contention (1964) that obvious attempts to ingratiate oneself will be less successful than subtle attempts.

Here again, culture may also play a role. One study on the effects of cultural background on perceptions of attraction involved showing Japanese and American subjects a series of slides of a Japanese confederate who smiled frequently or infrequently while displaying an open or closed body position. Americans rated the confederate as most attractive when she smiled frequently and displayed an open posture. By contrast, Japanese observers rated her as most attractive when she smiled frequently but used a closed body position (McGinley, Blau, & Takai, 1984). Perceptions of attractiveness are clearly affected by cultural perspectives.

Dominance cues are a fourth class of nonverbal behaviors promoting attractiveness. Accentuating dominance-related elements of energy, strength, and "panache" may add to a person's charisma and sexual appeal (Dabbs, 1994). But this may only work for men. A series of studies in which men and women were shown engaging in high-dominance or low-dominance behaviors found that only men benefited from exhibiting dominance; women were not seen as more attractive when they did so. High dominance consisted of sitting close to a target in a relaxed, asymmetrical posture with slight backward leaning and gesturing frequently but nodding infrequently. Low dominance consisted of more distant seating, symmetrical posture, greater postural tension, slightly forward body leaning with head partially bowed, frequent nodding and gazing toward the floor, but infrequent gesturing. The dominance pattern improved only impressions of sexual attractiveness—not likability. Moreover, related behaviors patterns—being aggressive or domineering—did not have the same positive effect. However, other research has confirmed that more postural relaxation, which is one component of the dominance profile, conveys greater sociability (Burgoon et al., 1990; see also Raines et al., 1990a, 1990b; Sadalla, Kenrick, & Vershore, 1987.)

Three vocal behaviors often equated with dominance are *turn length, response latencies* (pauses between speakers), *loudness,* and *fluency.* Research on duration of turns and response latencies suggests that moderate-length turns and latencies, or turns and latencies matching those of the receiver, are preferable for promoting social attractiveness (Baskett & Freedle, 1974; Stang, 1973; Street, 1982, 1984). As for loudness, moderation also appears to be the best policy: voices ranging from soft to moderately loud are perceived as more sociable (Pearce & Brommel, 1972; Ray, 1986; Scherer, 1979a). In the case of fluency, greater fluency combined with greater pleasantness is most effective in promoting impressions of sociability (Burgoon et al., 1990).

In sum, a wide variety of kinesic, vocalic, haptic, and proxemic code elements foster impressions of social attraction and liking. Attractive apparel and appearance, including good grooming; smiles and pleasant facial expressions and voices; greater immediacy, including close proximity, touch, high degrees of gaze, and postural openness; moderate postural relaxation; vocal variety, including pitch and tempo variety, but moderate loudness and talk time; and backchanneling all contribute to favorable impressions—along such dimensions as friendliness, sociability, and likability. So do use of turn lengths, response latencies, and tempos that are similar to those of audience members. However, these patterns have been studied primarily in North American culture and may differ in other cultures, since other cultures differ in their standards of attractiveness and their norms for immediacy, dominance, and deference displays. Additionally, men may have more tactics at their disposal than women do.

Managing Impressions of Credibility and Power Concerns about communicators' *credibility* (also called *ethos*) can be traced to the ancient Greek philosophers and classical rhetoricians—the historical roots of communication as a discipline. Contemporary treatments of credibility conceive of it as a set of judgments made by receivers about a sender. Although fostering credibility is often an end in itself, it is frequently designed to enable a communicator to achieve other objectives, such as social influence (see Chapter 14) and comprehension (see Chapter 6).

Research has turned up numerous dimensions of credibility, but there is limited agreement on which are most central. Within the field of communication, the most widely recognized are these five: (1) *Competence* concerns apparent expertise and knowledge; (2) *Character,* also called *trustworthiness,* concerns basic traits such as honesty, benevolence, and reliability; (3) *Composure* relates to the appearance of poise and relaxation or anxiety and tension; (4) *Extroversion,* also called *dynamism,* relates to energy and gregariousness; and (5) *Sociability* relates to the kinds of judgments discussed above with regard to friendliness and social attraction. Credibility, then, is a composite of several judgments, including the impression management strategy of trustworthiness and possibly incorporating Tedeschi and Norman's (1985) strategies of status and prestige, which are often equated with, or manifested through, displays of competence and composure. Impressions of power and dominance may also be conveyed by status, competence, and dynamism cues.

Because we have already addressed sociability, our emphasis here will be on how nonverbal cues foster impressions of power and favorable impressions along the other dimensions of credibility. Because of the historical interest in credibility, and because of its applicability to communication contexts ranging from dyads and small groups to corporate image and public and political arenas, it has spawned voluminous research and writing. Most of the research has been conducted within a single code (e.g., vocal, kinesic) and focused on one or two behaviors at a time. What follows is a summary of the major findings within each code.

The lion's share of attention has centered on vocal cues. One of the most extensively studied is *tempo* or *rate.* The preponderance of research shows that faster speaking enhances perceptions related to competence, status, and dominance, such as intelligence, objectivity, and knowledgeability (Aronovitch, 1976; Buller & Aune, 1988a; Crown, 1980; Giles & Street, 1985; Gunderson & Hopper, 1976; Mehrabian & Williams, 1969; Pearce & Brommel, 1972; Ray, 1966; Smith et al., 1975; Stewart & Ryan, 1982; Street & Brady, 1982). Other research shows that rapid tempo also conveys greater dynamism (Addington, 1971; Brown, Strong, & Rencher, 1973, 1974; but see Giles, Henwood, Coupland, Harriman, & Coupland, 1992, for an exception for younger speakers). Marketing research on the effects of time-compressed speech, which essentially speeds up the audio portion of a radio or television broadcast, also finds that faster tempo has beneficial effects (LaBarbera & MacLachlan, 1979; Machlachlan, 1979).

One caveat to this general argument in favor of rapid speech is that research on judgments related to character and composure has produced mixed findings: much of it favors a moderate or slower rate, perceived as more honest, people-oriented, benevolent, and composed (Brown, 1980; Brown et al., 1973, 1974, 1975; Burgoon, 1978a; Pearce & Conklin, 1971; Ray, 1986; Schwietzer, 1970; Smith et al., 1975; Woodall & Burgoon, 1983; but see also Miller, Maruyama, Beaber, & Valone, 1976). One possibility is that a curvilinear relationship exists, so that both slow and fast rates are less desirable than a moderate rate. Another possibility, borne out in several studies (Buller & Aune, 1986; Street & Brady, 1982; Street et al., 1983), is that tempo affects the various credibility dimensions differently. While a linear relationship exists between tempo and judgments of competence (faster is better), similarity to the listener's own speaking tempo mediates judgments of character, sociability, and composure. That is, people prefer a tempo similar to or slightly faster than their own: people who speak rapidly themselves will prefer rapid tempos, while those who speak slowly themselves will prefer slow tempos. Since most people speak at a moderate pace, a moderate tempo generally will emerge as the most preferred.

Two factors that can affect these judgments are context and mode of presentation. Negative perceptions of slow speaking rate can be canceled out if receivers can account favorably for it—for example, if it appears intended to help listeners understand a difficult or unfamiliar topic (Giles, Brown, & Thakerar, 1981). Speaking rate also has been shown to have more influence on judgments when listeners have access only to the audio channel (Woodall & Burgoon, 1983). When they have access to visual as well as audio information, tempo has less impact on credibility.

A second vocal feature affecting credibility and power is *pausing.* Two types of pausing that have been studied are pauses within turns, sometimes called *hesitation pauses,* and response latencies. Several studies have shown that shorter pauses of both types enhance credibility (Lay & Burron, 1968; Newman, 1982; Scherer, 1979c; Scherer, London, & Wolf, 1973; Siegman & Reynolds, 1982; Street, 1982). However, short latencies (1 second or less) may be best for appearing competent, while moderate latencies (1 to 3 seconds) may be best for appearing trustworthy (Baskett & Freedle, 1974).

Loudness is a third feature that affects credibility. Research indicates that increasing vocal volume or intensity up to a moderately high level increases a wide array of credibility judgments, including impressions of dominance, boldness, competence, emotional stability, and extroversion (Aronovitch, 1976; Burgoon, 1978a; Burgoon et al., 1990; Ray, 1986; Scherer, 1979c). There is one exception: a softer voice with varied pitch variety may be better for fostering judgments of benevolence.

Research on *pitch level* has been less consistent. Some evidence suggests that higher pitch promotes impressions of competence, dominance, and assertiveness (Scherer, 1978; Scherer et al., 1973). Other research suggests that higher pitch creates negative impressions and that deeper pitch is more credible (Apple et al., 1979; Brown et al., 1973, 1974). The conflicting findings may be due partly to different acceptable pitch ranges for male and female voices. Increases in male pitch may result in positive impressions; but at the point at which a man starts to sound like a woman, impressions may suffer. Research on *variety* in pitch and tempo, however, consistently shows that greater variation enhances credibility across the board, especially when coupled with faster tempo (Addington, 1971; Brown et al., 1973, 1974; Burgoon, 1978a; Burgoon et al., 1990; Ray, 1986; Scherer, 1979c).

Other vocal features that enhance credibility are *fluency, vocal pleasantness, utterance or turn length,* and *accent.* (Burgoon et al., 1990; Giles et al., 1992; Hayes & Meltzer, 1972; Miller & Hewgill, 1964; Scherer, 1979c; Sereno & Hawkins, 1967). For example, nonfluent speech may jeopardize competence and composure impressions but does not appear to diminish trustworthiness. Longer turns at talk are perceived positively in terms of competence and conscientiousness, but medium-length turns or turns matching the lengths of other conversants are best for enhancing sociability. Accented, nonstandard speech sounds more benevolent, but standard speech, especially with older sounding voices, conveys the most competence.

Two broader vocal styles that reflect a combination of vocal cues have been studied for their impact on credibility (Pearce & Brommel, 1971; Pearce & Conklin, 1971). One style, *conversational* delivery, has a smaller range of inflection, greater consistency in rate and pitch, less volume, and lower pitch. *Dynamic* style involves more pausing, higher pitch range, and more variations in volume. Conversational style results in perceptions of honesty and "people orientation," while dynamic delivery results in perceptions of tough-mindedness, task orientation, assertiveness, and confidence.

Finally, regional and ethnic dialects have been studied for their effects on perceptions. Although a dialect or accent includes variations in verbal behavior, variations in vocal behavior make up an accent as well (vocal qualities, pronunciations of various words, rate, etc.) The research on dialect and accent is extensive and will not be covered in detail here (for reviews, see Burgoon & Saine, 1978; Giles, 1979; Giles & Street, 1985; Giles et al., 1991; Ryan, 1979; Street & Hopper, 1982). Reviews of this literature lead to the following conclusions concerning accent and credibility: (1) Receivers generally perceive people with dominant or prestigious group accents and dialects as more competent, higher in status, more intelligent, and more successful; (2) People with regional or "inferior" group accents are perceived as trustworthy and likable and are preferred by ingroup members when in informal contexts such as neighborhood bars and homes but are not always rated highest by regional occupants; (3) The General American dialect (what is spoken in the midwest) is viewed as more credible and especially more competent than southern or New England dialects; (4) Speech with native accents is rated as more dynamic, more aesthetically pleasing and reflective of higher sociointellectual status than that of foreign-accented speech; and (5) Both blacks and whites rate speakers of standard English higher than speakers using nonstandard dialect.

Overall, the advice for someone who wants to appear poised, competent, and powerful is to speak rapidly, fluently and loudly with few pauses, with deep and varied pitch, with the preferred (General American) dialect and with long speaking turns, producing a dynamic communication style. However, if the goal is to give the impression of being social and trustworthy, a more conversational and slower style with nonstandard accents will work. Quite clearly, vocal cues have a strong effect on how others see us and how we see others. They affect impressions in educational, employment interview, therapeutic, and legal settings.

Among kinesic cues, one of the most potent is eye contact or gaze. Increased eye contact results in perceptions of dynamism, dominance, believability, and persuasiveness (Beebe, 1980; LaCrosse, 1975). Hemsley and Doob (1978), in a courtroom simulation study, found that witnesses who averted their gaze were perceived as less credible. Further, the defendant for whom the witness was testifying was also judged as more likely to be guilty. Similar results have been obtained in other studies (Kleck & Nuessle, 1968; LeCompte & Rosenfeld, 1971).

When gaze is combined with other immediacy cues, it further enhances power and credibility. Public speakers who use more immediacy and who are more expressive facially and gesturally are perceived as more extroverted and of better character, as well as more sociable.

Postural rigidity conveys lack of composure, whereas postural relaxation improves credibility and power impressions. Curiously, however, use of more rather than less self-adaptors is associated with perceptions of relaxation, suggesting that some degree of physical activation is desirable (Burgoon, et al., 1990). Finally, synchronizing gestures and head nods with the rhythm of speech enhances credibility (Woodall & Burgoon, 1981).

Several studies have demonstrated that proxemic variations have an impact on credibility perceptions. In one early study (Patterson & Sechrest, 1970), a curvilinear relationship between distance and social activity ratings (extroverted, dominant, aggressive) was found. Ratings were highest when confederates were 4 feet from the subjects and were lowest at distances of 2 feet and 6 feet. A series of studies designed to test a nonverbal expectations and violations model (to be discussed shortly) has also demonstrated that conversational distance affects credibility.

In an age of mass-media dominated political campaigns, most of us need not be reminded of the impact of physical appearance on perceptions of credibility. Political candidates pay a great deal of attention to physical appearance in an attempt to bolster their image and credibility. Even the news broadcasters who report on the candidates often take care that their physical appearance cues enhance their audience image as well as their audience share.

Several physical appearance factors are at work here. One is body type. Perhaps due to our culture's preference for thin females and muscular males, female ectomorphs and male mesomorphs are rated as most sociable (Toomb & Divers, 1972). Some studies on hair length (Andersen, Jensen, & King, 1972; Peterson & Curran, 1976) have found that short-haired men are rated more competent, dynamic, intelligent, masculine, mature, wise, and attractive than long-haired men.

Although there is little systematic and empirical evidence concerning effects of clothing on credibility, it is reasonable to believe that clothes have an impact. For example, in legal settings, astute trial lawyers have their clients dress so as to convey sincerity, believability, and innocence. Many people believe that dressing well and appropriately can make a difference in their status and credibility in an organization. Nowhere has this view been more effectively popularized than in John Molloy's *Dress for Success* books. Molloy (1975, 1977, 1988) offered very specific advice about the kind of cloth-

Gestures are important in enhancing a speaker's credibility.

ing choices that will work best in business settings. Unfortunately, there are two important drawbacks to Molloy's work. First, Molloy stated that his advice was based on research he and his associates conducted. However, his research methods, statistical analysis, and results are not well documented, so it is not possible to verify his advice. Second, his early advice was overly restrictive. In fairness, Molloy himself began to recognize the value of developing a wider range of clothing styles, to adapt better to particular audiences. His recent advice is that matching one's audience in dress style may be preferable to emphasizing power and competence (see Box 13-4).

Finally, chronemic code elements can potentially affect perceptions of credibility. One study (Baxter & Ward, 1975) asked secretaries what their impressions would be if someone arrived 15 minutes early, 15 minutes late, or on time for an appointment. Late arrivers were regarded as highly dynamic but low on competence, composure, and sociability. Prompt arrivers were considered the most competent, composed, and sociable but not very dynamic. Early arrivers were rated low on dynamism and only moderate on other dimensions. While these secretaries' views may not be representative of the whole population, the results do suggest that promptness overall has the best outcome for credibility.

As this review shows, a large number of cues from the vocalic, kinesic, proxemic, physical appearance, and chronemic codes can be used to enhance credibility and related impressions. In an attempt to make sense of the voluminous findings, Burgoon et al.

BOX 13-4

THE NEW DRESS CODE FOR SUCCESS

. . . Whereas [Molloy] championed the all-purpose power uniform in 1975, now he's advocating different suits for different folks.

"In the first book, I said *'this* is the right tie' and *'this* is the right suit,' " Molloy says. "Now the world is a little more sophisticated."

In the new version, Molloy gets very specific indeed. For instance, he advises the businessman traveling to Jacksonville, Florida, to wear a "midrange blue or gray suit with a blue shirt and striped tie"; a professional destined for St. Paul would do better in a dark-brown pinstripe.

For the salesman whose appointment is with a hip architect, Molloy's advice is to dress cleverly—in three shades of blue, for instance. If the client is a military man, the seller should avoid an off-putting gray suit and Ivy League tie.

This approach worked for Phil Dusenberry, chairman and chief creative officer of the New York advertising agency BBDO. When pitching the Apple computer account . . . , Dusenberry says his team "left our six-piece suits at home and dressed down—in sports jackets—for the presentation."

The folks at Apple wear jeans and open-collar shirts, "and we didn't want to come off as slick New Yorkers," Dusenberry says. It worked. BBDO landed the account.

Source: Sporkin, 1988, p. D2.

(1990) proposed that many specific nonverbal credibility cues can be grouped into substrategies related to *dominance or potency, pleasantness, immediacy*, and *arousal*. However, it should be evident that these substrategies do not affect different dimensions of credibility equally. For example, competence is conveyed through greater vocal and facial pleasantness and kinesic dominance through facial expressiveness. Character judgments are enhanced through the same cues plus kinesic-proxemic immediacy. Additionally, other nonverbal cues not mentioned above may have the potential to foster credibility, prestige, and apparent status. For example, as the discussion of status and dominance cues in Chapter 11 suggests, artifacts might be used for these purposes.

Expectancy Violations Theory

A common theme running through popular advice on communication and explicitly stated in Goffman's self-presentation theory is that to be a successful communicator requires conforming to social norms. Violators are supposedly regarded as deviant and evaluated negatively. Although this principle may seem intuitively appealing, evidence is coming to light that there may be occasions when nonverbal violations of expectations are a better strategy than conformity for enhancing credibility and attraction.

The genesis for this challenge to the claim that successful performances require conforming to norms and expectations was Burgoon and colleagues' initial forays into the realm of proxemic behavior (Burgoon, 1978b, 1983; Burgoon & Aho, 1982; Burgoon & Jones, 1976; Burgoon, Stacks, & Burch, 1982; Burgoon, Stacks, & Woodall, 1979). Their reviews of the literature turned up an apparent contradiction: people typically respond negatively to invasions of personal space but often respond positively to close interaction distances. Trying to make sense of this pattern led to the development of what was first called *nonverbal expectancy violations theory* and later *expectancy violations theory* (EVT). Over the past 15 years, EVT has been expanded to apply to numerous nonverbal behaviors and to interaction processes as well as outcomes. Here we look at EVT in terms of credibility and attraction. (Chapter 12 considers interaction patterns and Chapter 14 social influence.) The model is shown in Figure 13-1.

Four key elements in EVT are *expectancies, expectancy violations, communicator valence,* and *violation valence.* These combine to determine whether it is more advisable to adhere to norms and expectations (as suggested by self-presentation theory) or to violate them.

EVT begins with the assumption that people hold *expectancies*—enduring patterns of anticipated nonverbal (and verbal) behavior—about each other's communication (Burgoon & Walther, 1990; Olson, Roese, & Zanna, in press). These expectations are grounded largely in social norms but also take into account knowledge of another person's unique behavioral patterns. For example, men are expected to interact at farther distances than women, but you may know that a male friend of yours is even more distant than most. A combination of *communicator, relationship,* and *context* factors determine the expectancies. Features of communicators such as gender, age, and personality; features of relationships such as familiarity, cultural similarity, status, and liking; and

FIGURE 13-1
Expectancy violations theory.

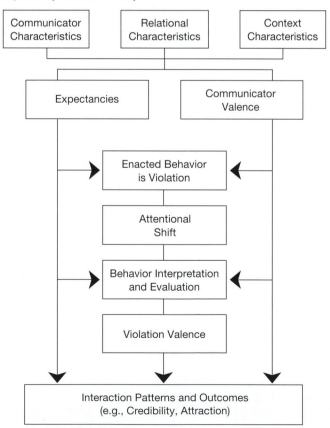

features of contexts such as physical setting, formality of the interaction, and conversational topic—all these feed into what is expected for a given interchange.

Expectations have both a *predictive* and a *prescriptive* component. They are predictive in the sense of reflecting what behavior is most typical; when we nod hello to people, we expect them to nod back. Expectations are prescriptive—or evaluative—in the sense of reflecting what is considered appropriate; we expect (prescribe) that people will not stare at us in public. Thus expectations represent a range of customary and preferred behavior. They may be specific to a culture, subculture, relationship, or situation; for example, Greeks expect interactions with their ingroup to be warm, cooperative, and trustworthy but expect interactions with outgroups to be hostile, competitive, and deceitful (Broome, 1990). Expectations will also vary in how wide or narrow the range of acceptable behavior is and how tentatively or certainly an expectancy is held. Still, EVT assumes that all communicative situations invoke expectancies.

When a communicator's behaviors fall within the expected range, they are said to *confirm* expectancies. When behaviors fall outside that range, they are called *expectancy violations, deviations,* or *disconfirmations.* Although EVT applies to situations in which people do what is expected, its main focus is on what happens when expectations are violated. Like other novel or vivid acts, violations are thought to draw a receiver's attention away from what is being said to the violation itself and to the person committing it. This shift of attention is thought to be part of an innate orientation response that may or may not be accompanied by heightened physiological arousal (Le Poire & Burgoon, 1994b, 1994c).

Heightened attention to the characteristics of the violator and the meaning of the violation brings into play another key factor: communicator reward valence, or more simply *communicator valence.* EVT assumes that we implicitly evaluate all communicators on a positive to negative continuum according to their apparent "reward value" for us. Someone who is physically attractive, has a great sense of humor, has high status, or gives us positive feedback, for instance, should be more positively regarded than someone who is physically repulsive, lacks a sense of humor, is of lower status, or gives us negative feedback. EVT posits that we consider the whole array of communicators' characteristics and arrive at a net assessment of their valence at a given point in time. Of course, positively valenced communicators should achieve more favorable impressions just by virtue of these characteristics. But their valence should also affect how we respond to any violations they commit.

Specifically, communicator valence may affect how we arrive at *violation valence.* According to EVT, when a communicator commits a violation, receivers attempt to make sense of it through a process of *interpretation* and *evaluation.* They try to determine its meaning, if any, and whether or not they like it. Suppose, for example, that while talking, an acquaintance unexpectedly moves very close to you. You might interpret the act as a relational message: interest or intimacy on the one hand, or dominance or aggression on the other. If the violation has multiple or ambiguous meanings (as this example does), EVT predicts that communicator valence will influence which meaning is selected: more favorable meanings will be attributed to positively valenced communicators than to negatively valenced communicators. In our example, if your acquaintance is someone you dislike, you might interpret closeness as a threat; if the acquaintance is someone you like, you might interpret it as a show of affiliation.

When behaviors have unambiguous meanings (e.g., averted gaze has mostly negative connotations), the interpretation may be the same for both kinds of communicators, but communicator valence can still make a difference in how the violation is evaluated. A move closer, for example, could be considered desirable or undesirable, depending on who commits it. You would probably welcome it from a person you regard positively but find it undesirable from a person you regard negatively. Some kinds of acts, such as increased attentiveness, might be welcome from both positively and negatively regarded communicators. In short, communicator valence doesn't guarantee what interpretations and evaluations are assigned to nonverbal violations, but it can influence both parts of the appraisal process.

The ultimate evaluation of a violation is whether it is *positive* or *negative*—and this in turn determines whether a violation helps or harms the communicator's image. EVT predicts that, relative to conformity, positive violations will enhance credibility, power, and attraction, and negative violations will reduce credibility, power, and attraction. Thus EVT proposes that some kinds of violations not only can have positive consequences but can also earn a better impression than doing what is normative or expected. This is contrary to the widespread claim that violations are necessarily negative and harmful to self-presentation (see, e.g., Olson et al., in press).

The idea that violations can have positive consequences may seem intuitively appealing, but just how practical and far-ranging is it? So far, research suggests that it applies in a variety of contexts and for a variety of behaviors; whether or not a violation is successful depends on what meanings are associated with it and who is committing it. One experiment is illustrative. Burgoon et al. (1982) examined attraction and credibility ratings of positively and negatively valenced confederates who violated or conformed to proxemic norms. In the context of a mock murder trial, subjects interacted with two confederates, one of whom presented the case for the prosecution and the other the case for the defense. Subjects were to decide at the end of the session which position they favored. During the discussion, one confederate moved closer or farther away, while the other remained stationary. In the "positive valence" conditions, both confederates were made to appear as physically attractive as possible, were introduced as having previous jury experience and a prestigious major, and expressed interest in the task. In the "negative valence" conditions, both were made to appear unattractive, claimed to have no jury experience, had an undisclosed major, and were unenthusiastic about the task. Consistent with EVT, positively valenced confederates were seen as more credible and attractive when they violated norms, especially when they moved farther away, as compared with maintaining the initial distance and as compared with the other confederate. Thus violations were a good strategy both for creating a positive impression and for looking better than the adversary. By contrast, the largest effect of violations by negatively valenced confederates was to confer greater credibility on the opponent—in other words, the contrast effect benefited the other person. Negatively valenced confederates were better off conforming to the expected distance.

Numerous other studies have tested effects of proxemic and other nonverbal violations, including violations related to gaze, touch, posture, immediacy, and involvement (Burgoon, 1983, 1991, 1993; Burgoon et al., 1986; Burgoon & Dillman, 1995; Burgoon & Hale, 1988; Burgoon & Le Poire, 1993; Burgoon, Le Poire, & Rosenthal, 1995; Burgoon, Manusov, Mineo, & Hale, 1985; Burgoon, Newton, Walther, & Baesler, 1989; Burgoon & Walther, 1990; Burgoon, Walther, & Baesler, 1992; Hale & Burgoon, 1984; Le Poire & Burgoon, 1994b). So far, the following conclusions seem warranted (with the caveat that they may apply only to western cultures, because that is where the tests have been conducted; see Burgoon, 1992a for a cross-cultural analysis):

1 *Proxemic violations improve impressions of positively valenced communicators but undermine impressions of negatively valenced communicators.* Probably, this is because numerous meanings are associated with close and far conversational distance, so that the valence of the communicator makes a big difference in how they are interpreted. Also, proximity, like other immediacy cues, has a strong potential for arousal. People may find this arousal pleasurable when it is associated with someone they like but unpleasant when it is associated with someone they dislike. However, a far distance coupled with either very tense or very relaxed posture is evaluated negatively; thus a positive violation can be transformed into a negative violation with the addition of other nonverbal cues.

2 *An unexpectedly high degree of gaze improves impressions and averted gaze harms impressions, regardless of communicator valence.* The reason is that maintaining gaze connotes interest, attention, friendliness, and composure, while averting gaze connotes lack of interest, nonreceptivity, noncomposure, and possibly disdain. In other words, in the United States and similar cultures, the multiple meanings associated with eye contact are largely positive, while the multiple meanings associated with avoidance of eye contact are largely negative; people prefer more gaze, regardless of who is gazing. This pattern is unlikely to hold true in cultures where averting the eyes is a sign of respect and where gazing too long or too directly is seen as overly forward and personal.

3 *Nonintimate brief touches, especially by positively valenced communicators, are positive violations that promote more favorable impressions.* Brief touches such as a handshake or a touch on the arm carry many favorable relational messages and are evaluated favorably. More intimate and informal touches, such as a touch on the face or an arm around the waist, are best when used by attractive, high-status, or female communicators.

4 *Violations that increase overall conversational involvement have positive effects, regardless of communicator valence, while violations that decrease involvement have negative effects.* Involvement, which is made up of numerous nonverbal cues, is fairly unambiguous and is desired in most conversational settings. High involvement is flattering to the recipient and carries such favorable relational meanings as receptivity, similarity, liking, composure, and dominance. It typically earns a communicator high marks for competence, character, composure, sociability, extroversion, social attractiveness, and task attractiveness. Significantly decreased involvement has the opposite effect, producing negative interpretations and reducing credibility and attraction.

5 *Immediacy violations, if extreme, may have negative effects regardless of communicator valence.* Nonimmediacy, like averted gaze, carries negative connotations, and the presence of multiple behaviors all conveying the same meaning reduces ambiguity. Extremely high immediacy, like proximity, may be highly arousing and disturbing except in intimate relationships. What counts as too much or too little immediacy will differ from culture to culture.

Other kinds of violations have yet to be studied, but it seems reasonable to predict that many violations of expectations about appearance, chronemics, and vocalics may foster favorable impressions. As faculty members, we have found ourselves responding positively when a student whom we are accustomed to seeing in casual attire arrives to class dressed formally, as if for a job interview. We tend to see the student in a new light, as more competent and poised than we had thought. The reverse can also be true. A corporate executive who dresses casually and colorfully in the midst of a sea of blue and gray suits may signal independence and power. This is akin to the principle of "idiosyncracy credit" found in the literature on small groups: people in positions of power have more latitude to deviate from the norms and may actually earn more latitude to do so by behaving differently from everyone else.

At the same time, behaviors that produce poor impressions may be better understood if we consider them as negative violations. Slow, halting speech may be a negative violation of the expectation that delivery will be fluent and rhythmic. In some cultures, excessive emotionality may violate the expectation that people withhold strong emotions in public. These examples suggest the potential value of viewing effects of many nonverbal behaviors through the lens of EVT.

FACTORS INFLUENCING THE SUCCESS OF IMPRESSION MANAGEMENT

The three major theoretical perspectives—self-presentation theory, impression management theory, and EVT—presented in this chapter have identified numerous principles and strategies that could be used to maximize favorable impressions. In practice, however, there are several limiting factors.

Individual Differences

One class of limiting factors is *individual differences.* The most important factors include social skills, or competence as a communicator, discussed in Chapter 1. (See Box 13-5 for an example.) An extensive body of research on social skills has shown that people who are better at encoding nonverbal messages and controlling their own nonverbal communication are more successful in fostering desired impressions (Friedman et al., 1988; Gallagher, 1992; Riggio, 1992; Riggio & Friedman, 1986; Riggio, Widaman, Tucker, & Salinas, 1991). Such people are typically more expressive and extroverted, and their communication style is more animated, expansive, dynamic, and coordinated; this makes them more likable and socially attractive. They also have a demeanor that inspires trust—an effect that has been called the *honest demeanor bias* (Zuckerman, Defrank, Hall, Larrance, & Rosenthal, 1979).

A related individual difference is self-monitoring. Self-monitors are sensitive to their self-presentation because they are concerned about the appropriateness of their social behavior (Snyder, 1974, 1979). They are more attentive to their own nonverbal and verbal communication, are better at expressing emotional states through the face and voice, and encode more skillfully to create favorable impressions (Giles & Street, 1985; Riggio,

BOX 13-5

THE NONVERBALLY SKILLFUL JOB APPLICANT

How do social skills translate into nonverbal behaviors? A study addressing this question looked at the nonverbal cues a job applicant could use to bolster an interviewer's perceptions of social skill and motivation, as well as the relationship between these cues and applicants' views of their own social skill and motivation (Gifford, Ng, & Wilkinson, 1985). Judgments being drawn about the applicants were similar to judgments of credibility, since perceptions of social skill and credibility are similar.

Results indicated that three nonverbal cues led to high perceptions of social skill by interviewers: gesturing during the interview for a brief amount of time, talking an average of 6.3 minutes when answering questions, and being dressed moderately formally. The cues were also strongly correlated with the applicants' own perceptions of their social skill, suggesting that self-confidence plays a role in these kinds of situations.

For the motivation judgments, interviewers and applicants differed on what nonverbal cues they relied on: interviewers relied on how much time the applicant spent talking, rate of gesturing, and smiling; applicants relied on body posture, dress, and gender. It is worthwhile for an applicant to know that interviewers infer motivation from talkativeness and friendliness. Effective use of these cues may be the most useful in creating a favorable impression and possibly obtaining an offer.

1992; Riggio & Friedman, 1986). Men seem to do this through greater speaking fluency, more gestures, and more body movement, while women do it primarily through facial expressiveness. But self-monitoring doesn't always lead to success. One study of courtship behavior found that highly self-monitoring men were seen as engaging and dominant, but highly self-monitoring women were seen as phony or arrogant, probably because they used too many flirtatious behaviors and gestures (Simpson et al., 1993). Anecdotally, we have all met people who make a great number of social mistakes and faux pas and others who are very smooth in social situations. Clearly, skill in projecting the right demeanor is the key.

Given that self-monitoring may affect skill in using nonverbal cues, we might wonder whether communicators know what kinds of impressions they are making. One study that addressed this question (DePaulo, Kenny, Hoover, Webb, & Oliver, 1987) found that participants in an interaction did know what impressions they were conveying, how those impressions changed over time and with different partners, and how their competence was perceived. Clearly, then, not only are communicators able to manage nonverbal cues to create impressions, but they are often aware of the impression they are creating.

At the same time, there are a number of individual constraints on what kinds of impressions are possible (DePaulo, 1991). Among these are individual physical characteristics and abilities. Short, stocky, baby-faced people and people with high-pitched voices may have difficulty creating a commanding presence; some facial physiognomies do not lend themselves to expressivity; slow, nonfluent speakers may be unable to speed up or omit hesitations. There are also automatic behaviors that are not easily controlled or feigned. Children may be unable to mask negative emotional states; competitors in a game may be unable to hide their elation at winning. Other constraints include individual differences in motivation to monitor and control behavior. Some of these differences are a function of maturation and experience. As children age, their knowledge of impression management grows, and they become more successful at concealing undesirable feelings and faking desirable expressions (see DePaulo, 1991, for a review of this research).

A second class of constraints on impression management includes *situational* and *cultural factors.* Cultural norms and expectations will naturally influence what kinds of public "performances" are considered acceptable and desirable. Additionally, as noted in Chapter 7, some situations are more suitable than others for impression management strategies and tactics. Impression management is appropriate in formal or goal-oriented situations, but it may be less appropriate in familiar, commonplace situations. To put it another way, going to a bank to talk to an officer about a loan is certainly a situation that calls for impression management; going to a local 7-Eleven for a Thirstbuster is not. Further work needs to be done to link situational analyses with impression management theory so that we can better specify which nonverbal strategies are most successful under different circumstances.

SUMMARY

Impression management addresses the ways in which senders control their nonverbal presentations to create desired images. Three major theories related to this communication function are (1) self-presentation theory, which advances a dramaturgic view of people's communication in public; (2) impression management theory, which incorporates strategies and tactics for creating successful impressions of attraction, likability, credibility, and prestige; and (3) expectancy violations theory, which focuses expressly on the effects of conforming or not conforming to expected nonverbal behavior patterns. All these theories offer principles for successful and failed performances, and extensive research has tested these various principles. Additionally, many other individual and situational factors such as social skills and cultural or situational norms have been analyzed that may place constraints on successful impression management. Many of the principles identified here can also be enlisted to accomplish social influence, discussed next.

SUGGESTED READINGS

Burgoon, J. K., & Hale, J. L. (1988). Nonverbal expectancy violations theory: Model elaboration and application to immediacy behaviors. *Communication Monographs 55,* 58–79.

DePaulo, B. M. (1991). Nonverbal behavior and self-presentation: A developmental perspective. In R. S. Feldman & B. Rimé (Eds.), *Fundamentals of nonverbal behavior* (pp. 351–397). Cambridge: Cambridge University Press.

Goffman, E. (1959). *The presentation of self in everyday life.* Garden City, NY: Doubleday.

Goffman, E. (1974). *Frame analysis.* New York: Harper & Row.

Kleinke, C. L. (1975). *First impressions: The psychology of encountering others.* Englewood Cliffs, NJ: Prentice-Hall.

O'Hair, D., Friedrich, G. W. Wiemann, J. M. & Weimann, M. O. (1995). *Competent communication.* New York: St. Martins.

Schlenker, B. R. (1980). *Impression management: The self-concept, social identity, and interpersonal relations.* Monterey, CA: Brooks/Cole.

Tedeschi, J. T., & Norman, N. (1985). Social power, self-presentation, and the self. In B. R. Schlenker (Ed.), *The self and social life* (pp. 293–322). New York: McGraw-Hill.

14

INFLUENCING OTHERS

All of us, apparently, are constantly trying to influence the people around us by means of sounds and movements we are unconscious of making. Correspondingly, all of us make some unconscious use of the cues presented to us by the people around us.

J. V. McConnell, L. Cutler, & B. McNeil

You can persuade a man only insofar as you can talk his language by speech, gesture, tonality, order, image, idea, identifying your way with his.

Kenneth Burke

In this chapter, we consider how nonverbal communication is used to influence others. Chapters 11, 12, and 13 examine how nonverbal cues are used to manage relationships, conversations, and impressions. Now we explore how people actively select their nonverbal communication to modify what others think and do.

Social influence has interested students of human communication for millennia. Aristotle was one of the earliest to write about how humans influence one another. Our own century has witnessed great interest in social influence reflected in the large amount of time, effort, and resources devoted to its study (Insko, 1967; Miller & Burgoon, 1978; Roloff & Miller, 1980). A good deal of this interest has been stimulated by the often notorious success of current and past attempts at social influence:

• *Item:* During World War II, an unimpressive man of diminutive stature was able to move the German populace to commit atrocities so horrible that many Germans later denied knowledge of or responsibility for them. The man who wielded such enormous influence—Adolf Hitler.

- *Item:* During the wars in Korea and Vietnam, hard-nosed, well-trained military men who became prisoners of war were coerced into renouncing their country and espousing the philosophical tenets of a foreign government. These changes in behavior and attitude were not a charade put on for the benefit of their captors. Prisoners, once released, often retained the views acquired during brainwashing.
- *Item:* In the past two decades, several religious cults have arisen in the United States. Followers of such leaders as the Reverend Sun Myung Moon and the Bhagwan Maharishi live in abject poverty while raising millions of dollars for their leaders through menial jobs. Psychological and social changes brought about in cult members are so striking that their relatives have hired agents to kidnap and "deprogram" them.
- *Item:* David Koresh, a self-proclaimed prophet of God, convinced a group of average Americans to join him in a compound in Waco, Texas. There he controlled every aspect of their psychological, social, and physical lives and convinced them that they were being persecuted by the government. This led to a gunfight with federal law enforcement personnel. Later, he ordered his followers to commit mass suicide by torching their compound rather than be captured. They complied and died.

In all these cases, certain psychological and physiological factors, as well as verbal strategies, enabled people to wield great power and make mass conversions. But a significant role was also played by the nonverbal strategies and tactics that these manipulators used to advance and reinforce their control. It is to such nonverbal strategies and tactics that this chapter is devoted.

THE NATURE OF SOCIAL INFLUENCE

Definition

Social influence is defined as one person's actions causing changes in another's thoughts and behaviors that would not have occurred in the absence of the actor's behaviors, or maintaining the target's way of thinking and behaving in the face of influence attempts from another source. We are most interested in the actor's communication behaviors and how those either change or reinforce a target's way of thinking and behaving.

Objectives

This definition makes several important assumptions. First, social influence is motivated behavior. The actor desires something from the target that would not occur if the communication did not take place. Three motivations are particularly important. (1) *Instrumental objectives* are the specific changes or lack of changes desired by the communicator; (2) *Interpersonal objectives* concern the establishment and maintenance of a particular interpersonal relationship; and (3) *Identity objectives* relate to the image projected by the influencer, such as credibility, dominance, expertise, and composure. These three motives are present in all attempts at social influence, but each fluctuates in importance. At times the three motivations compete with one another; at other times they complement one another; at still other times they are irrelevant to one another. An influ-

Jesse Jackson's gestures, facial expression, and posture, along with the surrounding artifacts, all contribute to the effectiveness of his persuasive messages.

encer's nonverbal and verbal communication is a product of how he or she reconciles the three motives (Clark, 1984; Clark & Delia, 1979; O'Keefe & Delia, 1982).

Strategic Behavior and Selection of Strategies

Another important assumption is that communication designed to influence is strategic: it is intentionally and purposely encoded (Edinger & Patterson, 1983; Patterson, 1983). The influencer (1) appraises the situation in which the influence attempt will occur, assessing important roles, norms, motives, and characteristics of the target; (2) develops a communication plan to achieve the desired outcome; (3) considers a diverse, differentiated repertoire of messages; (4) chooses a particular message and forgoes others; (5) monitors the success of this message; and (6) selects subsequent messages from the repertoire in response to the target's reactions and consistent with the situational appraisal and communication plan. Seibold, Cantrill, and Meyers (1994) labeled this the *strategic choice model* of social influence.

Although social influence is a deliberate process, not every move is consciously premeditated or enacted. Communicators tend to be more cognizant of their general goals and strategies than their specific ways of achieving them. Hence routinely enacted influence patterns may be intentional but occur at a low level of awareness.

Our approach to social influence also assumes that characteristics of communicators and situations affect the selection and success of influence messages. Expectancy violations theory (EVT), discussed in Chapters 12 and 13, illustrates how *communicator reward valence* frequently determines the success of nonverbal communication. The authority, dominance, status, and expertise of a source are likely to determine whether the target will comply with nonverbal influence messages, and the management of these images depends on the careful, deliberate display of nonverbal cues. Along with a source's image, the relationship between influencer and target can affect selection and consequences. Frequently, nonverbal cues during influence messages are designed to signal attraction, establish a relationship, indicate the current nature of the relationship (e.g., touching someone when asking for his or her help), or engender obligations to aid the partner.

Persuasibility of Targets

To this point, we have focused on the communicator who is attempting social influence; however, keep in mind that social influence is a two-way process. The target also enters the influence situation with instrumental, interpersonal, and identity motivations that must be reconciled in the target's decision to change or maintain behavior in response to influence messages (O'Keefe & Delia, 1982). Forsyth (1987) noted that the outcome of an attempt at social influence rests ultimately with the target, and sometimes the target's act of compliance or noncompliance is such an attempt in its own right.

Unfortunately, nonverbal behavior of targets has received scant attention. Petty, Wells, Heesacker, Brock, and Cacioppo (1983) found that recipients' posture affected their persuasibility. In two separate experiments, targets who reclined on a padded table were persuaded while receiving the persuasive message more than targets who stood. Reclining may present fewer distractions than standing, so reclining targets could pay closer attention to a message and respond favorably to a strong appeal. Standing also may increase targets' agitation and aggressiveness and perhaps heighten their sense of dominance in the situation, making them resist attempted influence.

Compresence

Although targets may show some natural resistance to attempts at influence, there is reason to believe that a competing predisposition toward being influenced is also operative. Researchers have uncovered a phenomenon called *compresence:* the mere presence of another person is arousing and can alter our behavior (Borden, 1980; Cottrell, 1972; Geen, 1980; Sanders, 1981; Zajonc, 1965, 1980). We are highly attentive to the presence of others and perform differently on tasks when spectators, coactors, or audiences are present, as compared with when we are alone. Because the mere presence of someone else is socially meaningful (Horn, 1974; Zajonc, 1980), our heightened awareness and orientation toward others may predispose us to being receptive to stimuli from them and ultimately to being influenced by them. One reason for this attentiveness to other humans is that the social actions of another person are less regular, systematic, and predictable than the actions of physical stimuli. Thus some measure of alertness is required when another person is present, and this sensitivity prepares a communicator to respond to the other's actions. This response—alertness—may in fact have given rise to our social norm of attention. Ignoring another person in our vicinity is considered socially inappropriate and can cause that person to withdraw, speak less, and rate us unfavorably (Geller, Goodstein, Silver, & Sternberg, 1974). The most important implication of compresence is that actor and target are attuned to each other's presence, and this may open up an opportunity for mutual influence.

NONVERBAL STRATEGIES OF SOCIAL INFLUENCE

In this section, we examine in detail how nonverbal cues are selected to exert social influence. We will focus on nonverbal strategies and tactics used to (1) project an image of authority, power, and credibility; (2) signal intimacy; (3) manipulate attractiveness; (4) signal interpersonal expectations; (5) evoke matching and compensation; (6) violate expectations so as to distract targets; (7) teach; and (8) reinforce, reward, and punish another person's behaviors.

Strategies That Project Power and Credibility

Perhaps the most pervasive strategies for influencing the thoughts, behaviors, and communication of others are those that rely on establishing an image of authority, expertise, or power. As discussed in Chapter 13, a major function of communication is to project a favorable image. Here self-presentation is not the end goal but is rather a means to the end of influencing others. Thus nonverbal patterns that foster an impression of power and credibility not only increase others' attraction to us, liking for us, and evaluations of us; they may also make others more receptive or susceptible to our influence. In analyzing how history's more notorious manipulators have come to power, one must give partial credit to their use of nonverbal messages of authority, dominance, power, or credibility.

Before discussing nonverbal cues signaling power, it is useful to consider what power is. *Power* is a relationally determined potential to influence another person that rests on the relevance of a communicator's resources and actions to the target. As relevance increases, the likelihood of influence increases (Tedeschi & Bonoma, 1972). For instance, because managers can determine raises and promotions, they are more powerful and their messages are more influential—but only for staff members who value raises and promotions. Their attempts at influence may be less powerful with those who don't value raises or promotions.

Power takes five forms: *reward power* (the ability to provide attractive rewards), *coercive power* (providing punishments), *expertise power* (based on knowledge of influencer relative to knowledge of target), *legitimate power* (authority conferred by a group or organization, to a role like teacher or president), and *referent power* (derived from target's attraction toward and desire to be similar to the influencer, e.g., charisma).

Authority, Expertise, Dominance, and Status   Among the most immediate and potent cues of authority and power are visible symbols such as uniforms, personal artifacts, and environmental trappings. Their potency resides partly in serving as an ever-present reminder of status during the course of an encounter and partly in the meanings we have come to associate with them.

Uniforms denote status and control of resources. They signal the ability to reward and bestow favors or to punish and take away valued commodities. Because the head-waiter in a restaurant controls whether we have a table by the window or by the kitchen, we become deferent and ingratiating. Because judges and police officers have the potential to levy severe penalties, we often become tense in their presence, acting as if we had just been caught with our hand in the cookie jar. Their clothing cues these responses, because we are conditioned to react to symbols of authority as clear markers of another's legitimate power and control.

Research demonstrates just how conditioned we are. In a landmark series of studies, Stanley Milgram explored how far people would go in obeying authority figures. His interest was prompted by trying to understand what mentality might lead people to commit the kinds of inhuman, heinous acts that the Germans committed under Hitler. Milgram (1963, 1974) devised an experiment in which one subject, assigned to the role of "teacher," was asked to administer increasingly intense electric shocks to another subject, given the role of "learner," whenever the learner gave wrong answers. In actuality, the learner was a confederate who did not really receive any shocks. Amazingly, the majority (65 percent) of teacher subjects continued to deliver shocks far past a supposedly dangerous level as long as the uniformed experimenter told them to do so—despite sometimes hearing the learner groan and plead for the shocks to stop before eventually lapsing into silence, and despite being told that the learner had a heart condition. Although Milgram was not directly testing the effects of clothing or artifacts, it is clear that the white lab coat and the trappings of the Yale University research laboratory where the experiments took place contributed to the subjects' blind obedience to these outrageous requests and to their willingness to disavow responsibility for their actions.

More direct evidence of the role of uniforms comes from a series of clever field experiments by Bickman (1971a, 1974a, 1974b). He dressed male accomplices in civilian clothes (sport coat and tie), a milkman's uniform (white shirt and pants carrying a basket with empty milk bottles), or a nondescript guard's uniform (consisting of a jacket and pants similar to a police uniform but with a different badge and insignia and no gun). The accomplice then approached passersby on a Brooklyn street and made one of three requests to see if uniforms would affect people's compliance. First, people were asked to pick up a small paper bag lying on the ground. If a person refused, the accomplice repeated the request and gave as justification that he had a bad back. In the second request, the accomplice pointed to a person standing by a parked car and said, "This fellow is overparked at the meter but doesn't have any change. Give him a dime!" If the subject didn't comply, the accomplice said he didn't have any change himself. In the third request, he told people standing at a bus stop that the "Bus Stop—No Standing" sign meant they couldn't stand there and had to move to the other side of the sign. If they refused to move, he told them it was a new law and the bus would not stop where they were standing. With all three requests, people were far more willing to comply when the request came from the uniformed guard than from the civilian or the milkman: 36 percent obeyed the guard, 20 percent obeyed the civilian, and 14 percent obeyed the milkman. In a later study that again asked pedestrians to give a dime for an expired parking meter, 83 percent obeyed when the person making the request was dressed as a guard, while only 46 percent obeyed when he was dressed as a civilian or a milkman, regardless of whether or not the requester watched to see that the respondent obeyed.

In another set of experiments, Bickman (1971b, 1974a) explored whether the social status implied by attire and personal possessions would affect people's honesty in complying with a request. He went to airport and train terminals and dressed his three male and three female accomplices in high-status clothing (suits and ties for men, dresses and a dress coat for women) or low-status clothing (working clothes and a lunch pail for men; inexpensive, unkempt skirts and blouses for women). The accomplices first placed a dime in an obvious place in a phone booth, waited for the next user of the phone to exit, and then approached, saying, "Excuse me, I think I might have left a dime in this phone booth a few minutes ago. Did you find it?" Regardless of the subject's age, race, sex, or status, far more people returned the money when the request came from a high-status person (77 percent complied) than from a low-status person (38 percent complied).

Follow-up research using questionnaires (Bickman, 1974a) showed that most people believed that they would not be influenced by a person's dress when responding to a trivial request. That is, they claimed they would not respond to illegitimate requests just because the person was wearing authoritative clothing.

These combined results reveal that despite what people claim they would do, most people are highly susceptible to influence when it is accompanied by clothing and artifacts as symbols of authority and status. The potency of such nonverbal cues is especially apparent when compared with their absence. The striking contrast effect is evident in Alexander Solzhenitsyn's chilling account of the ruthless treatment given Soviet prisoners en route to prison camps during the 1940s:

> "On your knees!" "Strip!" In these statutory orders of the convoy lay the basic power one could not argue with. After all, a naked person loses his self-assurance. He cannot straighten up proudly and speak as an equal to people who are still clothed. . . . Naked prisoners approach, carrying their possessions and the clothes they've taken off. A mass of armed soldiers surrounds them. It doesn't look as though they are going to be led to a prisoner transport but as though they are going to be shot immediately or put to death in a gas chamber—and in that mood a person ceases to concern himself with his possessions. The convoy does everything with intentional brusqueness, rudely, sharply, not speaking one word in an ordinary human voice. After all, the purpose is to terrify and dishearten. (Solzhenitsyn, 1973, p. 570)

The latter part of this excerpt highlights another nonverbal tactic for conveying power and authority—a harsh, dictatorial vocal tone. Although the "voice of authority" has not been studied directly, it appears that "confident" voices evoke more compliance from others. A confident voice has greater energy and volume, faster tempo, fewer and shorter pauses, higher and more varied pitch, more expressiveness, and greater fluency, and is perceived as more businesslike, professional, and impersonal (Scherer et al., 1973). Such vocal patterns have proved to be persuasive in public and interpersonal contexts. Others appear in Box 14-1.

BOX 14-1

APPLICATIONS: DO VOICES PERSUADE?

Do voices persuade? The answer is a resounding yes. Mehrabian and Williams (1969) identified four vocal cues that are both encoded and decoded as persuasive: louder amplitude, more intonation, greater fluency, and faster tempo. Studies of legal presentations and job interviews confirm the beneficial effects of loudness and fluency. They reveal that louder, more fluent voices communicate confidence, are more persuasive, and earn more favorable decisions (Erickson, Lind, Johnson, & O'Barr, 1978; Hollandsworth et al., 1979; Kimble & Seidel, 1991). Research specifically on nonfluencies (sentence corrections, slips of the tongue, repetitions, vocalized pauses, and stutters) indicates that nonfluent speech results in lower ratings of a speaker's competence (McCroskey & Mehrley, 1969; Miller & Hewgill, 1964; Sereno & Hawkins, 1967) and that this reduction in credibility often but not always translates into being less persuasive. In studies of public speaking, nonfluent speakers produced less attitude change and were rated as less persuasive than fluent speakers (Burgoon, Birk,

& Pfau, 1990; McCroskey & Mehrley, 1969), but Giesen (1973) and Sereno and Hawkins (1967) failed to find any differences.

Finally, faster tempos produce higher assessments of the speaker's expertise and competence and can be more persuasive (Buller & Aune, 1988, 1992; Buller & Burgoon, 1986; Buller, Le Poire, Aune, & Eloy, 1992; Miller et al., 1976; see Gundersen & Hopper, 1976, and Woodall & Burgoon, 1983, for exceptions). There is an upper limit to tempo (around 375 syllables per minute), after which judgments of competence plateau or even decrease (Buller & Aune, 1992), which may explain why Apple et al. (1979) found a moderately rapid tempo to be most persuasive. However, when influence is based on a speaker's character or social attractiveness, matching the speaker's tempo to the normal speaking tempo of the listener may improve persuasion. Similar tempos enhance perceptions of the speaker's immediacy, intimacy, and social attractiveness (Buller & Aune, 1988, 1992; Street, 1984; Street & Brady, 1982).

Expertise or competence can be communicated by physical appearance. Brownlow (1992; Brownlow & Zebrowitz, 1990) showed that people with mature faces are considered more expert than people with "baby faces." Moreover, when the speaker's expertise was called into question, speakers with mature faces were more persuasive (Brownlow, 1992). Presumably, casting doubt on a speaker's expertise caused receivers to rely on physical features to resolve their uncertainty, and their doubts were quelled by a mature face. Professional persuaders may rely on this. After reviewing 150 television commercials, Brownlow and Zebrowitz (1990) found that performers with mature faces were more likely to deliver persuasive appeals based on expertise.

In another study of advertising, spokeswomen for a household cleaner were rated as more expert when dressed appropriately for the product (i.e., wearing blue jeans, shirt, pullover sweater, shoes, and hair back in scarf) than when dressed inappropriately (i.e., wearing a long gown) (O'Neal & Lapitsky, 1991).

In one of the most detailed studies of the physical appearance cues associated with credibility, Rosenberg, Kahn, and Tran (1991) had receivers evaluate the competence, trustworthiness, and political demeanor of 210 women. These evaluations were then correlated with measurements of physical appearance cues. Women were evaluated as more competent if their eyes had a triangular or almond shape, their hair was cut short and worn down (rather than up), they appeared older, and they were formally and conservatively dressed with earrings and necklace. Their presumed competence also improved if they were photographed in front of a flat background of contrasting dark grays and whites. Many of these findings also applied in a political context: women who had more of these characteristics won mock elections when pitted against women who had fewer of them (Rosenberg et al., 1991).

A number of other kinesic and proxemic behaviors identified as persuasive by Mehrabian and Williams (1969) are typically used by dominant or high-status people and hence should qualify as appeals to authority, dominance, or status. Speakers attempting to be persuasive (1) make more eye contact with their listeners, (2) gesture more, (3) use more affirmative nods, (4) are more facially expressive, (5) engage in less self-manipulation, and (6) lean backward less. Females also exhibit less head and trunk swiveling. The first five cues are the same as those exhibited by speakers who are perceived as persuasive, and greater use of gaze is especially persuasive for women speaking from a far distance. Speakers also are seen as more persuasive if they adopt closer distances to their audience, are moderately relaxed (with women being slightly more tense than men), and for male speakers, adopt an indirect body orientation. Finally, greater perceived persuasiveness is correlated with more dominance behaviors, a finding that reinforces the dominant or authoritative nature of these nonverbal patterns.

Burgoon et al. (1990) confirmed many of these findings in a study of student public speakers who were evaluated by their classmates on their performance and whose nonverbal behaviors were coded by trained judges. These researchers found that persuasiveness increases the more a speaker shows expressiveness and immediacy, that is, makes more eye contact, exhibits more facial pleasantness, uses more illustrator gestures and fewer adaptor gestures, and leans backward less.

In another series of studies, Maslow, Yoselson, and London (1971) and Timney and London (1973) found similar results when comparing confident and doubtful speaking styles. In the first experiment, the experimenters paid an actor to use a confident, neutral, or doubtful communication style while miming a prerecorded tape of a legal argument. Students viewing the presentation rated the confident style—which consisted of rhythmic, forceful gestures, continuous eye contact (with the camera), and a relaxed posture—as more persuasive than the doubtful style. The doubtful style included fidgeting with a piece of paper, twirling a pencil, bringing the hand to the mouth, pulling at the shirt collar, avoiding eye contact, and sitting tensely erect. In the second experiment, subjects played jurors and tried to persuade one another about the correct verdict. In this case, only eye contact distinguished successful from unsuccessful persuaders—those who were more persuasive used more eye contact. The failure of other behaviors to make a difference across participants was probably due to the fact that everyone was trying to be persuasive.

Other research on gaze further demonstrates that longer gazes and greater amount of time spent gazing promote more attitude change and improve the overall effectiveness of a persuasive presentation, if the position advocated is not opposed to the listener's views (Burgoon et al., 1985; Edinger & Patterson, 1983; Giesen, 1973; Scherer, 1978). Gaze while speaking, as opposed to while listening, may be most important to persuasiveness (Linkey & Firestone, 1990). Moreover, gaze has been shown to be a powerful influence on other people's willingness to help someone or to comply with a request.

Kinesic and proxemic cues associated with persuasion are summarized by Betting-haus and Cody (1987), who conclude that

> there are a number of nonverbal behaviors that are *consistently* related to enhanced per-formance ratings in both public speaking and interview contexts: It is to the speaker's advantage to maintain eye contact, to nod, to smile, to illustrate, to avoid being too relaxed, and to refrain from using distracting adaptors. (p. 124)

These and the vocalic cues associated with persuasiveness are summarized in Table 14-1.

Finally, unidirectional (nonreciprocal) touch is a status and dominance cue that can be used to reinforce the influence of its user. As we will see shortly, it is a very effective means of eliciting behavioral change from others.

Character, Sociability, Composure, and Dynamism Akin to appeals to authority and competence are persuasive messages related to the other four dimensions of credi-bility: character, sociability, composure, and dynamism. It has been a long-standing assumption in communication that higher credibility leads to more attitude change and compliance. Psychologists likewise see perceptions of credibility of nonverbal behaviors as an important mediator of social influence (Edinger & Patterson, 1983). Yet increased credibility does not guarantee persuasion or compliance. What conclusions can we draw?

One is that overall strong delivery, coupled with strong arguments, is effective in changing attitudes. If a speaker has a weak message to begin with, delivery will make no difference; but if the verbal part of a message is sound, a strong nonverbal presentation will produce more attitude change than a weak one. Moreover, if both visual and vocal delivery are weak, the effect is particularly detrimental. Good delivery also produces higher credibility ratings, providing some support for a link between credibility and per-suasion (see McCroskey, 1972; Rosnow & Robinson, 1967).

The question is, what constitutes good delivery? Much of it is what has been described as a *confident* speaking style—vocal variety, fluency, good use of gestures, and eye contact. However, depending on what vocal, kinesic, and proxemic cues are combined, it is possible to create several alternative "good" delivery styles. Experiments contrasting conversational with dynamic delivery style (Pearce & Brommel, 1972; Pearce & Conklin, 1971), discussed in Chapter 13, did just that. Recall that in the con-versational speech version, the delivery was calm, slow, nonintense, consistent, deep-pitched, and soft. In the dynamic version, it was rapid, louder, higher pitched, and more varied. While the conversational style earned higher ratings of trustworthiness, honesty, sociability, likeableness, and professionalism, the two styles by themselves did not dif-fer in their effects on attitude change. Only when they were coupled with a high-credi-bility introduction for the speaker did delivery make a difference: a highly credible speaker using a dynamic style was most persuasive, while a low-credibility speaker using a dynamic style was least persuasive (Pearce & Brommel, 1972). These combined findings suggest that conversational style may be more appealing and effective if we are held in moderate or low esteem by our audience. If we are held in high esteem, we are better off using a dynamic style.

Other vocal research also demonstrates the advantage of more dynamic, expressive (i.e., louder, faster, more varied) speaking style, as do findings from kinesic research

TABLE 14-1
SUMMARY OF NONVERBAL PERSUASIVE BEHAVIORS

Cues encoded as persuasive	Cues decoded as persuasive	Cues actually achieving persuasion	Cues confirmed as credible
Vocalics			
greater fluency	greater fluency	greater fluency[a]	yes
faster tempo	faster tempo	faster tempo[a]	yes
more variety/intonation	more variety/intonation	more variety/intonation[a]	yes
louder/more intensity	louder	louder[a]	yes
	greater vocal pleasantness		yes
		strong delivery	yes
Kinesics			
greater gaze	greater gaze (especially women)	greater gaze (especially while speaking)[b]	yes
more nodding	more nodding	more nodding	
more facial activity	more facial pleasantness/ expressiveness		
less trunk swivel by women			
moderate relaxation	moderate relaxation		
		open body position	yes
more gesturing	more gesturing rhythmic gestures		
more self-adaptors[c]	fewer self- and object- adaptors		
Proxemics and Haptics			
more immediacy	more immediacy/affiliation		yes
	closer distance/distance violations[a]	closer and farther distance/ distance violations[a]	yes
	indirect body orientation by males	indirect body orientation by males	
less backward lean			
		brief touch, especially directed to women	

[a]Especially if speaker has positive reward valence.
[b]May backfire if speech is counterattitudinal.
[c]Only when audience is receptive.

that more gesturing and facial animation contribute to greater persuasiveness. The experiment by Burgoon et al. (1990), one of the few to combine several vocal and kinesic behaviors in the same study and to test their relationship to credibility and persuasion simultaneously, confirmed the link from kinesic expressiveness to credibility and perceived persuasiveness. Not only did greater expressiveness and immediacy increase persuasiveness, it also led to higher ratings on character, dynamism, and sociability. However, the study failed to find effects for tempo and loudness. Only vocal fluency and vocal pleasantness affected rated persuasiveness, and these voice qualities produced higher credibility ratings on composure and sociability (refer to Table 14-1).

Thus the jury is still out on how dynamic and forceful a speaker should be. This may depend on whether the speaker is held in high esteem by the audience. Also, it may be more effective to be kinesically dynamic than to be vocally forceful. Or it may be that a certain degree of animation and energy is desirable but being too assertive vocally and kinesically is not. Perhaps more important ultimately than dynamism is overall fluency and coordination of a presentation. Greater fluency contributes to intended, perceived, and actual persuasiveness.

With regard to physical appearance, Brownlow (1992; Brownlow & Zebrowitz, 1990) showed that people with "baby faces" were considered more trustworthy than people with mature faces. Also, people with "baby faces" were more persuasive than those with mature faces when their trustworthiness was questioned; and baby-faced actors were more likely to be in television commercials containing persuasive appeals that rely on the trustworthiness of the speaker. O'Neal and Lapitsky (1991) reported that appropriately dressed spokeswomen were considered more trustworthy than inappropriately dressed spokeswomen in advertisements for a household cleaner. Finally, according to Rosenberg et al. (1991), women who were rated as more trustworthy were more likely to have triangular, almond-shaped or upper-curve-shaped eyes, to smile, and to wear white clothes or clothes with a light pattern.

Brief, casual touch can increase perceptions of sociability. Burgoon et al. (1992) found that this was especially true when touch was directed toward females.

Strategies That Promote a Sense of Intimacy

Another major strategy for exerting influence is to use nonverbal messages to foster a more affiliative or intimate relationship and to rely on this as the basis for inducing changes in attitudes, behaviors, and communication patterns.

One difficulty in determining what behaviors establish intimacy is that many behaviors designated as immediacy and affiliation cues also have alternative meanings. For example, gaze may be interpreted as an affiliation or submission cue when used by and among women but as a threat or dominance cue when used by and among men (Burgoon et al., 1986; Valentine & Ehrlichman, 1979). Hence many of the nonverbal behaviors discussed in this section may in fact be efficacious not because they establish intimacy, as we are inferring, but because they express dominance, credibility, or all three. We have chosen to identify them as signals of intimacy, first, because they are the cues most commonly cited as promoting intimacy and, second, because the subjects or the experimenters in many of these studies have interpreted them in this way.

The primary behaviors that might foster intimacy and affiliation and that have been studied for their ability to change attitudes and behaviors are gaze; proximity and touch; body position, facial, gestural, and vocal expressiveness (including nods and smiles); and speaking tempo.

Gaze   We have already noted that increased gaze is effective in changing attitudes and is perceived as persuasive if the position one is advocating is agreeable to the subject. When the position advocated is counter to the audience's attitudes, use of too much gaze

Billy Sunday, a famous evangelist in the first part of the twentieth century, relied on dynamic gestures, posture, and movement to make his messages more forceful. Many evangelists today continue this preaching style.

may backfire (Giesen, 1973). When gaze is coupled with other affiliative cues such as close proximity, forward leaning, direct body orientation, and more gesturing, it not only promotes perceptions of persuasiveness, friendliness, and intimacy but also increases an applicant's chances of being offered a job (Burgoon et al., 1985; Forbes & Jackson, 1980; Imada & Hakel, 1977; LaCrosse, 1975; Washburn & Hakel, 1973).

One of the more interesting effects of prolonged gaze is on others' willingness to help. Several studies have explored whether staring at another person increases or decreases the likelihood of that person's offering assistance. In one experiment, a confederate carrying a cumbersome shopping bag dropped a stack of papers, apparently by accident. Regardless of whether the stare was straight or broken and accompanied or not accompanied by a smile, fewer passersby offered to help pick up the papers when they were stared at than when they were not. In a similar experiment, subjects working on a puzzle in a room with the researcher were more reluctant to help the researcher on a subsequent computer problem if he or she had stared at them (Horn, 1974).

Although these studies suggest that prolonged gaze may be an aversive behavior that is read as hostile or threatening, a recent meta-analysis by Segrin (1994) showed that gaze increased compliance in 12 studies. For example, Ellsworth and Langer (1976) used the same "bystander intervention" technique as Horn (1974), this time with a person in distress whose plight (a medical problem) and remedy were sometimes clear, sometimes not. When the nature of the problem and solution were clear, a stare increased the probability of a bystander's offering help. Gaze can increase the probability that people will return dimes left in a phone booth (Brockner, Pressman, Cabitt, & Moran, 1982; Kleinke, 1977) or help a falling person (Shotland & Johnson, 1978). When accompanied by a brief touch, it can increase compliance with a request to complete a survey (Hornik & Ellis, 1988). Moreover, staring produces greater compliance with a request than not staring when the request is legitimate. Kleinke (1980) sometimes coupled gaze with touch to produce a high-intimacy situation and found that men comply more with a high-intimacy approach than with a low-intimacy approach (no gaze or touch). However, with an illegitimate request, low intimacy is the more successful approach. Kleinke surmised that averting gaze when making an illegitimate request may win sympathy from others by appearing tactful, embarrassed, or humble. It may be that gaze avoidance appears less assertive. Krapfel (1988) found that, in general, requests were seen as less legitimate if pressed too assertively.

The gender of a potential helper also makes a difference. In female-female pairs, people offer more help in picking up dropped coins when eye contact is made, but in male-male pairs, they offer more help when there is no eye contact (Valentine & Ehrlichman, 1979). Also, eye contact with a brief hesitation increases willingness to help a female but decreases it for a male (Geller & Malia, 1981). Gaze coupled with touch did particularly well with women in the study by Hornik and Ellis (1988). Gaze may be a nonspecific activator whose interpretation and effects depend on the context (Ellsworth & Langer, 1976; Kleinke, 1977). Under some circumstances, prolonged gaze may serve as an affiliative cue in the form of a plea for help, while in other cases it may be seen as overly forward or aggressive behavior.

A final way in which gaze facilitates influence is in altering other people's communication behavior—again, with gender differences. Direct gaze by a partner causes women to make more intimate, self-disclosive statements but causes men to become less intimate, even though they think they have become more so. Conversely, averting gaze reduces females' level of verbal intimacy and increases males' disclosiveness (Ellsworth & Ross, 1975).

Proximity and Touch Like gaze, proximity and touch can have generally positive consequences (Segrin, 1994), but this effect can be reduced or reversed in some circumstances. Audiences pay more attention to a speaker at an intermediate distance but are more persuaded by the speech the farther away the speaker is. At close and far distances, audiences focus more on the speaker's appearance (Albert & Dabbs, 1970); that is, they are distracted from the content of the speech. However, when it comes to persuading someone to hire you, we have already seen that close proximity is the best strategy, partly because it is among a set of behaviors conveying greater warmth and enthusiasm (Imada & Hakel, 1977).

Distancing and touch also affect helping behavior and compliance. Buller (1987) found that compliance with a request to sign a petition increased when the petitioner moved closer to the target than when the petitioner did not move from the normative distance or moved farther away. In a series of four field experiments, Konečni et al.

(1975) tested the effects of invading or not invading the personal space of pedestrians waiting at crosswalks on their willingness to return a lost object. They found not only that violations of personal space prompt people to cross the intersection faster—an indication that a violation is arousing, threatening, or both—but also that they reduce helping behavior, especially if the violation is prolonged and the lost object to be returned is of little value (e.g., a pencil as opposed to a set of keys). Greatest helping occurred at an intermediate distance (5 feet); helping was considerably lower at very close and very far distances. Smith and Knowles (1979) pursued these findings in two additional field experiments using a modified version of the "pedestrian violation" format. In one version, the violator either had a plausible explanation for the violation (carrying an open sketch pad with a partially completed sketch of the intersection) or no apparent explanation (the sketch pad was held closed at the side). A noninvading confederate who was the one in need of help was also present half the time. In the second experiment, subjects were asked to complete a questionnaire following the encounter. Results showed that when there is no apparent justification for an invasion, pedestrians cross the street faster, regard the invasion as inappropriate, and are less willing to return a dropped pen to either the invader or the noninvading bystander than when the invader has a reason for being close by or when no invasion occurs. These conditions, involving violations by strangers, conform to expectancy violations theory, which predicts that violations by nonrewarding others produce more negative consequences than conformity does.

Other studies in what could be considered high-reward conditions present opposite results. Baron and Bell (1976), who originally set out to substantiate that proximity reduces helping behavior, found instead that experimenters approaching diners in a cafeteria obtained greater willingness to help with a research project when the experimenters approached them at a 1 1/2-foot distance than a 3-foot distance. A follow-up study showed that closer distance communicates a greater need for help and greater friendliness, a conclusion consistent with our inference that gaze and proximity may appeal to basic affiliation motives. A subsequent study by Baron (1978) further demonstrated, as Kleinke (1980) also found, that the close approach worked only when the request was legitimate; with an illegitimate request, a far distance was preferable. By contrast, Glick, DeMorest, and Hotze (1988) reported that changes in proximity were relevant only for outgroups (people who appeared to be in a different social group from the recipient), not for ingroups. In their study, female confederates dressed as "punkers" (i.e., an outgroup) increased compliance from female shoppers by adopting a far distance rather than normal or close distances. Compliance was not affected by the proximity adopted by female confederates who appeared to be dressed similarly to the female shoppers (i.e., an ingroup). Reports from the female shoppers reveal that farther distances by the "outgroup" confederate reduced shoppers' anxiety about being approached.

In sum, close proximity may reduce persuasion, helping, and compliance when the communicator is nonrewarding, makes an illegitimate request, or distracts the receiver; but it may increase helping and compliance otherwise. Far distances may be effective in situations where the nonrewarding communicator evokes anxiety or fear. Touch most often elicits helping and compliance (see Box 14-2).

Finally, effects of proximity on communication behavior are mixed. Some research finds that subjects write more intimate disclosures for a surveyor standing 1 foot away rather than 2 feet away (Cozby, 1974). Other research finds that physical closeness has

---

BOX 14-2

APPLICATIONS: A TOUCHING REQUEST FOR HELP

Touching typically increases people's willingness to help and to comply with a request (Segrin, 1994). In one of the first studies of this effect, Kleinke (1977) found that people were more willing to return "lost" dimes when the requester touched than when the requester did not. Others have found that touch increases people's willingness to sign petitions or complete questionnaires, to assist with scoring inventories (especially if the request was by a female to a female), and to help an interviewer pick up dropped questionnaires, regardless of whether the task is easy or difficult (Crusco & Wetzel, 1984; Goldman & Fordyce, 1983; Patterson et al., 1986; Willis & Hamm, 1980). It also increases airline passengers' liking for flight attendants and their perceived safety (Wycoff & Holley, 1990).

Touch can even overcome negative feelings to improve compliance. Goldman, Kiyohara, and Pfannensteil (1985) created a "foot-in-the-door" situation in which a first confederate asked for a small favor. Later, a second confederate made a larger request. The first confederate either reacted positively to the receiver's compliance by saying, "You have been very helpful," or reacted negatively by saying, "You are not very helpful." When the first confederate reacted negatively, compliance with the second request was higher if the second confederate touched the receiver than if he or she did not. Goldman et al. concluded that touch ameliorated the receiver's unfavorable feelings produced by the first confederate's negative reactions.

Finally, Paulsell and Goldman (1984) discovered a slight sex difference: males increased helping behavior if touched, no matter where they were touched (shoulder, upper arm, lower arm, or hand). Women were especially likely to increase assistance when touched on the lower or upper arm.

Only one study (Stockwell & Dye, 1980) failed to find an effect for touch. Conclusion: Touching helps.

---

a dampening affect on the amount and nature of intimate verbal behavior (Dietch & House, 1975; Greenberg, 1976; Sundstrom, 1975). Intermediate distances may be best: unacquainted dyads divulge more intimate information, descriptively and qualitatively, at 4 feet than at either 2 or 16 feet (Morton, 1974).

Body Position   As we have seen, more forward lean and more direct body orientation, as part of a set of affiliative cues, are associated with greater persuasiveness (LaCrosse, 1975). Body posture may function in the same way. One study found that an open body position, in which limbs are turned outward from the trunk, engenders more attitude change, is evaluated more positively, and is seen as more active than a closed position (McGinley, LeFevre, & McGinley, 1975). However, when the target holds attitudes similar to those advocated by the communicator, a closed position may be preferable (McGinley et al., 1978).

Another way body position influences others is in affecting their communication style. When an interviewer leans forward, the interviewee displays expressive behaviors, speech patterns, and emotional reactions indicative of rapport (Bond & Shiraishi, 1974).

Facial, Gestural, and Vocal Expressiveness   As with other affiliative cues, more smiling, nodding, and gesturing are associated with greater persuasiveness and with greater success as a job applicant (Edinger & Patterson, 1983; Forbes & Jackson, 1980;

LaCrosse, 1975; Maslow et al., 1971; Timney & London, 1973). Thus greater expressiveness and pleasantness seem to facilitate influence.

Speaking Tempo   Speakers can also enhance their relationship with the receiver by adjusting their tempo to match the receiver's normal rate of speech (Buller & Aune, 1988, 1992; Buller & Burgoon, 1986; Buller et al., 1992). In two experiments, Buller and his colleagues (Buller & Aune, 1988; Buller & Burgoon, 1986) reported that receivers who were good decoders of vocal cues preferred a faster rate, saw it as more immediate and intimate, and were more willing to comply with fast-paced requests. By contrast, poor decoders of vocal cues preferred a slower rate, saw it as more intimate and immediate, and were more likely to comply with such a request. Because good decoders also spoke more quickly themselves, whereas poor decoders spoke more slowly (in the second experiment), Buller and Aune (1988) concluded that a speech-accommodation effect is at work—people prefer speech tempos most like their own and consider speakers with similar rates to be more socially attractive. Buller and Aune (1992) provided further confirmation of this accommodation effect in a third study. They also speculated that the favorable relational interpretations attributed to similar tempos, especially those of greater immediacy, created obligations to comply with the request because favorable relationships are based on the exchange of favors that fulfill partners' needs (Roloff, 1987; Roloff, Janiszewski, McGrath, Burns, & Manrai, 1988). A fourth experiment (Buller et al., 1992) confirmed the role of obligations by showing that perceptions of greater social attractiveness engendered by similar tempo produced more compliance when the speaker directly benefited. (Roloff claimed that between strangers, obligations affect only help given to the requester, not help given to someone else like a spouse, friend, or group for whom the requester may ask for help.) When the speaker did not benefit, increased perceptions of dominance and status associated with faster tempos improved compliance.

Strategies That Maximize Attractiveness

Another strategy that may allow a communicator to exert influence is to maximize one's attractiveness to the target. Although physical attractiveness does not invariably override other elements of a message, such as arguments or credibility (Chaiken, Eagly, Sejwacz, Gregory, & Christensen, 1978; Maddux & Rogers, 1980; Mills & Aronson, 1965), there is evidence that being physically attractive can help one's case.

Consider a few experiments that have confirmed this. In one set of experiments, a woman gives the same speech to two different audiences, altering only her appearance. For one audience, she is made to look unattractive with messy hair, oily skin, no makeup, a faint mustache, and loose, ill-fitting clothing. For the other audience, she has clean, neat hair, makeup, and fashionable clothing. When she makes clear her intent to persuade, the attractive speaker is somewhat more persuasive with a male audience than when she is unattractive or does not explicitly attempt to persuade (Mills & Aronson, 1965). In another type of study, students deliver persuasive messages to passersby on campus, asking them to complete an attitude survey and sign a petition banning meat at lunch and dinner on campus. Canvassers independently judged more attractive have

Here is the same communicator made to look attractive and unattractive. Which appearance is likely to be more persuasive?

greater success in getting their petitions signed and also obtain more agreement on the survey (Chaiken, 1979). A later version of this study finds that the persuasiveness of the communicator is complicated by the sex composition of the dyad (communicator and target) and by anticipated future interactions. In a third variation, the same written speech, which is either supported by evidence or not, is attributed to an attractive male undergraduate or an unattractive but expert middle-age professor. Whereas the professor is more persuasive when using evidence than when not using it, the attractive undergraduate is equally persuasive with the female audience with or without evidence; this indicates that physical attractiveness alone can be sufficient to exert influence and that other variables, such as arguments, are relevant primarily when influence is based on expertise rather than attractiveness (Norman, 1976). Other studies using photographs of the supposed author of a persuasive message have found that more attractive communicators obtain more changes of opinion (Horai, Naccari, & Fatoullah, 1974; Snyder & Rothbart, 1971) and compliance (Krapfel, 1988). One study with children also showed that attractive children are more influential with their peers (Dion & Stein, 1978).

These experiments affirm that attractiveness can significantly affect people's susceptibility to influence. Why does it work? Bettinghaus and Cody (1987) offered this answer:

While credibility causes attitude change primarily because of the apparent validity of the recommended position and the evidence presented, attitude change produced by an attractive source is caused, apparently, by our desire to identify with and be liked by good-looking persons. . . . Attractive sources influence us because of their attractiveness, not because of message content. That is, since we identify with, and desire approval from, attractive sources, we respond to *them,* not the messages. (p. 95)

This concept of *identification* may be an important cognitive heuristic or convenient rule of thumb for recipients as they try to decide whether or not to comply with a request (Pallak, 1983). Numerous studies find that people who are well-groomed and attired in conventional, formal, high-status clothing are more successful in getting others to sign petitions, to accept political literature, to make change, or to pick them up when hitch-hiking than if they are wearing unconventional attire (Bickman, 1971b; Crassweller, Gordon, & Tedford, 1972; Darley & Cooper, 1972; Keasy & Tomlinson-Keasy, 1973; MacNeil & Wilson, 1972; Raymond & Unger, 1972; Segrin, 1994). The Clean for Gene movement in the 1968 presidential primary, in which college students campaigning for Senator Eugene McCarthy dressed conventionally, was based on this principle (Darley & Cooper, 1972).

In the most direct tests of this identification process, Pallak, Murroni, and Koch (1983) showed that an attractive communicator was more persuasive than an unattractive one when delivering an emotional message, but attractiveness was irrelevant to the outcome of a rational message. Other measures showed that targets were more likely to evaluate the communicator rather than the message when receiving the emotional message. In another study, Pallak (1983) showed that when the salience of an attractive communicator was reduced, strength of message predicted persuasion, but when the salience of an attractive communicator was increased, persuasion increased, targets thought more about the communicator, and strength of message was unrelated to changes in opinion.

Interestingly, DeBono (1992) was able to produce a similar effect with a pleasant perfume. Initially, targets were either exposed or not exposed to a pleasant perfume. They were then asked to read an advertisement with either an attractive or unattractive spokesperson. The ad contained either a strong or a weak persuasive appeal. The attractiveness of the spokesperson influenced the opinions of targets in the "scent" condition (the attractive spokesperson was more persuasive), but the strength of the message affected the opinions of targets in the "no scent" condition (the stronger message produced more change in opinion). DeBono concluded that the pleasant perfume put listeners in a favorable mood so that they processed the message heuristically and relied on the speaker's attractiveness when evaluating the persuasive appeal.

Other research, however, finds that similarity of dress between communicator and target is more persuasive. For example, Hensley (1981) found that a well-dressed solicitor gained more compliance at an airport but less compliance at a bus stop than a more casually dressed solicitor. The hypothesis is that people whose dress is more similar to their targets or is more conventional will receive more compliance and less aggression, because similarity is reinforcing (Harris et al., 1983; Hensley, 1981).

Another factor is self-presentation. One study reports that people are less willing to seek help from an attractive source as opposed to an unattractive source, unless it is a woman seeking help from an attractive man (Nadler, Shapira, & Ben-Itzhak, 1982). The researchers argued that people's concern with self-presentation affects their behavior, and they are willing to appear needy only when they are anonymous, expect no future interaction, or recognize the helper's role. If concern about presenting oneself favorably affects willingness to seek help from attractive people, it may also affect willingness to comply with requests for help from attractive people. It is possible that the desire to win the approval of attractive people may lead to greater willingness to comply with their requests.

While all this evidence paints a rosy picture for attractive people, one must be cautious not to make a blanket assumption that attractive people are always more influential. Rosenberg, Bohan, McCafferty, and Harris (1986) found that less physically attractive men had higher "congressional demeanor" and received more votes in mock elections than more physically attractive men. Overly attractive men may not appear as credible as less attractive men. Also, credibility may be more important when people assess the legislative potential of a political candidate—notwithstanding recent laments that most elections degenerate into popularity contests.

Poor appearance also may establish expectations that increase compliance with some requests for help. In one study, a poorly dressed requester received more help than a well-dressed requester when asking for directions to a thrift shop, but not when asking for directions to a tennis club (Juhnke et al., 1987). The combination of poor dress and thrift shop may have created a perception of financial plight and increased the legitimacy of the request or the perceived social responsibility of the target.

Another consideration is the juxtaposition of expectations set up by appearance and actual behavior. Cooper, Darley, and Henderson (1974) reported that householders interviewed on a tax issue by students who looked like hippies became more favorable toward the position they advocated and toward college students in general, as compared with their reaction when they were interviewed by students who looked like straight-arrows. The explanation offered is that appearance led them to expect to dislike the student and that listening to someone they disliked created dissonance, causing them to change their attitude. An experiment by McPeek and Edwards (1975) similarly suggests that unconventional appearance can sometimes produce positive results. A long-haired, unconventional speaker was more persuasive than the conservative-looking speaker when arguing against using marijuana, no doubt because his appearance set up negative expectations that were positively violated by his atypical message. These findings indicate that more attractive or conventional appearance is not always the best strategy, particularly when appearance can be used strategically in setting up violations of expectations. We will return to the violations strategy shortly.

One additional consideration is that attractive people may alter other elements of their communication style so that appearance alone does not account for their success. Singer (1964) had male undergraduates rate photographs of 192 first-year women on physical attractiveness and then compared the ratings with the grades the women received. Consistent with his hypothesis, more attractive women received higher grades, but only if they were firstborns. Observations and interviews revealed that these women were more likely to talk to their male professors after class, make appointments with them, and sit in the front of the room—in other words, to be more manipulative. A follow-up study

(Singer & Lamb, 1966) confirmed that firstborn women are more concerned with their appearance, more accurate in describing themselves, and more likely to distort their own measurements toward the ideal when they think no one will verify their answers. The study by Chaiken (1979) involving signing of petitions found that the more attractive solicitors were judged friendlier, talked somewhat faster, and were more fluent. Dion and Stein (1978) likewise found not only that attractive children were more successful than unattractive children in influencing their peers but also that they used different interaction styles. It is likely, therefore, that attractive communicators have an overall style that effuses confidence and charisma, further reinforcing the effect of their physical attractiveness. To understand the role of attractiveness fully, we must ultimately take into account the whole person—static cues of appearance and attire, and more dynamic elements of demeanor.

Strategies That Signal Expectations

Another strategy of social influence is use of nonverbal communication to signal interpersonal expectations. Communicators enter every interaction with expectations about the partner's personality, attitudes, and behavior. These expectations shape the messages that are encoded and the interpretation of partner's messages. Expectations about strangers are based largely on stereotypes associated with the impressions we form about them. As stereotypes, they are oversimplified and overgeneralized (Snyder, Tanke, & Berscheid, 1977). When relationships develop, expectations become more elaborate and specific to the partner and continue to exert considerable influence on selection and interpretation of messages.

With regard to social influence, an important result is that holding expectations can cause a communicator to select verbal and nonverbal messages that covertly signal these expectations. (See Box 14-3 for an example.) Moreover, behaviors that signal expectations often cause the target's behaviors to conform with the source's expectations. This form of influence has been labeled the *self-fulfilling prophecy* (Merton, 1948; Rosenthal, 1981; Snyder, 1992; Snyder et al., 1977; Word, Zanna, & Cooper, 1974). An interesting characteristic of this form of influence is that the communicator is often unaware of it.

Evidence for the effect of expectations can be traced back to the remarkable feats of Clever Hans in 1911. Hans was a horse that could apparently spell, read, and solve mathematical problems; he tapped out the answers with his hoof. A committee even certified that Hans received no clues from his questioners. However, eventually a man named Pfungst was able to demonstrate that Hans was using minute head and eye movements from the questioners as cues. When a question was posed, the questioner looked at Hans's hoof, since that was where the answer would appear. When Hans approached the correct answer, the questioner would inadvertently move his head or eyes upward or simply flare his nostrils. This was all Hans needed to know to stop tapping (Pfungst, 1911). The scientific community did not recognize until the 1960s that the same thing happens between people.

Robert Rosenthal (1976, 1985, 1993; Harris & Rosenthal, 1985; Rosenthal & Jacobson, 1968) conducted an extended analysis of the ways in which people signal expecta-

BOX 14-3

IS JUSTICE BLIND? SIGNALING EXPECTATIONS IN THE COURTROOM

[Covert cues] have a strong impact in key relationships such as those between judge and jury, physician and patient, or teacher and student.

Indeed, the tacit communication of expectations between one person and another are found, in many cases, to make all the difference between success or failure in various kinds of endeavors.

How a judge gives his instructions to a jury was perceived to double the likelihood that the jury would deliver a verdict of guilty or not guilty—even when on the surface the judge's demeanor seemed perfectly impartial. . . .

[A] judicial study, reported in . . . The Stanford Law Review is believed to be one of the first scientific tests of the courtroom lore that the judge's attitudes, even if never openly expressed, are often crucial to a trial's outcome. One striking finding concerned trials in which the judge knew that the defendant had a record of previous felonies, a fact that a jury, by law, is not allowed to know

unless the defendant takes the stand. When the judges were aware of past felonies, the Stanford study found, their final instructions to juries were lacking in warmth, tolerance, patience and competence. . . .

"Judges can't come out and say 'This defendant is guilty,' " said Peter Blanck, who did the study. "But they may say it subtly, nonverbally—even if that message is inadvertent.". . .

[Blanck] said he believed that most of the biasing elements he found in his research were unintended. He sees his study as a first step in helping judges to neutralize their hidden messages, as well as, one day, providing lawyers with a new basis for challenging verdicts.

"If judges became sensitized to the problem, they could learn to be more impartial in their demeanor," Dr. Blanck said.

Source: Goleman, 1986, pp. C1, C6.

tions. He and other researchers explored numerous verbal and nonverbal behaviors that may help signal expectations (see, e.g., Babad, Bernieri, & Rosenthal, 1989; Blanck & Rosenthal, 1984; Duncan, Rosenberg, & Finkelstein, 1969; Duncan & Rosenthal, 1968; Scherer, Rosenthal, & Koivumaki, 1972). Rosenthal (1973) originally offered a four-factor theory of the communication of expectations about performance (e.g., expectations held by a teacher about the probable performance of a student). When communicators, like teachers, supervisors, or clinicians, expect superior performance from a student, employee, or client, they tend to treat that other person in four special ways. (1) They create a warmer socioemotional *climate* for the other person; (2) They give the other person more *feedback* on how he or she is performing; (3) They *input* more information and more difficult information to the other person; (4) They give the other person more opportunities to perform, that is, to produce *output.* More recently, this model has been simplified to just two factors. Communicators change *affect* shown toward the target person and degree of *effort* expended on behalf of the target person.

Nonverbal communication plays a large role in this process. In a meta-analysis of 135 experiments on communication of expectations, Harris and Rosenthal (1985) showed that communicators increased immediacy cues (i.e., encoded greater eye contact, closer conversational distance, more smiling, and more nodding) when they held higher expectations for others. In turn, immediacy cues (eye contact, distance, and smiling) increased the likelihood that the target would match these expectations. Harris and Rosenthal also reported that when performance expectations were high, communicators engaged in more frequent and longer interactions with target persons (perhaps providing them with more opportunities for input and output), and more frequent and longer inter-actions increased matching of preinteractional expectations by targets. Other nonverbal cues (such as vocal cues) may be important, too, but researchers have yet to examine them (Harris & Rosenthal, 1985).

Studies have examined personality factors and social skills associated with the like-lihood of signaling expectations. For instance, Sullins, Friedman, and Harris (1985) found that teachers who were more expressive but low self-monitors were most likely to communicate performance expectations to their students. By contrast, teachers who were more expressive and high self-monitors were least likely to communicate performance expectations. Blanck and Rosenthal (1984), however, reported that inexpressive and incompetent counselors at a summer camp were more likely to signal performance expectations through vocal cues than more expressive, competent counselors. Those who are less concerned with their own behavior and less adept may be unaware of the extent to which they can communicate performance expectations. Harris (1989; Harris & Rosenthal, 1986) reported that counselors who scored higher on dogmatism and need for order were more likely to bias their clients toward the counselors' performance expectations. Cooper and Hazelrigg (1988) showed that experimenters were more likely to bias experimental subjects if they had a higher need for social influence, while sub-jects were more likely to be biased by experimenters if they scored higher on a measure of "influenceability" and had better decoding skills. Snyder (1992) suggested that com-municators with higher needs for control and order may feel a greater need to predict the target persons' behavior, and so they behave in accordance with their expectations to reduce their uncertainty about the targets.

The influence of interpersonal expectations has also been investigated in social inter-actions. Mark Snyder (Snyder & Swann, 1978; Snyder et al., 1977) explained that social stereotypes channel the communicator's behaviors in the interaction in ways that cause the target's behavior to confirm the stereotypes. Snyder argued that expectations create predictions or hypotheses about the target's future behavior that communicators set out to test through their own verbal and nonverbal messages. Communicators' hypothesis-testing messages signal their expectations and must be dealt with by the target. Fre-quently, the target's method of dealing with the messages is to present behaviors that confirm the communicators' original expectations. Behavioral confirmation then leads the communicators to conclude that their initial expectations were correct. For exam-ple, say a student named Bob has a problem with his class schedule at State University and must see the assistant registrar to clear it up. A friend, Sally, tells Bob that the assis-tant registrar is aloof and does not seem concerned with students' problems (in our terms, nonimmediate). With these expectations, Bob enters the assistant registrar's office and adopts a very nonimmediate nonverbal pattern—indirect body orientation, back-ward leaning, little smiling, and less eye contact. The assistant registrar responds to Bob's nonimmediate pattern by being nonimmediate and uninvolved in return. Bob leaves the interaction satisfied that Sally was correct: the assistant registrar is an uncar-ing, unfeeling bureaucrat. Bob's fundamental error is his failure to recognize that the registrar's nonimmediacy cues were not a signal of indifference but a response to his own nonverbal message.

Snyder's research demonstrated this process empirically. He found that men who thought they were talking with attractive women in phone conversations were more sociable, sexually warm, interesting, independent, bold, outgoing, humorous, obvious, socially adept, attractive, confident, and animated than men who believed they were talking with less attractive women. Further, women in the "high attractiveness" condition were themselves more sociable, poised, humorous, and adept than women in the "low attractiveness" condition, regardless of their actual attractiveness (Snyder et al., 1977). In a second experiment, Snyder and Swann (1978) manipulated their subjects' expectations that a partner would be hostile or not hostile. Subjects who expected the partner to be hostile were more hostile themselves than subjects who expected the partner not to be hostile. Moreover, subjects' hostility produced hostility in the partner, thereby confirming the subjects' expectations.

From a similar perspective, Word et al. (1974) reasoned that interracial attitudes and expectations would cause white interviewers to be less immediate with black interviewees, which would in turn produce less immediacy by black interviewees. As predicted, white interviewers were less immediate with black interviewees than white interviewees, and black interviewees were less immediate when a white interviewer was less immediate than when a white interviewer was more immediate. These data, however, should be viewed with caution, since these two findings were derived in separate experiments. That is, the reduction in black interviewees' immediacy was observed in response to experimental manipulation of interviewers' level of immediacy rather than the natural reduction in immediacy observed among interviewers interacting with black and white applicants.

Snyder (1992) later contended that the entire process of communicating expectations can be understood by considering interactants' motivations in conversations in which expectations are signaled. He argued that expectations are most likely to be signaled when the communicators are principally motivated by the need to gain information about the target persons in order to get to know them better. Signaling preconceived expectations about target persons' performance is another way of creating order and increasing predictability about the target persons—both important aspects of obtaining social information. Also, communicators who have a tendency to control conversations and a high need to bring order to information and events should expend more effort to gather information and consequently be more likely to signal their expectations to target persons. On the other hand, target persons are more likely to confirm the communicators' expectations when their primary goal is to get along well with communicators. By conforming to the expectations signaled by communicators, the target persons facilitate social interaction, even by conforming to unfavorable expectations.

Strategies That Exploit Reciprocity and Compensation

A special case of signaling expectations—or sometimes their opposites—is the use of interaction patterns to influence someone else. In Chapter 12, we introduced patterns of reciprocity and compensation. Communicators at times strategically choose to reciprocate or compensate expected nonverbal patterns from interaction partners in an effort to change the targets' undesirable nonverbal communication and to reward desirable nonverbal communication (Edinger & Patterson, 1983). Coutts et al. (1980) manipulated expectations about a female partner by having her agree or disagree with the subject's opinions in an initial interaction. In a subsequent interaction, the partner either increased her immediacy (by gazing more and adopting a more direct body orientation) or did not change it. Subjects displayed a reciprocal immediacy pattern when the confederate initially disagreed with them, increasing their own immediacy when the confederate increased immediacy. Reciprocity, though, was not accompanied by favorable impressions of the confederate. Coutts et al. speculated that reciprocity may have been used as a reward for the unexpected increase in immediacy by the disagreeable partner or as a signal that her higher involvement was a more appropriate level of involvement.

Ickes, Patterson, Rajecki, and Tanford (1982) conducted two experiments in which, before interacting with a partner, subjects were told to expect the partner to be either friendly or unfriendly and similar in personality and pleasant to talk with (experiment 1) or dissimilar and unpleasant (experiment 2). In experiment 1, communicators who expected a friendly interaction style displayed a reciprocal pattern by sitting closer and initiating communication more frequently. In contrast, communicators expecting an unfriendly style displayed a compensatory pattern of greater positive affect, immediacy, and nonverbal involvement. However, compensating communicators retained an unfavorable impression of the partner, suggesting that compensation did not indicate liking or attraction but was designed to influence the partner's expected style of behavior. Experiment 2 had similar results. Communicators who expected a dissimilar, unpleasant partner encoded a compensatory nonverbal pattern of greater involvement—greater facial pleasantness, gaze, and talking time and a more direct body orientation. Again, compensation was an attempt to influence the partner's behavior and not a result of liking or attraction, since compensating communicators rated the partner unfavorably. Honeycutt (1989) likewise reported that communicators who expected their conversational partner to be unfriendly initiated more talk throughout the conversation, vocalized more in the first minute, and said that they compensated more for the partner's failure to talk than communicators who expected the partner to be friendly or who received no preinteraction information about the partner.

Burgoon, LePoire, and Rosenthal (1995) offered four possible explanations for these behavioral patterns. According to the first explanation, *expectancy signaling,* senders inadvertently and unintentionally encode behavior matching what they anticipate from the receiver, and the receiver confirms the expectation by displaying the expected behavior. This explanation is most consistent with the expectancy effects discussed in the preceding section; it predicts that receivers should reciprocate the nonverbal behavior displayed by senders. The second explanation is *expectancy-based modeling of desired behavior.* This explanation proposes that communicators compensate for expected unpleasant communication by modeling the desired behavior, anticipating that the target will then reciprocate. Findings of Ickes et al. and Honeycutt fit this explanation. By contrast, the third explanation, *communication-based modeling and reinforcement of desired behavior,* says that a sender's behavior is determined more by the receiver's actual communication pattern than by expectations about that pattern. Communicators react to receivers' behavior on the basis of their own conversational goals. Burgoon et al. speculated that an overriding goal in initial interactions is to have a comfortable, pleasant, nonconfrontational exchange. Thus communicators should reciprocate a pleasant behavioral pattern from a receiver and compensate for an unpleasant one. Findings by Burgoon et al. and Coutts et al. support this explanation. The fourth explanation is derived from Burgoon's *expectancy violations theory,* which we take up more fully in the following section. In brief, it predicts that regardless of initial expectations, pleasant interaction patterns should be interpreted as positive and result in reciprocity of pleasant nonverbal behavior. By contrast, unpleasant nonverbal behavior by an interactant who is expected to be pleasant should be labeled negatively and result in compensation in order to restore the previous level of pleasantness. Finally, unpleasant behavior by someone who is expected to be unpleasant is a negative violation but produces a reciprocal decrease in pleasantness by the communicator.

Strategies That Violate Expectations

As discussed in Chapter 13, one consideration in maximizing self-presentation is whether or not to conform to expectations. Just as nonverbal violations of expectations may sometimes increase a communicator's perceived attractiveness and credibility, they may also sometimes improve a communicator's chances of being persuasive, getting hired for a job, obtaining assistance, or altering someone else's communication style.

According to expectancy violations theory (EVT), people develop expectations about the nonverbal behaviors of others; violations of those expectations arouse and distract, shifting attention toward the communicator and relationship characteristics; and labeling a violation as negative or positive depends on (1) reward valence of the communicator, (2) direction and magnitude of the violation, and (3) interpretation and evaluation of the violation. Negative violations should hinder attitude change, compliance, helping behavior, and other forms of influence; positive violations should facilitate these outcomes.

In the first study to test the effect of distance violations on persuasion, Burgoon, Stacks, and Burch (1982) had three-person groups deliberate a murder trial. Subjects interacted with two confederates presenting opposite sides of the case. The confederates were either highly rewarding (both with a prestigious major, previous jury experience, interest in the task, well-groomed appearance, and attractive) or nonrewarding (undisclosed major, no previous experience, no interest in the task, and physically unattractive). In each threesome, one confederate moved in very close or moved much farther away after the discussion had started, while the other confederate remained stationary. Results showed that subjects were more likely to accept the position advocated by the "high reward" communicators and to rate them persuasive when they engaged in a violation, especially a far violation, than when they conformed to the originally established, normative distance. Violators were also more persuasive than equally rewarding nonviolators. In other words, a communicator was better off engaging in a violation, both compared with himself or herself when following the norm and compared with another equally rewarding person who conformed to distance expectations. By contrast, violations did not have much impact on actual acceptance of the message for "low reward" confederates, but they were seen as less persuasive when they violated distance norms than when they conformed. They were also seen as less persuasive than nondeviating confederates. These results show that violations for a positively valenced person may gain ground absolutely and relative to other communicators present who do not violate. The converse is true for negatively valenced communicators.

A second series of studies by Burgoon and Aho (1982) considered whether distance violations affect a salesperson's communication behavior and willingness to comply with a simple request (to use a telephone). Student experimenters approached salespeople and asked for help with a purchase or interviewed them about consumer behavior. When the experimenters were rewarding (e.g., were interested in purchasing a big-ticket item, dressed more formally and attractively, or verbally indicated their expertise), salespeople were much more helpful and willing to comply with the phone request, showed greater interest in the experimenter, smiled more, talked more, and spent more time with the customer than when experimenters were nonrewarding (e.g., were interested in a low-priced purchase, dressed as if lower in status, or lacked expertise). Distance violations also induced salespeople to show more interest and talk more loudly with "high reward" experimenters. When the violator was low in reward value, salespeople talked less, spoke more loudly, and showed more tension as the experimenter moved farther away. Finally, distance violations produced evidence of arousal in the targets, who also appeared more distracted. These arousal and distraction effects were consistent with the predictions of the model.

Many of the earlier experiments that found distance adjustments to affect persuasion and helping behavior can also be interpreted as fitting a violations model. In the cases where the violator was a stranger or there was no apparent explanation for a violation, it can be assumed that such encounters qualified as nonrewarding. Hence one would predict, from this theory, that distance violations such as invasions of personal space should produce less helping behavior or persuasion. Conversely, when the violation could be justified or seen as rewarding (e.g., by giving positive feedback or behaving enthusiastically), greater helpfulness and persuasiveness should have occurred. That is exactly what was found in the experiments by Baron (1978), Baron and Bell (1976), Imada and Hakel (1977), Konečni et al. (1975), and Smith and Knowles (1979).

Violations of proxemic expectations alone may be sufficient to improve persuasiveness by increasing the arousal experienced by the target (Patterson, 1983). In one study (Buller, 1987), confederates adopted either close, normative, or far distances when requesting that subjects sign a petition. Close distances produced the most compliance with the request, whereas compliance decreased in the normative and far conditions. This effect of close distances occurred even though the rewarding nature of the confederates was not manipulated. Buller concluded that violations of proxemic expectations that signal increased involvement arouse targets, who decide to comply with the request to reduce this arousal.

Three studies (Burgoon, et al., 1986; Burgoon, Manusov, Mineo, & Hale, 1985; Manusov, 1984) tested the effects of gaze violations on willingness to hire a job applicant. One experiment (Burgoon et al., 1985) found that nearly continuous or normal gaze produced the greatest likelihood of being endorsed for the job, while averted gaze lowered one's prospects. The two other studies failed to find any effects on hiring. However, if the findings on attraction and credibility are considered, it appears that averted gaze is a negative violation, regardless of who commits it, while high degrees of gaze serve as a positive violation for most communicators.

In a more recent experiment (Burgoon & Le Poire, 1993), communicator reward valence and preinteraction expectations were manipulated by attributing to a target confederate either positive or negative personal attributes and an engaging, easy communication style or a detached and difficult one. Subsequently, the confederate either exhibited an involved-pleasant or uninvolved-unpleasant communication style that served to confirm expectations for some subjects but violate them for others. Results showed that preinteraction expectations continued to influence evaluations of the target person and his or her behavior, but that positive violations by targets intensified the credibility and attraction subjects assigned to them relative to communication that conformed to expectations.

Finally, research on dress reveals that deviant dress can sometimes be successful in achieving influence if it is coupled with something else that serves as a positive violation. For example, if a nonconformist appearance sets up negative expectations, a well-presented verbal message or an unexpected message may serve as a positive violation, enhancing persuasiveness. When there is no contrasting positive information, deviant dress most often produces less compliance and helping behavior than conformist dress.

At this juncture, the research evidence on expectancy violations with regard to social influence suggests the following conclusions. Violations of expectations arouse and distract recipients, shifting greater attention to the violator and the meaning of the violation itself (Buller, 1986; Burgoon & Hale, 1988). People who can assume they are well regarded by their audience (e.g., are more credible, have higher status, or are more attractive) are safer engaging in violations than people who are poorly regarded when attempting to influence others. The reward valence of the communicator can be especially significant when the violation is likely to be ambiguous or is open to multiple interpretations which are not uniformly positive or negative (e.g., conversational proximity and touch). When violations have relatively consensual meanings and valences (e.g., gaze and nonverbal involvement), they produce similar persuasive effects regardless of the reward valence of the communicator.

Strategies That Reinforce Learning

The earlier discussion of how nonverbal behaviors can signal expectations points out that the classroom is an environment in which influence often occurs. Nonverbal communication can affect learning in more overt ways than simply by signaling teachers' expectations (for reviews, see Andersen, 1986, and Smith, 1979). A teacher's nonverbal immediacy behaviors can affect students' attitudes and feelings toward a subject area (Andersen, 1979). More eye contact, smiling, vocal expressiveness, physical proximity, appropriate touching, leaning toward a student, gesturing, overall body movement, and relaxation communicate liking and positive affect toward students and the educational experience (Andersen, 1979, 1986). Students respond to teachers' immediacy behaviors by developing positive attitudes toward the content area being taught, by becoming more likely to take courses in the content area in the future (Andersen, 1979; Andersen, Norton, & Nussbaum, 1981; Kearney et al., 1985; McDowell et al., 1980; Plax et al., 1986), by being more motivated to study (Frymier, 1993), and, according to students' own perceptions, by actually learning more (Gorham, 1988; Richmond et al., 1986; Woolfolk & Brooks, 1985). Studies of Inuit and Caucasian children found that a warmer teaching style—smiling, close distances, touch, and direct body orientation—

increased learning for both groups of children (Kleinfeld, 1973, 1974). This style may be effective when instructing people outside classroom environments as well. Hudson and Blane (1985) found that children were most likely to follow instructions from their mothers when learning a new task if the mothers were more immediate (stood closer, squatted or kneeled to be at child's level, engaged in greater eye contact) and vocally pleasant.

If you reflect on your own educational experience, these findings are not surprising. One of the factors that probably influenced you to continue taking courses in a certain area is an instructor who was very positive, enthusiastic, and approachable. The relationship between an instructor's immediacy and a student's positive attitude also suggests that the opposite can happen: instructors who do not display immediacy cues may turn students off a given area of content, resulting in students' having negative attitudes toward the content and being less likely to continue study in that area.

Maintaining students' attention is essential for effective teaching. The classroom environment is itself a crucial determinant of attention. Yet many classrooms are poorly designed and may actually be distracting. The windowless classroom, an innovation intended to reduce distractions from outdoors (and to reduce heating costs), has failed to improve learning and has resulted in less pleasant moods on the part of students (Karmel, 1965). Open classroom designs, also intended to aid learning, have likewise impaired attention by not providing enough privacy for groups of students and by allowing too much noise (Rivlin & Rothenberg, 1976). It has been argued that learning environments should tend toward simplicity, as too many stimuli can prove distracting (see Fisher et al., 1984). One study confirmed that greater learning occurs in less complex settings (Porteous, 1972). Ideally, one would like to strike a balance between environments that are too complex and distracting and environments that are so simple and bland as to be boring. It is possible that type of learning (rote versus experiential versus semantic-based) and complexity of the material to be learned may determine level of attention and environmental stimulation needed.

Color and intensity of lighting also may affect attention and learning. German experimenters found that placing children in brightly colored playrooms increased their IQ by 12 points, while those placed in white, black, or brown rooms lost 14 IQ points (cited in Silden, 1973). Presumably, the color of the environment affected their general level of alertness and mental quickness. Look at the colors in your classroom the next time you're there. Do they help keep you mentally alert or are they so bland that they decrease your performance?

In another investigation (Sadesky, 1974), subjects received the highest scores on a multiple-choice test after interacting in a room with either low-intensity red lighting or medium-intensity blue lighting. Test scores were lowest when high-intensity white light was used. If an attention effect was at work in this study, high-intensity white light might be distracting. Such an effect seems plausible, as there are many reflective surfaces (white paper, floor tile) in typical classrooms off which white light may bounce, creating distraction. This may explain the popularity of florescent lighting, which delivers a softer, less reflective white light, in classrooms.

Another way in which nonverbal cues may facilitate learning has to do with their regulative function (Andersen, 1986). As we noted earlier, regulatory cues serve to keep conversants on track and can therefore enhance learning. As in informal conversation, these cues regulate who speaks when, for how long, and on what topic, although in the classroom the regulation process is a bit more formal. Skillful use of regulative cues by an instructor can apportion floor time fairly among students, prompt some students to speak and limit others, keep students' comments on the topic, and provide a better over-all flow for class discussion. The upshot of these regulative effects is to make the material being discussed in class more comprehensible for students.

Nonverbal behaviors also can enhance a productive and supportive classroom climate by signaling instructors' power and status (Andersen, 1986; Plax et al., 1986; Richmond et al., 1985). Because we often like powerful people, who are in a position to reward us, nonverbal cues that send power and status messages can increase students' liking for an instructor. Greater liking in turn can enhance student motivation and cognitive learning. As Andersen (1986) pointed out, nonverbal power and status messages may be especially effective because they can be nonoffensive ways of indicating power and status. However, an instructor's verbal behavior, in both style and content, must be congruent with nonverbal power and status messages; over time, students pick up on inconsistent or unconvincing messages.

Finally, modeling is an important method of learning, especially among young children. It might be considered a special case of reciprocity, but modeling is so fundamental to learning that we include it in this section. A number of experiments have produced evidence that children and adults adopt behaviors they see modeled (Bandura, 1965, 1977). Children who watched an adult display aggressive behavior toward a doll later exhibited the same behavior in free play and were more violent than children who did not witness the model's behavior. In another study, Zimmerman and Brody (1975) showed that black and white children who observed a black child and a white child interacting on film adopted the interaction style they saw. When they observed the models interacting in a warm fashion, the children played closer together, faced each other more directly, and engaged in more eye contact than they did after observing the models interacting in a cold manner.

Modeling may also operate among older children and adults in novel situations and situations characterized by uncertainty. In such situations, communicators may look to the behavior of others for examples of appropriate behavior. For example, a new employee may observe and attempt to imitate the expressive behavior of a senior employee in a task situation. A new student may model the physical appearance of established students to conform to the norms of the university context. Modeling is more likely to occur when either the model or the observer is reinforced (Bandura, 1977; Tan, 1986). Hence modeling should be more successful if the communicator has a favorable image, and less successful if the communicator has an unfavorable image.

Modeling as a response also may manipulate behavior. Bates (1973) found that children who modeled the behavior of male college students attempting to teach basketball moves received more positive verbal and nonverbal responses than children instructed not to model the college students' behavior. Modeling, then, may be selected as a method of flattery and a way to obtain approval from others.

Box 14-4 gives an example of shaping in the classroom.

> **BOX 14-4**
>
> ### APPLICATIONS: SHAPING BEHAVIOR NONVERBALLY
>
> Sara is attempting to explain to her fifth-grade class-mates how Egyptians mummified their dead. As she begins her explanation, the teacher looks at her expectantly; as Sara proceeds correctly, the teacher nods frequently. When Sara begins to make an error, the teacher cocks her head and narrows her eyes. Sara revises her statement; the teacher smiles and Sara continues. At the conclusion of Sara's presentation, the teacher gives another reassuring smile and praises Sara warmly for her informative talk. That night, Sara delightedly repeats her newfound knowledge to her parents, without error.
>
> This vignette illustrates the use of nonverbal cues to achieve influence. The teacher's kinesic cues served as positive and negative feedback, which shaped Sara's behavior and ultimately reinforced her learning of the material.

Strategies That Reward and Punish

Nonverbal behaviors may be used quite effectively to shape other people's knowledge, attitudes, and behavior, outside as well as inside the classroom. Basic strategies include positive or negative feedback that reinforces someone's actions and more negative cues, such as threat displays, that serve as punishment.

Positive and Negative Feedback   Positive and negative nonverbal feedback are forms of observable responses to someone else's behavior, designed to maintain or change that behavior. Two forms of positive nonverbal feedback can be distinguished: positive and negative reinforcement. *Positive reinforcement* is a set of rewarding nonverbal cues presented after a desired behavior occurs. *Negative reinforcement* is a set of negative nonverbal cues that the target tries to escape or avoid by exhibiting the desired behavior. The key outcome of both types of reinforcement is the increase or maintenance of a particular behavior. Negative feedback, also called *punishment,* is a set of negative nonverbal cues presented after some behavior by the target, with the goal of decreasing that behavior. Educators argue that positive feedback is preferable to negative feedback, because positive feedback both rewards the target and informs the target about the appropriate, desired behavior. Negative feedback simply punishes undesirable behavior. Many people have difficulty managing negative feedback effectively and at the same time fail to realize how often they communicate negative feedback to others who behave undesirably.

It has generally been assumed that smiles, nods, forward leaning, frequent gaze, touching, approving vocal cues, and the like serve as positive feedback. Frowns, scowls, knitted brows, reduced eye contact, neutral and negative facial expressions, angry or cold vocal tones, and silence serve as negative reinforcement if they function to increase a desired behavior and punishment if they function to extinguish or reduce undesired behavior.

Evidence supports the beneficial effects of positive feedback. When male and female interviewers nod their heads, smile, or both, they also increase the number of feeling and self-reference statements they make (Hackney, 1974). When teachers use nonverbal approval cues (smiling and touch), students increase their attention in class (Kazdin & Klock, 1973). Positive nonverbal patterns increase children's play activity (Jacunska-Iwinska, 1975), self-disclosure, and ratings of a source's attractiveness (Woolfolk & Woolfolk, 1974). Positive nonverbal feedback—increased smiling, eye contact, positive facial expressions, and positive vocalic cues—from a counselor increases clients' interest in trying to make changes to solve their problems (Bourget, 1977). In turn, when clients use increased eye contact, forward leaning, nodding, gesturing, and verbal reinforcers in response to counselors' feeling statements, counselors make more such statements (Lee, Hallberg, Hassard, & Haase, 1979).

Positive nonverbal feedback does not always work in expected ways. Experiments by Banks (1974), Isenberg and Bass (1974), and Furbay (1965) failed to find any reinforcing effects on subjects' speech production, intelligence test scores, learning, and persuasion. It seems that the specific combination of nonverbal cues and their relationship to the verbal message determine the reinforcing effect of positive nonverbal feedback. Stewart and Patterson (1973) found that thematic responses by subjects increased most when eye contact was coupled with greater distance. Greene (1977) found that closer proximity increased compliance with a counselor's recommendations only when coupled with accepting verbal feedback. When coupled with neutral feedback, increased proximity reduced compliance, perhaps because it transmitted an inconsistent or mixed message. The combination of proximity and accepting verbal feedback was a more consistent and powerful reinforcing message.

In much of the research just reported, positive feedback was compared with no feedback or negative feedback. Thus these experiments, which show increased behavior following positive feedback, also provide evidence of decreased behavior following negative or less positive feedback. Taken together, the research indicates that the most effective positive nonverbal reinforcement cues are eye contact, smiling, and nodding, and changes in proximity are important to the extent that they complement verbal and nonverbal feedback (Edinger & Patterson, 1983).

Communicators often seek to obtain reinforcing behaviors from others. Rosenfeld (1966a, 1966b) found that when asked to seek approval from a target, people increased their smiling, nodding, gesturing, and duration of utterances. They also reduced the display of adaptors but increased the number of speech disturbances. Further, targets interacting with communicators who sought their approval provided them with more positive feedback, particularly in the form of more smiling. Seeking approval may involve two processes discussed earlier. First, many cues can also be used as positive nonverbal feedback cues; when used to seek approval, they may signal interpersonal expectations that are fulfilled by the target's subsequent positive feedback. Second, strategies for seeking approval may rely on the norm of reciprocity. Targets may be predisposed to reciprocate the positive cues displayed by communicators who seek approval.

Threat Cues   Threat cues are another evaluative nonverbal message. However, rather than being designed exclusively to punish the target's behavior, threat cues are often encoded to inhibit future behavior and to cause the target to leave the environment. The ability of threat cues to influence a target's behavior lies in their arousing, aversive nature, often resulting in flight. Drawing on Hediger's theory of *critical flight distance*

(1950), Ginsburg et al. (1977) held that if the environment allows flight as an adaptive response, one may flee when threatened or display submissive behaviors that dissipate the threat, such as lowering the head, avoiding eye contact, or increasing conversational distance. If flight is not an option, because of physical or social constraints, aggressive responses, such as a reciprocal threat display or actual physical aggression, may be more adaptive. Ginsburg et al. showed that children in a small, physically constrained playground were more aggressive toward each other than children in a larger, less constrained playground. Similar findings were reported some 60 years ago by Jersild and Markey (1935) and Murphy (1937). The upshot of all this is that threat cues arouse targets. In coping with an aversive arousal, targets choose the most adaptive response, either some form of flight or a reciprocal display of aggression.

Alexander Solzhenitsyn's chilling description (1973) of how Russian prisoners were treated en route to prison camps during the 1940s, excerpted earlier in this chapter, demonstrates some of the ruthless, effective ways in which nonverbal threat cues have been used to elicit desired behavior. Brusque movements and loud, threatening voices are very familiar to us from films, where they form part of the repertoire of stock dictators, military leaders, and gangsters. Of course, these methods are not just media fantasies. They exist in real life, and they need not be blatant to work. A slight innuendo in a voice can make a child stop whining or an assembly line worker buy an unwanted lottery ticket from a supervisor. Battered wives have reported that they knew when their husbands intended to beat them by their tone of voice.

As noted in our discussion of intimacy cues, the eyes are powerful threat cues. The infamous Rasputin was alleged to have gained his great command over men and women through his penetrating, almost hypnotic stare. Charles Manson's eyes were the subject of much comment and apprehension during his trial; even his lawyer, Vincent Bugliosi, said that he found something frightening in Manson's steady gaze. If a stranger has ever held eye contact with you too long, you know how uncomfortable and disconcerting that can be.

Several investigations confirm that prolonged staring is aversive and interpreted as threatening (Edinger & Patterson, 1983; Ellsworth & Carlsmith, 1973; Ellsworth et al., 1972; Geller & Malia, 1981; Patterson, 1983). Cross-species comparisons show staring to be a frequent component of threat displays in primates. Staring is often observed immediately preceding an attack or as a substitute for an attack. In humans, staring may take on special significance because it is a very salient interpersonal stimulus that demands a response. Staring is less threatening if the appropriate response is readily apparent. When situational or relational cues do not indicate an appropriate response, staring is more threatening, evokes more tension in the target, and increases the target's motivation to escape the situation. Flight, which removes the aversive staring stimulus, then becomes negatively reinforced (Ellsworth & Carlsmith, 1973; Ellsworth et al., 1972).

Several laboratory and field experiments provide support for staring as a threat. Kidd (1975) found that staring reduced a target's aggressiveness. Ellsworth and Carlsmith (1973) reported that when a confederate stared at an angered subject, the subject reduced the level of electric shock supposedly being delivered to the confederate. An earlier field experiment by Ellsworth et al. (1972) showed that when a confederate stared at a driver

Charles Manson was
infamous for his
threatening stare.

who was waiting at a stoplight, the driver drove much faster across the intersection after the light changed to green.

For staring to be an effective threat cue, it is necessary that it be unwavering. That is, constant staring at another person can engender anxiety and escape. However, if the stare vacillates, its impact is severely curtailed (Ellsworth & Carlsmith, 1973; Geller & Malia, 1981; Schlenker, 1980). A vacillating stare may signal uncertainty or weakness by the communicator. Targets then may feel that they can resist or punish the communicator. In Ellsworth and Carlsmith's experiment, vacillating stares increased the severity of shocks supposedly delivered by subjects to the staring confederate. Geller and Malia found that a brief hesitation in staring reduced the assistance given to male confederates. Staring may be a more relevant threat cue for males, so vacillation did more harm to male than female confederates in this study (see also our earlier discussion of the 1979 experiment by Valentine and Ehrlichman).

Kinesic cues are also used in threat displays. In Chapters 2 and 11, we noted that showing the tongue can be a threat cue, particularly when one wants to be left alone or wants others to keep their distance (Horn, 1973). The same behavior appears among apes and monkeys. Certain emblems, particularly those with negative or obscene meanings (e.g., "the finger") and those that connote power (e.g., a clenched fist), are frequently used as threat displays. Forceful gestures are also included in many threat displays, as are hostile, negative facial expressions. It should come as no surprise that staring is a dominant component in a facial expression of anger.

Finally, physical appearance cues can be threatening. Physical size, both muscle mass and height, can be used to threaten others. The cliché, "I wouldn't want to meet that guy in a dark alley," attests to the threatening nature of some physical appearance cues. Greater size connotes a greater ability to control the environment, including others (Kitahara, 1985).

SUMMARY

This chapter has examined the multifaceted role of nonverbal communication in achieving social influence. It began with the assumption that communicators strategically select their nonverbal messages to influence others. One set of nonverbal messages is designed to project an image of authority, power, and credibility. A second set of nonverbal messages relies on establishing an intimate relationship between the communicator and the target. Communicators use nonverbal cues to signal affiliation, liking, and immediacy. Often physical appearance cues are manipulated to influence the communicator's attractiveness on the assumption that beauty persuades. Interpersonal expectations about the target's behavior are important in the social influence process, because communicators can subtly and unknowingly signal these expectations to targets, who may fulfill them. In interpersonal relationships, communicators also employ patterns of nonverbal behavior that reciprocate or compensate the nonverbal pattern employed by the target in order to change the target's behavior. Further, communicators can violate nonverbal expectations to improve persuasiveness and compliance or to distract attention to favorable communicator characteristics. Nonverbal behaviors are also crucial when teaching others. A final group consists of nonverbal messages that signal positive and negative evaluations to targets to maintain, change, or inhibit behavior. This group of messages includes positive and negative nonverbal feedback and nonverbal threat cues.

SUGGESTED READINGS

Bickman, L. (1974, April). Social roles and uniforms: Clothes make the person. *Psychology Today, 7,* 48–51.

Buller, D. B., & Aune, R. K. (1988). The effects of vocalics and nonverbal sensitivity on compliance: A speech accommodation theory explanation. *Human Communication Research, 14,* 301–332.

Burgoon, J. K. (1995). Cross-cultural and intercultural applications of expectancy violations theory. In R. L. Wiseman (Ed.), *Intercultural Communication Theory* (Vol. 19, pp. 194–214). Thousand Oaks, CA: Sage.

Cialdini, R. B. (1988). *Influence: Science and practice,* 2d ed. Glenview, IL: Scott, Foresman.

Edinger, J. A., & Patterson, M. L. (1983). Nonverbal involvement and social control. *Psychological Bulletin, 93,* 30–56.

Harris, M. J., & Rosenthal, R. (1985). Mediation of interpersonal expectancy effects: 31 meta-analyses. *Psychological Bulletin, 97,* 363–386.

Pallak, S. R., Murroni, E., & Koch, J. (1983). Communicator attractiveness and expertise, emotional versus rational appeals, and persuasion: A heuristic versus systematic processing interpretation. *Social Cognition, 2,* 122–141.

Petty, R. E., Wells, G. L., Heesacker, M., Brock, T. C., & Cacioppo, J. T. (1983). The effects of recipient posture on persuasion: A cognitive response analysis. *Personality and Social Psychology Bulletin, 9,* 209–222.

Rosenberg, S. W., Kahn, S., & Tran, T. (1991). Creating a political image: Shaping appearance and manipulating the vote. *Political Behavior, 13,* 345–367.

Rosenthal, R. (1985). Nonverbal cues in the mediation of interpersonal expectancy effects. In A. W. Siegman & S. Feldstein (Eds.), *Multichannel integrations of nonverbal behavior* (pp. 105–128). Hillsdale, NJ: Erlbaum.

Snyder, M. (1992). Motivational foundations of behavioral confirmation. In M. P. Zanna (Ed.), *Advances in experimental social psychology* (Vol. 25, pp. 67–114). New York: Academic.

Wiemann, J. M. (1985). Power, status, and dominance: Interpersonal control and regulation in conversation. In R. L. Street, Jr., & J. N. Cappella (Eds.), *Sequence and pattern in communicative behavior* (pp. 85–102). London: Arnold.

15

DECEIVING OTHERS

The face is the mirror of the mind, and the eyes, without speaking, confess the secrets of the heart.

St. Jerome

Most people assume that interpersonal interactions are truthful and believe that deceit is reprehensible and immoral. But deception—intentional, strategic management of information by a sender to foster a false belief or conclusion by the receiver—is an integral part of everyday life. Deception can be indispensable for maximizing rewards, negotiating relationships, and managing one's image (Bok, 1978; Buller & Burgoon, 1994; Burgoon, Buller, Guerrero, Afifi, & Feldman, in press; Knapp & Comadena, 1979; Lippard, 1988; Turner, Edgley, & Olmstead, 1975; Wolk & Henley, 1970; Zuckerman, DePaulo, & Rosenthal, 1981). It is a highly adaptive, competent communication strategy that some researchers have argued might have arisen through natural selection (Camden, Motley, & Wilson, 1984; Kraut, 1980; Leakey & Lewin, 1978).

THE NATURE OF NONVERBAL DECEPTION

Deception, broadly conceived as a method of controlling information, is a communication strategy; its morality is determined by the motives of the deceiver. It is so common that in one study, in which the participants were asked to keep a log of their conversations, only about one-third of the exchanges were found to be entirely honest (i.e., did not contain verbal expressions that controlled information) (Turner et al., 1975).

People deceive for the same reasons they tell the truth: deception is functional (Camden et al., 1984; Lindskold & Walters, 1983; Metts & Chronis, 1986; Turner et al.,

1975). As Table 15-1 shows, motives for deception have to do with basic needs, affiliation, self-esteem, cognitive consistency, and entertainment. Moreover, deception can benefit a conversational partner or a third person, as well as the sender, although benefit to oneself may be the most common motive (Camden et al., 1984; Ekman, 1985; Metts & Chronis, 1986).

It seems that men and women differ in their use of, and motives for, deceit. Men may feel that deceit is more permissible than women do. Women's lies may be motivated more than men's by affiliation, especially when they are trying to avoid relationships. Women may also deceive more than men to benefit a partner, especially to protect a partner's self-esteem. Men may lie more to protect their own self-esteem in general and to protect their image when conversing with a woman (Camden et al., 1984; Lindskold & Walters, 1983; Metts & Chronis, 1986). Although these gender differences may apply only to young adults, they suggest that the sexes differ in their approach to deception.

Defining Deception

Typically, *deception* is defined as an intentional, conscious act that "fosters in another person a belief or understanding which the deceiver considers false" (Zuckerman,

TABLE 15-1
MOTIVES FOR DECEPTION

Camden, Motley, and Wilson	Metts and Chronis
I. Basic needs	I. Partner-focused motives
A. Acquisition of resources	A. Avoid hurting partner
B. Protection of resources	B. Regulate or constrain partner's self-image
II. Affiliation	C. Permissible deception owing to partner's previous deception
A. Positive	D. Maintain partner's face or self-esteem
1. Initiate interaction	E. Uncertain about partner's attitudes, feelings, preferences, etc.
2. Continue interaction	F. Concern for partner's mental or physical state
3. Avoid relational conflict	G. Protect partner's relationship with a third party
4. Obligatory acceptance	H. Avoid worrying partner
B. Negative	II. Self-focused motives
1. Avoid social interaction	A. Self would suffer "stress" and abuse from partner
2. Leave taking	B. Protect partner's presumed image of self
C. Conversational control	C. Enhance self-image
1. Redirect conversation	D. Fear of being resented for telling truth
2. Avoid self-disclosure	E. Protect or retain own resources
III. Self-esteem	F. Ensure continued reward or service from partner
A. Competence	G. Issue too trivial
B. Taste	H. Issue too private to tell or forbidden to tell
C. Social desirability	I. Own feelings too confused to express
IV. Other	III. Relationship-focused motives
A. Reduction of dissonance	A. Avoid conflict
B. Practical joke	B. Avoid relational trauma
C. Exaggeration for effect	C. Avoid unpleasant, repetitive episodes
	D. Avoid violation of role expectation

Sources: Adapted from Camden, Motley, & Wilson, 1984; Metts & Chronis, 1986.

DePaulo, & Rosenthal, 1981, p. 3). This definition rules out self-deception, intentionally transparent lies (sarcasm, joking, and social amenities), and statements mistakenly identified as lies (information that the sender believes is true but is actually false). In practice, deception can be achieved in various ways. Senders can manipulate messages in terms of (1) completeness, (2) directness or relevance, (3) clarity, (4) personalization, and (5) veridicality (Burgoon, Buller, Guerrero, Afifi, & Feldman, in press; see also McCornack's *information manipulation theory*, 1992). These dimensions of deception apply primarily to the central message, which is usually verbal. Accompanying this central message, however, are two messages that rely extensively on nonverbal behavior: ancillary messages designed to bolster the credibility of sender and message and inadvertent cues that signal psychological reactions such as arousal, affect, and cognitive processing. Unfortunately, most research on deception has focused on messages in which veridicality or honesty is manipulated, although recent investigations have focused on other forms such as equivocation and concealment (see, e.g., Bavelas, Black, Chovil, & Mullett, 1990; Buller, Burgoon, Buslig, & Roiger, 1994, in press; Buller, Burgoon, White, & Ebesu, 1994).

Theoretical Approaches to Nonverbal Deception

The Leakage Hypothesis   Research on nonverbal behaviors of deceivers occurred as early as the 1920s (see, e.g., English, 1926; Goldstein, 1923), but it began in earnest with a study by Ekman and Friesen (1969a). Ekman and Friesen offered a *leakage hypothesis* of behavior in deceptive messages: deceivers attempt to control their nonverbal presentations to avoid giving the receivers any behavioral clues that deception is occurring *(deception cues)* or any clues to the nature of their true feelings *(leakage cues).* The success of such attempts at control is determined by senders' internal reactions to the deception and by the controllability, sending capacities, and external feedback of the nonverbal channels.

Ekman and Friesen speculated that when people deceive, they experience some internal emotional reaction. Such reactions generally are negative, taking the form of guilt and anxiety about the possibility of detection. However, deceivers can also experience overeagerness and "delight" about duping someone. Generalized arousal accompanying these emotions and anxiety may then be automatically exhibited by the deceiver.

The controllability and sending capacities of the nonverbal channels determine whether a particular channel will display cues to internal reactions. *Controllability* relates to an encoder's awareness of cues in a channel and ability to recall, repeat, or specifically display a planned sequence of cues. *Sending capacity* concerns how many different messages can be sent, how quickly they can be sent, and how visible and salient they are in a channel. The extent to which a receiver attends to, comments on, reacts to, and holds a person responsible for messages in a channel determines the external feedback an encoder receives to a channel. Deceivers are less likely to display nonverbal cues reflecting internal reactions in channels that are highly controllable, have a large sending capacity, and receive extensive external feedback.

There is a *leakage hierarchy,* then, among the various nonverbal channels (Buller & Burgoon, 1994; DePaulo, Stone, & Lassiter, 1985a; DePaulo, Zuckerman, & Rosenthal, 1980b; Ekman & Friesen, 1969a, 1974; Zuckerman & Driver, 1985). Facial cues are thought to be least likely to leak information about deception because (1) encoders are highly aware of them; (2) such cues are highly visible, can send many different messages, and can send messages rapidly; and (3) receivers are likely to attend and react to facial cues. Bodily cues are more likely to leak information because they are less controllable, have a lower sending capacity, and receive less external feedback. Many characteristics of vocalic cues suggest that they would be less likely to leak information about deception: senders obtain excellent internal feedback and can control the larynx; vocalic cues are able to transmit rapidly a wide range of messages; and receivers attend and react to vocalic cues. However, for reasons not fully understood, vocalic cues actually leak as much as body cues (DePaulo et al., 1980a; Zuckerman & Driver, 1985). The automatic link between internal affective reactions and vocalic cues may be particularly strong, and encoders may pay less attention to the vocalic portion of speech than is commonly assumed. Finally, the verbal channel is considered least likely to leak clues to deception; however, several studies show that this assumption, too, might be somewhat in error (Buller, Burgoon, Buslig, & Roiger, 1994, in press; DePaulo, Zuckerman, & Rosenthal, 1980a; Knapp, Hart, & Dennis, 1974; Littlepage & Pineault, 1978, 1981; Zuckerman & Driver, 1985).

The Four-Factor Theory   Zuckerman, DePaulo, and Rosenthal (1981) extended the leakage hypothesis by proposing four factors that influence displays of cues: (1) *attempted control*, (2) *arousal*, (3) *affective reactions*, and (4) *cognitive processing*. Deceivers attempt to control their nonverbal display, but owing to differences in internal feedback, sending capacities, and external feedback, attempted control produces more deliberate and inconsistent presentations. Deceivers will experience autonomic arousal that can produce changes such as dilated pupils, faster blinking, higher vocal pitch, and more speech disturbances. Like Ekman and Friesen, Zuckerman et al. suggested that deceivers experience affective reactions, most commonly guilt and anxiety, which are reflected in their nonverbal display. Deceivers may exhibit less pleasant facial expressions and vocalic cues, more adaptors, and less immediacy (i.e., less eye contact, less direct body orientation, less proximity, and fewer illustrators). Finally, deception requires more cognitive effort than telling the truth, and this effort can be reflected in more pauses during speech, increased response latencies (time from the end of a question to the beginning of a response), more dilation of the pupils, and fewer illustrators.

Research to identify behaviors associated with nonverbal leakage has produced mixed findings. For instance, among vocalic cues, three studies found that pitch increased during deception, but another study found that pitch did not discriminate honesty from deception. Liars have been found to talk for shorter periods than truth tellers in three studies, but in another experiment they did not differ in time spent talking. Likewise, two studies reported that deception was associated with more speech errors, but this association was not found in a third study (deTurck & Miller, 1985; Ekman, Friesen, O'Sullivan, & Scherer, 1980; Ekman, Friesen, & Scherer, 1976; Knapp et al., 1974; Kraut, 1978; Matarazzo, Weins, Jackson, & Manaugh, 1970; Mehrabian, 1971a; Motley, 1974; Streeter, Krauss, Geller, Olson, & Apple, 1977; Zuckerman, DeFrank, Hall, Larrance, & Rosenthal, 1979). Similar inconsistencies emerged from research on the kinesic channel, specifically in positivity of facial cues, amount of eye contact, and frequency of gesturing (deTurck & Miller, 1985; Ekman & Friesen, 1972; Ekman et al., 1976; Feldman, Devin-Sheehan, & Allen, 1978; Hocking & Leathers, 1980; Knapp et al., 1974; Kraut, 1978; Matarazzo et al., 1970; McClintock & Hunt, 1975; Mehrabian, 1971a, 1972; Riggo & Friedman, 1983; Zuckerman, Larrance, Hall, DeFrank, & Rosenthal, 1979).

Not surprisingly, some researchers have claimed that nonverbal cues are unreliable indicators of deception, and thus that receivers use them (if at all) only to confirm suspicions of either deception or truth, not to discriminate between deceivers and truth tellers (Kraut, 1978, 1980). Other scholars, however, take issue with this position, asserting that some consistency in cue display has been shown. In three extensive reviews of the data on cues to actual deception, Zuckerman, DePaulo, and Rosenthal (1981; DePaulo et al., 1985a; Zuckerman & Driver, 1985) showed that several nonverbal cues are, in fact, consistently related to deception. They found that 58 percent of behaviors examined in two or more studies consistently discriminated deceivers from truth tellers (see Table 15-2). Deceivers display increased pupil dilation, faster rates of blinking, more adaptors, more segments of body behavior, and fewer segments of facial behavior. The last two of these variables are related to how much deliberate control is exercised over cues in a channel. Naturally occurring segments of behavior generally decrease as deliberate control increases. Thus liars' facial cues are more deliberate and controlled than their body cues. Deceivers' voices are characterized by shorter answers, more errors, more hesitations, and higher pitch. Finally, there is more discrepancy between the nonverbal channels during deception than during truthful communication.

Interpersonal Deception Theory Two of the authors of this textbook have formulated a more comprehensive theory of deception in interpersonal exchange, *interpersonal deception theory* (IDT), synthesizing fundamental assumptions about interpersonal communication and deceptive communication (Buller & Burgoon, in press; Burgoon & Buller, 1994). IDT proposes that deception must be viewed as a communication process embedded in contextual and relational factors. Among the most important of these is an *interactive* (rather than noninteractive) context.

In IDT, deception is a series of moves and countermoves by both deceiver and receiver. Behaviors and interpretations by both are a function of (1) their communication goals, expectations, and skills; (2) contextual and relational factors; and (3) each other's behavior during the interaction. Thus, to understand the behavior of deceivers, one must consider the actions of receivers. According to IDT, senders monitor receivers' behavior for signs that their messages are believed or suspected. When receivers appear skeptical or suspicious, senders adjust their behavior to appear more credible. Hence, receivers can be their own worst enemy when attempting to verify senders' messages.

Moreover, behaviors by deceivers are enacted within the context of norms and expectations of interpersonal exchange, which often prescribe behavior that is at odds with the behavior witnessed in research on deception in largely noninteractive contexts. For instance, interpersonal interactions usually are characterized by a relatively high degree of nonverbal immediacy, affiliation cues, expressiveness, reciprocity of nonverbal

TABLE 15-2
NONVERBAL BEHAVIORS ASSOCIATED WITH DECEPTION

Nonverbal behavior	Associated with actual deception	Stereotypically associated with deception	Decoded as deception
Kinesic			
Pupil dilation	+	+	×
Gaze	0	−	−
Blinking	+	+	×
Smiling	0	+	−
Facial segmentation	−	×	×
Head movements	0	+	×
Gestures	0	0	×
Shrugs	0	+	×
Adaptors	+	+	0
Foot and leg movements	0	+	×
Postural shifts	0	+	+
Body segmentation	+	×	×
Vocalic			
Response latency	0	+	+
Response length	−	+	0
Speech rate	0	+	−
Speech errors	+	+	+
Speech hesitations	+	+	+
Pitch	+	+	+
Channel discrepancy	+	×	×

Note: + indicates that the behavior increased during actual deception, was believed to increase during deception, or increased in association with attributions of deception; − indicates that the behavior decreased during actual deception, was believed to decrease during deception, or decreased in association with attributions of deception; 0 indicates that a change in the behavior was not related to actual deception, beliefs about deception, or attributions of deception; × indicates that the role of the behavior was not investigated.

behavior, and well-coordinated conversational behavior. In a noninteractive context, by contrast, research implies that deceivers are withdrawn, uninvolved, anxious, uncomfortable, and conversationally impaired. Thus deceivers' behavior in interpersonal interchanges is likely to be the product of norms and behavioral tendencies in normal interpersonal exchange and of their attempts to bolster their credibility and avoid revealing their deceit.

The remainder of this chapter is organized around several issues and principles from IDT. In the section on deception displays, we begin by reviewing what nonverbal behaviors are used strategically to enhance a deceiver's credibility and what behaviors unintentionally leak the deception. We then consider how preinteractional and interactional factors influence the deceiver's nonverbal behavior. In the section on detecting deception and suspicion, we consider how receivers sense deception and how senders, in turn, sense this suspicion. The issue of accuracy in detection is considered at length. Behaviors associated with judgments of dishonesty and suspicion are also identified.

DECEPTION DISPLAYS

Strategic Behavior and Nonstrategic Leakage

The distinction in IDT between strategic behavior and nonstrategic leakage built upon work by Knapp et al. (1974) and Miller and Burgoon (1982). Deceivers strategically encode some behaviors to authenticate a message or to protect themselves or a relationship. At the same time, they inadvertently leak information about psychological processes (Buller & Burgoon, 1994, in press).

Three classes of *strategic behavior* are evident:

1 *Information management.* Predominantly linguistic. Used to modify the extent to which a message is complete, clear, relevant, veridical, and personal. Nonverbal behavior in this category conveys uncertainty and vagueness, withholds information (i.e., reticence), expresses nonimmediacy, and indicates insincerity.
2 *Image management.* Verbal and nonverbal behaviors used to make oneself appear poised, pleasant, and under control, in order to communicate competence, truthworthiness, and openness.
3 *Behavior management.* Mainly nonverbal actions designed to prevent leakage and detection, often by suppressing and restraining behavior that might expose ulterior motives. If carried to an extreme, behavior management can produce overcontrolled, rigid presentations, inexpressiveness, and lack of spontaneity.

Nonstrategic leakage includes:

1 *Arousal and nervousness.* Display of nonverbal cues that betray a heightened state of physiological arousal.
2 *Negative or dampened affect.* Verbal and nonverbal behaviors that leak unpleasant emotions or lack of emotion, possibly associated with guilt and embarrassment at deceiving.
3 *Noninvolvement.* Strategic performances have inadvertent by-products—an overcontrolled, rigid presentation; inexpressiveness; less spontaneous, less immediate verbal and nonverbal presentations that communicate less altercentrism.
4 *Performance decrements.* Extreme and nonnormative verbal and nonverbal behavior, awkward conversation, and discrepancies between channels that yield awkward, substandard communication, possibly resulting from increased cognitive effort or excessive motivation.

Our own research has found evidence for both strategic and nonstrategic activity during deception. For example, deceivers manage information by being brief and hesitant, manage behavior by being nonverbally nonimmediate, and manage image through increased pleasantness and relaxation over time. At the same time, they leak nervousness, arousal, and negative affect (at least initially); show nonfluencies; and convey poor

FRANK AND ERNEST   by Bob Thaves

Reprinted by permission of NEA, Inc.

impressions (Buller & Aune, 1987; Buller, Burgoon, Buslig, & Roiger, 1994; Buller, Burgoon, White, & Ebesu, 1994; Buller, Strzyzewski, & Comstock, 1991; Burgoon & Buller, 1994; Burgoon, Buller, Dillman, & Walther, 1995; Burgoon, Buller, Guerrero, Afifi, & Feldman, in press).

Preinteractional Factors Affecting Cue Displays

The general profile of nonverbal behavior during deception is modified substantially in actual communication by several preinteraction factors. These include communicators' personalities, motivation, age, and communication skills; their relationship with one another; and their opportunity to plan deceit.

Personality Two personality traits—Machiavellianism and self-monitoring—have received the most attention.

Machiavellian deceivers are highly manipulative and see lying as a justifiable means to an end; thus they should not experience the negative internal reactions that less Machiavellian liars experience. Further, Machiavellian senders are more skilled at controlling their spontaneous presentation; hence they should be more successful liars (Christie & Geis, 1970; DePaulo & Rosenthal, 1979b; Geis & Moon, 1981; Knapp & Comadena, 1979; O'Hair, Cody, & McLaughlin, 1981). However, the actual evidence for these assumptions is mixed. In some studies, highly Machiavellian liars engaged in more eye contact than less Machiavellian liars, exaggerated dishonest displays ("hammed"), were less likely to confess when accused, and were believed more by receivers. Some studies, though, found no differences between Machiavellian and less Machiavellian liars (DePaulo & Rosenthal, 1979b; Exline, Thibaut, Hickey, & Gumpert, 1970; Geis & Moon, 1981; Knapp et al., 1974; O'Hair et al., 1981).

Self-monitoring has to do with the ability to control expressive behavior (Snyder, 1974). Self-monitoring should make people more effective deceivers, but here again, results are mixed. Elliot (1979), Hemsley (1977), Krauss, Geller, and Olson (1976), and Lippa (1976) reported that "high self-monitors" were less detectable deceivers than "low self-monitors." Zuckerman, DeFrank, Hall, Larrance, and Rosenthal (1979), however, found that high self-monitors were more detectable than low self-monitors, and Zuckerman, DePaulo, and Rosenthal (1981) concluded that self-monitoring does not consistently affect the ability to deceive.

Another personality trait—*public self-consciousness*—has also been related to deception. Publicly self-conscious people are overly concerned with the appropriateness of their social behavior. Riggio, Tucker, and Widaman (1987) argued that such people would be more anxious when deceiving and that this would disrupt their performance. As they expected, these individuals did become less verbally fluent, made less eye contact and fewer head movements, and showed more emotional reactions when deceiving than less publicly self-conscious communicators.

Other personality characteristics that may be associated with the ability to deceive include *dominance, extroversion,* and *exhibitionism.* Riggio and Friedman (1983) reported that dominant, extroverted, and exhibitionistic deceivers control their nervous movements and increase their facial animation more than deceivers low in these traits. Reduction in nervous movements and increased facial animation mislead receivers.

Motivation   As we noted earlier, deception is undertaken for the same purposes as truthful communication. However, motivation may affect *how* deception is enacted (Buller & Burgoon, in press). For example, Metts and Chronis (1986) found that falsification is most common when deception is motivated by a desire to avoid hurting a partner, avoid relational trauma, or protect the deceiver's image. Also, deceit that is motivated by a desire to aid a partner or a third person, or simply to be polite, may involve less nonstrategic leakage because it provokes less apprehension about being detected (Buller & Burgoon, 1994).

The motivation to succeed at deceiving may be both beneficial and deleterious. We have observed that deceivers who are more motivated are judged by observers to be more successful than moderately motivated or unmotivated deceivers, possibly because they engage in strategic behaviors that bolster credibility (Burgoon, Buller, & Guerrero, 1995). However, some researchers claim that too much motivation to deceive can backfire—a "motivation impairment effect." Deceivers who are given incentives to deceive will attempt to manage their demeanor and are said to succeed at the verbal level but overcontrol nonverbal behavior, producing inconsistent presentations and poor conversational performances; they decrease blinking, have more neutral facial expressions, make fewer head movements, use fewer adaptors, make fewer postural shifts, provide shorter responses to questions, and talk more slowly (Bauchner, Brandt, & Miller, 1977; DePaulo & Kirkendol, 1989; DePaulo, Kirkendol, Tang, & O'Brien, 1988; DePaulo, Lanier, & Davis, 1983; Exline et al., 1970; Zuckerman et al., 1981; Zuckerman & Driver, 1985).

Age   Ability to deceive successfully increases with age (DePaulo et al., 1985a; Feldman & White, 1980; Zuckerman, DePaulo, & Rosenthal, 1981). It seems to increase during fourth and fifth grade, and this increase continues through high school. Very young children have no strategies; they leak cues and are easy to detect. The first real

strategy to emerge is naturalistic reproduction of emotions. This is followed by *hamming*—an ability to exaggerate affect. Hamming involves facial and body cues but not vocal cues, which remain leaky (DePaulo & Rosenthal, 1979b; DePaulo et al., 1985a). Children are successful liars primarily with peers and adult strangers; they have difficulty deceiving their parents (Allen & Atkinson, 1978; DePaulo et al., 1985b; Morency & Krauss, 1982). Finally, girls show an increasing ability to control facial cues with age, but a decreasing ability to control body cues. Boys show just the opposite tendencies (Feldman & White, 1980).

Communication Skills   Developmental changes suggest that successful deception is a skill. You probably know people who are good liars and people who are always caught at their lies. You yourself may be very adept at lying, or you may avoid lying because you are usually found out. Research on deception clearly shows that some people are consistently successful while others are consistently detected (Kraut, 1978; Miller & Burgoon, 1982; Zuckerman, Larrance, Spiegel, & Klorman, 1981).

Communication skills affect deception by influencing senders' ability to encode behavior that looks "normal." For example, in one study, people who had more social control (i.e., skills involving verbal self-presentation or role playing) were considered more believable when sending truthful and deceptive messages. People with more emotional control (i.e., skills involving the regulation of nonverbal affect displays) were more believable when telling the truth, but not when deceiving (Riggio, Tucker, & Throckmorton, 1987). A second study showed that people who could role-play effectively were also more fluent deceivers than unskilled people (Riggio, Tucker, & Widaman, 1987). Finally, our own research shows that senders who were more expressive nonverbally and had more verbal control but were *less* expressive verbally were the most believable. Skilled communicators were more fluent and less hesitant (Burgoon, Buller, & Guerrero, 1995). Communication skills may account for the "demeanor bias" observed by Zuckerman, DePaulo, and Rosenthal (1981)—some people looked truthful, whereas others looked and sounded deceitful.

Familiarity   People have information about one another that they can use when crafting lies. There are three types of familiarity. (1) *Informational* familiarity is background information about partners derived from a history of interactions or from third parties; (2) *Behavioral* familiarity is knowledge of partners' typical behavioral routines or general knowledge about typical deception cues, gained through training and experience; and (3) *Relational* familiarity consists of expectations about the other person based on the state of the relationship with that person.

Familiarity may improve our ability to detect deception or, in the case of relational familiarity, may alter our expectations about truthfulness. Thus deceivers react to familiarity by altering their performances. For instance, we observed that deceivers altered their nonverbal activity, nervousness, pleasantness, and kinesic expressivity when deceiving expert as opposed to novice interviewers. However, the exact pattern of behavior depended on whether deceivers falsified, equivocated, or concealed information (Buller, Burgoon, White, & Ebesu, 1994). As Box 15-1 illustrates, relational familiarity also makes a difference.

BOX 15-1

APPLICATIONS: DECEIVING FRIENDS AND LOVERS

Deception is no less common in conversations with intimates such as best friends, lovers, and spouses than it is in interactions with strangers. But motives for deception may differ in these relationships. Whereas strangers may be motivated mostly by, say, a desire to date an attractive partner, intimates have far more at stake (DePaulo, Stone, & Lassiter, 1985b). Friends, dating partners, and spouses deceive to avoid harming a partner, to protect a partner's imago, and to avoid conflict. Dating partners and spouses often also lie to protect a partner's self-esteem, but friends rarely cite this motive. Dating partners are more likely than spouses and friends to deceive to avoid relational trauma. Friends deceive to protect their resources, and dating partners deceive to protect their relationships; spouses are unlikely to deceive for either of these reasons (Metts & Chronis, 1986; Metts & Hippensteele, 1988).

Relational familiarity also affects behavior during deception. Compared with strangers, relational partners seem to monitor and control their nonverbal behavior during deception, particularly cues of arousal, negative affect, and immediacy (Buller & Aune, 1987). For instance, senders in one experiment were more expressive, less dominant, and less formal; reduced their random movement; and gave briefer answers when deceiving acquaintances than when telling them the truth. In contrast, senders showed fewer changes when deceiving strangers, with the exception that they were more dominant and displayed more random movement when deceiving as opposed to telling the truth to strangers.

Perhaps people are willing to take control of conversations when lying to strangers and are less concerned with nonverbal leakage than they are when deceiving friends. These patterns may make it more difficult to detect when someone we care for is lying to us.

Planning   Ability to plan a deception also seems to increase success by allowing more control over the nonverbal display, although its effect is not as great as that of motivation. Compared with lies that receive little or no planning, planned lies are characterized by increased pupil dilation, more smiling, less gesturing, more postural shifts, shorter response latencies, fewer unfilled pauses, shorter response lengths, and faster speech. Reduction in response latencies may be particularly important. However, two of the other cues encoded during planned lies correspond to actual cues of lying: increased pupil dilation and shorter response lengths. Thus planning does not result in complete control of the nonverbal display (Buller, Burgoon, White, Buslig, & Ebesu, 1995; di Battista, 1995; Littlepage & Pineault, 1979; O'Hair et al., 1981; Zuckerman, DePaulo, & Rosenthal, 1981; Zuckerman & Driver, 1985).

Interactional Factors Affecting Cue Displays

The behavioral profile of deception is fluid and dynamic. Deceivers modify and adapt their performances to the changing landscape of interaction. They make choices about how to manage the information in their central deception messages—for example, whether to falsify, equivocate, or conceal—and these choices precipitate a set of nonverbal behaviors. Deceivers also monitor receivers' reactions for indications of whether their messages have been accepted or have provoked skepticism or suspicion. When acceptance is evident, deceivers continue their initial performances; when suspicion is signaled, deceivers alter their behavior to bolster their credibility.

Type of Deception   Researchers have focused on one type of deception—falsification—almost to the exclusion of others. Actually, however (as we discussed earlier), senders can perpetrate several types of deception by managing how complete, clear, direct, relevant, personal, and veridical a message will be. The more common combinations are falsifying information, mixing truthful and dishonest information, exaggerating truthful information, concealing information, and misdirecting conversations away from particular information (Bavelas, Black, Chovil, & Mullett, 1990; Buller & Burgoon, 1994; Buller, Burgoon, White, & Ebesu, 1994; Burgoon, Buller, Guerrero, Afifi, & Feldman, in press; Hopper & Bell, 1984; Metts & Chronis, 1986; Metts & Hippensteele, 1988).

The choice of one type of deception over another may entail a particular set of nonverbal behaviors. Type of deception may affect apprehension of detection and motivation to succeed; for example, falsification may increase apprehension because it violates the expectation of honesty. Also, different types of deception may require different communication skills; for example, equivocation may place more cognitive demands on senders, who must tread a fine line between truth and deception.

Consistent with this speculation, we observed that senders appear vaguer, briefer, more hesitant, more defensive, and less active (they show less random movement and less nodding) when equivocating than when falsifying or concealing information. Random movement, though, was higher when senders falsified than when they concealed. Random movement in this case may have indicated more arousal when falsifying than when concealing, consistent with the notion that violations of the norm for truth increase apprehension (Buller, Burgoon, White, & Ebesu, 1994). Another investigation focusing primarily on equivocation described senders as less dominant, more kinesically expressive, less vocally expressive, and less pleasant when equivocating than when telling the truth. Reduced dominance may be a strategy for information management; kinesic expressivity may be a deliberate attempt to project a favorable image; and less vocal expressivity and less pleasantness may be nonstrategic leakage (Buller, Burgoon, Buslig, & Roiger, 1994).

Suspicion   Receivers frequently reveal nonverbally skepticism or suspicion—that is, their own belief, without proof or evidence sufficient to warrant certainty, that a communicator's speech or actions may be duplicitous. This information can be used by deceivers to modify their performance and improve their credibility.

How is suspicion signaled? Receivers may strategically manage their performance in an attempt to increase their ability to detect deception but at the same time leak nonstrategic behavior indicative of conversational impairment. Suspicious receivers seem to strategically take more control of, and become more involved in, the conversation, perhaps to steer it into areas in which they feel more confident about evaluating senders' credibility. However, receivers may try to temper their dominance with a positive, accepting demeanor. By being more pleasant and accepting, receivers may hope to make their attempts at control more palatable to senders and also avoid telegraphing their suspicions. However, suspicion may provoke anxiety about the sender's honesty and induce more cognitive effort to evaluate the sender's credibility, and this can interfere with the smooth management of conversation. For example, suspicious receivers have been observed to speak faster and less clearly and exhibit longer response latencies, more awkward turn switches, more disfluencies, more kinesic tension, and negative affect. Of course, as with deception, suspicion displays are influenced by preinteractional factors such as relational and behavioral familiarity and interactional factors such as type of deception (Buller, Strzyzewski, & Comstock, 1991; Burgoon, Buller, Dillman, & Walther, 1995; Burgoon, Buller, Ebesu, Rockwell, & White, in press; Toris & DePaulo, 1985).

In turn, a receiver's suspicion provokes changes in a sender's performance. Senders under suspicion report performing poorly; are more vague, uncertain, and reticent; reduce expressivity, activity, and nodding; reveal negative affect (but may smile longer); appear nervous; increase random movements; suffer performance decrements; and face the receiver more (Buller, Strzyzewski, & Comstock, 1991; Burgoon, Buller, Dillman, & Walther, in press; Burgoon, Buller, Ebesu, Rockwell, & White, in press; Toris & DePaulo, 1985). These findings suggest that suspicion provokes arousal and negative affect and impairs conversational performance—all of which may be inadvertently signaled. At the same time, however, senders under suspicion may attempt to restrain their behavior to avoid leakage and may become more vigilant (by facing the other). Strategic actions may be most successful when a receiver's suspicion is high. In a study by Burgoon, Buller, Dillman, and Walther (1995), senders were more pleasant, immediate, and relaxed under high suspicion than under moderate suspicion.

Some of the senders' reactions, however, may come about because they get caught up in patterns of reciprocity that typify interpersonal conversations. Senders may become more pleasant and immediate under increased suspicion because receivers also become more pleasant and involved. However, compensation can also arise when suspicion is present. For example, senders appear to respond to the increased dominance of a suspicious receiver by becoming more submissive, perhaps hoping that if they behave meekly, the receiver will not continue to press them for answers (Burgoon, Buller, Ebesu, Rockwell, & White, in press).

This pattern of moves and countermoves on the part of suspicious receivers and deceptive senders shows that suspicion can backfire, undermining receivers' ability to detect deception. On the one hand, deceivers can use feedback about suspicion to come up with more believable answers and convey a more credible demeanor. On the other hand, changes provoked by suspicion can produce an "Othello error," making truthful senders appear deceptive (Bond & Fahey, 1987; Burgoon, Buller, Ebesu, Rockwell, & White, in press). This is not to say that suspicion cannot help receivers. Suspicion may stimulate subtle indications of deceit and make it more difficult for deceivers to offset the negative by-products of their strategic manipulation of information, image, and behavior.

DETECTING DECEPTION AND SUSPICION

We have seen that receivers may become suspicious and that senders may adjust to such suspicions, but all this depends on the ability to *detect* deception and suspicion. Research has focused extensively on the receiver's skill at detecting deception. When the choice is limited to truth versus deception, people detect deception only slightly better than they would if they simply guessed. However, when judgments are measured along an "honesty-dishonesty" continuum, people see deceptive performances as less honest or sincere (Burgoon, Buller, Ebesu, & Rockwell, 1994; DePaulo & Kirkendol, 1989; DePaulo, Le May, & Epstein, 1991), though they are unwilling to label them "dishonest." Furthermore, several factors influence people's detection abilities, not always in beneficial ways. Much less is known about how senders detect suspicion.

Accuracy in Detecting Deceit

Across most studies of detecting deception, accuracy is only slightly above chance when receivers have access to only the deceiver's nonverbal behavior. That is, receivers would be almost as accurate if they relied entirely on guessing (DePaulo et al., 1985a; Hocking et al., 1979; Hocking & Leathers, 1980; Knapp & Comadena, 1979; Kraut, 1980; Miller & Burgoon, 1982; Stiff & Miller, 1986; Zuckerman, DePaulo, & Rosenthal, 1981). Kraut (1980) found that in 10 studies, accuracy ranged from 36 percent to 72 percent and averaged only 57 percent (50 percent is chance accuracy). Likewise, Miller and Burgoon (1982) reported that in six experiments, accuracy ranged from 46 percent to 64 percent. Receivers are even less accurate when it comes to detecting a deceiver's underlying affect: usually, they decode the emotion the deceiver intends to convey rather than the true emotion the deceiver is hiding. Thus accuracy at detecting deception cues (i.e., cues that deception is occurring) exceeds accuracy at detecting leakage cues (i.e., cues to the true state of affairs) (DePaulo & Rosenthal, 1979b).

A certain level of inaccuracy may be functional in everyday interactions. Being unaware of deception may at times be beneficial—safer, easier, quicker. People who are too sensitive to deception may be less popular and have less satisfying relationships than less sensitive people. Norms of polite interaction often lead people to place more weight on meanings intended by senders than on covert, leaked information. Further, it may be instrumental to assume truthfulness so that one can make inferences to fill in the gaps in messages. In many interactions, therefore, people usually believe that a sender is being truthful (Buller & Burgoon, 1994; Burgoon, Buller, Ebesu, & Rockwell, 1994; DePaulo, 1981; DePaulo et al., 1980a; DePaulo & Rosenthal, 1979a; DePaulo, Rosenthal, Green, & Rosenkrantz, 1982; DePaulo et al., 1985a; Goffman, 1959; Knapp & Comadena, 1979; Kraut, 1978; Rosenthal & DePaulo, 1979b; Stiff & Miller, 1986).

Lack of skill at detection may also be a function of the inferential process by which receivers perceive deception. In everyday interaction, detecting deception is a two-step process: a receiver must perceive and attend to relevant cues and then interpret those cues. Deception is only one possible interpretation (Zuckerman, DePaulo, & Rosenthal, 1981). Nonverbal cues do not indicate deception directly; rather, they strategically signal management of information, image, and behavior and inadvertently signal arousal, negative affect, and heightened cognitive processing. Thus a receiver must make an inferential leap from these perceptions to deception. Receivers may be reluctant to attribute deception simply on the basis of senders' behavior without contextual cues that strongly suggest intent to deceive, because deception is socially unfavorable. Instead, receivers may make "safer" interpretations, such as ambivalence, discrepancy, tension, or indifference (DePaulo, Rosenthal, Green, & Rosenkrantz, 1982). Also, receivers may fail to correct early impressions of a sender if later information suggests deception (Gilbert, 1989; Gilbert & Osborne, 1989; Gilbert, Pelham, & Krull, 1988). Finally, receivers may use judgmental heuristics or "rules of thumb" that do not match the actual form of lies. If receivers are unable to sense changes indicative of deception, or if the validity of a statement is difficult to determine, they may instead make educated guesses based on the content of the message. Receivers may consider a statement deceptive if it is unexpected (*infrequency* rule), if it is amenable to a "reality check" (*falsifiability* rule), or if it is accompanied by particularly noticeable nonverbal behaviors (*nonverbal conspicuousness* rule) (Fiedler, 1989; Fiedler & Walka, 1993). See Figure 15-1 for examples of inaccurate cues to deception suggested by Vaught early in this century.

Receivers' apparent inaccuracy at detection also may be a result of methods used to measure detection skills. Often, the truthfulness of any given utterance is a matter of degree rather than an "on-off" variable. Hence, receivers may opt for leniency when forced to choose simply between "truth" or "lie." Also, experimental participants usually make judgments about honesty at the end of interactions, a method that may overlook variations in honesty across multiple statements.

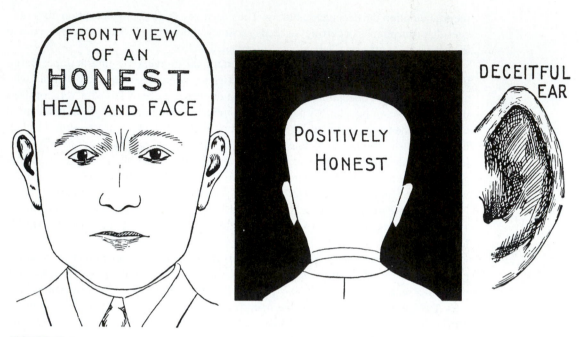

FIGURE 15-1
Deception and the ability to detect it have fascinated people for a long time. Unfortunately, knowledge of the cues that reveal deception has often been imperfect. For example, early in this century, L. A. Vaught was convinced that the shape of the head, face, and ears reveal the liar.

Studies using continuous measurement strategies and methods that obtain judgments for each response have shown that receivers are, in fact, more sensitive to changes in the credibility of senders and messages during deception than studies using dichotomous choices suggest. In such studies, receivers do evaluate deceptive messages as less honest than truthful ones. However, receivers continue to be reluctant to attribute dishonesty to senders; their judgments decline on the "honesty" end of the continuum but usually are not transferred to the "dishonest" end (Buller & Hunsaker, in press; Buller, Strzyzewski, & Hunsaker, 1991; Burgoon, Buller, Ebesu, & Rockwell, 1994; DePaulo et al. 1991).

Accuracy in Recognizing Suspicion

Senders show some ability to detect suspicion when it is present (Burgoon, Buller, Dillman, & Walther, 1995; Burgoon, Buller, Ebesu, Rockwell, & White, in press). However, in Buller, Strzyzewski, and Comstock's experiment (1991), senders did not accurately attribute suspicion to receivers in the "suspicion" condition. It may be that the weakness of the "suspicion" manipulation in this study produced fewer cues to deception. It is also possible that receivers tried to hide their suspicions by asking follow-up questions that did not indicate skepticism about the senders' responses. Senders did perceive more suspicion when the number of negative or skeptical follow-up questions increased.

Preinteractional Factors Affecting Accuracy

As with senders, receivers' perceptions are influenced by preinteractional factors, including their familiarity with the deceiver and their age and sex.

Behavioral and Relational Familiarity   Earlier in this chapter, we described three types of familiarity—informational, behavioral, and relational. Research has documented that behavioral and relational familiarity have pronounced effects on detecting deception.

Behavioral familiarity takes three forms. We can become familiar with someone else's "honest" or normal pattern of interaction through exposure to a sample of his or her behavior. This can improve our ability to detect deception because many behavioral indicators of deception represent changes from honest behavior (Bond, Omar, Pitre, Lashley, Skaggs, & Kirk, 1992; Buller & Burgoon, in press). Behavioral familiarity can also arise from training in cues associated with deception or from experience with deception behaviors in general (as in the case of professionals in investigatory agencies).

Research on the first two types of behavioral familiarity—exposure and training— typically has shown some gain in accuracy in detecting deception (Brandt, Miller, & Hocking, 1980a, 1980b, 1982; deTurck, Harszlak, Bodhorn, & Texter, 1990; Manstead, Wagner, & MacDonald, 1986; Mongeau, 1988; Zuckerman, Koestner, & Colella, 1985). However, when behavioral familiarity takes the form of expertise, in which training is coupled with experience, it can become counterproductive. Research has shown that experts such as law enforcement officers, judges, and customs agents, like laypeople, are often no more accurate than chance and may even be less accurate than nonexperts (Burgoon, Buller, Ebesu, & Rockwell, 1994; DePaulo & Pfeifer, 1986; Ekman & Friesen, 1974; Ekman & O'Sullivan, 1991; Kohnken, 1987; Kraut & Poe, 1980) (see also Box 15-2). Experts appear to be especially poor at judging emotional deception. They are slightly better at judging information and even better at judging opinions (Ekman, O'Sullivan, & Frank, 1994). Some researchers claim, however, that receivers are less likely to attribute dishonesty to lies about subjective opinions than to lies about facts (Fiedler & Walka, 1993).

There are several reasons why expertise fails to improve accuracy. For one, expertise often entails other factors, including occupational factors—for example, age, high motivation, and access to other senders of information (Kalbfleisch, 1992). Also, experts may receive little corrective feedback from a false negative (believing a dishonest person to be honest). During actual communication, moreover, they seldom receive feedback from a false positive (believing an honest person to be dishonest) and so may become overconfident. Experts also may find it safer to adopt a "lie bias" in order not to miss liars, even at the expense of doubting truth tellers, and suspicion simply heightens this tendency. Together, these factors may impair their judgment by producing chronic suspicion or at least decreasing the "truth bias" observed in novices (Burgoon, Buller, Ebesu, & Rockwell, 1994; DePaulo et al., 1985a).

BOX 15-2

FALLIBLE CUSTOMS INSPECTORS

Do customs inspectors have a secret formula for detecting deception? Not likely. Despite their experience, in a simulation they and a group of untrained adults used identical commonsense signs of nervousness in deciding whom to search for contraband—and were equally unsuccessful in fingering smugglers.

Through newspaper advertisements, social psychologists Robert Kraut and Donald Poe recruited 39 United States customs inspectors from three ports of entry along the border of New York State and Canada [and] 49 adults with occupations ranging from housepainter to cook.

Because federal officials forbade making tapes of real customs inspections, the inspectors and amateurs had to judge a simulated inspection arranged by Kraut and Poe and complete with smugglers. The researchers paid passengers waiting in the Syracuse, New York, airport $2.50 for participating and hid "contraband," such as bags of white powder and cameras, on half the group. The researchers urged the participants to try passing inspection without being selected for a search . . . and offered a $100 prize to "the most convincing traveler."

The amateur and professional inspectors agreed on half the travelers. To identify the behavior they might have used in making their decisions, Kraut and Poe had coders categorize smugglers and nonsmugglers on the basis of 15 verbal and nonverbal cues that had helped people in previous studies detect deception. The inspectors turned out to have tapped people whom the coders had noted shifting their weight from foot to foot, swaying back and forth, hesitating before responding to questions, giving very brief answers, and avoiding eye contact. These nervous nellies tended to be young, lower-class travelers.

Source: From *Psychology Today,* March 1981, p. 27.

Relational familiarity has also received considerable attention from researchers. Several early studies found that acquaintances, friends, and intimates make more accurate judgments of truthfulness than strangers do (Bauchner, 1978; Comadena, 1982; Kalbfleisch, 1985; McBurney & Comadena, 1992; Miller, Bauchner, Hocking, Fontes, Kaminski, & Brandt, 1981; Miller, deTurck, & Kalbfleisch, 1983). These gains in accuracy come about because of increased knowledge about background and habits and firsthand experience with individual interaction styles (i.e., behavioral familiarity).

However, several investigations have documented that the opposite also occurs. Acquaintances, friends, and intimates often ascribe more truth to their relational partners than strangers do, because relational familiarity creates a positive bias—people are more tolerant of, or favorable toward, those with whom they have a personal relationship (Buller, 1987; Buller, Strzyzewski, & Comstock, 1991; Burgoon, 1992b; Burgoon, Buller, Ebesu, & Rockwell, 1994; McCornack & Parks, 1986). McCornack and Parks (1986) held that in well-developed relationships, detectors become rigid and confident in their judgments of honesty, adopting a "truth bias" that reduces accuracy. Buller (1987) took a slightly different tack, suggesting that positive relational valence produces an "overattribution effect" (E. E. Jones, 1979; Jones & Harris, 1967; Quattrone, 1982). Initial positive impressions of acquaintances anchor subsequent attributions about a message. Thus, in the face of information that contradicts initial positive impressions of acquaintances, interpretations of messages change less than they should from an objective analysis of the contradictory information. Zuckerman, Koestner, Colella, and Alton (1984) and Zuckerman, Fischer, Osmum, Winkler, and Wolfson (1987) demonstrated that the overattribution effect can occur in judgments of honesty.

In sum, your intimate partners and close friends may be successful when deceiving you because you are likely to believe their messages. If, however, contextual cues are present that warn you about possible deception, you may be able to detect it because you are familiar with their truthful behavior—although suspicion may cause you simply to seek cues confirming their truthfulness rather than cues that would uncover deceit.

Age   A receiver's age is another important factor in detection. Young children do not have the same understanding of moral values; cultural, social, and interpersonal norms; or experience with deception as adults. Therefore, they cannot be expected to make the same attributions about deception (DePaulo et al., 1985a; Piaget, 1965). DePaulo, Jordan, Irvine, and Laser (1982) found that as age increases, a child's ability to detect ambivalence, discrepancies, and deception increases. Further, the researchers identified a developmental progression in these ratings. Younger children (sixth- to eighth-graders) distinguished deceptive messages from truthful messages solely on the basis of affect expressed in them. That is, younger children rated the emotion expressed in truthful messages as more extreme than the emotion expressed in deceptive messages. Slightly older children (tenth-graders) were able to discriminate deceptive and truthful messages on the presence or absence of mixed feelings. The oldest children (twelfth-graders) separated deceptive messages and truthful messages in their judgments of deception. These children, though, were less accurate than younger children at detecting leakage cues (interpreting a liar's true emotion). It may be that older children learn a norm for politeness that causes them to interpret the emotional meaning intended by the sender even though they suspect that a message is false. Younger children, who are unaware of this norm and who are not able to decode mixed messages or deception cues, decode the emotional content of the nonverbal cues more accurately (DePaulo, Jordan, Irvine, & Laser, 1982; Rosenthal & DePaulo, 1979b).

Gender   Gender is also a factor in detection. For example, Rosenthal and DePaulo (1979b) reported that the norm of politeness seems to be stronger among women than men. Women are more likely than men to decode the meaning intended by the sender. Also, women's greater visual primacy implies that they are less likely to attend to leaky body and voice cues. Women, therefore, may be less accurate detectors of deception and less likely to decode leakage cues.

Interactional Factors Affecting Accuracy

Features of the interaction itself help determine whether receivers will be sensitive to deception. In particular, accuracy is influenced by the communication channel on which receivers rely for clues to deceit, the degree of suspicion provoked in receivers, and the way in which receivers go about questioning senders.

Channel Reliance   Body and vocalic cues should display deception more than facial cues. It follows, then, that receivers who attend to body and vocalic cues will detect deception more accurately than receivers who attend to the face. This is exactly what happens. Receivers who can see only a deceiver's body are more accurate detectors than receivers who see only the deceiver's face (DePaulo et al., 1985a; Ekman & Friesen, 1974; Riggio & Friedman, 1983; Zuckerman, DePaulo, & Rosenthal, 1981). Similarly, receivers exposed to vocalic cues are more accurate than receivers exposed to facial cues and are sometimes more accurate than receivers exposed only to body cues. Accuracy is lower when receivers have access to only facial cues—as would be expected, since senders have greater control over these cues (DePaulo, Lassiter, & Stone, 1982; DePaulo et al., 1985a; DePaulo et al., 1980b; Ekman & Friesen, 1974; Feldman, 1976; Hocking et al., 1979; Littlepage & Pineault, 1979; Maier & Thurber, 1968; Riggio & Friedman, 1983; Zuckerman, Amidon, Bishop, & Pomerantz, 1982; Zuckerman, DePaulo, & Rosenthal, 1981; Zuckerman, Larrance, Spiegel, & Klorman, 1981).

Thus receivers should pay more attention to leakier channels such as the body and voice. However, in actual conversations receivers seem to do just the opposite. Buller, Strzyzewski, and Hunsaker (1991) and Buller and Hunsaker (in press) showed that receivers who interacted with a deceiver paid more attention to facial cues and less attention to vocalic cues than observers of the conversations. Moreover, receivers who interacted with deceivers assigned different interpretations to the same behavior than observers did—interpretations that misled them into believing the person was telling the truth.

Attention to the verbal portion of a deceiver's presentation may be more advantageous than relying entirely on nonverbal cues. Although IDT and the motivation impairment hypothesis claim that senders manage verbal behavior to enhance credibility and that the verbal channel, consequently, may be least revealing of deceit (Buller & Burgoon, in press; DePaulo & Kirkendol, 1989), some research showed that accuracy is highest when receivers have access to the deceiver's verbal channel alone or along with nonverbal channels (DePaulo et al., 1985a; DePaulo et al., 1980a; Hocking et al., 1979; Zuckerman, DePaulo, & Rosenthal, 1981).

These results may appear counterintuitive. One might think that the verbal channel is less likely to leak information about deception than nonverbal channels because of its sending capacity, senders' ability to control it, and attention senders and receivers pay to it. However, deceivers display many changes indicative of deceit in their verbal messages, especially verbal nonimmediacy (e.g., more leveling terms and modifiers), lack of specificity (fewer self- and group references), and more humorous, negative, and irrelevant statements (Buller, Burgoon, Buslig, & Roiger, 1994, in press; DePaulo et al., 1985a; Zuckerman, DePaulo, & Rosenthal, 1981; Zuckerman & Driver, 1985). Implausible, self-serving, and ingratiating responses also can clue receivers to deception (DePaulo et al., 1985b; Kraut, 1978; Riggio & Friedman, 1983).

Finally, juxtaposition of nonverbal and verbal cues may be critical to accuracy. Kraut (1978) asserted that receivers first judge the veracity of a verbal statement, then search the nonverbal channels for confirming evidence. In his study, receivers who observed a long pause before a statement they considered false were more convinced of the sender's

Charles Van Doren answered question after question correctly on the quiz show *21* in 1956. Van Doren's performance, depicted in the 1994 movie *Quiz Show,* was later exposed as a hoax, a masterpiece of deception.

duplicity. For receivers who considered the same statement true, the long pause reinforced their belief.

Receivers' Suspicion   The notion that suspicious receivers should be better detectors is intuitively appealing. However, very little research has examined the effects of receivers' suspicion on detecting deception, and the research that has been conducted has yielded inconclusive findings. Some studies found that suspicion failed to improve accuracy and decreased receivers' confidence in their judgments (Buller & Hunsaker, in press; Toris & DePaulo, 1985). McCornack and Levine (1990) found that moderate suspicion increased accuracy, whereas Zuckerman, Spiegel, DePaulo, and Rosenthal (1982) found that suspicion decreased accuracy in decoding positive affect.

The reason for these inconsistencies may be that receivers' suspicion affects their accuracy in sometimes contradictory ways. First, it may affect how receivers process information from senders. It may help overcome the "truth bias" most people bring to interactions (Buller & Hunsaker, in press; Buller, Strzyzewski, & Hunsaker, 1991; Kalbfleisch, 1992; Levine & McCornack, 1991; Riggio, Tucker, & Throckmorton, 1987), although some people may be more suspicious by nature, and suspicion only heightens their skepticism (Levine & McCornack, 1989). Reducing truth bias is a double-edged sword: people who are wary and vigilant may become more accurate at detecting deceptive messages, but they may simultaneously become less accurate at detecting truthful messages.

Suspicion may also increase receivers' attention to vocalic and body cues, making them more accurate. A study by Zuckerman, Spiegel, DePaulo, and Rosenthal (1982) showed that suspicious receivers relied less on facial cues and more on vocalic cues than unsuspicious receivers. Suspicious receivers were also more sensitive to channel discrepancies, which often arise in deceptive messages. However, in these experiments, receivers were not able to discount facial cues entirely. This suggests that in multichannel nonverbal presentations, receivers find it difficult to attend only to the cues in a single channel. This may explain why detection is more difficult in a face-to-face interaction than, for example, an interaction by intercom or telephone, where only vocalic cues are present (Feldman, 1976; Feldman, Jenkins, & Popoola, 1979; Krauss et al., 1976). It is also important to note that a recent study by Buller and Hunsaker (in press) failed to confirm that suspicious receivers rely more on vocalic cues and less on facial cues than unsuspicious receivers; instead, they merely evaluated all messages as less honest than unsuspicious receivers did.

Another reason for the inconsistent effects of suspicion is that (as we outlined earlier) receivers may telegraph their suspicions, allowing senders to adapt and appear more credible. Further, messages of skepticism or suspicion can make truth tellers look dishonest.

Finally, the effect of suspicion is influenced by other factors in the communication setting. Burgoon, Buller, Ebesu, and Rockwell (1994) found that suspicion impaired detection by expert interviewers (i.e., instructors from a military intelligence school) apparently by exacerbating their lie bias. Suspicion also caused receivers to ascribe less honesty to strangers and more honesty to acquaintances. It seems that with acquaintances the presumption of truth is highly resilient, causing receivers to search for "truth" in messages. Finally, suspicion was more beneficial with senders who equivocated but was harmful with senders who concealed or omitted the truth. Equivocal messages may have appeared plausible to unsuspicious receivers but failed to withstand scrutiny by suspicious receivers. Suspicion may have provoked senders to become even more reticent when concealing information, increasing the difficulty of detection.

Overall, it is apparent that suspicion is not always advantageous. If the goal is to avoid being deceived but not to identify truthful messages, a healthy dose of skepticism is helpful. However, skepticism with friends may not do the trick. By contrast, if one needs to identify both deceptive and truthful messages, suspicion does not help. This is especially true if one signals that suspicion to senders.

Type of Questioning   To discern a sender's truthfulness, receivers may use a variety of strategies, including different types of questions to probe for more information. Once again, intuitively it would seem to make sense that probing for additional information can help us detect deception; however, several studies have found that asking probing (follow-up) questions does not in itself improve accuracy (Buller, Comstock, Aune, & Strzyzewski, 1989; Buller, Strzyzewski, & Comstock, 1991; Stiff & Miller, 1986). It appears that when senders are probed, they alter their performances to appear more credible, especially if receivers express a negative or skeptical reaction (Buller, Strzyzewski, & Comstock, 1991; Kalbfleisch, 1992; Stiff & Miller, 1986).

A better strategy may be to ask questions that catch deceivers off-guard and cause them to divulge information or leak nonverbal cues before they are able to monitor and manage their behavior. As we noted earlier, spontaneous lies are less successful than planned lies because deceivers are less able to control their nonverbal behaviors when caught unaware (deTurck & Miller, 1990; Miller, deTurck, & Kalbfleisch, 1983; O'Hair et al., 1981; Zuckerman & Driver, 1985). Two tactics for catching deceivers off-guard are asking unexpected questions and returning to previous questions later in the sequence (Burgoon, Buller, Ebesu, & Rockwell, 1994; McBurney & Comadena, 1992; O'Hair, Cody, Wang, & Chao, 1990). Our recent research shows that these questioning strategies can be successful, depending on relational and behavioral familiarity between receivers and senders. Unexpected questions can be advantageous, but only for novice interviewers and mostly when they interview acquaintances. Expert interviewers did not gain as much accuracy with unexpected questions, but they were somewhat more accurate when they returned to a previous question with an acquaintance. Senders, however, were least accurate detecting deception overall when they returned to a previous question, especially when interviewing strangers.

Test your understanding of these principles of deception detection in the scenario presented in Box 15-3.

Behaviors Affecting Judgments of Deception and Suspicion

To explain poor detection, researchers have examined nonverbal cues that receivers rely on in making attributions of deception and truth. It appears that receivers hold beliefs

---

BOX 15-3

APPLICATIONS: CATCHING A LIAR

Last month, you ordered a new bicycle for commuting to and from your classes, including your class in non-verbal communication. Unfortunately, after 6 weeks the bike has still not arrived. What's more, you're beginning to suspect that the salesperson is not being honest with you. She first told you that the bike would arrive in a week, but today, when you call to see if the bike is in, she tells you that it will arrive next week. What would you do in order to determine most accurately whether or not the salesperson is deceiving you?

1 Tell her that you are coming to the bike shop this afternoon to talk with her about the delay.
2 Over the phone, continue quizzing her about the reasons for the delay.
3 Accuse her of deceiving you and see what she says.
4 Go unannounced to the bike shop 2 days from now, taking along a friend, and ask her when the bike will arrive.

If you choose option 1, you will probably reduce your chance of detecting deceit. By forewarning the salesperson of your coming visit, you give her a chance to spend some time planning her defense. She will be more relaxed when talking to you this afternoon, and you will be less likely to detect arousal cues.

If you choose option 2, you will tend to increase your chance of detecting deceit. Remember, the voice is among the most leaky nonverbal channels. This fact also works against option 1. People tend to focus on facial cues in a face-to-face conversation, so confronting her at the shop may distract you from other important cues.

Option 3 is not a particularly good strategy. Granted, it is conducted over the phone, and vocal cues are often very telling. However, a direct accusation of deceit may produce a negative reaction from the salesperson that will be difficult to distinguish from the arousal and negative emotions produced by deception.

Option 4 is a potentially successful strategy. The salesperson will probably not expect to see you 2 days from now particularly if you sound satisfied with her explanation today. Thus you may catch her off-guard, forcing her to create spontaneous deceptions that are more likely to be accompanied by nonverbal clues. (However, remember that unexpected questions do not seem to be advantageous with strangers.) Taking a friend along is a good idea, because observers of conversations are less likely to rely on facial cues. Also, your friend may be a more accurate detector than you are.

---

about how a deceiver will behave. Some of these beliefs are accurate and some are not. Further, a receiver's beliefs or stereotypes about deception cues differ somewhat from the cues that are actually associated with the receiver's attribution of deception.

Stereotypical Cues to Deception   Several investigations surveyed people about what nonverbal cues they believe are encoded by liars (Hemsley, 1977; Hocking & Leathers, 1980; Hocking, Miller, & Fontes, 1978). In the most extensive survey of receivers' stereotypes, Zuckerman, Koestner, and Driver (1981) reported that respondents thought deceivers would gaze less; have dilated pupils; blink more rapidly; smile, move the head, shrug, move the feet and legs, and shift posture more; and use more adaptors. With regard to voices, these respondents believed that deceivers would have longer response latencies, longer responses, faster speech rates, more errors and hesitations, and higher pitches. Most of these are classified as nonstrategic leakage. The respondents seemed to overlook the fact the deceivers use strategic management of information, image, and behavior. As you can see from referring back to Table 15-2, these stereotypes do not correspond completely to actual behavior changes accompanying deception.

Cues Decoded as Deception   Although stereotypes exist about how deceivers behave, receivers do not rely on them entirely when judging veracity. Further, the cues that receivers actually do rely on do not correspond exactly with a deceiver's behavior, although they are somewhat more dependable than the general stereotypes. Zuckerman and Driver (1985) reported a less than perfect correlation ($r = .64$) between cues associated with actual deception and cues associated with attributions of deception. Receivers' judgments are complicated by alterations in deceivers' performances produced by the preinteractional and interactional factors outlined earlier.

The right-hand column in Table 15-2 lists the cues Zuckerman and Driver found to be associated most with *attributions* of deception. It is apparent that receivers rely on a small number of nonverbal behaviors for such attributions. They are more likely to think a sender is lying when they observe less eye contact, less smiling, more postural shifts, longer response latencies, slower speech, frequent speech errors and hesitations, and higher-pitched voices. Once again, these are all inadvertent cues signaling increased arousal, negative affect, noninvolvement, or performance decrements. Only increased speech errors and hesitations and higher pitch were accurate indicators of deception across several studies. The remaining behavioral changes are not dependable indicators of deception.

Miller and Burgoon (1982) also concluded that receivers frequently ignore or are misled by gestures, facial cues, speech rate, and response length. Riggio and Friedman (1983) found similar processes of faulty attribution; their receivers attributed deception to senders who made less eye contact and showed more nervous behaviors and more facial animation. These attributions, however, were incorrect: in that study, liars actually made more eye contact and showed fewer nervous behaviors and less facial animation. The only dependable cue that receivers picked up on was body adaptors: deceivers did use more body adaptors, and receivers did attribute more deceit to senders who used more body adaptors. Riggio et al. (1987) reported that observers considered senders less believable when the senders encoded less verbal fluency, more positive affect, less head movement, and less eye contact. Socially skilled senders, though, effectively controlled their fluency and head movements to appear more believable. Finally, Buller, Strzyzewski, and Hunsaker (1991) and Buller and Hunsaker (in press) showed that both participants in conversations and observers of conversations rely on erroneous nonverbal cues. For instance, participants relied on smiling, head nodding, and head shaking when judging deception, yet these behaviors were not altered by deception. Likewise, observers relied more on interruptions, "talkovers," and response latencies, but talkovers and response latencies did not change with deception. Further, observers mistakenly attributed more honesty to senders who decreased interruptions; it was the deceivers who actually made fewer interruptions (Buller, Strzyzewski, & Hunsaker, 1991).

Why do receivers have incorrect theories about deceptive behavior? Hocking and Leathers (1980) speculated that senders are also aware of these stereotypes and try to inhibit behaviors that would cause a receiver to perceive deception. This idea is at the heart of Buller and Burgoon's assertion in IDT (1994, in press) that deceivers engage in strategic management of image and behavior.

Also, as we noted earlier in our discussion of behavioral familiarity, receivers do not seem to learn through experience, because they do not always obtain the feedback necessary to change their faulty theories (Burgoon, Buller, Ebesu, & Rockwell, 1994; DePaulo et al., 1985a). For example, with some partners in conversations, you neither suspect nor attribute deception and are unlikely ever to find out if you are wrong. At other times, you may be suspicious but conclude that the person is telling the truth even though the person is lying; again, you receive improper feedback. Only when you successfully detect deception or perceive deception and subsequently find out that you were misled do you have a chance to modify your theories. And even in such cases you may not be completely aware of the cues you originally relied on. Moreover, if your correct judgments were based on incorrect stereotypes and you merely "got lucky," that will reinforce an inaccurate process which is likely to fail in the future.

Fiedler and Walka (1993) showed that accuracy could be improved if the receiver was informed about the diagnostic value of seven reliable nonverbal indicators of deception obtained from Zuckerman and Driver's meta-analysis (i.e., was informed that these cues are associated with deception): (1) disguised smiling, (2) lack of eye movement, (3) adaptors, (4) higher pitch, (5) speech hesitations, (6) filled pauses, and (7) channel discrepancies. This further supports the idea that people can be trained to use cues accurately.

Cues Decoded as Suspicion   Asking what behaviors produce suspicion in a receiver is another way of asking what cues produce judgments of deceit. The answer once again is abnormal, "fishy-looking" behavior (Bond et al., 1992; Burgoon, Buller, Ebesu, Rockwell, & White, in press; Burgoon, Buller, Guerrero, & Feldman, 1994). Two studies have specifically related perceptions of suspicion to senders' behavior. Burgoon (1992b) found that receivers reported more suspicion when senders were more distant, less pleasant vocally, less relaxed vocally, more nervous, and more uncertain and vague. Receivers interpreted such behavior as conveying less immediacy, positive affect, composure, and receptivity-trustworthiness. A follow-up study likewise reported that receivers were more suspicious when senders displayed less pleasantness, involvement, vocal expressiveness, and composure. All these behaviors constitute nonstrategic leakage by senders and probably create an "abnormal" style, given the expectation of pleasantness and involvement in interpersonal conversations. Receivers, though, also reported being more suspicious when senders were too glib, that is, more fluent and smoother in their conversation management. So, too much behavioral or image management may backfire on deceivers.

SUMMARY

Deception is a frequent, essential, adaptive strategy in human communication. In many conversations, communicators depart from the truth by being incomplete, irrelevant, dishonest, impersonal, and unclear. Deception is motivated by needs for resources, affiliation desires, relational considerations, and self-esteem requirements, and it is these motives that determine the morality of a particular deception.

Research on deception has failed to reveal a consistent profile of nonverbal behaviors that signal deception. Deceivers engage in strategic information, image, and behavior management and inadvertently leak arousal, negative or dampened affect, noninvolvement, and impaired communication performances. However, the exact combination of cues depends on the conversational and relational context, preinteractional expectations, knowledge, goals, motivations, communication skills, and interactional features such as the type of deception and receiver suspicion.

Receivers often evaluate deceptive messages as less honest but are reluctant to attribute dishonesty to senders. Consequently, they are relatively inaccurate judges of deception. These evaluations often are based on faulty judgments about what behaviors actually signal deception. Senders, on the other side of the interaction, sense receiver suspicion when it is present. Receivers' ability to detect deception depends on the communication channels they rely on to judge deception, their suspicion, their behavioral and relational familiarity with the senders, their age and sex, the method of questioning they use, and the type of deception enacted by senders.

SUGGESTED READINGS

Camden, C., Motley, M. T., & Wilson, A. (1984). White lies in interpersonal communication: A taxonomy and preliminary investigation of social motivations. *Western Journal of Speech Communication, 48,* 309–325.

Bond, C. R., Omar, A., Pitre, V., Lashley, B. R., Skaggs, L. M., & Kirk, C. T. (1992). Fishy-looking liars: Deception judgment from expectancy violation. *Journal of Personality and Social Psychology,* 63, 969–977.

Buller, D. B., & Burgoon, J. K. (1994). Deception: Strategic and nonstrategic behavior. In J. Daly & J. Wiemann (Eds.), *Strategic interpersonal communication* (pp. 191–224). Hillsdale, NJ: Erlbaum.

Buller, D. B., & Burgoon, J. K. (in press). Interpersonal deception theory. *Communication Theory.*

Burgoon, J. K., Buller, D. B., Ebesu, A. S., & Rockwell, P. (1994). Interpersonal deception: V. Accuracy in deception detection. *Communication Monographs, 61,* 303–325.

Burgoon, J. K., Buller, D. B., Ebesu, A. S., Rockwell, P., & White, C. H. (in press). Testing interpersonal deception theory: Effects of suspicion on communication behaviors and perceptions. *Communication Theory.*

DePaulo, B. M., & Pfeifer, R. L. (1986). On the job experience and skill at detecting deception. *Journal of Applied Social Psychology, 16,* 249–267.

DePaulo, B. M., Stone, J. I., & Lassiter, G. D. (1985). Deceiving and detecting deceit. In B. R. Schlenker (Ed.), *The self and social life* (pp. 323–370). New York: McGraw-Hill.

Ekman, P. (1985). *Telling lies.* New York: Norton.

Ekman, P., & Friesen, W. V. (1969). Nonverbal leakage and clues to deception. *Psychiatry, 32,* 88–105.

Ekman, P., & O'Sullivan, M. (1991). Who can catch a liar? *American Psychologist, 46,* 913–920.

Knapp, M. L., & Comadena, M. E. (1979). Telling it like it isn't: A review of theory and research on deceptive communications. *Human Communication Research, 5,* 270–285.

Miller, G. R., & Stiff, J. B. (1993). *Deceptive communication*. Newbury Park, CA: Sage.

Zuckerman, M., DePaulo, B. M., & Rosenthal, R. (1981). Verbal and nonverbal communication of deception. In L. Berkowitz (Ed.), *Advances in experimental social psychology* (Vol. 14, pp. 1–59). Orlando, FL: Academic.

Zuckerman, M., & Driver, R. E. (1985). Telling lies: Verbal and nonverbal correlates of deception. In A. W. Siegman & S. Feldstein (Eds.), *Multichannel integrations of nonverbal behavior* (pp. 129–148). Hillsdale, NJ: Erlbaum.

REFERENCES

Abelson, R. P., & Sermat, V. (1962). Multidimensional scaling of facial expressions. *Journal of Experimental Psychology, 63,* 564–554.

Abrahamson, M. (1966). *Interpersonal accommodation.* New York: Van Nostrand.

Ackerman, D. (1990). *A natural history of the senses.* New York: Random House.

Acking, C. A., & Kuller, R. (1972). The perception of an interior as a function of its colour. *Ergonomics, 15,* 645–654.

Acton, W. I. (1970). Speech intelligibility in a background noise and noise-induced hearing loss. *Ergonomics, 13,* 546–554.

Addington, D. W. (1968). The relationship of selected vocal characteristics to personality perception. *Speech Monographs, 35,* 492–503.

Addington, D. W. (1971). The effect of vocal variations on ratings of source credibility. *Speech Monographs, 38,* 242–247.

Ahmed, S. M. S. (1980). Reactions to crowding in different settings. *Psychological Reports, 46,* 1279–1284.

Ahrentzen, S., & Evans, G. W. (1984). Distraction, privacy, and classroom design. *Environment and Behavior, 16,* 437–454.

Aiello, J. R. (1987). Human spatial behavior. In D. Stokols & I. Altman (Eds.), *Handbook of environmental psychology* (Vol. 1, pp. 389–504). New York: Wiley.

Aiello, J. R., & Aiello, T. D. (1974). The development of personal space: Proxemic behavior of children 6 through 16. *Human Ecology, 2,* 177–189.

Aiello, J. R., & Cooper, R. E. (1972). Use of personal space as a function of social affect. *Proceedings of the 80th Annual Convention of the American Psychological Association, 7*(1), 207–208.

Aiello, J. R., DeRisi, D. T., Epstein, Y. M., & Karlin, R. A. (1977). Crowding and the role of interpersonal distance preference. *Sociometry, 40,* 271–282.

Aiello, J. R., Epstein, Y. M., & Karlin, R. A. (1975). Effects of crowding on electrodermal activity. *Sociological Symposium, 14,* 43–57.

Aiello, J. R., & Jones, S. E. (1971). Field study of the proxemic behavior of young school children in three subcultural groups. *Journal of Personality and Social Psychology, 19,* 351–356.

Aiken, L. R. (1963). The relationship of dress to selected measures of personality in undergraduate women. *Journal of Social Psychology, 59,* 119–128.

Akert, R. M., & Panter, A. T. (1988). Extraversion and the ability to decode nonverbal communication. *Personality and Individual Differences, 9,* 965–972.

Albert, S., & Dabbs, J. M., Jr. (1970). Physical distance and persuasion. *Journal of Personality and Social Psychology, 15,* 265–270.

Albert, S., & Kessler, S. (1978). Ending social encounters. *Journal of Experimental Social Psychology, 14,* 541–553.

Alberts, J. K. (1989). A descriptive taxonomy of couples' complaint interactions. *Southern Communication Journal, 54,* 125–143.

Alexander, I. E., & Babad, E. Y. (1981). Returning the smile of the stranger: Within-culture and cross-cultural comparisons of Israeli and American children. *Genetic Psychology Monographs, 103,* 31–77.

Alfred, G. H., Harper, J. M., Wadham, R. A., & Woolley, B. H. (1981). Expanding the frontiers of interaction research. In E. E. Filsinger & R. A. Lewis (Eds.), *Assessing marriage* (pp. 160–170). Newbury Park, CA: Sage.

Allen, V. L., & Atkinson, M. L. (1978). Encoding of nonverbal behavior by high-achieving and low-achieving children. *Journal of Educational Psychology, 70,* 298–305.

Allport, F. H. (1924). *Social psychology.* Boston: Houghton Mifflin.

Allport, G. W., & Cantril, H. (1934). Judging personality from voice. *Journal of Social Psychology, 5,* 37–54.

Allport, G. W., & Vernon, P. E. (1937). *Studies in expressive movement.* New York: Hafner.

Als, H., Tronick, E., & Brazelton, T. B. (1979). Analysis of face-to-face interaction in infant-adult dyads. In M. E. Lamb, S. J. Suomi, & G. R. Stephenson (Eds.), *Social interaction analysis* (pp. 33–76). Madison: University of Wisconsin Press.

Altman, I. (1971). Ecological aspects of interpersonal functioning. In A. H. Esser (Ed.), *Behavior and environment: The use of space by animals and men* (pp. 291–306). New York: Plenum.

Altman, I. (1975). *The environment and social behavior.* Monterey, CA: Brooks/Cole.

Altman, I., & Chemers, M. M. (1980). *Culture and environment.* Monterey, CA: Brooks/Cole.

Altman, I., & Haythorn, W. W. (1967). The ecology of isolated groups. *Behavioral Science, 12,* 169–182.

Altman, I., Nelson, P. A., & Lett, E. E. (1972). The ecology of home environments. *Man-Environment Systems, 2,* 189–191.

Altman, I., Taylor, D. A., & Wheeler, L. (1971). Ecological aspects of group behavior in social isolation. *Journal of Applied Social Psychology, 1,* 76–100.

Altman, I., & Vinsel, A. M. (1977). Personal space: An analysis of E. T. Hall's proxemics framework. In I. Altman & J. F. Wohlwill (Eds.), *Human behavior and environment: Advances in theory and research* (Vol. 2, pp. 181–259). New York: Plenum.

Amabile, T. M., & Kabat, L. G. (1982). When self-descriptions contradict behavior: Actions do speak louder than words. *Social Cognition, 1,* 311–335.

Ambady, N., & Rosenthal, R. (1993). Half a minute: Predicting teacher evaluations from thin slices of nonverbal behavior and physical attractiveness. *Journal of Personality and Social Psychology, 64,* 431–441.

Anderson, J. F. (1979). The relationship between teacher immediacy and teaching effectiveness. In B. Ruben (Ed.), *Communication Yearbook 3.* New Brunswick, NJ: Transaction.

Andersen, J. F. (1986). Instructor nonverbal communication: Listening to our silent messages. In J. M. Civikly (Ed.),

Communicating in college classrooms: New directions for teaching and learning (pp. 41–49). San Francisco: Jossey-Bass.

Andersen, J. F., Andersen, P. A., & Jensen, A. D. (1979). The measurement of nonverbal immediacy. *Journal of Applied Communication Research, 7,* 153–180.

Andersen, J. F., Andersen, P. A., & Landgraf, J. (1985, May). *The development of nonverbal communication competence in childhood.* Paper presented at the annual meeting of the International Communication Association, Honolulu.

Andersen, J. F., Andersen, P. A., & Lustig, M. W. (1987). Opposite sex touch avoidance: A national replication and extension. *Journal of Nonverbal Behavior, 11,* 89–109.

Andersen, J. F., Norton, R. W., & Nussbaum, J. F. (1981). Three investigations exploring relationships between perceived teacher communication behaviors and student learning. *Communication Education, 30,* 377–392.

Andersen, P. A. (1985). Nonverbal immediacy in interpersonal communication. In A. W. Siegman & S. Feldstein (Eds.), *Multichannel integrations of nonverbal behavior* (pp. 1–36). Hillsdale, NJ: Erlbaum.

Andersen, P. A. (1989, May). *A cognitive valence theory of intimate communication.* Paper presented at the conference of the International Network on Personal Relationships, Iowa City, IA.

Andersen, P. A. (1991). When one cannot not communicate: A challenge to Motley's traditional communication postulates. *Communication Studies, 42,* 309–325.

Andersen, P. A., & Andersen, J. F. (1984). The exchange of nonverbal intimacy: A critical review of dyadic models. *Journal of Nonverbal Behavior, 8,* 327–349.

Andersen, P. A., Andersen, J. F., Wendt, N. J., & Murphy, M. A. (1981, May). *The development of nonverbal communication behavior in school children, grades K–12.* Paper presented at the annual meeting of the International Communication Association, Minneapolis.

Andersen, P. A., Garrison, J. P., & Andersen, J. F. (1979). Implications of a neurophysiological approach for the study of nonverbal communication. *Human Communication Research, 6,* 72–89.

Andersen, P. A., Guerrero, L. K., Buller, D. B., & Jorgensen, P. F. (1995, May). *The arousal-immediacy link: A critical test of three theories of nonverbal immediacy exchange.* Paper presented at the annual meeting of the International Communication Association, Albuquerque.

Andersen, P. A., Jensen, T. A., & King, L. B. (1972). *The effects of homophilous hair and dress styles on credibility and comprehension.* Paper presented at the annual meeting of the International Communication Association, Atlanta.

Andersen, P. A., & Liebowitz, K. (1978). The development and nature of the construct touch avoidance. *Environmental Psychology and Nonverbal Behavior, 3,* 89–106.

Andersen, P. A., & Sull, K. K. (1985). Out of touch, out of reach: Tactile predispositions as predictors of interpersonal distance. *Western Journal of Speech Communication, 49,* 57–72.

Anderson, C. A. (1989). Temperature and aggression: Ubiquitous effects of heat on occurrence of human violence. *Psychological Bulletin, 106,* 1161–1173.

Anderson, J. R. (1980). *Cognitive psychology and its implications.* New York: Freeman.

Anderson, N. H., & Jacobson, A. (1965). Effect of stimulus inconsistency and discounting instructions in personality impression formation. *Journal of Personality and Social Psychology, 2,* 531–539.

Andrew, R. J. (1972). The information potentially available in mammal displays. In R. A. Hinde (Ed.), *Nonverbal communication* (pp. 179–204). Cambridge: Cambridge University Press.

Anttila, R. (1972). *An introduction to historical and comparative linguistics.* New York: Macmillan.

Apple, W. (1979). *Perceiving emotion in others: Integration of verbal, nonverbal and contextual cues.* Unpublished doctoral dissertation, Columbia University.

Apple, W., & Hecht, K. (1982). Speaking emotionally: The relation between verbal and vocal communication of affect. *Journal of Personality and Social Psychology, 42,* 864–875.

Apple, W., Streeter, L. A., & Krauss, R. M. (1979). Effects of pitch and speech rate on personal attributions. *Journal of Personality and Social Psychology, 37,* 715–727.

Arce, C. H., Murguia, E., & Frisbie, W. P. (1987). Phenotype and life chances among Chicanos. *Hispanic Journal of Behavioral Sciences, 9,* 19–32.

Archer, D., & Akert, R. M. (1977). Words and everything else: Verbal and nonverbal cues in social interpretation. *Journal of Personality and Social Psychology, 35,* 443–449.

Archer, D., & Costanzo, M. (1988). *The interpersonal perception task (IPT).* Berkeley: University of California Media Extension Center.

Ardrey, R. (1966). *The territorial imperative.* New York: Atheneum.

Ardrey, R. (1970). *African genesis.* New York: Dell.

Argyle, M. (1969). *Social interaction.* New York: Atherton.

Argyle, M. (1972a). Non-verbal communication in human social interaction. In R. A. Hinde (Ed.), *Nonverbal communication* (pp. 243–268). Cambridge: Cambridge University Press.

Argyle, M. (1972b). *The psychology of interpersonal behaviour* (2d ed.). Baltimore: Penguin.

Argyle, M. (1975). *Bodily communication.* London: Methuen.

Argyle, M. (1979). Sequences in social behaviour as a function of the situation. In G. P. Ginsburg (Ed.), *Emerging strategies in social psychological research* (pp. 11–37). New York: Wiley.

Argyle, M., Alkema, F., & Gilmour, R. (1971). The communication of friendly and hostile attitudes by verbal and nonverbal signals. *European Journal of Social Psychology, 1,* 385–402.

Argyle, M., & Cook, M. (1976). *Gaze and mutual gaze.* Cambridge: Cambridge University Press.

Argyle, M., & Dean, J. (1965). Eye contact, distance, and affiliation. *Sociometry, 28,* 289–304.

Argyle, M., Furnham, A., & Graham, J. A. (1981). *Social situations.* Cambridge: Cambridge University Press.

Argyle, M., & Kendon, A. (1967). The experimental analysis of social performance. In L. Berkowitz (Ed.), *Advances in experimental social psychology* (pp. 55–91). New York: Academic.

Argyle, M., Lalljee, M., & Cook, M. (1968). The effects of visibility on interaction in a dyad. *Human Relations, 21,* 3–17.

Argyle, M., Salter, V., Nicholson, H., Williams, M., & Burgess, P. (1970). The communication of inferior and superior attitudes by verbal and non-verbal signals. *British Journal of Social and Clinical Psychology, 9,* 221–231.

Aries, E. J. (1982). Verbal and nonverbal behavior in single-sex and mixed-sex groups: Are traditional sex-roles changing? *Psychological Reports, 51,* 127–134.

Aronovitch, C. D. (1976). The voice of personality: Stereotyped judgments and their relation to voice quality and sex of speaker. *Journal of Personality and Social Psychology, 33,* 255–270.

Aronson, E., & Linder, D. (1965). Gain and loss of esteem as determinants of interpersonal attractiveness. *Journal of Experimental Social Psychology, 1,* 156–171.

Asch, S. E. (1946). Forming impressions of personality. *Journal of Abnormal and Social Psychology, 41,* 258–290.

Auvine, B., Densmore, B., Extrom, M., Poole, S., & Shanklin, M. (1978). *A manual for group facilitators.* Madison, WI: Center for Conflict Resolution.

Axelrod, J. (1980). *The effect of sex-role attitude, status and sex of the addressee on the nonverbal communication of women.* Unpublished doctoral dissertation, New York University.

Babad, E., Bernieri, F., & Rosenthal, R. (1989). Nonverbal communication and leakage in the behavior of biased and unbiased teachers. *Journal of Personality and Social Psychology, 56,* 89–94.

Badzinski, D. M., & Pettus, D. M. (1994). Nonverbal involvement and sex: Effects on jury decision making. *Journal of Applied Communication Research, 22,* 309–321.

Baglan, T., & Nelson, D. J. (1982). A comparison of the effects of sex and status on the perceived appropriateness of nonverbal behaviors. *Women's Studies in Communication, 5,* 29–38.

Bakker, C. B., & Bakker-Rabdau, M. K. (1985). *No trespassing! Explorations in human territoriality.* San Francisco: Chandler & Sharp.

Bandler, R., & Grinder, J. (1979). *Frogs into princes.* Moab, UT: Real People.

Bandura, A. (1965). Influence of models' reinforcement contingencies on the acquisition of imitative responses. *Journal of Personality and Social Psychology, 1,* 589–595.

Bandura, A. (1977). *Social learning theory.* Englewood Cliffs, NJ: Prentice-Hall.

Banks, D. L. (1974). A comparative study of the reinforcing potential of verbal and nonverbal cues in a verbal conditioning paradigm. (Doctoral dissertation, University of Massachusetts). *Dissertation Abstracts International, 35,* 2671A. (University Microfilms No. 74-25,819)

Banse, R., & Scherer, K. R. (1994). *Acoustic profiles in vocal emotion expression.* Unpublished manuscript, Humboldt University, Berlin, Germany.

Barak, A., Patkin, J., & Dell, D. M. (1982). Effects of certain counselor behaviors on perceived expertness and attractiveness. *Journal of Counseling Psychology, 29,* 261–267.

Bargh, J. A. (1989). Conditional automaticity: Varieties of automatic influence in social perception and cognition. In J. S. Uleman & J. A. Bargh (Eds.), *Unintended thought* (pp. 3–51). New York: Guilford.

Barner-Barry, C. (1980). The structure of young children's authority relationships. In D. R. Omark, F. F. Strayer, & D. G. Freedman (Eds.), *Dominance relations* (pp. 177–190). New York: Garland.

Barnlund, D. C. (1975). Communicative styles in two cultures: Japan and the United States. In A. Kendon, R. M. Harris, & M. R. Key (Eds.), *Organization of behavior in face-to-face interaction* (pp. 427–456). The Hague: Mouton.

Baron, R. A. (1978). Invasions of personal space and helping: Mediating effects of invader's apparent need. *Journal of Experimental Social Psychology, 14,* 304–312.

Baron, R. A. (1986). Self-presentation in job interviews: When there can be "too much of a good thing." *Journal of Applied Social Psychology, 16,* 16–28

Baron, R. A., & Bell, P. A. (1976). Physical distance and helping: Some unexpected benefits of "crowding in" on others. *Journal of Applied Social Psychology, 6,* 95–104.

Barrett, K. C. (1993). The development of nonverbal communication of emotion: A functionalist perspective. *Journal of Nonverbal Behavior, 17,* 145–170.

Barroso, F., Freedman, N., Grand, S., & Van Meel, J. (1978). Evocation of two types of hand movements in information processing. *Journal of Experimental Psychology, 4,* 321–329.

Bar-Tal, D., & Saxe, L. (1976). Perceptions of similarly and dissimilarly attractive couples and individuals. *Journal of Personality and Social Psychology, 33,* 772–781.

Baskett, G. D., & Freedle, R. O. (1974). Aspects of language pragmatics and the social perception of lying. *Journal of Psycholinguistic Research, 3,* 117–131.

Basow, S. A. (1991). The hairless ideal: Women and their body hair. *Psychology of Women Quarterly, 15,* 83–96.

Bass, B. M., & Klubeck, S. (1952). Effects of seating arrangement on leaderless group discussions. *Journal of Abnormal and Social Psychology, 47,* 724–727.

Batchelor, J. P., & Goethals, G. R. (1972). Spatial arrangements in freely formed groups. *Sociometry, 35,* 270–279.

Bates, E., Thal, D., Fenson, L., Whitesell, K., & Oakes, L. (1989). Integrating language and gesture in infancy. *Developmental Psychology, 25,* 1004–1019.

Bates, J. E. (1973). *The effects of a child's imitation versus nonimitation on adults' verbal and nonverbal positivity.* Unpublished doctoral dissertation, University of California, Los Angeles.

Bateson, G. (1935). Culture contact and schismogenesis. *Man, 35,* 178–183.

Bateson, G. (1958). *Naven* (2d ed.). Stanford, CA: Stanford University Press.

Bateson, M. C. (1975). Mother-infant exchanges: The epigenesis of conversational interaction. *Annals of the New York Academy of Sciences, 263,* 101–113.

Bauchner, J. E. (1978). *Accuracy in detecting deception as a function of level of relationship and communication history.* Unpublished doctoral dissertation, Michigan State University.

Bauchner, J. E., Brandt, D. R., & Miller, G. R. (1977). The truth-deception attribution: Effects of varying levels of information availability. In B. R. Ruben (Ed.), *Communication yearbook 1* (pp. 229–243). New Brunswick, NJ: Transaction Books.

Bauer, E. A. (1973). Personal space: A study of blacks and whites. *Sociometry, 36,* 402–408.

Baum, A., & Greenberg, C. I. (1975). Waiting for a crowd: The behavioral and perceptual effects of anticipated crowding. *Journal of Personality and Social Psychology, 32,* 671–679.

Baum, A., Harpin, R. E., & Valins, S. (1975). The role of group phenomena in the experience of crowding. *Environment and Behavior, 7,* 185–198.

Baum, A., Riess, M., & O'Hara, J. (1974). Architectural variants of reaction to spatial invasion. *Environment and Behavior, 6,* 91–100.

Baum, A., & Singer, J. E. (1982). *Advances in environmental psychology. 4: Environment and health.* Hillsdale, NJ: Erlbaum.

Bavelas, J. B. (1983). Situations that lead to disqualification. *Human Communication Research, 9,* 130–145.

Bavelas, J. B. (1990). Behaving and communicating: A reply to Motley. *Western Journal of Speech Communication, 54,* 593–602.

Bavelas, J. B. (1994). Gestures as part of speech: Methodological implications. *Research on Language and Social Interaction, 27,* 201–221.

Bavelas, J. B., Black, A., Chovil, N., Lemery, C. R., & Mullett, J. (1988). Form and function in motor mimicry: Topographic evidence that the primary function is communicative. *Human Communication Research, 14,* 275–300.

Bavelas, J. B., Black, A., Chovil, N., & Mullett, J. (1990). *Equivocal communication.* Newbury Park, CA: Sage.

Bavelas, J. B., Black, A., Lemery, C. R., & Mullett, J. (1986). "I *show* how you feel": Motor mimicry as a communicative act. *Journal of Personality and Social Psychology, 50,* 322–329.

Bavelas, J. B., Chovil, N., Lawrie, D. A., & Wade, A. (1992). Interactive gestures. *Discourse Processes, 15,* 469–489.

Bavelas, J. B., & Coates, L. (1992). How do we account for the mindfulness of face-to-face dialogue? *Communication Monographs, 59,* 301–305.

Bavelas, J. B., Hagen, D., Lane, L., & Lawrie, D. A. (1989, May). *Interactive gestures and a systems theory of conversation.* Paper presented at the annual meeting of the International Communication Association, San Francisco.

Baxter, J. C. (1970). Interpersonal spacing in natural settings. *Sociometry, 33,* 444–456.

Baxter, J. C., & Deanovitch, B. F. (1970).

Anxiety effects of inappropriate crowding. *Journal of Consulting and Clinical Psychology, 35,* 174–178.

Baxter, J. C., Winters, E. P., & Hammer, R. E. (1968). Gestural behavior during a brief interview as a function of cognitive variables. *Journal of Personality and Social Psychology, 8,* 303–307.

Baxter, L., & Ward, J. (1975, December). Cited in "Newsline." *Psychology Today, 28.*

Baxter, L. A. (1988). A dialectic perspective on communication strategies in relationship development. In S. Duck (Ed.), *Handbook of personal relationships: Theory, research, and interventions* (pp. 257–288). Chichester, UK: Wiley.

Bayes, M. A. (1970). *An investigation of the behavioral cues of interpersonal warmth.* Unpublished doctoral dissertation, University of Miami.

Bayes, M. A. (1972). Behavioral cues of interpersonal warmth. *Journal of Consulting and Clinical Psychology, 39,* 333–339.

Beattie, G. W. (1981a). A further investigation of the cognitive interference hypothesis of gaze patterns during conversation. *British Journal of Social Psychology, 20,* 243–248.

Beattie, G. W. (1981b). Interruption in conversational interaction and its relation to the sex and status of the interactants. *Linguistics, 21,* 742–748.

Becker, F. D. (1973). Study of spatial markers. *Journal of Personality and Social Psychology, 26,* 439–445.

Beebe, S. A. (1980). Effects of eye contact, posture and vocal inflection upon credibility and comprehension. *Australian SCAN: Journal of Human Communication, 7–8,* 57–70.

Beekman, S. (1975). *Sex differences in nonverbal behavior.* Paper presented at the annual meeting of the American Psychological Association, Chicago.

Beier, E. G. (1974). Nonverbal communication: How we send emotional messages. *Psychology Today, 8*(5), 52–59.

Beier, E. G., & Sternberg, D. P. (1977). Subtle cues between newlyweds. *Journal of Communication, 27*(3), 92–97.

Beighley, K. C. (1952). An experimental study of the effect of four speech variables on listener comprehension. *Speech Monographs, 19,* 249–258.

Beighley, K. C. (1954). An experimental study of three speech variables on listener comprehension. *Speech Monographs, 21,* 248–253.

Bell, P. A., & Barnard, W. A. (1984). Effects of heat, noise, and sex of subject on a projective measure of personal space permeability. *Perceptual and Motor Skills, 59,* 422.

Bem, S. L. (1974). The measurement of psychological androgyny. *Journal of Consulting and Clinical Psychology, 42,* 155–162.

Bem, S. L. (1981). Gender schema theory: A cognitive account of sex typing. *Psychological Review, 88,* 354–364.

Berenbaum, H., & Rotter, A. (1992). The relationship between spontaneous facial expressions of emotion and voluntary control of facial muscles. *Journal of Nonverbal Behavior, 16,* 179–190.

Berger, C. R. (1977). The covering law perspective as a theoretical basis for the study of human communication. *Communication Quarterly, 25,* 7–18.

Berger, C. R. (1979). Beyond initial interaction: Uncertainty, understanding, and the development of interpersonal relationships. In H. Giles & R. St. Clair (Eds.), *Language and social psychology* (pp. 122–144). Oxford: Blackwell.

Berger, C. R., & Bradac, J. J. (1982). *Language and social knowledge: Uncertainty in interpersonal relations.* London: Arnold.

Berger, C. R., & Calabrese, R. J. (1975). Some explorations in initial interaction and beyond: Toward a developmental theory of interpersonal communication. *Human Communication Research, 1,* 99–112.

Berger, C. R., & Knowlton, S. (1994, July). *The hierarchy principle in strategic communication.* Paper presented at the annual meeting of the International Communication Association, Sydney, Australia.

Berman, H. J., Shulman, A. D., & Marwit, S. J. (1976). Comparison of multidimensional decoding of affect from audio, video, and audio-video recordings. *Sociometry, 39,* 83–89.

Berman, P. W., & Smith, V. L. (1984). Gender and situational differences in children's smiles, touch, and proxemics. *Sex Roles, 10,* 347–356.

Bernieri, F. J., Reznick, J. S., & Rosenthal, R. (1988). Synchrony, pseudosynchrony, and dissynchrony: Measuring the entrainment process in mother-infant interactions. *Journal of Personality and Social Psychology, 54,* 243–253.

Bernieri, F. J., & Rosenthal, R. (1991). Interpersonal coordination: Behavior matching and interactional synchrony. In R. S. Feldman & B. Rimé (Eds.), *Fundamentals of nonverbal behavior* (pp. 401–432). Cambridge: Cambridge University Press.

Berry, D. S. (1990a). Vocal attractiveness and vocal babyishness: Effects on stranger, self, and friend impressions. *Journal of Nonverbal Behavior, 14,* 141–153.

Berry, D. S. (1990b). What can a moving face tell us? *Journal of Personality and Social Psychology, 58,* 1004–1014.

Berry, D. S. (1991). Accuracy in social perception: Contributions of facial and vocal information. *Journal of Personality and Social Psychology, 61,* 298–307.

Berry, D. S. (1992). Vocal types and stereotypes: Joint effects of vocal attractiveness and vocal maturity on person perception. *Journal of Nonverbal Behavior, 16,* 41–54.

Berry, D. S., Hansen, J. S., Landry-Pester, J. C., & Meier, J. A. (1994). Vocal determinants of first impressions of young children. *Journal of Nonverbal Behavior, 18,* 187–197.

Berry, D. S., & McArthur, L. Z. (1986). Perceiving character in faces: The impact of age-related craniofacial changes on social perception. *Psychological Bulletin, 100,* 3–18.

Berscheid, E., Dion, K. K., Walster, E. H., & Walster, G. W. (1971). Physical attractiveness and dating choice: Tests of the matching hypothesis. *Journal of Experimental Social Psychology, 7,* 173–189.

Berscheid, E., & Walster, E. H. (1969, 1978). *Interpersonal attraction* (2d ed.). Reading, MA: Addison-Wesley.

Berscheid, E. & Walster, E. H. (1972, September). Beauty and the best. *Psychology Today, 5,* 42–46, 74.

Berscheid, E., & Walster, E. H. (1974). Physical attractiveness. In L. Berkowitz (Ed.), *Advances in experimental social psychology* (Vol. 7, pp. 158–215). New York: Academic.

Berscheid, E., Walster, E. H., & Bohrnstedt, G. (1973, November). Body image: The happy American body. *Psychology Today, 7,* pp. 119–131.

Bettinghaus, E. P., & Cody, M. J. (1987). *Persuasive communication.* New York: Holt, Rinehart and Winston.

Bickman, L. (1971a). Effect of different uniforms on obedience in field situations. *Proceedings of the 79th Annual American Psychological Association Convention,* 359–360.

Bickman, L. (1971b). The effect of social status on the honesty of others. *Journal of Social Psychology, 85,* 87–92.

Bickman, L. (1974a). The social power of a uniform. *Journal of Applied Social Psychology, 4,* 47–61.

Bickman, L. (1974b). Social roles and uniforms: Clothes make the person. *Psychology Today, 7* (11), 48–51.

Biglan, A., Hops, H., Sherman, L., Friedman, L. S., Arthur, J., & Osteen, V. (1985). Problem-solving interactions of depressed women and their husbands. *Behavior Therapy, 16,* 431–451.

Billings, A. (1979). Conflict resolution in distressed and nondistressed married couples. *Journal of Consulting and Clinical Psychology, 47,* 368–376.

Birdwhistell, R. (1955). Background to kinesics. *ETC., 13,* 10–18.

Birdwhistell, R. (1970). *Kinesics and context: Essays on body motion communication.* Philadelphia: University of Pennsylvania Press.

Birren, F. (1950). *Color psychology and color therapy.* New York: McGraw-Hill.

Birren, F. (1952). Emotional significance of color preference. *American Journal of Occupational Therapy, 6,* 61–65, 72, 88.

Bjorklund, D. F. (1987). A note on neonatal imitation. *Developmental Review, 7,* 86–92.

Blake, J., & Dolgoy, S. J. (1993). Gestural development and its relation to cognition during the transition to language. *Journal of Nonverbal Behavior, 17,* 87–102.

Blake, J., McConnell, S., Horton, G., & Benson, N. (1992). The gestural repertoire and its evolution over the second year. *Early Development and Parenting, 1,* 127–136.

Blake, R., Rhead, C. C., Wedge, B., & Mouton, J. S. (1956). Housing architecture and social interaction. *Sociometry, 19,* 133–139.

Blanck, P. D., Buck, R., & Rosenthal, R. (Eds.) (1986). *Nonverbal communication in the clinical context.* University

Park: Pennsylvania State University Press.

Blanck, P. D., & Rosenthal, R. (1984). Mediation of interpersonal expectancy effects: Counselor's tone of voice. *Journal of Educational Psychology, 76,* 418–426.

Blanck, P. D., Rosenthal, R., & Vannicelli, M. (1986). Talking to and about patients: The therapist's tone of voice. In P. D. Blanck, R. Buck, & R. Rosenthal (Eds.), *Nonverbal communication in the clinical context* (pp. 99–143). University Park: Pennsylvania State University Press.

Blonston, G. (1985, July/August). The translator. *Science,* 79–85.

Bloom, L. J., Weigel, R. G., & Trautt, G. M. (1977). Therapeugenic factors in psychotherapy: Effects of office decor and subject-therapist sex pairing on perception of credibility. *Journal of Consulting and Clinical Psychology, 45*(5), 867–873.

Boderman, A., Freed, D. W., & Kinnucan, M. T. (1972). "Touch me, like me": Testing an encounter group assumption. *Journal of Applied Behavioral Science, 8,* 527–533.

Boggs, D. H., & Simon, J. R. (1968). Differential effect of noise on tasks of varying complexity. *Journal of Applied Psychology, 52,* 148–153.

Boice, R., & Monti, P. M. (1982). Specification of nonverbal cues for clinical assessment. *Journal of Nonverbal Behavior, 7,* 79–94.

Bok, S. (1978). *Lying: Moral choice in public and private life.* New York: Pantheon.

Bok, S. (1982). *Secrets: On the ethics of concealment and revelation.* New York: Pantheon.

Bond, C. F., Jr., & Fahey, W. E. (1987). False suspicion and the misperception of deceit. *British Journal of Social Psychology, 26,* 41–46.

Bond, C. R., Omar, A., Pitre, U., Lashley, B. R., Skaggs, L. M., & Kirk, C. T. (1992). Fishy-looking liars: Deception judgment from expectancy violation. *Journal of Personality and Social Psychology, 63,* 969–977.

Bond, M. H., & Komai, H. (1976). Targets of gazing and eye contact during interviews: Effects on Japanese nonverbal behavior. *Journal of Personality and Social Psychology, 34,* 1276–1284.

Bond, M. H., & Shiraishi, D. (1974). The effect of interviewer's body lean and status on the nonverbal behavior of interviewees. *Japanese Journal of Experimental Social Psychology, 13,* 11–21.

Boomer, D. S. (1965). Hesitation and grammatical encoding. *Language and Speech, 8,* 148–158.

Boomer, D. S. (1978). The phonemic clause: Speech unit in human communication. In A. W. Siegman & S. Feldstein (Eds.), *Nonverbal behavior and communication* (pp. 245–262). Hillsdale, NJ: Erlbaum.

Boomer, D. S., & Dittmann, A. T. (1962). Hesitation pauses and juncture pauses in speech. *Language and Speech, 5,* 215–220.

Borden, R. J. (1980). Audience influence. In P. B. Paulus (Ed.), *Psychology of group influence* (pp. 99–131). Hillsdale, NJ: Erlbaum.

Borod, J. C., & Koff, E. (1990). Lateralization for facial emotional behavior: A methodological perspective. *International Journal of Psychology, 25,* 157–177.

Bossley, M. I. (1976). Privacy and crowding: A multidisciplinary analysis. *Man-Environment Systems, 6,* 8–19.

Boucher, J. D., & Ekman, P. (1975). Facial areas and emotional information. *Journal of Communication, 25* (2), 21–29.

Boulding, K. E. (1968). Am I a man or a mouse—or both? In M. F. A. Montagu (Ed.), *Man and aggression* (pp. 83–90). London: Oxford University Press.

Bourget, L. G. C. (1977). Delight and information specificity as elements of positive interpersonal feedback (Doctoral dissertation, Boston University). *Dissertation Abstracts International, 38,* 1946B–1947B. (University Microfilms No. 77–21,580)

Boyatzis, C. J., & Satyaprasad, C. (1994). Children's facial and gestural decoding and encoding: Relations between skills and with popularity. *Journal of Nonverbal Behavior, 18,* 37–55.

Boyatzis, C. J., & Watson, M. W. (1993). Preschool children's symbolic representation of objects through gestures. *Child Development, 64,* 729–735.

Brady, A. T., & Walker, M. B. (1978). Interpersonal distance as a function of situationally induced anxiety. *British Journal of Social and Clinical Psychology, 17,* 127–133.

Brandt, D. R. (1980). A systematic approach to the measurement of dominance in human face-to-face interaction. *Communication Quarterly, 28,* 31–43.

Brandt, D. R., Miller, G. R., & Hocking, J. E. (1980a). Effects of self-monitoring and familiarity on deception detection. *Communication Quarterly, 28,* 3–10.

Brandt, D. R., Miller, G. R., & Hocking, J. E. (1980b). The truth-deception attribution: Effects of familiarity on the ability of observers to detect deception. *Human Communication Research, 6,* 99–110.

Brandt, D. R., Miller, G. R., & Hocking, J. E. (1982). Familiarity and lie detection: A replication and extension. *Western Journal of Speech Communication, 46,* 276–290.

Brannigan, C. R., & Humphries, D. A. (1972). Human non-verbal behavior: A means of communication. In N. G. Blurton Jones (Ed.), *Ethological studies of child behavior* (pp. 37–64). London: Cambridge University Press.

Brault, G. J. (1962). Kinesics and the classroom: Some typical French gestures. *French Review, 36,* 374–382.

Brazelton, T. B., Tronick, E., Adamson, L., Als, H., & Wise, S. (1975). Early mother-infant reciprocity. In M. A. Hofer (Ed.), *Parent-infant interaction, Ciba Foundation Symposium 33* (pp. 137–168). Amsterdam: Elsevier.

Breed, G., & Ricci, J. S. (1973). "Touch me, like me": Artifact? *Proceedings of the 81st Annual Convention of the American Psychological Association, 8,* 153–154.

Brend, R. M. (1975). Male-female intonation patterns in American English. In B. Thorne & N. Henley (Eds.), *Language and sex: Difference and dominance* (pp. 84–87). Cambridge, MA: Newbury House.

Brislin, R. W., & Lewis, S. A. (1968). Dating and physical attractiveness: Replication. *Psychological Reports, 22,* 976.

Briton, N. J., & Hall, J. A. (1995). Gender-based expectancies and observer judgments of smiling. *Journal of Nonverbal Behavior, 19,* 49–65.

Broadstock, M., Borland, R., & Gason, R. (1992). Effects of suntan on judgments of healthiness and attractiveness by adolescents. *Journal of Applied Psychology, 22,* 157–172.

Broch, H. (1964). *The sleepwalkers: A triology.* New York: Pantheon.

Brockner, J., Pressman, B., Cabitt, J., & Moran, P. (1982). Nonverbal intimacy, sex, and compliance: A field study. *Journal of Nonverbal Behavior, 6,* 253–258.

Brodey, W. M. (1969). Information exchange in the time domain. In W. Gray, F. J. Diehl, & N. D. Rizzo (Eds.), *General systems theory and psychiatry* (pp. 220–243). Boston: Little, Brown.

Brody, E. B. (1963). Color and identity conflict in young boys. *Psychiatry, 26,* 188–201.

Broekmann, N. C., & Moller, A. T. (1973). Preferred seating position and distance in various situations. *Journal of Counseling Psychology, 20,* 504–508.

Brooks, A. D. (1975). *Responses to three American dialects.* Paper presented at the AILA Congress, Stuttgart, West Germany.

Broome, B. J. (1990). "Palevome": Foundations of struggle and conflict in Greek interpersonal communication. *Southern Communication Journal, 55,* 260–275.

Brown, B. L. (1980). Effects of speech rate on personality attributions and competency evaluations. In H. Giles, W. P. Robinson, & P. M. Smith (Eds.), *Language: Social psychological perspectives* (pp. 293–300). Oxford: Pergamon.

Brown, B. L., Strong, W. J., & Rencher, A. C. (1973). Perceptions of personality from speech: Effects of manipulations of acoustic parameters. *Journal of the Acoustical Society of America, 54,* 29–35.

Brown, B. L., Strong, W. J., & Rencher, A. C. (1974). Fifty-four voices from two: The effects of simultaneous manipulations of rate, mean fundamental frequency and variance of fundamental frequency on ratings of personality from speech. *Journal of the Acoustical Society of America, 55* (2), 313–318.

Brown, B. L., Strong, W. J., & Rencher, A. C. (1975). Acoustic determinants of perceptions of personality from speech. *International Journal of the Sociology of Language, 6,* 11–32.

Brown, C. E., Dovidio, J. F., & Ellyson, S. L. (1990). Reducing sex differences in visual displays of dominance: Knowledge is power. *Personality and Social Psychology Bulletin, 16,* 358–368.

Brownlow, S. (1992). Seeing is believing: Facial appearance, credibility, and attitude change. *Journal of Nonverbal Behavior, 16,* 101–115.

Brownlow, S., & Zebrowitz, L. A. (1990). Facial appearance, gender, and credibility in television commercials. *Journal of Nonverbal Behavior, 14,* 51–60.

Bruneau, T. J. (1973). Communicative silences: Forms and functions. *Journal of Communication, 23,* 17–46.

Bruneau, T. J. (1979). The time dimension in intercultural communication. In D. Nimmo (Ed.), *Communication yearbook 3* (pp. 169–181). New Brunswick, NJ: Transaction.

Bruneau, T. J. (1980). Chronemics and the verbal-nonverbal interface. In M. R. Key (Ed.), *The relationship of verbal and nonverbal communication* (pp. 101–118). New York: Mouton.

Brunetti, F. A. (1972). Noise, distraction, and privacy in conventional and open school environments. In W. J. Mitchell (Ed.), *Environmental design: Research and practice* (Vol. 1, pp. 12.2.1–12.2.6). Los Angeles: University of California Press.

Buck, J. (1968). The effects of Negro and White dialectical variations upon attitudes of college students. *Speech Monographs, 35,* 181–186.

Buck, R. (1975). Nonverbal communication of affect in children. *Journal of Personality and Social Psychology, 31,* 644–653.

Buck, R. (1976). A test of nonverbal receiving ability: Preliminary studies. *Human Communication Research, 2,* 162–171.

Buck, R. (1977). Nonverbal communication of affect in preschool children: Relationships with personality and skin conductance. *Journal of Personality and Social Psychology, 35,* 225–236.

Buck, R. (1979a). Individual differences in nonverbal sending accuracy and electrodermal responding: The externalizing-internalizing dimension. In R. Rosenthal (Ed.), *Skill in nonverbal communication: Individual differences* (pp. 140–170). Cambridge, MA: Oelgeschlager, Gunn & Hain.

Buck, R. (1979b). Measuring individual differences in the nonverbal communication of affect: The slide-viewing paradigm. *Human Communication Research, 6,* 47–57.

Buck, R. (1980). Nonverbal behavior and the theory of emotion: The facial feedback hypothesis. *Journal of Personality and Social Psychology, 38,* 811–824.

Buck, R. (1981). The evolution and development of emotion expression and communication. In S. S. Brehm, S. M. Kassin, & F. X. Gibbons (Eds.), *Developmental social psychology* (pp. 127–151). New York: Oxford University Press.

Buck, R. (1982, February). *A theory of spontaneous and symbolic expression: Implications for facial lateralization.* Paper presented at the annual meeting of the International Neuropsychological Society, Pittsburgh.

Buck, R. (1984). *The communication of emotion.* New York: Guilford.

Buck, R. (1988). Nonverbal communication: Spontaneous and symbolic aspects. *American Behavioral Scientist, 31,* 341–354.

Buck, R. (1991). Social factors in facial display and communication: A reply to Chovil and others. *Journal of Nonverbal Behavior, 15,* 155–161.

Buck, R., Losow, J. I., Murphy, M. M., & Costanzo, P. (1992). Social facilitation and inhibition of emotional expression and communication. *Journal of Personality and Social Psychology, 63,* 962–968.

Buck, R., Miller, R. E., & Caul, W. F. (1974). Sex, personality and physiological variables in the communication of emotion via facial expression. *Journal of Personality and Social Psychology, 30,* 587–596.

Buck, R., Savin, V. J., Miller, R. E., & Caul, W. F. (1972). Nonverbal communication of affect in humans. *Journal of Personality and Social Psychology, 23,* 362–371.

Bugental, D. E. (1974). Interpretations of naturally occurring discrepancies between words and intonation: Modes of inconsistency resolution. *Journal of Personality and Social Psychology, 30,* 125–133.

Bugental, D. E., Henker, B., & Whalen, C. K. (1976). Attributional antecedents of verbal and vocal assertiveness. *Journal of Personality and Social Psychology, 34,* 405–411.

Bugental, D. E., Kaswan, J. W., & Love, L. R. (1970). Perceptions of contradictory meanings conveyed by verbal and nonverbal channels. *Journal of Person-*

ality and Social Psychology, 16, 647–655.

Bugental, D. E., Kaswan, J. W., Love, L. R., & Fox, M. N. (1970). Child versus adult perception of evaluative messages in verbal, vocal, and visual channels. *Developmental Psychology, 2,* 367–375.

Bugental, D. E., Love, L. R. & Gianetto, R. M. (1971). Perfidious feminine faces. *Journal of Personality and Social Psychology, 17,* 314–318.

Bugental, D. E., Love, L. R., Kaswan, J. W., & April, C. (1971). Verbal-nonverbal conflict in parental messages to normal and disturbed children. *Journal of Abnormal Psychology, 77,* 6–10.

Buller, D. B. (1983). *Deception detection and the passive receiver: Are we assuming too little?* Paper presented at the annual meeting of the Eastern Communication Association, Ocean City, MD.

Buller, D. B. (1986). Distraction during persuasive communication: A meta-analytic review. *Communication Monographs, 53,* 91–114.

Buller, D. B. (1987). Communication apprehension and reactions to proxemic violations. *Journal of Nonverbal Behavior, 11,* 13–25.

Buller, D. B., & Aune, R. K. (1987). Nonverbal cues to deception among intimates, friends, and strangers. *Journal of Nonverbal Behavior, 11,* 269–290.

Buller, D. B., & Aune R. K. (1988). The effects of vocalics and nonverbal sensitivity on compliance: A speech accommodation theory explanation. *Human Communication Research, 14,* 301–332.

Buller, D. B., & Aune, R. K. (1992). The effects of speech rate similarity on compliance: Application of communication accommodation theory. *Western Journal of Communication, 56,* 37–53.

Buller, D. B., & Burgoon, J. K. (1986). The effects of vocalics and nonverbal sensitivity on compliance: A replication and extension. *Human Communication Research, 13,* 126–144.

Buller, D. B., & Burgoon, J. K. (1994). Deception: Strategic and nonstrategic communication. In J. A. Daly & J. M. Wiemann (Eds.), *Strategic interpersonal communication.* (191–224). Hillsdale, NJ: Erlbaum.

Buller, D. B., & Burgoon, J. K. (in press). Interpersonal deception theory. *Communication Theory.*

Buller, D. B., Burgoon, J. K., Buslig, A., & Roiger, J. (1994). Interpersonal deception: VIII. Further analysis of nonverbal and verbal correlates of equivocation from the Bavelas et al. (1990) research. *Journal of Language and Social Psychology, 13,* 396–417.

Buller, D. B., Burgoon, J. K., Buslig, A., & Roiger, J. (in press). Testing interpersonal deception: The language of interpersonal deception. *Communication Theory.*

Buller, D. B., Burgoon, J. K., White, C., Buslig, A., & Ebesu, A. S. (1995, November). *Interpersonal deception: XIV. Effects of planning on verbal and nonverbal behavior during deception.* Paper presented at the annual meeting of the Speech Communication Association, San Antonio.

Buller, D. B., Burgoon, J. K., White, C., & Ebesu, A. S. (1994). Interpersonal deception: VII. Behavioral profiles of falsification, concealment, and equivocation. *Journal of Language and Social Psychology, 13,* 366–395.

Buller, D. B., Comstock, J., Aune, R. K., & Strzyzewski, K. D. (1989). The effect of probing on deceivers and truthtellers. *Journal of Nonverbal Behavior, 13,* 155–169.

Buller, D. B., & Hunsaker, F. (in press). Interpersonal deception: XIII. Suspicion and the truth-bias of conversational participants. In J. Aitken (Ed.), *Intrapersonal communication processes reader.* Westland, MI: McNeil.

Buller, D. B., Le Poire, B. A., Aune, R. K., & Eloy, S. V. (1992). Social perceptions as mediators of the effect of speech rate similarity on compliance. *Human Communication Research, 19,* 286–311.

Buller, D. B., Strzyzewski, K. D., & Comstock, J. (1991). Interpersonal deception: I. Deceivers' reactions to receivers suspicions and probing. *Communication Monographs, 58,* 1–24.

Buller, D. B., Strzyzewski, K. D., & Hunsaker, F. G. (1991). Interpersonal deception: II. The inferiority of conversational participants as deception detectors. *Communication Monographs, 58,* 25–40.

Buller, M. K., & Buller, D. B. (1987). Physicians' communication style and patient satisfaction. *Journal of Health and Social Behavior, 28,* 375–388.

Bullis, C., & Horn, C. (1995). Get a little closer: Further examination of nonverbal comforting strategies. *Communication Reports, 8,* 10–117.

Burgess, J. W. (1983). Developmental trends in proxemic spacing behavior between surrounding companions and strangers in casual groups. *Journal of Nonverbal Behavior, 7,* 158–169.

Burggraf, C. S., & Sillars, A. L. (1987). A critical examination of sex differences in marital communication. *Communication Monographs, 54,* 276–294.

Burgoon, J. K. (1978a). Attributes of the newscaster's voice as predictors of his credibility. *Journalism Quarterly, 55,* 276–281, 300.

Burgoon, J. K. (1978b). A communication model of personal space violations: Explication and an initial test. *Human Communication Research, 4,* 129–142.

Burgoon, J. K. (1980). Nonverbal communication in the 1970s: An overview. In D. Nimmo (Ed.), *Communication yearbook 4* (pp. 179–197). New Brunswick, NJ: Transaction.

Burgoon, J. K. (1982). Privacy and communication. In M. Burgoon (Ed.), *Communication yearbook 6* (pp. 206–249). Beverly Hills, CA: Sage.

Burgoon, J. K. (1983). Nonverbal violations of expectations. In J. M. Wiemann & R. P. Harrison (Eds.), *Nonverbal interaction* (pp. 77–111). Beverly Hills, CA: Sage.

Burgoon, J. K. (1985a). Nonverbal signals. In M. L. Knapp & G. R. Miller (Eds.), *Handbook of interpersonal communication* (pp. 344–390). Beverly Hills, CA: Sage.

Burgoon, J. K. (1985b). The relationship of verbal and nonverbal codes. In B. Dervin & M. J. Voight (Eds.), *Progress in communication sciences* (Vol. 6, pp. 263–298). Norwood, NJ: Ablex.

Burgoon, J. K. (1986, February). *Expectancy violations: Theory, research and critique.* Paper presented at the annual meeting of the Western Speech Communication Association, Tucson, AZ.

Burgoon, J. K. (1991). Relational message interpretations of touch, conversational distance, and posture. *Journal of Nonverbal Behavior, 15,* 233–259.

Burgoon, J. K. (1992a). Applying a comparative approach to nonverbal expectancy violations theory. In J. Blumler, K. E. Rosengren, & J. M. McLeod (Eds.), *Comparatively speaking: Communication and culture across space and time* (pp. 53–69). Newbury Park, CA: Sage.

Burgoon, J. K. (1992c). Spatial relationships in small groups. In R. S. Cathcart & L. A. Samovar (Eds.), *Small group communication: A reader* (6th ed., pp. 287–300). Dubuque, IA: Brown.

Burgoon, J. K. (1992d). Spatial relationships in small groups. In K. S. Cathcart & L. A. Samovar (Eds.), *Small group communication: A reader* (6th ed., pp. 287–300). Dubuque: Brown.

Burgoon, J. K. (1993). Interpersonal expectations, expectancy violations, and emotional communication. *Journal of Language and Social Psychology, 12,* 30–48.

Burgoon, J. K. (1994). Nonverbal signals. In M. L. Knapp & G. R. Miller (Eds.), *Handbook of interpersonal communication* (2d ed., pp. 229–285). Newbury Park, CA: Sage.

Burgoon, J. K. (1995). Cross-cultural and intercultural applications of expectancy violations. In R. L. Wiseman (Ed.), *Intercultural communication theory* (Vol. 19, pp. 194–214). Thousand Oaks, CA: Sage.

Burgoon, J. K., & Aho, L. (1982). Three field experiments on the effects of violations of conversational distance. *Communication Monographs, 49,* 71–88.

Burgoon, J. K., Birk, T., & Pfau, M. (1990). Nonverbal behaviors, persuasion, and credibility. *Human Communication Research, 17,* 140–169.

Burgoon, J. K., & Buller, D. B. (1994). Interpersonal deception: III. Effects of deceit on perceived communication and nonverbal behavior dynamics. *Journal of Nonverbal Behavior, 18,* 155–184.

Burgoon, J. K., Buller, D. B., Dillman, L., & Walther, J. (in press). Interpersonal deception: IV. Effects of suspicion on perceived communication and nonverbal behavior dynamics. *Human Communication Research.*

Burgoon, J. K., Buller, D. B., Ebesu, A., & Rockwell, P. (1994). Interpersonal deception: V. Accuracy in deception detection. *Communication Monographs, 61,* 303–325.

Burgoon, J. K., Buller, D. B., Ebesu, A., Rockwell, P., & White, C. (in press). Testing interpersonal deception: Effects of suspicion on communication behaviors and perceptions. *Communication Theory.*

Burgoon, J. K., Buller, D. B., & Guerrero, L. K. (1995). Interpersonal deception: IX. Effects of social skill and nonverbal communication on deception success and detection accuracy. *Journal of Language and Social Psychology, 14,* 289–311.

Burgoon, J. K., Buller, D. B., Guerrero, L. K., Afifi, W., & Feldman, C. (in press). Interpersonal deception: XII. Information management dimensions underlying deceptive and truthful messages. *Communication Monographs.*

Burgoon, J. K., Buller, D. B., Guerrero, L. K., & Feldman, C. (in press). Interpersonal deception: VI. Effects of preinteractional and interactional factors on deceiver and observer perceptions of deception success. *Communication Studies.*

Burgoon, J. K., Buller, D. B., Hale, J. L., & deTurck, M. A. (1984). Relational messages associated with nonverbal behaviors. *Human Communication Research, 10,* 351–378.

Burgoon, J. K., Buller, D. B., & Woodall, W. G. (1989). *Nonverbal communication: The unspoken dialogue.* New York: HarperCollins.

Burgoon, J. K., & Coker, D. A. (1987, May). *Nonverbal expectancy violations and conversational involvement.* Paper presented at the annual meeting of the International Communication Association, New Orleans.

Burgoon, J. K., Coker, D. A., & Coker, R. A. (1986). Communicative effects of gaze behavior: A test of two contrasting explanations. *Human Communication Research, 12,* 495–524.

Burgoon, J. K., & Dillman, L. (1995). Gender, immediacy and nonverbal communication. In P. J. Kalbfleisch & M. J. Cody (Eds.), *Gender, power and communication in human relationships* (pp. 63–81). Hillsdale, NJ: Erlbaum.

Burgoon, J. K., Dillman, L., & Stern, L. A. (1993). Adaptation in dyadic interaction: Defining and operationalizing patterns of reciprocity and compensation. *Communication Theory, 3,* 295–316.

Burgoon, J. K., & Hale, J. L. (1984). The fundamental topoi of relational communication. *Communication Monographs, 51,* 193–214.

Burgoon, J. K., & Hale, J. L. (1987a, May). *Nonverbal expectancy violations: Model elaboration and application to immediacy behaviors.* Paper presented at the annual meeting of the International Communication Association, Montreal.

Burgoon, J. K., & Hale, J. L. (1987b). Validation and measurement of the fundamental themes of relational communication. *Communication Monographs, 54,* 19–41.

Burgoon, J. K., & Hale, J. L. (1988). Nonverbal expectancy violations: Model elaboration and application to immediacy behaviors. *Communication Monographs, 55,* 58–79.

Burgoon, J. K., & Jones, S. B. (1976). Toward a theory of personal space expectations and their violations. *Human Communication Research, 2,* 131–146.

Burgoon, J. K., Kelley, D. L., Newton, D. A., & Keeley-Dyreson, M. P. (1989). The nature of arousal and nonverbal indices. *Human Communication Research, 16,* 217–255.

Burgoon, J. K., & Koper, R. J. (1984). Nonverbal and relational communication associated with reticence. *Human Communication Research, 10,* 601–626.

Burgoon, J. K., & Langer, E. (1995). Language, fallacies, and mindlessness-mindfulness. In B. R. Burleson (Ed.), *Communication yearbook 18* (105–132). Newbury Park, CA: Sage.

Burgoon, J. K., & Le Poire, B. A. (1993). Effects of communication expectancies, actual communication, and expectancy disconfirmation on evaluation of communicators and their communication behavior. *Human Communication Research, 20,* 67–96.

Burgoon, J. K., Le Poire, B. A., & Rosenthal, R. (1995). Effects of preinteraction expectancies and target communication on perceiver reciprocity and compensation during dyadic interaction. *Journal of Experimental Social Psychology, 31,* 287–321.

Burgoon, J. K. Manusov, V., Mineo, P., & Hale, J. L. (1985). Effects of eye gaze on hiring credibility, attraction, and relational message interpretation.

Journal of Nonverbal Behavior, 9, 133–146.

Burgoon, J. K., & Newton, D. A. (1991). Applying a social meaning model to relational message interpretations of conversational involvement: Comparing observer and participant perspectives. *Southern Communication Journal 56,* 96–113.

Burgoon, J. K., Newton, D. A., Walther, J. A., Baesler, E. J. (1989). Nonverbal expectancy violations and conversational involvement. *Journal of Nonverbal Behavior 13,* 97–120.

Burgoon, J. K., Olney, C. A., & Coker, R. (1988). The effects of communicator characteristics on patterns of reciprocity and compensation. *Journal of Nonverbal Behavior, 11,* 146–165.

Burgoon, J. K., Parrott, R., Le Poire, B. A., Kelley, D. L., Walther, J. B., & Perry, D. (1989). Maintaining and restoring privacy through communication in different types of relationships. *Journal of Social and Personal Relationships, 6,* 131–158.

Burgoon, J. K., Pfau, M., Parrott, R., Birk, T., Coker, R., & Burgoon, M. (1987). Relational communication, satisfaction, compliance-gaining strategies, and compliance in communication between physicians and patients. *Communication Monographs, 54,* 307–324.

Burgoon, J. K., & Saine, T. J. (1978). *The unspoken dialogue: An introduction to nonverbal communication.* Boston: Houghton-Mifflin.

Burgoon, J. K., Stacks, D. W., & Burch, S. A. (1982). The role of interpersonal rewards and violations of distancing expectations in achieving influence in small groups. *Communication, Journal of the Communication Association of the Pacific, 11,* 114–128.

Burgoon, J. K., Stacks, D. W., & Woodall, W. G. (1979). A communicative model of violations of distancing expectations. *Western Journal of Speech Communication, 43,* 153–167.

Burgoon, J. K., Stern, L. A., & Dillman, L. (1995). *Interpersonal adaptation: Dyadic interaction patterns.* Cambridge: Cambridge University Press.

Burgoon, J. K., & Walther, J. B. (1990). Nonverbal expectancies and the consequences of violations. *Human Communication Research, 17,* 232–265.

Burgoon, J. K., Walther, J. B., & Baesler, E. J. (1992). Interpretations and conse-

quences of interpersonal touch. *Human Communication Research, 19,* 237–263.

Burley, T. D. (1972). *An investigation of the roles of imagery, kinesthetic cues and attention in tactile nonverbal communication.* Unpublished doctoral dissertation, University of Tennessee, Knoxville.

Burns, J. (1972). Development and implementation of an environmental evaluation and redesign process for a high school science department. In W. J. Mitchell (Ed.), *Environmental design: Research and practice* (Vol. 1, pp. 12.3.1–12.3.9). Los Angeles, University of California Press.

Burns, K. L., & Beier, E. G. (1973). Significance of vocal and visual channels in the decoding of emotional meaning. *Journal of Communication, 23,* 118–130.

Burris, P. A. (1982, November). *An interactionist view of small group leadership: Studies of influence relationships and leadership perception.* Paper presented at the annual convention of the Speech Communication Association, Louisville, KY.

Bush, L. E., II (1973). Individual differences in multidimensional scaling of adjectives denoting feelings. *Journal of Personality and Social Psychology, 25,* 50–57.

Buslig, A. L. S. (1991). *Architects' and laypeople's preceptions of interaction environments.* Unpublished master's thesis, University of Arizona.

Butler, D., & Geis, F. L. (1990). Nonverbal affect responses to male and female leaders: Implications for leadership evaluations. *Journal of Personality and Social Psychology, 58,* 48–59.

Byers, P., & Byers, H. (1972). Nonverbal communication and the education of children. In C. B. Cazden, V. P. John, & D. Hymes (Eds.), *Functions of language in the classroom* (pp. 3–31). New York: Teachers College Press.

Byrne, D. (1961). The influence of propinquity and opportunities for interaction on classroom relationships. *Human Relations, 14,* 63–70.

Byrne, D., Baskett, G. D., & Hodges, L. (1971). Behavioral indicators of interpersonal attraction. *Journal of Applied Social Psychology, 1,* 137–149.

Byrne, D., Ervin, C. R., & Lamberth, J. (1970). Continuity between the experi-

mental study of attraction and real-life computer dating. *Journal of Personality and Social Psychology, 16,* 157–165.

Byrne, D., London, O., & Reeves, K. (1968). The effects of physical attractiveness, sex, and attitude similarity on interpersonal attraction. *Journal of Personality, 36,* 259–272.

Cacioppo, J. T., Bush, L. K., & Tassinary, L. G. (1992). Microexpressive facial actions as a function of affective stimuli: Replication and extension. *Personality and Social Psychology Bulletin, 18,* 515–526.

Cahnman, W. J. (1968). The stigma of obesity. *Sociological Quarterly, 9,* 283–299.

Calhoun, J. B. (1962). Population density and social pathology. *Scientific American, 206,* 139–148.

Calhoun, J. B. (1966). The role of space in animal sociology. *Journal of Social Issues, 22,* 46–58.

Calhoun, J. B. (1970). Space and the strategy of life. *Ekistics, 29,* 425–437.

Camden, C., Motley, M. T., & Wilson, A. (1984). White lies in interpersonal communication: A taxonomy and preliminary investigation of social motivations. *Western Journal of Speech Communication, 48,* 309–325.

Campbell, J. (1982). *Grammatical man.* New York: Simon & Schuster.

Camras, L. A. (1977). Facial expressions used by children in a conflict situation. *Child Development, 48,* 1431–1435.

Camras, L. A. (1980a). Animal threat displays and children's facial expressions: A comparison. In D. R. Omar, F. F. Strayer, & D. G. Freedman (Eds.), *Dominance relations: An ethological view of human conflict and social interaction* (pp. 124–127). New York: Garland STPM.

Camras, L. A. (1980b). Children's understanding of facial expressions used during conflict encounters. *Child Development, 51,* 879–885.

Camras, L. A. (1982). Ethological approaches to nonverbal communication. In R. S. Feldman (Ed.), *Development of nonverbal behavior in children* (pp. 3–28). New York: Springer-Verlag.

Camras, L. A. (1984). Children's verbal and nonverbal communication in a conflict situation. *Ethology and Sociobiology, 5,* 257–268.

Camras, L. A., Sullivan, J., & Michel, G.

(1993). Do infants express discrete emotions? Adult judgments of facial, vocal, and body actions. *Journal of Nonverbal Behavior, 17,* 171–186.

Caplan, F. (1973). *The first twelve months of life.* New York: Grosset & Dunlap.

Cappella, J. N. (1981). Mutual influence in expressive behavior: Adult-adult and infant-adult dyadic interaction. *Psychological Bulletin, 89,* 101–132.

Cappella, J. N. (1983). Conversational involvement: Approaching and avoiding others. In J. M. Wiemann & R. P. Harrison (Eds.), *Nonverbal interaction* (pp. 113–148). Beverly Hills, CA: Sage.

Cappella, J. N. (1984). The relevance of microstructure of interaction to relationship change. *Journal of Social and Personal Relationships, 1,* 239–264.

Cappella, J. N. (1985). The management of conversations. In M. L. Knapp & G. R. Miller (Eds.), *Handbook of interpersonal communication* (pp. 393–438). Beverly Hills, CA: Sage.

Cappella, J. N. (1987). Interpersonal communication: Definitions and questions. In C. R. Berger & S. Chaffee (Eds.), *Handbook of communication science* (pp. 184–238). Beverly Hills, CA: Sage.

Cappella, J. N. (1991). The biological origins of automated patterns in human interaction. *Communication Theory, 1,* 4–35.

Cappella, J. N. (1994). The management of conversations. In M. L. Knapp & G. R. Miller (Eds.), *Handbook of interpersonal communication* (pp. 380–419). Newbury Park, CA: Sage.

Cappella, J. N. (in press). Dynamic coordination of vocal and kinesic behavior in dyadic interaction: Methods, problems, and interpersonal outcomes. In J. Watt & C. A. Van Lear (Eds.), *Cycles and dynamic patterns in communication processes.* Newbury Park: Sage.

Cappella, J. N., & Greene, J. O. (1982). A discrepancy-arousal explanation of mutual influence in expressive behavior for adult-adult and infant-adult dyadic interaction. *Communication Monographs, 49,* 89–114.

Cappella, J. N., & Greene, J. O. (1984). The effects of distance and individual differences in arousability on nonverbal involvement: A test of discrepancy-arousal theory. *Journal of Nonverbal Behavior, 8,* 259–286.

Cappella, J. N., & Palmer, M. T. (1990). The structure and organization of verbal and non-verbal behavior: Data for models of production. In H. Giles & W. P. Robinson (Eds.), *Handbook of Language and Social Psychology* (pp. 141–161). Chichester: Wiley.

Cappella, J. N., & Planalp, S. (1981). Talk and silence sequences in informal conversations: III. Interspeaker influence. *Human Communication Research, 7,* 117–132.

Carroll, J. M. (1975). *Confidential information sources: Public and private.* Los Angeles: Security World.

Casey, R. J., & Fuller, L. L. (1994). Maternal regulation of children's emotions. *Journal of Nonverbal Behavior, 18,* 57–89.

Cash, T. F. (1988). The psychology of cosmetics: A research bibliography. *Perceptual and Motor Skills, 66,* 455–460.

Cassotta, L., Feldstein, S., & Jaffe, J. (1964). AVTA: A device for automatic vocal transaction analysis. *Journal of Experimental Analysis of Behavior, 7,* 99–104.

Castellow, W. A., Wuensch, K. L., & Moore, C. H. (1990). Effects of physical attractiveness on plaintiff and defendant sexual harassment judgments. *Journal of Social Behavior and Personality, 5,* 547–562.

Cate, R. M., & Lloyd, S. A. (1992). *Courtship.* Newbury Park, CA: Sage.

Cathcart, D., & Cathcart, R. (1976). The Japanese social experience and concept of groups. In L. A. Samovar & R. E. Porter (Eds.), *Intercultural communication: A reader* (2nd ed., pp. 58–66). Belmont, CA: Wadsworth.

Chaikin, A. L., Derlega, V. J., & Miller, S. J. (1976). Effects of room environment on self-disclosure in a counseling analogue. *Journal of Counseling Psychology, 23,* 479–481.

Chaikin, A. L., Sigler, E., & Derlega, V. J. (1974). Nonverbal mediators of teacher expectancy effects. *Journal of Personality and Social Psychology, 30,* 144–149.

Chaiken, S. (1979). Communicator physical attractiveness and persuasion. *Journal of Personality and Social Psychology, 37,* 1387–1397.

Chaiken, S., Eagly, A. H., Sejwacz, D., Gregory, W. L., & Christensen, D. (1978). Communicator physical attractiveness as a determinant of opinion change. *JSAS Catalog of Selected Documents in Psychology, 8* (Ms. No. 1639).

Chance, M. R. A. (1967). Attention structures as the basis of primate rank orders. *Man, 2,* 503–518.

Chapin, F. S. (1951). Some housing factors related to mental hygiene. *Journal of Social Issues, 7,* 164–171.

Chapman, A. J. (1975). Eye contact, physical proximity and laughter: A reexamination of the equilibrium model of social intimacy. *Social Behavior and Personality, 3,* 143–155.

Chapple, E. D. (1970). *Cultural and biological man: Exploration in behavioral anthropology.* New York: Holt, Rinehart and Winston.

Charlesworth, W. R., & Kreutzer, M. A. (1973). Facial expressions of infants and children. In P. Ekman (Ed.), *Darwin and facial expression* (pp. 91–168). New York: Academic.

Charney, E. J. (1966). Psychosomatic manifestation of rapport in psychotherapy. *Psychosomatic Medicine, 28,* 305–315.

Chawla, P., & Krauss, R. M. (1994). Gesture and speech in spontaneous and rehearsed narratives. *Journal of Experimental Social Psychology, 30,* 580–601.

Cherry, C. (1957, 1964). *On human communication.* Cambridge, MA: MIT Press.

Chovil, N. (1991). Social determinants of facial displays. *Journal of Nonverbal Behavior, 15,* 141–154.

Chovil, N., & Fridlund, A. J. (1991). Why emotionally cannot·equal sociality: Reply to Buck. *Journal of Nonverbal Behavior, 15,* 163–168.

Christenfeld, N., Schachter, S., & Bilous, F. (1991). Filled pauses and gestures: It's not coincidence. *Journal of Psycholinguistic Research, 20,* 1–10.

Christian, J. J., Flyer, V., & Davis, D. E. (1961). Phenomena associated with population density. *Proceedings of the National Academy of Sciences, 47*(4), 428–449.

Christie, R., & Geis, F. L. (1970). *Studies in Machiavellianism.* New York: Academic.

Ciolek, T. M. (1983). The proxemics lexicon: A first approximation. *Journal of Nonverbal Behavior, 8,* 55–79.

Claiborn, C. D. (1979). Counselor verbal intervention, nonverbal behavior, and social power. *Journal of Counseling Psychology, 26,* 378–383.

Clark, H. H., & French, J. W. (1981). Telephone goodbyes. *Language in society, 10,* 1–19.

Clark, M. S., Milberg, S., & Erber, R. (1984). Effects of arousal on judgments of others' emotions. *Journal of Personality and Social Psychology, 46,* 551–560.

Clark, R. A. (1984). *Persuasive messages.* New York: Harper & Row.

Clark, R. A., & Delia, J. G. (1979). Topoi and rhetorical competence. *Quarterly Journal of Speech, 65,* 187–206.

Clevenger, T., Jr. (1991). Can one not communicate? A conflict of models. *Communication Studies, 42,* 340–353.

Cliff, N., & Young, F. W. (1968). On the relation between unidimensional judgments and multidimensional scaling. *Organizational Behavior and Human Performance, 3,* 269–285.

Clifford, M. M., & Walster, E. H. (1973). The effect of physical attractiveness on teacher expectation. *Sociology of Education, 46,* 248–258.

Clore, G. L., Wiggins, N. H., & Itkin, S. (1975a). Gain and loss in attraction: Attributions from nonverbal behavior. *Journal of Personality and Social Psychology, 31,* 706–712.

Clore, G. L., Wiggins, N. H., & Itkin, S. (1975b). Judging attraction from nonverbal behavior: The gain phenomenon. *Journal of Consulting and Clinical Psychology, 43,* 491–497.

Cloudsley-Thompson, J. L. (1981). Time sense of animals. In J. T. Fraser, *The voices of time* (2d ed., pp. 296–311). Amherst: University of Massachusetts Press.

Cochran, C. D., Hale, W. D., & Hissam, C. P. (1984). Personal space requirements in indoor versus outdoor locations. *Journal of Psychology, 117,* 121–123.

Cody, M. J., & McLaughlin, M. L. (1985). The situation as a construct in interpersonal communication research. In M. L. Knapp & G. R. Miller (Eds.), *Handbook of interpersonal communication* (pp. 263–312). Beverly Hills, CA: Sage.

Cohen, A., & Starkweather, J. (1961). Vocal cues to the identification of language. *American Journal of Psychology, 74,* 90–93.

Cohen, A. A. (1977). The communicative functions of hand illustrators. *Journal of Communication, 27,* 54–63.

Cohen, A. A., & Harrison, R. P. (1973). Intentionality in the use of hand illustrators in face-to-face communication situations. *Journal of Personality and Social Psychology, 28,* 276–279.

Cohen, S., & Weinstein, N. (1981). Nonauditory effects of noise on behavior and health. *Journal of Social Issues, 37,* 36–70.

Coker, D. A., & Burgoon, J. K. (1987). The nature of conversational involvement and nonverbal encoding patterns. *Human Communication Research, 13,* 463–494.

Cole, P. M. (1986). Children's spontaneous control of facial expression. *Child Development, 57,* 1309–1321.

Collett, P. (1971). On training Englishmen in the non-verbal behavior of Arabs: An experiment on intercultural communication. *International Journal of Psychology, 6,* 209–215.

Collins, A. M., & Loftus, E. F. (1975). A spreading-activation theory of semantic processing. *Psychological Review, 82,* 407–428.

Collins, B. E., & Guetzkow, H. (1964). *A social psychology of group processes.* New York: Wiley.

Comadena, M. E. (1982). Accuracy in detecting deception: Intimate and friendship relationships. In M. Burgoon (Ed.), *Communication Yearbook 6* (pp. 446–472). Beverly Hills, CA: Sage.

Compton, N. H. (1962). Personal attributes of color and design preferences in clothing fabrics. *Journal of Psychology, 54,* 191–195.

Condon, J. C., & Kurata, K. (1974). *In search of what's Japanese about Japan.* Tokyo, Japan: Shufunotomo.

Condon, J. C., & Yousef, F. (1975). *An introduction to intercultural communication.* Indianapolis: Bobbs-Merrill.

Condon, W. S. (1976). An analysis of behavior organization. *Sign Language Studies, 13,* 285–318.

Condon, W. S., & Ogston, W. D. (1966). Sound film analysis of normal and pathological behavior patterns. *Journal of Nervous and Mental Disease, 143,* 338–347.

Condon, W. S., & Ogston, W. D. (1967). A segmentation of behavior. *Journal of Psychiatric Research, 5,* 221–235.

Condon, W. S., & Sander, L. W. (1974). Synchrony demonstrated between movement of the neonate and adult speech. *Child Development, 45,* 456–462.

Cook, M. (1970). Experiments on orientation and proxemics. *Human Relations, 23,* 61–76.

Cook, M. (1979). *Perceiving others: The psychology of interpersonal perception.* London: Methuen.

Coombs, R. H., & Kenkel, W. F. (1966). Sex differences in dating aspirations and satisfaction with computer-selected partners. *Journal of Marriage and the Family, 28,* 62–66.

Cooper, C. L., & Bowles, D. (1973). Physical encounter and self-disclosure. *Psychological Reports, 33,* 451–454.

Cooper, H., & Hazelrigg, P. (1988). Personality moderators of interpersonal expectancy effects: An integrative research review. *Journal of Personality and Social Psychology, 55,* 937–949.

Cooper, J., Darley, J. M., & Henderson, J. E. (1974). On the effectiveness of deviant- and conventional-appearing communicators: A field experiment. *Journal of Personality and Social Psychology, 29,* 752–757.

Copeland, J. B., Shapiro, D., Williams, E., & Matsumoto, N. (1987, February). How to win over a Japanese boss. *Newsweek, 109,* 46–48.

Cordwell, J. M. (1976). Human arts of transformation. *CTFA Cosmetic Journal, 8,* 22–28.

Corso, J. F. (1977). Auditory perception and communication. In J. E. Birren & K. W. Schaie (Eds.), *Handbook of the psychology of aging* (pp. 535–553). New York: Van Nostrand Reinhold.

Cortes, J. B., & Gatti, F. M. (1965). Physique and self-description of temperament. *Journal of Consulting Psychology, 29,* 432–439.

Cortes, J. B., & Gatti, F. M. (1970, October). Physique and propensity. *Psychology Today, 4,* pp. 32–34, 42–44.

Cory, C. T. (1983, February 17). Crosstalk. *Psychology Today,* p. 22.

Costanzo, F. S., Markel, N. N., & Costanzo, R. R. (1969). Voice quality profile and perceived emotion. *Journal of Counseling Psychology, 16,* 267–270.

Costanzo, M., & Archer, D. (1989). Interpreting the expressive behavior of others: The Interpersonal Perception Task (IPT). *Journal of Nonverbal Behavior, 13,* 225–245.

Cottrell, N. B. (1972). Social facilitation. In C. G. McClintock (Ed.), *Experimental social psychology* (pp. 185–236). New York: Holt, Rinehart and Winston.

Coupland, N. (1984). Accommodation at work: Some phonological data and their implications. *International Journal of the Sociology of Language, 46,* 49–70.

Cousins, N. (1979). *Anatomy of an illness as perceived by the patient: Reflecting on healing and regeneration.* New York: Norton.

Coutts, L. M., & Schneider, F. W. (1976). Affiliative conflict theory: An investigation of the intimacy equilibrium and compensation hypothesis. *Journal of Personality and Social Psychology, 34,* 1135–1142.

Coutts, L. M., Schneider, F. W., & Montgomery, S. (1980). An investigation of the arousal model of interpersonal intimacy. *Journal of Experimental Social Psychology, 16,* 545–561.

Cozby, P. C. (1974). *Some recent research on self-disclosure processes.* Paper presented at the annual meeting of the American Psychological Association, New Orleans.

Craig, R. T. (1978). Cognitive science: A new approach to cognition, language, and communication. *Quarterly Journal of Speech, 64,* 439–467.

Craik, F. I. M., & Lockhart, R. S. (1972). Levels of processing: A framework for memory research. *Journal of Verbal Learning and Verbal Behavior, 11,* 671–684.

Crane, D. R., Dollahite, D. C., Griffin, W., & Taylor, V. L. (1987). Diagnosing relationships with spatial distance: An empirical test of a clinical principle. *Journal of Marital and Family Therapy, 13,* 307–310.

Crassweller, P., Gordon, M. A., & Tedford, W. H., Jr. (1972). An experimental investigation of hitchhiking. *Journal of Psychology, 82,* 43–47.

Crawford, C. C., & Michael, W. (1927). An experiment in judging intelligence by the voice. *Journal of Educational Psychology, 18,* 107–114.

Cronkhite, G. (1986). On the focus, scope, and coherence of the study of human symbolic activity. *Quarterly Journal of Speech, 72,* 231–246.

Crown, C. L. (1980). Impression formation and the chronography of dyadic interactions. In M. Davis (Ed.), *Interaction rhythms: Periodicity in communicative behavior* (pp. 225–248). New York: Human Sciences.

Crusco, A. H., & Wetzel, C. G. (1984). The midas touch: The effects of interpersonal touch on restaurant tipping. *Personality & Social Psychology Bulletin, 10,* 512–517.

Crystal, D. (1969). *Prosodic systems and intonation in English.* Cambridge: Cambridge University Press.

Cuceloglu, D. M. (1970). Perception of facial expressions in three different cultures. *Ergonomics, 13,* 93–100.

Cuceloglu, D. M. (1972). Facial code in affective communication. In D. C. Speer (Ed.), *Nonverbal communication* (pp. 395–407). Beverly Hills, CA: Sage.

Cupchik, G. C. (1973). Expression and impression: The decoding of nonverbal affect. *Dissertation Abstracts International, 33,* 5536B.

Cupchik, G. C., & Poulos, C. X. (1984). Judgments of emotional intensity in self and others: The effects of stimulus context, sex, and expressivity. *Journal of Personality and Social Psychology, 46,* 431–439.

Cushman, D., & Whiting, G. C. (1972). An approach to communication theory: Toward consensus on rules. *Journal of Communication, 22,* 217–238.

Custrini, R. J., & Feldman, R. S. (1989). Children's social competence and nonverbal encoding and decoding of emotion. *Journal of Clinical Child Psychology, 18,* 336–342.

Cutler, W. B., Preti, G., Krieger, A., Huggins, G. R., Garcia, C. R., & Lawley, H. J. (1986). Human axillary secretions influence women's menstrual cycles: The role of donor extract from men. *Hormones and Behavior, 20,* 463–473.

Dabbs, J. M., Jr. (1969). Similarity of gestures and interpersonal influence. *Proceedings of the 77th Annual Convention of the American Psychological Association, 4,* 337–338.

Dabbs, J. M., Jr. (1994, October). *Testosterone and marriage: Like a rhino and a carriage.* Paper presented at the annual meeting of the Society for Experimental Social Psychology, Lake Tahoe, NV.

Dabbs, J. M., Evans, M. S., Hopper, C. H., & Purvis, J. A. (1980). Self-monitors in conversation: What do they monitor? *Journal of Personality and Social Psychology, 39,* 278–284.

D'Alessio, M., & Zazzatta, A. (1986). Development of self-touching behavior in childhood. *Perceptual and Motor Skills, 63,* 243–253.

Daley, J. P. (1973). *The effects of crowding and comfort on interaction behavior and membership satisfaction in small groups.* Paper presented at the annual meeting of the International Communication Association, Montreal.

Daly, E. M., Lancee, W. J., & Polivy, J. (1983). A conical model for the taxonomy of emotional experience. *Journal of Personality and Social Psychology, 45,* 443–457.

Daly, J. A., Hogg, E., Sacks, D., Smith, M., & Zimring, L. (1983). Sex and relationship affect social self-grooming. *Journal of Nonverbal Behavior, 7,* 183–189.

d'Angeljan, A., & Tucker, G. R. (1973). Sociolinguistic correlates of speech style in Quebec. In R. Shuy & R. Fasold (Eds.), *Language attitudes: Current trends and prospects* (pp. 1–27). Washington, DC: Georgetown University Press.

Danziger, K. (1976). *Interpersonal communication.* Oxford: Pergamon.

Darley, J. M., & Cooper, J. (1972). The "Clean for Gene" phenomenon: The effect of students' appearance on political campaigning. *Journal of Applied Social Psychology, 2,* 24–33.

Darwin, C. (1965). *The expression of the emotions in man and animals.* Chicago: University of Chicago Press. (Original work published 1872.)

D'Augelli, A. R. (1974). Nonverbal behavior of helpers in initial helping interactions. *Journal of Counseling Psychology, 21,* 360–363.

Davidson, L. G. (1950). Some current folk gestures and sign languages. *American Speech, 25,* 3–9.

Davies, D. (1990, June). Traveller's tales. *Far Eastern Economic Review, 148,* 32.

Davis, D. E. (1971). Physiological effects of continued crowding. In A. H. Esser (Ed.), *Behavior and environment* (pp. 133–147). New York: Plenum.

Davis, R. C. (1961). Physiological responses as a means of evaluating information. In A. D. Biderman & H. Zimmer (Eds.), *The manipulation of human behavior* (pp. 142–168). New York: Wiley.

Davitz, J. R. (1964). *The communication of emotional meaning.* New York: McGraw-Hill.

Davitz, J. R., & Davitz, L. J. (1959). The communication of feelings by content-free speech. *Journal of Communication, 9,* 6–13.

Dean, L. M., Willis, F. N., & Hewitt, J.

(1975). Initial interaction distance among individuals equal and unequal in military rank. *Journal of Personality and Social Psychology, 32,* 294–299.

Dean, L. M., Willis, F. N., & Rinck, C. M. (1978). *Patterns of interpersonal touch in the elderly.* Paper presented at the annual meeting of the Western Psychological Association, San Francisco.

DeBono, K. G. (1992). Pleasant scents and persuasion: An information processing approach. *Journal of Applied Psychology, 22,* 910–919.

Delia, J. G. (1972). Dialects and the effects of stereotypes on interpersonal attraction and cognitive processes in impression formation. *Quarterly Journal of Speech, 58,* 285–297.

Denham, S. A., & Grout, L. (1993). Socialization of emotion: Pathway to preschoolers' emotional and social competence. *Journal of Nonverbal Behavior, 17,* 205–227.

DePaulo, B. M. (1981). Success at detecting deception: Liability or skill? *Annals of the New York Academy of Sciences, 364,* 245–255.

DePaulo, B. M. (1991). Nonverbal behavior and self-presentation: A developmental perspective. In R. S. Feldman & B. Rimé (Ed.), *Fundamentals of nonverbal behavior* (pp. 351–397). Cambridge: Cambridge University Press.

DePaulo, B. M. (1992). Nonverbal behavior and self-presentation. *Psychological Bulletin, 111,* 203–243.

DePaulo, B. M., Jordan, A., Irvine, A., & Laser, P. S. (1982). Age changes in the detection of deception. *Child Development, 53,* 701–709.

DePaulo, B. M., Kenny, D. A., Hoover, C. W., Webb, W., & Oliver, P. V. (1987). Accuracy of person perception: Do people know what kinds of impressions they convey? *Journal of Personality and Social Psychology, 52,* 303–315.

DePaulo, B. M., & Kirkendol, S. E. (1989). The motivational impairment effect in the communication of deception. In J. Yuille (Ed.), *Credibility assessment* (pp. 51–70). Deurne, Belgium: Kluwer.

DePaulo, B. M., Kirkendol, S. E., Tang, J., & O'Brien, T. P. (1988). The motivation impairment effect in the communication of deception: Replications and extensions. *Journal of Nonverbal Behavior, 12,* 177–202.

DePaulo, B. M., Lanier, K., & Davis, T.

(1983). Detecting the deceit of the motivated liar. *Journal of Personality and Social Psychology, 45,* 1096–1103.

DePaulo, B. M., Lassiter, G. D., & Stone, J. I. (1982). Attentional determinants of success at detecting deception and truth. *Personality and Social Psychology Bulletin, 8,* 273–279.

DePaulo, B. M., LeMay, C. S., & Epstein, J. A. (1991). Effects of importance of success and expectations for success on effectiveness at deceiving. *Personality and Social Psychology Bulletin, 17,* 14–24.

DePaulo, B. M., & Pfeifer, R. (1986). On-the-job experience and skill at detecting deception. *Journal of Applied Social Psychology, 16,* 249–267.

DePaulo, B. M., & Rosenthal, R. (1979a). Ambivalence, discrepancy, and deception in nonverbal communication. In R. Rosenthal (Ed.), *Skill in nonverbal communication: Individual differences* (pp. 204–248). Cambridge, MA: Oelgeschlager, Gunn & Hain.

DePaulo, B. M., & Rosenthal, R. (1979b). Telling lies. *Journal of Personality and Social Psychology, 37,* 1713–1722.

DePaulo, B. M., Rosenthal, R., Eisenstat, R. A., Rogers, P. L., & Finkelstein, S. (1978). Decoding discrepant nonverbal cues. *Journal of Personality and Social Psychology, 36,* 313–323.

DePaulo, B. M., Rosenthal, R., Finkelstein, S., & Eisenstat, R. A. (1979). The developmental priority of the evaluative dimension in perceptions of nonverbal cues. *Environmental Psychology and Nonverbal Behavior, 3,* 164–171.

DePaulo, B. M., Rosenthal, R., Green, C. R., & Rosenkrantz, J. (1982). Diagnosing deceptive and mixed messages from verbal and nonverbal cues. *Journal of Experimental Social Psychology, 18,* 433–446.

DePaulo, B. M., Stone, J. I., & Lassiter, G. D. (1985a). Deceiving and detecting deceit. In B. R. Schlenker (Ed.), *The self and social life* (pp. 323–370). New York: McGraw-Hill.

DePaulo, B. M., Stone, J. I., & Lassiter, G. D. (1985b). Telling ingratiating lies: Effects of target sex and target attractiveness on verbal and nonverbal deceptive success. *Journal of Personality and Social Psychology, 48,* 1191–1203.

DePaulo, B. M., Zuckerman, M., & Rosenthal, R. (1980a). Detecting deception: Modality effects. In L. Wheeler (Ed.),

Review of personality and social psychology (Vol. 1, pp. 125–162). Beverly Hills, CA: Sage.

DePaulo, B. M., Zuckerman, M., & Rosenthal, R. (1980b). The deceptions of everyday life. *Journal of Communication, 30,* 216–218.

Deprez, K., & Persoons, K. (1984). On the identity of Flemish high school students in Brussels. *Journal of Language and Social Psychology, 3,* 273–296.

Derlega, V. J., & Chaikin, A. L. (1977). Privacy and self-disclosure in social relationships. *Journal of Social Issues, 33,* 102–122.

Derlega, V. J., Metts, S., Petronio, S., & Margulis, S. T. (1993). *Self-disclosure.* Newbury Park, CA: Sage.

Desor, J. A. (1972). Toward a psychological theory of crowding. *Journal of Personality and Social Psychology, 21,* 79–83.

Despert, J. L. (1941). Emotional aspects of speech and language development. *International Journal of Psychiatry and Neurology, 105,* 193–222.

deTurck, M. A., Harszlak, J. J., Bodhorn, D. J., & Texter, L. A. (1990). The effects of training social perceivers to detect deception from behavioral cues. *Communication Quarterly, 38,* 189–199.

deTurck, M. A., & Miller, G. R. (1985). Deception and arousal: Isolating the behavioral correlates of deception. *Human Communication Research, 12,* 181–202.

deTurck, M. A., & Miller, G. R. (1990). Training observers to detect deception effects of self-monitoring and rehearsal. *Human Communication Research, 16,* 603–620.

Deutsch, M. (1973). *The resolution of conflict: Constructive and destructive processes.* New Haven, CT: Yale University Press.

Deutsch, M., & Collins, M. (1951). *Interracial housing: A psychological evaluation of a social experiment.* Minneapolis: University of Minnesota Press.

DeVito, J. A. (1989). *The interpersonal communication book* (5th ed.). New York: Harper & Row.

Dew, A., & Ward, C. (1993). The effects of ethnicity and culturally congruent and incongruent nonverbal behaviors on interpersonal attraction. *Journal of Applied Psychology, 23,* 1376–1389.

Dew, D., & Jensen, P. J. (1977). *Phonetic processing: The dynamics of speech.* Columbus, OH: Merrill.

di Battista, P. (1995, May). *Preparation, familiarity, control, and deceivers' responses to challenges of their truthfulness.* Paper presented at the annual meeting of the International Communication Association, Albuquerque.

Diehl, C. F., White, R. C., & Satz, P. H. (1961). Pitch change and comprehension. *Speech Monographs, 28,* 65–68.

Dietch, J., & House, J. (1975). Affiliative conflict and individual differences in self-disclosure. *Representative Research in Social Psychology, 6,* 69–75.

Dillard, J. L. (1972). *Black English.* New York: Random House.

Dillman, L. (1994). *Untangling the web of interconnectedness.* Unpublished doctoral dissertation, University of Arizona.

DiMatteo, M. R., Prince, L. M., & Hays, R. (1986). Nonverbal communication in the medical context: The physician-patient relationship. In P. D. Blanck, R. Buck, & R. Rosenthal (Eds.), *Nonverbal communication in the clinical context* (pp. 74–98). University Park: Pennsylvania State University Press.

Dindia, K. (1987). The effects of sex of subject and sex of partner on interruptions. *Human Communication Research, 13,* 345–371.

Dion, K. K. (1972). Physical attractiveness and evaluations of children's transgressions. *Journal of Personality and Social Psychology, 24,* 207–213.

Dion, K. K., Berschied, E., & Walster, E. (1972). What is beautiful is good. *Journal of Personality and Social Psychology, 24,* 285–290.

Dion, K. K., Pak, A. W., & Dion, K. L. (1990). Stereotyping physical attractiveness. *Journal of Cross-Cultural Psychology, 21,* 158–179.

Dion, K. K., & Stein, S. (1978). Physical attractiveness and interpersonal influence. *Journal of Experimental and Social Psychology, 14,* 97–108.

Dittmann, A. T. (1972a). The body movement-speech rhythm relationship as a cue to speech encoding. In A. W. Siegman & B. Pope (Eds.), *Studies in dyadic communication* (pp. 135–151). New York: Pergamon.

Dittmann, A. T. (1972b). *Interpersonal messages of emotion.* New York: Springer.

Dittmann, A. T. (1978). The role of body movement in communication. In A. W. Siegman & S. Feldstein (Eds.), *Nonverbal behavior and communication* (pp. 69–95). Hillsdale, NJ: Erlbaum.

Dittmann, A. T., & Llewellyn, L. G. (1967). The phonemic clause as a unit of speech decoding. *Journal of Personality and Social Psychology, 6,* 341–349.

Dolin, D., & Booth-Butterfield, M. (1993). Reach out and touch someone: Analysis of nonverbal comforting responses. *Communication Quarterly, 41,* 383–393.

Doob, L. W. (1971). *Patterning of time.* New Haven, CT: Yale University Press.

Dosey, M. A., & Meisels, M. (1969). Personal space and self-protection. *Journal of Personality and Social Psychology, 11,* 93–97.

Douty, H. I. (1963). Influence of clothing on perception of persons. *Journal of Home Economics, 55,* 197–202.

Dovidio, J. F., Brown, C. E., Heltman, K., Ellyson, S. L., & Keating, C. F. (1988). Power displays between women and men in discussions of gender-linked tasks: A multichannel study. *Journal of Personality and Social Psychology, 55,* 580–587.

Dovidio, J. F., & Ellyson, S. L. (1982). Decoding visual dominance behavior: Attributions of power based on the relative percentages of looking while speaking and looking while listening. *Social Psychology Quarterly, 45,* 106–113.

Dovidio, J. F., & Ellyson, S. L. (1985). Patterns of visual dominance behavior in humans. In S. L. Ellyson & J. F. Dovidio (Eds.), *Power, dominance, and nonverbal behavior* (pp. 129–150). New York: Springer-Verlag.

Drummond, K. (1989). A backward glance at interruptions. *Western Journal of Speech Communication, 53,* 150–166.

Dubos, R. (1965). *Man adapting.* New Haven, CT: Yale University Press.

Duck, S. (1994). Strategems, spoils, and a serpent's tooth: On the delights and dilemmas of personal relationships. In W. R. Cupach & B. H. Spiteberg (Eds.), *The dark side of interpersonal communication* (pp. 3–24). Hillsdale, NJ: Erlbaum.

Duker, S. (1974). *Time compressed speech: An anthology and bibliography* (Vol. 3). Metuchen, NJ: Scarecrow.

Duncan, S. D., Jr. (1972). Some signals and rules for taking speaking turns in conversations. *Journal of Personality and Social Psychology, 23,* 283–292.

Duncan, S. D., Jr. (1974). On the structure of speaker-auditor interaction during speaking turns. *Language in Society, 2,* 161–180.

Duncan, S. D., Jr. (1975). Interaction units during speaking turns in dyadic, face-to-face conversations. In A. Kendon, R. Harris, & M. R. Key (Eds.), *The organization of behavior in face-to-face interaction* (pp. 199–213). The Hague: Mouton.

Duncan, S. D., Jr., & Fiske, D. W. (1977). *Face-to-face interaction: Research, methods, and theory.* Hillsdale, NJ: Erlbaum.

Duncan, S. D., Jr., & Fiske, D. W. (1985). *Interaction structure and strategy.* Cambridge: Cambridge University Press.

Duncan, S. D., Jr., Rosenberg, M. J., & Finkelstein, J. (1969). The paralanguage of experimenter bias. *Sociometry, 32,* 207–219.

Duncan, S. D., Jr., & Rosenthal, R. (1968). Vocal emphasis in experimenters' instruction reading as unintended determinant of subjects' responses. *Language and Speech, 11,* 20–26.

Eagly, A. (1987). *Sex differences in social behavior: A social role interpretation.* Hillsdale, NJ: Erlbaum.

Eakins, B. W., & Eakins, R. G. (1978). *Sex differences in human communication.* Boston: Houghton Mifflin.

Edelmann, R. J., & Hampson, S. E. (1981a). Embarrassment in dyadic interaction. *Social Behavior and Personality, 9,* 171–177.

Edelmann, R. J., & Hampson, S. E. (1981b). The recognition of embarrassment. *Personality and Social Psychology Bulletin, 7,* 109–116.

Edinger, J. A., & Patterson, M. L. (1983). Nonverbal involvement and social control. *Psychological Bulletin, 93,* 30–56.

Edney, J. J. (1972). Property, possession and permanence: A field study in human territoriality. *Journal of Applied Social Psychology, 3,* 275–282.

Edney, J. J. (1976). Human territories: Comment on functional properties. *Environment and Behavior, 8,* 31–47.

Edney, J. J., & Buda, M. A. (1976). Distinguishing territoriality and privacy: Two studies. *Human Ecology, 4,* 283–296.

Edney, J. J., & Jordan-Edney, N. L. (1974). Territorial spacing on a beach. *Sociometry, 37,* 92–103.

Educational Facilities Laboratories (1965). *Profiles of significant schools: Schools without walls.* New York: Author.

Edwards, D. J. A. (1981). The role of touch in interpersonal relations: Implications for psychotherapy. *South African Journal of Psychology, 11,* 29–37.

Edwards, D. J. A. (1984). The experience of interpersonal touch during a personal growth program: A factor analytic approach. *Human Relations, 37,* 769–780.

Efran, J. S. (1968). Looking for approval: Effects on visual behavior of approbation from persons differing in importance. *Journal of Personality and Social Psychology, 10,* 21–25.

Efran, M. G. (1974). The effect of physical appearance on the judgment of guilt, interpersonal attraction and severity of recommended punishment in a simulated jury task. *Journal of Experimental Research in Personality, 8,* 45–54.

Efron, D. (1972). *Gesture, race and culture.* The Hague: Mouton.

Eibl-Eibesfeldt, I. (1971). *Love and hate: The natural history of behavioral patterns* (G. Strachan, Trans.). New York: Holt, Rinehart and Winston.

Eibl-Eibesfeldt, I. (1972, 1979). Similarities and differences between cultures in expressive movements. In R. A. Hinde (Ed.), *Nonverbal communication* (pp. 297–314). Cambridge: Cambridge University Press. Reprinted in S. Weitz (Ed.), *Nonverbal communication* (2d ed., pp. 37–48). New York: Oxford University Press.

Eibl-Eibesfeldt, I. (1973). The expressive behavior of the deaf-and-blind born. In M. von Cranach & I. Vine (Eds.), *Social communication and movement* (pp. 163–194). New York: Academic.

Eibl-Eibesfeldt, I. (1975). *Ethology: The biology of behavior.* New York: Holt, Rinehart and Winston.

Eisenberg, A. M., & Smith, R. R., Jr. (1971). *Nonverbal communication.* Indianapolis: Bobbs-Merrill.

Eisendorfer, C., & Wilkie, F. (1972). Auditory changes. *Journal of the American Geriatrics Society, 20,* 377–382.

Ekman, P. (1971). Universal and cultural differences in facial expressions of emotion. In J. K. Cole (Ed.), *Nebraska symposium on motivation* (pp. 207–

283). Lincoln: University of Nebraska Press.

Ekman, P. (1973). Cross-cultural studies of facial expression. In P. Ekman (Ed.), *Darwin and facial expression: A century of research in review* (pp. 169–222). New York: Academic.

Ekman, P. (1975, September). The universal smile: Face muscles talk every language. *Psychology Today, 9,* pp. 35–39.

Ekman, P. (1976). Movements with precise meanings. *Journal of Communication, 26,* 14–26.

Ekman, P. (1978). Facial expression. In A. W. Siegman & S. Feldstein (Eds.), *Nonverbal behavior and communication* (pp. 97–116). Hillsdale, NJ: Erlbaum.

Ekman, P. (1980). Asymmetry in facial expression. *Science, 209,* 833–834.

Ekman, P. (1985). *Telling lies.* New York: Norton.

Ekman, P., & Friesen, W. V. (1967). Head and body cues in the judgment of emotion: A reformulation. *Perceptual and Motor Skills, 24,* 711–724.

Ekman, P., & Friesen, W. V. (1969a). Nonverbal leakage and clues to deception. *Psychiatry, 32,* 88–106.

Ekman, P., & Friesen, W. V. (1969b). The repertoire of nonverbal behavior: Categories, origins, usage, and coding. *Semiotica, 1,* 49–98.

Ekman, P., & Friesen, W. V. (1972). Hand movements. *Journal of Communication, 22,* 353–374.

Ekman, P., & Friesen, W. V. (1974). Detecting deception from the body or face. *Journal of Personality and Social Psychology, 29,* 288–298.

Ekman, P., & Friesen, W. V. (1975). *Unmasking the face.* Englewood Cliffs, NJ: Prentice-Hall.

Ekman, P., & Friesen, W. V. (1976). Measuring facial movement. *Environmental Psychology and Nonverbal Behavior, 1,* 56–75.

Ekman, P., & Friesen, W. V. (1978). *Investigator's guide to the Facial Action Coding System, part II.* Palo Alto, CA: Consulting Psychologists Press.

Ekman, P., & Friesen, W. V. (1982). Felt, false and miserable smiles. *Journal of Nonverbal Behavior, 6,* 238–252.

Ekman, P., Friesen, W. V., & Ancoli, S. (1980). Facial signs of emotional experience. *Journal of Personality and Social Psychology, 39,* 1125–1134.

Ekman, P., Friesen, W. V., & Ellsworth, P. (1972). *Emotion in the human face.* New York: Pergamon.

Ekman, P., Friesen, W. V., O'Sullivan, M., & Scherer, K. R. (1980). Relative importance of face, body and speech in judgments of personality and affect. *Journal of Personality and Social Psychology, 38,* 270–277.

Ekman, P., Friesen, W. V., & Scherer, K. R. (1976). Body movement and voice pitch in deceptive interaction. *Semiotica, 16,* 23–27.

Ekman, P., Friesen, W. V., & Tomkins, S. S. (1971). Facial affect scoring technique: A first validity study. *Journal of Communication, 3,* 37–58.

Ekman, P., Hager, J. C., & Friesen, W. V. (1981). The symmetry of emotional and deliberate facial actions. *Psychophysiology, 18,* 101–106.

Ekman, P., Levinson, R. W., & Friesen, W. V. (1983). Autonomic nervous system activity distinguishes among emotions. *Science, 221,* 1208–1210.

Ekman, P., & Oster, H. (1979). Facial expression of emotion. *Annual Review of Psychology, 30,* 527–554.

Ekman, P., & O'Sullivan, M. (1991). Who can catch a liar? *American Psychologist, 46,* 913–920.

Ekman, P., O'Sullivan, M., & Frank, M. (1994, October). *Detecting deception from demeanor.* Paper presented at the annual meeting of the Society for Experimental Social Psychology, Incline Village, CA.

Ekman, P., Roper, G., & Hager, J. C. (1980). Deliberate facial movement. *Child Development, 1,* 886–891.

Ekman, P., Sorenson, E. R., & Friesen, W. V. (1969). Pan-cultural elements in facial displays of emotion. *Science, 164,* 86–88.

Elashoff, J. D., & Snow, R. E. (1971). *Pygmalian reconsidered: A case study in statistical inference: Reconsideration of the Rosenthal & Jacobsen data on teacher expectancy.* Worthington, OH: Jones.

Elliot, G. C. (1979). Some effects of deception and level of self-monitoring on planning and reacting to a self-presentation. *Journal of Personality and Social Psychology, 37,* 1282–1292.

Ellis, D. G. (1982). Language and speech communication. In M. Burgoon (Ed.), *Communication yearbook 6* (pp. 34–62). Beverly Hills, CA: Sage.

Ellis, D. G. (1992). Syntactic and pragmatic codes in communication. *Communication Theory, 2,* 1–23.

Ellis, D. S. (1967). Speech and social status in America. *Social Forces, 45,* 431–451.

Ellsworth, P. C., & Carlsmith, J. M. (1973). Eye contact and gaze aversion in an aggressive encounter. *Journal of Personality and Social Psychology, 28,* 280–292.

Ellsworth, P. C., Carlsmith, J. M., & Henson, A. (1972). The stare as a stimulus to flight in human subjects: A series of field experiments. *Journal of Personality and Social Psychology, 21,* 302–311.

Ellsworth, P. C., & Langer, E. J. (1976). Staring and approach: An interpretation of the stare as a nonspecific activator. *Journal of Personality and Social Psychology, 33,* 117–122.

Ellsworth, P. C., & Ludwig, L. M. (1972). Visual behavior in social interactions. *Journal of Communication, 22,* 375–403.

Ellsworth, P. C., & Ross, L. (1975). Intimacy in response to direct gaze. *Journal of Experimental Social Psychology, 11,* 592–613.

Ellyson, S. L., & Dovidio, J. F. (1985). Power, dominance, and nonverbal behavior: Basic concepts and issues. In S. L. Ellyson & J. F. Dovidio (Eds.), *Power, dominance, and nonverbal behavior* (pp. 1–27). New York: Springer-Verlag.

Ellyson, S. L., Dovidio, J. F., & Corson, R. L. (1981). Visual behavior differences in females as a function of self-perceived expertise. *Journal of Nonverbal Behavior, 5,* 164–171.

Ellyson, S. L., Dovidio, J. F., Corson, R. L., & Vinicur, D. L. (1980). Visual behavior in female dyads: Situational and personality factors. *Social Psychology Quarterly, 43,* 328–336.

Elman, D., Schulte, D. C., & Bukoff, A. (1977). Effects of facial expression and stare duration on walking speed: Two field experiments. *Environmental Psychology and Nonverbal Behavior, 2,* 93–99.

Elzinga, R. H. (1975). Nonverbal communication: Body accessibility among the Japanese. *Psychologia, 18,* 205–211.

Emde, R. N. (1984). Levels of meaning for infant emotions: A biosocial view. In K. R. Scherer & P. Ekman (Eds.), *Approaches to emotion* (pp. 77–107). Hillsdale, NJ: Erlbaum.

Engebretson, D., & Fullman, D. (1972). Cross-cultural differences in territoriality: Interaction distances of Native Japanese, Hawaii Japanese, and American Caucasians. In L. A. Samovar & R. E. Porter (Eds.), *Intercultural communication: A reader* (pp. 220–226). Belmont, CA: Wadsworth.

English, H. B. (1926). Reaction-time symptoms of deception. *American Psychologist, 37,* 428–429.

Epstein, A., & Ulrich, J. H. (1966). The effect of high- and low-pass filtering on the judged vocal quality of male and female speakers. *Quarterly Journal of Speech, 52,* 267–272.

Epstein, C. F. (1986). Symbolic segregation: Similarities and differences in the language and non-verbal communication of women and men. *Sociological Forum, 1,* 27–49.

Epstein, Y. M., & Karlin, R. A. (1975). Effects of acute experimental crowding. *Journal of Applied Social Psychology, 5,* 34–53.

Epstein, Y. M., Woolfolk, R. L., & Lehrer, P. M. (1981). Physiological, cognitive, and nonverbal responses to repeated exposure to crowding. *Journal of Applied Social Psychology, 11,* 1–13.

Erickson, B., Lind, E. A., Johnson, B. C., & O'Barr, W. M. (1978). Speech style and impression formation in a court setting: The effects of "powerful" and "powerless" speech. *Journal of Experimental Social Psychology, 14,* 266–279.

Erickson, F. (1975). One function of proxemic shifts in face-to-face interaction. In A. Kendon, R. Harris, & M. Key (Eds.), *Organization of behavior in face-to-face interaction* (pp. 175–187). The Hague: Mouton.

Erickson, F. (1979). Talking down: Some cultural sources of miscommunication in interracial interviews. In A. Wolfgang (Ed.), *Nonverbal behavior: Applications and cultural implications* (pp. 99–126). New York: Academic.

Erickson, F., & Shultz, J. (1982). *The counselor as gatekeeper: Social interaction in interviews.* New York: Academic.

Eschenbrenner, A. J., Jr. (1971). Effects of intermittent noise on the performance of a complex psychomotor task. *Human Factors, 13,* 59–63.

Esser, A. H. (1971). Social pollution. *Social Education, 35*(1), 10–18.

Esser, A. H. (1972). A biosocial perspective on crowding. In J. F. Wohlwill & D. H. Carson (Eds.), *Environment and the social sciences: Perspectives and applications* (pp. 15–28). Washington, DC: American Psychological Association.

Evans, G. W., & Eichelman, W. (1976). Preliminary models of conceptual linkages among proxemic variables. *Environment and Behavior, 9,* 87–116.

Evans, G. W., & Howard, R. B. (1973). Personal space. *Psychological Bulletin, 80,* 334–344.

Evans, G. W., & Lovell, B. (1979). Design modification in an open-plan school. *Journal of Educational Psychology, 71,* 41–49.

Exline, R. V. (1963). Explorations in the process of person perception: Visual interaction in relation to competition, sex, and the need for affiliation. *Journal of Personality, 31,* 1–20.

Exline, R. V. (1972). Visual interaction: The glances of power and preference. In J. D. Cole (Ed.), *Nebraska symposium on motivation* (Vol. 19, pp. 163–206). Lincoln: University of Nebraska Press.

Exline, R. V. (1985). Multichannel transmission of nonverbal behavior and the perception of powerful men: The presidential debates of 1976. In S. L. Ellyson, & J. F. Dovidio (Eds.), *Power, dominance, and nonverbal behavior* (pp. 183–206). New York: Springer-Verlag.

Exline, R. V., Ellyson, S. L., & Long, B. (1975). Visual behavior as an aspect of power role relationships. In P. Pliner, L. Krames, & T. Alloway (Eds.), *Nonverbal communication of aggression* (pp. 21–52). New York: Plenum.

Exline, R. V., & Fehr, B. J. (1978). Applications of semiosis to the study of visual interaction. In A. W. Siegman & S. Feldstein (Eds.), *Nonverbal behavior and communication* (pp. 117–158). Hillsdale, NJ: Erlbaum.

Exline, R. V., Gray, D., & Schuette, D. (1965). Visual behavior in a dyad as affected by interview content and sex of respondent. *Journal of Personality and Social Psychology, 1,* 201–209.

Exline, R. V., Thibaut, J., Hickey, C., & Gumpert, P. (1970). Visual interaction in relation to Machiavellianism and an unethical act. In P. Christie & F. Geis (Eds.), *Studies in Machiavellianism* (pp. 53–75). New York: Academic.

Exline, R. V., & Winters, L. C. (1965). Affective relations and mutual glances in dyads. In S. S. Tomkins & C. E. Izard (Eds.), *Affect, cognition, and personality* (pp. 319–350). New York: Springer-Verlag.

Fairbanks, G., Guttman, N., & Miron, M. (1957). Effects of time compression upon the comprehension of connected speech. *Journal of Speech and Hearing Disorders, 22,* 10–19.

Fay, P. J., & Middleton, W. G. (1940). Judgment of intelligence from the voice as transmitted over a public address system. *Sociometry, 3,* 186–191.

Feinman, J. A., & Feldman, R. S. (1982). Decoding children's expressions of affect. *Child Development, 53,* 710–716.

Feldman, R. E. (1968). Response to compatriots and foreigners who seek assistance. *Journal of Personality and Social Psychology, 10,* 202–214.

Feldman, R. S. (1976). Nonverbal disclosure of teacher deception and interpersonal affect. *Journal of Educational Psychology, 68,* 807–816.

Feldman, R. S., Devin-Sheehan, L., & Allen, V. L. (1978). Nonverbal cues as indicators of verbal dissembling. *American Educational Research Journal, 15,* 217–231.

Feldman, R. S., Jenkins, L., & Popoola, O. (1979). Detection of deception in adults and children via facial expressions. *Child Development, 50,* 350–355.

Feldman, R. S., & White, J. B. (1980). Detecting deception in children. *Journal of Communication, 30,* 121–139.

Feldstein, S., & Welkowitz, J. (1978). A chronography of conversation: In defense of an objective approach. In A. W. Siegman & S. Feldstein (Eds.), *Nonverbal behavior and communication* (pp. 329–378). Hillsdale, NJ: Erlbaum.

Felipe, N. J., & Sommer, R. (1966). Invasions of personal space. *Social Problems, 14,* 206–214.

Fernández-Dols, J. M., Wallbott, H., & Sanchez, F. (1991). Emotion category accessibility and the decoding of emotion from facial expression and context. *Journal of Nonverbal Behavior, 15,* 107–123.

Ferris, S. H., Crook, T., Clark, E.,

McCarthy, M., & Rae, D. (1980). Facial recognition memory deficits in normal aging and senile dementia. *Journal of Gerontology, 35,* 707–714.

Festinger, L. (1951). Architecture and group membership. *Journal of Social Issues, 7,* 152–163.

Festinger, L., Schachter, S., & Back, K. (1950). *Social pressures in informal groups: A study of human factors in housing.* New York: Harper & Row.

Feyereisen, P. (1987). Gestures and speech, interactions and separations: A reply to McNeill (1985). *Psychological Review, 94,* 493–498.

Feyereisen, P. (1991). Brain pathology, lateralization, and nonverbal behavior. In R. S. Feldman & B. Rimé (Eds.), *Fundamentals of nonverbal communication* (pp. 31–70). Cambridge: Cambridge University Press.

Fichten, C. S., Tagalakis, V., Judd, D., Wright, J., & Amsel, R. (1992). Verbal and nonverbal communication cues in daily conversations and dating. *Journal of Social Psychology, 132,* 751–769.

Fiedler, K. (1989). Suggestion and credibility: Lie detection based on content-related cues. In V. Gheorghiu, P. Netter, H. J. Eysenck, & R. Rosenthal (Eds.), *Suggestibility, theory, and research* (pp. 323–335). New York: Springer.

Fiedler, K., & Walka, I. (1993). Training lie detectors to use nonverbal cues instead of global heuristics. *Human Communication Research, 20,* 199–223.

Firestone, I. J. (1977). Reconciling verbal and nonverbal models of dyadic communication. *Environmental Psychology and Nonverbal Behavior, 2,* 30–43.

Fisher, B. A. (1978). *Perspectives on human communication.* New York: Macmillan.

Fisher, B. A. (1980). *Small group decision making* (2d ed.). New York: McGraw-Hill.

Fisher, J. D., Bell, P. A., & Baum, A. (1984). *Environmental psychology* (2d ed.). New York: Holt, Rinehart and Winston.

Fisher, J. D., & Byrne, D. (1975). Too close for comfort: Sex differences in response to invasions of personal space. *Journal of Personality and Social Psychology, 32,* 15–21.

Fisher, J. D., Rytting, M., & Heslin, R. (1976). Hands touching hands: Affective and evaluative effects of an inter-

personal touch. *Sociometry, 39,* 416–421.

Fitzpatrick, M. A., Mulac, A., & Dindia, K. (1994, July). *Convergence and reciprocity in male and female communication patterns in spouse and stranger interaction.* Paper presented at the Fifth International Conference on Language and Social Psychology, Brisbane, Australia.

Folger, J. P., & Woodall, W. G. (1982). Nonverbal cues as linguistic context: An information processing view. In M. Burgoon (Ed.), *Communication Yearbook 6* (pp. 63–91). Beverly Hills, CA: Sage.

Forbes, R. J., & Jackson, P. R. (1980). Non-verbal behaviour and the outcome of selection interviews. *Journal of Occupational Psychology, 53,* 65–72.

Forgas, J. P. (1976). The perception of social episodes: Categorical and dimensional representations in two different social milieus. *Journal of Personality and Social Psychology, 33,* 199–209.

Forgas, J. P. (1978). The effects of behavioural and cultural expectation cues on the perception of social episodes. *European Journal of Social Psychology, 8,* 203–213.

Forgas, J. P. (1979). *Social episodes: The study of interaction routines.* London: Academic.

Forston, R. F., & Larson, C. U. (1968). The dynamics of space: An experimental study in proxemic behavior among Latin Americans and North Americans. *Journal of Communication, 18,* 109–116.

Forsyth, D. R. (1987). *Social psychology.* Monterey, CA: Brooks/Cole.

Forsyth, G. A., Kushner, R. I., & Forsyth, P. D. (1981). Human facial expression judgment in a conversational context. *Journal of Nonverbal Behavior, 6,* 115–130.

Fortenberry, J. H., Maclean, J., Morris, P., & O'Connell, M. (1978). Mode of dress as a perceptual cue to deference. *Journal of Social Psychology, 104,* pp. 139–140.

Foulke, E., & Sticht, T. G. (1969). Review of research on the intelligibility and comprehension of accelerated speech. *Psychological Bulletin, 72,* 50–62.

Fraenkel, D. L. (1983). The relationship of empathy in movement to synchrony, echoing, and empathy in verbal interactions. *American Journal of Dance Therapy, 6,* 31–48.

Fraiberg, S. (1971). Intervention in infancy: A program for blind infants. *Journal of the American Academy of Child Psychiatry, 10,* 381–405.

Frank, L. K. (1957). Tactile communication. *Genetic Psychology Monographs, 56,* 204–255.

Frank, L. K. (1971). Tactile communication. In H. A. Bosmajian (Ed.), *The rhetoric of nonverbal communication* (pp. 34–56). Glenview, IL: Scott, Foresman.

Frank, L. K. (1972). Cultural patterning of tactile experiences. In L. A. Samovar & R. E. Porter (Eds.), *Intercultural communication: A reader* (pp. 200–204). Belmont, CA: Wadsworth.

Freedman, D. G. (1969, October). The survival value of the beard. *Psychology Today, 3,* pp. 36–39.

Freedman, J. L. (1975). *Crowding and behavior.* San Francisco: Freeman.

Freedman, J. L., Levy, A. S., Buchanan, R. W., & Price, J. (1972). Crowding and human aggressiveness. *Journal of Experimental Social Psychology, 8,* 528–548.

Freedman, N. (1972). The analysis of movement behavior during the clinical interview. In A. Siegman & B. Pope (Eds.), *Studies in dyadic communication* (pp. 153–175). New York: Pergamon.

Freedman, N., & Steingart, I. (1975). Kinesic internalization and language construction. *Psychoanalysis & Contemporary Science, 4,* 355–403.

French, J. R. P., Jr., & Raven, B. (1959). The bases of social power. In D. Cartwright (Ed.), *Studies in social power* (pp. 150–167). Ann Arbor, MI: Institute for Social Research.

French, P., & von Raffler Engel, W. (1973). The kinesics of bilingualism. Unpublished manuscript, Vanderbilt University. Cited in M. LaFrance & C. Mayo (1978), *Moving bodies.* Monterey, CA: Brooks/Cole.

Fretz, B. R., Corn, R., Tuemmler, J. M., & Bellet, W. (1979). Counselor nonverbal behaviors and client evaluations. *Journal of Counseling Psychology, 26,* 304–311.

Frick, R. W. (1985). Communicating emotion: The role of prosadic features. *Psychological Bulletin, 97,* 412–429.

Frick, R. W. (1986). The prosadic expression of anger: Differentiating threat and frustration. *Aggressive Behavior, 12,* 121–128.

Fridlund, A. J. (1991). Evolution and facial action in reflex, social motive, and paralanguage. *Biological Psychology, 32,* 3–100.

Fridlund, A. J. (1994). *Human facial expression: An evolutionary view.* San Diego: Academic.

Fridlund, A. J., Kenworthy, K. G., & Jaffey, A. K. (1992). Audience effects in affective imagery: Replication and extension to dysphoric imagery. *Journal of Nonverbal Behavior, 16,* 191–212.

Fridlund, A. J., Sabini, J. P., Hedlund, L. E., Schaut, J. A., Shenker, J. I., & Knauer, M. J. (1990). Social determinants of facial expressions during affective imagery: Displaying to the people in your head. *Journal of Nonverbal Behavior, 14,* 113–137.

Friedman, H. S. (1978). The relative strength of verbal versus nonverbal cues. *Personality and Social Psychology Bulletin, 4,* 147–150.

Friedman, H. S. (1979a). The concept of skill in nonverbal communication: Implications for understanding social interaction. In R. Rosenthal (Ed.), *Skill in nonverbal communication: Individual differences* (pp. 2–27). Cambridge, MA: Oelgeschlager, Gunn & Hain.

Friedman, H. S. (1979b). The interactive effects of facial expressions of emotion and verbal messages on perceptions of affective meaning. *Journal of Experimental Social Psychology, 15,* 453–469.

Friedman, H. S. (1979c). Nonverbal communication between patients and medical practitioners. *Journal of Social Issues, 35,* 82–99.

Friedman, H. S., & Miller-Herringer, T. (1991). Nonverbal display of emotion in public and in private: Self-monitoring, personality, and expressive cues. *Journal of Personality and Social Psychology, 61,* 766–775.

Friedman, H. S., Prince, L., Riggio, R. E., & DiMatteo, M. R. (1980). Understanding and assessing nonverbal expressiveness: The Affective Communication Test. *Journal of Personality and Social Psychology, 39,* 333–351.

Friedman, H. S., Riggio, R. E., & Casella, D. F. (1988). Nonverbal skill, personal charisma, and initial attraction. *Personality and Social Psychology Bulletin, 14,* 203–211.

Friesen, W. V. (1972). *Cultural differences in facial expressions in a social situation: An experimental test of the concept of display rules.* Unpublished doctoral dissertation, University of California, San Francisco.

Friesen, W. V., Ekman, P., & Wallbott, H. (1979). Measuring hand movements. *Journal of Nonverbal Behavior, 4,* 97–112.

Frieze, I., & Ramsey, S. (1976). Nonverbal maintenance of traditional sex roles. *Journal of Social Issues, 32,* 133–141.

Fromme, D. K., & Beam, D. C. (1974). Dominance and sex differences in nonverbal responses to differential eye contact. *Journal of Research in Personality, 8,* 76–87.

Fromme, D. K., Jaynes, W. E., Taylor, D. K., Hanold, E. G., Daniell, J., Rountree, R., & Fromme, M. L. (1989). Nonverbal behaviors and attitudes toward touch. *Journal of Nonverbal Behavior, 13,* 3–14.

Frymier, A. B. (1993). The impact of teacher immediacy on students' motivation: Is it the same for all students? *Communication Quarterly, 41,* 454–464.

Fugita, S. S. (1974). Effects of anxiety and approval on visual interaction. *Journal of Personality and Social Psychology, 29,* 586–592.

Fugita, S. S., Wexley, K. N., & Hillery, J. M. (1974). Black-white differences in nonverbal behavior in an interview setting. *Journal of Applied Social Psychology, 4,* 343–350.

Fujimoto, E. K. (1971). *The comparative power of verbal and nonverbal symbols.* Unpublished doctoral dissertation, Ohio State University.

Fujita, B. N., Harper, R. G., & Wiens, A. N. (1980). Encoding-decoding of nonverbal emotional messages: Sex differences in spontaneous and enacted expressions. *Journal of Nonverbal Behavior, 4,* 131–145.

Fulcher, J. S. (1942). "Voluntary" facial expression in blind and seeing children. *Archives of Psychology, 38,* No. 272.

Furbay, A. L. (1965). The influence of scattered versus compact seating on audience response. *Speech Monographs, 32,* 144–148.

Furnham, A., & Argyle, M. (1981). *The psychology of social situations: Selected readings.* New York: Pergamon.

Furno-Lamude, D. (1991). Dimensions of psychological time and favorite TV personalities. *Social Behavior and Personality, 19,* 277–288.

Gales, A., Spratt, G., Chapman, A. J., & Smallbone, A. (1975). EEG correlates of eye contact and interpersonal distance. *Biological Psychology, 3,* 237–245.

Galgan, R. J., Mable, H. M., Ouellette, T. M., & Balance, W. D. G. (1989). Body image distortion and weight preoccupation in college women. *College Student Journal, 23,* 13–15.

Gallaher, P. E. (1992). Individual differences in nonverbal behavior: Dimensions of style. *Journal of Personality and Social Psychology, 63,* 133–145.

Gallois, C., & Markel, N. M. (1975). Turn taking: Social personality and conversational style. *Journal of Personality and Social Psychology, 31,* 1134–1140.

Garcia, S., Stinson, L., Ickes, W., & Bissonnette, V. (1991). Shyness and physical attractiveness in mixed-sex dyads. *Journal of Personality and Social Psychology, 61,* 35–49.

Garfinkel, H. (1964). Studies of the routine grounds of everyday activities. *Social Problems, 11,* 225–250.

Garner, P. H. (1972). *The effects of invasion of personal space on interpersonal communication.* Unpublished manuscript, Illinois State University, Normal.

Garratt, G. A., Baxter, J. C., & Rozelle, R. M. (1981). Training university police in black-American nonverbal behaviors: An application to police-community relations. *Journal of Social Psychology, 113,* 217–229.

Gatewood, J. B., & Rosenwein, R. (1981). Interactional synchrony: Genuine or spurious? A critique of recent research. *Journal of Nonverbal Behavior, 6,* 12–29.

Geen, R. G. (1980). The effects of being observed on performance. In P. B. Paulus (Ed.), *Psychology of group influence* (pp. 62–97). Hillsdale, NJ: Erlbaum.

Geis, F. L., & Moon, T. H. (1981). Machiavellianism and deception. *Journal of Personality and Social Psychology, 41,* 766–775.

Geiselman, R. E., & Bellezza, F. S. (1976). Long-term memory for speaker's voice and source location. *Memory and Cognition, 4,* 483–489.

Geiselman, R. E., & Bellezza, F. S. (1977). Incidental retention of speaker's voice. *Memory and Cognition, 5,* 658–665.

Geiselman, R. E., & Crawley, J. M. (1983). Incidental processing of speaker characteristics: Voice as connotative information. *Journal of Verbal Learning and Verbal Behavior, 22,* 15–23.

Geldhard, F. A. (1960). Some neglected possibilities of communication. *Science, 131,* 1583–1587.

Geller, D. M., Goodstein, L., Silver, M., & Sternberg, W. C. (1974). On being ignored: The effects of the violation of implicit rules of social interaction. *Sociometry, 37,* 541–556.

Geller, D. M., & Malia, G. P. (1981). The effects of noise on helping behavior reconsidered. *Basic and Applied Social Psychology, 2,* 11–25.

Gewirtz, J. L., & Boyd, E. F. (1976). Mother-infant interaction and its study. In H. W. Reese (Ed.), *Advances in child development and behavior* (Vol. 11, pp. 141–163). New York: Academic.

Gibbons, K., & Gwynn, T. K. (1975). A new theory of fashion change: A test of some predictions. *British Journal of Social and Clinical Psychology, 14,* 1–9.

Giesen, J. M. (1973). *Effects of eye contact, attitude agreement, and presentation mode on impressions and persuasion.* Unpublished doctoral dissertation, Kent State University, Kent, OH.

Giesen, M., & McClaren, H. A. (1976). Discussion, distance and sex: Changes in impressions and attraction during small group interaction. *Sociometry, 39,* 60–70.

Gifford, R. (1982). Projected interpersonal distance and orientation choices: Personality, sex, and social situation. *Social Psychology Quarterly, 45,* 145–152.

Gifford, R. (1991). Mapping nonverbal behavior on the interpersonal circle. *Journal of Personality and Social Psychology, 61,* 279–288.

Gifford, R., Ng, C. F., & Wilkinson, M. (1985). Nonverbal cues in the employment interview: Links between applicant qualities and interviewer judgments. *Journal of Applied Psychology, 70,* 729–736.

Gilbert, B. O. (1991). Physiological and nonverbal correlates of extraversion, neuroticism, and psychoticism during active and passive coping. *Personality and Individual Differences, 12,* 1325–1331.

Gilbert, D. T. (1989). Thinking lightly about others: Automatic components of the social inference process. In J. S. Uleman & J. A. Bargh (Eds.), *Unintended thought* (pp. 189–211). New York: Guilford.

Gilbert, D. T., & Osborne, R. E. (1989). Thinking backward: Some curable and incurable consequences of cognitive busyness. *Journal of Personality and Social Psychology, 57,* 940–949.

Gilbert, D. T., Pelham, B. W., & Krull, D. S. (1988). On cognitive busyness: When person perceivers meet persons perceived. *Journal of Personality and Social Psychology, 54,* 733–740.

Gilbert, G. S., Kirkland, K. D., & Rappoport, L. (1977). Nonverbal assessment of interpersonal affect. *Journal of Personality Assessment, 41,* 43–48.

Giles, H. (1973a). Accent mobility: A model and some data. *Anthropological Linguistics, 15,* 87–105.

Giles, H. (1973b). Communicative effectiveness as a function of accented speech. *Speech Monographs, 40,* 330–331.

Giles, H. (1977). Social psychology and applied linguistics: Towards an integrative approach. *ILT: Review of Applied Linguistics, 33,* 27–40.

Giles, H. (1979). Ethnicity markers in speech. In K. R. Scherer & H. Giles (Eds.), *Social markers in speech* (pp. 251–290). Cambridge: Cambridge University Press.

Giles, H. (1980). Accommodation theory: Some new directions. In S. de Silva (Ed.), *Aspects of linguistic behavior* (pp. 105–136). York: University of York Press.

Giles, H., Bourhis, R. Y., & Taylor, D. M. (1977). Towards a theory of language in ethnic group relations. In H. Giles (Ed.), *Language, ethnicity, and intergroup relations* (pp. 307–348). London: Academic.

Giles, H., Brown, B. L., & Thakerar, J. N. (1981). *The effects of speech rate, accent, and context on the attribution of a speaker's personality characteristics.* Unpublished manuscript, University of Bristol.

Giles, H., Coupland, N., & Coupland, J.

(1991). Accommodation theory: Communication, context, and consequence. In H. Giles, J. Coupland, & N. Coupland (Eds.), *Contexts of accommodation: Developments in applied sociolinguistics* (pp. 1–68). Cambridge: Cambridge University Press.

Giles, H., Henwood, K., Coupland, N., Harriman, J., & Coupland, J. (1992). Language attitudes and cognitive mediation. *Human Communication Research, 18,* 500–527.

Giles, H., & Powesland, P. F. (1975). *Speech style and social evaluation.* London: Academic.

Giles, H., & Smith, P. M. (1979). Accommodation theory: Optimal levels of convergence. In H. Giles & R. St. Clair (Eds.), *Language and social psychology* (pp. 45–65). Baltimore: University Park Press.

Giles, H., & Street, R. L., Jr. (1985). Communicator characteristics and behavior. In M. L. Knapp & G. R. Miller (Eds.), *Handbook of interpersonal communication* (pp. 205–261). Beverly Hills, CA: Sage.

Gillespie, D. L. (1978). *The effects of status differentiation on selected nonverbal behaviors at settled distances.* Unpublished doctoral dissertation, University of California, Berkeley.

Gillespie, D. L., & Leffler, A. (1983). Theories of nonverbal behavior: A critical review of proxemics research. In R. Collins (Ed.), *Sociological theory* (pp. 120–153). San Francisco: Jossey-Bass.

Ginsburg, H. J., Pollman, V. A., Wauson, M. S., & Hope, M. L. (1977). Variation of aggressive interaction among male elementary school children as a function of changes in spatial density. *Environmental Psychology and Nonverbal Behavior, 2,* 67–75.

Gitter, A. G., Black, H., & Fishman, J. E. (1975). Effect of race, sex, nonverbal communication and verbal communication on perception of leadership. *Sociology and Social Research, 60,* 46–57.

Givens, D. B. (1978). The nonverbal basis of attraction: Flirtation, courtship, and seduction. *Psychiatry, 41,* 346–359.

Givens, D. B. (1983). *Love signals.* New York: Crown.

Glasgow, G. M. (1952). A semantic index of vocal pitch. *Speech Monographs, 19,* 64–68.

Glass, D. C., & Singer, J. E. (1972). Behavioral after effects of unpredictable and uncontrollable aversive events. *American Scientist, 80,* 457–465.

Glass, D. C., Singer, J. E., & Friedman, L. N. (1969). Psychic cost of adaptation to an environmental stressor. *Journal of Personality and Social Psychology, 12,* 200–210.

Glick, P., DeMorest, J. A., & Hotze, C. A. (1988). Keeping your distance: Group membership, personal space, and requests for small favors. *Journal of Applied Social Psychology, 18,* 315–330.

Goffman, E. (1959). *The presentation of self in everyday life.* Garden City, NY: Anchor/Doubleday.

Goffman, E. (1961a). *Asylums: Essays on the social situation of mental patients and other inmates.* Garden City, NY: Anchor/Doubleday.

Goffman, E. (1961b). *Encounters: Two studies in the sociology of interaction.* Indianapolis: Bobbs-Merrill.

Goffman, E. (1963). *Behavior in public places.* New York: Free Press.

Goffman, E. (1967). *Interaction ritual: Essays on face-to-face behavior.* Garden City, NY: Anchor/Doubleday.

Goffman, E. (1969). *Strategic interaction.* Philadelphia: University of Pennsylvania Press.

Goffman, E. (1971). *Relations in public: Microstudies of the public order.* New York: Basic.

Goffman, E. (1974). *Frame analysis.* New York: Harper & Row.

Goffman, E. (1976). *Gender advertisements.* New York: Harper & Row.

Goldberg, G. N., Kiesler, C. A., & Collins, B. E. (1969). Visual behavior and face-to-face distance during interaction. *Sociometry, 32,* 43–53.

Goldberg, K. Y., & Bajcsy, R. (1984). Active touch and robot perception. *Cognition and Brain Theory, 7,* 199–214.

Goldberg, M. L. (1980). *Effects of shifts in listeners' looking behavior upon speakers' verbal and nonverbal immediacy behavior: A test of affiliative conflict and intimacy-arousal models.* Unpublished doctoral dissertation, University of Miami.

Goldberg, S., & Lewis, M. (1969). Play behavior in the year-old infant: Early sex differences. *Child Development, 40,* 21–31.

Goldberg, S., & Rosenthal, R. (1986). Self-touching behavior in the job interview: Antecedents and consequences. *Journal of Nonverbal Behavior, 10,* 65–80.

Goldhaber, G. M. (1983). *Organizational communication* (3d ed.). Dubuque, IA: Brown.

Goldman, M., & Fordyce, J. (1983). Prosocial behavior as affected by eye contact, touch, and voice expression. *Journal of Social Psychology, 121,* 125–129.

Goldman, M., Kiyohara, O., & Pfannensteil, D. A. (1985). Interpersonal touch, social labeling, and the foot-in-the-door effect. *Journal of Social Psychology, 125,* 143–147.

Goldman-Eisler, F. (1961a). A comparative study of two hesitation phenomena. *Language and Speech, 4,* 18–26.

Goldman-Eisler, F. (1961b). Hesitation and information in speech. In C. Cherry (Ed.), *Information theory.* London: Butterworths.

Goldman-Eisler, F. (1968). *Psycholinguistics: Experiments in spontaneous speech.* New York: Academic.

Goldstein, E. R. (1923). Reaction times and the consciousness of deception. *American Journal of Psychology, 34,* 562–581.

Goleman, D. (1986, April 8). Studies point to power of nonverbal signals. *New York Times,* pp. C1, C6.

Goleman, D. (1991, May 7). Kids who got hugs found to be happy adults. (Tucson) *Arizona Daily Star,* pp. 1C, 3C.

Gonzales, A., & Zimbardo, P. G. (1985, March). Time in perspective. *Psychology Today,* pp. 21–26.

Gonzales, G. E. (1982). *Nonverbal behavior and person perception in dyads of varied sex and ethnicity.* Unpublished doctoral dissertation, University of California, Santa Cruz.

Goodenough, F. L. (1932). Expression of the emotions in a blind-deaf child. *Journal of Abnormal and Social Psychology, 27,* 328–333.

Goodwin, S. W., & Acredolo, L. P. (1993). Symbolic gesture versus word: Is there a modality advantage for onset of symbol use? *Child Development, 64,* 688–701.

Gorer, G. (1968). Ardrey on human nature: Animals, nations, imperatives. In M. F. A. Montagu (Ed.), *Man and aggression* (pp. 74–82). London: Oxford University Press.

Gorham, J. (1988). The relationship between verbal teacher immediacy behaviors and student learning. *Communication Education, 37,* 40–53.

Gottlieb, A. (1980). Touching and being touched. *Mademoiselle, 88,* 80–81, 167, 174.

Gottman, J. M. (1979). *Marital interaction: Experimental investigations.* New York: Academic.

Gottman, J. M., & Levenson, R. W. (1992). Marital processes predictive of later dissolution: Behavior, physiology, and health. *Journal of Personality and Social Psychology, 63,* 221–233.

Gottman, J. M., Markman, H., & Notarius, C. (1977). The topography of marital conflict: A sequential analysis of verbal and nonverbal behavior. *Journal of Marriage and the Family, 39,* 461–477.

Gouldner, A. W. (1960). The norm of reciprocity: A preliminary statement. *American Sociological Review, 25,* 161–178.

Graham, J. A., & Heywood, S. (1975). The effects of elimination of hand gestures and of verbal codability on speech performance. *European Journal of Social Psychology, 5,* 189–195.

Greenbaum, P. E., & Rosenfeld, H. M. (1980). Varieties of touching in greetings: Sequential structure and sex-related differences. *Journal of Nonverbal Behavior, 5,* 13–25.

Greenberg, C. I. (1976). *Intimacy overload, intrusion, and behavior restriction: An interpersonal distance-equilibrium approach to the stressful experience of crowding.* Unpublished doctoral dissertation, Wayne State University, Detroit.

Greenberg, C. I., & Firestone, I. J. (1977). Compensatory responses to crowding: Effects of personal space intrusion and privacy reduction. *Journal of Personality and Social Psychology, 35,* 637–644.

Greenberg, E. (1979). *The effects of dominance on sex differences in nonverbal behavior in mixed-sex dyads.* Unpublished doctoral dissertation, New School for Social Research, New York.

Greene, L. R. (1977). Effects of verbal evaluative feedback and interpersonal distance on behavioral compliance. *Journal of Counseling Psychology, 24,* 10–14.

Griffitt, W. (1970). Environmental effects on interpersonal affective behavior: Ambient effective temperature and attraction. *Journal of Personality and Social Psychology, 15,* 240–244.

Griffitt, W., & Veitch, R. (1971). Hot and crowded: Influence of population density and temperature on interpersonal affective behavior. *Journal of Personality and Social Psychology, 17,* 92–98.

Guardo, C. J. (1969). Personal space in children. *Child Development, 40,* 143–151.

Guardo, C. J., & Meisels, M. (1971). Factor structure of children's personal space schemata. *Child Development, 42,* 1307–1312.

Gudykunst, W. B., & Kim, Y. Y. (1992). *Communicating with strangers: An approach to intercultural communication* (2d ed.). New York: McGraw-Hill.

Gudykunst, W. B., & Ting-Toomey, S. (1988). *Culture and interpersonal communication.* Newbury Park, CA: Sage.

Guerin, D. V. (1967). Implications of the communication process for school plant design. *Audiovisual Instruction, 12,* 815–817.

Guerrero, L. K. (1994, November). *Nonverbal immediacy and involvement in friendships and romantic relationships: Untangling the effects of communicator sex, target sex, and relationship type.* Paper presented at the annual meeting of the Speech Communication Association, New Orleans.

Guerrero, L. K., & Andersen, P. A. (1991). The waxing and waning of relational intimacy: Touch as a function of relational stage, gender and touch avoidance. *Journal of Social and Personal Relationships, 8,* 147–166.

Gump, P. V., & Good, L. R. (1976). Environments operating in open space and traditionally designed schools. *Journal of Architectural Research, 5,* 20–26.

Gunderson, D. F., & Hopper, R. (1976). Relationship between speech delivery and speech effectiveness. *Communication Monographs, 43,* 158–165.

Gurel, L. M., Wilbur, J. C., & Gurel, L. (1972). Personality correlates of adolescent clothing styles. *Journal of Home Economics, 64,* 42–47.

Gurevitch, Z. D. (1989). Distance and conversation. *Symbolic Interaction, 12,* 251–263.

Gutsell, L. M., & Andersen, J. F. (1980, April). *Perceptual and behavioral responses to smiling.* Paper presented at the annual meeting of the International Communication Association, Acapulco, Mexico.

Haase, R. F. (1970). The relationship of sex and instructional set to the regulation of interpersonal interaction distance in a counseling analogue. *Journal of Counseling Psychology, 17,* 233–236.

Haase, R. F., & Dimattia, D. (1976). Spatial environments and verbal conditioning in a quasi-counseling interview. *Journal of Counseling Psychology, 23,* 414–421.

Haase, R. F., & Tepper, D. T., Jr. (1972). Nonverbal components of empathetic communication. *Journal of Counseling Psychology, 19,* 417–424.

Hackney, H. (1974). Facial gestures and subject expression of feelings. *Journal of Counseling Psychology, 21,* 173–178.

Hadar, U. (1989). Two types of gesture and their role in speech production. *Journal of Language and Social Psychology, 8,* 221–228.

Hai, D. M., Khairullah, Z. Y., & Coulmas, N. (1982). Sex and the single armrest: Use of personal space during air travel. *Psychological Reports, 51,* 743–749.

Halberstadt, A. (1991). Toward an ecology of expressiveness: Family expressiveness in particular and a model in general. In R. S. Feldman & B. Rimé (Eds.), *Fundamentals of nonverbal communication* (pp. 106–160). Cambridge: Cambridge University Press.

Halberstadt, A. G., Grotjohn, D. K., Johnson, C. A., Furth, M. S., & Greig, M. M. (1992). Children's abilities and strategies in managing the facial display of affect. *Journal of Nonverbal Behavior, 16,* 215–230.

Halberstadt, A. G., Hayes, C. W., & Pike, K. M. (1988). Gender and gender role differences in smiling and communication consistency. *Sex Roles, 19,* 589–604.

Halberstadt, A. G., & Saitta, M. B. (1987). Gender, nonverbal behavior, and perceived dominance: A test of the theory. *Journal of Personality and Social Psychology, 53,* 257–272.

Halberstam, D. (1979). *The powers that be.* New York: Dell.

Halberstam, D. (1986). *The reckoning.* New York: Morrow.

Hale, J. L., & Burgoon, J. K. (1984). Models of reactions to changes in nonverbal immediacy. *Journal of Nonverbal Behavior, 8,* 287–314.

Hall, E. T. (1959, 1973). *The silent language.* Garden City, NY: Anchor/Doubleday.

Hall, E. T. (1963). A system for the notation of proxemic behavior. *American Anthropologist, 65,* 1003–1026.

Hall, E. T. (1966). *The hidden dimension* (2d ed.). Garden City, NY: Anchor/Doubleday.

Hall, E. T. (1974). *Handbook for proxemic research.* Washington, DC: Society for the Anthropology of Visual Communication.

Hall, E. T. (1976). *Beyond culture.* New York: Doubleday.

Hall, E. T. (1981). *Beyond culture.* Garden City, NY: Anchor/Doubleday.

Hall, E. T., & Whyte, W. F. (1966). Intercultural communication: A guide to men of action. In A. G. Smith (Ed.), *Communication and culture* (pp. 567–575). New York: Holt, Rinehart and Winston.

Hall, J. A. (1979). Gender, gender roles, and nonverbal communication skills. In R. Rosenthal (Ed.), *Skill in nonverbal communication: Individual differences* (pp. 32–67). Cambridge, MA: Oelgeschlager, Gunn & Hain.

Hall, J. A. (1980). Voice tone and persuasion. *Journal of Personality and Social Psychology, 38,* 924–934.

Hall, J. A. (1984). *Nonverbal sex differences: Communication accuracy and expressive style.* Baltimore: Johns Hopkins University Press.

Hall, J. A., & Halberstadt, A. G. (1986). Smiling and gazing. In J. S. Hyde & M. Linn (Eds.), *The psychology of gender: Advances through meta-analysis* (pp. 136–158). Baltimore: Johns Hopkins University Press.

Hall, J. A., Roter, D. L., & Rand, C. S (1981). Communication of affect between patient and physician. *Journal of Health and Social Behavior, 22,* 18–30.

Hall, J. A., & Vecchia, A. M. (1992). More "touching" observations: New insights on men, women, and interpersonal touch. *Journal of Personality and Social Psychology, 59,* 1155–1162.

Hamilton, M. L. (1973). Imitative behavior and expressive ability in facial expression of emotion. *Developmental Psychology, 8,* 138.

Hamner, K. C. (1981). Experimental evidence for the biological clock. In J. T. Fraser (Ed.). *The voices of time* (2d ed., pp. 281–295). Amherst: University of Massachusetts Press.

Hannan, T. E. (1992). An examination of spontaneous pointing in 20- to 50-month-old children. *Perceptual and Motor Skills, 74,* 651–658.

Hare, A., & Bales, R. F. (1963). Seating position and small group interaction. *Sociometry, 26,* 480–486.

Harlow, H. F. (1958). The nature of love. *American Psychologist, 13,* 673–685.

Harlow, H. F. (1959). Love in monkeys. *Scientific American, 200,* 68–74.

Harlow, H. F., & Harlow, M. K. (1962). The effect of rearing conditions on behavior. *Bulletin of the Meninger Clinic, 26,* 213–224.

Harlow, H. F., Harlow, M. K., & Hansen, E. W. (1963). The maternal affectional system of rhesus monkeys. In H. L. Rheingold (Ed.), *Maternal behaviors in mammals* (pp. 254–281). New York: Wiley.

Harlow, H. F., & Zimmerman, R. R. (1958). The development of affectional responses in infant monkeys. *Proceedings, American Philosophical Society, 102,* 501–509.

Harms, L. S. (1961). Listener judgments of status cues in speech. *Quarterly Journal of Speech, 47,* 164–168.

Harper, L., & Sanders, K. M. (1975). Preschool children's use of space: Sex differences in outdoor play. *Developmental Psychology, 11,* 119.

Harper, R. G. (1985). Power, dominance, and nonverbal behavior: An overview. In S. L. Ellyson & J. F. Dovidio (Eds.), *Power, dominance, and nonverbal behavior* (pp. 29–48). New York: Springer-Verlag.

Harper, R. G., Wiens, A. N., & Matarazzo, J. D. (1978). *Nonverbal communication: The state of the art.* New York: Wiley.

Harper, R. G., Wiens, A. N., & Matarazzo, J. D. (1979). The relationship between encoding and decoding of visual nonverbal emotional cues. *Semiotica, 28,* 171–192.

Harre, H., & Secord, P. F. (1972). *The explanation of social behavior.* Oxford: Blackwells.

Harrigan, J. A. (1985). Self-touching as an indicator of underlying affect and language processes. *Social Science and Medicine, 20,* 1161–1168.

Harrigan, J. A., Kues, J. R., Steffen, J. J., & Rosenthal, R. (1987). Self-touching and impressions of others. *Personality and Social Psychology Bulletin, 13,* 497–512.

Harrigan, J. A., Kues, J. R., & Weber, J. G. (1986). Impressions of hand movements: Self-touching and gestures. *Perceptual and Motor Skills, 63,* 503–516.

Harrigan, J. A., Oxman, T. E., & Rosenthal, R. (1985). Rapport expressed through nonverbal behavior. *Journal of Nonverbal Behavior, 9,* 95–110.

Harrigan, J. A., & Rosenthal, R. (1983). Physicians' head and body positions as determinants of perceived rapport. *Journal of Applied Social Psychology, 13,* 496–509.

Harrigan, J. A., & Rosenthal, R. (1986). Nonverbal aspects of empathy and rapport in physician-patient interaction. In P. D. Blanck, R. Buck, & R. Rosenthal (Eds.), *Nonverbal communication in the clinical context* (pp. 36–73). University Park: Pennsylvania State University Press.

Harrigan, J. A., Weber, J. G., & Kues, J. R. (1986). Attributions of self-touching performed in spontaneous and posed modes. *Journal of Social and Clinical Psychology, 4,* 433–446.

Harris, L. M., Gergen, K. J., & Lannamann, J. W. (1986). Aggression rituals. *Communication Monographs, 53,* 252–265.

Harris, M. B., James, J., Chavez, J., Fuller, M. L., Kent, S., Massanari, C., Moore, C., & Walsh, F. (1983). Clothing: Communication, compliance, and choice. *Journal of Applied Social Psychology, 13,* 88–97.

Harris, M. B., Ramsey, S., Sims, D., & Stevenson, M. (1974). Effects of uniforms on perceptions of pictures of athletes. *Perceptual and Motor Skills, 39,* 59–62.

Harris, M. J. (1989). Personality moderators of interpersonal expectancy effects: Replication of Harris and Rosenthal (1986). *Journal of Research in Personality, 23,* 381–397.

Harris, M. J. & Rosenthal, R. (1985). Mediation of interpersonal expectancy effects: 31 meta-analyses. *Psychological Bulletin, 97,* 363–386.

Harris, M. J., & Rosenthal, R. (1986). Counselor and client personality as determinants of counselor expectancy effects. *Journal of Personality and Social Psychology, 50,* 362–369.

Harris, R. M., & Rubenstein, D. (1975). Paralanguage, communication, and cognition. In A. Kendon, R. M. Harris, & M. R. Key (Eds.), *Organization of behavior in face-to-face interaction* (pp. 251–276). Chicago: Aldine.

Harrison, R. P. (1974). *Beyond words: An introduction to nonverbal communication.* Englewood Cliffs, NJ: Prentice-Hall.

Hartley, L. R., & Adams, R. G. (1974). Effect of noise on the Stroop test. *Journal of Experimental Psychology, 102,* 62–66.

Hartnett, J. J., Bailey, K. G., & Gibson, F. W., Jr. (1970). Personal space as influenced by sex and type of movement. *Journal of Psychology, 76,* 139–144.

Hastie, R., & Carlston, D. E. (1980). Theoretical issues in person memory. In R. Hastie, T. R. Ostrom, E. B. Ebbesen, R. S. Wyer, D. L. Hamilton, & D. E. Carlston (Eds.), *Person memory: The cognitive basis of social perception* (pp. 1–53). Hillsdale, NJ: Erlbaum.

Hastie, R., Ostrom, T. R., Ebbesen, E. B., Wyer, R. S., Hamilton, D. L., & Carlston, D. E. (1980). *Person memory: The cognitive basis of social perception.* Hillsdale, NJ: Erlbaum.

Hatfield, E., Cacioppo, J. T., & Rapson, R. (1994). *Emotional contagion.* Cambridge: Cambridge University Press.

Hatfield, E. E., & Sprecher, S. (1986). *Mirror, mirror . . . the importance of looks in everyday life.* Albany: State University of New York Press.

Haviland, J. M. (1977). Sex-related pragmatics in infants' nonverbal communication. *Journal of Communication, 27* (2), 80–84.

Haviland, S. E., & Clark, H. H. (1974). What's new? Acquiring new information as a process in comprehension. *Journal of Verbal Learning and Verbal Behavior, 13,* 512–521.

Hawad-Claudot, H. (1993). The veiled face and expressiveness among the Tuaregs. In F. Poyatos (Ed.), *Advances in non-verbal communication: Sociocultural, clinical, esthetic, and literary perspectives* (pp. 197–211). Amsterdam: Johns Benjamins.

Hayduk, L. A. (1978). Personal space: An evaluative and orienting overview. *Psychological Bulletin, 85,* 117–134.

Hayes, D., & Ross, C. E. (1987). Concern with appearance, health beliefs, and eating habits. *Journal of Health and Social Behavior, 28,* 120–130.

Hayes, D. P., & Meltzer, L. (1972). Interpersonal judgments based on talkative-

ness: I. Fact or artifact. *Sociometry, 35,* 538–561.

Hearn, G. (1957). Leadership and the spatial factor in small groups. *Journal of Abnormal and Social Psychology, 54,* 269–272.

Hecht, M. A., LaFrance, M., & Haertl, J. C. (1993, August). *Gender differences in smiling: A meta-analysis of archival data.* Paper presented at the 101st annual meeting of the American Psychological Association, Toronto.

Heckel, R. V. (1973). Leadership and voluntary seating choice. *Psychological Reports, 32,* 141–142.

Hediger, H. P. (1950). *Wild animals in captivity.* London: Butterworths.

Hediger, H. P. (1961). The evolution of territorial behavior. In S. L. Washburn (Ed.), *Social life of early man* (pp. 34–57). Chicago: Aldine.

Hegstrom, T. G. (1979). Message impact: What percentage is nonverbal? *Western Journal of Speech Communication, 43,* 134–142.

Heinberg, P. (1964). *Voice training for speaking and reading aloud.* New York: Ronald.

Heller, J. G., Groff, B. D., & Solomon, S. H. (1977). Toward an understanding of crowding: The role of physical attraction. *Journal of Personality and Social Psychology, 35,* 183–190.

Helson, H. (1964). *Adaptation-level theory.* New York: Harper & Row.

Hemsley, G. D. (1977). *Experimental studies in the behavioral indicants of deception.* Unpublished doctoral dissertation, University of Toronto.

Hemsley, G. D., & Doob, A. T. (1978). The effect of looking behavior on perceptions of a communicator's credibility. *Journal of Applied Social Psychology, 8,* 136–144.

Hendershot, J., & Hess, A. K. (1982). *Detecting deception: The effects of training and socialization levels on verbal and nonverbal cue utilization and detection accuracy.* Unpublished manuscript, Auburn University.

Henley, N., & Kramarae, C. (1991). Gender, power, and miscommunication. In N. Coupland, H. Giles, & J. M. Wiemann (Eds.), *"Miscommunication" and problematic talk* (pp. 18–43). Newbury Park, CA: Sage.

Henley, N. M. (1973). Status and sex: Some touching observations. *Bulletin of the Psychonomic Society, 2,* 91–93.

Henley, N. M. (1977). *Body politics:*

Power, sex, and nonverbal communication. Englewood Cliffs, NJ: Prentice-Hall.

Henley, N. M., & Freeman, J. (1975). The sexual politics of interpersonal behavior. In J. Freeman (Ed.), *Women: A feminist perspective* (pp. 391–401). Palo Alto, CA: Mayfield.

Henley, N. M., & Harmon, S. (1985). The nonverbal semantics of power and gender: A perceptual study. In S. L. Ellyson & J. F. Dovidio (Eds.), *Power, dominance, and nonverbal behavior* (pp. 151–164). New York: Springer-Verlag.

Henningsen, D. D. (1995, May). *A pattern violation model of nonverbal behavior and perceptions of deception.* Paper presented at the annual meeting of the International Communication Association, Albuquerque, NM.

Hensley, W. E. (1981). The effects of attire, location, and sex on aiding behavior: A similarity explanation. *Journal of Nonverbal Behavior, 6,* 3–11.

Heslin, R. (1974, May). *Steps toward a taxonomy of touching.* Paper presented at the annual convention of the Midwestern Psychological Association, Chicago.

Heslin, R. (1978). *Responses to touching as an index of sex-role norms and attitudes.* Paper presented at the American Psychological Association Symposium, Toronto.

Heslin, R., & Alper, T. (1983). Touch: A bonding gesture. In J. M. Wiemann & R. P. Harrison (Eds.), *Nonverbal interaction* (pp. 47–75). Beverly Hills, CA: Sage.

Heslin, R., & Boss, D. (1980). Nonverbal intimacy in airport arrival and departure. *Personality and Social Psychology Bulletin, 6,* 248–252.

Heslin, R., Nguyen, T. D., & Nguyen, M. L. (1983). Meaning of touch: The case of touch from a stranger or same sex person. *Journal of Nonverbal Behavior, 7,* 147–157.

Hess, E. H. (1975). The role of pupil size in communication. *Scientific American, 233,* 110–119.

Hess, E. H., & Polt, J. M. (1960). Pupil size as related to interest value of visual stimuli. *Science, 132,* 349–350.

Hess, U., Kappas, A., McHugo, G. J., Kleck, R. E., & Lanzetta, J. T. (1989). An analysis of the encoding and decoding of spontaneous and posed smiles:

The use of facial electromyography. *Journal of Nonverbal Behavior, 13,* 121–137.

Heston, J. K., & Garner, P. (1972, April). *A study of personal space and desk arrangement in the learning environment.* Paper presented at the annual meeting of the International Communication Association, Atlanta, GA.

Hewes, D. E., & Planalp, S. (1982). "There is nothing as useful as a good theory . . . ": The influence of social knowledge on interpersonal communication. In C. Berger & M. Roloff (Eds.), *Social cognition and communication* (pp. 107–150). Beverly Hills, CA: Sage.

Hewes, G. W. (1957). The anthropology of posture. *Scientific American, 196,* 123–132.

Hickson, M. L., III, & Stacks, D. W. (1985). *NVC: Nonverbal communication studies and applications.* Dubuque, IA: Brown.

Higginbotham, D. J., & Yoder, D. E. (1982). Communication within natural conversational interaction: Implications for severe communicatively impaired persons. *Topics in Language Disorders, 2,* 1–19.

Hill, S. D., & Smith, J. M. (1984). Neonatal responsiveness as a function of maternal contact and obstetrical drugs. *Perceptual and Motor Skills, 58,* 859–866.

Hillison, J. (1983). Communicating humanism nonverbally. *Journal of Humanistic Education and Development, 22,* 25–29.

Hilpert, F. P., Kramer, C., & Clark, R. A. (1975). Participants' perceptions of self and partner in mixed-sex dyads. *Central States Speech Journal, 26,* 52–56.

Hinchliffe, M. K., Hooper, D., Roberts, F. J., & Vaughan, P. W. (1975). A study of interaction between depressed patients and their spouses. *British Journal of Psychiatry, 126,* 164–172.

Ho, R., & Mitchell, S. (1982). Students' nonverbal reaction to tutors' warm/cold nonverbal behavior. *Journal of Social Psychology, 118,* 121–131.

Hockett, C. F. (1960). The origin of speech. *Scientific American, 203,* 86–96.

Hocking, J. E., Bauchner, J., Kaminski, E. P., & Miller, G. R. (1979). Detecting deceptive communication from verbal, visual, and paralinguistic cues. *Human Communication Research, 6,* 33–46.

Hocking, J. E., & Leathers, D. G. (1980). Nonverbal indicators of deception: A new theoretical perspective. *Communication Monographs, 47,* 119–131.

Hocking, J. E., Miller, G. R., & Fontes, N. E. (1978). Videotape in the courtroom. *Trial, 14,* 52–55.

Hoffman, S. A. (1988, February). The doctor as dramatist. *Newsweek,* p. 10.

Holahan, C. J. (1982). *Environmental psychology.* New York: Random House.

Hollandsworth, J. G., Jr., Kazelskis, R., Stevens, J., & Dressel, M. E. (1979). Relative contributions of verbal, articulative, and nonverbal communication to employment decisions in the job interview setting. *Personnel Psychology, 32,* 359–367.

Hollien, H., Dew, D., & Philips, P. (1971). Phonational frequency ranges of adults. *Journal of Speech and Hearing Research, 14,* 755–760.

Honeycutt, J. M. (1989). Effects of preinteraction expectancies on interaction involvement and behavioral responses in initial interaction. *Journal of Nonverbal Behavior, 13,* 25–36.

Honeycutt, J. M. (1991). The role of nonverbal behaviors in modifying expectancies during initial encounters. *Southern Communication Journal, 56,* 161–177.

Honkavaara, S. (1961). The psychology of expression: Dimensions in human perception. *British Journal of Psychology Monograph Supplements, 32,* 1–96.

Hooker, D. (1952). *The prenatal origin of behavior.* Lawrence: University of Kansas Press.

Hoots, M. A., McAndrew, F. T., & Francois, G. R. (1989). Decoding of gestures by kindergarten, first-, and third-grade children. *Journal of Genetic Psychology, 150,* 117–118.

Hooyman, N. R., & Kiyak, H. A. (1988). *Social gerontology.* Boston: Allyn & Bacon.

Hope, C. (1982). Caucasian female body hair and American culture. *Journal of American Culture, 5,* 93–99.

Hopper, R., & Bell, R. A. (1984). Broadening the deception construct. *Quarterly Journal of Speech, 70,* 288–302.

Horai, J., Naccari, N., & Fatoullah, E. (1974). The effects of expertise and physical attractiveness upon opinion agreement and liking. *Sociometry, 37,* 601–606.

Horatçsu, N., & Ekinci, B. (1992). Children's reliance on situational and vocal expression of emotions: Consistent and conflicting cues. *Journal of Nonverbal Behavior, 16,* 231–247.

Horn, P. (1973, June). Newsline. *Psychology Today, 7,* p. 92.

Horn, P. (1974, April). Newsline. *Psychology Today, 7,* p. 27.

Horn, P. (1975, January). Newsline. *Psychology Today, 8,* p. 28.

Horner, T. M. (1983). On the formation of personal space and self-boundary structures in early human development: The case of infant stranger reactivity. *Developmental Review, 3,* 148–177.

Hornik, J., & Ellis, S. (1988). Strategies to secure compliance for a mall intercept interview. *Public Opinion Quarterly, 52,* 539–551.

Hornstein, M. G. (1967). Accuracy of emotional communication and interpersonal compatibility. *Journal of Personality, 35,* 20–30.

Horowitz, M. J., Duff, D. F., & Stratton, L. O. (1964). Body-buffer zones. *Archives of General Psychiatry, 11,* 651–656.

Howells, L. T., & Becker, S. W. (1962). Seating arrangement and leadership emergence. *Journal of Abnormal and Social Psychology, 64,* 148–150.

Hudson, A., & Blane, M. (1985). The importance of nonverbal behavior in giving instructions to children. *Child and Family Behavior Therapy, 7*(2), 1–10.

Huon, G. F., Morris, S. E., & Brown, L. B. (1990). Differences between male and female preferences for female body size. *Australian Psychologist, 25,* 314–317.

Huston, T. L., & Vangelisti, A. L. (1991). Socioemotional behavior and satisfaction in marital relationships: A longitudinal study. *Journal of Personality and Social Psychology, 61,* 721–733.

Hutt, C., & Vaizey, M. J. (1967). Differential effects of group density on social behavior. *Nature, 209,* 1371–1372.

Huxley, A. (1954). *The doors of perception.* New York: Harper & Row.

Ickes, W. (1984). Compositions in black and white: Determinants of interaction in interracial dyads. *Journal of Personality and Social Psychology, 47,* 330–341.

Ickes, W., & Barnes, R. (1977). The role of sex and self-monitoring in unstructured dyadic interactions. *Journal of*

Personality and Social Psychology, 35, 315–330.

Ickes, W., Patterson, M. L., Rajecki, D. W., & Tanford, S. (1982). Behavioral and cognitive consequences of reciprocal versus compensatory responses to preinteraction expectancies. *Social Cognition, 1,* 160–190.

Ickes, W., Schermer, B., & Steeno, J. (1979). Sex and sex-role influences in same-sex dyads. *Social Psychology Quarterly, 42,* 373–385.

Iizuka, Y., Mishima, K., & Matsumoto, T. (1989). A study of the arousal model of interpersonal intimacy. *Japanese Psychological Research, 31,* 127–136.

Iliffe, A. H. (1960). A study of preferences in feminine beauty. *British Journal of Psychology, 51,* 267–273.

Imada, A. S., & Hakel, M. D. (1977). Influence of nonverbal communication and rater proximity on impressions and decisions in simulated employment interviews. *Journal of Applied Psychology, 62,* 295–300.

Insko, C. A. (1967). *Theories of attitude change.* Englewood Cliffs, NJ: Prentice-Hall.

Institute for Environmental Education. (1978). *User participation and requirements in planning Navajo school facilities in New Mexico* (Monograph #2). Albuquerque: University of New Mexico.

Isenberg, S. J., & Bass, B. A. (1974). Effects of verbal and nonverbal reinforcement on the WAIS performance of normal adults. *Journal of Consulting and Clinical Psychology, 42,* 467.

Ishii, S. (1973). Characteristics of Japanese nonverbal communicative behavior. *Communication, Journal of the Communication Association of the Pacific, 2,* 3.

Ittelson, W. H. (Ed.) (1973). *Environment and cognition.* New York: Seminar.

Ittelson, W. H., Proshansky, H. M., Rivlin, L. G., & Winkel, G. H. (1974). *An introduction to environmental psychology.* New York: Holt, Rinehart and Winston.

Izard, C. E. (1971). *The face of emotion.* Englewood Cliffs, NJ: Prentice-Hall.

Izard, C. E. (1972). *Patterns of emotion: A new analysis of anxiety and depression.* New York: Academic.

Izard, C. E. (1977). *Human emotions.* New York: Plenum.

Izard, C. E. (1978). Emotions as motivations: An evolutionary-developmental perspective. In R. A. Dienstbier (Ed.), *Nebraska symposium on motivation* (Vol. 25, pp. 163–200). Lincoln: University of Nebraska Press.

Izard, C. E. (1979). Facial expression, emotion and motivation. In A. Wolfgang (Ed.), *Nonverbal behavior: Applications and cultural implications* (pp. 31–49). New York: Academic.

Izard, C. E. (1981). Differential emotions theory and the facial feedback hypothesis of emotion activation: Comments on Tourangeau and Ellsworth's "The role of facial response in the experience of emotion." *Journal of Personality and Social Psychology, 40,* 350–354.

Jacobsen, N. S., Follette, W. C., & McDonald, D. W. (1982). Reactivity to positive and negative behavior in distressed and nondistressed marital couples. *Journal of Consulting and Clinical Psychology, 50,* 706–714.

Jacobson, M. B. (1981). Effects of victim's and defendant's physical attractiveness on subjects' judgments in a rape case. *Sex Roles, 7,* 247–255.

Jacunska-Iwinska, M. (1975). An experimental modification of the young child's level of activity. *Polish Psychological Bulletin, 6,* 27–35.

Jaffe, J., & Feldstein, S. (1970). *Rhythms of dialogue.* New York: Academic.

Jakobson, R. (1972). Motor signs for "yes" and "no." *Language in Society, 1,* 91–96.

James, P. B. (1969). *Children's interpretations of multi-channel communications conveying verbal and nonverbal meanings.* Unpublished doctoral dissertation, Ohio State University.

James, W. (1890). *The principles of psychology.* New York: Dover.

Janisse, M. P., & Peavler, W. S. (1974, February). Pupillary research today: Emotion in the eye. *Psychology Today, 7,* 60–73.

Janzen, S. A. (1984). *Empathic nurse's nonverbal communication.* Unpublished doctoral dissertation. University of Illinois, Chicago.

Jasper, C. R., & Klassen, M. L. (1990). Stereotypical beliefs about appearance: Implications for retailing and consumer issues. *Perceptual and Motor Skills, 71,* 519–528.

Jaworski, A. (1993). *The power of silence: Social and pragmatic perspectives.* Newbury Park, CA: Sage.

Jensen, J. V. (1985). Perspective on nonverbal intercultural communication. In L. A. Samovar & R. E. Porter (Eds.), *Intercultural communication: A reader* (3d ed., pp. 256–272). Belmont, CA: Wadsworth.

Jerison, H. J. (1959). Effects of noise on human performance. *Journal of Applied Psychology, 43,* 96–101.

Jersild, A. T., & Markey, F. V. (1935). Conflicts between preschool children. *Child Development Monographs, 21,* ix–181.

Johnson, D. W., McCarty, K., & Allen, T. (1976). Congruent and contradictory verbal and nonverbal communications of cooperativeness and competitiveness in negotiations. *Communication Research, 3,* 275–291.

Johnson, E. Y., & Lookingbill, D. P. (1984). Sunscreen use and exposure: Trends in the White population. *Archives of Dermatology, 120,* 727–731.

Johnson, H. G., Ekman, P., & Friesen, W. V. (1975). Communicative body movement: American emblems. *Semiotica, 15,* 335–353.

Johnson, J. D. (1987). Development of the communication and physical environment scale. *Central States Speech Journal, 38,* 35–43.

Johnson, K. L., & Edwards, R. (1991). The effects of gender and type of romantic touch on perceptions of relational commitment. *Journal of Nonverbal Behavior, 15,* 43–55.

Johnson, K. R. (1972). Black kinesics: Some non-verbal communication patterns in the black culture. In L. A. Samovar & R. E. Porter (Eds.), *Intercultural communication: A reader* (2d ed., pp. 181–189). Belmont, CA: Wadsworth.

Johnson, R. N. (1972). *Aggression in man and animals.* Philadelphia: Saunders.

Johnston, D. (1981, June). The pink jail. *Corrections Magazine,* 28–32.

Jones, E. E. (1964). *Ingratiation.* New York: Appleton-Century-Crofts.

Jones, E. E. (1979). The rocky road from acts to dispositions. *American Psychologist, 34,* 107–117.

Jones, E. E., & Harris, V. A. (1967). The attribution of attitudes. *Journal of Experimental Social Psychology, 3,* 1–24.

Jones, E. E., & Nisbett, R. E. (1972). The actor and the observer: Divergent perceptions of the causes of behavior. In

E. E. Jones, D. E. Kanouse, H. H. Kelley, R. E. Nisbett, S. Valins, & B. Weiner (Eds.), *Attribution: Perceiving the causes of behavior* (pp. 79–94). Morristown, NJ: General Learning.

Jones, E. E., & Pittman, T. S. (1982). Toward a general theory of strategic self-presentation. In J. Suls (Ed.), *Psychological perspectives on the self* (Vol. 1, pp. 231–262). Hillsdale, NJ: Erlbaum.

Jones, S. E. (1971). A comparative proxemics analysis of dyadic interaction in selected subcultures of New York City. *Journal of Social Psychology, 84,* 35–44.

Jones, S. E. (1984, November). *An exploratory study of sex differences in tactile communication.* Paper presented at the annual meeting of the Speech Communication Association, Chicago.

Jones, S. E. (1985). *A study of the validity of Jourard's tactile body-accessibility questionnaire.* Paper presented at the annual meeting of the Speech Communication Association, Denver.

Jones, S. E. (1986). Sex differences in touch communication. *Western Journal of Speech Communication, 50,* 227–241.

Jones, S. E. (1991). Problems of validity in questionnaire studies of nonverbal behavior: Jourard's tactile body-accessibility scale. *Southern Communication Journal, 56,* 83–95.

Jones, S. E., & Aiello, J. R. (1973). Proxemic behavior of black and white first-, third-, and fifth-grade children. *Journal of Personality and Social Psychology, 25,* 21–27.

Jones, S. E., & Yarbrough, A. E. (1985). A naturalistic study of the meanings of touch. *Communication Monographs, 52,* 19–56.

Jones, S. S., Collins, K., & Hong, H. (1991). An audience effect on smile production in 10-month-old infants. *Psychological Science, 2,* 45–49.

Jorgenson, D. O. (1975). Field study of the relationship between status discrepancy and proxemic behavior. *Journal of Social Psychology, 97,* 173–179.

Jourard, S. M. (1966a). An exploratory study of body accessibility. *British Journal of Social and Clinical Psychology, 5,* 221–231.

Jourard, S. M. (1966b). Some psychological aspects of privacy. *Law and Contemporary Problems, 31,* 307–318.

Jourard, S. M. (1971). *The transparent self.* New York: Van Nostrand Reinhold.

Jourard, S. M., & Friedman, R. (1970). Experimenter-subject "distance" and self-disclosure. *Journal of Personality and Social Psychology, 15,* 278–282.

Jourard, S. M., & Secord, P. F. (1955). Body-cathexis and personality. *British Journal of Psychology, 46,* 130–138.

Juhnke, R., Barmann, B., Vickery, K., Cunningham, M., Hohl, J., Smith, E., & Quinones, J. (1987). Effects of attractiveness and nature of request on helping behavior. *Journal of Social Psychology, 127,* 317–322.

Julien, D., Markman, H. J., & Lindahl, K. M. (1989). A comparison of a global and a microanalytic coding system: Implications for future trends in studying interactions. *Behavioral Assessment, 11,* 81–100.

Jurich, A. P., & Jurich, J. A. (1974). Correlations among nonverbal expressions of anxiety. *Psychological Reports, 34,* 199–204.

Kahlbaugh, P. E., & Haviland, J. M. (1994). Nonverbal communication between parents and adolescents: A study of approach and avoidance behaviors. *Journal of Nonverbal Behavior, 18,* 91–113.

Kalbfleisch, P. J. (1985). Accuracy in deception detection: A quantitative review (Doctoral dissertation, Michigan State University). *Dissertation Abstracts International, 45,* 46112B.

Kalbfleisch, P. J. (1992). Deceit, distrust, and the social milieu: Application of deception research in a troubled world. *Journal of Applied Communication Research, 20,* 308–334.

Kalymun, M. (1989). Relationships between sensory decline among the elderly and the physical environment: Implications for health care. *Rhode Island Medical Journal, 79,* 161–167.

Karmel, L. J. (1965). Effects of windowless classroom environment on high school students. *Perceptual and Motor Skills, 20,* 277–278.

Katz, A. M., & Katz, V. T. (1983). Introduction to nonverbal communication. In A. M. Katz & V. T. Katz (Eds.), *Foundations of nonverbal communication: Readings, exercises and commentary* (pp. xv–xvii). Carbondale: Southern Illinois Press.

Katz, D. (1937). *Animals and men.* White Plains, NY: Longman.

Katz, L. M. (1994, December 6). A touch of frost after Cold War thaw. *USA Today,* p. 10A.

Kauffman, L. E. (1971). Tacesics, the study of touch: A model for proxemic analysis. *Semiotica, 4,* 149–161.

Kazdin, A. E., & Klock, J. (1973). The effect of nonverbal teacher approval on student attentive behavior. *Journal of Applied Behavior Analysis, 6,* 643–654.

Kearney, P., Plax, T. G., & Wendt-Wasco, N. J. (1985). Teacher immediacy for affective learning in divergent college classes. *Communication Quarterly, 33,* 61–74.

Keasy, C. B., & Tomlinson-Keasy, C. (1973). Petition signing in a naturalistic setting. *Journal of Social Psychology, 89,* 313–314.

Keating, C. F. (1985). Human dominance signals: The primate in us. In S. L. Ellyson & J. F. Dovidio (Eds.), *Power, dominance, and nonverbal behavior* (pp. 89–108). New York: Springer-Verlag.

Keeley-Dyreson, M. P., Bailey, W., & Burgoon, J. K. (1988, May). *The effect of stress on decoding of kinesic and vocalic channels.* Paper presented at the annual meeting of the International Communication Association, New Orleans.

Keeley-Dyreson, M., Burgoon, J. K., & Bailey, W. (1991). The effects of stress and gender on nonverbal decoding accuracy in kinesic and vocalic channels. *Human Communication Research, 17,* 584–605.

Keiser, G., & Altman, I. (1976). Relationship of nonverbal behavior to the social penetration process. *Human Communication Research, 2,* 147–161.

Keith, V. M., & Herring, C. (1991). Skin tone and stratification in the black community. *American Journal of Sociology, 97,* 760–778.

Kellermann, K. (1992). Communication: Inherently strategic and primarily automatic. *Communication Monographs, 59,* 288–300.

Kellermann, K., & Lim, T. (1990). The conversation MOP: Part 3. Timing of scenes in discourse. *Journal of Personality and Social Psychology, 59,* 1163–1179.

Kellermann, K., Reynolds, R., & Chen, J. B. (1991). Strategies of conversational retreat: When parting is not sweet sorrow. *Communication Monographs, 58,* 362–383.

Kelley, J. (1969, May). *Dress as non-verbal communication.* Paper presented at the annual conference of the American Association for Public Opinion Research.

Kelvin, P. (1973). A social-psychological examination of privacy. *British Journal of Social and Clinical Psychology, 12,* 248–261.

Kemper, S. (1994). Elderspeak: Speech accommodations to older adults. *Aging and Cognition, 1,* 17–28.

Kemper, S., Vandeputte, D., Rice, K., & Cheung, H. (in press). Speech accommodation during a referential communication task. *Journal of Language and Social Psychology.*

Kemper, T. D. (1984). Power, status, and emotions: A sociological contribution to a psychophysiological domain. In K. R. Scherer & P. Ekman (Eds.), *Approaches to emotion* (pp. 369–383). Hillsdale, NJ: Erlbaum.

Kendon, A. (1967). Some functions of gaze-direction in social interaction. *Acta Psychologica, 26,* 22–63.

Kendon, A. (1975). Some functions of the face in a kissing round. *Semiotica, 15,* 299–334.

Kendon, A. (1978). Looking in conversation and the regulation of turns at talk: A comment on the papers of G. Beattie and D. R. Rutter et al. *British Journal of Social and Clinical Psychology, 17,* 23–24.

Kendon, A. (1980). Gesticulation and speech: Two aspects of the process of utterance. In M. R. Key (Ed.), *The relationship of verbal and nonverbal communication* (pp. 207–227). The Hague: Mouton.

Kendon, A. (1983). Gesture and speech: How they interact. In J. M. Wiemann & R. P. Harrison (Eds.), *Nonverbal interaction* (pp. 13–45). Beverly Hills, CA: Sage.

Kendon, A. (1990). *Conducting interaction: Patterns of behavior in focused encounters.* Cambridge: Cambridge University Press.

Kendon, A. (1994). Do gestures communicate? *Research on Language and Social Interaction, 27,* 175–200.

Kendon, A., & Ferber, A. (1973). A description of some human greetings. In R. P. M. Michael & J. H. Crook (Eds.), *Comparative ecology and behavior of primates* (pp. 591–668). New York: Academic.

Kennedy, C. W., & Camden, C. (1981).

Gender differences in interruption behavior: A dominance perspective. *International Journal of Women's Studies, 4,* 18–25.

Kennedy, C. W., & Camden, C. (1983). Interruptions and nonverbal gender differences. *Journal of Nonverbal Behavior, 8,* 91–108.

Kennedy, R. (1943). Premarital residential propinquity. *American Journal of Sociology, 48,* 580–584.

Kenner, A. N., & Katsimaglis, G. (1993). Gender differences in proxemics: Taxi-seat choice. *Psychological Reports, 72,* 625–626.

Kenny, D. A., Horner, C., Kashy, D. A., & Chu, L. (1992). Consensus at zero acquaintance: Replication, behavioral cues, and stability. *Journal of Personality and Social Psychology, 62,* 88–97.

Kenrick, D. (1994, October). *From genes to brains to love affairs: Searching for evolved cognitive mechanisms underlying close relationships.* Presentation to the annual meeting of the Society of Experimental Social Psychology, Lake Tahoe, NV.

Kent, R. D., & Burkhard, R. (1981). Changes in acoustic correlates of speech production. In D. Beasley & G. Davis (Eds.), *Aging: Communication processes and disorders* (pp. 47–62). New York: Grune & Strattorn.

Kent, S. (1991). Partitioning space: Cross-cultural factors influencing domestic spatial segmentation. *Environment and Behavior, 23,* 438–473.

Kesey, K. (1963). *Sometimes a great notion.* New York: Bantam.

Key, M. R. (Ed.). (1980). *The relationship of verbal and nonverbal communication.* The Hague: Mouton.

Kidd, R. F. (1975). Pupil size, eye contact, and instrumental aggression. *Perceptual and Motor Skills, 41,* 538.

Kikuchi, T. (1994, July). *Effects of backchannel convergence on a speaker's speech rate and track-checking behavior.* Paper presented at the annual meeting of the International Communication Association, Sydney, Australia.

Kimble, C. E., Forte, R. A., & Yoshikawa, J. C. (1981). Nonverbal concomitants of enacted emotional intensity and positivity: Visual and vocal behavior. *Journal of Personality, 49,* 271–283.

Kimble, C. E., & Seidel, S. D. (1991). Vocal signs of confidence. *Journal of Nonverbal Behavior, 15,* 99–106.

King, P. (1987). *Power and communication.* Prospect Heights, IL: Waveland.

King, M. G. (1966). Interpersonal relations in preschool children and average approach distance. *Journal of Genetic Psychology, 109,* 109–116.

Kintsch, W. (1974). *The representation of meaning in memory.* Hillsdale, NJ: Erlbaum.

Kira, A. (1966). *The bathroom: Criteria for design.* New York: Center for Housing and Environmental Studies, Cornell University.

Kira, A. (1970). Privacy and the bathroom. In H. M. Proshansky, W. H. Ittleson, & L. G. Rivlin (Eds.), *Environmental psychology: Man and his physical setting* (pp. 269–275). New York: Holt, Rinehart & Winston.

Kitahara, M. (1985). Cognition of size and evolutionary advantage. *Psychology, 22,* 49–50.

Kleck, R. E. (1969). Physical stigma and task oriented interaction. *Human Relations, 22,* 53–60.

Kleck, R. E., & Mendolia, M. (1990). Decoding of profile versus full-face expressions of affect. *Journal of Nonverbal Behavior, 14,* 35–49.

Kleck, R. E., & Nuessle, W. (1968). Congruence between the indicative and communicative functions of eye-contact in interpersonal relations. *British Journal of Social and Clinical Psychology, 7,* 241–246.

Kleinfeld, J. S. (1973). Effects of nonverbally communicated personal warmth on intelligence test performance of Indian and Eskimo adolescents. *Journal of Social Psychology, 91,* 149–150.

Kleinfeld, J. S. (1974). Effects of nonverbal warmth on learning of Eskimo and white children. *Journal of Social Psychology, 92,* 3–90.

Kleinke, C. L. (1977). Compliance to requests made by gazing and touching experimenters in field settings. *Journal of Experimental Social Psychology, 13,* 218–223.

Kleinke, C. L. (1980). Interaction between gaze and legitimacy of request on compliance in a field setting. *Journal of Nonverbal Behavior, 5,* 3–12.

Kleinke, C. L., Lenga, M. R., Tully, T. B., Meeker, F. B., & Staneski, R. A. (1976). *Effect of talking rate on first impressions of opposite-sex and same-sex interactions.* Paper presented at the annual meeting of the Western Psychological Association, Los Angeles.

Kleinke, C. L., Meeker, F. B., & LaFong, C. (1974). Effects of gaze, touch, and use of name on evaluation of "engaged" couples. *Journal of Research in Personality, 7,* 368–373.

Klopf, D. W., Thompson, C. A., Ishii, S., & Sallinen-Kuparinen, A. (1991). Nonverbal immediacy differences among Japanese, Finnish, and American university students. *Perceptual and Motor Skills, 73,* 209–210.

Knapp, M. L. (1972). *Nonverbal communication in human interaction.* New York: Holt, Rinehart and Winston.

Knapp, M. L. (1978). *Nonverbal communication in human interaction* (2d ed.). New York: Holt, Rinehart and Winston.

Knapp, M. L. (1983a). Dyadic relationship development. In J. M. Wiemann & R. P. Harrison (Eds.), *Nonverbal interaction* (pp. 179–207). Beverly Hills CA: Sage.

Knapp, M. L. (1983b). *The study of nonverbal behavior vis-à-vis human communication theory.* Paper presented at the 2d International Conference on Nonverbal Behavior, Toronto.

Knapp, M. L. (1984a). *Interpersonal communication and human relationships.* Boston: Allyn & Bacon.

Knapp, M. L. (1984b). The study of nonverbal behavior vis-à-vis human communication theory. In A. Wolfgang (Ed.), *Nonverbal behavior: Perspectives, applications, and intercultural insights* (pp. 15–40). Toronto: Hogrefe.

Knapp, M. L. (1985). The study of physical appearance and cosmetics in Western culture. In J. A. Graham & A. M. Kligman (Eds.), *The psychology of cosmetic treatments* (pp. 45–76). New York: Praeger.

Knapp, M. L., & Comadena, M. E. (1979). Telling it like it isn't: A review of theory and research on deceptive communications. *Human Communication Research, 5,* 270–285.

Knapp, M. L., & Hall, J. A. (1992). *Nonverbal communication in human interaction.* Fort Worth, TX: Harcourt Brace Jovanovich.

Knapp, M. L., Hart, R. P., & Dennis, H. S. (1974). An exploration of deception as a communication construct. *Human Communication Research, 1,* 15–29.

Knapp, M. L., Hart, R. P., Freidrich, G. W., & Shulman, G. M. (1973). The rhetoric of goodbye: Verbal and nonverbal correlates of human leave-taking. *Speech Monographs, 40,* 182–198.

Knapp, M. L., Wiemann, J. M., & Daly, J. A. (1978). Nonverbal communication: Issues and appraisal. *Human Communication Research, 4,* 271–280.

Knower, F. H. (1945). Studies in the symbolism of voice and action, V: The use of behavioral and tonal symbols as tests of speaking achievement. *Journal of Applied Psychology, 29,* 229–235.

Knowles, E. S. (1972). Boundaries around social space: Dyadic responses to an invader. *Environment and Behavior, 4,* 437–445.

Knowles, E. S. (1973). Boundaries around group interaction: The effect of group size and member status on boundary permeability. *Journal of Personality and Social Psychology, 26,* 327–331.

Knowles, E. S. (1980). An affiliative conflict theory of personal and group spatial behavior. In P. B. Paulus (Ed.), *Psychology of group influence* (pp. 133–188). Hillsdale, NJ: Erlbaum.

Knudsen, H. R., & Muzekari, L. H. (1983). The effects of verbal statements of context on facial expressions of emotion. *Journal of Nonverbal Behavior, 7,* 202–212.

Kohnken, G. (1987). Training police officers to detect deceptive eyewitness statements: Does it work? *Social Behaviour, 2,* 1–17.

Konečni, V. J., Libuser, L., Morton, H., & Ebbesen, E. B. (1975). Effects of a violation of personal space on escape and helping responses. *Journal of Experimental Social Psychology, 11,* 288–299.

Korda, M. (1975). *Power! How to get it, how to use it.* New York: Ballantine.

Kowal, S., O'Connel, D. C., & Sabin, E. J. (1975). Development of temporal patterning and vocal hesitations in spontaneous narratives. *Journal of Psycholinguistic Research, 4,* 195–207.

Krapfel, R. E. (1988). Customer complaint and salesperson response: The effect of the communication source. *Journal of Retailing, 64,* 181–198.

Krauss, R., Morrel-Samuels, P., & Colasante, C. (1991). Do conversational hand gestures communicate? *Journal of Personality and Social Psychology, 61,* 743–754.

Krauss, R. M., Apple, W., Morency, N., Wenzel, C., & Winton, W. (1981). Verbal, vocal, and visible factors in judgments of another's affect. *Journal of Personality and Social Psychology, 40,* 312–319.

Krauss, R. M., Fussell, S. R., & Chen, Y. (in press). Coordination of perspective in dialogue: Intrapersonal and interpersonal processes. In I. Markovà & S. Collins (Eds.), *Mutualities in dialogue.* Cambridge: Cambridge University Press.

Krauss, R. M., Geller, V., & Olson, C. (1976, September). *Modalities and cues in the detection of deception.* Paper presented at the annual meeting of the American Psychological Association, Washington, DC.

Kraut, R. E. (1978). Verbal and nonverbal cues in the perception of lying. *Journal of Personality and Social Psychology, 36,* 380–391.

Kraut, R. E. (1980). Humans as lie detectors: Some second thoughts. *Journal of Communication, 30*(4), 209–216.

Kraut, R. E., & Poe, D. (1980). On the line: The deception judgements of customs inspectors and laymen. *Journal of Personality and Social Psychology, 39,* 784–798.

Kraut, R. E., Thompson, A., & Lewis, S. H. (1980). *Listener responsiveness, deception, and semantic structure in conversation.* Unpublished manuscript, Cornell University.

Krieger, L. M. (1994, May 15). California moves to assist voters who select candidates by looks. *Arizona Daily Star,* p. A1.

Krivonos, P. D., & Knapp, M. L. (1975). Initiating communication: What do you say when you say hello? *Central States Speech Journal, 26,* 115–125.

Krout, M. H. (1935). Autistic gestures: An experimental study in symbolic movement. *Psychological Monographs, 46,* 1–119.

Krout, M. H. (1942). *Introduction to social psychology.* New York: Harper & Row.

Krout, M. H. (1954a). An experimental attempt to determine the significance of unconscious manual symbolic movements. *Journal of General Psychology, 51,* 93–120.

Krout, M. H. (1954b). An experimental attempt to produce unconscious manual symbolic movements. *Journal of General Psychology, 51,* 121–152.

Krout, M. H. (1971). Symbolism. In H. A. Bosmajian (Ed.), *The rhetoric of nonverbal communication* (pp. 15–33). Glenview, IL: Scott, Foresman.

Kunihiro, M. (1976). The Japanese language and intercultural communication. *Japan Interpreter, 10,* 267–283.

LaBarbera, P., & MacLachlan, J. (1979). Time compressed speech in radio advertising. *Journal of Marketing, 43,* 30–36.

LaBarre, W. (1947). The cultural basis of emotions and gestures. *Journal of Personality, 16,* 49–68.

LaBarre, W. (1972). Paralinguistics, kinesics, and cultural anthropology. In L. A. Samovar & R. E. Porter (Eds.), *Intercultural communication: A reader* (2d ed., pp. 172–180). Belmont, CA: Wadsworth.

LaCrosse, M. B. (1975). Nonverbal behavior and perceived counselor attractiveness and persuasiveness. *Journal of Counseling Psychology, 22,* 563–566.

LaFrance, M. (1979). Nonverbal synchrony and rapport: Analysis by the cross-lag panel technique. *Social Psychology Quarterly, 42,* 66–70.

LaFrance, M. (1985a). Postural mirroring and intergroup relations. *Personality and Social Psychology Bulletin, 11,* 207–217.

LaFrance, M. (1985b). The school of hard knocks: Nonverbal sexism in the classroom. *Theory into Practice, 24,* 40–44.

LaFrance, M., & Broadbent, M. (1976). Group rapport: Posture sharing as a nonverbal indicator. *Group and Organizational Studies, 1,* 328–333.

LaFrance, M., Hecht, M. A., & Noyes, A. (1994, October). *Who's smiling now? A meta-analysis of sex differences in smiling.* Paper presented at the annual meeting of the Society of Experimental Social Psychology, Lake Tahoe, NV.

LaFrance, M., & Ickes, W. (1981). Postural mirroring and interactional involvement: Sex and sex-typing effects. *Journal of Nonverbal Behavior, 5,* 139–154.

LaFrance, M., & Mayo, C. (1976). Racial differences in gaze behavior during conversations: Two systematic observational studies. *Journal of Personality and Social Psychology, 33,* 547–552.

LaFrance, M., & Mayo, C. (1978a). Cultural aspects of nonverbal communication. *International Journal of Intercultural Relations, 2,* 71–89.

LaFrance, M., & Mayo, C. (1978b). *Moving bodies.* Monterey, CA: Brooks/Cole.

LaFrance, M., & Mayo, C. (1979). A review of nonverbal behaviors of women and men. *Western Journal of Speech Communication, 43,* 96–107.

Laird, J. D. (1974). Self-attribution of emotion: The effects of expressive behavior on the quality of emotional experience. *Journal of Personality and Social Psychology, 29,* 475–486.

Lakoff, R. (1973). Language and woman's place. *Language in Society, 2,* 45–79.

Lamb, M. E., Suomi, S. J., & Stephenson, G. R. (1979). *Social interaction analysis: Methodological issues.* Madison: University of Wisconsin Press.

Lamb, T. A. (1981). Nonverbal and paraverbal control in dyads and triads: Sex or power differences? *Social Psychology Quarterly, 44,* 49–53.

Lambert, W. E., Hodgson, R. C., Gardner, R. C., & Fillenbaum, S. (1960). Evaluational reactions to spoken languages. *Journal of Abnormal and Social Psychology, 60,* 44–51.

Landis, B. (1970). Ego boundaries. *Psychological Issues* (Monograph No. 24). New York: International Universities Press.

Langer, E. J. (1989). *Mindfulness.* Reading, MA: Addison-Wesley.

Langer, E. J., & Imber, L. (1980). Role of mindlessness in the perception of deviance. *Journal of Personality and Social Psychology, 39,* 360–367.

Langer, E. J., & Saegert, S. (1977). Crowding and cognitive control. *Journal of Personality and Social Psychology, 35,* 175–182.

Lanzetta, J. T., Cartwright-Smith, J., & Kleck, R. E. (1976). Effects of nonverbal dissimulation on emotional experience and autonomic arousal. *Journal of Personality and Social Psychology, 33,* 354–370.

Lass, N. L., & Davis, M. (1976). An investigation of speaker height and weight identification. *Journal of the Acoustical Society of America, 60,* 700–707.

Laver, R. H. (1981). *Temporal man.* New York: Praeger.

Lavrakas, P. J. (1975). Female preferences for male physiques. *Journal of Research in Personality, 9,* 324–333.

Lawton, M., & Nahemoir, L. (1973). Ecology and the aging process. In C. Eisdorfer & M. Lawton (Eds.), *The psychology of adult development and aging* (pp. 619–714). Washington, DC: American Psychological Association.

Lay, C. H., & Burron, B. F. (1968). Perception of the personality of the hesitant speaker. *Perceptual and Motor Skills, 26,* 951–956.

Leach, E. (1968). Don't say "boo" to a goose. In M. F. A. Montagu (Ed.), *Man and aggression* (pp. 65–73). London: Oxford University Press.

Leach, E. (1972). The influence of cultural context on non-verbal communication in man. In R. A. Hinde (Ed.), *Non-verbal communication* (pp. 315–344). Cambridge: Cambridge University Press.

Leaf, A. (1973, Sept.). Getting old. *Scientific American, 229,* 45–52.

Leakey, R. E., & Lewin, R. (1978). *People of the lake: Mankind and its beginnings.* Garden City, NY: Anchor/Doubleday.

Leary, T. (1957). *Interpersonal diagnosis of personality.* New York: Ronald.

Leathers, D. G. (1976). *Nonverbal communication systems.* Boston: Allyn & Bacon.

Leathers, D. G. (1979). The impact of multichannel message inconsistency on verbal and nonverbal decoding behaviors. *Communication Monographs, 46,* 88–100.

LeCompte, W. F., & Rosenfeld, H. M. (1971). Effects of minimal eye contact in the instruction period on impressions of the experimenter. *Journal of Experimental Social Psychology, 7,* 211–220.

Lee, D. Y., Hallberg, E. T., Hassard, J. H., & Haase, R. F. (1979). Client verbal and nonverbal reinforcement of counselor behavior: Its impact on interviewing behavior and postinterview evaluation. *Journal of Counseling Psychology, 26,* 204–209.

Leffler, A., Gillespie, D. L., & Conaty, J. C. (1982). The effects of status differentiation on nonverbal behavior. *Social Psychology Quarterly, 45,* 153–161.

Leibman, M. (1970). The effects of sex and race norms on personal space. *Environment and Behavior, 2,* 208–248.

Leighton, A. H., & Leighton, D. C. (1944). *The Navaho door: An introduction to Navaho life.* Cambridge, MA: Harvard University Press.

Le Poire, B. A., & Burgoon, J. K. (1994a). *Participant and observer perceptions of relational messages associated with nonverbal involvement and pleasantness.* Manuscript submitted for publication.

Le Poire, B. A., & Burgoon, J. K.

(1994b). Two contrasting explanations of involvement violations: Expectancy violations theory versus discrepancy arousal theory. *Human Communication Research, 20,* 560–591.

Le Poire, B. A., & Burgoon, J. K. (1994c). *Useful of the "orientation response" for theories of nonverbal involvement violations: The orienting versus arousal debate.* Manuscript submitted for publication.

Levelt, W. J. M. (1989). *Speaking: From intention to articulation.* Cambridge, MA: MIT Press.

Leventhal, H., Nerenz, D. R., & Leventhal, E. (1982). Feelings of threat and private views of illness: Factors in dehumanization in the medical care system. In A. Baum & J. E. Singer (Eds.), *Advances in environmental psychology: Environment and health* (Vol. 4, pp. 85–114). Hillsdale, NJ: Erlbaum.

Levin, H., Silverman, I., & Ford, B. L. (1967). Hesitations in children's speech during explanation and description. *Journal of Verbal Learning and Verbal Behavior, 6,* 560–564.

Levine, M. H. (1972). *The effects of age, sex, and task on visual behavior during dyadic interaction.* Unpublished doctoral dissertation, Columbia University, New York.

Levine, R., & Wolff, E. (1985, March). Social time: The heartbeat of culture. *Psychology Today,* 28–35.

Levine, T. R., & McCornack, S. R. (1989, November). *Distinguishing between types of suspicion and measuring predisposition toward suspicion: Two studies validating a measure of trait suspicion.* Paper presented at the annual meeting of the Speech Communication Association, San Francisco.

Levine, T. R., & McCornack, S. A. (1991). The dark side of trust: Conceptualizing and measuring types of communicative suspicion. *Communication Quarterly, 39,* 325–340.

Levy, P. (1964). The ability to express and perceive vocal communication of feeling. In J. R. Davitz (Ed.), *Communication of emotional meaning* (pp. 43–56). New York: McGraw-Hill.

Lewin, K. (1935). *A dynamic theory of personality.* New York: McGraw-Hill.

Lewinski, R. H. (1938). An investigation of individual responses to chromatic illumination. *Journal of Psychology, 6,* 6.

Lewis, M. (1972). Parents and children: Sex-role development. *School Review, 80,* 229–240.

Lewis, M., & Goldberg, S. (1969). Perceptual-cognitive development in infancy: A generalized expectancy model as a function of the mother-infant interaction. *Merrill-Palmer Quarterly, 15,* 81–100.

Leyhausen, P. (1971). Dominance and territoriality as complemented in mammalian social structure. In A. H. Esser (Ed.), *Behavior and environment* (pp. 22–33). New York: Plenum.

Libby, W. L., Jr. (1970). Eye contact and direction of looking as stable individual differences. *Journal of Experimental Research in Personality, 4,* 303–312.

Lieberman, P. (1967). *Intonation, perception, and language.* Cambridge, MA: MIT Press.

Lindskold, S., & Walters, P. S. (1983). Categories for acceptability of lies. *Journal of Social Psychology, 120,* 129–136.

Linkey, H. E., & Firestone, I. J. (1990). Dyad dominance composition effects, nonverbal behaviors, and influence. *Journal of Research in Personality, 24,* 206–215.

Lipman, A. (1970). Territoriality: A useful architectural concept? *Royal Institute of British Architects Journal, 77,* 68–70.

Lippa, R. (1976). Expressive control and the leakage of dispositional introversion-extraversion during role-played teaching. *Journal of Personality, 44,* 541–559.

Lippard, P. V. (1988). "Ask me no questions, I'll tell you no lies": Situational exigencies for interpersonal deception. *Western Journal of Speech Communication, 52,* 91–103.

Liska, J. (1986). Symbols: The missing link? In J. G. Else & P. Lee (Eds.), *Proceedings of the Tenth Congress of the International Primatological Society: Vol. 3. Primate ontogeny, cognition, and social behavior.* Cambridge: Cambridge University Press.

Liska, J. (1988, July). *Dominance-seeking strategies in primates: An evolutionary perspective.* Paper presented at the Twelfth Congress of the International Primatological Society, Brasilia, Brazil.

Little, K. B. (1965). Personal space. *Journal of Experimental Social Psychology, 1,* 237–247.

Little, K. B. (1968). Cultural variations in social schemata. *Journal of Personality and Social Psychology, 10,* 1–7.

Littlepage, G., & Pineault, T. (1978). Verbal, facial, and paralinguistic cues to the detection of truth and lying. *Personality and Social Psychology Bulletin, 4,* 461–464.

Littlepage, G. E., & Pineault, M. A. (1979). Detection of deceptive factual statements from the body and the face. *Personality and Social Psychology Bulletin, 5,* 325–328.

Littlepage, G., & Pineault, T. (1981). Detection of truthful and deceptive interpersonal communication across information transmission modes. *Journal of Social Psychology, 114,* 57–68.

Lochman, J. E., & Allen, G. (1981). Nonverbal communication of couples in conflict. *Journal of Research in Personality, 15,* 253–269.

Lockard, J. S., Allen, D. J., Schiele, B. J., & Wiemer, M. J. (1978). Human postural signals: Stance, weight-shifts and social distance as intention movements to depart. *Animal Behaviour, 26,* 219–224.

Lomranz, J., & Shapira, A. (1974). Communicative patterns of self-disclosure and touching behavior. *Journal of Psychology, 88,* 223–227.

Lomranz, J., Shapira, A., Choresh, N., & Gilat, Y. (1975). Children's personal space as a function of age and sex. *Developmental Psychology, 11,* 541–545.

Loo, C. (1972). The effects of spatial density on the social behavior of children. *Journal of Applied Social Psychology, 4,* 172–181.

Loo, C., & Smetana, J. (1978). The effects of crowding on the behavior and perception of 10-year-old boys. *Environmental Psychology and Nonverbal Behavior, 2,* 226–249.

Lord, T., & Kasprzak, M. (1989). Identification of self through olfaction. *Perceptual and Motor Skills, 69,* 219–224.

Lott, D. F., & Sommer, R. (1967). Seating arrangements and status. *Journal of Personality and Social Psychology, 7,* 90–94.

Loveday, L. (1991). Pitch, politeness, and sexual role: An explanatory investigation into the pitch correlates of English and Japanese politeness formulae. *Language and Speech, 24,* 71–88.

Ludemann, P. M., & Nelson, C. A. (1988). Categorical representation of facial expressions by 7-month-old infants. *Developmental Psychology, 24,* 492–501.

Lüscher, M. (1971). *The Lüscher color test* (I. Scott, Trans.). New York: Washington Square Press/Pocket Books.

Lyman, S. M., & Scott, M. B. (1967). Territoriality: A neglected sociological dimension. *Social Problems, 15,* 236–249.

Lyons, J. (1972). Human language. In R. A. Hinde (Ed.), *Non-verbal communication* (pp. 49–85). Cambridge: Cambridge University Press.

Mabry, E. A., & Kaufman, S. (1973, April). *The influence of sex and attraction on seating positions in dyads.* Paper presented at the annual meeting of the International Communication Association, Montreal.

Mach, R. S. (1972). *Postural carriage and congruency as nonverbal indicators of status differentials and interpersonal attraction.* Unpublished doctoral dissertation, University of Colorado.

Mackey, W. C. (1976). Parameters of the smile as a social signal. *Journal of Genetic Psychology, 129,* 125–130.

MacLachlan, J. (1979, November). What people really think of fast talkers. *Psychology Today, 13,* 113–117.

MacLachlan, J. (1981, April). *New Developments in time compression.* Paper presented at the annual meeting of the American Psychological Association, Pittsburgh.

MacLachlan, J., & LaBarbera, P. (1978). Time-compressed TV commercials. *Journal of Advertising Research, 18,* 11–15.

MacLachlan, J., & Siegel, M. H. (1980). Reducing the cost of TV commercials by use of time compressions. *Journal of Marketing Research, 17,* 52–57.

MacNeil, L., & Wilson, B. (1972). *Effects of clothing and hair length on petition-signing behavior.* Unpublished manuscript, Illinois State University, Normal.

Maddux, J. E., & Rogers, R. W. (1980). Effects of source expertness, physical attractiveness, and supporting arguments on persuasion: A case of brains over beauty. *Journal of Personality and Social Psychology, 39,* 235–244.

Magnusson, D. (1971). An analysis of situational dimensions. *Perceptual and Motor Skills, 32,* 851–867.

Magnusson, D. (1978). *On the psychological situation.* Stockholm: University of Stockholm Reports.

Maier, N. R. F., & Thurber, J. A. (1968). Accuracy of judgments of deception when an interview is watched, heard, and read. *Personnel Psychology, 21,* 23–30.

Maier, R. A., & Ernest, R. C. (1978). Sex differences in the perception of touching. *Perceptual and Motor Skills, 46,* 577–578.

Maines, D. R. (1977). Tactile relationships in the subway as affected by racial, sexual, and crowded seating situations. *Environmental Psychology and Nonverbal Behavior, 2,* 100–108.

Maisonneuve, J., Palmade, G., & Fourment, C. (1952). Selective choices and propinquity. *Sociometry, 15,* 135–140.

Major, B. (1981). Gender patterns in touching behavior. In C. Mayo & N. M. Henley (Eds.), *Gender and nonverbal behavior* (pp. 15–37). New York: Springer-Verlag.

Major, B., & Heslin, R. (1982). Perceptions of cross-sex and same-sex nonreciprocal touch: It is better to give than to receive. *Journal of Nonverbal Behavior, 6,* 148–162.

Major, B., Schmidlin, A. M., & Williams, L. (1990). Gender patterns in social touch: The impact of setting and age. *Journal of Personality and Social Psychology, 58,* 634–643.

Major, B., & Williams, L. (1980). *Frequency of touch by sex and race: A replication of some touching observations.* Unpublished manuscript, State University of New York, Buffalo.

Malandro, L. A., & Barker, L. (1983). *Nonverbal communication.* Reading, MA: Addison-Wesley.

Mallory, E., & Miller V. (1958). A possible basis for the association of voice characteristics and personality traits. *Speech Monographs, 25,* 255.

Mann, J. M. (1959). The effect of interracial contact on sociometric choices and perceptions. *Journal of Social Psychology, 50,* 143–152.

Mansfield, E. (1973). Empathy: Concept and identified psychiatric nursing behavior. *Nursing Research, 22,* 525–530.

Manstead, A. S. R., Wagner, H. L., & MacDonald, C. J. (1986). Deceptive and nondeceptive communications: Sending experience, modality, and individual abilities. *Journal of Nonverbal Behavior, 10,* 147–167.

Manusov, V. L. (1984). *Nonverbal violations of expectations theory: A test of gaze behavior.* Unpublished thesis, Michigan State University, East Lansing.

Manusov, V. (1990). An application of attribution principles to nonverbal behavior in romantic dyads. *Communication Monographs, 57,* 104–118.

Manusov, V. (1991). Perceiving nonverbal messages: Effects of immediacy and encoded intent on receiver judgments. *Western Journal of Speech Communication, 55,* 235–253.

Manusov, V. (1992, November). *Intentionality attributions for naturally occurring nonverbal behaviors in romantic dyads.* Paper presented at the annual meeting of the Speech Communication Association, Chicago.

Manusov, V. (1994, February). *Reacting to changes in nonverbal behaviors: Relational satisfaction and adaptation patterns in romantic dyads.* Paper presented at the Western States Communication Association, San Jose, CA.

Manusov, V., & Rodriguez, J. S. (1989). Intentionality behind nonverbal messages: A perceiver's perspective. *Journal of Nonverbal Behavior, 13,* 15–24.

Marche, T. A., & Peterson, C. (1993). The development and sex-related use of interruption behavior. *Human Communication Research, 19,* 388–408.

Markel, N. N. (1969). Relationship between voice-quality and MMPI profiles in psychiatric patients. *Journal of Abnormal Psychology, 74,* 61–66.

Markel, N. N. (1975). Coverbal behavior associated with conversational turns. In A. Kendon, R. Harris, & M. R. Key (Eds.), *Organization of behavior in face-to-face interaction* (pp. 189–197). The Hague: Mouton.

Markel, N. N., Long, J. F., & Saine, T. J. (1976). Sex effects in conversational interaction: Another look at male dominance. *Human Communication Research, 2,* 356–364.

Markel, N. N., Phillis, J. A., Vargas, R., & Howard, K. (1972). Personality traits associated with voice types. *Journal of Psycholinguistic Research, 1,* 249–255.

Markel, N. N., Prebor, L. D., & Brandt, J. F. (1972). Biosocial factors in dyadic communication: Sex and speaking intensity. *Journal of Personality and Social Psychology, 23,* 11–13.

Markman, H. J., & Floyd, F. (1980). Possibilities for the prevention of marital discord: A behavioral perspective. *American Journal of Family Therapy, 8,* 29–48.

Markman, H. J., Notarius, C. I., Stephen, T., & Smith, R. J. (1981). Behavioral observation systems for couples: The current status. In E. E. Filsinger & R. A. Lewis (Eds.), *Assessing marriage* (pp. 197–216). Beverly Hills, CA: Sage.

Marks, L. E. (1975, June). Synesthesia: The lucky people with mixed-up senses. *Psychology Today, 9,* 48–52.

Marshall, N. J. (1972). Privacy and environment. *Human Ecology, 1,* 93–110.

Martin, J. G. (1964). Racial ethnocentrism and judgment of beauty. *Journal of Social Psychology, 63,* 59–63.

Martin, J. (1986, March 16). "Miss Manners." *Knoxville News-Sentinel,* p. 32.

Maslow, C., Yoselson, K., & London, H. (1971). Persuasiveness of confidence expressed via language and body language. *British Journal of Social and Clinical Psychology, 10,* 234–240.

Massie, H. N. (1978). Blind ratings of mother-infant interaction in home movies of prepsychotic and normal infants. *American Journal of Psychiatry, 135,* 1371–1374.

Matarazzo, J. D., & Wiens, A. N. (1972). *The interview: Research on its anatomy and structure.* Chicago: Aldine.

Matarazzo, J. D., Wiens, A. N., Jackson, R. H., & Manaugh, T. S. (1970). Interviewee speech behavior under conditions of endogenously-present and exogenously-induced motivational states. *Journal of Clinical Psychology, 26,* 141–148.

Matarazzo, J. D., Wiens, A. N., & Saslow, G. (1965). Studies in interviewer speech behavior. In L. Krasner & L. P. Ullmann (Eds.), *Research in behavior modification. New developments and implications* (pp. 179–210). New York: Holt, Rinehart and Winston.

Matsumoto, D. (1989). Face, culture, and judgments of anger and fear: Do the eyes have it? *Journal of Nonverbal Behavior, 13,* 171–189.

Matsumoto, D. (1991). Cultural influences on facial expressions of emotion. *Southern Communication Journal, 56,* 128–137.

Matsumoto, D., & Assar, M. (1992). The effects of language on judgments of universal facial expressions of emo-

tion. *Journal of Nonverbal Behavior, 16,* 85–100.

Matsumoto, D., & Kishimoto, H. (1983). Developmental characteristics in judgments of emotion from nonverbal vocal cues. *International Journal of International Relations, 7,* 415–424.

Matthews, R. W., Paulus, P. B., & Baron, R. A. (1979). Physical aggression after being crowded. *Journal of Nonverbal Behavior, 4,* 5–17.

Mattingly, I. M. (1966). Speaker variation and vocal tract size. *Journal of the Acoustical Society of America, 39,* 1219.

Mayo, C., & LaFrance, M. (1978). On the acquisition of nonverbal communication: A review. *Merrill Palmer Quarterly, 24,* 213–228.

McAdams, D. P., Jackson, R. J., & Kirshnit, C. (1984). Looking, laughing, and smiling in dyads as a function of intimacy motivation and reciprocity. *Journal of Personality, 52,* 261–273.

McBrayer, D. J., Johnson, W. R., & Purvis, D. (1992). Gestural behavior: Causes and questions. *Perceptual and Motor Skills, 74,* 239–242.

McBride, G. (1971). Theories of animal spacing: The role of flight, fight and social distance. In A. H. Esser (Ed.), *Behavior and environment* (pp. 53–68). New York: Plenum.

McBride, G. (1975). Interactions and the control of behavior. In A. Kendon, R. M. Harris, & M. R. Key (Eds.), *Organization of behavior in face-to-face interaction* (pp. 415–425). The Hague: Mouton.

McBride, G., King, M. G., & James, J. W. (1965). Social proximity effects on galvanic skin responses in adult humans. *Journal of Psychology, 61,* 153–157.

McBurney, D. L., & Comadena, M. E. (1992, November). *An examination of the McCormack and Parks model of deception detection.* Paper presented at the annual meeting of the Speech Communication Association, Chicago.

McCain, G., Cox, V. C., & Paulus, P. B. (1976). The relationship between illness complaints and degree of crowding in a prison environment. *Environment and Behavior, 8,* 283–290.

McCallum, R., Rusbult, C. E., Hong, G. K., Walden, T. A., & Schopler, J. (1979). Effects of resource availability and importance of behavior on the experience of crowding. *Journal of*

Personality and Social Psychology, 37, 1304–1313.

McCarrick, A. K., Manderscheid, R. W., & Silbergeld, S. (1981). Gender differences in competition and dominance during married-couples group therapy. *Social Psychology Quarterly, 44,* 164–177.

McCarthy, P. (1988, January). Mind openers. *Psychology Today,* p. 16.

McCauley, C., Coleman, G., & DeFusco, P. (1978). Commuters' eye contact with strangers in city and suburban train stations: Evidence of short-term adaptation to interpersonal overload in the city. *Environmental Psychology and Nonverbal Behavior, 2,* 215–225.

McClintock, C. C., & Hunt, R. G. (1975). Nonverbal indicators of affect and deception in an interview setting. *Journal of Applied Social Psychology, 5,* 54–67.

McClintock, M. K. (1971). Menstrual synchrony and suppression. *Nature, 229,* 244–245.

McConnell, J. V., Cutler, L., & McNeil, B. (1958). Subliminal stimulation: An overview. *American Psychologist, 13,* 235.

McConnell-Ginet, S. (1974). *Intonation in a man's world.* Paper presented at the annual meeting of the American Anthropological Association, Mexico City.

McCormick, E. J. (1976). *Human factors in engineering and design.* New York: McGraw-Hill.

McCornack, S. A. (1992). Information manipulation theory. *Communication Monographs, 59,* 1–16.

McCornack, S. A., & Levine, T. R. (1990). When lovers become leery: The relationship between suspicion and accuracy in detecting deception. *Communication Monographs, 57,* 219–230.

McCornack, S. A., & Parks, M. R. (1986). Deception detection and relationship development: The other side of trust. In M. L. McLaughlin (Ed.), *Communication yearbook 9* (pp. 377–389). Beverly Hills CA: Sage.

McCroskey, J. C. (1972). *An introduction to rhetorical communication.* Englewood Cliffs, NJ: Prentice-Hall.

McCroskey, J. C., & Mehrley, R. S. (1969). The effects of disorganization and nonfluency on attitude change and source credibility. *Speech Monographs, 36,* 13–21.

McDowall, J. J. (1978a). Interactional

synchrony: A reappraisal. *Journal of Personality and Social Psychology, 36,* 963–975.

McDowall, J. J. (1978b). Microanalysis of filmed movement: The reliability of boundary detection by observers. *Environmental Psychology and Nonverbal Behavior, 3,* 77–88.

McDowell, E. E., McDowell, C. E., & Hyerdahl, J. (1980, October). *A multivariate study of teacher immediacy, effectiveness and student attentiveness at the junior high and senior high levels.* Paper presented at the annual meeting of the Speech Communication Association, New York.

McDowell, K. V. (1973). Accommodations of verbal and nonverbal behaviors as a function of the manipulation of interaction distance and eye contact. *Proceedings of the 81st Annual Convention of the American Psychological Association, 8,* 207–208.

McGinley, H., Blau, G., & Takai, M. (1984). Attraction effects of smiling and body position: A cultural comparison. *Perceptual and Motor Skills, 58,* 915–922.

McGinley, H., LeFevre, R., & McGinley, P. (1975). The influence of a communicator's body position on opinion change in others. *Journal of Personality and Social Psychology, 31,* 686–690.

McGinley, H., McGinley, P., & Nicholas, K. (1978). Smiling, body position, and interpersonal attraction. *Bulletin of the Psychonomic Society, 12,* 21–24.

McGlone, R. E. (1966). Vocal pitch characteristics of children aged one to two years. *Speech Monographs, 33,* 178–181.

McGlone, R. E., & Hollien, H. (1963). Vocal pitch characteristics of aged women. *Journal of Speech and Hearing Research, 6,* 164–170.

McHarg, I. (1963). Man and his environment. In L. J. Dahl (Ed.), *The urban condition* (pp. 57–58). New York: Basic.

McHugo, G. J., Lanzetta, J. T., & Bush, L. K. (1991). The effect of attitudes on emotional reactions to expressive displays of political leaders. *Journal of Nonverbal Behavior, 15,* 19–41.

McLaughlin, M. L. (1984). *Conversation: How talk is organized.* Beverly Hills, CA: Sage.

McLuhan, M., & Fiore, Q. (1967). *The medium is the massage.* New York: Random House.

McMahan, E. M. (1976). Nonverbal communication as a function of attribution in impression formation. *Communication Monographs, 43,* 287–294.

McMillan, J. R., Clifton, A. K., McGrath, D., & Gale, W. S. (1977). Women's language: Uncertainty or interpersonal sensitivity and emotionality? *Sex Roles, 3,* 545–559.

McMullan, G. R. (1974). *The relative contribution of selected nonverbal behaviors to the communication of empathy in a counseling interview.* Unpublished doctoral dissertation, West Virginia University, Morgantown.

McNeill, D. (1970). *The acquisition of language: The study of developmental psycholinguistics.* New York: Harper & Row.

McNeill, D. (1979). *The conceptual basis of language.* Hillsdale, NJ: Erlbaum.

McNeill, D. (1985). So you think gestures are nonverbal? *Psychological Review, 92,* 350–371.

McNeill, D. (1987). So you *do* think gestures are nonverbal! Reply to Feyereisen (1987). *Psychological Review, 94,* 499–504.

McNeill, D. (1992). *Hand and mind: What gestures reveal about thought.* Chicago: University of Chicago Press.

McNeill, D., Cassell, J., & McCullough, K. (1994). Communicative effects of speech-mismatched gestures. *Research on Language and Social Interaction, 27,* 223–237.

McNeill, D., & Levy, E. (1982). Conceptual representations in language activity and gesture. In R. J. Jarvella & W. Klein (Eds.), *Speech, place, and action: Studies in deixis and related topics* (pp. 271–295). Chichester, England: Wiley.

McPeek, R. W., & Edwards, J. D. (1975). Expectancy disconfirmation and attitude change. *Journal of Social Psychology, 96,* 193–208.

Mead, M. (1975). Review of *Darwin and facial expression: A century of research in review* by P. Ekman. *Journal of Communication, 25*(1), 209–213.

Mechanic, D. (1972). Social psychologic factors affecting the presentation of bodily complaints. *New England Journal of Medicine, 286,* 1132–1139.

Meditch, A. (1975). The development of sex-specific speech patterns in young children. *Anthropological Linguistics, 17,* 421–433.

Meerloo, J. A. M. (1955). Archaic behav-

ior and the communicative act. *Psychiatric Quarterly, 29,* 60–73.

Meerloo, J. A. M. (1970). *Along the fourth dimension.* New York: Harper & Row.

Mehrabian, A. (1967). Orientation behaviors and nonverbal attitude communication. *Journal of Communication, 17,* 324–332.

Mehrabian, A. (1968a, September). Communication without words. *Psychology Today, 2,* 52–55.

Mehrabian, A. (1968b). Inference of attitude from the posture, orientation, and distance of a communicator. *Journal of Consulting and Clinical Psychology, 32,* 296–308.

Mehrabian, A. (1968c). Relationship of attitude to seated posture, orientation, and distance. *Journal of Personality and Social Psychology, 10,* 26–30.

Mehrabian, A. (1969). Significance of posture and position in the communication of attitude and status relationships. *Psychological Bulletin, 71,* 359–372.

Mehrabian, A. (1970a). A semantic space for nonverbal behavior. *Journal of Consulting and Clinical Psychology, 35,* 248–257.

Mehrabian, A. (1970b). When are feelings communicated inconsistently? *Journal of Experimental Research in Personality, 4,* 198–212.

Mehrabian, A. (1971a). Nonverbal betrayal of feelings. *Journal of Experimental Research in Personality, 5,* 64–73.

Mehrabian, A. (1971b). Verbal and nonverbal interaction of strangers in a waiting situation. *Journal of Experimental Research in Personality, 5,* 127–138.

Mehrabian, A. (1972). *Nonverbal communication.* Chicago: Aldine-Atherton.

Mehrabian, A. (1976). *Public places and private spaces: The psychology of work, play, and living environments.* New York: Basic.

Mehrabian, A. (1981). *Silent messages: Implicit communication of emotions and attitudes* (2d ed.). Belmont, CA: Wadsworth.

Mehrabian, A., & Diamond, S. G. (1971). Seating arrangement and conversation. *Sociometry, 34,* 281–289.

Mehrabian, A., & Ferris, S. R. (1967). Inference of attitudes from nonverbal communication in two channels. *Journal of Consulting Psychology, 31,* 248–252.

Mehrabian, A., & Friar, J. T. (1969). Encoding of attitude by a seated communicator via posture and position cues. *Journal of Consulting and Clinical Psychology, 33,* 330–336.

Mehrabian, A., & Ksionzky, S. (1970). Models for affiliative and conformity behavior. *Psychological Bulletin, 74,* 110–126.

Mehrabian, A., & Ksionzky, S. (1972). Categories of social behavior. *Comparative Group Studies, 3,* 425–436.

Mehrabian, A., & Russell, J. A. (1974). *An approach to environmental psychology.* Cambridge, MA: MIT Press.

Mehrabian, A., & Wiener, M. (1967). Decoding of inconsistent communications. *Journal of Personality and Social Psychology, 6,* 108–114.

Mehrabian, A., & Williams, M. (1969). Nonverbal concomitants of perceived and intended persuasiveness. *Journal of Personality and Social Psychology, 13,* 37–58.

Meisels, M., & Guardo, C. J. (1969). Development of personal space schemata. *Child Development, 40,* 1167–1178.

Meltzer, L., Morris, W. N., & Hayes, D. P. (1971). Interruption outcomes and vocal amplitude: Explorations in social psychophysics. *Journal of Personality and Social Psychology, 18,* 392–402.

Meltzoff, A. N., & Moore, M. K. (1989). Imitation in newborn infants: Exploring the range of gestures imitated and the underlying mechanisms. *Developmental Psychology, 25,* 954–962.

Menyuk, P. (1971). *The acquisition and development of language.* Englewood Cliffs, NJ: Prentice-Hall.

Menyuk, P. (1972). *The development of speech.* New York: Bobbs-Merrill.

Merton, R. K. (1948). The self-fulfilling prophecy. *Antioch Review, 8,* 193–210.

Metts, S., & Chronis, H. (1986, May). *An exploratory investigation of relational deception.* Paper presented at the annual meeting of the International Communication Association, Chicago.

Metts, S., & Hippensteele, S. (1988). *Characteristics of deception in close relationships.* Paper presented at the annual meeting of the Western Speech Communication Association, San Diego.

Michael, G., & Willis, F. N., Jr. (1969). The development of gestures in three subcultural groups. *Journal of Social Psychology, 79,* 35–41.

Michener, J. A. (1980). *The covenant.* New York: Fawcett Crest.

Milgram, S. (1963). Behavioral study of obedience. *Journal of Abnormal and Social Psychology, 67,* 371–378.

Milgram, S. (1970). The experience of living in cities. *Science, 167,* 1461–1468.

Milgram, S. (1974). *Obedience to authority: An experimental view.* New York: Harper & Row.

Millar, F. E., & Rogers, L. E. (1976). A relational approach to interpersonal communication. In G. R. Miller (Ed.), *Explorations in interpersonal communication* (pp. 87–104). Beverly Hills, CA: Sage.

Miller, A. (1970). Role of physical attractiveness in impression formation. *Psychonomic Science, 19,* 241–243.

Miller, A. G., Ashton, W. A., McHoskey, J. W., & Gimbel, J. (1990). What price attractiveness? Stereotype and risk factors in suntanning behavior. *Journal of Applied Social Psychology, 20,* 1272–1300.

Miller, G. A. (1956). The magical number seven, plus or minus two: Some limits on our capacity for processing information. *Psychological Review, 63,* 81–97.

Miller, G. R., Bauchner, J. E., Hocking, J. E., Fontes, N. E., Kaminski, E. P., & Brandt, D. R. (1981). ". . . and nothing but the truth": How well can observers detect deceptive testimony? In B. D. Sales (Ed.), *Perspectives in law and psychology. 3: The jury, judicial, and trial process.* New York: Plenum.

Miller, G. R., & Burgoon, J. K. (1982). Factors affecting witness credibility. In N. L. Kerr & R. M. Bray (Eds.), *The psychology of the courtroom* (pp. 169–194). New York: Academic.

Miller, G. R., & Burgoon, M. (1978). Persuasion research: Review and commentary. In B. Rubin (Ed.), *Communication yearbook 2* (pp. 29–47). New Brunswick, NJ: Transaction.

Miller, G. R., deTurck, M. A., & Kalbfleisch, P. J. (1983). Self-monitoring, rehearsal, and deceptive communication. *Human Communication Research, 10,* 97–117.

Miller, G. R., & Hewgill, M. A. (1964). The effect of variations in nonfluency on audience ratings of source credibility. *Quarterly Journal of Speech, 50,* 36–44.

Miller, G. R., & Steinberg, M. (1975). *Between people.* Chicago: Science Research Associates.

Miller, N., Maruyama, G., Beaber, R. J., & Valone, K. (1976). Speed of speech and persuasion. *Journal of Personality and Social Psychology, 34,* 615–624.

Miller, R. A. (1982). *Japan's modern myth: The language and beyond.* Tokyo: Weatherhill.

Mills, J., & Aronson, E. (1965). Opinion change as a function of the communicator's attractiveness and desire to influence. *Journal of Personality and Social Psychology, 1,* 73–77.

Mischel, W. (1968). *Personality and assessment.* New York: Wiley.

Mischel, W. (1979). On the interface of cognition and personality: Beyond the person-situation debate. *American Psychologist, 34,* 740–754.

Mitchell, G. (1975). What monkeys tell us about human violence. *The Futurist, 9,* 75–80.

Mitchell, G., & Maple, T. L. (1985). Dominance in nonhuman primates. In S. L. Ellyson & J. F. Dovidio (Eds.), *Power, dominance, and nonverbal behavior* (pp. 49–66). New York: Springer-Verlag.

Mobbs, N.A. (1969). Eye contact and introversion-extroversion. Cited in A. Kendon & M. Cook, The consistency of gaze patterns in social interaction. *British Journal of Psychology, 60,* 481–494.

Modigliani, A. (1971). Embarrassment, facework, and eye contact: Testing a theory of embarrassment. *Journal of Personality and Social Psychology, 17,* 15–24.

Moe, J. D. (1972). Listener judgments of status cues in speech: A replication and extension. *Speech Monographs, 39,* 144–147.

Molloy, J. T. (1975). *Dress for success.* New York: Warner.

Molloy, J. T. (1977). *The woman's dress for success book.* Chicago: Follett.

Mongeau, P. A. (1988, February). *Would I lie to you, honey? If I did, would you be able to tell? Deception detection accuracy in ongoing relationships.* Paper presented at the annual meeting of the Western Speech Communication Association, San Diego.

Montagu, A. (1971). *Touching: The human significance of the skin.* New York: Columbia University Press.

Montagu, A. (1978). *Touching: The human significance of the skin* (2d ed.). New York: Harper & Row.

Montagu, M. F. A. (1968). The new

litany of "innate depravity," or original sin revisited. In M. F. A. Montagu (Ed.), *Man and aggression* (pp. 3–17). New York: Oxford University Press.

Montepare, J. M., Goldstein, S. B., & Clausen, A. (1987). The identification of emotions from gait information. *Journal of Nonverbal Behavior, 11,* 33–42.

Montepare, J. M., & Zebrowitz-McArthur, L. (1987). Perceptions of adults and children with childlike voices in two cultures. *Journal of Experimental Social Psychology, 23,* 331–349.

Moore, H. A., & Porter, N. K. (1988). Leadership and nonverbal behaviors of hispanic females across school equity environments. *Psychology of Women Quarterly, 12,* 147–163.

Moore, H. T., & Gilliland, A. R. (1921). The measurement of aggressiveness. *Journal of Applied Psychology, 5,* 97–118.

Moore, W. E. (1939). Personality traits and voice quality deficiencies. *Journal of Speech and Hearing Disorders, 4,* 33–36.

Morency, N. L., & Krauss, R. M. (1982). Children's nonverbal encoding and decoding of affect. In R. S. Feldman (Ed.), *Development of nonverbal behavior in children* (pp. 181–199). New York: Springer-Verlag.

Morford, M., & Goldin-Meadow, S. (1992). Comprehension and production of gesture in combination with speech in one-word speakers. *Journal of Child Language, 19,* 559–580.

Morley, I. E., & Stephenson, G. M. (1969). Interpersonal and interparty exchange: A laboratory simulation of an industrial negotiation at the plant level. *British Journal of Psychology, 60,* 543–545.

Morris, D. (1967). *The naked ape.* New York: McGraw-Hill.

Morris, D. (1971). *Intimate behavior.* New York: Random House.

Morris, D. (1977). *Manwatching: A field guide to human behavior.* New York: Abrams.

Morris, D. (1985). *Bodywatching.* New York: Crown.

Morris, D. (1994). *Bodytalk: The meaning of human gestures.* New York: Crown.

Morris, D., Collett, P., Marsh, P., & O'Shaughnessy, M. (1979). *Gestures.* New York: Stein & Day.

Morsbach, H. (1973). Aspects of nonverbal communication in Japan. *Journal of Nervous and Mental Disease, 157,* 262–277.

Morton, T. L. (1974). *The effects of acquaintance and distance on intimacy and reciprocity.* Unpublished master's thesis, University of Utah, Salt Lake City.

Mosby, K. D. (1978). *An analysis of actual and ideal touching behavior as reported on a modified version of the body accessibility questionnaire.* Unpublished doctoral dissertation, Virginia Commonwealth University.

Motley, M. T. (1974). Acoustic correlates of lies. *Western Speech, 38,* 81–87.

Motley, M. T. (1986). Consciousness and intentionality in communication: A preliminary model and methodological approaches. *Western Journal of Speech Communication, 50,* 3–23.

Motley, M. T. (1990). On whether one can(not) communicate: An examination via traditional communication postulates. *Western Journal of Speech Communication, 54,* 1–20.

Motley, M. T. (1991). How one may not communicate: A reply to Andersen. *Communication Studies, 42,* 326–339.

Motley, M. T., Camden, C. T., & Baars, B. J. (1981). Toward verifying the assumptions of laboratory-induced slips of the tongue: The output-error and editing issues. *Human Communication Research, 8,* 3–15.

Moyer, D. M. (1975). The development of children's ability to recognize and express facially posed emotion. *Dissertation Abstracts International, 35,* 5622.

Mueser, K. T., Grau, B. W., Sussman, S., & Rosen, A. J. (1984). You're only as pretty as you feel: Facial expression as a determinant of physical attractiveness. *Journal of Personality and Social Psychology, 46,* 469–478.

Mulac, A. (1989). Men's and women's talk in same-gender and mixed-gender dyads: Power or polemic? *Journal of Language and Social Psychology, 8,* 249–270.

Mulac, A., Hanley, T. D., & Prigge, D. Y. (1974). Effects of phonological speech foreignness upon three dimensions of attitude of selected American speakers. *Quarterly Journal of Speech, 60,* 411–420.

Mulac, A., Studley, L. B., Wiemann, J. W., & Bradac, J. J. (1987). Male/

female gaze in same-sex and mixed-sex dyads: Gender-linked differences and mutual influence. *Human Communication Research, 13,* 323–344.

Murphy, L. B. (1937). *Social behavior and child personality.* New York: Columbia University Press.

Murray, D. C. (1971). Talk, silence and anxiety. *Psychological Bulletin, 75,* 244–260.

Murray, R. P., & McGinley, H. (1972). Looking as a measure of attraction. *Journal of Applied Social Psychology, 2,* 267–274.

Mysak, E. D. (1959). Pitch and duration characteristics of older males. *Journal of Speech and Hearing Research, 2,* 46–54.

Nadler, A., Shapira, R., & Ben-Itzhak, S. (1982). Good looks may help: Effects of helper's physical attractiveness and sex of helper on males' and females' help-seeking behavior. *Journal of Personality and Social Psychology, 42,* 90–99.

Natale, M. (1975). Convergence of mean vocal intensity in dyadic communication as a function of social desirability. *Journal of Personality and Social Psychology, 32,* 790–804.

Natale, M., Entin, E., & Jaffe, J. (1979). Vocal interruptions in dyadic communication as a function of speech and social anxiety. *Journal of Personality and Social Psychology, 37,* 865–878.

Navarre, D. (1982). Posture sharing in dyadic interaction. *American Journal of Dance Therapy, 5,* 28–42.

Neal, A., & Wilson, M. L. (1989). The role of skin color and features in the black community: Implications for black women and therapy. *Clinical Psychology Review, 9,* 323–333.

Nerbonne, G. P. (1967). *The identification of speaker characteristics on the basis of aural cues.* Unpublished doctoral dissertation, Michigan State University, East Lansing.

Nesbitt, P. D., & Steven, G. (1974). Personal space and stimulus intensity at a southern California amusement park. *Sociometry, 37,* 105–115.

Neufeld, R. W. J. (1975). A multidimensional scaling analysis of schizophrenics' and normals' perceptions of verbal similarity. *Journal of Abnormal Psychology, 84,* 498–507.

Neufeld, R. W. J. (1976). Simultaneous processing of multiple stimulus dimensions among paranoid and nonparanoid schizophrenics. *Multivariate Behavioral Research, 11,* 425–441.

Newman, H. M. (1982). The sounds of silence in communicative encounters. *Communication Quarterly, 30,* 142–149.

Newman, O. (1972). *Defensible space: Crime prevention through urban design.* New York: Collier.

Newton, D. A., & Burgoon, J. K. (1990). Nonverbal conflict behaviors: Functions, strategies, and tactics. In D. A. Cahn (Ed.), *Intimates in conflict: A communication perspective* (pp. 77–104). Hillsdale, NJ: Erlbaum.

Newtson, D. A. (1973). Attribution and the unit of perception of ongoing behavior. *Journal of Personality and Social Psychology, 28,* 28–38.

Newtson, D. A., & Engquist, G. (1976). The perceptual organization of ongoing behavior. *Journal of Experimental Social Psychology, 12,* 436–450.

Newtson, D. A., Engquist, G., & Bois, J. (1977). The objective basis of behavior units. *Journal of Personality and Social Psychology, 35,* 847–862.

Nguyen, M. L., Heslin, R., & Nguyen, T. D. (1976). The meaning of touch: Sex and marital status differences. *Representative Research in Social Psychology, 7,* 13–18.

Nguyen, T., Heslin, R., & Nguyen, M. L. (1975). The meaning of touch: Sex differences. *Journal of Communication, 25* (3), 92–103.

Nikodym, N., & Simonetti, J. L. (1987). Personal appearance: Is attractiveness a factor in organizational survival and success? *Journal of Employment Counseling, 24,* 69–78.

Nisbett, R., & Ross, L. (1980). *Human inference: Strategies and shortcomings of social judgment.* Englewood Cliffs, NJ: Prentice-Hall.

Noesjirwan, J. (1978). A laboratory study of proxemic patterns of Indonesians and Australians. *British Journal of Social and Clinical Psychology, 17,* 333–334.

Nolan, M. J. (1975). The relationship between verbal and nonverbal communication. In G. J. Hanneman & W. J. McEwen (Eds.), *Communication and behavior* (pp. 98–118). Reading, MA: Addison-Wesley.

Noller, P. (1980a). Gaze in married couples. *Journal of Nonverbal Behavior, 5,* 115–129.

Noller, P. (1980b). Misunderstandings in marital communication: A study of couples' nonverbal communication. *Journal of Personality and Social Psychology, 39,* 1135–1148.

Noller, P. (1984). *Nonverbal communication and marital interaction.* Oxford, U.K.: Pergamon.

Noller, P. (1985). Video primacy—a further look. *Journal of Nonverbal Behavior, 9,* 28–47.

Noller, P. (1993). Gender and emotional communication in marriage: Different cultures or different social power? *Journal of Language and Social Psychology, 12,* 92–112.

Norman, R. (1976). When what is said is important: A comparison of expert and attractive sources. *Journal of Experimental Social Psychology, 12,* 294–300.

Norton, R. (1983). *Communicator style: Theory, applications, and measures.* Newbury Park, CA: Sage.

Norum, G. A., Russo, N. J., & Sommer, R. (1967). Seating patterns and group tasks. *Psychology in the Schools, 4,* 276–280.

Norwood, P. E. (1979). *The effects of personality, sex and race variables on touching behavior.* Unpublished doctoral dissertation, Virginia Commonwealth University.

Nowicki, S., & Duke, M. P. (1994). Individual differences in the nonverbal communication of affect: The diagnostic analysis of nonverbal accuracy scale. *Journal of Nonverbal Behavior, 18,* 9–35.

Nussbaum, J. F., Thompson, T., & Robinson, J. D. (1989). *Communication and aging.* New York: Harper & Row.

Octigan, M., & Niederman, S. (1979). Male dominance in conversation. *Frontiers, 4,* 50–54.

Odom, R. D., & Lemond, C. M. (1972). Developmental differences in the perception and production of facial expressions. *Child Development, 43,* 359–369.

O'Hair, D., Allman, J., & Gibson, L. A. (1991). Nonverbal communication and aging. *Southern Communication Journal, 56,* 147–160.

O'Hair, D., Cody, M. J., Wang, X., & Chao, E. Y. (1990). Vocal stress and deception detection among Chinese. *Communication Quarterly, 38,* 158–169.

O'Hair, D., Friedrich, G. W., Wiemann, J. M., & Wiemann, M. O. (1995). *Competent communication.* New York: St. Martin's Press.

O'Hair, H. D., Cody, M. J., & McLaughlin, M. L. (1981). Prepared lies, spontaneous lies, Machiavellianism, and nonverbal communication. *Human Communication Research, 7,* 325–340.

O'Keefe, B. J., & Delia, J. G. (1982). Impression formation and message production. In M. E. Roloff & C. R. Berger (Eds.), *Social cognition and communication* (pp. 33–72). Beverly Hills, CA: Sage.

O'Leary, M. J., & Gallois, C. (1985). The last ten turns: Behavior and sequencing in friends' and strangers' conversational findings. *Journal of Nonverbal Behavior, 9,* 8–27.

Olsen, R. (1978). *The effect of the hospital environment.* Unpublished doctoral dissertation, City University of New York.

Olson, J. M., Roese, N. J., & Zanna, M. P. (in press). Expectancies. In E. T. Higgins & A. W. Kruglanski (Eds.), *Social psychology: Handbook of basic principles.* New York: Guilford.

O'Neal, G. S., & Lapitsky, M. (1991). Effects of clothing as nonverbal communication on credibility of the message source. *Clothing and Textiles Research Journal, 9*(3), 28–34.

Oregon Project Dayshoot Photographs (1984). *One average day.* U.S.A.: Western Imprints Press of the Oregon Historical Society.

Orr, D. B. (1968). Time compressed speech—a perspective. *Journal of Communication, 18,* 288–292.

Ortony, A. (1978). Remembering, understanding, and representation. *Cognitive Science, 2,* 53–69.

Osmond, H. (1957). Function as the basis of psychiatric ward design. *Mental Hospitals, 8,* 23–32.

Oster, H., & Ekman, P. (1978). Facial behavior in child development. In W. A. Collins (Ed.), *Minnesota symposia on child psychology* (pp. 231–276). Hillsdale, NJ: Erlbaum.

O'Sullivan, M. (1983). Measuring individual differences. In J. Wiemann & R. P. Harrison (Eds.), *Nonverbal interaction* (pp. 243–270). Beverly Hills, CA: Sage.

Packwood, W. T. (1974). Loudness as a variable in persuasion. *Journal of Counseling Psychology, 21,* 1–2.

Paivio, A. (1971). *Imagery and verbal processes.* New York: Holt, Rinehart and Winston.

Pallak, S. R. (1983). Salience of a communicator's physical attractiveness and persuasion: A heuristic versus systematic processing interpretation. *Social Cognition, 2,* 158–170.

Pallak, S. R., Murroni, E., & Koch, J. (1983). Communicator attractiveness and expertise, emotional versus rational appeals, and persuasion: A heuristic versus systematic processing interpretation. *Social Cognition, 2,* 122–141.

Palmer, M. T., & Simmons, K. B. (1993, November). *Interpersonal intentions, nonverbal behaviors and judgments of liking: Encoding, decoding, and consciousness.* Paper presented at the annual meeting of the Speech Communication Association, Miami.

Parham, I. A., Feldman, R. S., Oster, G. D., & Popoola, O. (1981). Intergenerational differences in nonverbal disclosure of deception. *Journal of Social Psychology, 113,* 261–269.

Parke, R. D., & Swain, D. B. (1979). Children's privacy in the home: Developmental, ecological, and child-rearing determinants. *Environment and Behavior, 11,* 87–104.

Parks, R., & Burgess, E. (1924). *Introduction to the science of sociology.* Chicago: University of Chicago Press.

Parrott, R., & Le Poire, B. (1988, February). *The pediatrician's voice: Impact on the pediatrician-parent relationship.* Paper presented at the annual meeting of the Western Speech Communication Association, San Diego.

Parsons, C. K., & Liden, R. C. (1984). Interviewer perceptions of applicant qualifications: A multivariate field study of demographic characteristics and nonverbal cues. *Journal of Applied Psychology, 69,* 557–568.

Pastalan, L. A. (1970). Privacy as an expression of human territoriality. In L. A. Pastalan & D. H. Carson (Eds.), *Spatial behavior of older people* (pp. 88–101). Ann Arbor: University of Michigan Press.

Patterson, A. H. (1978). Territorial behavior and fear of crime in the elderly. *Environmental Psychology and Nonverbal Behavior, 2,* 131–144.

Patterson, M. L. (1973a). Compensation in nonverbal immediacy behaviors: A review. *Sociometry, 36,* 237–252.

Patterson, M. L. (1973b). Stability of nonverbal immediacy behaviors. *Journal of Experimental Social Psychology, 9,* 97–109.

Patterson, M. L. (1976). An arousal model of interpersonal intimacy. *Psychological Review, 83,* 235–245.

Patterson, M. L. (1977). Interpersonal distance, affect, and equilibrium theory. *Journal of Social Psychology, 101,* 205–214.

Patterson, M. L. (1983). *Nonverbal behavior: A functional perspective.* New York: Springer-Verlag.

Patterson, M. L. (1985). Social influences and nonverbal exchange. In S. L. Ellyson & J. F. Dovidio (Eds.), *Power, dominance, and nonverbal behavior* (pp. 207–217). New York: Springer-Verlag.

Patterson, M. L. (1987). Presentational and affect-management functions of nonverbal involvement. *Journal of Nonverbal Behavior, 11,* 110–122.

Patterson, M. L. (1990). Functions of non-verbal behavior in social interaction. In H. Giles & W. P. Robinson (Eds.), *Handbook of language and social psychology* (pp. 101–120). Chichester: Wiley.

Patterson, M. L. (1991). A functional approach to nonverbal exchange. In R. S. Feldman & B. Rimé (Eds.), *Fundamentals of nonverbal behavior* (pp. 458–495). Cambridge: Cambridge University Press.

Patterson, M. L. (1995). A parallel process model of nonverbal communication. *Journal of Nonverbal Behavior, 19,* 3–29.

Patterson, M. L., Jordan, A., Hogan, M. B., & Frerker, D. (1981). Effects of nonverbal intimacy on arousal and behavioral adjustment. *Journal of Nonverbal Behavior, 5,* 184–198.

Patterson, M. L., Mullens, S., & Romano, J. (1971). Compensatory reactions to spatial intrusion. *Sociometry, 34,* 114–121.

Patterson, M. L., Powell, J. L., & Lenihan, M. G. (1986). Touch, compliance and interpersonal affect. *Journal of Nonverbal Behavior, 10,* 41–50.

Patterson, M. L., & Schaeffer, R. E. (1977). Effects of size and sex composition on interaction distance, participation, and satisfaction in small groups. *Small Group Behavior, 8,* 433–442.

Patterson, M. L., & Sechrest, L. B. (1970). Interpersonal distance and impression formation. *Journal of Personality, 38,* 161–166.

Paulsell, S., & Goldman, M. (1984). The effect of touching different body areas on prosocial behavior. *Journal of Social Psychology, 122,* 269–273.

Paulus, P. B., Annis, A. B., Seta, J. J., Schkade, J. K., & Matthews, R. W. (1976). Density does affect task performance. *Journal of Personality and Social Psychology, 34,* 248–253.

Paunonen, S. V., Jackson, D. N., & Keinonen, M. (1990). The structured nonverbal assessment of personality. *Journal of Personality, 58,* 481–502.

Pear, T. H. (1931). *Voice and personality.* London: Chapman and Hall.

Pearce, W. B. (1971). The effect of vocal cues on credibility and attitude change. *Western Speech, 35,* 176–184.

Pearce, W. B. (1976). The coordinated management of meaning: A rules-based theory of interpersonal communication. In G. R. Miller (Ed.), *Explorations in interpersonal communication* (pp. 17–36). Beverly Hills, CA: Sage.

Pearce, W. B., & Brommel, B. J. (1972). Vocalic communication in persuasion. *Quarterly Journal of Speech, 58,* 298–306.

Pearce, W. B., & Conklin, F. (1971). Nonverbal vocalic communication and perception of a speaker. *Speech Monographs, 38,* 235–241.

Pedersen, D. M. (1973). Developmental trends in personal space. *Journal of Psychology, 83,* 3–9.

Pei, M. (1965). *The story of language* (2d ed.). Philadelphia: Lippincott.

Pellegrini, R. J. (1973). The virtue of hairiness. *Psychology Today, 6,* 14.

Pellegrini, R. J. (1989). Beardedness as a stimulus variable: Note on methodology and meta-analysis of impression-formation data. *Perceptual and Motor Skills, 69,* 161–162.

Pellegrini, R. J., & Empey, J. (1970). Interpersonal spatial orientation in dyads. *Journal of Psychology, 76,* 67–70.

Pellegrini, R. J., Schauss, A. G., & Miller, M. E. (1978). Room color and aggression in a criminal detention holding cell: A test of the "tranquilizing pink" hypothesis. *Journal of Orthomolecular Psychiatry, 10,* 174–181.

Pendleton, K. L., & Snyder, S. S. (1982). Young children's perceptions of nonverbally expressed "preference": The effects of nonverbal cue, viewer age, and sex of viewer. *Journal of Nonverbal Behavior, 6,* 220–237.

Pendry, L. F., & Macrae, C. N. (1994). Stereotypes and mental life: The case of the motivated but thwarted tactician. *Journal of Experimental Social Psychology, 30,* 303–325.

Perdue, V. P., & Connor, J. M. (1978). Patterns of touching between preschool children and male and female teachers. *Child Development, 49,* 1258–1262.

Perlmutter, K. B., Paddock, J. R., & Duke, M. P. (1985). The role of verbal, vocal, and nonverbal cues in the communication of evoking message styles. *Journal of Research in Personality, 19,* 31–43.

Peterson, K., & Curran, J. C. (1976). Trait attribution as a function of hair length and correlates of subjects' preferences for hair style. *Journal of Psychology, 93,* 331–339.

Peterson, P. (1976). An investigation of sex differences in regard to nonverbal body gestures. In B. Eakins, G. Eakins, & B. Lieb-Brilhard (Eds.), *Siscom '75: Women's (and men's) communication* (pp. 20–27). Falls Church, VA: Speech Communication Association.

Petitto, L. A., & Marentette, P. F. (1991). Babbling in the manual mode: Evidence for the ontogeny of language. *Science, 251,* 1493–1496.

Petty, R. E., Wells, G. L., Heesacker, M., Brock, T. C., & Cacioppo, J. T. (1983). The effects of recipient posture on persuasion: A cognitive response analysis. *Personality and Social Psychology Bulletin, 9,* 209–222.

Pfungst, O. (1911). *Clever Hans (the horse of Mr. von Osten): A contribution to experimental, animal, and human psychology.* New York: Holt, Rinehart and Winston.

Philpott, J. S. (1983). *The relative contribution to meaning of verbal and nonverbal channels of communication: A meta-analysis.* Unpublished master's thesis, University of Nebraska.

Piaget, J. (1965). *The moral judgment of the child.* New York: The Free Press.

Piaget, J. (1981). Time perception in children. In J. T. Fraser, *The voices of time* (2d ed., pp. 202–216). Amherst: University of Massachusetts Press.

Pike, G. R., & Sillars, A. L. (1985). Reciprocity of marital communication. *Journal of Social and Personal Relationships, 2,* 303–324.

Pinaire-Reed, J. A. (1979). Interpersonal attraction: Fashionability and perceived similarity. *Perceptual and Motor Skills, 48,* 571–576.

Pisano, M. D., Wall, S. M., & Foster, A. (1986). Perceptions of nonreciprocal touch in romantic relationships. *Journal of Nonverbal Behavior, 10,* 29–40.

Pitcairn, T. K., & Eibl-Eibesfeldt, I. (1976). Concerning the evolution of nonverbal communication in man. In M. E. Hahn & E. C. Simmel (Eds.), *Communicative behavior and evolution* (pp. 81–113). New York: Academic.

Pittam, J., & Scherer, K. R. (1993). Vocal expression and communication of emotion. In M. Lewis & J. M. Haviland (Eds.). *Handbook of emotions* (pp. 185–197). New York: Guilford.

Pittenger, R. E., Hockett, C. F., & Danehy, J. J. (1960). *The first five minutes.* Ithaca, NY: Martineau.

Planalp, S., & Tracy, K. (1980). Not to change the topic but . . . : A cognitive approach to the management of conversation. In D. Nimmo (Ed.), *Communication yearbook 4* (pp. 237–258). New Brunswick, NJ: Transaction.

Plax, T. G., Kearney, P., McCroskey, J. C., & Richmond, V. P. (1986). Power in the classroom VI: Verbal control strategies, nonverbal immediacy, and affective learning. *Communication Education, 35,* 43–55.

Plazewski, J. G., & Allen, V. L. (1985). The effect of verbal content on children's encoding of paralinguistic affect. *Journal of Nonverbal Behavior, 9,* 147–159.

Plutchik, R. (1962). *The emotions: Facts, theories, and a new model.* New York: Random House.

Plutchik, R. (1980). *Emotion: A psycho-evolutionary synthesis.* New York: Harper & Row.

Poling, T. H. (1978). Sex differences, dominance, and physical attractiveness in the use of nonverbal emblems. *Psychological Reports, 43,* 1087–1092.

Porteous, C. W. (1972). *Learning as a function of molar environmental complexity.* Unpublished master's thesis, University of Victoria, British Columbia.

Porter, C. P. (1991). Social reasons for skin tone preferences of black school-age children. *American Journal of Orthopsychiatry, 61,* 149–154.

Porter, R. H., Cernoch, J. M., & Balogh, R. D. (1985). Odor signatures and kin recognition. *Physiology and Behavior, 34,* 445–448.

Porter, R. H., Cernoch, J. M., & McLaughlin, F. J. (1983). Maternal recognition of neonates through olfactory cues. *Physiology and Behavior, 30,* 151–154.

Porter, R. H., Matochik, J. A., & Makin, J. W. (1983). The role of familiarity in the development of social preferences in spiny mice. *Behavioural Processes, 9,* 241–254.

Porter, R. H., & Moore, J. D. (1981). Human kin recognition by olfactory cues. *Physiology and Behavior, 27,* 493–495.

Posner, M. I., Nissen, M. J., & Klein, R. M. (1976). Visual dominance: An information-processing account of its origins and significance. *Psychological Review, 83,* 157–171.

Powell, R. G., & Harville, B. (1990). The effects of teacher immediacy and clarity on instructional outcomes: An intercultural assessment. *Communication Education, 39,* 341–353.

Poyatos, F. (1983). *New perspectives in nonverbal communication.* New York: Pergamon.

Poyatos, F. (1984). Linguistic fluency and verbal-nonverbal cultural fluency. In A. Wolfgang (Ed.), *Nonverbal behavior: Perspectives, applications, intercultural insights* (pp. 431–459). Lewiston, NY: Hogrefe.

Poyatos, F. (1991). Parlinguistic qualifiers: Our many voices. *Language and Communication, 11,* 181–195.

Poyatos, F. (1992). Audible-visual approach to speech. In F. Poyatos (Ed.), *Advances in nonverbal communication* (pp. 41–57). Amsterdam: Johns Benjamins.

Poyatos, F. (1993). *Paralanguage: A linguistic and interdisciplinary approach to interactive speech and sounds.* Amsterdam: Johns Benjamins.

Prescott, J. W. (1975). Body pleasure and the origins of violence. *Futurist, 9,* 64–74.

Priest, R. F., & Sawyer, J. (1967). Proximity and peership: Bases of balance in interpersonal attraction. *American Journal of Sociology, 72,* 633–649.

Proshansky, H. M., & Altman, I. (1979). Overview of the field. In W. P. White (Ed.), *Resources in environment and behavior* (pp. 3–36). Washington, DC: American Psychological Association.

Proshansky, H. M., Ittelson, W. H., & Rivlin, L. G. (1970). Freedom of choice and behavior in a physical setting. In H. M. Proshansky, W. H. Ittelson, & L. G. Rivlin (Eds.), *Environmental psychology: Man and his physical setting* (pp. 173–183). New York: Holt, Rinehart and Winston.

Prosser, M. H. (1978). *The cultural dialogue: An introduction to intercultural communication.* Boston: Houghton Mifflin.

Public Broadcasting System [Broadcast] (1984). Signs and signals: The discovery of animal behavior. *Nature,* January 22, 1984.

Purcell, A. T. (1986). Environmental perception and affect: A schema discrepancy model. *Environment and Behavior, 18,* 3–30.

Putman, W. B., & Street, R. L. (1984). The conception and perception of non-content speech performance: Implications for speech-accommodation theory. *International Journal of the Sociology of Language, 46,* 97–114.

Quattrone, G. A. (1982). Overattribution and unit formation: When behavior engulfs the person. *Journal of Personality and Social Psychology, 42,* 593–607.

Raines, R. S., Hechtman, S. B., & Rosenthal, R. (1990a). Nonverbal behavior and gender as determinants of physical attractiveness. *Journal of Nonverbal Behavior, 14,* 253–267.

Raines, R. S., Hechtman, S. B., & Rosenthal, R. (1990b). Physical attractiveness of face and voice: Effects of positivity, dominance, and sex. *Journal of Applied Social Psychology, 20,* 1558–1578.

Ramsey, S. J. (1976). Prison codes. *Journal of Communication, 26,* 39–45.

Ramsey, S. J. (1981). The kinesics of femininity in Japanese women. *Language Sciences, 3,* 104–123.

Ramsey, S. J. (1983, May). *Double vision: Nonverbal behavior East and West.* Paper presented at the Second International Conference on Nonverbal Behavior, Toronto.

Ramsey, S. J., & Birk, J. (1983). Training North Americans for interaction with Japanese: Considerations of language and communication style. In R. Brislin & D. Landis (Eds.), *The handbook of intercultural training: Vol. III. Area studies in intercultural training* (pp. 227–259). New York: Pergamon.

Rapoport, A. (1982). *The meaning of the built environment: A nonverbal communication approach.* Beverly Hills, CA: Sage.

Rapoport, A. (1990). *The meaning of the built environment: A nonverbal communication approach.* Tucson: University of Arizona.

Ray, G. B. (1986). Vocally cued personality prototypes: An implicit personality theory. *Communication Monographs, 53,* 266–276.

Raymond, B. J., & Unger, R. K. (1972). The apparel oft proclaims the man: Cooperation with deviant and conventional youths. *Journal of Social Psychology, 87,* 75–82.

Reade, M. N., & Smouse, A. D. (1980). Effect of inconsistent verbal-nonverbal communication and counselor response mode on client estimate of counselor regard and effectiveness. *Journal of Counseling Psychology, 27,* 546–553.

Reece, M. M., & Whitman, R. N. (1961). Warmth and expressive movements. *Psychological Reports, 8,* 76.

Reece, M. M., & Whitman, R. N. (1962). Expressive movements, warmth, and verbal reinforcement. *Journal of Abnormal and Social Psychology, 64,* 234–236.

Reed, C. (1981). *The impact of consistent-inconsistent combinations of visual and verbal cues on communication of empathy and genuineness in the therapeutic situation.* Unpublished doctoral dissertation. Texas Tech University, Lubbock.

Reed, S. K. (1982). *Cognition: Theory and applications.* Monterey, CA: Brooks/Cole.

Reifman, A. S., Larrick, R. P., & Fein, S. (1991). Temper and temperature on the diamond: The heat-aggression relationship in major league baseball. *Personality and Social Psychology Bulletin, 17,* 580–585.

Reilly, S. S., & Muzekari, L. H. (1979). Responses of normal and disturbed adults and children to mixed messages. *Journal of Abnormal Psychology, 88,* 203–208.

Reinert, J. (1971). What your sense of time tells you. *Science Digest, 69,* 8–12.

Reis, H. T., Wilson, I. M., Monestere, C., Bernstein, S., Clark, K., Seidl, E., Franco, M., Gioioso, E., Freeman, L., & Radoane, K. (1990). What is smiling is beautiful and good. *European Journal of Social Psychology, 20,* 259–267.

Reiss, M., & Rosenfeld, P. (1980). Seating preferences as nonverbal communication: A self-presentational analysis.

Journal of Applied Communications Research, 8, 22–30.

Reizenstein, J. E. (1982). Hospital design and human behavior: A review of the recent literature. In A. Baum & J. E. Singer (Eds.), *Advances in environmental psychology: Environment and health* (Vol. 4, pp. 137–169). Hillsdale, NJ: Erlbaum.

Remland, M. S., & Jones, T. S. (1989). The effects of nonverbal involvement and communication apprehension on state anxiety, interpersonal attraction, and speech duration. *Communication Quarterly, 37,* 170–183.

Remland, M. S., Jones, T. S., & Brinkman, H. (1991). Proxemic and haptic behavior in three European countries. *Journal of Nonverbal Behavior, 15,* 215–232.

Restak, R. M. (1979). *The brain: The last frontier.* Garden City, NY: Anchor/Doubleday.

Ricci Bitti, P. E. (1993). Facial and manual components of Italian symbolic gestures. In F. Poyatos (Ed.), *Advances in non-verbal communication: Sociocultural, clinical, esthetic, and literary perspectives* (pp. 187–196). Amsterdam: Benjamins.

Ricci Bitti, P. E., & Poggi, I. (1991). Symbolic nonverbal behavior: Talking through gestures. In R. S. Feldman & B. Rimé (Eds.), *Fundamentals of nonverbal communication* (pp. 433–457). Cambridge: Cambridge University Press.

Richmond, V. P., Gorham, J. S., & McCroskey, J. C. (1986). The relationships between selected immediacy behavior and cognitive learning. In M. McLaughlin (Ed.). *Communication Yearbook 10* (pp. 574–590). Beverly Hills CA: Sage.

Richmond, V. P., McCroskey, J. C., Kearney, P., & Plax, T. (1985, November). *Power in the classroom VII: Linking behavior alteration techniques to cognitive learning.* Paper presented at the annual meeting of the Speech Communication Association, Denver.

Richmond, V. P., McCroskey, J. C., & Payne, S. K. (1987). *Nonverbal behavior in interpersonal relations.* Englewood Cliffs, NJ: Prentice-Hall.

Ridgeway, C. L., Berger, J., & Smith, L. (1985). Nonverbal cues and status: An expectation states approach. *American Journal of Sociology, 90,* 955–978.

Riggio, R. E. (1986). Assessment of basic social skills. *Journal of Personality and Social Psychology, 51,* 649–660.

Riggio, R. E. (1992). Social interaction skills and nonverbal behavior. In R. S. Feldman (Ed.), *Applications of nonverbal behavioral theories and research* (pp. 3–30). Hillsdale, NJ: Erlbaum.

Riggio, R. E., & Friedman, H. S. (1982). The interrelationships of self-monitoring factors, personality traits, and nonverbal skills. *Journal of Nonverbal Behavior, 7,* 33–45.

Riggio, R. E., & Friedman, H. S. (1983). Individual differences and cues to deception. *Journal of Personality and Social Psychology, 45,* 899–915.

Riggio, R. E., & Friedman, H. S. (1986). Impression formation: The role of expressive behavior. *Journal of Personality and Social Psychology, 50,* 421–427.

Riggio, R. E., Friedman, H. S., & DiMatteo, M. R. (1981). Nonverbal greetings: Effects of the situation and personality. *Personality and Social Psychology Bulletin, 7,* 682–689.

Riggio, R. E., Messamer, J., & Throckmorton, B. (1991). Social and academic intelligence: Conceptually distinct but overlapping constructs. *Personality and Individual Differences, 12,* 695–702.

Riggio, R. E., Throckmorton, B., & DePaola, S. (1990). Social skills and self-esteem. *Personality and Individual Differences, 11,* 799–804.

Riggio, R. E., Tucker, J., & Throckmorton, D. (1987). Social skills and deception ability. *Personality and Social Psychology Bulletin, 13,* 568–577.

Riggio, R. E., Tucker, J., & Widaman, K. F. (1987). Verbal and nonverbal cues as mediators of deception ability. *Journal of Nonverbal Behavior, 11,* 126–145.

Riggio, R. E., Watring, K., & Throckmorton, B. (1993). Social skills, social support, and psychosocial adjustment. *Personality and Individual Differences, 15,* 275–280.

Riggio, R., Widaman, K., & Friedman, H. S. (1985). Actual and perceived emotional sending and personality correlates. *Journal of Nonverbal Behavior, 9,* 69–83.

Riggio, R., Widaman, K. F., Tucker, J. S., & Salinas, L. (1991). Beauty is more than skin deep: Components of attractiveness. *Basic and Applied Social Psychology, 12,* 423–429.

Rimé, B., & Schiaratura, L. (1991). Gesture and speech. In R. S. Feldman & B. Rimé (Eds.), *Fundamentals of nonverbal behavior* (pp. 239–281). Cambridge: Cambridge University Press.

Rinn, W. E. (1984). The neuropsychology of facial expression: A review of the neurological and psychological mechanisms for producing facial expressions. *Psychological Bulletin, 95*(1), 52–77.

Rinn, W. E. (1991). Neuropsychology of facial expression. In R. S. Feldman & B. Rimé (Eds.), *Fundamentals of nonverbal communication* (pp. 3–30). Cambridge: Cambridge University Press.

Riseborough, M. G. (1981). Physiographic gestures as decoding facilitators: Three experiments exploring a neglected facet of communication. *Journal of Nonverbal Behavior, 5,* 172–183.

Ritts, V., Patterson, M. L., & Tubbs, M. E. (1992). Expectations, impressions, and judgments of physically attractive students: A review. *Review of Educational Research, 62,* 413–426.

Rivlin, L. G., & Rothenberg, M. (1976). The use of space in open classrooms. In H. M. Proshansky, W. H. Ittelson, & L. G. Rivlin (Eds.), *Environmental psychology: People and their physical settings* (2d ed.) (pp. 479–490). New York: Holt, Rinehart and Winston.

Roberts, M. (1987, June). No language but a cry. *Psychology Today, 21,* 57–58.

Robson, K. S. (1967). The role of eye-to-eye contact in maternal-infant attachment. *Journal of Child Psychology and Psychiatry, 8,* 13–25.

Rodin, J., Solomon, S. K., & Metcalf, J. (1978). Role of control in mediating perceptions of density. *Journal of Personality and Social Psychology, 36,* 988–999.

Roedell, W. C., & Slaby, R. G. (1977). The role of distal and proximal interaction in infant social preference formation. *Developmental Psychology, 13,* 266–273.

Rogers, W. T. (1978). The contribution of kinesic illustrators toward the comprehension of verbal behavior within utterances. *Human Communication Research, 5,* 54–62.

Rohles, F. H. (1967, June). Environmental psychology: A bucket of worms. *Psychology Today, 1,* 55–63.

Rohles, F. H. (1971). Thermal sensations of sedentary man in moderate temperatures. *Human Factors, 13,* 553–560.

Roll, S. A., Crowley, M. A., & Rappl, L. E. (1985). Client perceptions of counselors' nonverbal behavior: A reevaluation. *Counselor Education and Supervision, 24,* 234–243.

Roloff, M. E. (1987). Communication and reciprocity within intimate relationships. In M. E. Roloff & G. R. Miller (Eds.), *Interpersonal processes: New directions in communication research* (pp. 11–38). Newbury Park, CA: Sage.

Roloff, M. E., & Berger, C. R. (1982). Social cognition and communication: An introduction. In M. E. Roloff & C. R. Berger (Eds.), *Social cognition and communication* (pp. 9–32). Beverly Hills, CA: Sage.

Roloff, M. E., Janiszewski, C. A., McGrath, M. A., Burns, C. S., & Manrai, L. A. (1988). Acquiring resources from intimates: When obligation substitutes for persuasion. *Human Communication Research, 14,* 364–396.

Roloff, M. E., & Miller, G. R. (1980). *Persuasion: New directions in theory and research.* Beverly Hills, CA: Sage.

Rom, A. (1979). *Comparison of nonverbal and verbal communicative skills of language impaired and normal speaking children.* Unpublished doctoral dissertation, Wayne State University.

Romano, J. M., & Bellack, A. S. (1980). Social validation of a component model of assertive behavior. *Journal of Consulting and Clinical Psychology, 48,* 473–490.

Roos, P. D. (1968). Jurisdiction: An ecological concept. *Human Relations, 21,* 75–84.

Rosa, E., & Mazur, A. (1979). Incipient status in small groups. *Social Forces, 58,* 18–37.

Rosekrans, R. L. (1955). Do gestures speak louder than words? *Collier's, 135,* 56–57.

Roseman, I. (1984). Cognitive determinants of emotions: A structural theory. In P. Shaver (Ed.), *Review of personality and social psychology: Vol. 5. Emotions, relationships, and health* (pp. 11–36). Beverly Hills CA: Sage.

Rosenberg, S. W., Bohan, L., McCafferty, P., & Harris, K. (1986). The image and the vote: The effect of candidate presentation on voter preference. *American Journal of Political Sciences, 30,* 108–126.

Rosenberg, S. W., Kahn, S., & Tran, T. (1991). Creating a political image: Shaping appearance and manipulating the vote. *Political Behavior, 13,* 345–367.

Rosencranz, M. L. (1962). Clothing symbolism. *Journal of Home Economics, 54,* 18–22.

Rosencranz, M. L. (1965). Sociological and psychological approaches to clothing research. *Journal of Home Economics, 57,* 26–29.

Rosenfeld, H. M. (1965). Effect of approval-seeking induction on interpersonal proximity. *Psychological Reports, 17,* 120–122.

Rosenfeld, H. M. (1966a). Approval-seeking and approval-inducing functions of verbal and nonverbal responses in the dyad. *Journal of Personality and Social Psychology, 4,* 597–605.

Rosenfeld, H. M. (1966b). Instrumental affiliative functions of facial and gestural expressions. *Journal of Personality and Social Psychology, 4,* 65–72.

Rosenfeld, H. M. (1978). Conversational control functions of nonverbal behavior. In A. W. Siegman & S. Feldstein (Eds.), *Nonverbal behavior and communication* (pp. 291–328). Hillsdale, NJ: Erlbaum.

Rosenfeld, L. B., & Civikly, J. M. (1976). *With words unspoken: The nonverbal experience.* New York: Holt, Rinehart and Winston.

Rosenfeld, L. B., Kartus, S., & Ray, C. (1976). Body accessibility revisited. *Journal of Communication, 26* (3), 27–30.

Rosenfeld, L. B., & Plax, T. G. (1977). Clothing as communication. *Journal of Communication, 27,* 24–31.

Rosenthal, R. (1973). The mediation of Pygmalion effects: A four-factor "theory." *Papua New Guinea Journal of Education, 9,* 1–12.

Rosenthal, R. (1976). *Experimenter effects in behavioral research* (enlarged ed.). New York: Irvington.

Rosenthal, R. (1981). Pavlov's mice, Pfungst's horse, and Pygmalion's PONS: Some models for the study of interpersonal expectancy effects. In T. A. Sebeok & R. Rosenthal (Eds.), *The Clever Hans phenomenon: Communication with horses, whales, apes, and people* (pp. 182–198). New York: Annals of the New York Academy of Sciences.

Rosenthal, R. (1985). Nonverbal cues in the mediation of interpersonal expectancy effects. In R. L. Street, Jr., & J. N. Cappella (Eds.), *Sequence and pattern in communicative behavior* (pp. 85–102). London: Arnold.

Rosenthal, R. (1993). Interpersonal expectations: Some antecedents and some consequences. In P. D. Blanck (Ed.), *Interpersonal expectations: Theory, research, and applications* (pp. 3–24). Paris: Cambridge University Press.

Rosenthal, R., & DePaulo, B. M. (1979a). Expectancies, discrepancies, and courtesies in nonverbal communication. *Western Journal of Speech Communication, 43,* 76–95.

Rosenthal, R., & DePaulo, B. M. (1979b). Sex differences in accommodation in nonverbal communication. In R. Rosenthal (Ed.), *Skill in nonverbal communication: Individual differences* (pp. 68–103). Cambridge, MA: Oelgeschlager, Gunn & Hain.

Rosenthal, R., Hall, J. A., DiMatteo, M. R., Rogers, P. L., & Archer, D. (1979). *Sensitivity to nonverbal communication: The PONS test.* Baltimore: Johns Hopkins University Press.

Rosenthal, R., & Jacobson, L. (1968). *Pygmalion in the classroom: Teacher expectation and pupils' intellectual development.* New York: Holt, Rinehart and Winston.

Rosenwasser, S. M., Adams, V., & Tansil, K. (1983). Visual attention as a function of sex and apparel of stimulus object: Who looks at whom? *Social Behavior and Personality, 11,* 11–15.

Rosnow, R. L., & Robinson, E. J. (1967). *Experiments in persuasion.* New York: Academic.

Royal, D. C., & Hays, W. L. (1959). Empirical dimensions of emotional behavior. *Acta Psychologica, 15,* 419.

Rubin, M. E. Y. (1977). *Differences between distressed and nondistressed couples in verbal and nonverbal communication codes.* Unpublished doctoral dissertation, Indiana University.

Rubin, R. B. (1982). Assessing speaking and listening competence at the college level: The Communication Competency Assessment Instrument. *Communication Education, 31,* 19–32.

Rubin, Z. (1970). Measurement of romantic love. *Journal of Personality and Social Psychology, 16,* 265–273.

Ruesch, J., & Kees, W. (1956). *Nonverbal communication: Notes on the visual perception of human relations.* Berkeley: University of California Press.

Ruesch, J., & Kees, W. (1970). Function and meaning in the physical environment. In H. M. Proshansky, W. H. Ittelson, & L. G. Rivlin (Eds.), *Environmental psychology: Man and his physical setting* (pp. 141–153). New York: Holt, Rinehart and Winston.

Russell, J. A. (1978). Evidence of convergent validity on the dimensions of affect. *Journal of Personality and Social Psychology, 36,* 1152–1168.

Russell, J. A. (1980). A circumplex model of affect. *Journal of Personality and Social Psychology, 39,* 1161–1178.

Russell, J. A. (1983). Pancultural aspects of the human conceptual organization of emotions. *Journal of Personality and Social Psychology, 45,* 1281–1288.

Russell, J. A., & Bullock, M. (1985). Multidimensional scaling of emotional facial expressions: Similarity from preschoolers to adults. *Journal of Personality and Social Psychology, 48,* 1290–1298.

Russell, J. A., & Steiger, J. H. (1982). The structure in persons' implicit taxonomy of emotions. *Journal of Research in Personality, 16,* 447–469.

Russell, M. J. (1976). Human olfactory communication. *Nature, 260,* 520–522.

Russo, N. F. (1967). Connotation of seating arrangement. *Cornell Journal of Social Relations, 2,* 37–44.

Russo, N. F. (1975). Eye contact, interpersonal distance, and the equilibrium theory. *Journal of Personality and Social Psychology, 31,* 497–502.

Rutter, D. R., Pennington, D. C., Dewey, M. E., & Swain, J. (1984). Eye contact as a chance product of individual looking: Implications for the intimacy model of Argyle and Dean. *Journal of Nonverbal Behavior, 8,* 250–258.

Rutter, D. R., & Stephenson, G. M. (1979). The functions of looking: Effects of friendship on gaze. *British Journal of Social and Clinical Psychology, 18,* 203–205.

Rutter, D. R., Stephenson, G. M., Ayling, K., & White, P. A. (1978). The timing of looks in dyadic conversation. *British Journal of Social and Clinical Psychology, 17,* 17–21.

Ryan, E. B. (1979). Why do low-prestige language varieties persist? In H. Giles & R. N. St. Clair (Eds.), *Language and social psychology* (pp. 145–157). Oxford: Basil Blackwell.

Ryan, E. B. (1994, July). *Language and aging: Social cognitive studies of intergenerational communication.* Paper presented at the 5th International Conferences on Language and Social Psychology, Brisbane, Australia.

Ryan, E. B., Bourhis, R. Y., & Knops, U. (1991). Evaluative perceptions of patronizing speech addressed to elders. *Psychology and Aging, 6,* 442–450.

Ryan, E. B., & Cole, R. (1990). Evaluative perceptions of interpersonal communication with elders. In H. Giles, N. Coupland, & J. Weimann (Eds.), *Communication, health, and the elderly* (pp. 172–190). Manchester, U.K.: University of Manchester Press.

Saarni, C. (1979). Children's understanding of display rules for expressive behavior. *Developmental Psychology, 15,* 424–429.

Saarni, C. (1982). Social and affective functions of nonverbal behavior: Developmental concerns. In R. S. Feldman (Ed.), *Development of nonverbal behavior in children* (pp. 123–147). New York: Springer-Verlag.

Sabatelli, R. M., Buck, R., & Dreyer, A. (1980). Communication via facial cues in intimate dyads. *Personality and Social Psychology Bulletin, 6,* 242–247.

Sabatelli, R. M., & Rubin, M. (1986). Nonverbal expressiveness and physical attractiveness as mediators of interpersonal perceptions. *Journal of Nonverbal Behavior, 10,* 120–133.

Sabourin, T. C., Infante, D. A., & Rudd, J. E. (1993). Verbal aggression in marriages: A comparison of violent, distressed but nonviolent, and nondistressed couples. *Human Communication Research, 20,* 245–267.

Sachs, J., Lieberman, P., & Erickson, D. (1973). Anatomical and cultural determinants of male and female speech. In R. W. Shuy & R. W. Fasold (Eds.), *Language attitudes: Current trends and prospects* (pp. 74–84). Washington, DC: Georgetown University Press.

Sackeim, H. A., Gur, R. C., & Saucy, M. C. (1978). Emotions are expressed more intensely on the left side of the face. *Science, 202,* 434–435.

Sacks, H., Schegloff, E., & Jefferson, G. (1974). A simplest systematics for the organization of turn-taking for conversation. *Language, 50,* 696–735.

Sacks, O. W. (1985). *The man who mistook his wife for a hat and other clinical tales.* New York: Summit.

Sadalla, E. K., Kenrick, D. T., & Vershure, B. (1987). Dominance and het-

erosexual attraction. *Journal of Personality and Social Psychology, 52,* 730–738.

Sadalla, E. K., & Sheets, V. L. (1993). Symbolism in building materials: Self-presentational and cognitive components. *Environment and Behavior, 25,* 155–180.

Sadalla, E. K., Vershure, B., & Burroughs, J. (1987). Identity symbolism in housing. *Environment and Behavior, 19,* 569–587.

Sadesky, G. A. (1974). *The effects of lighting color and intensity on small group communication.* Paper presented at the annual convention of the International Communication Association, New Orleans.

Sainsbury, P. (1955). Gestural movement during psychiatric interview. *Psychosomatic Medicine, 17,* 458–469.

Saitz, R. L., & Cervenka, E. J. (1972). *Handbook of gestures: Colombia and the United States.* The Hague: Mouton.

Samovar, L. A., & Porter, R. E. (1985). *Intercultural communication: A reader* (2nd ed.). Belmont, CA: Wadsworth.

Sanders, G. S. (1981). Driven by distraction: An integrative review of social facilitation theory and research. *Journal of Experimental Social Psychology, 17,* 227–251.

Sanders, M., Gustanski, J., & Lawton, M. (1974). Effect of ambient illumination on noise level of groups. *Journal of Applied Psychology, 59,* 527–528.

Sandhu, D. S. (1984). *The effects of mirroring vs. nonmirroring of clients' nonverbal behaviors on empathy, trustworthiness, and positive interaction in cross-cultural counseling dyads.* Unpublished doctoral dissertation, Mississippi State University, Jackson.

Sapir, E. (1928). The unconscious patterning of behavior in society. In E. S. Dummer (Ed.), *The unconscious* (pp. 114–142). New York: Knopf.

Schachter, S., Christenfeld, N., Ravina, B., & Bilous, F. (1991). Speech disfluency and the structure of knowledge. *Journal of Personality and Social Psychology, 60,* 362–367.

Schachter, S., & Singer, J. E. (1962). Cognitive, social, and physiological determinants of emotional state. *Psychological Review, 69,* 379–399.

Schaefer, E. S., & Plutchik, R. (1966). Interrelationships of emotions, traits, and diagnostic constructs. *Psychological Reports, 18,* 399–419.

Schaeffer, G. H., & Patterson, M. L. (1980). Intimacy, arousal, and small group crowding. *Journal of Personality and Social Psychology, 38,* 283–290.

Schank, R. C., & Abelson, R. P. (1977). *Scripts, plans, goals, and understanding: An inquiry into human knowledge structures.* Hillsdale, NJ: Erlbaum.

Scheflen, A. E. (1964). The significance of posture in communication systems. *Psychiatry, 27,* 316–331.

Scheflen, A. E. (1965). Quasi-courtship behavior in psychotherapy. *Psychiatry, 28,* 245–257.

Scheflen, A. E. (1967). On the structuring of human communication. *American Behavioral Scientist, 10,* 8–12.

Scheflen, A. E. (1971). Living space in an urban ghetto. *Family Process, 10,* 429–450.

Scheflen, A. E. (1974). *How behavior means.* Garden City, NY: Anchor Books/Doubleday.

Scheflen, A. E., & Scheflen, A. (1972). *Body language and the social order: Communication as behavior control.* Englewood Cliffs, NJ: Prentice-Hall.

Schegloff, E., & Sacks, H. (1973). Opening up closings. *Semiotica, 8,* 289–327.

Schenck-Hamlin, W. J., Wiseman, R. L., & Georgacarakos, G. N. (1982). A model of properties of compliance-gaining strategies. *Communication Quarterly, 30,* 92–100.

Scherer, K. R. (1978). Personality inference from voice quality: The loud voice of extroversion. *European Journal of Social Psychology, 8,* 467–487.

Scherer, K. R. (1979a). Acoustic concomitants of emotional dimensions: Judging affect from synthesized tone sequences. In S. Weitz (Ed.), *Nonverbal communication* (2d ed., pp. 249–253). New York: Oxford University Press.

Scherer, K. R. (1979b). Personality markers in speech. In K. R. Scherer & H. Giles (Eds.). *Social markers in speech* (pp. 147–209). Cambridge: Cambridge University Press.

Scherer, K. R. (1979c). Voice and speech correlates of perceived social influence in simulated juries. In H. Giles & R. St. Clair (Eds.), *Language and social psychology* (pp. 88–120). Oxford: Blackwell.

Scherer, K. R. (1980). The functions of nonverbal signs in conversation. In R. N. St. Clair (Ed.), *The social psycho-*

logical contexts of language (pp. 225–244). Hillsdale, NJ: Erlbaum.

Scherer, K. R. (1982a). Emotion as process: Function, origin and regulation. *Social Science Information, 21,* 555–570.

Scherer, K. R. (1982b). Methods of research on vocal communication: Paradigms and parameters. In K. R. Scherer & P. Ekman (Eds.), *Handbook of methods in nonverbal behavior research* (pp. 136–198). Cambridge: Cambridge University Press.

Scherer, K. R. (1992). What does facial expression express? In K. T. Strongman (Ed.), *International Review of Studies on Emotion* (Vol. 2, pp. 139–165). New York: Wiley.

Scherer, K. R. (1994). Affect bursts. In S. H. M. van Goozen, N. E. Van de Poll, & J. A. Sergeant (Eds.), *Emotions: Essays on emotion theory* (pp. 161–193). Hillsdale, NJ: Erlbaum.

Scherer, K. R., Banse, R., Wallbott, H. G., & Goldbeck, T. (1991). Vocal cues in emotion encoding. *Motivation and Emotion, 15,* 123–148.

Scherer, K. R., London, H., & Wolf, J. J. (1973). The voice of confidence: Paralinguistic cues and audience evaluation. *Journal of Research in Personality, 7,* 31–44.

Scherer, K. R., & Oshinsky, J. S. (1977). Cue utilization in emotion attribution from auditory stimuli. *Motivation and Emotion, 1,* 331–346.

Scherer, K. R., Rosenthal, R., & Koivumaki, J. (1972). Mediating interpersonal expectancies via vocal cues: Differential speech intensity as a means of social influence. *European Journal of Social Psychology, 2,* 163–176.

Scherer, K. R., Scherer, U., Hall, J. A., & Rosenthal, R. (1977). Differential attribution of personality based on multichannel presentation of verbal and nonverbal cues. *Psychological Research, 39,* 221–247.

Scherer, S. E. (1974). Proxemic behavior of primary school children as a function of their socioeconomic class and subculture. *Journal of Personality and Social Psychology, 29,* 800–805.

Scherer, S. E. (1978). The influence of linguistic style, interpersonal distance and gaze on attitude acquisition (Doctoral dissertation, University of Toronto). *Dissertation Abstracts International, 38,* 4479B.

Schlenker, B. R. (1980). *Impression management.* Monterey, CA: Brooks/Cole.

Schlosberg, H. (1952). The description of facial expressions in terms of two dimensions. *Journal of Experimental Psychology, 44,* 229–237.

Schlosberg, H. (1954). Three dimensions of emotion. *Psychological Review, 61,* 81–88.

Schneirla, T. C. (1965). Aspects of stimulation and organization in approach/withdrawal processes underlying vertebrate behavior development. *Advances in the Study of Behavior, 1,* 1–74.

Schneirla, T. C. (1968). Instinct and aggression. In M. F. A. Montagu (Ed.), *Man and aggression* (pp. 59–64). New York: Oxford University Press.

Schulz, R., & Barefoot, J. (1974). Nonverbal responses and affiliative conflict theory. *British Journal of Social and Clinical Psychology, 13,* 237–243.

Schutz, W. C. (1958). *FIRO: A three dimensional theory of interpersonal behavior.* New York: Holt, Rinehart and Winston.

Schwartz, B. (1968). The social psychology of privacy. *American Journal of Sociology, 73,* 741–752.

Schwartz, B., Tesser, A., & Powell, E. (1982). Dominance cues in nonverbal behavior. *Social Psychology Quarterly, 45,* 114–120.

Schwartz, M. F., & Rine, H. E. (1968). Identification of speaker sex from isolated whispered vowels. *Journal of the Acoustical Society of America, 44,* 1736–1737.

Schwartz, T. (1974). *The responsive chord.* Garden City, NY: Anchor/Doubleday.

Schweitzer, D. A. (1970). The effect of presentation on source evaluation. *Quarterly Journal of Speech, 56,* 33–39.

Scott, A. L. (1988). Human interaction and personal boundaries. *Journal of Psychosocial Nursing, 26,* 23–27.

Scott, A. L. (1994). *What exactly did you mean to say?* Unpublished manuscript, University of Arizona, Tucson.

Scott, A. L. (in press). A beginning theory of the state and trait of personal space boundaries. *Perspectives of Psychiatric Care.*

Seay, T. A., & Altekruse, M. K. (1979). Verbal and nonverbal behavior in judgments of facilitative conditions. *Journal of Counseling Psychology, 26,* 108–119.

Sebeok, T. A. (1964). Indiana University conference on paralinguistics and kinesics. In T. A. Sebeok, A. S. Hayes,

& M. C. Bateson (Eds.), *Approaches to semiotics* (pp. TK). The Hague: Mouton.

Sebeok, T. A., Hayes, A. S., & Bateson, M. C. (1964). *Approaches to semiotics.* The Hague: Mouton.

Sechrest, L. (1969). Nonreactive assessment of attitudes. In E. P. Willems & H. L. Raush (Eds.), *Naturalistic viewpoints in psychological research* (pp. 147–161). New York: Holt, Rinehart and Winston.

Segrin, C., & Abramson, L. Y. (1994). Negative reactions to depressive behaviors: A communication theories analysis. *Journal of Abnormal Psychology, 103,* 655–668.

Seibold, D. R., Cantrill, J. G., & Meyers, R. A. (1985). Communication and interpersonal influence. In M. L. Knapp & G. R. Miller (Eds.), *Handbook of interpersonal communication* (pp. 551–611). Beverly Hills, CA: Sage.

Selye, H. (1956). *The stress of life.* New York: McGraw-Hill.

Sereno, K. K., & Hawkins, G. J. (1967). The effects of variations in speakers' nonfluency upon audience ratings of attitude toward the speech topic and speakers' credibility. *Speech Monographs, 34,* 58–64.

Seta, J. J., Paulus, P. B., & Schkade, J. K. (1976). Effects of group size and proximity under cooperative and competitive conditions. *Journal of Personality and Social Psychology, 34,* 47–53.

Shaffer, D. R., & Sadowski, C. (1975). [An investigation of territorial invasion in a barroom environment.] This table is mine: Respect for marked barroom tables as a function of gender of spatial marker and desirability of locale. *Sociometry, 38,* 408–419.

Shapiro, J. G. (1968). Responsivity to facial and linguistic cues. *Journal of Communication, 18,* 11–17.

Shaw, M. E. (1981). *Group dynamics: The psychology of small group behavior* (3d ed.). New York: McGraw-Hill.

Shennum, W. A., & Bugental, D. B. (1982). The development of control over affective expression in nonverbal behavior. In R. S. Feldman (Ed.), *Development of nonverbal behavior in children* (pp. 101–122). New York: Springer-Verlag.

Shepard, R. N. (1962). The analysis of proximities: Multidimensional scaling with an unknown distance function. *Psychometrika, 27,* 125–140, 219–246.

Sheppard, W. C., & Lane, H. L. (1968).

Development of the prosodic features of infant vocalizing. *Journal of Speech and Hearing Research, 11,* 94–108.

Shively, C. (1985). The evolution of dominance hierarchies in nonhuman primate society. In S. L. Ellyson & J. F. Dovidio (Eds.), *Power, dominance, and nonverbal behavior* (pp. 67–88). New York: Springer-Verlag.

Shotland, R. L., & Johnson, M. P. (1978). Bystander behavior and kinesics: The interaction between the helper and victim. *Environmental Psychology and Nonverbal Behavior, 2,* 181–190.

Shuter, R. (1976). Proxemics and tactility in Latin America. *Journal of Communication, 26,* 46–52.

Shuter, R. (1977). A field study of nonverbal communication in Germany, Italy, and the United States. *Communication Monographs, 44,* 298–305.

Shuter, R. (1979). A study of nonverbal communication among Jews and Protestants. *Journal of Social Psychology, 109,* 31–41.

Shuter, R. (1984, September 2). The new rules of global competition. *New York Times,* p. F1.

Siegman, A. W. (1976). *The effects of cognition on hesitation phenomena in speech.* Paper presented at the Interdisciplinary Conference on Perspectives on Language, University of Louisville, KY.

Siegman, A. W. (1978). The telltale voice: Nonverbal messages of verbal communication. In A. W. Siegman & S. Feldstein (Eds.), *Nonverbal behavior and communication* (pp. 183–243). Hillsdale, NJ: Erlbaum.

Siegman, A. W. (1979). The voice of attraction: Vocal correlates of interpersonal attraction in the interview. In A. W. Siegman & S. Feldstein (Eds.), *Of speech and time* (pp. 89–114). Hillsdale, NJ: Erlbaum.

Siegman, A. W. (1985). Expressive correlates of affective states and traits. In A. W. Siegman & S. Feldstein (Eds.), *Multichannel integrations of nonverbal behavior* (pp. 37–68). Hillsdale, NJ: Erlbaum.

Siegman, A. W., & Pope, B. (1965). Effects of question specificity and anxiety producing messages on verbal fluency in the initial interview. *Journal of Personality and Social Psychology, 4,* 188–192.

Siegman, A. W., & Reynolds, M. (1982). Interviewer-interviewee nonverbal

communications: An interactional approach. In M. A. Davis (Ed.), *Interaction rhythms: Periodicity in communication behavior* (pp. 249–278). New York: Human Sciences.

Sigelman, C. K., & Adams, R. M. (1990). Family interactions in public: Parent-child distance and touching. *Journal of Nonverbal Behavior, 14,* 63–76.

Sigelman, C. K., & Davis, P. J. (1978). Making good impressions in job interviews: Verbal and nonverbal predictors. *Education and Training of the Mentally Retarded, 13,* 71–77.

Silden, I. (1973, December). Psychological effects of office planning. *Mainliner,* pp. 30–34.

Sillars, A. L., Coletti, S. F., Parry, D., & Rogers, M. A. (1982). Coding verbal conflict tactics: Nonverbal and perceptual correlates of the "avoidance-distributive-integrative" distinction. *Human Communication Research, 9,* 83–95.

Sillars, A. L., Pike, G. R., Jones, T. J., & Redmon, K. (1983). Communication and conflict in marriage. In R. N. Bostrom (Ed.), *Communication yearbook 7* (pp. 414–429). Beverly Hills, CA: Sage.

Silveira, J. (1972). Thoughts on the politics of touch. *Women's Press, 1,* 13.

Simmel, G. (1950). Secrecy and group communication. In K. H. Wolff (Ed. and Trans.), *The sociology of George Simmel* (pp. 330–375). Glencoe, IL: Free Press.

Simonds, J. O. (1961). *Landscape architecture.* New York: McGraw-Hill.

Simpson, J. A., Gangestad, S. W., & Biek, M. (1993). Personality and nonverbal social behavior: An ethological perspective of relationship initiation. *Journal of Experimental Social Psychology, 29,* 434–461.

Singer, J. E. (1964). The use of manipulative strategies: Machiavellianism and attractiveness. *Sociometry, 27,* 128–151.

Singer, J. E., & Lamb, P. F. (1966). Social concern, body size, and birth order. *Journal of Social Psychology, 68,* 143–151.

Slane, S., & Leak, G. (1978). Effects of self-perceived nonverbal immediacy behaviors on interpersonal attraction. *Journal of Psychology, 98,* 241–248.

Smith, A. (1983). Nonverbal communication among black female dyads: An assessment of intimacy, gender, and

race. *Journal of Social Issues, 39* (3), 55–67.

Smith, B. L., Brown, B. L., Strong, W. J., & Rencher, A. C. (1975). Effects of speech rate on personality perception. *Language and Speech, 18,* 145–152.

Smith, B. L., Wasowicz, J., & Preston, J. (1987). Temporal characteristics of the speech of normal elderly adults. *Journal of Speech and Hearing Research, 30,* 522–529.

Smith, C. A., & Ellsworth, P. C. (1985). Patterns of cognitive appraisal in emotion. *Journal of Personality and Social Psychology, 48,* 813–838.

Smith, D. E., Willis, F. N., & Gier, J. A. (1980). Success and interpersonal touch in a competitive setting. *Journal of Nonverbal Behavior, 5,* 26–34.

Smith, H. A. (1979). Nonverbal communication in teaching. *Review of Educational Research, 49,* 631–672.

Smith, H. J., Archer, D., & Costanzo, M. (1991). "Just a hunch": Accuracy and awareness in person perception. *Journal of Nonverbal Behavior, 15,* 3–18.

Smith, M. J., Reinheimer, R. E., & Gabbard-Alley, A. (1981). Crowding, task performance, and communicative interaction in youth and old age. *Human Communication Research, 7,* 259–272.

Smith, R. J., & Knowles, E. S. (1979). Affective and cognitive mediators of reactions to spatial invasions. *Journal of Experimental Social Psychology, 15,* 437–452.

Smith, S., & Haythorn, W. W. (1972). The effects of compatability, crowding, group size, and leadership seniority on stress, anxiety, hostility, and annoyance in isolated groups. *Journal of Personality and Social Psychology, 22,* 67–69.

Smith, W. J. (1974). Displays and messages in intraspecific communication. In S. Weitz (Ed.), *Nonverbal communication: Readings with commentary* (pp. 331–340). New York: Oxford University Press.

Smith, W. J., Chase, J., & Lieblich, A. K. (1974). Tongue-showing: A facial display of humans and other primate species. *Semiotica, 11,* 201–246.

Smith-Hanen, S. S. (1977). Effects of nonverbal behaviors on judged levels of counselor warmth and empathy. *Journal of Counseling Psychology, 24,* 87–91.

Smutkupt, S., & Barna, L. (1976). Impact of nonverbal communication in an intercultural setting: Thailand. In F.

Casmir (Ed.), *International and intercultural communication annual* (Vol. 3, pp. 130–138). Falls Church, VA: Speech Communication Association.

Snyder, M. (1974). Self-monitoring of expressive behavior. *Journal of Personality and Social Psychology, 30,* 526–537.

Snyder, M. (1979). Self-monitoring processes. In L. Berkowitz (Ed.), *Advances in experimental social psychology* (Vol. 12, pp. 85–128). New York: Academic.

Snyder, M. (1992). Motivational foundations of behavioral confirmation. In M. P. Zanna (Ed.), *Advances in experimental social psychology* (Vol. 25, pp. 67–114). New York: Academic.

Snyder, M., & Rothbart, M. (1971). Communicator attractiveness and opinion change. *Canadian Journal of Behavioral Science, 3,* 377–387.

Snyder, M., & Swann, W. B., Jr. (1978). Behavioral confirmation in social interaction: From social perception to social reality. *Journal of Experimental Social Psychology, 14,* 148–162.

Snyder, M., Tanke, E. D., & Berscheid, E. (1977). Social perception and interpersonal behavior: On the self-fulfilling nature of social stereotypes. *Journal of Personality and Social Psychology, 35,* 656–666.

Snyder, R. A., & Sutker, L. W. (1977). The measurement of the construct of dominance and its relationship to nonverbal behavior. *Journal of Psychology, 97,* 227–230.

Sobelman, S. A. (1973). *The effects of verbal and nonverbal components on the judged level of counselor warmth.* Unpublished doctoral dissertation, American University, Washington, DC.

Sohl, R., & Carr, A. (Eds.). (1970). *The gospel according to Zen.* New York: New American Library. (Originally published in P. Reps. (1957). *Zen flesh, Zen bones.* Tokyo: Tuttle.)

Solomon, D., & Yeager, J. (1969a). Determinants of boys' perceptions of verbal reinforcers. *Developmental Psychology, 1,* 637–645.

Solomon, D., & Yeager, J. (1969b). Effects of content and intonation on perceptions of verbal reinforcers, *Perceptual and Motor Skills, 28,* 319–327.

Solzhenitsyn, A. (1973). *The gulag archipelago.* New York: Harper & Row.

Sommer, R. (1959). Studies in personal space. *Sociometry, 22,* 247–260.

Sommer, R. (1961). Leadership and group geography. *Sociometry, 24,* 499–510.

Sommer, R. (1962). The distance for comfortable conversation: A further study. *Sociometry, 25,* 111–116.

Sommer, R. (1965). Further studies in small group ecology. *Sociometry, 28,* 337–348.

Sommer, R. (1966). Man's proximate environment. *Journal of Social Issues, 22,* 59–70.

Sommer, R. (1968). Intimacy ratings in five countries. *International Journal of Psychology, 3,* 109–114.

Sommer, R. (1969). *Personal space: The behavioral basis of design.* Englewood Cliffs, NJ: Prentice-Hall.

Sommer, R. (1970). The ecology of privacy. In H. M. Proshansky, W. H. Ittelson, & L. G. Rivlin (Eds.), *Environmental psychology: Man and his physical setting* (pp. 256–266). New York: Holt, Rinehart and Winston.

Sommer, R. (1971). Spatial parameters in naturalistic research. In A. H. Esser (Ed.), *Behavior and environment: The use of space in animals.* (pp. 281–290). New York: Plenum.

Sommer, R. (1974a). Studies of small group ecology. In R. S. Cathcart & L. A. Samovar (Eds.), *Small group communication: A reader* (pp. 283–293). Dubuque, IA: Brown.

Sommer, R. (1974b). *Tight spaces: Hard architecture and how to humanize it.* Englewood Cliffs, NJ: Prentice-Hall.

Sommer, R., & Becker, F. D. (1969). Territorial defense and the good neighbor. *Journal of Personality and Social Psychology, 11,* 85–92.

Sommers, S. (1984). Reported emotions and conventions of emotionality among college students. *Journal of Personality and Social Psychology, 46,* 207–215.

Sorrentino, R. M., & Boutillier, R. G. (1975). The effect of quantity and quality of verbal interaction on ratings of leadership ability. *Journal of Experimental Research in Personality, 11,* 403–411.

Soskin, W. F., & John, V. P. (1963). The study of spontaneous talk. In R. G. Barker (Ed.), *The stream of behavior* (pp. 228–287). Englewood Cliffs, NJ: Prentice-Hall.

Spain, C. (1985). *Reflective eye positions as indicators of cognitive information processing within an English and Spanish speaking sample.* Unpublished master's thesis, University of New Mexico, Albuquerque.

Spiegel, J. P., & Machotka, P. (1974). *Messages of the body.* New York: Free Press.

Spignesi, A., & Shor, R. E. (1981). The judgment of emotion from facial expressions, contexts and their combination. *Journal of General Psychology, 104,* 41–58.

Spitzberg, B. H., & Capuch, W. R. (1989). *Handbook of interpersonal competence research.* New York: Springer-Verlag.

Sporkin, E. (1988, January 12). The new dress code for success. *USA Today,* p. D.2.

Springer, S. P., & Deutsch, G. (1981). *Left brain, right brain.* New York: Freeman.

Stacks, D. W. (1982, May). *Hemispheric and evolutionary use: A re-examination of verbal and nonverbal communication and the brain.* Paper presented at the annual meeting of the Eastern Communication Association, Hartford, CT.

Stacks, D. W., & Burgoon, J. K. (1981). The role of nonverbal behaviors as distractors in resistance to persuasion in interpersonal contexts. *Central States Speech Journal, 32,* 61–73.

Stafford, L., & Daly, J. A. (1984). Conversational memory: The effects of recall mode and memory expectancies on remembrances of natural conversations. *Human Communication Research, 10,* 379–402.

Staley, C. C., & Cohen, J. L. (1988). Communicator style and social style: Similarities and differences between the sexes. *Communication Quarterly, 36,* 192–202.

Stamp, G. H., & Knapp, M. L. (1990). The construct of intent in interpersonal communication. *Quarterly Journal of Speech, 76,* 282–299.

Stang, D. J. (1973). Effect of interaction rate on ratings of leadership and liking. *Journal of Personality and Social Psychology, 27,* 405–408.

Starkweather, J. A. (1964). Variations in vocal behavior. In D. M. Rioch & E. A. Weinstein (Eds.), *Disorders of communication* (pp. 424–449). Baltimore: Waverly.

Stea, D. (1965, Autumn). Territoriality, the interior aspect: Space, territory, and human movements. *Landscape,* pp. 13–17.

Stea, D. (1970). Space, territory and human movements. In H. M. Proshansky, W. H. Ittelson, & L. G. Rivlin (Eds.), *Environmental psychology: Man and his physical setting* (pp. 37–42). New York: Holt, Rinehart and Winston.

Stead, B. A., & Zinkhan, G. M. (1986). Service priority in department stores: The effects of customer gender and dress. *Sex Roles, 15,* 601–611.

Stechler, G., & Latz, E. (1966). Some observations on attention and arousal in the human infant. *Journal of the American Academy of Child Psychology, 5,* 517–525.

Steinzor, B. (1950). The spatial factor in face-to-face discussion groups. *Journal of Abnormal and Social Psychology, 45,* 552–555.

Stephan, F. F. (1952). The relative rate of communication between members of small groups. *American Sociological Review, 17,* 482–486.

Stephenson, G. M., Ayling, K., & Rutter, D. R. (1976). The role of visual communication in social exchange. *British Journal of Social and Clinical Psychology, 15,* 113–120.

Stern, D. N. (1971). A micro analysis of mother-infant interaction. *Journal of the American Academy of Child Psychiatry, 10,* 501–517.

Stern, D. N. (1980). *The first relationship: Mother and infant.* Cambridge, MA: Harvard University Press.

Stewart, D. J., & Patterson, M. L. (1973). Eliciting effects of verbal and nonverbal cues on projective test responses. *Journal of Consulting and Clinical Psychology, 41,* 74–77.

Stewart, M. A., & Ryan, E. B. (1982). Attitudes toward younger and older adult speakers: Effects of varying speech rates. *Journal of Language and Social Psychology, 1,* 91–110.

Stier, D. S., & Hall, J. A. (1984). Gender differences in touch: An empirical and theoretical review. *Journal of Personality and Social Psychology, 47,* 440–459.

Stiff, J. B. (1986). Cognitive processing of persuasive message cues: A meta-analytic review of the effects of supporting information on attitudes. *Communication Monographs, 53,* 75–89.

Stiff, J. B., & Miller, G. R. (1986). "Come to think of it . . .": Interrogative probes, deceptive communication, and deception detection. *Human Communication Research, 12,* 339–358.

Stifter, C. A., & Grant, W. (1993). Infant responses to frustration: Individual differences in the expression of negative affect. *Journal of Nonverbal Behavior, 17,* 187–204.

Stine, E. A., Wingfield, A., & Myers, S. D. (1990). Age differences in processing information from television news: The effects of bisensory augmentation. *Journal of Gerontology, 45,* 1–8.

Stinson, L., & Ickes, W. (1992). Empathic accuracy in the interactions of male friends versus male strangers. *Journal of Personality and Social Psychology, 62,* 787–797.

Stockwell, S. R., & Dye, A. (1980). Effects of counselor touch on counseling outcomes. *Journal of Counseling Psychology, 27,* 443–446.

Stokols, D. (1972). A social-psychological model of human crowding phenomena. *Journal of the American Institute of Planners, 38,* 72–84.

Stokols, D. (1976). The experience of crowding in primary and secondary environments. *Environment and Behavior, 8,* 49–85.

Stokols, D., Rall, M., Pinner, B., & Schopler, J. (1973). Physical, social, and personal determinants of the perception of crowding. *Environment and Behavior, 5,* 87–117.

Streeck, J. (1993). Gestures as communication: 1. Its coordination with gaze and speech. *Communication Monographs, 60,* 275–299.

Streeck, J. (1994). Gestures as communication: 2. The audience as co-author. *Research on Language and Social Interaction, 27,* 239–267.

Street, R. L., Jr. (1982). Evaluation of noncontent speech accommodation. *Language and Communication, 2,* 13–31.

Street, R. L., Jr. (1983). Noncontent speech convergence in adult-child interactions. In R. N. Bostrom (Ed.), *Communication yearbook 7* (pp. 369–395). Beverly Hills, CA: Sage.

Street, R. L., Jr. (1984). Speech convergence and speech evaluation in fact-finding interviews. *Human Communication Research, 11,* 139–169.

Street, R. L., Jr. (1990). The communicative functions of paralanguage and prosody. In H. Giles & W. P. Robinson (Eds.), *Handbook of language and social psychology* (pp. 121–140). Chichester: Wiley.

Street, R. L., Jr., & Brady, R. M. (1982). Speech rate acceptance ranges as a factor of evaluative domain, listener speech rate, and communication context. *Communication Monographs, 49,* 290–308.

Street, R. L., Jr., Brady, R. M., & Putman, W. B. (1983). The influence of speech rate stereotypes and rate similarity on listeners' evaluations of speakers. *Journal of Language and Social Psychology, 2,* 37–56.

Street, R. L., Jr., & Cappella, J. N. (1989). Social and linguistic factors influencing adaptation in children's speech. *Journal of Psycholinguistic Research, 18,* 497–519.

Street, R. L., Jr., & Giles, H. (1982). Speech accommodation theory: A social cognitive approach to language and speech behavior. In M. Roloff & C. Berger (Eds.), *Social cognition and communication* (pp. 193–226). Beverly Hills, CA: Sage.

Street, R. L., Jr., & Hopper, R. (1982). A model of speech style evaluation. In E. B. Ryan & H. Giles (Eds.), *Attitudes towards language variation: Social and applied contexts* (pp. 175–188). London: Arnold.

Streeter, L. A., Krauss, R. M., Geller, V., Olson, C., & Apple, W. (1977). Pitch changes during attempted deception. *Journal of Personality and Social Psychology, 35,* 345–350.

Strodtbeck, F. L. (1951). Husband-wife interaction over revealed differences. *American Sociological Review, 16,* 468–473.

Strodtbeck, F. L., & Hook, L. H. (1961). The social dimensions of a twelve-man jury table. *Sociometry, 24,* 397–415.

Strodtbeck, F. L., & Mann, R. D. (1956). Sex role differentiation in jury deliberations. *Sociometry, 19,* 3–11.

Strongman, K. T., & Champness, B. G. (1968). Dominance hierarchies and conflict in eye contact. *Acta Psychologica, 28,* 376–386.

Sullins, E. S. (1989). Perceptual salience as a function of nonverbal expressiveness. *Personality and Social Psychology Bulletin, 15,* 584–595.

Sullins, E. S., Friedman, H. S., & Harris, M. J. (1985). Individual differences in expressive style as a mediator of expectancy communication. *Journal of Nonverbal Behavior, 9,* 229–238.

Summerfield, A. B., & Lake J. A. (1977). Non-verbal and verbal behaviors associated with parting. *British Journal of Psychology, 68,* 133–136.

Summerhayes, D. L., & Suchner, R. W. (1978). Power implications of touch in male-female relationships. *Sex-roles, 4,* 103–110.

Sundstrom, E. (1975). An experimental study of crowding: Effects of room size, intrusion, and goal blocking on nonverbal behavior, self-disclosure, and self-reported stress. *Journal of Personality and Social Psychology, 32,* 645–654.

Sundstrom, E. (1978). A test of equilibrium theory: Effects of topic intimacy and proximity on verbal and nonverbal behavior in pairs of friends and strangers. *Environmental Psychology and Nonverbal Behavior, 3,* 3–16.

Sundstrom, E., & Altman, I. (1976). Interpersonal relationships and personal space: Research review and theoretical model. *Human Ecology, 4,* 47–67.

Sundstrom, E., & Sundstrom, M. G. (1977). Personal space invasions: What happens when the invader asks permission? *Environmental Psychology and Nonverbal Behavior, 2,* 76–82.

Sunnafrank, M. (1986). Predicted outcome value during initial interactions: A reformulation of uncertainty reduction theory. *Human Communication Research, 13,* 3–33.

Sussman, N. M., & Rosenfeld, H. M. (1982). Influence of culture, language, and sex on conversational distance. *Journal of Personality and Social Psychology, 42,* 66–74.

Swap, W. C., & Rubin, J. Z. (1983). Measurement of interpersonal orientation. *Journal of Personality and Social Psychology, 44,* 208–219.

Sybers, R., & Roach, M. E. (1962). Clothing and human behavior. *Journal of Home Economics, 54,* 184–187.

Sykes, R. E. (1983). Initial interaction between strangers and acquaintances: A multivariate analysis of factors affecting choice of communication partners. *Human Communication Research, 10,* 27–53.

Tajfel, H. (1981). *Human groups and social categories: Studies in social psychology.* Cambridge: Cambridge University Press.

Talese, G. (1969). *The kingdom and the power.* New York: World Publishing.

Tan, A. S. (1986). Social learning of aggression from television. In J. Bryant & D. Zillman (Eds.), *Perspectives on media effects* (pp. 41–55). Hillsdale, NJ: Erlbaum.

Taylor, L. C., & Compton, N. H. (1968). Personality correlates of dress conformity. *Journal of Home Economics, 60,* 653–656.

Tedeschi, J. T. (Ed.). (1981). *Impression management theory and social psychological research.* New York: Academic.

Tedeschi, J. T., & Bonoma, T. V. (1972). Power and influence: An introduction. In J. T. Tedeschi (Ed.), *The social influence processes* (pp. 1–49). Chicago: Aldine.

Tedeschi, J. T., & Norman, N. (1985). Social power, self-presentation, and the self. In B. R. Schlenker (Ed.), *The self and social life* (pp. 293–322). New York: McGraw-Hill.

Tedeschi, J. T., & Reiss, M. (1981). Identities, the phenomenal self, and laboratory research. In J. T. Tedeschi (Ed.), *Impression management theory and social psychological research* (pp. 3–22). New York: Academic.

Tepper, D. T., Jr. (1972). *The communication of counselor empathy, respect and genuineness through verbal and nonverbal channels.* Unpublished doctoral dissertation, University of Massachusetts.

Tepper, D. T., Jr., & Haase, R. F. (1978). Verbal and nonverbal communication of facilitative conditions. *Journal of Counseling Psychology, 25,* 35–44.

Thakerar, J. N., & Giles, H. (1981). They are—so they spoke: Noncontent speech stereotypes. *Language and Communication, 1,* 255–261.

Thakerar, J. N., Giles, H., & Cheshire, J. (1982). Psychological and linguistic parameters of speech accommodation theory. In C. Fraser & K. R. Scherer (Eds.), *Advances in the social psychology of language* (pp. 205–255). Cambridge: Cambridge University Press.

Thal, D. J., & Tobias, S. (1992). Communicative gestures in children with delayed onset of oral expressive vocabulary. *Journal of Speech and Hearing Research, 35,* 1281–1289.

Thalhofer, N. N. (1980). Violation of a spacing norm in high social density. *Journal of Applied Social Psychology, 10,* 175–183.

Thayer, S. (1969). The effect of interpersonal looking duration on dominance judgments. *Journal of Social Psychology, 79,* 285–286.

Thayer, S. (1986). Touch: Frontier of intimacy. In S. Thayer (Ed.), The psychology of touch (special issue). *Journal of Nonverbal Behavior, 10,* 7–11.

Thayer, S. (1988, March). Close encounters. *Psychology Today,* pp. 31–36.

Thayer, S., & Schiff, W. (1974). Observer judgment of social interaction: Eye contact and relationship inferences. *Journal of Personality and Social Psychology, 30,* 110–114.

Theologus, G. C., Wheaton, G. R., & Fleishman, E. A. (1974). Effects of intermittent, moderate intensity noise stress on human performance. *Journal of Applied Psychology, 59,* 539–547.

Thompson, D. E., & Aiello, J. R. (1988, August). *Male and female managers: Effects of nonverbal communication style.* Paper presented at the annual meeting of the Academy of Management, Anaheim, CA.

Thompson, D. F., & Meltzer, L. (1964). Communication of emotional intent by facial expression. *Journal of Abnormal and Social Psychology, 68,* 129–135.

Thorpe, W. H. (1972). The comparison of vocal communication in animals and man. In R. A. Hinde (Ed.), *Nonverbal communication* (pp. 27–48). Cambridge: Cambridge University Press.

Thrasher, F. M. (1927). *The gang.* Cited in Abrahamson, M. [1966]. *Interpersonal accommodation.* Princeton, NJ: Van Nostrand.

Tiersma, P. M. (1993). Nonverbal communication and the freedom of "speech." *Wisconsin Law Review, 6,* 1525–1589.

Timney, B., & London, H. (1973). Body language concomitants of persuasiveness and persuasibility in dyadic interaction. *International Journal of Group Tensions, 3,* 48–67.

Ting-Toomey, S. (Ed.). (1994). *The challenge of facework: Cross-cultural and interpersonal issues.* Albany: State University of New York Press.

Tomkins, S. S. (1962). *Affect, imagery, consciousness: Vol. 1. The positive affects.* New York: Springer-Verlag.

Tomkins, S. S. (1963). *Affect, imagery, consciousness: Vol. 2. The negative affects.* New York: Springer-Verlag.

Tomkins, S. S. (1981). The role of facial response in the experience of emotion: A reply to Tourangeau and Ellsworth. *Journal of Personality and Social Psychology, 40,* 355–357.

Toomb, J. K., & Divers, L. T. (1972, April). *The relationship of somatotype to source credibility.* Paper presented at the annual convention of the International Communication Association, Atlanta.

Toomb, J. K., Quiggins, J. G., Moore, D. L., MacNeil, L. B., & Liddell, C. M. (1972, April). *The effects of regional dialects on initial source credibility.* Paper presented at the annual convention of the International Communication Association, Atlanta.

Toris, C., & DePaulo, B. M. (1985). Effects of actual deception and suspiciousness of deception on interpersonal perceptions. *Journal of Personality and Social Psychology, 47,* 1063–1073.

Tourangeau, R., & Ellsworth, P. C. (1979). The role of facial response in the experience of emotion. *Journal of Personality and Social Psychology, 37,* 1519–1531.

Trager, G. L. (1958). Paralanguage: A first approximation. *Studies in Linguistics, 13,* 1–12.

Trager, G. L. (1961). The typology of paralanguage. *Anthropological Linguistics, 3,* 17–21.

Tremine, N. T., & Izard, C. E. (1988). Infants' responses to their mothers' expressions of joy and sadness. *Developmental Psychology, 24,* 223–229.

Trevarthen, C. (1984). Emotions in infancy: Regulators of contact and relationships with persons. In K. R. Scherer & P. Ekman (Eds.), *Approaches to emotion* (pp. 129–157). Hillsdale, NJ: Erlbaum.

Trippett, F. (1981, January 5). Man of the year. *Time,* pp. 13–14.

Trippett, F. (1981, December 21). Hard times for the status-minded. *Time,* p. 90.

Trout, D. L., & Rosenfeld, H. M. (1980). The effect of postural lean and body congruence on the judgment of psychotherapeutic rapport. *Journal of Nonverbal Behavior, 4,* 176–190.

Tseëlon, E. (1992). What is beautiful is bad: Physical attractiveness as stigma. *Journal for the Theory of Social Behavior, 22,* 295–309.

Tucker, J. S., & Friedman, H. S. (1993). Sex differences in nonverbal expressiveness: Emotional expression, personality, and impressions. *Journal of Nonverbal Behavior, 17,* 103–117.

Tulving, E., & Thomson, D. M. (1973). Encoding specificity and retrieval processes in episodic memory. *Psychological Review, 80,* 359–380.

Tulving, E., & Watkins, M. (1975). Structure of memory traces. *Psychological Review, 82,* 261–275.

Turner, R. E., Edgley, C., & Olmstead, G. (1975). Information control in conversations: Honesty is not always the best policy. *Kansas Journal of Speech, 11,* 69–89.

Valentine, M. E., & Ehrlichman, H. (1979). Interpersonal gaze and helping behavior. *Journal of Social Psychology, 107,* 193–198.

Valins, S., & Baum, A. (1973). Residential group size, social interactions and crowding. *Environment and Behavior, 5,* 421–439.

Vande Creek, L., & Watkins, J. T. (1972). Responses to incongruent verbal and nonverbal emotional cues. *Journal of Communication, 22,* 311–316.

van Hooff, J. A. R. A. M. (1972). A comparative approach to the phylogeny of laughter and smiling. In R. A. Hinde (Ed.), *Non-verbal communication* (pp. 209–238). Cambridge: Cambridge University Press.

Vaught, L. A. (1902). *Vaught's practical character reader.* Chicago: Vaught-Rocine.

Vickroy, S. C., Fisher, C. D., & Shaw, J. B. (1982). Effects of temperature, clothing, and task complexity on task performance and satisfaction. *Journal of Applied Psychology, 67,* 97–102.

Vine, I. (1975). Territoriality and the spatial regulation of interaction. In A. Kendon, R. M. Harris, & M. R. Key (Eds.), *Organization of behavior in face-to-face interaction* (pp. 357–387). The Hague: Mouton.

Vinsel, A., Brown, B. B., Altman, I., & Foss, C. (1980). Privacy regulation, territorial displays, and effectiveness of individual functioning. *Journal of Personality and Social Psychology, 39,* 1104–1115.

von Cranach, M., & Ellgring, J. H. (1973). Problems in the recognition of gaze direction. In M. von Cranach & I. Vine (Eds.), *Social communication and movement* (pp. 419–443). New York: Academic.

Vrij, A., & Winkel, F. W. (1991). Cultural differences in Dutch and Surinam nonverbal behavior: An analysis of simulated police/citizen encounters. *Journal of Nonverbal Behavior, 15,* 169–184.

Vrij, A., & Winkel, F. W. (1992). Cross-cultural police-citizen interactions: The influence of race, beliefs, and nonver-

bal communication on impression formation. *Journal of Applied Psychology, 22,* 1546–1559.

Wada, M. (1990). The effect of interpersonal distance change on nonverbal behaviors: Mediating effects of sex and intimacy levels in a dyad. *Japanese Psychological Research, 32,* 86–96.

Wagner, H. L., Buck, R., & Winterbotham, M. (1993). Communication of specific emotions: Gender differences in sending accuracy and communication measures. *Journal of Nonverbal Behavior, 17,* 29–53.

Wagner, H. L., MacDonald, C. J., & Manstead, A. S. R. (1986). Communication of individual emotions by spontaneous facial expressions. *Journal of Personality and Social Psychology, 50,* 737–743.

Wahlers, K. J. (1976). *An investigation of the effects of selected inconsistent verbal/nonverbal messages on channel preference.* Unpublished doctoral dissertation, Florida State University.

Waid, W. M., & Orne, M. T. (1981). Cognitive, social, and personality processes in the physiological detection of deception. In L. Berkowitz (Ed.), *Advances in experimental social psychology* (Vol. 14, pp. 61–106). New York: Academic.

Waitzkin, H. (1984). Doctor-patient communication: Clinical implications of social scientific research. *Journal of the American Medical Association, 252,* 2441–2446.

Walden, T. A., Nelson, P. A., & Smith, D. E. (1981). Crowding, privacy, and coping. *Environment and Behavior, 13,* 205–224.

Waldron, J. (1975). Judgment of like-dislike from facial expression and body posture. *Perceptual and Motor Skills, 41,* 799–804.

Walker, M. B., & Trimboli, C. (1984). The role of nonverbal signals in coordinating speaking turns. *Journal of Language and Social Psychology, 3,* 257–272.

Walker, R. N. (1963). Body build and behavior in young children: II. Body build and parents' ratings. *Child Development, 34,* 1–23.

Walker-Tyson, J. (1981, May 31). These cons weren't surprised: Riot. *Detroit Free Press,* pp. 1B, 4B.

Walster, E., Aronson, V., Abrahams, D., & Rottman, L. (1966). Importance of physical attractiveness in dating behavior. *Journal of Personality and Social Psychology, 4,* 508–516.

Walther, J. B. (1995, May). *Computer-mediated communication: Impersonal, interpersonal, and hyperpersonal communication.* Paper presented to the annual meeting of the International Communication Association, Albuquerque, NM.

Walther, J. B. (in press). Relational aspects of computer-mediated communication: Experimental observations over time. *Organizational Science.*

Walther, J. B., Anderson, J. F., & Park, D. (1994). Interpersonal effects in computer-mediated interaction: A meta-analysis of social and anti-social communication. *Communication Research, 21,* 460–487.

Walther, J. B., & Burgoon, J. K. (1992). Relational communication in computer-mediated interaction. *Human Communication Research, 19,* 50–88.

Walther, J. B., & Tidwell, L. C. (1994, November). *Nonverbal cues in computer-mediated communication, and the effects of chronemics on relational communication.* Paper presented at the annual meeting of the Speech Communication Association, New Orleans.

Ward, C. D. (1968). Seating arrangement and leadership emergence in small discussion groups. *Journal of Social Psychology, 74,* 83–90.

Warner, R. M., Malloy, D., Schneider, K., Knoth, R., & Wilder, B. (1987). Rhythmic organization of social interaction and observer ratings of positive affect and involvement. *Journal of Nonverbal Behavior, 11,* 57–74.

Warren, C., & Laslett, B. (1977). Privacy and secrecy—conceptual comparison. *Journal of Social Issues, 33,* 43–51.

Washburn, P. V., & Hakel, M. D. (1973). Visual cues and verbal content as influences on impressions formed after simulated employment interviews. *Journal of Applied Psychology, 58,* 137–141.

Wass, H. (1973). Pupil evaluation of teacher messages in three channels of communication. *Florida Journal of Educational Research, 15,* 46–52.

Watkins, M. J., Ho, E., & Tulving, E. (1976). Context effects in recognition memory for faces. *Journal of Verbal Learning and Verbal Behavior, 15,* 505–517.

Watkins, M. J., & Tulving, E. (1975). Episodic memory: When recognition

fails. *Journal of Experimental Psychology: General, 104,* 5–29.

Watson, O. M. (1970). *Proxemic behavior: A cross-cultural study.* The Hague: Mouton.

Watson, O. M., & Graves, T. D. (1966). Quantitative research in proxemic behavior. *American Anthropologist, 68,* 971–985.

Watson, W. H. (1975). The meanings of touch: Geriatric nursing. *Journal of Communication, 25,* 104–112.

Watzlawick, P., Beavin, J. H., & Jackson, D. D. (1967). *Pragmatics of human communication: A study of interactional patterns, pathologies, and paradoxes.* New York: Norton.

Webb, J. T. (1969). Subject speech rates as a function of interviewer behavior. *Language and Speech, 12,* 54–67.

Webb, J. T. (1972). Interview synchrony: An investigation of two speech rate measures. In A. W. Siegman & B. Pope (Eds.), *Studies in dyadic communication* (pp. 115–133). New York: Pergamon.

Webb, S. D. (1978). Privacy and psychosomatic stress: An empirical analysis. *Social Behavior and Personality, 6,* 227–234.

Webster, R. L., Steinhardt, M. H., & Senter, M. G. (1972). Changes in infants' vocalizations as a function of differential acoustic stimulation. *Developmental Psychology, 7,* 39–43.

Wegner, D. M., & Vallacher, R. R. (1977). *Implicit psychology: An introduction to social cognition.* New York: Oxford University Press.

Weisfeld, G. E., & Linkey, H. E. (1985). Dominance displays as indicators of a social success motive. In S. L. Ellyson & J. F. Dovidio (Eds.), *Power, dominance, and nonverbal behavior* (pp. 109–128). New York: Springer-Verlag.

Weitz, S. (1976). Sex differences in nonverbal communication. *Sex Roles, 2,* 175–184.

Welkowitz, J., & Feldstein, S. (1969). Dyadic interactions and induced differences in perceived similarity. *Proceedings of the 78th Annual Convention of the American Psychological Association, 5,* 387–388.

Welkowitz, J., & Kuc, M. (1973). Interrelationships among warmth, genuineness, empathy, and temporal speech patterns in interpersonal interaction. *Journal of Consulting and Clinical Psychology, 41,* 472–473.

Werner, C. M., & Haggard, L. M. (1985). Temporal qualities of interpersonal relationships. In M. L. Knapp & G. R. Miller (Eds.), *Handbook of interpersonal communication* (pp. 59–99). Beverly Hills, CA: Sage.

Werner, C. M., Peterson-Lewis, S., & Brown, B. B. (1989). Inferences about homeowner's sociability: Impact of Christmas decorations and other cues. *Journal of Environmental Psychology, 9,* 279–296.

West, C. (1979). Against our will: Male interruptions of females in cross-sex conversation. *Annals of the New York Academy of Sciences, 327,* 81–97.

West, C., & Zimmerman, D. H. (1977). Women's place in everyday talk: Reflections on parent-child interaction. *Social Problems, 24,* 521–529.

West, C., & Zimmerman, D. H. (1982). Conversational analysis. In K. R. Scherer & P. Ekman (Eds.), *Handbook of methods in nonverbal behavior research* (pp. 506–541). Cambridge: Cambridge University Press.

West, C., & Zimmerman, D. H. (1983). Small insults: A study of interruptions in cross-sex conversations between unacquainted persons. In B. Thorne, C. Kramarae, & N. Henley (Eds.), *Language, gender, and society* (pp. 102–117). Rowley, MA: Newbury House.

Westin, A. (1970). *Privacy and freedom.* New York: Atheneum.

Wexner, L. B. (1954). The degree to which colors (hues) are associated with mood-tones. *Journal of Applied Psychology, 38,* 432–435.

Wheeless, L. R. (1971). Some effects of time-compressed speech on persuasion. *Journal of Broadcasting, 15,* 415–420.

Whitbourne, S. K. (1985). *The aging body: Physiological changes and psychological consequences.* New York: Springer-Verlag.

Whitcher, S. J., & Fisher, J. D. (1979). Multidimensional reaction to therapeutic touch in a hospital setting. *Journal of Personality and Social Psychology, 37,* 87–96.

Whitehurst, T. C., & Derlega, V. J. (1985). Influence of touch and preferences for control on visual behavior and subjective responses. In S. L. Ellyson & J. F. Dovidio (Eds.), *Power, dominance, and nonverbal behavior* (pp. 165–182). New York: Springer-Verlag.

Whiting, B., & Edwards, C. (1973). A cross-cultural analysis of sex differences in the behavior of children aged three through 11. *Journal of Social Psychology, 91,* 171–188.

Whyte, W. F. (1943). *Street corner society: The structure of an Italian slum.* Chicago: University of Chicago Press.

Wiemann, J. M. (1973). *An exploratory study of turn-taking in conversations: Verbal and nonverbal behavior.* Unpublished master's thesis, Purdue University, West Lafayette, IN.

Wiemann, J. M. (1974). *An experimental study of visual attention in dyads: The effects of four gaze conditions on evaluations by applicants in employment interviews.* Paper presented at the annual convention of the Speech Communication Association, Chicago.

Wiemann, J. M. (1977). Explication and test of a model of communicative competence. *Human Communication Research, 3,* 195–213.

Wiemann, J. M. (1985). Power, status and dominance: Interpersonal control and regulation in conversation. In R. L. Street & J. N. Cappella (Eds.), *Sequence and pattern in communicative behavior* (pp. 85–102). London: Arnold.

Wiemann, J. M., & Knapp, M. L. (1975). Turn-taking in conversations. *Journal of Communication, 25,* 75–92.

Wiener, M., Devoe, S., Rubinow, S., & Geller, J. (1972). Nonverbal behavior and nonverbal communication. *Psychological Review, 79,* 185–214.

Wiener, M., & Mehrabian, A. (1968). *Language within language: Immediacy, a channel in verbal communication.* Englewood Cliffs, NJ: Prentice-Hall.

Wiggers, M. (1982). Judgments of facial expressions of emotion predicted from facial behavior. *Journal of Nonverbal Behavior, 7,* 101–116.

Wilkinson, R. (1969). Some factors influencing the effect of environmental stressors upon performance. *Psychological Bulletin, 72,* 260–272.

Williams, S. J., & Willis, F. N. (1978). Interpersonal touch among preschool children at play. *Psychological Record, 28,* 501–508.

Willis, F. N. (1966). Initial speaking distance as a function of the speakers' relationship. *Psychonomic Science, 5,* 221–222.

Willis, F. N., Jr., & Briggs, L. F. (1992). Relationship and touch in public settings. *Journal of Nonverbal Behavior, 16,* 55–63.

Willis, F. N., & Hamm, H. K. (1980). The use of interpersonal touch in securing compliance. *Journal of Nonverbal Behavior, 5,* 49–55.

Willis, F. N., & Hoffman, G. E. (1975). Development of tactile patterns in relation to age, sex, and race. *Developmental Psychology, 11,* 866.

Willis, F. N., & Reeves, D. L. (1976). Touch interactions in junior high students in relation to sex and race. *Developmental Psychology, 12,* 91–92.

Willis, F. N., Reeves, D. L., & Buchanan, D. R. (1976). Interpersonal touch in high school relative to sex and race. *Perceptual and Motor Skills, 43,* 843–847.

Willis, F. N., & Rinck, C. M. (1983). A personal log method for investigating interpersonal touch. *Journal of Psychology, 113,* 119–122.

Willis, F. N., Rinck, C. M., & Dean, L. M. (1978). Interpersonal touch among adults in cafeteria lines. *Perceptual and Motor Skills, 47,* 1147–1152.

Willis, F. N., & Williams, S. J. (1976). Simultaneous talking in conversation and sex of speakers. *Perceptual and Motor Skills, 43,* 1067–1070.

Willson, A., & Lloyd, B. (1990). Gender vs. power: Self-posed behavior revisited. *Sex Roles, 23,* 91–99.

Wilson, G. D. (1966). Arousal properties of red versus green. *Perceptual and Motor Skills, 23,* 947–949.

Wilson, P. R. (1968). Perceptual distortion of height as a function of ascribed academic status. *Journal of Social Psychology, 74,* 97–102.

Wilson, T., Wiemann, J. M., & Zimmerman, D. H. (1984). Models of turn taking in conversational interaction. *Journal of Language and Social Psychology, 3,* 159–183.

Winkel, F. W., & Vrij, A. (1990). Nonverbal behavior in a cross-cultural dyad: The frequency and effects of gaze aversion in police-black encounters. *Social Behaviour: An International Journal of Applied Psychology, 5,* 335–350.

Winton, W. M. (1986). The role of facial response in self-reports of emotion: A critique of Laird. *Journal of Personality and Social Psychology, 50,* 808–812.

Wish, M. (1979). Dimensions of dyadic communication. In S. Weitz (Ed.), *Nonverbal communication: Readings with commentary* (2d ed., pp. 371–378). New York: Oxford University Press.

Wish, M., Deutsch, M., & Kaplan, S. J. (1976). Perceived dimensions of interpersonal relations. *Journal of Personality and Social Psychology, 33,* 409–420.

Wolfe, M., & Laufer, R. (1974). The concept of privacy in childhood and adolescence. In S. T. Margulis (Ed.), *Privacy* (pp. 29–54). Stony Brook, NY: Environmental Design Research Association.

Wolff, P., & Gutstein, J. (1972). Effects of induced motor gestures on vocal output. *Journal of Communication, 22,* 277–288.

Wolk, R., & Henley, A. (1970). *The right to lie.* New York: Wyden.

Wood, B. S. (1981). *Children and communication: Verbal and nonverbal language development* (2d ed.). Englewood Cliffs, NJ: Prentice-Hall.

Wood, M. H. (1985). Learning disabilities and human sexuality. *Academic Therapy, 20,* 543–547.

Woodall, W. G. (1984, May). *Attitude and comprehension processes: Some unexamined and re-examined relations.* Paper presented at the annual meeting of the International Communication Association, San Francisco.

Woodall, W. G., & Burgoon, J. K. (1981). The effects of nonverbal synchrony on message comprehension and persuasiveness. *Journal of Nonverbal Behavior, 5,* 207–223.

Woodall, W. G., & Burgoon, J. K. (1983). Talking fast and changing attitudes: A critique and clarification. *Journal of Nonverbal Behavior, 8,* 126–142.

Woodall, W. G., Burgoon, J. K., & Markel, N. N. (1980). The effects of facial-head cue combinations on interpersonal evaluations. *Communication Quarterly, 28* (3), 47–55.

Woodall, W. G., Davis, D. K., & Sahin, H. (1983). From the boob tube to the black box: Television news comprehension from an information processing perspective. *Journal of Broadcasting, 27,* 1–23.

Woodall, W. G., & Folger, J. P. (1981). Encoding specificity and nonverbal cue context: An expansion of episodic memory research. *Communication Monographs, 48,* 39–53.

Woodall, W. G., & Folger, J. P. (1985). Nonverbal cue context and episodic memory: On the availability and endurance of nonverbal behaviors as retrieval cues. *Communication Monographs, 52,* 319–333.

Woodhead, M. M. (1964). Searching of a visual display in intermittent noise. *Journal of Sound and Vibration, 1,* 157–161.

Woodhead, M. M. (1966). An effect of noise on the distribution of attention. *Journal of Applied Psychology, 50.* 296–299.

Woolbert, C. (1920). The effects of various models of public reading. *Journal of Applied Psychology, 4,* 162–185.

Woolfolk, A. E., & Brooks, D. M. (1985). The influence of teachers' nonverbal behavior on students' perceptions and performance. *Elementary School Journal, 85,* 513–528.

Woolfolk, R. L., & Woolfolk, A. E. (1974). Effects of teacher verbal and nonverbal behaviors on student perceptions and attitudes. *American Educational Research Journal, 11,* 297–303.

Worchel, S. (1986). The influence of contextual variables on interpersonal spacing. *Journal of Nonverbal Behavior, 10,* 230–254.

Worchel, S., & Teddlie, C. (1976). The experience of crowding: A two-factor theory. *Journal of Personality and Social Psychology, 34,* 30–40.

Worchel, S., & Yohai, S. M. L. (1979). The role of attribution in the experience of crowding. *Journal of Experimental Social Psychology, 15,* 91–104.

Word, C. O., Zanna, M. P., & Cooper, J. (1974). The nonverbal mediation of self-fulfilling prophecies in interracial interaction. *Journal of Experimental Social Psychology, 10,* 109–120.

Wright, G. (1981). *Building the dream: A social history of housing in America.* Cambridge, MA: MIT Press.

Wycoff, E. G., & Holley, J. D. (1990). Effects of flight attendants' touch upon airline passengers' perceptions of the attendant and the airline. *Perceptual and Motor Skills, 71,* 932–934.

Wylie, L., & Stafford, R. (1977). *Beaux gestes: A guide to French body talk.* Cambridge, MA: Undergraduate Press.

Yerkes, R. M., & Dodson, J. D. (1908). The relation of strength of stimulus to rapidity of habit-formation. *Journal of Comparative and Neurological Psychology, 18,* 459–482.

Yngve, V. H. (1970). On getting a word in edgewise. In M. A. Campbell et al. (Eds.), *Papers from the sixth regional meeting, Chicago Linguistics Society.* Chicago: University of Chicago Press.

Zabel, R. (1979). Recognition of emotions in facial expressions by emotionally disturbed and nondisturbed children. *Psychology in the Schools, 16,* 119–126.

Zahn, G. L. (1973). Cognitive integration of verbal and vocal information in spoken sentences. *Journal of Experimental Social Psychology, 9,* 320–334.

Zaidel, S. F., & Mehrabian, A. (1969). The ability to communicate and infer positive and negative attitudes facially and vocally. *Journal of Experimental Research in Personality, 3,* 233–241.

Zajonc, R. B. (1965). Social facilitation. *Science, 149,* 269–274.

Zajonc, R. B. (1980). Compresence. In P. B. Paulus (Ed.), *Psychology of group influence* (pp. 35–60). Hillsdale, NJ: Erlbaum.

Zebrowitz-McArthur, L., & Montepare, J. M. (1989). Contributions of a babyface and a child-like voice to impressions of moving and talking faces. *Journal of Nonverbal Behavior, 13,* 189–203.

Zeilik, M. (1985a). A reassessment of the fajada butte solar marker. *Archaeoastronomy, 9,* 69–85.

Zeilik, M. (1985b). Sun shrines and sun symbols in the U.S. southwest. *Archaeoastronomy, 9,* 86–96.

Zimmerman, B. J., & Brody, G. H. (1975). Race and modelling influences on the interpersonal play patterns of boys. *Journal of Educational Psychology, 67,* 591–598.

Zimmerman, D. H., & West, C. (1975). Sex roles, interruptions and silences in conversation. In B. Thorne & N. Henley (Eds.), *Language and sex: Difference and dominance* (pp. 105–129). Cambridge, MA: Newbury House.

Zuckerman, M., Amidon, M. D., Bishop, S. E., & Pomerantz, S. D. (1982). Face and tone of voice in the communication of deception. *Journal of Personality and Social Psychology, 43,* 347–357.

Zuckerman, M., DeFrank, R. S., Hall, J. A., Larrance, D. T., & Rosenthal, R. (1979). Facial and vocal cues of deception and honesty. *Journal of Experimental Social Psychology, 15,* 378–396.

Zuckerman, M., DePaulo, B. M., & Rosenthal, R. (1981). Verbal and nonverbal communication of deception. In L. Berkowitz (Ed.), *Advances in experimental social psychology* (Vol. 14, pp. 1–59). New York: Academic.

Zuckerman, M., & Driver, R. E. (1985). Telling lies: Verbal and nonverbal correlates of deception. In A. W. Siegman & S. Feldstein (Eds.), *Multichannel integrations of nonverbal behavior* (pp. 129–148). Hillsdale, NJ: Erlbaum.

Zuckerman, M., & Driver, R. E. (1989). What sounds beautiful is good: The vocal attractiveness stereotype. *Journal of Nonverbal Behavior, 13,* 67–82.

Zuckerman, M., Driver, R. E., & Koestner, R. (1982). Discrepancy as a cue to actual and perceived deception. *Journal of Nonverbal Behavior, 7,* 95–100.

Zuckerman, M., Fischer, S. A., Osmun, R. W., Winkler, B. A., & Wolfson, L. R. (1987). Anchoring in lie detection revisited. *Journal of Nonverbal Behavior, 11,* 4–12.

Zuckerman, M., Hall, J. A., DeFrank, R. S., & Rosenthal, R. (1976). Encoding and decoding of spontaneous and posed facial expressions. *Journal of Personality and Social Psychology, 34,* 966–977.

Zuckerman, M., Hodgins, H., & Miyake, K. (1990). The vocal attractiveness stereotype: Replication and elaboration. *Journal of Nonverbal Behavior, 14,* 97–112.

Zuckerman, M., Koestner, R., & Colella, M. J. (1985). Learning to detect deception from three communication channels. *Journal of Nonverbal Behavior, 9,* 188–194.

Zuckerman, M., Koestner, R., Colella, M. J., & Alton, A. O. (1984). Anchoring in the detection of deception and leakage. *Journal of Personality and Social Psychology, 47,* 301–311.

Zuckerman, M., Koestner, R., & Driver, R. E. (1981). Beliefs about cues associated with deception. *Journal of Nonverbal Behavior, 6,* 105–114.

Zuckerman, M., Larrance, D. T., Hall, J. A., DeFrank, R. S., & Rosenthal, R. (1979). Posed and spontaneous communication of emotion via facial and vocal cues. *Journal of Personality, 47,* 712–733.

Zuckerman, M., Larrance, D. T., Spiegel,

N. H., & Klorman, R. (1981). Controlling nonverbal displays: Facial expressions and tone of voice. *Journal of Experimental Social Psychology, 17,* 506–524.

Zuckerman, M., Lipets, M. S., Koivumaki, J. H., & Rosenthal, R. (1975). Encoding and decoding nonverbal cues of emotion. *Journal of Personality and Social Psychology, 32,* 1068–1076.

Zuckerman, M., & Miyake, K. (1993). The attractive voice: What makes it so? *Journal of Nonverbal Behavior, 17,* 119–135.

Zuckerman, M., Miyake, K., & Hodgins, H. S. (1991). Cross-channel effects of vocal and physical attractiveness and their implications for interpersonal perception. *Journal of Personality and Social Psychology, 60,* 545–554.

Zuckerman, M., Spiegel, N. H., DePaulo, B. M., & Rosenthal, R. (1982). Nonverbal strategies for decoding deception. *Journal of Nonverbal Behavior, 6,* 171–187.

CREDITS

TEXT, TABLES, BOXES, AND FIGURES (LISTED BY PAGE NUMBER)

3 Silent Meaning by William S. Cohen in THE NEW YORK TIMES, July 23, 1985. Copyright © 1985 by The New York Times Company. Reprinted by permission. **7** Box 1-2: From KINESICS AND CONTEXT: ESSAYS ON BODY MOTION COMMUNICATION by Ray L. Birdwhistell, 1970. Reprinted by permission of the University of Pennsylvania Press. **23** Fig 1-2: From Similarities and Differences Between Cultures in Expressive Movements by I. Eible-Eibesfeldt, in NON-VERBAL COMMUNICATION, edited by R.A. Hinde, 1972. Copyright © 1972 Cambridge University Press. Reprinted by permission. **34** Box 2-1: From ZEN FLESH, ZEN BONES by Paul Reps, 1957. Reprinted by permission of Charles E. Tuttle Co., Inc. **37** Fig 2-1: From The Anthropology of Posture by G.W. Hewes. Copyright © 1957 by Scientific American, Inc. All rights reserved. Reprinted by permission. **40** Fig 2-2: Redrawn from Ray L. Birdwhistell, KINESICS AND CONTEXT: ESSAYS ON BODY MOTION COMMUNICATION (Philadelphia: University of Pennsylvania Press, 1970). **55** Fig 2-4: Drawing by Richard Geiger from MANWATCHING by Desmond Morris, first published in Great Britain by Jonathan Cape Ltd., London; planned and produced by Equinox (Oxford) Ltd. In cooperation with Jonathan Cape Ltd., 1977. Reprinted by permission. **73** Box 3-1: From Parent Is Seen as Key to Happiness by Daniel Goleman in THE NEW YORK TIMES, April 18, 1991. Copyright © 1991 by The New York Times Company. Reprinted by permission. **81** Box 3-2: From Joyce Walker-Tyson, THE DETROIT FREE PRESS, 5/31/81. Reprinted by permission. **91** Fig 3-1: From A System for the Notation of Proxemic Behavior by E. T. Hall. Reproduced by permission of the American Anthropological Association from AMERICAN ANTHROPOLOGIST 65:5, 1963. Not for further reproduction. **98** Fig 3-2: From RESPONSES TO TOUCHING AS AN INDEX OF SEX ROLE NORMS AND ATTITUDES by R. Heslin. Washington, D.C.: American Psychological Association. Copyright 1978 by the American Psychological Association. Reprinted by permission. **99** Box 3-5: From Embraceable USA—by Region from USA TODAY, May 31, 1985. Copyright 1985, USA TODAY. Reprinted with permission. **101** Tab 3-2: From BODY POLITICS: POWER, SEX, AND NONVERBAL COMMUNICATION (p. 105) by N. Henley. Copyright © 1977 by Simon & Schuster, Inc. Reprinted by permission of Simon & Schuster, Inc. **102** Tab 3-3: From A Naturalistic Study of the Meanings of Touch by S. E. Jones and A. E. Yarborough, 1985, COMMUNICATION MONOGRAPHS, 52, pp. 28–35. Reprinted by permission. **115** Tab 4-1: From THE UNSPOKEN DIALOGUE: AN INTRODUCTION TO NONVERBAL COMMUNICATION (p. 110) by J.K. Burgoon and T. Saine, 1978. Boston: Houghton Mifflin. **126** Tab 4-2: From Time in Perspective by A. Gonzalez and P.G. Zimbardo in PSYCHOLOGY TODAY, March 1985. Reprinted with permission from PSYCHOLOGY TODAY MAGAZINE. Copyright © 1985 (PT Partners, L.P.) **130** Hagar the Horrible cartoon reprinted with special permission of King Features Syndicate. **140** Hagar the Horrible cartoon reprinted with special permission of King Features Syndicate. **167** Box 6-1: From THE MAN WHO MISTOOK HIS WIFE FOR A HAT by Oliver Sacks. Copyright © 1970, 1981, 1983, 1984, 1985 by Oliver Sacks. Reprinted by permission of Simon & Schuster, Inc. **182** Box 6-3: From Conversational Amnesia by C.T. Cory in PSYCHOLOGY TODAY, February 1983. Reprinted by permission. **186** Box 6-4: From Helping Elders Get the Message by S. Chollar in PSYCHOLOGY TODAY, May 1988. Reprinted by permission. **194** Fig 7-1: From LANDSCAPE ARCHITECTURE: A MANUAL OF SITE PLANNING AND DESIGN by J. O. Sidmonds. Copyright © 1961 by F.W. Dodge Corporation. Used with permission of McGraw-Hill Book Company. **200** From Human Territories: Comment on Functional Properties by J. Edney in ENVIRONMENT AND BEHAVIOR, 8 (1976), pp. 31–47. Copyright © 1976 by Human Sciences Press. Reprinted by permission of Sage Publications, Inc. **203** Box 7-3: From Prison Codes by S.J. Ramsey in JOURNAL OF COMMUNICATION, 1976. Reprinted by permission of Oxford University Press. **206** Fig 7-3: From LANDSCAPE ARCHITECTURE: A MANUAL OF SITE PLANNING AND DESIGN by J. O. Sidmonds. Copyright © 1961 by F.W. Dodge Corporation. Used with permission of McGraw-Hill Book Company. **219** Fig 8-1: From a drawing by Larry Ratzkin in GESTURES by D. Morris, P. Collett, P. Marsh and M. O'Shaughnessy, 1979, London: Jonathan Cape Ltd. Copyright 1979 by Jonathan Cape Ltd. Reprinted by permission. **221** Fig 8-2: From The Kinesics of Femininity in Japanese Women, by S. J. Ramsey, 1981, LANGUAGE SCIENCES, 3, pp. 108–110. Reprinted by permission. **254** Box 9-1: From Height, Weight Affect Salary, Researchers Say as appeared in TUCSON CITIZEN, March 2, 1987. Reprinted by permission of AP Newsfeatures. **267** Tab 9-1: From The relationship of selected vocal characteristics to personality perceptions by D. W. Addington in SPEECH MONOGRAPHS, 35, 1968. Reprinted by permission. **275** Box 10-1: From Associated Press, June 3, 1985. Reprinted by permission. **277** Tab 10-2: From AFFECT, IMAGERY, CONSCIOUSNESS, Vol. 1: THE POSITIVE AFFECTS and Vol. 2: THE NEGATIVE AFFECTS by S. S. Tomkins, 1962–1963, New York: Springer-Verlag; Universal and Cultural Differences in Facial Expressions of Emotions, by P. Ekman in J.K. Cole (Ed.), 1971, NEBRASKA SYMPOSIUM ON MOTIVATION, Vol. 19(Pp. 207–283), Lincoln: University of Nebraska Press; HUMAN EMOTIONS by C. E. Izard, 1977, New York: Plenum. Reprinted with permission of the publisher. **277** Fig 10-2: From A Conical Model for the Taxonomy of Emotional Experience by E.M. Daly, W.J. Lancee, and J. Polivy, 1983, JOURNAL OF PERSONALITY AND SOCIAL PSYCHOLOGY, 45, pp. 443–457. Copyright 1983 by the American Psychological Association. Reprinted by permission of the authors. **280** Fig 10-3: Ekman, P. (1971). Universal and cultural differences in facial expressions of emotion. In J.K. Cole (Ed.), NEBRASKA SYMPOSIUM ON MOTIVATION (pp. 207–283). Lincoln, NE: University of Nebraska Press. Reprinted by permission. **285** Tab 10-3: Adapted from Facial Affect Scoring Technique: A First Validity Study, by P. Ekman, W.V. Friesen, and S. S. Tomkins, 1971, JOURNAL OF COMMUNICATION 21, 37–58; Facial Areas and Emotional Information, by J. D. Boucher and P. Ekman, 1975, JOURNAL OF COMMUNICATION, 25(2), 21–29. Reprinted by permission of Oxford University Press. **287** Tab 10-4: Adapted from Cue Utilization in Emotion Attribution from Auditory Stimuli, by K. R. Scherer and J. S. Oshinsky, 1977, MOTIVATION AND EMOTION, I(4), p. 340. Reprinted by permission. **291** Tab 10-5: Adapted from Judgments of Facial Expressions of Emotion Predicted from Facial Behavior, by M. Wiggers, 1982, JOURNAL OF NONVERBAL BEHAVIOR, 7, 101–116. Reprinted by permission. **294** Tab 10-6: Adapted from The Communication of Feelings by Content-free Speech, by J.R. Davitz and L. J. Davitz, 1959, JOURNAL OF COMMUNICATION, 9, 6–13. Reprinted with permission of International Communication Association. **300** Tab 11-1: From INTERPERSONAL COMMUNICATION AND HUMAN RELATIONSHIPS 2E by Knapp, M.L. and Vangelisti, A. L. Copyright © 1992 Allyn & Bacon. Reprinted by permission. **310** Tab 11-2: From BODY POLITICS (p. 181) by Nancy M. Henley, 1977, Englewood Cliffs, NJ: Prentice-Hall. Reprinted by permission. **311** From THE NEW YORK TIMES, September 2, 1984. Copyright © 1984 by The New York Times Company. Reprinted by permission. **311** From Hard Times for the Status-Minded by Frank Trippett in TIME, December 21, 1981. Copyright © 1981 Time Inc. Reprinted by permission. **314** Fig 11-1: From Patterns of Visual Dominance Behavior in Humans, by J.F. Dovidio and S.L. Ellyson in POWER, DOMINANCE, AND NONVERBAL BEHAVIOR (pp. 135–139), edited by J.F. Dovidio and S.L. Ellyson, 1985, New York: Springer Verlag, Inc. Copyright 1985 by Springer Verlag, Inc. Reprinted with permission of Springer Verlag. **322** Box 11-4: From Miss Manners by J. Martin, THE KNOXVILLE NEWS-SENTINAL, March 16, 1986. MISS MANNERS reprinted by permission of United Feature Syndicate, Inc. **332** Fig 11-2: From HOW BEHAVIOR MEANS by A.E. Scheflen, 1974, New York: Science Publishers, Inc. Copyright 1974 by Science Publishers, Inc. Reprinted by permission. **341** Box 12-1: Reprinted with permission from PSYCHOLOGY TODAY magazine, January 1988. Copyright © 1988 (PT Partners, L.P.). **345** Tab 12-1: From The Rhetoric of Goodbye: Verbal and Nonverbal Correlates of Human Leave-taking, by M.L. Knapp, R. P. Hart, G. W. Friedrich, & G.M. Shulman, 1973, SPEECH MONOGRAPHS, 40, 191. Reprinted with permission. **347** Fig 12-1: Adapted from RHYTHMS OF DIALOGUE (p. 20) by J. Jaffe and S. Feldstein, 1970, Orlando, Florida: Academic Press, Inc. Copyright 1970 by Academic Press, Inc. Reprinted with the permission of Academic Press. **365** Box 13-1: CEO image can make or break firm from USA TODAY, August 18, 1995. Copyright 1995, USA TODAY. Reprinted with permission. **371** Box 13-2: (Permission pending—tentative credit) From The Doctor as Dramatist by S. A. Hoffman, as appeared in NEWSWEEK, February 1, 1988. Reprinted by permission. **385** Box 13-4: From The new dress code for success by Elizabeth Sporkin in USA TODAY, January 12, 1988. Copyright 1988, USA TODAY. Excerpted with permission. **414** Box 14-3: From Studies point to power of nonverbal signals by Daniel Goleman in THE NEW YORK TIMES, April 8, 1986. Copyright © 1986 by The New York Times Company. Reprinted by permission. **430** Tab 15-1: Adapted from White Lies in Interpersonal Communication: A Taxonomy and Preliminary Investigation of Social Motivations, by C. Camden, M.T. Motley, and A. Wilson, 1984, WESTERN JOURNAL OF SPEECH COMMUNICATION, 48, 309–325; AN EXPLORATORY INVESTIGATION OF RELATIONAL DECEPTION, by S. Mettsk and H. Chronis, paper presented to the annual meeting of the International Communication Association, Chicago, 1986. Reprinted by permission. **446** Box 15-2: From PSYCHOLOGY TODAY, March 1981. Reprinted with permission from PSYCHOLOGY TODAY MAGAZINE, Copyright © 1981 (Sussex Publishers, Inc.).

PHOTOGRAPHS (LISTED BY PAGE NUMBER)

16 Ulrike Welsch **17** Left, Fujifotos/Image Works; right, Don Rutledge/Picture Cube **25** T. Michaels/Image Works; **43** Top left, Joel Gordon; bottom left, Mike Malyszko/FPG; right, Elizabeth Crews/Image Works; **62** All except bottom right, AP/Wide World; bottom right, Bob Daemmrich/Stock, Boston; **70** AP/Wide World; **77** Left, Andy Levin/Photo Researchers; right, Jen & Des Bartlett/Photo Researchers **95** Left, AP/Wide World; right, Spencer Grant/Photo Researchers; **106** Ulrike Welsch; **110** Paolo Koch/Photo Researchers; **119** Top left, Emilio A. Mercado/Picture Cube; bottom left, Rameshwar Das/Monkmeyer; top right, Karlson/Picture Cube; bottom right, Jeff Dunn/Picture Cube; **138** Alan Borrud **156** Left, AP/Wide World; right, Reuter/Bettmann; **171** Joel Gordon; **176** Donald C. Dietz/Stock, Boston; **200** Left, Gerard Fritz/Monkmeyer; right, Joel Gordon; **220** Karlson/Picture Cube; **227** Top left, Joel Gordon; top right, W. Lüthy/FPG; bottom left, Marcello Bertinetti/Photo Researchers; bottom right, George Holton/Photo Researchers; **233** Bottom left, Stuart Cohen/Comstock; bottom right, Dave Driscoll/Photo Researchers; **253** Ulrike Welsch **262** Top, Jennings/Image Works; bottom left, Rick Mansfield/Image Works; bottom right, Spencer Grant/Photo Researchers; **272** AP/Wide World; **284** Paul Ekman, Department of Psychiatry, University of California, San Francisco **299** Ogust/Image Works; **308** Michael Kagen/Monkmeyer; **319** AP/Wide World; **325** Left, W. Hill, Jr./Image Works; bottom, Joel Gordon; right, Ellis Herwig/Picture Cube; **342** Tony Velez/Image Works; **348** Steven Bloch Photo; **353** Joel Gordon **370** AP/Wide World; **372** Will McIntyre/Photo Researchers **378** AP/Wide World; **384** Joel Gordon; **395** Katherine McGlynn/Image Works; **405** AP/Wide World; **426** and **449** UPI/Bettmann

NAME INDEX

SUBJECT INDEX